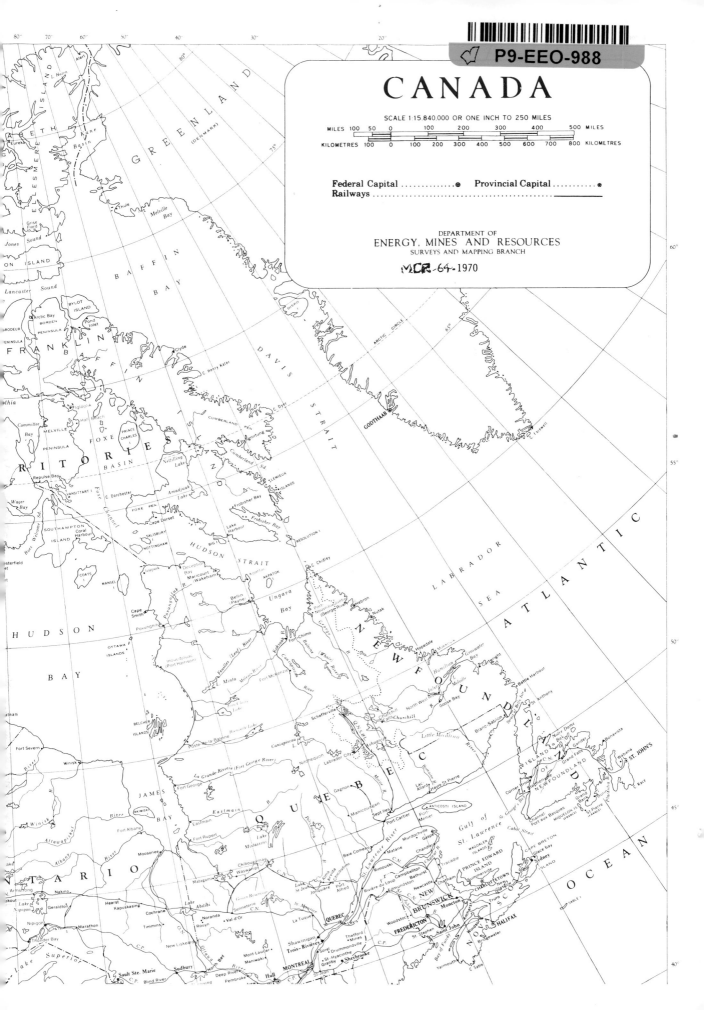

Enjoy my "Gold"!
"Sourdough"
Phillip G. Allen
1993

PHILLIP E. ALLEN

315, 8905 - 184 Street

Edmonton, AB   T5T 1T8

(403) 487-9062

Phillip Allen sharing a memorable moment with Canadian poet Robert W. Service, at the International Reunion and Convention of Alaska and Yukon Sourdoughs, celebrating the 50th anniversary of the *Trail of '98.*
Hotel Vancouver, B.C. August 12–15, 1948

Monte Carlo

Feb 26 '54

Dear Mr. Allen,

Thanks for
your greeting card and the
picture of your nice family
& their house in our neighborhood.
I proud written to books -
B. Also I prefer my
more recent ones as they
reflect my philosophy of
living and point paths to
happiness.

Greetings

(Canadian Poet).   Robert Service,

ONE CAME LATE

A true unsponsored story of one Canadian with a tremendous 'Love of Life' and 'Lust for Adventure'. . . stowing away on an aircraft with a simple grubstake, headed into the vast and sometimes uncharted Northland, his desire: to re–trek and re–live the 'Gold Trails of '98' made famous by Robert W. Service. . . all this with only a clarinet, a typewriter and. . . a dime!

Printed in Edmonton, Alberta, Canada

This, personal narrative of the North during 1947 is written in the language or parlance of the people and races of the period. Personal affront must not be taken due to current changes in nomenclature by the peoples or our governments in the process of change and human rights in Canada.

The Author in his reliving the vigorous and sometimes unmapped Trails of '98, set out in search of truth by total participation and personal exposure during his Odyssey of six months, six thousand miles, on a dime, graduating from 'Cheechako' to 'Sourdough' by journeys end.

Phillip Allen
1992

Drifting

I seem to just keep drifting
Through narrow aisles of life,
Where many other weary men
Have trod, and laughed at strife.

Thro' highways and thro' byways
Of endless, cloudy thought;
Sometimes off the narrow path
Another world I've sought.

Down robust rivers I have sped...
On to the waterfalls;
I've portaged with my fellow men
Through Nature's hanging halls.

I've travelled with the mighty Drake;
With Columbus, sailed the seas;
Have shot the rapids with La Salle;
Just drifters — all of these.

Endlessly I travel on...
On wanton wings of thought.
Seeking only happiness
That other men have sought!

P.E. Allen
British Columbia,
Canada
March 18, 1943

Acknowledgments

Roy Inglangasuk, my Eskimo friend whose mother I knew in Aklavik before he did; and his wife Jackie, for gratuitous hours of computering "One Came Late".

Bob Walls, computer wiz and teacher.

Ron Swan, computer and correction expert.

Bob & Evelyn of Alphatel, who guided and fulfilled all the author's wishes and odd requests in the final DeskTop Publishing of his Northern Narrative.

Jan, also of Alphatel, computer format and final Desktop editor whose patience and creativity gave form to "The Book".

The entire staff of Quality Color Press Inc. Edmonton, Alberta, Canada who shared the final making of a dream, a beautiful reality.

Lerena Greig	—Sales and P.R. Consultant
Gerry Dotto	—Artist and Cover Design
Alice Hjort	—Publishing Co-ordinator

Brent Anderson, Wetaskiwin, Alberta, photographer, whose time, patience and printing skill, turned the Author's hundreds of photographs into the desired visual story accompanying the narrative.

Department of Energy, Mines and Resources Canada for the use of Map MCR 64 Copyright 1970.

McGraw Hill Ryerson Ltd., for the use of some of poet Robert W. Service's words.

Finally, a big Northern "Thank You" to all those not mentioned or photographed during the "The Adventure Of My Life" who are the unheralded "Ships That Pass In The Night".

Sincerely, 'Sourdough'

Phillip Allen

Dedications

To the wonderful, accepting and generous spirit of all the people of the High North with whom the Cheechako shared food, lodgings, hardships and laughter, in the pursuit of his Odyssey: to trek the entire Gold Trails of '98 through their beautiful but sometimes harsh domain; the knowledge and secrets of survival therein, he came to know through their kinship and unselfish nature inbred by a respect for a land which surely "Does not choose its people; but merely eliminates the weaklings"

To Jan, without whose love, concern and unselfish devotion in typing a long—since, neglected narrative, brought forth this true, long—overdue experience for the sharing with others.

To Helen, a Kindered Spirit who shares our love of the North, in ardent addiction during two years re—editing "The Book".

The author, absorbed in the 'Complete Poems of Robert W. Service', finds inspiration during the early days of his Odyssey: The *Gold Trails of '98* – waiting for the ice to 'Go Out'.

Yellowknife, Northwest Territories

"...It is doubtful if a single person has repeated this full exploit since the turn of the century. . ."

Pierre Berton
—Klondike—
—The Last Great Gold Rush—
:first edition 1958
:revised edition 1972

ONE ——

CAME

—— *LATE*

A Pictorial Travelogue of the Gold Rush Trails of '98 as relived by the Author from April 23, 1947 covering 6,000 miles in 6 months on a dime.

ONE CAME LATE.........PHILLIP ALLEN.

ONE CAME LATE.........PHILLIP ALLEN.

CHAPTER ONE

UNSETTLED

It was a misty, chilly Wednesday morning that I clambered aboard the transport. With me was a complete outfit: sleeping bag, Ojibway snowshoes, rifle, more than one man's share of one hundred percent wool clothing (I was determined to cheat the persistent cold, the scourge of the North), my faithful typewriter and a ten–cent piece.

The pilot had said: "We leave at seven; if you happen to be aboard it's none of my business!" It was seven; I was aboard; and it was none of his business. But the feeling of successful crime did not come 'til we dashed at the misty runway, devouring it like some ravenous, prehistoric monster till nothing remained but space. There was no turning back then.

As the motors echoed their challenge to the morning silence I put my past where it belonged, and, as the present was taking good care of itself at the hands of the generous pilot, I set my thoughts to imagining what the future held in store for me.

Seven–fifteen: the plane had proven its challenge along the east–west runway. As I glanced below I caught another perspective of Edmonton awakening to the warm touch of the sun's fingers gently prodding its populace to another day of routine work. Silently saying farewell for what I intended to be an indefinite period I thought of Mackenzie, La Salle, Henry Hudson, Fraser, Thompson... how they had entered the vast unknown which is still as vast, but less unknown. As it was to them, so it was to me: a bothersome question mark. But here I was in this the twentieth century, flying into country that thirty years ago heard not the echo of persistent motors; saw not such strange birds circle and land on the frozen lakes; but a land that knew only of the canoe and dogteam–indispensable companions of the traveller in the North.

Too, I thought of progress, realizing the ease with which I was travelling. I was aware also that later it would be paid for in 'rough sledding'. So I entertained no qualms as to the future. Then, as though my mind was not content to probe the unknown, thoughts flashed back to the few weeks previous. My bout with the University of Alberta, the final succumbing to the temptress– Adventure, anxious days of preparation, the quickly advancing spring, disappointment at the airport and that final happy day. Oh! How it all haunted me suddenly. I smiled inwardly, safely away from its confusion, as that unforgettable morning in the French class took shape vividly....

It was spring–very early spring. In fact the snow had scarce been softened by a persistent sun. I had arisen at my usual late hour stealing last precious moments from the clock, gorged a bowl of cereal, downed hastily a glass of milk and simultaneously bolted for the door. Darkness hung about as Dawn tried hard to shove it aside. Fresh snow crunched under my feet as I churned it in my haste to reach the Campus. Entered, how good the warm air of the inner halls felt: the sprint up the stairs (five at a time)... sliding on the freshly waxed floor untouched by classes at this early hour; the plunge through the door that stood ajar at the end of the hall; slumping in a front seat, overcome by the sudden change in temperature. How pleasantly sleepy one felt. Then an imperative voice crashed the din of an oversized class buzzing with last night's events, or the morning's assignment.

"Venez–ici!....Venez ici!" and the jowls of Monsieur Sonet, Professeur de Francais, University of Alberta, shook from the vibration of the words. The ebullient gentleman in the torn, black gown had entered the classroom, banged the door and assumed his eight o'clock position behind the desk. Carelessly flapping open his beaten text he continued tossing excited phrases at the drowsy class. Suddenly, as if the desire to instruct was too tedious a chore, he pushed the text to arms length and, leaning over the desk, smiled quizzically as he said: "My wife made za coffee ziss morning. Eet was gooood coffee too! I am feeling gooood, so I tell you about France. Would you like zat better heh?"

1

It takes very little to turn one's mind to the past. With the Frenchman I returned overseas; the classroom was infinity. He continued … "and zen I come to Edmonton… 'e was a good town… 'e treat me good, yes… I reemember when za sermometer drop to seexty below and za ice hang heavy on my wheesskers." I had come to Edmonton too. It was cold; damn cold. Now, looking out the window, nothing but a frozen, white blanket stretched for miles. Wonder what's beyond that low horizon? I chided myself. Think you'll ever take a fling in that direction? Bet you haven't got the guts! answered the Devil of Pessimism. Say, it would be a grand challenge, wouldn't it? returned Optimism. Used to be at the turn of the century… why not now? Impossible! Foolish thought! Crazy! answered the Doubter.

Laughter filled the room. The gay Frenchman, swinging his cassock about him like a Roman descending from a dais, leaped from his chair to the floor…. "Now back to za lesson. Tout a fini! Tout a fini!" We became a French class once more. But seeds had been sown that morning.

Goodbye Books – Hello Klondike!

Events happened rapidly after that. "It's up to you fella," said a benign professor to a bewildered student … but I do admire a man who can make his own decisions." "Well, I've just made mine!" A kindly smile spread over Dean Hardy's face. He said one word: "Good!" We shook hands firmly; he returned to the manuscript he was checking; I turned and passed from his office. Lighthearted, whistling a jazz tune, books under arm, I stepped lightly from the University for the last time. But mine was a feeling of extreme joy as with my Bachelor of Bewilderment I stepped boldly from the campus into the rugged avenue of Adventure.

The next were uncertain days, what with trying to sell gold stocks to an already exploited people; accepting the taunts from my fellow classmates who considered me a deserter from the ranks. (Little did they realize how they drove me on, saying: "You mean you'd chuck a degree?…. You'll never make it North!…. What about security?") Inwardly I answered each jest: 'To Hell with the degree—I want wisdom above all!… we'll see, give me time and opportunity… security is only in the mind!'

Spring had at last found its way northward. The last vestiges of winter lay in shaded gutters and on the north side of buildings in the form of dirty mud cakes. Kicking a piece of this substance I slid into the office of Kenwood and Kenwood one day. It was no more than one of those friendly visits that prairie folk are wont to pay one another.

"Good morning!" came the cheery greeting from Mike Power—youthful apprentice to the business. "What's on your mind?" "Oh, nothing special," I said, knowing full well how recently I had wondered to whom that part of me really belonged. "Just makin' the rounds," I added. Wishing to change the subject, I brought in the obvious comment on the weather.

It was fully fifteen minutes before our morning discourse had run the usual gamut of topics. Echoes of Rabelaisian laughter brought the parley to a close. I turned to go. A full−length, wall map caught my eye. It was Canada above the 53rd parallel. Ideas had been unconsciously banding in my head as I tramped the busy

Al Hartley & Self
Yellowknife Gold Syndicate

streets of Edmonton; but little notice had been taken of them. Now the call welled up strong in my breast. So two armies clashed; Imagination completely overwhelming its sinister opponent, Reason. Then and there my decision was made: I would re−trek the Gold *Trails of '98.*

Edmonton is undisputedly the Gateway to the Northland. Whoever has visited it in winter must surely have sensed the Call of the North. The city has long been the jumping−off−point for trappers, traders, prospectors and ne'er−do−well adventurers seeking individual fortunes in the cold, mysterious hinterlands stretching from this once Fort town to the far−reaching Arctic Ocean some two thousand miles distant. As the days passed I had seen faint traces of intrigue in the mukluks, moccasins, fur parkas, beards, and the occasional dogteam−not uncommon sights in this still frontier city; smelt the enticing aroma of Adventure lurking behind these garments; and I saw aircraft take off and head into the White North...somewhere, someplace that I knew I must visit to satisfy this strong urge for Freedom. Impatience was mounting; I was coming. Of that I was definite.

Grubstake

The pilot might well be called one of this gay breed of men who venture North. For years the bush−pilot has kept the thin connection between civilization and the outposts, where only a Mountie, a Hudson's Bay trader and an Oblate Priest spend the long silent winter−a winter that prolongs its stay well into June, when spring and summer come and go in their quick tease and the loneliness of winter hangs over all life once more. Added to this hardy breed today are the Ferry pilots and their huge transports carrying daily freight−loads to the vast, virgin Northwest Territories.

Another week came and went with its accompanying disappointments. "Sorry!.... No chance!.... Maybe there'll be a flight next week...Just left this morning!"echoed and re−echoed in my mind. In fact I began to feel at home with negation. However, in the meantime I was busy. I was re−organizing my kit. "Maybe another woolen shirt?" suggested ruddy Owen Hargreaves. "How about some more dried fruit bars? ...Might get caught in the Yukon−never know!", chimed Jack Dick. As a new week dragged on I made fast friends with these two veterans of the North; and I learned much that was to be of value later. Then one day their secretary, Coral, uttered the last "check". I tossed everything into the duffel bag, yanked on the rope and tied it securely. Rolling the whole into a corner with the rest of my gear I straightened up, panting. An ear−to−ear smile greeted me. Yes, Owen had guessed the answer; and I remembered clearly his parting words: "Good luck to you, boy!" That was Tuesday evening.

My reverie was split suddenly by the roar of a motor. It was Wednesday. Looking out I discovered that spring had not penetrated all of the land. Far below the scenery turned from brown to white, and the rivers ceased to flow. But as the cold increased the conversation became warmer. I found myself with interesting company. We were fourteen from all walks of life and all parts of Canada. As I was later to learn: "The North doesn't choose its people, it merely eliminates the weaklings." In retrospect I have often wondered just how many of that motley collection remained unweeded.

Several miles flew by before the chilly atmosphere was broken by the warmth of conversation. "How much was your fare?", came the odd query from a fellow passenger, rather old, I thought, to be hitting the Road to Adventure. "About the same as yours,"I retaliated, thinking quickly and smiling inwardly. Apparently satisfied, he continued, as we huddled on sacks of flour and boxes of freight, watching the endless miles of white scenery pass the frosted windows: "I'm from Toronto; I'm headed North to try a fling at the bigger money." An air pocket broke the thread momentarily. We gathered ourselves up from amongst the flour, the sugar, and sides of beef.

My friend was a plump, good—natured fellow. He talked and I listened to his many tales of rum—running on the east coasts of Canada and the U.S.A. Smiling with inward pride, he said: "I was on the boats in my early teens and at twenty—one had made myself a net income of thirty—thousand dollars in three years." The highlight of his exploits was a chase by the police patrol into shore, at which point it was discovered another patrol boat was making its exodus from the river mouth. "This led us to one alternative — a getaway to sea," he continued. "Turning out and down the coast we beat it with tracer bullets skimming over our heads and on the water. But we made a neat getaway," he climaxed boastfully. Conversation moved to his wife and family, dying off with his decision (like most others aboard) to get rich quick, if not quicker.

'Dakota' North

As the white miles slipped carelessly by, more conversations emanated. Another Torontonian, engaged to be married, found his pocket too empty for the final plunge, his mission turning out to be none other than mercenary. An ex—navy engineer who must have enjoyed the few hours' stopover in Edmonton (if the smell of alcohol emitted when he spoke at close range could be suggestive of anything) related a few of his most vivid nautical experiences. The cold apparently not penetrating this semi—fortified individual, he leaned back on the sacks and, chuckling to himself over an Irish encounter, passed into an enviable doze. Still another, rising accidentally after the hotel clerk's negligence, found himself running to the airport without breakfast. Consequently, he continued to substitute his necessity with cigarette after cigarette. Imagining the disappointment his stomach must have been suffering, I proffered a morsel of an H & D concentrated chocolate bar that I had stowed away for emergency. Seemingly satisfied, he settled back with the other sleepy bundles as the drone of motors took over once more....

The hours above had been very pleasant as the shadow of our aircraft flitted over a small portion of the thousands of lakes that comprise this mysterious North. Far below, the ancient Athabasca River, flowing with the sureness of spring and already well on its way to capacity, cut a proud figure through the spruce—dotted landscape as it accepted greedily the fast—melting snow, vanishing gradually into the moisture of its former self. Lac La Biche below...Lesser Slave on the

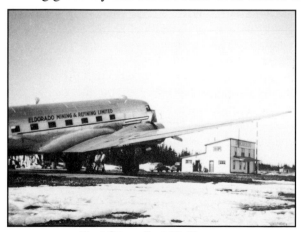

First Stop—Fort McMurray

extreme left, passed away with distance while a hundred transient clouds came between the sun and the terrain, their shadows gamboling with that of our aircraft projected on the snow—white screen below.

"What's that down there?", came the voice of one who was not lost in slumber. He pointed anxiously to a settlement surrounded in a blanket of snow, its rooftops gleaming in the April sunshine. Bodies stirred, blinked, rubbed themselves to increase the circulation. "What the hell's all the racket for?", came the unmistakable voice of the inebriate. Managing momentary control of his jelly—like mass, he joined us at the windows. A quick circuit (as though the pilot was anxious to land and be on his way again), a series of bumps, a flurry of wet snow past the plastic windows...we came to a sudden stop. About two hundred miles due north we had reached Fort McMurray.

Climbing out of the doorway into the nine o'clock sunshine I was greeted by a windsock fluttering above a white frame building. This is the entire airport! Entering into conversation I gathered that it was the only serviceable runway during the unusual cold spell that struck the entire country in 1947. Glancing at the short landing strip I was thoroughly convinced of the old adage concerning small things. Two bags and their owners are deposited, a short exchange of banter between the attendant and pilot as they check the engine, and once more our angry machine roars, paws the ground, eats up another runway (this one white) and throws itself into space...

Glad of my all−wool raiment I huddled with the remaining passengers, all like so many more pieces of freight to be unloaded at a certain destination. From far below the endless vista of frozen, white wastes appeared through a clear spot on the frosted windows, dotted here and there with a clump of thin spruce and occasionally cut by a snakelike river winding its way into infinity. The heads of those aboard lolled with the drowsiness accompanying cold, the engines droned monotonously and the miles passed on.... Only when one flies over this country can it be realized that spring in Edmonton is not spring two hundred miles North. It is a gradual tapering off into winter. So as the miles increased the lakes were replaced by tons of snow, soon to melt like their brothers farther south and seek their own courses in life, away from the homes in which they were nurtured. Over the ice− bound Athabasca River...Lake Athabasca...Fort Chipewyan−one time headquarters for Alexander Mackenzie, discoverer of the Mackenzie River waterway to the Arctic in 1789. And then like boa constrictors twisting and turning, the Peace and Slave riverbeds appeared, caught in the merciless throes of winter. Following somewhat the course of the latter, a mile above, we were led to another tiny settlement barely discernible but for the reflections of sunlight on tin roofs.

Second Stop−Fort Smith
Northwest Territories

Eleven o'clock. We 'bump down' at the second important stop on our aerial Trail of '98: Fort Smith. Only slightly larger than the last airport it boasts as improvements: a nose hangar, larger gas pump and a C.P.A. waiting room for passengers. Our stay here is slightly longer and the warmth of the waiting room is greatly appreciated. At this point I lose most of my travelling companions. They depart for mines and logging camps far in the bush, accessible only by plane− one of which, to my surprise, rather impolitely and without any delay, picks them up and disappears over the snow−ridden hills beyond. I feel a sudden void. The small handful left climb aboard, assume their former positions among the cargoes and wait. A foreboding silence reigns over us as though we have lost forever some of our ranks, knowing full well that we may be next. We await with our thoughts for the guillotine blades of the propellers to cut the air again.

Well over half way to our destination we became airborne. The atmosphere within the 'craft became colder. Below, the endless stretches of snow continued, broken only by sporadic spruce and animal tracks in endless quantities. It was a pleasant relief when the shores of Great Slave Lake came into view, stretching for miles on either side of our ship, beyond the horizon to the west, where it merged with the sky, giving no hint as to where lake ended and sky began.

"Gee, I'd hate to be those guys below!" said one of us. Once more we massed at the windows to see what broke the white monotony. 'Cat−trains' are a common sight in this country, being the only other commercial means of entering the frozen reaches. There below I caught my first sight of one such outfit, stranded half way across the lake in the path of the severest winds. Then I remembered the exciting broadcasts earlier this spring describing the tragic fate that overcame more than one such train. In desperation they burned the truck boxes and all wood available from their loads in an effort to keep warm. Perhaps this is an unfortunate, I reflected, not envying its isolated position.

Workhorses North
Yellowknife, Northwest Territories

More snow, spruce and the endless bleak rock that had appeared as we coursed northward, greeted us. But when was Yellowknife going to break the monotony? I had heard much about this gold−camp; but to the Outsider impressions are many and varied. Since the boom in '39 an endless amount of stories (enlarged, as are so often the tales of mining and prospecting camps) had filtered to the Gateway City. These naturally aroused the curiosity of the adventurous and of times confused the general public who must rely for their news on the word of mouth of those intent on selling gold and oil stocks; or perhaps on the general 'guff' that manages through the Moccasin Telegraph to reach the ears of those unable to tear away from their established roots. I had heard, thought, but now I waited... waited for the sight of more tin roofs reflecting the sun's rays skyward. Then it happened. With question marks cluttering my brain we passed over Yellowknife Bay...the Horseshoe. The faint outline of buildings assured me we were here at last. Questions marks grew. Altitude fell. I braced myself for a shaky landing.

Tumbling from a loaded Douglas the most outstanding building one first sees is the Yellowknife Hotel, still clad in its original coat of paint, now a drab yellow. A varied assortment of all sized and coloured buildings fall off from the heights, ending at the base of the Old Townsite in a large, elongated, white building, its red roof emblazoned with three huge, white letters: C.P.A. Feelings are mixed as I lug my baggage over the snow to the office. Civilization, as the Outside is jocularly called, is behind me. I am alone. A feeling of isolation creeps over me. But I beat it off with a reassuring glance at the assortment of aircraft lining the edge of the bay, each bush−pilot fondling his own Norseman, Taylorcraft, Cub, Fox Moth, Hornet, Husky or Anson−not unlike nurses fussing over newborn. Then I am initiated to the din that will soon become a part of the daily symphony of Yellowknife. A Norseman taking off deafens my ears with its unmerciful roar which, echoing back and forth across the bay, pursues me to the door of the Canadian Pacific Airlines.

Gold Boom Town
Yellowknife, Northwest Territories

CHAPTER TWO

GOLD BOOM TOWN

You meet such friendly people in Northern towns. Dropping my bag to the floor I was met by the smiles of several curious onlookers. Inquiring about the place, I met Don Cameron. "A good home−cooked meal? Try Ruth's place, up the hill", he proffered. A friend made, I passed along the bottom street.

On the left stands the Hudson's Bay Company. It is not the mere trading post generally associated with such settlements but a modern store serviced by a mixed staff. Civilization's wasting no time pushing North, I thought. Next appears the Post Office, as busy a place as any in town (with the exception, of course, of the beverage hall), occupying a site on the waterfront farther south. Turning up the hill leading to the business section a well−laden billboard informs me that a theatre is in existence. Adjacent appear the Wildcat Cafe and the Canadian Bank of Commerce. Slowly my old impressions are shattered one by one. The next turn reveals Joe's Barber Shop complete

The Honourable Company

with pole, the Yellowknife Rooms, Busy Bee Cafe and Ruth's Roving Hornet. This is my immediate destination without further delay. An Oblate priest had said to me some time later: "When the belly is full the rest of the world looks all right". With a similar thought in mind, I desire that Yellowknife present its best. So the door of Ruth's banged shut on the hungry vagabond.

Ruth's Roving Hornet is a small, homey cafe overlooking the west bay. While Ruth patters back and forth serving between intervals in the kitchen, I find myself scanning the panorama from this vantage point. An endless procession of aircraft come and go, their noises and unmistakable colours as individual as the swarthy pilots who fly them. They carry freight and passengers to such outposts as Diversified, Lexindin, North Inca and Peg Tantellum mines; returning two−hourly for another mixed cargo, periodically unloading core boxes filled with possible rich colours awaiting the verdict of the local assayer.

No More Barter

"You're just a little late for dinner", came a voice lacking in feminine timidity. I was jerked from my spell, at the same time receiving a small improvised menu. Being an Outsider I had ample reason to be surprised as I surveyed the A La Carte list of dishes. This is what met my scrutiny:

Cream of Tomatoe Soup	.20
Tomatoe Juice	.15

Sandwiches

Combination Salad	1.00
Hamburger	.50
Liverworst & Onions	.50
Denver	.50
Peanut Butter	.50
Cheese	.40
Cold Veal	.40

Pies

Apple—Raisin—Banana Cream	.25

Outside, the inflation and cost of living is soaring; in the North it has soared! But there is a compensation for all things, or a fairly good reason somewhere if there isn't. This I discovered later when receiving $1.00 per hour for labour wages. So I had soup, lettuce and tomato, a piece of pie and milk (always in Klim form). It was not until I had picked my teeth, chatted with an oldtimer and had several glimpses of aircraft churning their way along the frozen bay that I realized I was the proud possessor of a dime. My original stake was 10 cents. I had started with determination. But this would not pay the $1.25 bill! I felt uneasy. Already aware of the warmth of the people, I approached Ruth and gave my plot away. "Oh, that's all right", she said benignly, "You'll have some money in a day or so." Thus I first witnessed the trusting nature of Northerners. Smiling largely, like a boy caught in a prank, I assured Ruth I intended to stay in the settlement for some time; and with this I made for the door. Broad Street claimed me. As I walked from The Hornet I thought of the T—Bone steak that could be circulating within me had I been back in Edmonton. I decided then to try all eating houses till I knew exactly where I stood in the realm of food. Such was my culinary introduction to Yellowknife.

Main Street—Yellowknife

Contented inwardly for the time being, I surveyed the street scene. There was the office of McDougall & Wheeler—Brokers, the Coffee Shop, the Imperial Bank of Canada built entirely of logs, and the Yellowknife Hotel mothering it from the heights of rock on which the original townsite is constructed. Nothing irregular disturbed the tranquility of the main street.

Yellowknife is a 'boom—town' only slightly *reminiscent of earlier gold—rush settlements in the Yukon and Alaska during the fabulous year of 1898. No six—guns ride the flanks of bewhiskered prospectors, although beards are not uncommon sights; no great mobs mull and push their way down the lone street or lean on outer railings; no music drifts from cheap dance halls with swinging doors.* But there is an audible din coming from the top of the town. Interested, I strolled upwards. From a square, unpainted board building comes the familiar 'Song of the Inebriates' in its unintelligible drone...crescendo... diminuendo...crescendo...rising and falling with the opening of the outer door.

Then it all happened: as though the Powers—That—Be had read my thoughts, a human carcass came hurtling through the open door with the accompaniment of another vocal crescendo from within. Then all was silence but for the bitter curses of the unfortunate prospector. Picking himself up from the snow he turned, and with feeble railery tossed his last insults at the shabby building, then trudged, a loose figure, down the hill. There was life in Yellowknife after all! Here is the social centre for the males of this gold town. Here is where the long winter hours are passed with lies, liquid and braggadosio. Here is where more gold mines are discovered than anywhere else in the Northwest Territories! It is the hard−living prospector's winter home where he spends most of his time and all of his money earned the previous summer. Little is it realized, but the owner, Bert Ingraham, has the richest mine in the vicinity−a liquid gold mine running in one continual shift−the Yellowknife Hotel.

So absorbed had I become in the community life that I had plumb forgotten accommodation for the night. I was a man without a home or a bed. But it was not night yet. Something will crop up, I assured my ever−optimistic self. It always does. So I continued my perusal with a visit to an address scrawled hastily on an envelope before my Edmonton departure. It read: Don Thompson, Bush Pilot, Yellowknife, N.W.T.

Another 'Pole' North

"Don's away today. He's in one day and out the next", said the plump, jovial clerk in the office. "Guess I'll see him later", I said, disappointed. It is always pleasant to know one person in a strange place. I knew no one. "Where're ya bunkin?", asked Bert without prompting. "Dunno yet", I admitted frankly. "How'd ya like to use Don's bunk for the night? He won't mind". Seeing an ounce of nocturnal security I grabbed at the favour. But I did not expect the next remark. "By the way", said Bert, eyeing me curiously, "you look new here; might need a couple of bucks to see you till you get

connected... It'll get you something to eat, anyway." I thought with a start: 'Who told him I only had a dime?' Why this sudden gesture of generosity? What Samaritan is this? I realized one thing: I was in the North! So it is true, what they say about this country.

As darkness fell I felt completely at home. We talked far into the evening....It was midnight when sleeping bags and narrow bunks claimed the man from Outside and the clerk from Toronto. How much in the way of a Northerner he was in *his* short six months. How long would it take for the country to tell on me? The coal−oil lamp flickered...glowed a short moment...and became part of the night. A faint snore from across the shack was all that filled the silence.

Eaglespread Architecture

The chill of a northern morning brought us about early. Unconcerned as to shaving for the next long while, I groped for warmth from the tin firepot. With meals as I had discovered them the day before, there was but one alternative. I must get to work, and quick! Thanking Bert for the night, I started out the office door when a voice halted me in my tracks. "You look pretty hefty...how'd you like a job?" What sort of a land was this? Where was I? Could seven−hundred miles make this much difference? "Well, do you want it or not?" demanded the man in the loud, checkered shirt.

My old−time flame Lady Luck was still tagging along. Within the hour I was loading aircraft. I was an essential part of all that activity I had witnessed from the Hornet the day before. For the time being my future looked quite certain.

The days came and went. So did the endless procession of aircraft. Dozens accepted and discharged their odd cargoes of oil, gasoline, timbers, core boxes and all shapes and forms of food packed especially for Northerners. It was seldom a pleasant task loading these aerial monsters, but oh! the satisfaction as each winged its way towards the horizon; and, too, the delightful momentary rest.

First Job

As Fate unerringly designs, I am thrown once more into the company of men who have dreams—dreams like any man's dreams of going somewhere and doing something. "How'd you like to shack up with me?", asked the guy on the other side of an oil barrel. Grunting, I affirmed with a strained "Sure 'nuff". I was about ready to flop in my bed under the Big Dipper. "I've got a tenthouse...only half in use. You might as well share the heat with me", said my new found friend, Alec. And that's how my 'home' for the next while came to be.

Home Sweet Home

**Tom Dornboss
Dutch Waterbearer**

It is interesting to notice one's feeling of security immediately a roof covers the head, a fire glows red in the stove. With shelter above, a fire glowing, some food in the apple—box cupboard, and a cosy sleeping robe to crawl into when the embers died, I became aware of myself formulating new plans. 'But why so soon?' I asked myself. 'And before you're settled?' But the Goddess of Impulse knew better than to answer. She knew it was that hidden voice, that lure of the wind and snow, the combination of forces that offer pleasant resistance to some men. It had smelled me out already! Knowing I was to be its willing victim, I let the plans merge into their own crazy network.

I slept well on this my second night in the most—talked—of town in Canada. Morning found me eager to commence what plans I had laid earlier in the year. I must act soon, for already the sun and moon are dual possessors of the heavens, I reminded myself. This to a Northerner is a sure sign of spring.

Every frontier town has its characters. Yellowknife is no exception. Among the oldtimers that one is likely to meet is Tom Dornboss, the Watercarrier. A tall, red—faced Dutchman, he is invariably seen in any part of the community carrying two pails of water dangling from a crude yoke slung across his shoulders. As I watched the old man trudging up the incline of Broad Street, content to labour in his official capacity of town waterbearer, it was not hard to place him beside the dykes in his native garb, clopping over the cobblestones in clogs, carrying in his dilatory manner the dual buckets hanging from the crude yoke familiar to peasants of European countries. Tom let me in on a little of his present and past as we walked. "I hail from Groningen, Holland. Forsook it many years ago," he said, setting the pails to rest on the snow. "I am quite content here to carry water for 25 cents a pail and look after my few claims. I read much on the world situation in my bachelor cabin." With much of his hard Dutch accent still intact, Tom pipes: "It is a good country. A man can work hard if he wants to and when he desires, with no one to boss him all the time!" Thus another freedom lover has found his haven in this northerly mining town.

As I consumed a steak in the Pioneer Lunch under the proprietorship of short, corpulent Joe Gerhard, I enjoyed listening to the travels of Jack Amos. Between bites he said: "Been followin' the frontiers since I was a kid....from Mexico to Alaska. In fact, I came north from Texas as a Ranger." And here he is, single and carefree, a jack−of−all trades who does his share of gold−seeking. Without a doubt Jack is still following the last frontier of Canada perhaps still farther north than Yellowknife. It was such little scraps of conversation, day by day, that brought out the character of these northerners. And day by day they began to take a hold of me.

Wizened Pete Schwartz, typified by his battered, well ventilated hat with turned−up brim, quite reminiscent of western stage coach drivers, is another of the familiar faces seen about the gold town. Always on the go, he darts here and there talking 'gold talk' or joking over a meal in Joe's. I had just finished one of these humorous conversations and one of Joe's steaks in the company of Pete; sauntered outside into the clear air when the sound of music greeted my ears. "What's that?" I asked. "Oh, *that* damnable noise you mean! Why, that's our blacksmith down the road. You can hear him for miles but he's quite a guy, Felix is." I needed no further introduction. There is no Longfellow chestnut tree in the Canadian north; but Yellowknife has the person of Felix Grenier to add a little character to this settlement as he sends his notes from the anvil and the smoke from his forge to the senses of the townspeople.

Felix, as can be guessed, is a Frenchman. He was born in a village near Avignon. With the dormant wanderlust hidden in most of us coming to life, he found himself in America travelling as a blacksmith and labourer. Clang! went the hammer on the anvil, followed by a brief pause as I stood in the light seeping through the doorway. Up went the wide moustache in a naturally friendly smile. "Hello there! You make a lot of noise for one man", I challenged. "But eet's my vork", he half apologized; and laughter filled the smithy.

Conversation became as warm as the fire amongst the coals and I dared ask a few questions. "Are you married?", to which came the terse comment: "No sireeee:... I am single and happy. A man is a damn fool to marry these days." In the free−speaking manner of his

Out to Lunch

Felix Grenier
Village Blacksmith

11

race, he continued: "I have lived my life. I am happy. They say I have a good twenty years to go; but I know different," came forth with the resignation of a true philosopher. "I am seventy," he continued, smiling with satisfaction as though he had already fooled life with his three score and ten, his walrus moustache moving in unison with the many wrinkles. "I just need four or five thousand dollars and I shall return to France and die there. It will be enough!" he said, with a note of finality. With this the bent figure clad in his familiar black hat and soiled apron trudged towards the waterfront swinging a pail with the abandon of a man twenty years his junior.

Father Gathay
Order of Mary Immaculate

Gesticulating impulsively as he climbed the Broad Street hill, the black−robed figure of a priest wound its way upwards. I waited. He reached the summit. "Kinda tough on an old man", I challenged, hoping for a retort from the bearded gentleman. It came with the speed of the northwind that he has bucked for the past few years. "Now listen, my son..." and behind the whiskers I sensed a broad smile. Here was the first of the Roman Catholic Oblate Order that I met. His name was Father Gathay, a name well known throughout the North. Many years he has spent in this country among the Indians. "What brought you here as a pioneer priest?" I asked. In his jocular manner, stroking his long black beard, he said abruptly: "I was too wild for Belgium!" Satisfied at the priest's frankness, I let well enough alone.

We walked together to the Mission. In a comfortable chair I heard parts of an extremely interesting life bared. Gathay, a six footer, is proud of his fifty−two years hidden well behind the superfluous growth of whiskers. A native of Belgium, he waited ten years to join the Oblate Order. Hardships appeared a part of the daily diet, as the Father, with eyes and mind into the past, recalled: "I travelled about 400 miles a week by dogteam throughout my scattered parish of Great Slave Lake. That was in my early days. There I baptised the first white baby." As the visible lines on his face became concentrated, he leaned forward in his chair. "Much of my time I was alone with the dog team..." He trailed off as though away over the Great White Wilderness on a mission of goodwill. "But I cannot tell you all!....I must pack!....Time!....Time!....Time!. It is our best friend and worst enemy".

From other lips I gleaned more of his peculiar background. "Understand he lost his folks in the First Great War," said the prospector. "Shot in front of his face. Pushed in a trench to be buried. Yeah, they claim it's so! A German officer seeing the young lad in the lineup pulled him away by the arm saying: "You're too young to die!" "Guess its a good thing too, cause we shore enjoy his company. Some of them long, cold winter nights he plays cards with us. (He was an entertaining magician, all the time spying on the Jerries till the war ended.) Always wins too! But of course he gives the winnin's back....Wouldn't be like a priest to keep 'em." Busy preparing to go Outside, I took no more of the Father's time, saying I would call later at his request, and departed. However, it was later that afternoon I was to accost this energetic man again. He was bound for the Consolidated Mining and Smelting Company's hospital to make his goodwill rounds. Before we had gone two blocks I realized that here was a walker. "Climb in" came a voice as an auto halted... "might as well give those dogs a rest", shouted a Mounted Policeman. We did. But in the process the priest found himself seated precariously upon a confiscated case of beer. Suggestively he chimed: "It's a good thing there are a few of us around to keep them out of trouble", winking at me, a twinkle in his eye. Once more this northern brand of humour, so vital, hit the mark. That was the last I was to see of Father Gathay.

As I mentioned before, it was my luck that I should fall amongst adventurers. With one week's work behind me and its equivalent in hard cash resulting from the arduous efforts of cargo loading, I managed to convince a Half−Breed (one of the crew of locals who appeared sporadically when the necessity for funds compelled them to labour) that he was wasting his time in the endless pursuits common to so many of the males of Yellowknife. As for myself, I was eager to pick up the loose and worn threads of the *Trail of '98.*

Plans came to completion. It was decided that we should meet early in the morning at my tent. The grubstake procured from the local Hudson's Bay Company lay packed, awaiting a bearer. Innumerable tinned goods (the most common form of food in this country) comprised the stake. This, I thought, did not look too healthy in ratio to the gradually melting snow. "Wish we had the equivalent in drymeat (caribou strips sun dried and smoked) and I'd also feel better about the dogs", said the native. "Well, let's wait till we have to…. I'd like to be initiated gradually", I said. My initiation was not long in coming….

The Law Goes North

Freddie Mercredi and Family

A Familiar 'Husky!'　　　　　**Where All The Gold Stops**

CHAPTER THREE

BRIEF INTERLUDE

Saturday morning at seven I was awakened by a knock on the door and the unheralded entry of my companion−to−be. Smiling gingerly, the native queried: "All set to go?" These were the words I had listened for all week. Was I dreaming? Was I awake? This same morning I had arranged the haversack and such travelling necessities in a pile. In the meantime, curled up in my robe, I awaited the doubtful arrival of Fred Mercredi, who had once before postponed the trip. With the local dance in full swing, the carousing high and tribal visitors aplenty, I had resigned myself to another delay. But here he was, asking me if I was ready! One leap and I stood before him fully clothed with only my sleeping bag to push into its obstinate container. Tying a knot on the top I threw it with the other luggage, turned to my friend, saying: "Well...let's

get!" Suddenly I remembered: I had put aside a 'starter'. Waking my slumbering tentmate I bade him have a quick shot as a temporary parting toast. It went three ways, and two of us made toward the dogsled waiting on the bank of Yellowknife Bay. Eager whines and anxious howls made me run with excitement. I would not be satisfied till the sled was in motion and the water tank at the zenith of the townsite disappeared with distance.

All Set to 'Mush'

"*Mush!*" yelled the 'Breed. "Hang on!" he threw my way. One word was all that was necessary for Ben, Blackie, Ring and Skookum. Snow flew; runners swished over the crisp morning crust of frost; the dogs whined with eagerness. We were off!

On the Trail

Two miles later we rounded the last island; turning to the sou'west the water tank and Yellowknife disappeared. Negus Mine, puffing black smoke and belching rude, mechanical noises on its graveyard shift, came into view. Miles passed swiftly and civilization, it seemed, was behind us.

As the sun climbed the snow became soft. Tongues began to hang; the 'Breed cursed; I was in ecstasy. "We'll have to pull up till night when the snow hardens," came from the mouth of my friend who was continually eyeing the surface in perplexed fashion, trotting beside the sled to ease the burden. "Got no 'leases'(runners)...makes sledding tough...not fair to my dogs," he gasped, between breaths. "We'll stop at the cabin ahead...want you to meet the fellow there; he's quite a character." So we spotted signs of life at the cabin nestled amongst a thousand islands. A small figure waves us in. Ben, sensing a rest, quickened the pace. His brothers caught the lead. We scraped to a halt on the rocky surface at the door of the cabin.

A small man garbed in 'leathertops' into which his pants were carelessly tucked, a coat sweater and a once fawn ski—cap, stood smiling at us. Our introduction was brief; the handshake offered, firm. "What're you doing 'traipsin' around this country?" came the expected query. "Just doin' some real down—to—earth living," I retorted, a smile of devilment crossing my face. Something seemed to stir, then flicker within the man. His weatherbeaten face took on another expression and the bluest eyes I've ever seen looked into the past of his own hazardous youth. "Guess we can stay till nightfall and make some 'leases' for the sled, D'Arcy?" interrupted the third party. "Yes, Yes,

The D'Arcy Ardens

...come on in...there's fish for the dogs down the yard apiece." There are some men who are too modest to mention their contributions to a fast—changing world. Here I decided was one of those Oldtimers (as they like to be called) who could tell a few. He assured me I would still be able to find plenty to see and do. I daresay his optimism, which has not been dulled by the years, was the first real encouragement proffered so far. I knew right off that his company would be appreciated in our short stay and sensed he would have enough stories to keep an interested audience listening until a chill crept into the room and the embers needed reshuffling.

Lunch time proved my suspicions. "Pull up a chair, fellows...might as well get one good meal under your belts...you've got a lot of distance to cover," invited the little man. His wife placed us accordingly, set steaming dishes in front of large appetites and an air of pleasantness filled the room and the ensuing conversation.

There is a humorous saying in the North that a white man after three years in the country either goes crazy or marries an Indian wife. Well, D'Arcy is very sane and has a wonderful Indian wife. "This is all of my family that are around at present," he said, glancing from the head of the table at his wife, daughter and adopted Eskimo boy (saved from infanticide during an Eskimo famine). "The four boys are all out working or hunting...but it looks more like normal with you fellows here. Go ahead, just reach for anything you want, we're not proud." Minutes passed and I waited for the conversation to change to his past. Then, as though my thoughts were read, he pushed his Time magazine to the window sill, looked up momentarily, then said: "It was a queer turn of events that landed me in these parts." Cutting into the tender caribou steak on the plate before me, I looked up. "I was about eighteen when I landed in the Yukon in the capacity of Government surveyor in 1900, if I remember rightly. Anyway, it was just after the big Klondike Gold Rush...things were still roarin' then, and before I knew it we were in that famous town. Guess I'm getting ahead of myself?..." "Anyhow, getting back to my home in Ottawa. I'd finished school and college and had an opportunity to complete the crew of 23 of an expedition to the Arctic under Captain Bernier. But when I discovered they were all Frenchmen, I declined the offer. Couldn't see two years in the lonely Arctic in the company of 23 'frogs' talking their native tongue the whole time...oh no, not me. So I accepted an office job, but soon bored with the routine which became a matter of 'signing in' in the morning, I asked the boss for a change. "The only field work left is in the Yukon," he said sternly. "Then send me there!" I said.

"So you find me in Dawson, finally, after laying a few boundary lines along the Alaska—Yukon sector. It was some city, it was; six—guns were not yet outlawed, exchange was in gold dust, saloons were really saloons—sawdust on the floor, a brass rail to perch your foot on and songs from the line of chorus girls as they thumped their can—can to the accompaniment of tinny music and boisterous approval of the bewhiskered old prospectors just in from the bush for the first time in months...what a time everybody had!" The caribou made a second round as the weatherbeaten face temporarily lost its wrinkles.

"Dawson at that time had a population of about 30,000 of which some 2,000 were dance—hall girls eager to entertain an easily entertained audience of pioneers in the gay halls, where many a 'poke' was dumped down the back of a charming lady's abbreviated evening dress, the gold dust scattering widely in all directions on the sawdust floor. Next morning the floorsweeper would sift the mixture, floating the sawdust to the top, leaving a good sized 'find' as residue," D'Arcy says, with one of those hearty chuckles that wrinkles his face, the extra—blue eyes nearly losing themselves. "There were more floorsweepers in Dawson City than prospectors. It was as proud a vocation as any other, and certainly more highly paid than many! No dollar bills were to be seen in the city; for the gold poke, coming usually in the $100.00 and $200.00 sizes, did away with such civilized means of exchange. The gold dust from the placer claims would be brought into a bank or store, weighed, discounted for its percentage of black sand and dumped into bins accordingly. Many a time we wondered about the clerk's finger, but I guess he had to live too, for they were never paid too much.

"Jack London? Yes, come to think of it I did meet him at Nome. He had already gained fame for his dare—devil luck at running the Whitehorse Rapids in the original headlong rush. Everyone thought well of him, and he could look after himself should a ruckus start, but mind you he was not an instigator of trouble"...

Unabashed, the little man went on to tell of the infamous Klondike City across the river of that name, from Dawson. "500 or so little buildings housed an equal number of good—time girls...far superior in class to the modern 'loose girl'...they'd never steal your wallet if you treated them like women...yes, there was some fine women among them." One didn't quite know where his mind and thoughts were, but he must have re—crossed the swing bridge to Dawson; for a moment elapsed as he pulled at a caribou rib, continuing: "They were courageous women who ventured into that God—forsaken country eager to share the adventure with the menfolk. There were no finer women in the world than those who ventured to Dawson in them days...baronesses, countesses, duchesses from all over the world, Europe especially...they were real women!" he said with nostalgic admiration.

"A wonderful meal, Mother" said the Oldtimer pushing his chair back from the table. "And some interesting experiences, too," I said. "Maybe if you come back this way you can stay awhile and I'll tell you a few more yarns about my associations with Dr. Anderson and Stefansson, the two Arctic explorers, far inside the Arctic Circle...about other experiences in the Northwest Territories around Bear Lake, Dease Bay, Cameron Bay, Coppermine, Coronation Gulf and Victoria Island, where I lived in close communion with the Eskimo...oh, there's so darn much, but say, you'd better get those leases on that sled...the days aren't getting any colder!" In a moment empty dishes had full possession of the table.

Here is a man who lives close to Nature in a Northern Garden of Eden which is a cross between Jack Miner's Sanctuary and the Martin Johnson home at Lake Paradise, Africa. It is equally surrounded by wildlife of every description (that very day the last of the caribou heading north for the summer migration passed within close range of the cabin). D'Arcy and his wife became elated in describing the vast herds of caribou that fill the entire bay and how they have shot them from the doorstep. As Martin and Osa Johnson became attached to their elephant friends, so have the Ardens a deep respect for their migratory friends, the caribou.

A Northern Garden of Eden

D'Arcy is a surveyor, geologist, trapper, prospector, fisherman and an at—home politician with a concern for world affairs which he garners from his favourite magazines: Time, Newsweek and the Reader's Digest. But this is as far as his regard for the Outside goes. When I asked him if he ever wanted to return to civilization I received a similar reply to the one given Fullerton Waldo back in the 1920's. "Define your Civilization!" There he is still, as happy a man as one would want to meet, living on the border of ever—outward—pushing Canada and his vast beloved Northland.

Yes, I would re—visit D'Arcy Arden. It was a must.

"That'll have to do," grunted Freddie the halfbreed, flopping the dogsled over on its new 'leases'. Looking from my blistered palm (worn out from turning screws) to my companion, a smile broke over my sweating countenance. It was silent admiration for native ingenuity. "It's getting cooler too. Wind's coming up," I said with optimism. "Let's get out of here then...I'm getting damned restless." He had spoken for both of us as we made ready to depart.

"Sure you've got everything?" queried the kindly D'Arcy, appearing at the cabin door. "Better take a few extra fish; and by the way, I see you haven't a 'tarp'. Can't travel without shelter in Spring...it rains now and then, you know." Pulling a series of half hitches to the criss—crossed roped binding everything neatly in the Mackenzie sled, the native looked about him, glancing anxiously toward the western horizon. These are moments that white men can respect. So I left full judgement to him. "Looks right...we'll head straight for that island way out in the bay." It was an exciting moment. We were about to slip into the Great White Wilderness. "Well, Allen, don't forget my invitation; and Mercredi, look after the Cheechako." "He's big enough to look after himself," retorted my friend with one of his broad halfbreed smiles. "Mush!..mush!"and before any further exchange of words could take place the dogs yelped with excitement, snow flew in all directions and a steady *swish, swish* of sled runners announced our departure. I turned once, when the pace was established, to see D'Arcy and his wife waving from the open cabin door. Then a glistening sheet of white claimed us.

This afternoon I fully realized just what the Call of the North is. It is a silent beckoning from all the inanimate that stretches for so many miles in every direction, keeping one optimistic and the mind ever alert, wondering what is around the next bend or bared shoulder or rock clothed only in a sparse cape of spruce. The incessant white gives one a feeling of smallness, throwing a challenge at dogs and driver, the only visible life and moving object in miles. A hot sun and melting snow are the odds stacked against one reaching his destination on time.

I can best describe the North as a challenge. It is that to all, and especially to eager youth intent on making its own discoveries. To buck the wind, to travel with wet feet all day and ignore them, to bear the steady glare of sun on snow which causes the cursed snow—blindness, to rely on a team of dogs and oneself when others aren't present to call upon, to make and eat one's own bannock, to be independent, and most of all to be out in the open, free to commune mentally and physically with Mother Nature who gives no mercy: she is your best friend and worst enemy.

The white miles slid behind the runners and stretched far ahead. My native companion and myself alternated positions, running behind or riding the well—laden sled, at intervals. Four dogs, eager as their master for the trail, hung their tongues low, panting with the unison of their gait. With that peace of mind one suddenly discovers with freedom, I leaned back on the load and drew a few hasty conclusions. Already I felt a part of this vastness.

Hour after hour the landscape changes slightly. Great Slave Lake branches Northwest towards Fort Rae; the jagged shoreline gives way to a deep bay which will, in turn, give way to a creek just beginning to melt, enticing the muskrats to venture into the bright sunlight. Now and then a few drying bones and a caribou head tell their own story. Fresh caribou caches appear frequently — the animals minus a few choice parts such as the liver, brains or tongue (the part of the animal most cherished by the Indians).

Fort Rae Named after Dr. John Rae, surgeon to the Hudson's Bay Company, who travelled overland on foot some 20,000 miles and walked 7,500 miles of Arctic coastline—an all time record of discovery. However, his greatest discovery in 1856 was that of the remains of the lost Sir John Franklin expedition and their resorting to cannnibalism as verified by the Eskimo. Thus he claimed the &10,000 reward established by the British government.

I have forgotten to mention an incident shortly after we left the Arden home. We had decided to pull up for tea because of the sticky snow. As the pot boiled and the dogs rested on the rocks (on which the sled is usually drawn if convenient), the sound of bells came to our ears. Looking far to the east we could see nothing, for an island stood in the line of vision. Then above the bells came the cussings, yellings and encouragements of the driver downwind to our campsite. His identity was established as he came closer, his dogs' tails high and they pulling with eagerness a wide, wooden sled (the only one like it in the vicinity) atop of which sat a small figure, legs dangling to the side.

Once more we sipped tea and exchanged words with D'Arcy Arden. From his pocket he produced a pair of forgotten sunglasses. An hour later this thoughtful gent waved farewell, his happy dogs bouncing back on the trail they had come, the voice of their master carrying pleasantly back to us as he enjoyably cussed his dogs (a habit with most men on the trail). I thought to myself: "I'll bet it was a good opportunity for D'Arcy to leave his domestic labours, board his sled and get out into the open." The measure of thoughtfulness common to Northerners had been demonstrated again.

As the day progressed towards evening we had an unexpected but rather pleasant surprise. Two Breed trappers—Dodd Lafferty and Ernie Camsell—on the hunt for a creek, met us. "Know any good creeks?" asked one. "Haven't had much luck yet," added the other. "No, but we might as well all travel together." So two became four as we cut off the scattered islands at the junction of the lake arm.

Evening advanced to twilight; twilight to dusk; dusk to the semi—darkness of early spring in the Northland. Our dogteam became a moving silhouette rising and falling with the irregularity of the trail. A pleasant eeriness invaded the haunting loneliness of everything. Was I dreaming? No, that was impossible, for we had not slept yet...

Meeting Dodd Lafferty and Ernie Camsell

It was so strange to see the sun rising while the moon still rode on high. Stranger still was the speed at which it ascended. Gazing at the early morning scene with a certain awe, I realized just how much of the day's early beauty most of us ordinarily miss. Although I would not prescribe a 4 a.m. rising for everyone, I shall never forget the dual lighting in the High North as the round, rose sun broke its reflected prismatic colours and began its ascent into a cold, grey dawn.

We had travelled all night and here it was, the lull before all living creatures stir with the welcome warmth of the sun. All this time I had watched the changing pageant of colours: the blackish greys, so ominous, began to soften with the addition of white from the nor'east. The nun—grey sky of early morn has a beauty all its own—a kind of charcoal etching. The gay mauves, reds, oranges and yellows of evening have exchanged their costumes for the dance of morning: a slow, changing panorama of steel and battleship grey.

Beauty soon fades with fatigue. The dogs, slowed to a crawl by slushy snow and unable to stand any longer, we chose the first clearing for our halt. It happened to be a barren rock; but who cared? The dogs fell asleep in the harness and their masters soon followed suit. Then out of the dawn came an irksome voice. A noisome crow, unable to sleep, let all living creatures know of his troubles as he voiced his grievance to the morning. Disturbed, we echoed ours in return and sleep overcame us one by one.

A late morning and a hot sun found us on the move again, eager to give the dogs the benefit of the frosty snow. Fish caches are a common sight on the lake. As we passed a large one later this morning we knew Big Rock to be close at hand. (This was the bay wherein lay a creek in which, it had been rumoured, dwelt an abundance of muskrats.) "That's where a party spent the entire winter fishing...but the fish are rotting 'cause of no boxes to ship them out," said one of the natives. As I stood there surveying the endless miles of timber, an obvious absurdity struck Reason between the eyes. I thought: Canada saturated with timber...post—war unemployment...thousands dying of starvation in other corners of the globe. Somehow it didn't add up.

Pete Baker's cabin is a welcome sight for any traveller looking for a change in the landscape. It lies in the centre of an Indian encampment. "Want to meet some Dogribs?" asked my friend. "Sure, but I don't imagine much conversation will pass between us," I suggested. Grinning, all four of us forgot about Pete's supply cabin and entered an Indian dwelling. Speaking dialect, my breed friends make acquaintance, informing them that I am a policeman looking for stolen fish. Innocent of the goings−on, I am told I must act the part. So a policeman I am today! Frightened, they make assurances of their ignorance of such activities. Later the air rang with the laughter of three halfbreeds at the expense of a phony policeman. Still later the act was repeated and I was forced to carry the litigate role further, convincing another family of ten huddled about on the floor I was a Mountie on a routine inspection. "How is the 'ratting' (muskrat hunting) in these parts?" I asked, trying unsuccessfully to ease the tension. In their innocence they rushed to show me the volume of caribou drymeat hung from the ceiling. Another volume of Northern laughter resounded over the snows and, knowing the efficiency of the moccasin telegraph, I felt sure of being a marked man at all future villages enroute.

In late May the snow melts fast and one must proceed mostly at night, resting up during the heat of the day. So it came about that we spent the afternoon cooking a large meal in Pete's cabin, thereafter sleeping off the effects of a hard night and a huge repast. Realizing our own provisions, which we had originally planned for a three−day trip to Fort Rae, were now low, we 'borrowed' enough necessities for baking bannock (flour, baking powder, and butter−the Cheechako recipe), left the usual note of thanks and pushed across the Bay.

Indian settlements can be the most putrid spots imaginable. So far I was unable to praise those I had seen. They were all littered with rotting fish, moulting caribou hides and the entrails of a season's kill strewn about the encampment amongst old bones and tin cans discarded at random. I had also noticed the sled dogs completely neglected, lying in their own filth, some in pools of water and all without fresh water to drink as they unenergetically shifted their skinny carcasses to another uncomfortable position in the hot sun. I was later to see further ill−treatment at the hands of their masters, who don't hesitate to lay the whip and boot to their canines, prodding the 'wheel dog' (nearest the sled) unceasingly.

Quite contradictory to these previous observations, we pulled into as clean a campsite in which I ever hope to see Indians dwelling. The very whiteness of the tent spoke for the rest of the camp and its occupants. An old Indian offers us hospitality and while another of the sleds takes on runners, I commence to make use of the stove and utensils generously offered by the man's squaw. Characteristic of the dwelling is the huge bannock browning itself slowly in a frying pan. Removing this 'moon', as they so often call them, and placing it in a box with others, the smiling squaw gave me her bashful cue to proceed.

In Whiteman fashion (which is rather clumsy at first), I fashioned a crude 'moon', placed a pot of tea to boil and prepared an equally crude but satisfying supper for our insatiable entourage, under the amused glances of the Indian family, who, periodically, didn't refrain from chuckling at the Cheechako.

Our culinary procedure over, the Dogribs showed us a teepee where they informed us (by means of a halfbreed interpreter) that we could stay the night. We had reached a unanimous conclusion that the snow was still too soft to proceed. Then the thought occurred to us: why not 'borrow' two more dogs to overcome the strain? So the bartering began. I turned from my partner, Fred, to the interpreter, to the aged Indian, and back again several times before realizing we could buy one for five dollars. Five dollars? Our suspicions were aroused as we inspected the timid fellow. Not content, my partner harnessed him with the team, took off over the snow and reappeared in five minutes, the dogs panting with the sudden dash. "We'll take 'im'," said the Breed coming to a stop, "providing you throw in a harness and lend us another dog and harness." Several more altercations, more glances and the gnarled hunter, raising his head from thought, assented with a large nod. "Got four more to add to this?" queried Fred, unraveling a soiled bill from his pocket. "Yeah...but it's the last," I returned, handing him the sum total of my monetary gains.

"Never mind, you won't starve while you're with me; and there's always Indians who'll give you a fish or two." I was gradually becoming used to this lack of fear of any crisis, travelling with such ingenious and keen company. I mumbled assent and again eyed the dog suspiciously. The deal was completed, the Indian counting each bill as he arranged them, whereupon Indian, interpreter and trapper adjourned to the tent, where, it was suggested that I play a little music in appreciation of services. I was doubtful as I reached into the bottom of the grub sack for my clarinet.

Indians like music very much. As I blew I noted quizzical glances at the long, black stick. It must have been a novelty, for they giggled. Unable to interpret their actions I played on, wondering as to the appreciation. *Home Sweet Home* was changed to *Teepee Smoky Teepee* a half an hour later and whether it was the music that did not soothe the savage breast or the plain fickleness of Indians, I shall never know; but we did not get the extra dog and harness!

There is no use arguing with an Indian. He will always win in his quiet, sullen manner, and there is no power in the North (other than the tabooed liquor) that can make him change his mind.

With Indian children falling asleep all around us we decided ourselves to turn in. Assuring the Indian that everything was all right we departed for the adjacent teepee offered us. Pushing the remaining embers of a fire outside the door, and lining the frozen ground with spruce boughs we crammed ourselves together. Gazing at the rack of drymeat that hung over our heads I thought of my empty wallet, gloated momentarily over 'Fiver'—the five dollar bargain just struck—and slumbered.

It was a very small hour of the morning that found us re—rolling our sleeping bags. A bright moon peaked around the teepee. An Indian dog howled mournfully at the rotund bannock as it waned in the gradually greying sky. A faint light flickered in an adjacent teepee. A dim figure motioned me in that direction. Entering the smoky interior I discovered a very ancient squaw squatted on the ground, huddled in tattered clothing and dirty blankets, her face in the smoke rising from the fire. "My mother very sick...what can you do, Dazzio?" came the plaintive query from the daughter who had beckoned me, (Dazzio referring to the growth of whiskers, in Indian tongue).

Here I mused; for were not the Indians once the finest of physical specimens immune to such ailments as the common cold? Moved by the pathetic situation of the old woman, who sniffed and blew her nose continually, I offered my own personal formula, so simple that I felt a little embarrassed at telling her to get plenty of fresh air and sunshine. She thanked me, grateful of someone's interest. I wished her well as I executed a hasty departure.

CHAPTER FOUR

AN UNEXPECTED VISITOR

Following a map of the North country is not easy for a neophyte, and as we weaved in and out of the Slave Archipelago I wondered if not only I was temporarily lost. Our search was for a point named Trout Rock. Finally stopping for a four power consultation we agreed on an advance. So it was that late morning found us aware of our mistake, far beyond the illusive Rock. 'Fiver', our new buy, proved quite independent at climbing into his own traces but insisted he would rather go south. As we backtracked, one at least was happy as he filled the harness well in his anxiety to go in the direction of his old home. Completely confused by an ignorance of the countryside and the doubtfulness of the party, I felt exultation at the sight of a bay tapering far back, and of running water. Surely, here would be home for awhile? At that debatable moment a lone fox flashed by with incredible speed, not staying long enough for an introduction or a bullet; his long bushy tail swinging like a windsock in the slipstream behind him. This timely incident proved the turning point of all doubts. Already I was pleased with another beautiful sunrise as the shepherd−like sun gradually broke up the grey morning sky in a continual show; then came the joyous shouts of the Halfbreed: "There's the creek...see the pushups!" pointing to the conical hive−like mounds of the muskrat dwelling, peering just above the snow. I set my thoughts to dry boots, rest, a warm fire and food. Raising a temporary shelter with the aid of eight hands is a simple matter, so home and dinner were not long in nearing completion.

Then suddenly I found myself in a new capacity. Having only one pair of waterproof boots between we two it was decided (by Fred) that he use them for the wet sport of chasing muskrats along the melting stream. With no alternative I found myself the cook. Eager for the hunt the three 'Breeds disappeared, for how long and where I knew not. So I accepted with resignation my culinary position.

This was where my career as a Cheechako began. Now a Cheechako, according to Robert W. Service, is 'a man who uses baking powder in his bannock'. Not wanting to sacrifice the altitude of my bannocks, which

Spring Cleaning and Drying

had so far proven a gamble, I fell pathetically in with all the others who are not eligible for the rank of Sourdough, because necessity has not forced us to eliminate this ingredient−one distinguishing factor between novice and oldtimer.

With a battered volume of Jack London's *White Fang*, the complete poems of Robert Service and an aging volume, *Down The Mackenzie*, by Fullerton Waldo, perchanced upon at the Arden home, I settled down for a week of bannocks and books; caring for five sled−dogs and potting occasionally with a rifle that rested within close reach, at the thousands of ducks that dared fly into our sanctuary.

Spring in the North is altogether different from that season elsewhere. It comes suddenly in civilization where a million footsteps help the sun on its day−shift, and the chinook winds blow their warm breath of evening. Here, spring evolves slowly where the only footsteps are those of straying caribou, a lone fox or wolf, or the zig−zag imprints of sled−dogs beside which now and then a human tread is cast. Sitting outside the tent in the quiet of early afternoon I listened and watched the creatures of nature commencing their spring songs and busy activities. The stream cracks periodically as a piece of ice breaks loose, releasing a suffocating breath. It is saturated

23

with sea—gulls which seem out of place in the free water of the stream, while high overhead flock upon flock of ducks and geese come and go in an endless succession of V's, in pairs or mateless. A pleasant refrain, falling from overhead, bids me look skyward where a Rainbird, the northern equivalent of an English skylark, flutters; the touching poem of Shelley finds words here in the white stillness of the Canadian North. A minute sparrow flits among the willows; while darting to and fro' with equivalent speed are the squirrels, chattering as they slip up a spruce, run to the end of an overhanging bough and mock the rest of the world from their safe distance.

Fatigue, a low fire and a pot o' tea are conducive to story telling. These three and we four came together one evening in the smoky atmosphere of our Indian bivouac. It had been a good day for muskrats and wet feet. The time was ripe for vocal intercourse. But such gross exaggeration I never dreamed of as I absorbed the tales and learned another Northern lesson. To each experience, multiplied with the telling, comes a weird hyperbolic addition to which is added a similar experience by another trapper until the story crumbles with its own distortion; a hearty laugh shatters the dead spell under which the entire audience has fallen. (Since this first imaginative episode I have refused to take seriously any statement made by anyone north of the 60th parallel.) It started in a legitimate manner with: "I was Rat—trapping on a creek once and all I had was a #3 trap…" and ended after many additions and interruptions with something like, "we evacuated the creek vicinity because of too many bulldozers bogged down in our efforts to raise the huge muskrats,"—which had grown with each additional phrase. With all eyes focused questioningly on the Cheechako for reaction, I lifted the teapot from the makeshift stove and pushed past the tent flap into the twilight, dumped the remaining leaves, and chuckled to myself as their laughter died and a new story circulated about the dimly lit tent. Across the creek came the only other sound…the crazy mocking of a loon.

As I sat one afternoon absorbing the sun and Service's *Trail of '98*, a movement in the distance attracted my attention. Someone was invading our hunting grounds. As he came within earshot I heard him mumbling in Indian dialect. So following the unwritten law of the North I invited him to cross the creek, which had now become waist deep, and stop for awhile. Fishing for a shallow spot, the bronzed figure, clad in 'waders' and holding his rifle above his head, ploughed through the current, climbed the bank and mumbled in guttural sounds a few words in English. Shaking hands I returned the words, inviting him to remove his wet clothes. He hung his socks over the fire in customary fashion and partook of the macaroni and bannock, our sole remaining food stuffs save for a scant bag of rice, rolled oats and one tin of Spam, the latter unknown to my native friend (hidden by me in case of emergency).

There we were, Dogrib and Whiteman, managing only occasionally to understand one another verbally, but more often with gesticulations.

I managed to piece the disjointed words together, discovering that his wife, who was quite pretty, died a short time ago and once more he was a lone—wolf out looking for a few 'rats'. He had no food with him and I marvelled at the nonchalance with which Indians travel, armed only with a rifle and sometimes only a little 'drymeat' jammed in a pocket. Here in the last frontier I realized, then, that man can still live from the land as was the primordial design. 'How long his natural supply will last is only a matter of time and events, I mused. With great satisfaction I entertained one of Nature's children who rely only slightly on civilization for survival, but if needs—be could quite easily (with a greater degree of hardship) secure his food by natural means.

Sipping our tea, little was said; but our silence was broken as he jumped up, reaching for his rifle. In the semi—darkness of the lengthening day he had seen through the tent flap the slight movement of a muskrat swimming about under water, near its 'pushup'. No time and bullets were wasted. A few minutes later another 'rat' hung drying on its wooden stretcher. The meal was resumed and climaxed by a cigar which had been presented to me and which I now offered to my Redskin guest. Smiling broadly, there was no doubt of his enjoying such a rarity, which I satisfied myself with smelling; the pungent aroma brought visions of the city into the North with each fresh puff he took. It was the contrast that was suddenly enjoyable; but the city was well behind me now.

Food is the all—important commodity in this country, whether it be the prospector's retinue of canned foodstuffs, the trapper's bannock and tea or the Indian's drymeat. As the days passed so our food vanished and it was voted we set course for Fort Rae. The dogfood, which is a fish a day per dog, had diminished accordingly. Not only this...the snow had melted all round us and without a canoe in the spring thaw one begins to feel stuck. Overburdened with deficiencies we began breaking−up camp. It was a pleasant feeling to move again, and Fort Rae seemed to spell romance and adventure.

"Mush, you hounds!" yelled Fred in a friendly manner and we hit the waist−high water which trapped us well back from the creek mouth. *Splash!* went the dogs, sleds, 'Breeds and Cheechako. In a spray of spring moisture we emerged, soaked, on the far bank. The dogs, not content to remain wet, shook themselves continually, so it was futile to wring out our own garments till once out of this morass. Then came another unsuspected surprise, as I swatted a monstrous mosquito. "You haven't seen anything yet," chortled a 'Breed as another pest made its spring debut. "You'd better arm yourself with plenty of D.D.T., a net and, by the way, don't cut those whiskers you're growing." "Why, the dirty little dive bomber," I yelled, slapping another of large proportions that managed to get through those self−same whiskers.

Again on the Big Ice (as they call Great Slave Lake in its frozen condition) sitting contentedly behind the dogs a wave of satisfaction overcomes me. Struck by the spaciousness of our surroundings I sigh with contentment, looking westward at a panorama that might not stir the heart of an Englishman, used to the cultural beauties of his island countryside, and feelings form thoughts. 'This is only beauty for those reared in the land,' I reflect, 'and such as see her enchanting form in space, stalwart spruce and rugged challenging countryside clothed in snow as far as the eye can see.' Then the time came for parting. With no wine to toast one another 'good luck' I groped in a concealed corner of a kit bag, bringing forth a tin of plums. "Surprise, fellas!" I chuckled, punching the top crudely with a hunting knife. "Why, you've been holding out on us, you rat!" shot Fred, making for the precious dessert. "Knew you'd thank me sooner or later." So the tin went the rounds, passed over the Indian's left shoulder and rattled to a stop on the glare ice. As we casually met, so we departed: the 'Breeds in search of a likely creek, the Indian (gosh knows where?) and my French−Indian companion, Mercredi, and myself, the Cheechako, to the isolated outpost of Fort Rae.

'Glare ice' is what the traveller most desires at this time of year. It comes with the chill of night, leaving a thin crust on the snow's wet surface. Men and beasts felt happy with the easy going; miles flew in our wake; white miles stretched to our fore. Life felt exceptionally good.

"Gettin' hungry?" asked the native after what seemed days on the sheen, white surface. "I can always eat...you know that!" I replied. "How about you?" "I'm concerned chiefly about the dogs...haven't eaten since last night...should be a camp ahead somewhere." "Well, what's that to the right?" I pointed, "a mirage?" "Say, you're learnin' fast," came the answer. "It's what I've been looking for the last hour." "*Yoo*," yelled the Breed, and the dogs sighting the shoreline, needed no further encouragement. In fact, I think they smelled fish long before we did.

"Anyone home?" I yelled. "Anyone home?"...came the echo. "Try some Indian on them," I suggested. But the echo came back in Indian. No life appeared. All that greeted us were overturned canoes, empty cabins surrounded by the remains of slaughtered caribou and the stillness so contrary to Indian encampments, where the ceaseless barking and howling of dogs is always a sufficient welcome for any stranger. Sighting the fishhouse there was but one thing to do. So in the customary manner we 'borrowed' enough for the hungry hounds, replaced the wire latch and retraced our footsteps to the beach. Never did five fish disappear down five throats so fast. We were on our way again.

Afternoon and heat walked hand in hand that day; so close to a gait that we were forced to pull up. It is very essential to stop where there is an abundance of dry timber, for storms arise out of nowhere in quick order. A patch of dead spruce, a stretch of bare rock, what could be more convenient? This was no mirage. In fact it turned out to be a temporary paradise. The rocks were warm and flat, perfect for drying our wet gear; the ice along the shoreline broken sufficient for drinking water and there amongst the rocks lay heated pools of water. "Dishwashing will be a pleasure today," I said, smiling at the find. "You and your damned cleanliness...you'll fergit it soon...you wait!"

"Furthermore, let's think of eating," he added, untying the dogs who wasted no time taking advantage of the hot rocks and slumber. "Eat what?" I replied, holding up the small bag of rice and oatmeal. "Mix it up anyway...with a little coffee, we won't know the difference." So it was mixed, eaten with imagination and I, not able to resist the convenience, set to the dishes, while a snore from the sleeping bag on the warm flat rock told its own tale. Stripped to the most meager piece of clothing and stretched out, like the dogs, the Cheechako prepared to do likewise. Once again a crow, breaking the silence with his raucous *caw*, complained of his troubles; but refusing to hear tell of them I slid into the land of Nod along with my pal and five dogs...

"Hello there!" a brusque voice called. My dreams were shattered. Crisp from the hot sun's merciless beating I felt like I cracked as I raised to an elbow, returning the salutation with a questioning: "Hello?" "Is there plenty of dry wood there?" were his next words, drawing his team to a stop. Answering in the affirmative, I invited the heavy−set trapper to stop for tea. The going too hard for the dogs, his decision was made quickly. At this point I could no longer withhold a chuckle, glancing from the huge form clad in a backwood's shirt to the odd−looking load on his sled, pulled by five large dogs. It resembled a sailboat in the last stages of disintegration, weatherbeaten beyond weather beatings. Sail and boat shared the same fate. "Where the hell are you going with that beaten−up wreck?" I asked, and the laughter that followed filled the still air, awakening my companion. For the next five minutes we heard more descriptive adjectives than necessary to describe any one sailing vessel. They came between uncontrollable spasms of laughter as the huge bulk shook and his face wrinkled from ear to ear. Such was our introduction to the infectiously good−natured Charlie Sanders, who, pulling a section of the sail from its winding about the spruce pole mast, displayed a flour sack sewed on to the rotting sail. This was too much and we three, bursting into a last volley of laughter that raised the ears of the tired dogs, settled to the warmth of campfire and a good strong cup of tea.

One of the pleasures of travelling in this White Wilderness is the chance meetings that invariably occur, especially for the lone trapper who for days has had no one to talk to but his dogs. Some of the more independent shun the company of others, but most like nothing better than to exchange stories over a crackling fire after the sun has set, sipping a hot cup of tea with friends. Such was the mutual pleasure of all three as we huddled close to the lapping flames, surrounded by curled−up dogs, a chilly wind and good humour. "She's a goin' to snow like hell tonight," shouted Charlie, finishing his tea and slinging his 'tarp' against the wind. Crouched warmly behind the makeshift shelter the conversation continued, the dogs creeping within the narrow limits of the shelter under the watchful eye of the trapper. "You see dem...dey're not so domb...oh no!...wheech reminds me...I tell you about de time when I was out of food for myself and de dogs...oh dat was bad for awhile! No caribou anyvere...da termometer was at a Northern low and a blizzard, she obliterate da trail...yeah, I'll nevare fergit dat time...Oh no! Dat God damn leader, he not want to follow da trail...(he know perfectly well where it is)" he reflected, chuckling and wrinkling his bronzed face till the twinkling eyes were barely discernable. "It vas eder me or da dogs...and I did not want to die jus yet! Den I get mad...I show dat leader who was master...I string him up in a tree by de forefeet and I lay a few across hees back."   It would sound brutal to anyone who does not realize the thin line between life and death when a 60 below blizzard is blowing, no campsight can be found, food is low and there is no other human being within miles, and to add to this the plain stubbornness, sometimes, of the dogs who possess the uncanny ability to orient themselves. This is no time to be soft.

Absorbed in thought, staring distantly into the glowing flame, Charlie, connecting the story, says humourously: "He follow da trail after dat and we make eet okay...But dat God damn leader,"he mumbled to himself, poking the fire with a stick as he reminisced.

As the black curtain of night slowly fell on the dim−lit scene and the fire had lashed itself into mere embers that ceased to struggle for life, the last story came to a dramatic close. It had been one succession of intriguing yarns of frozen snows, no caribou−run, stubborn dogs, no fish, a broken sled, wet matches, a pregnant Indian girl stranded by spring floods; first with Charlie narrating, then Fred the 'Breed retaliating. All the while the Cheechako sat silent, listening, absorbing.

Charlie, we learned, was headed for Waite Island with the nondescript craft brought from Yellowknife for an old optimistic prospector, sole inhabitant of the island. One of the unfortunate fishermen who spent the entire winter fishing and was unable to export because of the lack of boxes; he had turned to jobbing and some trapping. Undaunted, however, he had well—laid plans for summer. This in turn led to the European situation and the starving, which was climaxed by a few episodes of the trapper's youth in Czeckoslovakia. His short army career during the Revolution there and his eventual flight to Canada, where he began trapping and living the life of a free man in the spacious North. His description of the political upheaval and chaos of Europe in that era resembled all too closely the present condition of the mulling millions still searching for a free way of life. As I reflected on life and its complications on that side of the ocean, and looked over the burning embers at the carefree trapper Charlie Sanders, I was satisfied to think of him as having found his freedom.

Four a.m. It is time to shove off once more. Charlie, awake after a restless night, turns in his sleeping robe as our sled scrapes the rocks, "See you fellas in Fort Rae," and we slid on to the fluffy surface of Great Slave Lake again. Charlie's forecast had been exact. Swishing into another sunrise, the early morning belongs to us with its original colour scheme. It is this that I first look for in the long course of daily events. Still as eager for its ascent, I am reminded of very youthful days when, anxiously rising at six, I would slip from the house (unmindful of my mother's warnings) to the neighbour's sloping, cellar door and lap up those first, warm, welcome rays. Now with an equal fervor and as youthful a spirit, I find myself playing the same game; but this time from a dogsled. Within five minutes it is above the horizon, red as the coals of a fireplace, showing with dignity the true East. Nature's eiderdown soon melted with the touch of the red fingers stretching over the horizon; slush soon became the ordeal of the day. Noon came and went as did the first dried fruit bar cached away for emergency. A handful of rolled oats remained. Having portaged past Old Fort, the (consoling) original site, saving dogs and men fatiguing miles, my companion became familiar with the country. "Should be an Indian settlement somewhere near," he said, eyeing the fjorded coastline. Consulting the map, no markings of these nomadic folk serve as a clue. They would follow the 'game' naturally; but where was the game?

Tired, wet and with the thought of our meager rolled oats to pacify the growing hunger, we followed the shoreline in hopes of sighting an Indian encampment. Rae was yet some fifteen miles distant, our goal for the night. "What's that?" exclaimed my acute—eared friend, stopping the sled. "Didn't hear a damned thing," I retorted, knowing full well of the deceiving tendency of mirages and sounds in the surrounding vastness. "You're dreaming again," I chuckled. "Like hell...see a bobbing on the horizon behind?" "Well I'll be...people...real live people!" Sleigh bells jingling their happy melody crescendo'd on the winds. As good fortune had so far had it, we were once again in company. This

Indian Fish Rack

time it was three. A motley group, they were introduced as Dodd Lafferty, Ernie Camsell and Joe Beaulieu, his Indian friend. "Just returning from a hunt," I caught in the admixture of Dogrib, Indian and English that followed. Some conclusion was reached, for the load was divided. I found myself riding with Dodd; the gnarled old French—Indian 'Breed. He still remembered some French and between chats and encouraging quips to his dogs we exchanged badly mauled phrases; I in my best book—learned style; he in his seldom used French—Canadian. With that enlightenment that comes with good company we wended our way through the islands, Ernie's sled in the lead. The dogs, too, forget their fatigue of plodding through slush as they leaned against the traces, tongues hanging low; the bouncing bells set a rhythmic gait over the great, white stillness.

For an hour the sun−devils danced on the horizon. It became painful to look directly at the glittering white; but what else was there to view except the sky? I forgot the pains that weighed the eyeballs as we stopped at a fresh caribou cache, visible in the snow beside a sled trail. Thoughts of juicy caribou steak took the place of oatmeal in more than one mind.

Hooked on Caribou

Now all we needed was wood for the fire. It was keen−eyed Dodd who pointed to a woody point in the distance. Once again the dogs sensed the meaning of their masters. Minutes found them resting while we cut wood, sliced a side of ribs and hung wet socks over the crackling heat to dry. These are pleasant moments on the trail. This was to be cherished forever by me. Here was my initiation to barbeque caribou ribs. As the whole side of ribs hung close to the flames on a spit my hunger grew, unbearably. "Try this," said Ernie, tossing what looked like a burnt shoe−tongue. This preceded a piece of caribou fat cut in the same crude manner. Here was my introduction to another Northern delicacy−Drymeat. I daresay it is something that one develops a taste for; but hungry as I was I began chewing. The fat slid down with the same effect as that from Pork and Beans and I was relieved when the ribs were browned, putting the 'drymeat' in a pocket for future chewing.

The repast over, I remembered something that without a doubt sealed the new friendship, topped such a delectable session and sent each on his way in good spirits. Digging to the bottom of a kitbag, there it was, unbroken and inviting. All faces beamed at the surprise. "Seagram's 83…and you said nothing you !!#!@*," announced my companion. More appreciated than anything in a land where the chill nips the body to the bone, we toasted the health of each other. "Good hunting," said the Indian tossing the empty into a snowbank.

Partings in the North are often as sudden as the accosting. Exchanging sleds, Dodd headed back toward the South, while we three continued in the direction of Rae. Late afternoon saw Joe Beaulieu's cabin, a familiar landmark come into view on the right limit of the Marion River. The week had been generally warm and to our surprise we found the ice in its last stages of disintegration. Poling ahead of the team each reached the security of the Big Ice where the river

End of the Trail

joined the bay. As any tired traveller welcomes habitation, so we welcomed the towering spire of the Roman Catholic Mission pointing majestically toward the heavens. These characteristic steeples are like a welcome light on a stormy night; a white sheet on an empty sea; a camel trail on the hot desert sands. "*Mush!*" yelled the 'Breed as the dogs, sighting the settlement, yelped and strained in the harness. How we welcomed Fort Rae!

CHAPTER FIVE

ISOLATED OUTPOST–FORT RAE

Skies are grey as we approach, conveying a rather dismal solitude to the impressionist, and bringing out the smallness and isolation of this northerly community. Churches sometimes have the effect of drawing one into the past. Whether it be their long struggle for survival or the sacrifice through the years that they suggest, I can never quite fathom. As we crossed the expanse of the Bay my mind is with the first priest of the order struggling through the snows to convey the Whiteman's religion to the Indian, and struggling financially to raise funds for the construction of the silent, victorious Mission that looks far out over the surrounding countryside. It casts its religious challenge, holding high a beckoning hand for those who are miles away. So it beckoned to us, coupled with the echo of its bells, not unlike (I imagine) the peeling of those of Old Fort Gary ringing through the still prairie air as they beckoned the pioneers, scattered far and wide on their homesteads, to the safety of the Fort in times of Indian uprisings. And I felt like Mackenzie, forging North with renewed optimism.

The dullness of the elements was soon exchanged for the brightness of the fire in the cabin of Joe Beaulieu, on the Southwest point of Fort Rae, my new home. Caribou sizzled in the frying pan, steam emanated from the drying rack above, while warm conversation permeated the room. Completing the feast with a wassail of Hassell's Olive Blossom Rum (saved for just such a gathering, I presume), the company dispersed. The 'Breed went visiting, Joe remained to skin his day's catch of muskrats and I on an inspection of the Fort, to pay my respects and the greetings of Father Gathy in Yellowknife to the Fathers at the Mission.

The hour was getting on as I clomped over the crude wooden bridge to what appeared the centre of the community. A light in the frame building marked Post Office flickered, silhouetting a figure seated at the window. I was enticed to meet the owner, just for a talk on general topics. It was thus that I met the jovial priests of the settlement under Father LaPerriere, who officiates in the dual capacity of Father and Post Master of Fort Rae.

Knocking, I wasted little time on the doorstep as a rush to the door demonstrated the occupants' desire to receive company. Father Trassard and Brother Korpel were introduced with energetic handshakes. One glance was sufficient to take in the simple interior. Three small rooms, each with its single bed, a six–by–six mail–box–sized Post Office with no more than a dozen pigeon holes and the main rotunda containing three chairs, centred by a stove, round about which, no doubt, on long winter nights, many tales are spun into the complicated yarns so typical of this strange land. There naturally would be no tobacco chewing (with its eventual result directed at the hot stove), for

Old Fort Rae

this is a house of religion. A small mission occupies the upper storey for use when congregations are small. Such was my simple introduction to three very interesting European priests who forsook the bowels of civilization to become Oblates in the Northern wastes of a pioneer country.

"Ave a seat," beckoned the white–bearded Father LaPierre in broken English, "an tell uzz everything from ze Outside." It is with keen interest that those on the Inside listen to any newcomer for small clues to the latest goings–on in the Outside World. Radio reception is poor and newspapers are outdated. Living their own day–to–day existence, there is no need to know, or care, about the fluctuations of the Outside which really have no direct bearing on the lives of these isolated folk. However, appearance of a new face in such communities is a local source of great interest. Realizing this, I tried my best to entertain my three hosts, who had drawn closer to the rotund stove, and who were trying just as hard to make me at home in Fort Rae. As the words filtered throughout the room, the history of each man slowly unfolded itself. "I vas born een France," commented the head Father, "an I come to zee Norzwest Terreetories some forty—four year ago as a member of zee O.M.I. (Oblate Order of Mary Immaculate) to Fort Resolution. Since, I 'ave been to manee outposts all over zee country," he added, the beard of many of these years receiving an habitual stroke. "When I was in Monreau zey all stare at me so much, zat I go to zee barber shop and shave eet all off!" he chuckles, waving his hands in wide, French gestures. "I onlee been out about three times...when you are here as long as I 'ave been, you cannot leave zee countree." This then is the Call of the North; the beckoning to the pioneer spirit; the love of freedom from society. "I think I understand, Father. I already feel this." "Ahhh...zat ees goot...zen you do understand, yes," smiled the Father.

**Fathers and Brothers of O.M.I.
(Oblate Order of Mary Immaculate)**

"See zis map on zee wall," he pointed; "I veel show you where ve are, and where all our missions are too. Oh yes...we hav' manee...all overe." Yes, it is faith; that alone builds many things and molds countries, I thought to myself, glancing again at the sprawling North on paper, and I see the mold only as a tinker's dam, not yet saturated with the necessary ingredients for the final casting. I feel I would like it to remain as it is, semi—virgin and uncast: for, once stigmatized by the sting of modern civilization, I see the marring roots of evil spreading their destroying tentacles. However, one consolation: it will be as it is for many years to come—the Hudson's Bay Co. posts, lone Missions and the bartering Indians; here is where Red and White merge, each extracting something from the other, good or bad; each clinging to the innate.

Thoughts are brought to words once more as the Father says, "I 'ave about 700 people in the deestrict, the population of zee Fort being about feefty." Happily, the old man comments on the Faroud Hospital, built in the 30's, how it has helped his people so much against T.B. "You must visit the Sisters dere...dey are very kind." Father Trassard, also a short plump man, but with a dark beard and brown eyes, had said little, but interpolated in a brief pause. "I too am from France...I 'ave been here about seexteen year now, but we talk in French, eh, eet is so much easierr...you speak it, no?" I stumbled over a few stock French phrases, ill—organized; his brown eyes twinkled and the concerned brow relaxed as he gave way to sudden laughter upon recognition of his native tongue, little short of guillotined. Laughter in the North is more than contagious. As it spread through the building and died, a third voice, hitherto saying little, but nodding in assent or negation, made itself heard.

"My whole name is Brother A. Theodore Y. Korpel. It is long, but I have to like it anyway," he smiled. "I am the latest to arrive at the Mission...only (how do you say it...is that correct?) eight months ago. My home was in Holland," he added, with a mixture of English, French and his native Dutch. "I cannot understand your country...so much snow and winter. And to make eet worse, I land here for what they say is the worst in many years. They tell me I will get used to it. I know I shall. I have to!" he smiled. The Brother is a young man with plump countenance, very quick to react in his efforts to become adjusted to the country, especially in efforts of speech. "I did not know English before...I am doing, okay?" stopping to receive verification of proper usage. Nodding, I desired him to continue, which he did. "During the war I played mute, then they place me in the kitchen to aid the cook," he said with a sly smile. "When the belly is full the rest of the world looks good, No?" This gave occasion for another bout of laughter followed by more grotesque tales of tyranny, which since have been revealed publicly. "I 'ave travelled all of Holland, most of Europe and here I am now...stuck in the North,"he added, with slight consternation over his maladjustment. "But, never have I seen so much continuous sunshine," he exclaimed, all smiles. "Time will tell...we all feel that way at first,"assures Father LaPierre. It is indeed a life of privation and the acid—test for men of religion. Nevertheless, six months has made the Brother keenly interested in the life and customs, although Holland, his native land, still remains dominant in his mind, even in its post—war garments. A student of language, he has started to sort out the difficult Dogrib tongue. "Here is where my linguistic abilities halt," I said to the Brother, reflecting on previous Chinese barriers that confronted me, deciding at that time to stick with: "Hello, Charlie...I would like my laundry...thank you," departing with the parcel tucked under an arm. Another burst of mirth brought us all to our feet. Time had flown. "I shall leave while I am still appreciated," said the Cheechako, as the clock struck nine. "Bon nuit, mon ami...bon nuit...bon nuit," bade the three priests with broad smiles. "By the way,"smiles the Father, "you'd better grow some whiskers, you have a long way to go." Resisting no longer, I politely asked the Father if he minded I feel his beard. "No....No...," he invited. I felt like the pilgrim who, on a visit to the Pope, was so enthralled by the good man's growth of whiskers that he asked the unusual favour of stroking the most pious man's beard. It too was granted.

Another round of laughter mingled with, "Bon nuit, mon ami!" "Bon nuit!" "Bon Nuit!" from the three priests and the door closed on the setting sun. It was setting wide across the Nor'western horizon in a natural arch, its easternmost tip marking the spot where in but a short while the aurora would ascend, igniting the fading illumination, bearing the torch for another day. The rickety bridge creaked with the heavy feet of the tired traveller; a hungry Indian dog howled in the distance, as the Cheechako plodded toward the log, mud hut on the banks of Marion Lake, satisfied with his first impressions of Fort Rae.

Sunday brought new experiences. "Go ahead, try some," taunted the 'Breed, tossing part of a sizzling muskrat on a plate under my nose. Closely resembling duck in its richness, I satisfied the pangs of hunger and again headed for the center of the Fort, basked in the sunshine of a bright May morning. Standing on the rocks overlooking the creek, winding its way through the heart of the village, the echoing peel of a small bell caught my ear. There in the distance stood the black—robed Father La Perriere assisted by an eager young follower, tugging the rope that led to the belfry and the bell that shattered the Sunday morning silence. I stood quietly observing. Again I returned to Old Fort Garry with the poet who caught the true settler spirit. As those bells had results, so had this one. A disjointed procession wound its way from the Indian village on the remote edge of town. They might just as well have been Chaucer's pilgrims wending their way over the snow toward their Canterbury. The bells ceased their calling; the last of the Indian family trailed into the Mission house followed closely by the Father. All was silence.

"Hello there! Watcha doin?" asked the stranger. "Just enjoying your little town," I replied. "I'm Jack Wilson of the Hudson's Bay Trading Post...been here some years now. Me an' Mac (that's my assistant) look after things here." "Well, it sure doesn't look like much to look after," I retorted. "You'd be surprised all the work these blamed Indians can stir up...course we're single and that means washin' and all that stuff...you know?" "Yeah...I know all about that!" Timing my meanderings, I arrive at the scene of the Mission as the benediction ends. Posing Indians for a photograph is one of those things called 'difficulties', what with thumb—sucking squaws, bashful children and wondering males. But with a degree of trouble and three large smiles from my religious friends of the previous evening, I, rather more voluntary than Richard Halliburton in the role of the Involuntary Monk when stranded at Mount Athos, heard the shutter click on what I hoped would represent a cross—section of Fort Rae.

I mentioned the Faround Hospital previously. It was this afternoon that the proposed visit matured. With warm welcomes I met the Grey Nuns of the Far North. I first met smiling Mother Gadbord on entry. She, showing me about the 35—bed hospital with its own operating room, stopped at the door of the special southwest sunrooms. "She's ridden with T.B.," said the Mother, "but she smiles happily, anyway." "Bonjour. Comment allez—vous?" I asked, in my best French. "Tres bien, merci!" came the surprised reply. "They learn fast," smiled the Mother, pleased with her pupil.

31

A visit to the lunch room was in order (and, I daresay, timely). Here I was to receive a pleasant surprise. Baked that day was a huge plate of peanut−butter cookies, long since a favorite with me. Wishing to express thanks personally, I asked to be led to the kitchen. It was here I met the cook, Sister Pearson. Complimenting her at coming close to my mother's recipe, I wittily suggested I would return again on the day of my departure. Delighted as any woman, she insisted I take more then, which could be answered only one way for they were too 'civilized' to resist. (It later happened that she did not forget the jest and had it not been for a sly, hungry sled−dog I would have headed south well armed with peanut−butter cookies.)

Resuming our trek through the immaculate halls we met the remainder of the staff: Sisters Gaudette, Roberge and Comeau. A final climb to the rooftop for a panoramic view of the settlement realized the beauty of these outposts−their picturesque simplicity, lost in an endless blanket of white. "Beautiful, isn't it?" remarked the Father; "Now maybe you can understand why we cannot leave?" It was then that I did. "I would like to stay longer, too, Father," I agreed, "but I have to go. I have a date with the *Trails of '98* and the Klondike." "Yes, you are young, my boy...see all you can," he added encouragingly. At this we descended to the outside, leaving the good nuns to their daily tasks.

Sunday in an isolated northern outpost is sufficient reason for a gathering of the Whites. This week it was at the home of Grant McMillan, the other fur trader. Thus it was that I joined the gathering for Sunday dinner. I immediately forgot my remote surroundings and was soon 'at home', surrounded by relatives gathered for the big meal of the day. The only clue as to the North is the dehydrated potatoes and Moose steak, which I could not discern at a glance from any other. In attendance were the two men of the Hudson's Bay staff, two R.C.M.P. of the local detachment and the McMillan family of four. Northern stories naturally went their round with the intrusion of later news from the South forwarded by the Cheechako.

As we departed from a sociable evening, I said, "...then I can say I have dined with the elite of Fort Rae," which the senior policeman, Bill Coombs, corrected with: "You have dined *with Fort Rae*!" and the essential Northern humour passed with us into the night.

The wooden bridge and I became nocturnal friends, answering one another with hollow echoes that fled over the melting snows. In the west the tardy sun was bending in its mauve arch. Toward the east and the Indian camp was silence: the dogs had finished their nightly chorals to the moon. On the shoreline of the melting lake in its lone vigil stood the cabin, silhouetted against the west, awaiting the Cheechako. He came, slid into his sleeping robe, rolled over and drifted from all things mundane.

Next morning the entire scene had changed. Fort Rae had re−donned her winter garment of snow and was being lashed by a cold wind. Suddenly I felt what the entire settlement must feel in the dead of winter − the claustrophobic isolation. Snow twisted, turned, fell and rose, obliterating vision completely. We might as well have been in the Arctic. Then through the white maelstrom came the anxious bark of dogs. "Something's up!" said a 'Breed... "wind isn't blowing from the village." It was an hour before we could make out the trouble. Already the hot week's sun had split the lake ice, cutting off all traffic from the settlement. It wasn't a happy thought as we stood helpless on this side while dogs whined and Indians yelled in vain on the other. Finally an Indian, seeing their plight, rushed to the scene with a canoe. As the snow continued to whistle in all directions activity back and forth continued; when it cleared hours later a dogsled and unharnessed dogs were all that remained in sight. "What could be going on?" I asked myself. The sad story reached the cabin the next night. Misfortune had dealt another pat hand. A young Indian girl of twenty, ridden with tuberculosis and pregnant, was too far gone to stand the ordeal. She and the baby died leaving her mourning family, who had arrived on the scene in time, completely bewildered. For days they moved like living ghosts through the village...utterly lost. So another case of the Indians severest ailment (causing their highest mortality) found its belated end (through the neglect of someone, somewhere) in the sanctuary of the Whiteman's hospital. Perhaps it is better this way?

Today the Mission looks especially immaculate, clothed in the unexpected snow, which seemed to come as a warning...as though Nature was reminding us that she has first and final word in the North. Here, moreso, the weather has a direct bearing on the lives of everyone, controlling the activity of the day. Although the country is governed from Ottawa, the unchallenged ruler is the weatherman! More or less confined, native friends set to another pastime—a game of 'craps'. Where they learned it is one of those mysteries; but play it!...why, were it not for their skins I would have sworn they were part of the American Negro Army that had been left behind. "Come on seven!" "Shoot the works!" and "Little Joe!" came forth in Dogrib, Cree, French, English and a mixture of all, as the two devils hit the log floor, came to a stop and a muskrat skin changed hands.

I had left the cabin as the Indian was about to throw in an all—out 'toss' to regain his losses. Returning hours later after a social evening in the well—booked Hudson's Bay Company staff house, I was surprised at the results.

There sat the Indian, dejected, in a corner, his last possessions, a suitcase and haversack, gone. Such a merciless game! I awoke next morning to another surprise. We were now four. Sometime during the night a visiting Indian friend had entered in his light—footed manner, camping in true Indian fashion on the floor.

The morning found him eyeing my sleeping robe, gibbering in Dogrib, accompanied by gesticulations toward my mobile bed. Upon interpretation I find he wants me to quote a price. Wondering what he thinks I shall use for my journey, and knowing he cares less, I defend my property with blunt refusal. He in turn suggests it might burn. Thwarting this, I suggest, "so will this one!" (thumbing another robe). We all see the humour (including the Indian) and laugh at the foolish one—sided deal.

So the days came and went; Spring was around the corner and against the side of each building; the 'Breeds were scheming amongst themselves and hunting was temporarily retarded by 'visiting'. We were unknowingly being cut off from the South by the thaw. There was nothing to do but wait. So I set to a little visiting on my own.

On one such visit I was amazed at the sundry tasks performed by the priests of the mission, who, I soon discovered, are Jacks—of—all Trades. My matin call finds them in overalls, laying the keel for a boat which is for pleasure, and to set their fish nets from which they will draw their winter supply. Gazing at the crude skill of the artisans one wonders if they have any prep—courses or a pre—knowledge of what is demanded of a religious man spreading the good word northward. "We mus' do everysing,"said Father LaPerriere, glancing up from his wood chiselling. Looking towards the hospital, I could see Brother Korpel piling wood and the Father's words hit home.

To Build A Better Boat

Time on my hands. Life looked sweet. Relaxing against the sunny side of the cabin I found a spot where I could silently marvel at the serene surroundings. Spring came around the corner again today. Crows are cawing; our dogs, restless, howl occasionally; the mission bell tolls; ice in the lake cracks, a piece sliding asunder bringing Summer that much closer. The village becomes alive, seemingly shaking off its heavy robes of winter, worn for seven long months. Yes, the days would be long and filled with much action now. There was no doubt about that.

'The Indian camp; I haven't paid it a visit yet', I reminded myself. 'Probably like all the others'? I imagined, crossing the bridge under which the water bubbled mirthfully. These people prefer to live apart from the Whites. Crossing the village, over the creek again I came face to face with innumerable log dwellings built in similar pattern, several teepees and an odd assortment of fish hung inverted from the crude racks. Dogs howled and barked at my approach. This was taken for granted, I now more familiar with Indian encampments. A cautious canine skulked from the doorstep as I knocked, paused a brief moment and then entered without hesitation. This is a well—established custom which omits the formalities. However, habit has left its mark on me, hence the hesitation. Handshakes are unnecessary as a squaw points to a chair in a dark corner. I am reminded that 'actions speak louder than words' in this instance. What good were English words, anyhow? The occupants huddle in squalid conditions saying nothing but the odd unintelligible guttural sounds. Elders affectionately paw and fondle their children habitually; the boys lie about sucking on cigarette after cigarette, one, no more than eight, holding his own with the family in this department. They enjoy music always, and proffering some peanuts, they accepted, listening intently as I strummed an aged cowboy song on the guitar. Lights are seldom bothered with, and as a draft sneaks in the wall behind me I refuse to think what it must be like in the sixty−below weather.

Natives of the North

Having run out of tunes a dusky damsel winds the gramophone, as common an article in their dwellings as the pictures of Jesus hanging above their beds. With uncertain moanings it picks up speed, repeats a line, clicks as it passes a crack on each round and scrapes its whining way to the chorus. Smiles appear and disappear on some faces as the cowboy sings words of love to his lady. Others, like deadpans, show no emotions while a child giggles with misunderstanding.

I chuckled inwardly as the words of Service's Chippewayan, Roll−in−the−Mud, drifted into the room: 'You've brought us canned beef, an' it's now my belief that this here's a case of 'canned man'.' Then the needle faltered, crossed the record at a dizzy pace and the voice ground to a mournful stop. Laughter came from every invisible corner of the room and as it too died I found my own voice amongst the others. Again I was struck by the freedom from care and worry of this simple−living people; again it left its indelible impression. Partings conform to the same nonchalance as entries. Whether they understood or not I thanked them for their hospitalities and departed.

Thursday, May 15th, dawned bright again, with peels of the bell echoing through the village. 'What can this mean on a weekday?' I asked myself, moving toward the calendar on the opposite wall. Ascension Sunday, it read on the Catholic Calendar. It would be another main event, I knew, so I dressed hurriedly to attend the service. Any event, no matter how small, brings a variation to the settlement, be it a dog falling through the ice or a small morsel about a Lafferty, Mercredi or a Beaulieu or some other well−known character within a large radius. This surely would give rise to some form of gossip, I thought, slamming the door and heading on my daily amble through the village.

Nine−fifty−nine saw me pulling the bell−pull in a very uneven and irreligious fashion. Then I discovered that in a ringing a simple bell there too is an art. With a slight interference by the Brother who's duty it was to call the flock, my off−beat bell−pulling came to a halt. "We mus' reach them all, you see,"he said jokingly, demonstrating with a final pull. We followed the last of the congregation into the tiny mission above the Post Office.

As I climbed the steps to the second floor wherein lies the chapel, I can see Indian and 'Breed faces lining the rear wall. Scanning the pew, I note a vacant place, seating myself on the wooden bench beside them, a Catholic for the nonce. On the left side of the small interior are the squaws, wearing for the occasion their best black shawls spread over head and shoulders. They kneel or squat in their moccasined feet beside their rubbers, placed neatly side by side. Behind them in a pew sit four of the Grey Nuns from the hospital while the fifth, beside the altar pumps the wheezing organ which is sufficient to lead the chanting and humming (the latter adopted by the Indians as a substitute for the Latin and French). The men have taken their place on the right, some squatting, others sitting. The altar is well decorated, immaculately white with candles all aglow. A green light flicks below the impressive statue of the Virgin Mary. Marvellously imitated flowers adorn the tableau above the I.H.S. painted in gold letters near the base of the altar.

Father Trassard conducts the main portion of the service, assisted by Brother Korpel, while the aging Father LaPerriere, seated on the right of the altar, clicks two hinged sticks when it is time to change the ritual. Father Trassard is dressed seemingly equivalent to Pope Pius himself and all this I feel must surely have a profound effect upon the converts, who have learned to respect, and accept the Roman Catholic religion.

At the rear are the 'Breeds, lining the entire pew. They appear less serious about the religion, although they be as good Catholics. It was not hard to conclude that natives have good voices, for as the hymns came and went they joined in with anxiety, one feminine voice high above the rest plucking the stratospheric notes too high for the hallowed group. Then followed the half–hour sermon in French, which reached the majority including the cheechako, who managed to grasp the occasional phrase.

One hour of ups and downs with the Father clicking the sticks to mark the changes and the larger portion of the congregation leaves. "Where's everyone going?" I asked in ignorance of the procedure. "Oh, it is benediction, which only some take," explained my adjacent native friend. So I descended with the majority to the welcome sunlight below, where all congregated and gossiped about the event of the day.

My attendance was rewarded with a pleasant offering–an invitation to dine with the priests. With the beckoning of a bell marking 11:30 we hastened away, I in possession of a valuable memoir of Ascension Sunday in Fort Rae–a Chippewayan Indian prayer book (out of the small stock printed in far off Belgium) signed with the compliments of the Fathers.

One week: I feel like a citizen of Fort Rae. Another day and I would have been a prisoner of the Fort as the river channel widened and snow disappeared by the hour. It had been a pleasant stay living in the environment of this mixture of people brought together by the common denominator, trade; but the spirit of adventure called from within. I must prepare to go, regardless of my 'Breed friends' decision. That might take days to make and I trusted not my fortune completely to the fickle nature of a Half–Breed mind. Yes, I was decided; I would leave tomorrow. But I had a shocking surprise to receive yet!

A Prayer for All

My first duty to perform was a visit to the Fathers to receive outgoing mail. "Hello dare...you going to get stranded weez us if you stay much longer," said Father LaPerriere, as I arrived on the scene of the boat–building. "Weel you take de mail with you wan you go?" "That's exactly what I've come for, Father, and of course, to bid farewell to you all," I said. "That ees kind of you, my son...but you mus' go soon, for summer lasts but a short while in thees contree...and your *Trails of '98* are long, no?" I laughed a little, knowing just how long they were to be. "Eet weel be a month before theee first plane lands on pontoons, you see?" The predicament suddenly became obvious. What work for one like me in such a tiny settlement? I had to go, I realized. Then a volley of what sounded like curses in a personal tongue resounded above the tapping of a hammer on the other end of the boat. A clamp fell to the rocks as the plank sprung free. Nailing the opposite end and trying again with the clamp the same thing happened; but the other end of the planking sprung free. Another volley of foreign language and I wondered. "I think that sounds close to the real thing, doesn't it Father?" I suggested. "Oh no!..no!...," he assured me, laughing: "I <u>always</u> say <u>that</u> when things go wrong." I still wonder what 'that', translated, might mean.

A quick round to the Colin MacDonald Trading Post, the Hudson's Bay and the Mounted Police home brought a handful of mail wrapped in an oilskin cover. Not forgetting the Grey Nuns, I recalled my jest of the previous visit. The moccasin telegraph proved most reliable. Somehow the

Sisters had caught wind of my date for departure. There was a large package of baking, wrapped and waiting. "The veree best to you," chimed the sisters, as I waved farewell. The jest had proven fruitful.

Then it happened. "You'll never get through alone!" said my friend, back at the cabin. "Alone?" I queried. "Yes..me and some friends are going ratting, North...I take the rifle...you have the dogs," he said, with presumed finality. "I'll take the rifle and the dogs," I challenged, regarding my weapon. "O.K....no rifle, no dogs!" he added. There we were getting nowhere as decision and indecision mounted. Eventually, we compromised: I took the dogs; he took the rifle. I was about to meet the North alone. 'How'll you get out of here? Supposing you can't get on the Big Ice?' said the voice of Pessimism. 'He'll manage alright,' answered the voice of Optimism. What about food? How about fish for the dogs?' Back and forth raced doubts and a restless night brought morning too soon. Sunshine and breakfast brought assurance. Suddenly, like a wave of comforting warmth, came the satisfying feeling of being on the move again...that feeling of being a something, if only an animated object refusing by unconscious natural forces to be still and accept. With this elated feeling I hitched the dogs and with the 'good luck' parting from my companions, bounded from the cabin−site over what remained of the sunstroked snows. "Mush," I yelled, and too−eager dogs lapped up distance.

Across the narrow wooden bridge for the last time; it echoed a thunderous farewell; and I came to a stop before the Post Office. "Hey"...you go by sled...you never make it...creek washed out below two miles...bad...veree bad! " said the Redskin trapper, wet to the hips. This was proof enough of the thaw. I was satisfied. "But there must be some way outa here?" I challenged. "I gotta get goin." At that moment the Goddess of Fortune waved her magical wand. "Come on in for some flapjacks, Cheechako," commanded a voice, loaded with good humour at the sight of my predicament. "We'll get you outa here somehow!" Sweating profusely, I accepted and as we sat around a stack of flapjacks Bill Coombs and Allen Dick decided my immediate future. "Should be able to pole out by now," suggested one. "You have to see about the oil barges down−water, anyway Al," replied the other. "Suppose you make it today, Sunday, nothin' much doin', and by the way better toss in a couple tins of meat...this guy hasn't a rifle!" And a large sized smile across the table gave away the feelings of the third party. "Well, how do you feel now?" asked the police corporal. "With a load of those flapjacks and news like I just heard, how else could I feel?" Half an hour later with the church bells peeling their own farewell, a boat loaded to prow with dogs, sled, grub, a Mounted Policeman, a trader and the Cheechako, pushed off from the shores of historic Fort Rae.

Minutes later, a motley crew, we poled, rowed and bailed our way out of sight of the isolated trading post, breaking the ice for our own Exodus. As the spire above the mission had first appeared in welcome, so it disappeared amongst the treetops, closing the Book of Adventure on an eventful week in the settlement sprawled beneath its silent vigil.

Caught In The Thaw

The journey to the Indian village and the Lake, seven miles distant, was not without event. "Look behind!" shouted the Mountie, poling vigorously amongst the ice floes. Turning, we saw what he meant. "She'll be on us in no time if we don't move fast," yelled Grant, the trader. With combined action we poled, pushed ice and fought to hold our own. The ice we had broken moved in behind us in a huge floe. "Hit for shore," said Al; and we did. Examining the terrain for a suitable portage to a nearby creek, an unmistakable din came to our ears. The dogs, tied to the seats of the boat, were hard at one another. By no means a fair fight, we raced to stop the possible carnage. A quick check showed a chewed ear and a bitten leg. Not too serious, was the verdict. We prepared for the portage.

Why dogs, seeing their burden—the sled—moving off without them' should be so desirous of following, is more than I can conceive. But follow they did. Half way across the stream with the sled in a canoe (discovered at the much—used portage), the Mountie shouted back, "Can you hold them?" "Sure," I yelled, and at that moment they bolted. Unable to hold five eager dogs who have had a week of rest, I stood breathless on the bank as they floundered in the harness, some swimming, some dragging, one heading off in his own direction. "*Mush!....Mush!*" the only encouragement I could offer, rang loud and far down the creek. As they reached the foremost shore I suddenly felt limp. Exhausted, I sagged to the bank. How many times had I envisaged myself walking to Yellowknife and accounting for five dogs. How glad I felt when the Great Slave Lake was reached; now it would be easy going once on the ice.

CHAPTER SIX

THE MAIL MUST GET THROUGH

Male farewells are generally brief. This one was no exception as I checked the map, shook hands with two swell fellows and with the loudest 'Mush!' I could muster, pushed through the hundred yards of open water that led to the solid ice beyond. "The mail must get through!" I laughed. Water splashed; dogs yelped with anxiety; I held on with both hands. Then the '*swish*' of crisp snow under sled runners came to my ears. A soothing feeling of security welled up inside. "You did it, Ben!...nice going, Blackie...atta boy Ring!...good old Skookum!...you're alright too, Fiver! (if you'd only keep the harness filled more often)," I said to each personally. They seemed to know I was with them—their new master. Dinner—hour having come and gone, I reached for some chocolate, headed the sled in the direction of Old Fort and settled myself on the dunnage as the eager dogs brought the silent point into gradual focus. The mail was going to get through!

My old urge to go somewhere takes complete command. I relax, wondering who is most eager, man or beast? There is certainly some energy to burn in all carcasses. A last wave and my ex—hosts pass out of

**Grant MᶜMillan and
Allan Dick**

sight. I am alone in the still, vast whiteness that reaches out in every direction with its luring distance, cheating the eye at every glance, but compensating also with its deceitful beauty. I am swallowed up, alive with the paradoxical life of the elements, shifting and changing in their impulsive dance upon and across the immaculate white stage, awesome and enthralling, lulling unarmed spectators with its Song of the Trail, the hours fleeting like careless minutes. How can one be alone with so much company; such versatile entertainers? Yet, I was alone; alone with five dogs, an axe, a frying pan and some grub.

Four o'clock in the afternoon: Sol was still running his long course high in the Northwest, surrounded by a fantail of cirro—cumulus clouds spreading with as splendorous a display of feathery appendages as the bird it so closely simulates. A cool wind assures of good travelling on the glazed surface. A commingled feeling of irresponsible self—sufficiency and irrepressible optimism, felt by a man as he throws his weight behind a string of eager dogs, pervades my person. 'Nothing can go wrong. Nothing will go wrong! There is always some way out,' I challenged unhearing ears. As I sat imagining all the improbable (yet, not impossible) things that can happen, I felt all the more secure with the life—giving (and life—taking) wilderness surrounding, broken only by the faintly audible '*swish*' of sled runners across glare ice. I had put the past behind me, in its proper place. Canine tongues were hanging out and their exerted puffing brought reason to the fore. My eager dogs were overdoing their good work. It was time to slacken the traces. "Whoa, Ben," I yelled at the lead, "you've all earned a rest...now have a good roll," I challenged, light—heartedly, jumping from the sled myself. Old Fort rose majestically in the foreground. Back along the horizon, where the sled runners slipped into infinity, dark green spruce agglomerated themselves in the fore of the district of Fort Rae; I thought again of an eventful week in a veritable 'beyond the beyond'. That was the last time we looked back.

So far I am amazed at the self—designed pace of my mongrels, but in retrospect I say "a fish a day and sleep anytime…why, you're all in fine fettle!" Listening ears hear the meaningless words, rising momentarily, falling as the words trail off. Later as the pace slackened I was to reflect once again; but this time on the season of the year.

It is well into spring and knowing that we all have our supine moments, I forgave them for their sin. I was in no rush: Why hurry? Yes —

> "Why hurry little river,
> Why hurry to the sea;
> There's nothing there to do,
> But to sink into the blue
> And all forgotten be…"

I put a boyhood poem to good practical usage as we sunk into the darkening blue of evening.

Alone on the 'Big Ice'

'Mush'—a word common to most dogs living north of latitude 60° put Old Fort a sled—length closer and my thoughts to wandering again as I watched the heavenly vicissitude. How blue the sky, how white the clouds and snow! Was I about to sacrifice civilization for its siren charms? No, surely it is only a passing thought; and a moment such as one wishes to cherish forever, came and went as I, 'yoo'ing and 'cha'ing' (right and left), cussing and mushing to the responding dogs, supped heavily of the Northern draught…not a worry in the world, a destination…but when? Not one of the six of us cared to answer.

Signs of life appear: fresh caribou tracks in the snow, a crow in a nearby tree, seagulls (seemingly displaced) sweeping, gliding, curving in their graceful aeronautics. Then the ruins of Old Fort came into view. Satisfied with the world and the distance covered, I decide to re—pioneer that ghost town. With psychic speed the dogs, always ready to 'cha' when land is to port, make for the island, once more rivals in eagerness. Six—thirty I officially claim Old Fort erecting (instead of the Fleur—de—lis) a camp fire from which the smell of cooking meat and the sound of boiling water proclaim supper is ready.

Any meal 'on the trail' is simple and sufficient. My pioneer meal, in front of the decaying ruins of the one—time Fort, lacked not in simplicity, leaving me with that satisfied feeling that nothing is wrong in the world. And there wasn't in my world! A tin of meat patties, Sunland (hard—tack) Pilot biscuits, Brookfield tinned butter from the convenient, flat, one—pound size tin done up especially for convenience, raspberry jam and my indispensable cocoa built from Klim powder comprised the repast on the once historical site. While on the subject of food I must mention that tea is the Northland 'standby' with everyone, and is as traditional as it is with Englishmen. Hanging my wet socks over the fire to dry for the next change, I relaxed in the pink sunset. Five dogs eyed me speculatively from their lying position, but they knew as well as I it was not time for their fish yet. Sparrows flit to and fro' while meadowlarks and spring's harbinger, a Robin, sing; I am singing too; inside, singing with contentment. Checking the well—worn map I set a goal past the right of Waite Island to the scattered reefs beyond. "All right, Ben" (a signal he had learned in his puppy days for rising, that I had heard Fred use), I said to the lead dog. On their feet and as anxious as I to be going, there was no hesitation. "Mush!…Mush!" and another post was vacated for the still beckoning reaches of the Big Lake.

'I am still running the gauntlet. The ice will surely be gone from the shores at the end of the journey?' This thought lingers in my mind, remembering well what happens when dogs take to water in harness. I don't exactly relish the thoughts that it kindles. There is but one thing to do: keep up the dog—trot my four—footed beasts of burden have lapsed into, and enjoy the splendor of sunset over Old Fort, flooding the countryside with its variegated pinks of evening. A cool wind assures good mileage as it freezes melted surface into glass. The dogs, in their desire to go south faster than north (why? I'll never know...unless, possibly they sense home?), aid too in this. They are not dumb; but like some wives we hear of who show more respect through subordination, they must be shown who is master. Ours is a 50−50 bargain so far, and I hope it will continue this way.

Settling myself once more in the sled, I turn my vision towards the rear; this is once when looking backward is profitable. The sun, round and redder than all Hades, is flooding the Western doorway as it slowly closes for the night. Gradually it changes, a veritable prism of colour, red, amber, mauve, amethyst, turquoise, weakening as it dilutes itself with night. Glancing only occasionally to the front, I fell victim to the western panorama for one hour, watching the last energies of the day spend themselves (much like overtired children, ready for the fall of night and rest) telling my unresponding canines how beautiful it is, wishing I did not have to hoard the entire scene. But I didn't feel guilty. There would be other nights; other sunsets; and other lone wolves to devour the most meaty morsel of the whole day.

Ten−thirty found us girdling Waite Island with Point−du−lac to the right. Waite Island has a sole inhabitant. His name is Jim Gode. He is a hermit living in a ramshackle cabin, content to retain and work his sixty claims, which he (like many a die−hard prospector) thinks is the 'real thing'. Time and our good speed forbade him a visit. "How is a man supposed to follow all these islands?" I asked my dogs, fumbling the map and hoping my guess was correct. "Only don't bother answering!" I added; "I'll rely on memory and instinct," folding the map and putting it in a pocket. With more confidence in myself than those behind, I felt overloaded with that vital 'traveller's optimism', feeling perfectly familiar with my present surroundings. "*Cha* Ben! Tomorrow is another day," I yelled at the pooches, sighting a likely clump of spruce for a campsite. So the day's successes and the dogsled came to a halt. "You've earned this," I muttered to each dog turning his collar sideways from a furry neck, tethering each to a nearby tree. "One for you...and one for you, Ring...and the biggest for you, Fiver. You did well today," I said to the understanding dogs who saw where the largest fish went. "Now a pot o' tea for you," I told myself, talking like a 'bushed' trapper. The day had proven more progressive than expected. Our reward was granted. Sleep.

With the mournful howl of a dog I had passed into slumber; with the same howl coming from a distance I greeted the warmth of a sunny morning. "Ten o'clock?....Surely not!" I answered myself. The snow was already melting. "I must have breakfast and be off," I told my canines, who pricked up their ears and understood. It was not long before the '*swish*' of runners coupled with the eager whining of five dogs sounded the getaway. It was about seventy−five miles to the cabin of D'Arcy Arden. "Will we make it today?" I asked the dogs, already into their best consistent pace; if they could speak I know they would say "We're sure as hell gonna' try!" So I turned Ben in the direction of home and the traces gave a responding tug. I knew we were going to make it.

Assuming my most casual posture on the bed roll in the sled I watched the clouds racing along with us. I had a long way to go; I might as well be comfortable.

It was about this time that I caught myself talking to the dogs, a habit common to most sled drivers. Each individual has his pet vocabulary, some falling within the bounds of censorship, while others have a few good words for their lifesavers in winter Down North. Bored with the vastness and silence, they utter such quips to their dogs as: "*Caribou! Caribou!*" which they understand only too well, perhaps from bringing them down on the run when no harness or tether impedes them; "*Ki!Ki!Ki!*" or "*Kee!..kee!..kee,*" in a high falsetto, and the popular high−toned vibration of the lips in a "*Brrrrrrrrrr*" all serve as encouragement. Others just talk about their destination, life, or a male's most common topic: women. All are excuses for talking to oneself, which in any man's language is supposed to be a bad sign. My topic of conversation was a Love of Life' that I felt as we cruised toward Whitebeach Point. It was a complete regard for this bright, white vastness that brought the Good and the Man to the surface. Such noble thoughts I could hide from no one. Feelings found words; words sought ears; and I felt the dogs understood as they continued to lean on the traces. I felt too sane to suspect myself of anything. I felt no loneliness on the trail, for, while on the move, I felt nothing to be lonely about. Occasionally a small memoir of civilization will linger and haunt the lone traveller who asks himself so often: 'Why do I stay in this goddam country?' But the lure is stronger than the man who has weathered the seasons, continually lured on till it is all a part of him. Then let him forsake it, like any man who forsakes a woman...she will continue to haunt him, regardless of space or distance. So nostalgia plays her small role, slipping in between curses and smooth talk to the dogs, or perhaps the light air of a once popular song.

Noon brought us to the Point, from which a clear view of the main arm of Great Slave could be seen. D'Arcy's cabin lay around that southeast point, I mused. "We're going to make it aren't we?" I asked the pooches: and if tail wagging meant 'yes' there was no doubt. Obsessed by the thought of a single tin of fruit in the pack, I could refrain no longer from digging it out. I sat munching hard—tack biscuits and plums, receiving now and then a look of envy from one dog, then another, raising his head at the tempting sounds of one making lunch. 'You know you can't eat while on the run!' I would say. The head would lower a degree, eyes looking wistfully in my direction.

Imagination has a loose rein in the Great White Wilderness. It is the common occurrence of most at sometime to imagine he hears sounds or sees strange objects. Just another part of this intriguing North, accepted for what it suggests. As we cleared the Point I discovered I was still not immune. "Did you hear that?"I asked Fiver, the wheel—dog. "Sounds like a Prairie freight train....Dammit if I ain't going' bugs too!" I accused myself. I sat up and listened. "Yes, there is no mistaking it...I grew up to the sound of those, hooting their way across Saskatchewan," I told the dogs. It was a pleasant reflection for the nonce. Then 'Cat—train' tracks (caterpillars for commercial hauling) coming into view brought my likeable hallucination to an end. The last snow to melt on the Big Ice exposed the tracks forming two distinct ridges which, winding crazily back and forth, would eventually lead to Yellowknife. "We're on the right track!" I yelled. *Mush*, Ben!" followed in unrestrained eagerness.

With hours to burn and not desiring to contact any more snow—blindness by watching diabolical heat waves dancing on their sheen stage, I reached for my battered volume of Robert W. Service poems and lay back in contented perusal. *The Call of The Wild....The Lone Trail....The Pines*; I hear it, I follow it and I see them.

> 'Have you known the Great White Silence, not a snow—gemmed tree (acquiver?)
> (Eternal truths that shame our soothing lies.)
> Have you broken trail on snowshoes? mushed your huskies up the river,
> Dared the unknown, led the way and clutched the prize?
> Have you marked the map's void spaces, mingled with the mongrel races,
> Felt the savage strength of brute in every thew?
> And though grim as hell the worst is, can you round it off with curses
> Then harken to the Wild—it's wanting you...'

Pausing to rest my eyes from the moving print, gazing into an infinity of white, I realize it 'has me'. Accepting the challenge, I encouragingly read on..."the Wild is calling, calling...let me go!"...and we slid over another mile of white, as lines from the Bohemian Bard's pen melted into reality.

> 'And sometimes it leads to the Northland
> And the scurvy softens your bones;
> And your flesh dints in like putty,
> And you spit out your teeth like stones...'

Passing over the Cat—Train tracks I felt thankful that they now bring a mixed diet to the settlements, which, in the early days fell prone to the dreaded scurvy because of lack of a proper diet. My bones wouldn't soften, my skin wouldn't dint like putty, and I didn't intend to spit out my teeth in the Northland. Reading on, I coursed the *Trail of '98* with the bard. "Just a few days and you'll be taking that Trail too," I threw at the dogs. Sorry, but that's where we part company...much as I like your style," I added, as we neared the S.E. Archipelago.

Hours pass, the sun beating mercilessly upon what must have looked like a tiny moving speck from a distance. With the proximity of the islands I put away the instilling verse of the Northern Bard and seek an opening between the many isles. The dogs have been faithful, never once slackening their rythmic trot, but hanging tongues told their own story. "Just another hour, Skookum," consoled the Cheechako, sighting the longest tongue. "*Cha*, Ben!" I commanded and without anymore encouragement the dogs, sighting land, doubled toward what they thought would be a rest. But alas, I had been too sure of my bearings. The sun, ever beguiling, had played its trick again. "Sorry, fellas, but you'll have to blame the sun!" I apologize as we head out again fast to the rim of the islands. "Surely, there must be a fresh trail somewhere?" I ask myself.

Then I saw it as plain as the very snow itself. Generously imprinted in the wet muck lay the unmistakable marks of the only sled of its kind in these parts. Simultaneously the dogs, picking up the trail, followed eagerly in the fresh path of the oldtimer, D'Arcy Arden. I had been afraid of a cul−de−sac amongst the islands. All fears were hastily dispelled as we ate up ground. Knowing man to be a creature of habit I felt sure it would lead to the place where D'Arcy hangs his hat. My surmise was to prove itself as the trail unfolded amongst the islands.

Then a new zeal overcame the dogs. Caribou bones are always an invitation to desert. And desert they did. With a volley of curses and all the disreputable words that a driver can muster, the Cheechako yelled at the impulsive canines who heedlessly made for the slim remains. More threats and yells; more scrimmaging through the left−offs. The next few minutes saw more than threats flying, and when the final count was taken I realized that not a one had failed to glean some fragment, a bone, dried skin or piece of moulting fur, trotting along the trail with the precious bits hanging where their tongues ought to hang. It was with scornful looks that they finally dropped their findings, under threat. Sorry to disappoint them at this stage of the game, I set to untangling the harness, the price paid for my curses and threats to the disobedient hounds. You can be sure we rounded each future deposit of caribou leftovers.

Ben, the lead dog (as though getting even), insisted he knew better than I as he strove to break his own trail. Ordinarily respecting the intelligence of a 'lead' I did nothing, till suddenly I discovered the plot. He was instigating a plan of stubbornness. One feels so often that the dogs know what the man is thinking. Today I had laid down a strick non−acceptance policy and the results had been too good to spoil. So it was that Ben received more than a curse, and, knowing exactly what I was thinking, returned to the trail which was followed without further event.

A still more welcome sight to the tired traveller than the wide sled tracks is the long, spruce−bordered Narrows at the end of which nestles the cabin of D'Arcy Arden. With an exuberant display of energy and as loud a '*Mush*' as can be extracted from my vocal chords, the encouraged dogs rush down the home stretch. So eager were they that by the time I had voiced a dozen "*Whoa's*" I discovered we were stranded on thin ice a hundred feet from shore, hailing D'Arcy Arden.

Too late to turn the dogs, there is but one course to take. Water splashes and troughs open like the waters of the Tiber to let the invader through. Wet, but safe, we hit the bank as the last loud 'Mush' echoes and dies in the hills beyond. With a smile and a handshake the little man says: "For a Cheechako, you're catching on fast!" "Well, I'll leave this frozen country a Sourdough or know why!" I responded. "You must be hungry? How far have you come?" "Left Waite Island about ten−thirty...been goin' steady since with a rest now and then for the dogs," I answered. "Well I'll be!...and it's seven−thirty now!" "Mother....come and hear this! I've got a surprise for you!" he shouted down the yard to his Indian wife. I was at home once more.

The dogs fed and bedded down and my clothing exchanged for dry garments, I found myself seated before a large meal of caribou steak and onions. "Give him another helping, Mother, he's earned it this day," said the gnarled oldtimer. "You looking good...beard and all," she said, refilling the plate. And the meal continued, broken only with the telling of tales which found the ears of a good listener, his wife and family. As the Coleman light died down, one by one we left the conversation of a sociable evening. Over saturated with the requisites of sleep, the Cheechako sought the inner folds of his sleeping bag...and he faintly remembered someone say: "Sleep as long as you like in the morning," and he thought, 'What a wonderful day...and there's another one tomorrow...'

Ben

Blackie

The Team—A Cheechako's Best Friends

Ring   Skookum   Fiver

CHAPTER SEVEN

THE ESKIMO MURDERS AND KLONDIKE ECHOES

The morrow dawned bright, as did each succeeding morning. D'Arcy, regular as clockwork in his visits to the 'shack' (his workshop overlooking the bay), opened the creaky door, saying: "Did I ever!...I should drive a dogteam more often." A hearty laugh gave way to a tale; an episode from his life. I listened from within my robe as he busied himself with the fire, sprayed flies in the window or sharpened a favorite knife. It was like opening a geography book and travelling away to another new frontier, for his was the era of frontiersmen. I began to feel personally in touch with Stefansson, Amundsen and the Arctic Regions of Banks Land, Coronation Gulf, Victoria Island, Coppermine and Herschel Island, all of which became a few miles distant. Told in the jargon of geologist–astronomer–surveyor, I felt the elemental closeness and importance of the wind, clouds and stars which play such a leading role in the life of the North. So each morning and each story was looked forward to with adventurous anticipation.

One morning I turned over in my sleeping bag and cocked an ear to the tale of the famous Doak murder of some years ago. "Cpl. William Andrew Doak was a very fine man," says D'Arcy, poking the fire, "and a close friend of mine." One day, a young Eskimo boy was travelling with his sister who carried a baby on her back. It was in the region of the Chopinar Islands and Hood River when suddenly a shot rang out. The girl collapsed, the bullet passing through the back of the baby into her breast. It was a tragic occurrence. No more was heard of the matter for awhile. But the following year a party of Eskimo was shooting lemming on the Barren Lands when a fellow Eskimo said to the murdered girl's brother: "There is the man who shot your sister...now is your chance!" So the boy shot. It too was fatal. A little later a man from the south country was hunting in the vicinity and the boy, fearing what he had done, became frightened. He thought it was the brother of the dead man, come to get him. In a fright he sought the aid of Cpl. Doak at the local police billet. Now Doak was lying down for a rest when the boy entered. His sidearms were slung on the wall from force of habit." Here D'Arcy explains, "the Eskimo at that time had no realization of the power of firearms." The lad, burdened with fear, took the sidearms from the wall. Next he tried to wake Doak with the rifle barrel. Bang! and the bullet passed into the thigh continuing to the heart. He had innocently shot the policeman. Doak, awaking with a shock, merely asked: "What are you doing?"...and fell dead. "Binder, another white man at the post, passed by the window. As he did so, he received a bullet from the rifle still held by the panic–stricken Eskimo... "It was too bad...Doak was a well–liked Corporal, and many felt the loss. Of course the whole thing boiled down to just another feud amongst the Eskimo, and their ignorance of the proper use of weapons. Judge Dube tried the case; but there's nothing much could be done...only put the guilty party on probation. They're an innocent people...don't mean to harm anyone; but they do have their feuds, which they settle in their own way." The Fire roaring warmly in the stove, I slid from my robe and commenced dressing. "They have some queer customs too; don't sew on the ice for fear of ruining their winter clothes. "Odd isn't it, but true in some tribes. They're very hospitable...are offended if you don't eat sumptuously. Each woman brings her offering into the igloo and you are obliged to accept of each." With a laugh D'Arcy continues: "Not so hot if you don't like fish...and they relish the taste of it months old, in fact, the older the better! It appeals to their peculiar taste. No wonder Stefansson had to eat ptarmigan feathers to keep it down...guess he brought up a few feathers at times too!" he chuckled heartily. "Did you know, Cheechako, that when you visit an Eskimo he gives you a warm reception...never seen anything like it...full privileges of the igloo: food, bed and the wives of the natives will mend or do your repairs during your stay. How's that for Northern hospitality?" he smiled. "And I thought yours was good!" I retorted. "For a long time I was curious to know the treatment given to the 'bad men' of the tribe as punishment for their crimes. Then one time I discovered it when visiting a distant tribe. It was grotesque! The prisoner was thonged about the neck and limbs. At a given signal he was dragged at an Eskimo pace (which is not a slow trot) over the Barrens. Such torture was swift and decisive...there was no doubt about that! So you see they have their native justice too."

As I dressed, the events of the Sourdough's life turned to the Klondike and Dawson City. My eventual goal being the heart of the Klondike, I turned a special ear to grasp whatever clue might assist me in re−living the world's greatest Gold Rush. *Fifty years faded and we were at the turn of the century again, mulling, pushing, slogging through the mud of First Avenue in Dawson City. As we stood in front of the Flora Dora Dance Hall D'Arcy leaned over to me and said: "Did ya hear about old Collins last night?" Paid a visit to Lousetown (he did...got drunk and somehow managed his way over to the new red−light district...across the river now, you know...anyway he meets up with a purty 'good time gal'...oh they's plentiful there still...anyhow, comes mornin' and he's looking for his poke...he knew he had a full 'un. So this 'easy acquaintance' sees him searching his clothes and d'you know what she did?...well, just to show you the honest character of some of them gals, she hands it to him, saying politely: "Here's your poke, I thought someone might steal it." Ho! Ho!...d'ya ever hear the likes of that? And he had $10,000 in the bloomin' thing!"* Back at the Arden homestead he added: "Course there's the good and bad everywhere, we all know that, but shows you the honest character of some of them gals. Betcha don't find much of that with your modern 'loose' gals?" he chuckled questioningly. And I smiled. This was one of those many humorous touches that brought a second volley of laughter, as he put away the flit gun and turned to sharpening his favorite pocket knife. "Yes...yes...it was sure a town; but I didn't stay there long. Sometimes wish I had of. By the way, when you get there (and I think you will by the looks of you and the way you got through that water t'other day) you may see the Regina Hotel, Ottawa House or the old Fairview Hotel...oh, there was so many I can't remember them all. And by the way, look up the Stipendary Magistrate while you're there. Gibbon's his name, and say 'hello' from all of us." I pulled on my parka and we left the shack for breakfast.

The day passed like any other day: dogs to be fed, fish to be brought from the nets, ground that was now visible to be raked clean. That afternoon I decided on a short hunt across the lake, with big intentions. The thaw had come fast this week and completed its demolition work on the entire lake behind the homestead. Hours later I returned home, eager to contribute my game to the evening meal. Throwing the bird on the floor I said boastfully: "Guess we have duck for supper!" Mrs. Arden and the entire household went into a spell of laughter. But the laugh was on me. "Mud Hens are no good to eat!" said the kindly woman, pointing at the limp bird and laughing all the more. "Well, a good try Cheechako," said the veteran, but you'll have to be more discriminate about your foul shooting!"

Supper time found me introduced to crushed drymeat and pink marrow, taken from caribou bones. A plate of brains sat before me and I dared not venture into it. "Go ahead," a voice encouraged..."it's the favorite of the Indians." "Well I'm not Indian, but I'll try some." It did have a very distinctive taste. With this hors d'oeuvre the meal progressed as the Oldtimer again became the centre of attraction with his delectable anecdotes, discharged between glances at the latest News Week. Chuckling in his inimitable fashion, he removes the black rimmed spectacles used for reading, and leaning towards his company as though plotting, says: "I'll never forget one incident while I was a government surveyor. One day the boss had said to go out and get a reading. So I packed my gear and set off. I found myself waiting for Polaris (North Star) to come into position. It's pretty hard to get at the right moment during the summer with the perpetual daylight," he added. "With this I could get the exact time and location for the shooting. A dead tree lay in my path of vision. So, with ample time on my hands and nothing better to do while I waited, I took my axe and began to lay low the darned thing. Three hours later I regained consciousness, shook myself and returned, slightly crestfallen, to camp." "Did you get it?" the chief asked. "I got it alright," I replied, removing my hat, "right here on the head!" It happened that the top of the rotten tree had broken off, descended on his skull and layed him out for three hours; consequently Polaris had passed and the day's work was in vain.

"Say, there's no prettier sight than to have a dog pack, each dog with his individual lead, strewn out on the Barrens, all within sight," he reminisces. "And speaking of the Barrens, there was once an infallible character who lived for years in that country...from a pretty good family too — Yorkshire, I believe! John Hornby was his name. Anyhow, after the war he was pretty restless...some thought he was a little off. He did act queer at times. I knew him well. He boasted that he would never starve on the Barren Lands. Last time I saw him he was headed on a new venture with another gent from a good family...name was James C. Critchell−Bullock...quite a handle, eh? Well, they must have spent a pretty hectic winter, the two of them...lived in a sand hole covered over with a tarp supported by poles. When the snows come in that country they blow away or bury everything. Well, somehow they survived the winter and went out via Hudson's Bay and the East. They made it too! Bullock since wrote a book called 'The Snow Man'...up on the shelf there!" He pointed to a collection of faded books. Hornby made another trip with a relative and a third party. That was his last. Untrue to his boast, he died of starvation. One by one they perished...it was horrible as told by the last one, in writing..."

Supper over, we climbed to the summit of the hill behind the house. The well−worn path wound its way amongst rocks and moss to the top, and puffing, D'Arcy says: "I come up here nearly every night with Mother and we spend long periods just gazing over the rugged country. Makes you feel like a king without artificial wealth doesn't it?...look at the lakes, inlets, and narrows...as far as your eye can see." We hear of Champlain and his thousand islands...well here is D'Arcy Arden and his thousand Islands, no less pretty, stretching away toward the south and west. "You've got a right to feel like a king," I said, struck by the panoramic beauty that unfolds itself from the heights to the Great Slave Lake, which is still garbed in whitish−blue to the horizon. "See the caribou out on the lake...must be the last of them...they passed in thousands just the other day," points out the little man at a speck in the white distance.

'Mother' Arden and Muskrats

It is truly a sanctuary. Ducks ripple the lake below, surrounded by a coulee of hay, sending ever−widening circles over the surface to lose themselves against the shore. Forboding rain clouds muster above, sending a soft evening shower down on the spring countryside. The air is suddenly cooled, birds chirp, scurrying for the shelter of their nests; greenstone adopts its brightest colour with the wet; a loon hoots crazily from the lake below, appearing at a different spot with each successive dive into the cloud−darkened surface and a bull frog completes the sound effects of evening.

Then the rain clouds disappeared, the last rays of the setting sun casting long spruce shadows over the tranquil ponds. A partridge, seemingly happy about the aftermath of the shower, 'drums' madly as he works himself into a frenzy about an answering mate. Consolidated Mine, smoking heavily over its daily drudge of extracting man's most−sought−for metal, is the one distracting sign of civilization, looming grotesquely above the horizon to the northeast.

"Now what do you think of the country?" asks the paladin. "Can't find words," I admitted, glowing with the inspiring strength of man close to Nature. We clambered from the heights. Darkness slowly descended upon us.

Over a cup of tea we sat around the long table discussing the world's problems, the merits of life in the North and once again conversation took a turn to the cold reaches of the Arctic. The Coleman lamp hissed as it gave off its brilliant illumination. Mrs. Arden, playing solitaire at the far end, glanced up now and then at a reminder of her years spent as a lone hunter with the 'Huskies', mentioning a time, a place, an interesting incident. The remainder of the family have their heads in books, the Eskimo boy playing on the floor. D'Arcy, imaginative, eager to find an interested ear, leans from his favourite place at the head of the table and speaks: "I remember the

Eskimo Murders very well. Perhaps it was before your time, (which it was)...about 1913 if memory serves me right...(Shortly after the spearing of Radford and Street—traders in Bathurst Inlet). The victims were two Roman Catholic priests — Fathers LaRoue and Rouviere. The priests were living amongst the Huskies (that's what we call the Esquimaux). Apparently they had some trouble convincing the tribesmen about Christianity...was a bad year too for game...you know what that means? They kill the young girls and boys in years of famine...oh yes, it is an old custom of the people: it's the old survival business. You see my adopted boy there?...it would have happened to him if I hadn't come along just when I did. "At any rate the Fathers decided to leave the tribe. They needed a guide to escort them on their way. this is where Sinnisiak and Uluksak came into the picture. Now, some Huskies have a strange superstition about the bush or South country inhabited by the Indians...it extended to a fear of the Indians themselves at one time and the two warred. It seems the two Eskimo became infuriated...they also had a personal disrespect for the attitude of Father Rouviere...he was quite overbearing and dogmatic in his manner...not too well liked. Eventually they reached the site of Bloody Falls where in 1711 Samuel Hearne stood and watched the Indians massacre the Eskimo. Here the Copper (blond) Eskimo did their treachery. Sinnisiak, coming behind the sled, shot Rouviere through the back, simultaneously motioning to his companion Uluksak to get Father La Roue...he did...stabbed him to death with a hunting knife. This done, the two superstitiously thought if the livers of the priests were consumed the virtues of the holy men would enter their own souls and their crime would be overlooked. The bloody ordeal over with, the Eskimo went their way and nothing was learned of the murder till...

...One day at Dease Bay I met some Huskies with white men's effects...my Indian friends recognized them as the clothing of the priests." At this point Mrs. Arden looked up from her losing game of solitaire and said in broken English and Indian, "Me too recognize black robe...one had bullet hole in back." "So the R.C.M.P. were contacted and a long search began for the truth and the criminals," continued D'Arcy as the lamp became dimmer (D'Arcy Arden was 'sworn in' as a constable with the R.C.M.P. search party). "Commander Perry sent La Nauze and two constables north to investigate. They went down the Peace and Slave Rivers thence down the MacKenzie to Fort Norman. That's where they met me on July 17. I was to lead them from there into Eskimo country. With a York boat and laden scows we battled rough waters for two months...when we reached Dease Bay on the remote shore of Great Bear Lake we camped for the winter." (This was the site of old Fort Confidence built by Dease and Simpson in Queen Victoria's Day). "In the meantime two other expeditions were organized to converge on the scene. Peter Beyts was ordered to take a ship from Halifax, proceed to Chesterfield Inlet, push west to Baker Lake, where he would then take to dogsled, crossing the Barren Lands to Bathurst Inlet. Corporal W.V. Bruce at the same time was to patrol from Fort MacPherson, along the Arctic Coast. Early May found us in the Dolphin and Union Straits. We began to hear rumours and picked up some clues; but no murderers were to be found. Then we met Corporal Bruce, off Cape Lambert, who confirmed the clues also; but still no culprits! Joining forces we began questioning the natives. It seemed hopeless, till one day, on questioning some Huskies, our interpretor, Ilvaruic, cried suddenly: "I'm on the track...their men know who murdered the priests...their names are Sinnisiak and Uluksak!" "So the party ventured to Victoria Island, where white law and order were unknown. Here on May 15th, we found the chief culprit — Sinnisiak." A bit of a sorcerer, he said, "I'll sink your boat if you try to take me away!" It was not until the 22nd that we discovered and arrested Uluksak on an island at the mouth of the Coppermine. With our prisoners we proceeded to Herschel Island, where we spent the winter of '16—17 at the northernmost R.C.M.P. outpost.

Meanwhile Beyts was struggling against the Arctic elements, living in misery. He sailed his small schooner through Atlantic storms to advance a base at Baker Lake. Falling short of his goal, he took to the open boats, rowing on into a brisk head—wind. Rough seas smashed the tiller and two oars, nearly capsizing the boat. So forty miles west of the new site he laid a depot. Caught in the ice, efforts were abandoned and he returned to the detachment. Determined, Corporal Beyts and Constable P.R. Conway with three natives, plodded on a heart—breaking patrol of 585 miles by dogteam, in trying to establish a cache on the Thelon River ready for the dash to Bathurst Inlet.

Cold and storms were appalling, game scarce and the dogs ate their harness. Six canines died; the wife of one native gave birth to a baby girl enroute. Worn out but successful Beyts placed the cache, never once dreaming of failure.

On March 21, 1917 Inspector F.H. French, another Arctic veteran, in company with Sergeant Major T.B. Caulkin and four Eskimo set out to complete the work begun by the overland patrol. Eight weeks later, five years after the killing of *Radford and Street, three years after Beyts left Halifax, they reached the Arctic in search of the killers. Finding them caught and hearing the stories of provocation, French gave the natives a good talking—to, explaining the white man's law.

October 16 found them commencing the return march across the dreaded Barrens. Supplies diminishing, French killed some dogs to feed the others, and proceeded. More dead dogs and more picked bones lined the trail. After three horrible weeks, about to starve to death, they spotted a herd of Musk Oxen. This was the happiest Christmas day of all their lives.

5,153 miles totalled the 'hazardous and dangerous journey', the Force's longest patrol and one of the longest Polar journeys on record." Pausing for a moment to link up the details, D'Arcy continued, seemingly as intrigued at memoirs as I was at such first—hand information.

"It was not till May 9th that we left the bleak outpost of Herschel. We were all rather glad to be on the move. Months later the party with the two Huskies reached Edmonton, Alberta. It must have been the most unique trial ever to be held in a Canadian court; and they the most colourful criminals.

Tried in the Supreme Court by a Chief Justice and jury of six, a verdict was reached. "Guilty of Murder....Sentence Death!" came the shocking result after lengthy deliberation. This was not final, though...the two Huskies, ignorant of proceedings, aroused so much pity that sentence was commuted to 'Life Imprisonment'. Still too harsh, sentence was eventually absolved, the Eskimos freed to return to their own land. Placed in the charge of Corporal and Mrs. Walters of Fort Resolution for a two—year period of probation, I understand they enjoyed life and became quite useful about the community, little realizing the seriousness of the crime they had committed. They were later returned to their native land.

Unfortunately the law was not impressed firmly upon the native minds. Two years later in Coronation Gulf, again murder flourished. One, Ahtak, killed his partner, Agluctuk, and, obviously dangerous, was himself murdered. The R.C.M.P. had to start all over again. Again the name of Uluksak came forth. Unbearably bossy, since his visit to the courts Outside, he was murdered by another.

Eskimo Wireless (Identical to Indian Telegraph) brought word to Inspector S.T. Wood of a terrible shooting at Kent Peninsula.

Radford and Street's murderers were never tracked down because of known maltreatment to the Eskimo people, and the costly experiences learned by the previous Eskimo murders.

Hanak, it appears, had threatened to kill some of the married men for their wives. Two others — Pugana and Tatamigana plotted to rid the village of him. The day came: Hanak ran amuck. When the shouting died and the elements were again master of the land, Hanak and four others lay dead. Soon Tatamigana turned on his partner in crime and persuaded another Eskimo to shoot him.

It was here that the well—liked and able Corporal Doak of Tree River entered the drama. Gathering the facts he 'brought in' Tatamigana and Alekomiak. Enroute the latter had frozen his feet, so Doak in his kindly way dressed them, allowing him certain liberties. At this point there is considerable controversy: some say it was ingratitude; others say it was ignorance of the proper use of weapons. At any rate the native shot Doak and ambushed the local trader, Binder, who was considered by some as a questionable character.

So the Pond Inlet Trials, probably the most original in Canada, commenced. In their own northern setting Tatamigana and Alekomiak were charged with murder. Both were hanged in a shed on Herschel Island. This was, without a doubt, the farthest north hanging in the history of the country. Eskimo uprisings in the earlier days were few; and when trouble occurred it was settled in its own tribal manner," continued D'Arcy. But with the introduction of firearms by the exploiting white man a new difficulty arose. So that's why the series of Eskimo murders followed the exchange, and misuse of the rifle became quite rampant.

*(Radford and Street's murderers were never tracked down because of the known maltreatment of the Eskimo people, and the costly experiences learned by the previous Eskimo murders.)

But in spite of all this (and I should know — I lived with them for years) I still say: "No finer specimens of humanity did God ever create — healthy in mind and body!"

The Coleman flickered — it had long since ceased to hiss objectionably and the children were asleep; Mrs. Arden had won a game of solitaire and put the cards aside; D'Arcy and myself caught one another yawning. "It's been a wonderful day and a very sociable evening. You're leaving tomorrow, so we'd better hit the hay!" "I'll probably dream of Eskimo all night," I said, as we reached the shack. "You could do worse...far worse," he said, handing me a lantern. "Good night, son...see you in the morning," and the door shut on the Cheechako as the oldtimer's footsteps died; in the distance...a dog howled...a mosquito buzzed...

Morning. Glorious sunshine. "Wondered when you'd get around to it," said the little figure I had left so few hours ago. He had apparently been busy for sometime in the shop, and now leaning over a book at his favorite window facing the bay, asked "D'ya ever read Kipling?" "Sometimes," I answered, "but I'm busy with Service now. Always have liked him since I could crawl...got a battered volume with me." "Listen to this!" he replied, as I dressed. And the lines from his favorite poem, *Lady Gloster*, flowed through the room. "It's hard to beat...damned hard to beat!" he emphasized, closing the book. We made our way to the last breakfast.

A week of adventurous morning conversations, warm spring days spent in this Utopia and sociable evenings with the family, gathered about the Coleman lamp, came to an end. I harnessed the eager dogs to the sled, which began to look out of place in the melted surroundings. However, the Big Ice was still intact. "Well, Cheechako, everything's ready. Guess you're eager for the *Trail of '98*? Don't get lost in the Rat Portage...it's tough in spots!" "After all those yarns, I've gotta see the Klondike for myself now," I returned, adjusting the gear. "Thanks for everything, D'Arcy, I won't forget." "You're welcome!" and with another loud "Mush!" the anxious dogs hit the slush and we skidded on to Great Slave Lake. The Oldtimer was soon left behind: Yellowknife lay ahead.

It was a feeling of reluctance mixed with joy that I rounded the point, mushed along the remaining ice and with a splash, cleared the melted edge to the dirt shore. My adventures were about to close; but others would soon begin.

Out of place already, the sled scratched its way to the Narrows. The dogs were loaded into a boat and I rowed to their Indian home, Latham Island. As neighbouring canines howled and barked their welcome, I unharnessed each dog, patted him on the head and tethered him to a nearby tree. "You were a swell team," I said, "and you brought the Cheechako home safely!" As tails wagged understandingly, I turned and retraced my steps to the mainland. The Lone Trail was behind; the Beaten Path lay ahead.

"Hi trapper!" Al cried at the tenthouse door. "Welcome home...good to have you back!...say, where'd you get that beard?" "It's kinda nice to be back, too; but I'm gonna miss those darned dogs, I'm thinking!" "Well sit down and tell us all about it...we thought you'd got lost!" "Well, after I left you that morning..."I started, and it was hours before the story came to a climax.

The veil of evening dropped slowly over the face of Yellowknife, the fiery west persisted in bathing the town and the West Bay dotted with sleeping, pontooned aircraft, in its vivid prismatic colours. Sounds lingered on the cool night air. A hungry Indian dog howled from Laytham Island, as though the moon were a bannock, its piercing tone trailing off into nothingness...

"Guess there's no place like home," came the sleepy voice from the inner folds of a sleeping bag. "What was that?" asked the other. No answer came from the still figure.

Safely Home   **Farewell Faithful Furry Friends**

Phil Looking   **Ingraham Hotel**
over Harbour and Hotel   **Bottles and Garbage Awaiting Spring Thaw Downhill**

Yellowknife Harbour and Huskie Aircraft

Phil Reading *'Trails of '98'*

Homemade Skidoo

Start of a Gold Mine

Giant Mine

CHAPTER EIGHT

GO NORTH YOUNG MAN!

June and Spring came to Yellowknife, with their balmy breezes, warm days and chilly nights. The streets (what precious few there were at that time) became slushy. Water began running down from the rock dome on which the original townsite is constructed, washing everything in its path past, under and into the cabins below. With no organized sewage disposal and the long winter, it is not surprising the amount and variety of objects that found the unfortunate cabins.

Music also came to Yellowknife. Robins began to sing; sparrows found this little town on the remote shore of Great Slave Lake; echoes from Felix Grenier's anvil passed through the open door of his blacksmith shop, were caught by the breezes, and whisked about the settlement...the wholesome music of labour.

The entire mining−town came to life. Motorboats resounded in their passage through the Narrows bound for the Consolidated and Negus Mines; the air was split by the roar of a Norseman winging its way to the bush−country with freight for Lexindin, Diversified or some adolescent mine; and the tapping of hammers arose from the Bay, where a hundred boats of all sizes received a new keel, a caulking, or just a fresh coat of paint. It is the healthy atmosphere of creation, which has so far raised Yellowknife from a few prospectors' cabins and Indian tents to the boom−town that it is; with a little imagination one can look into the future and perhaps see a huge northern metropolis fed by a never−ending stream of aircraft, crossing to all parts of the globe. The roar of a Piper Cub taking off brings one hastily back to reality, and Yellowknife back to the shacktown it is.

Yes, a new month had come at a quick pace around the corner. As the sun grew hotter by the day the throb from the heart of town increased. Jobs came and went as the Cheechako pocketed the money, dreaming of the day when he would board a boat for the trip down the Big River on the *Trail of '98*. For clarity it might be best to list the days and events as they occurred, taken from the soiled pages of his well−worn diary.

JUNE 1: Barges, frozen in deep water in the fall to prevent rotting, are gradually wiggling loose from their surrounding cellar of ice. Pontooned planes are chancing the narrow strip of water along the shore. A homemade Skidoo roars over the remaining snow past the Imperial Oil dump.

JUNE 3: Days are getting longer − we go to bed in broad daylight. Howling Indian dogs, buzzing mosquitoes, and diamond−drilling crews taking advantage of the light, make sleep difficult.

JUNE 4: Have reached the conclusion that it's the civilized pace which gives the receptive mind little time to devour its food properly.

JUNE 5: Am a painter today...The goddam mosquitoes and dogs have chosen midnight for their chorals.

JUNE 6: Still painting the Administrative Buildings ...mosquitoes getting larger by the day, appearing in relentless squadrons...dance job tonight...$20.00 more!

JUNE 7: Last day of painting...$30.00 closer to the Klondike!

New Boss—Charlie Sanders

JUNE 8: I'm a shipbuilder today, working on Charlie Sander's "Guy"…all aircraft are pontooned, now, kicking up one hell of a din day and night.

JUNE 9: Sees me still dabbling in the nautical groove…we add new gunwales and a keel. It is a pleasure to work about the waterfront as birds and planes soar by, 'kickers' roar incessantly while sun and clouds play their sheepish tricks…It is great to be alive surrounded by no time clock or boss burdened with ulcers, a nagging wife or the pressure of people trying vainly to beat time by keeping up with it…all I beat are a few boards with a large−size hammer. Today Charlie, enraged by something in the bow, cursed all heaven and hell from the inner depths of the boat. Then a hammering and ripping of timbers told their own story. Yanking the inner guts out with brute force (I chuckled from amidships as he appeared) saying: "Guess this is my bad day…nothing's gone right!" So he dropped his tools and left.

Two 'Guys'—One Making Shipshape

JUNE 10: Damn the mosquitoes! Their dive−bombing is too accurate…they get larger by the day…ice is all melted in Yellowknife Bay…won't be long now!

JUNE 11: Word came today that the *Distributor* is at Fort Smith waiting for the Big Ice to break…the *Sandy Jane* is to go to Norman Wells at breakup. Sunset has commenced to run into sunrise, its pageant of colour no less than wonderful!…Mosquitoes are getting the best of me. Out of work again but $24.00 closer to Dawson.

JUNE 12: Every boat in the bay, no matter how small, is undergoing some sort of repair. Meet Skipper Len McKinley of the *Sandy Jane*, and after a genial conversation he says: "I think I can fix you up right to Norman!" To add to this good luck, Chiefy, the engineer, gives me a job.

JUNE 13: Another dance — $20.00 more for the fund!

JUNE 14: Where else in the world are there such morning vistas?...I must be sure of passage, because the season is already late. How pleasant it is to see people going about their business in their own way without the rush, push and general cut—throating of city life. We're like one big happy family working aboard ship. Those at Sherriff's Novelty Shop and Lil's Lunch Counter across the street command a closeup view of such humourous irregularities as take place when a group of men work about a boat. The crew is complete. I go as a deckhand!

Indians at Trading Post

Ted Horton—Editor

JUNE 15: "Have you ever looked at Distance and wondered what's beyond?" is the thought as time grows shorter and anxiety unbearable.

JUNE 16: Today, after the rains, the entire countryside changed to its best spring greens. Grass, spruce buds and the indestructible muskeg seem to have grown an inch, while the birds all around don't hesitate to tell us about it. Raucous noises from an ancient gramophone break the serenity of evening...children shriek and play with their usual spring energies.

JUNE 17: *'Jane* has received her final coat of paint; the engines are ready!

JUNE 18: The *Radium King* is expected tomorrow…snow and ice disappear from the Bay…aircraft come and go all day in an incessant stream. They are certainly taking advantage of the Bay now…the wind blowing across from the Big Ice churns up the waters which in turn spank bottoms of boats and barges along shore, like mothers punishing their infants…pilots tinker with their craft, rub the sides gently, pat them here and there fondly with affection generally reserved for a woman.

Launching *Sandy Jane*

**1st Engineer—Skipper—
3rd Engineer—2nd Engineer**

Today the *Sandy Jane* was launched. There was a bustle at the dock. A large crowd had gathered. Shopkeepers gazed eagerly from across the road, temporarily halting business. My first thoughts as I arrived on the scene were: "Has she got trouble? Can't they float her?" Then she groaned, a skid timber creaked as the caterpillar tractor grunted and groaned, looking like an ant with too big a burden to push.

Suddenly a gap appeared between the ship and tractor. *'Jane* rushed down the smooth skids (greased with the cook's best lard) hit the water, sending a white spray bayward. Still undecided, she leaned, hesitated a moment, then straightened to a lady—like position. She was afloat! "She's ready for the Big River," yelled Skipper Len from the wheelhouse, "and I can't wait much longer!" he added, clutching the wheel. Sounds of approval came from the lips of the crew who had worked for days on the interior and exterior; a satisfied audience moved off one at a time; the tractor picked up its equipment and crawled off at a caterpillar's pace. A small cloud of dust settled as the community resumed its usual routine. Yes, our little lady is launched…we are now a floating crew.

JUNE 19: This morning was like a scene from a Jack London novel as the fog rolled into the Bay, looking not unlike San Francisco. After much talking, fussing and measuring, the rudders were finally placed. *Sandy Jane* was ready for her tryout. For weeks the crew have been impatient; but as we glided under our own power into the Bay the tension and impatience vanished. There is no doubt of our leaving within the week!

JUNE 20: Finishing touches were applied to our lady…smiles and laughter were everywhere as we took the afternoon easy…$80.00 more for the journey!

Consolidate Mine   **Negus Mine**

JUNE 21: The day off, I planned to visit D'Arcy Arden for the last time. Dropping out of sight of the 'Con' and Negus Mines, which puffed away arduously, the Indian Village across the Lake to the southeast and the ice floes broken off from the main ice body in the Great Slave Lake, I descended once more into the sanctuary of the Arden Paradise. Nature had deposited more than her quota of spring here.

Mine 'Claim Stake'

D'Arcy Arden and 40 Lb. Trout

The Arden Family

JUNE 22: I caught Whitefish, Coney and a 40–pound trout. Fishing, hunting, eating and drinking...what could be more pleasant?

JUNE 23: I bade a last farewell to the Oldtimer who shouted again: "You're welcome anytime, Cheechako! as the 'kicker' choked, sputtered and coughed itself into a consistent roar; the Arden family passed out of sight for good, around a rocky bend.

JUNE 24: Met Pete Baker, an Arab, born about 80 miles from Damascus...a trial run in the *Sandy Jane* to the Big Ice finds it three feet thick and impenetrable...I met Earl Harcourt of Yellowknife Transportation Company, owners of our staunch lady.

Hudson's Bay—M.V.S.*Radium King*   **'Beer Boat'—unloaded**
Deck Hands—loaded

JUNE 25: The event of the season! — the appearance of *Radium K*ing (the Beer Boat), officially clocked at the Negus Mine about 3:50 p.m.
(There is a lottery held as to the exact time each year that the first boat passes a given point — hundreds of dollars go to the winner.) A lot of dry souls lined the dock for the 'first arrival' of the season...we leave tomorrow!...Jollife Island was the scene of a big party tonight as the crew celebrated the good news.

At 10:30 on June 26th, the whistle, tooting for personal rather than legitimate reasons, echoed the crew's farewell to the humming little boom–town of Yellowknife in the Northwest Territories. I noticed particularly the day we departed. It couldn't be more perfect. White clouds hung from nothing, a hot sun warmed the metal deck and the waters were bluer than ever. All aboard had been restless for a week; now they stood quietly looking back at our wake. As we churned water, Jim, the cook, poked his head out of the galley door to see why his pots and pans had begun their nautical rhumba. "Well, at last!" he said with a sigh and a satisfied smile, whistling light–

heartedly as he returned to the depths of his galley.

It is hard to say who was the happiest as we sailed into the icy jaws of Great Slave Lake. The Skipper, Len, was beaming behind his wheel; Vital, the Indian pilot, smiled a broad native smile; beside him, as he read the waters, Axel, the Danish deckhand (and only rope—splicer aboard) hummed a popular tune as he twisted the wire rope; 'Chiefy', the chief engineer, pattered back and forth feeling piston heads, squirting oil, and wiping his hands with a soiled cloth each time he appeared on deck; the cook, Jim, continued to whistle light—heartedly a popular tune, as the agreeable smell of baking seeped through the screened window to the outer deck.

On the Water '*Trail of '98*'

The Cheechako was on the *Trail of '98*. He could be no happier!

"I think she's okay over there," yelled the Skipper from the wheelhouse after a few words passed between him and Vital — the keen pilot. "Keep well back on the barges...you might go overboard on one of those jolts," cried Earl Harcourt. And with a thud, followed by a shattering of a thousand mirrors of ice, we rammed the frozen blockade in the outer waters of the Great Slave Lake. Smiles came from the wheelhouse. "Never seen a better batterin' ram than that!" said a deckhand as the four steel barges in their most chivalrous manner cut a path for *Sandy Jane*.

Already the sun was lowering as we set course for Fort Smith on the Slave River, below the Big Lake. Its glorious colours prompted me to praise it. "So you like our country, do you!" answered Earl. "It's a part of me now...gets you after awhile. By the way, we're just taking a quick trip to Smith and we'll be on our way to Norman in a day or so...be back on your *Trails of '98* in no time." Northern conversations invariably turn to the country or some exciting incident therein. As we stood on the foremost barge in the face of a rising wind, flooded by the rosy glare from the west casting long shadows behind us, the modest man spoke again: "I've been fifteen years in the North...a lot of that spent around Bear Lake contracting logs, shooting caribou as grub for a mining camp, and did a little work under the ground too." At that moment a smile broke the rosy countenance, sending black shadows scattering across the weatherbeaten face. "Fell down a mine shaft once...lit on another gent at the bottom! I was paralyzed from the neck down," he laughed lightly. "At the hospital they jammed food down my throat; I could hardly turn my head to cuss the nurses...and couldn't get my hands free to shoot myself and alleviate the misery...yes, it was that bad!" We both laughed at the thought. "Lake looks pretty clear now!" he added, glancing like a sage over the waters so familiar to him... "but she might blow anytime, so be ready!" he suggested, and made off amongst the cargo on deck.

"Who the hell..." cried the Cheechako, as a spray of water shot through an aft' porthole. It was four—thirty. "On deck!...On deck!" yelled a rough voice from the head of the companionway. Five o'clock and all hands bounded to the deck, there to see the barges adrift, floundering helplessly or stuck on the mudflats of Slave Delta. This was my initiation to the hidden violence of Great Slave Lake. Mackenzie too had fought its treachery in 1789 on his journey to the Arctic.

It was with difficulty that we rounded up our barges. The winds continued to churn the waters into grey mud. We were now forced to tow the barges. Once within the narrow limits of the river they assumed their former position without further event.

Spring had certainly found its way to these southern Arctic regions. Mosquitoes became worse, abetted by horseflies. Flour, groceries, lumber, gasoline: all day we tramped with these, from the shore to the deck, like galley slaves, pausing occasionally to swat an ornery mosquito, down a drink of cold water or catch a breath. The heat of the day gave way to the cool of evening. "You can go ashore if you wish; but we leave at midnight!" said the skipper. No further invitation was needed. We would have a glimpse of the Fitzgerald Portage, for years the well−worn passage around the sixteen miles of treacherous waterfalls and rapids.

"Sixteen miles at this time of night is too much for shank's ponies," said one of the crew as we scaled the heights to the town of Fort Smith, the northern terminal of the portage. "Ten dollars will take you all there and back," said the squawman, expectantly. "Six dollars or nothing!" said the Cheechako, none too flush, and familiar with inflated tendencies. "O.K...pile in...but my wife and family are coming too!" "That's all right, as long as we get there." We boarded the broken−down taxi. "We're on the Hudson's Bay road," said our driver, with the mien of a sightseeing guide. "Other one a hundred yards away is the Northern Transportation Co.'s, built by the Ryan Brothers. You notice it joins this one at intervals," continued the Scotsman, his Indian wife managing the restless Breeds in the front. "During the war neither company would consent to the Americans using their stretch of road," he chuckled, hitting another bump and sending a shower of sand from the roof upon us. "So the Americans took over both roads, joining them by hundred−yard intersections...that showed them companies!" rang his brogue as we pulled to a stop at the townsite.

Fitzgerald, the southern terminus of the Portage, is practically a company town. The enormity of the machinery, sold to the Northern Transportation Co. when the Americans left, is amazing. Huge 'Dogs' & 'Cats' line the waterfront. Riverboats with barges, reaching the head of the rapids, are pulled from the waters by tractors, loaded on the 'dogs' and transported bodily over the sixteen miles of portage to Fort Smith, where they are re−launched, continuing to all points North.

Time being limited, we re−enter the misused auto with the Scot and his native family. "What's that?" I asked, pointing to a large, white, wooden cross erected against a spruce background overlooking the swirling waters. "Oh that!" replied the driver, "marks the spot where some priests were drowned when their small boat caught in the whirlpool and capsized. See that stuffed buffalo?" he pointed along the roadside. "For years that was the pride and joy of the old settler who shot and stuffed it. In his absence, the son neglected to fulfill his duties...and look at it now! ...this younger generation," he mumbled, eyeing the load of young bucks mirthfully. The ominous roar of the rapids rises above the motor as we return along the sandy road. "No one has ever run those rapids all the way, even an Indian!" exclaimed the gay Scot, swerving to miss a dog on the road. "Damn them!" he shouted, "why don't they fine them twenty−five cents and impound 'em with the R.C.M.P. like they do on our side?" "Perhaps they are more properly behaved in Alberta?" I suggested. We debarked in a cloud of sand at Fort Smith. Paying the man for the dusty ride we descended to our floating home. With that, a 'picaninny' ran along the street. 'No doubt of the recent American invasion, I thought. "May not go till seven a.m.," said the Dane. It was not long before the mosquito−bar was slung for the night. Sweet sleep soon overtook the tired crew.

The Dane had been well informed. "First sitting, you mugs!" yelled the cook down the hatch, next morning. One doesn't hesitate about food in this country, so the scramble was on. As the second sitting found their places the voice of the Skipper came from the wheelhouse. "Pull the shore cables...let's get outa this mosquito−ridden hole!" So we left our southern berth, claimed by the swift waters of the Slave River. We were on the *Trail of '98*! At least one heart was happy.

CHAPTER NINE

ON THE ALL–CANADIAN TRAIL OF '98 ONCE MORE

Belle Rock... a short stop...Fort Resolution...Res' Delta...and the turbulent waters of Great Slave slapped our starboard. It was a pleasant slap as the Skipper yelled from above: "Whadya think now, Cheechako?" "Same as you!" returned the novice; the two exchanged a laugh. *Sandy Jane* was taking the waves gracefully. Len and Vital kept her on course, scanning the Lake for reefs and the shoreline for bearings. "Egg Island to port...better pull up the barges...getting rougher!" shouted the Skipper over the mounting din of wind and waves. Buffalo Point...and with marked poles we sounded our way from the maddening lake to the calm waters of Hay River

A settlement appeared and disappeared with the transient fog, its Mission spire piercing the fleecy clouds without effect; an Indian canoe cut out of the low–lying mist on the river, about to ram our prow. "Look out!"...."Look out!" yelled a 'Breed deckhand. Paddling fiercely the Peterborough swerved and ran a short parallel course with the *Jane*. "Close, no?" shouted the Indian, his bronzed face flashing a broad smile, seemingly pleased with his agile maneouvre.

"Fish net to starboard," cried a deckhand, as he lifted his prize to the deck with the sounding pole. It was July 1st when we pitched the shore cables and tethered our Lady behind the Distributor, oldest of the original sternwheelers on the river, at the fogbound settlement of Hay River.

On July 2nd, we slipped past Big Island in the Archipelago, about to be claimed by the Big River. Red and black buoys guide us through the Providence Rapids rushing north at eleven m.p.h. "How we doin', Chiefy?" inquired the Skipper of the engineer who was on one of his deck walks. "About nine an hour," returned the latter. "Not bad"...said the voice from above, pleased.

The Mackenzie River claimed us. We were washed North at an incredible speed. 'How must the explorer of the river bearing this name have felt in his birchbark canoe?' I asked myself, scanning the ever–widening river in one glance. 'How could he have returned within the season in 102 days, against such a current?' I mused over the imponderables realizing that at the same tender age of twenty five years I was as unsullied, unperturbed and indifferent to hardship and adventure as he! A voice from above brought thoughts to a close and action to the deck. "Fort Providence next!" I beheld another majestic spire piercing the immeasurable morning blue.

Hudson's Bay Buildings
Fort Providence

Natives Watching the Event of the Season

'*Sandy Jane*' and Barge on Mackenzie River   **Indian School Children With The Father**

Father Jean Louis Michael and Doug Iveron—Second Engineer

Indian boys and girls, always delighted at such an event, line the banks, exchanging quips in native tongue to their 'breed friends aboard. Bounding ashore I met the head Father of the local mission halfway towards the boat. "Bon matin!...Bon matin!" he ejaculated in his native tongue. Catching the significance of my visit he continued about his life. "I am Father Jean Louis Michael an' I 'ave been for thirteen year here...Twenty seex een ze North altogeder. I come from France...you know Brittany?" "Oh, that is where the large horses come from," I replied. "No!no!no!" he shouted, laughing and gesticulating. "That ees Normandy...we are noted for small cows!" "Oh, slight mistake," I interjected. "Beeg mistake," he retorted and introduced me to Brother Vachon and another who accosted us along the path. "Dey are here five or seex year onlee!" "Our light plant is not working...perhaps you could feex it, maybe?" one asked. "No, but I know who can," I replied, and made off for the boat again, reappearing with Doug Iverson, the second engineer' who in time found the trouble. As the motor started its regular throb, three of the largest smiles I have ever seen broke on the faces of the holy men. Visiting the Mission School, to which the children come from miles around, we concluded our hasty visit. Our two native passengers, Jonas Lafferty and Baras Dechuard, aboard the gang—plank followed; a voice from the foremost barge yelled, "All clear, Len." Our native audience shouted farewells and waved us out of sight. We were Down North on the Big River.

Late afternoon found us at rest at Mills Lake, newly established headquarters of the Yellowknife Transportation Company. Mosquitoes also found us there. Unloading operations completed and the first swim of the year over, we resumed our journey along the broad Mackenzie, winding its ever—changing course through the heart of the Northwest Territories.

July 3rd. More rapids, the Narrows, and there on the south bank stood the welcoming settlement of Fort Simpson basking in the hot morning sun. Like any other of the Mackenzie trading posts, it presents at a distance the Roman Catholic Mission. On closer observance one sees the R.C.M.P. barracks, a hospital built in 1931, a wireless station and an individual trading post or two. "Take a half hour ashore, but no more!" said the Skipper as we tied up to the bank to discharge small cargo. As usual, I sought the Mission and the head—priest from whom the history and the interesting events of the settlement could invariably be procured. "Good morning, my son...I am Father Turcotte," proffered the kindly priest answering the door. "Where are you going weez all dose wheeskers?" came his second statement. "Just doing a little living," I remarked. He smiled at my levity and continued to answer the questions sent his way. "I came to zis countree in 1925, to Radium...Aklavik...and now here. So you see I am an oldtimer! Perhaps you would like to meet another of us?" "By all means!" I replied.

Fort Simpson

R.C.M.P. Barracks

Interrupting an overalled priest, who was chopping wood and wheeling it away in a barrow, the elder introduced me to Brother Gosling who arrived here and has remained, since 1936.

By this time the half hour was growing short. With a dash I reached the beach. I passed an Indian encampment along shore. "Bon−jour," said a dusky old warrior. Momentarily surprised, I stopped short, replied more than casually, and passed along to the waiting boat. 'The French have sure left their mark' I thought to myself.

Mile by mile the country was growing all the more intriguing. It was 9:30 a.m. as our Fairbanks engines churned the muddy waters.

Sisters of Mary Immaculate Hospital−1951

High on the bank above a tractor appeared, collected the crated engine from the ground and disappeared into the confines of the village. I had recognized the Brother behind the wheel, temporarily turned mechanic through necessity. I took off my hat to the Oblates again.

Barges Down the Mackenzie Below Fort Simpson

West Towards Nahanni Mountain Ridge

This afternoon the lowlands of the Mackenzie gave way to the Nahanni Mountains, looming like great, grey giants above the spruce and poplar below, their summits buried in white plumes of cloud. At four p.m. we pass Lone Point and the North Nahanni River, entrance to the legendary Headless Valley. The mountains, seemingly an arm's reach from the *'Jane*, are in reality about twenty−five miles distant. The only signs of habitation are sporadic cabins along the shore. Many small rivers and streams rush to join us here in our race to the Arctic.

'On…on…on…' the motors seemed to say as they throbbed through the night. Wrigley on the west limit came and went during the early hours. Morning, and another abundance of beautiful scenery disrobes before our expectant eyes: more trees, more incomparably blue sky, and still more cumulus clouds floating in their nether realms. Mountains, as rugged and challenging as any yet, rise in the background, their snow−capped crowns rubbing the clouds. 'Come and try us' they challenge. 'I'm coming, and I will,' I respond in thought. 'You must, if the Pacific is to be reached,' added the Devil of Adventure.

Ten−thirty a.m. we by−passed Fort Norman, Bear Rock, a veritable Gibralter on the Mackenzie, and the *Sikanni Chief*, another company boat, limping upstream on five of its six cylinders. "Cooks jumped too, at the Wells," yells one of the crew as she passed. We didn't envy her position. Then out of the spruce appears a radio station, an airport nearby and finally a vast cluster of shining oil tanks, reflecting the noon−day sun. This can be none other than Norman Wells, halfway down the Big River to the Arctic.

Bear Rock Below North Nahanni River   **'Sikanni Chief'**
Without a Cook

Norman Wells—Black Gold

"This is it, Cheechako!" said the Skipper, as he caught me eyeing my new 'home' approaching out of the distance. "Shouldn't be hard to catch a boat from here to Aklavik," he encouraged. We docked at the oil−town of the North.

Noon found my chores over with. Hoisting my kit to the shoulder I walked from the neatest little boat in which I have travelled. She and her crew were good company. So I signed−off the *Sandy Jane*. "Good luck, fella!" "Wish I were going, too!" "Don't lose yourself in that West country!" were the farewells that followed me up the riverbank. I was about to become a citizen of the Imperial Oil company−town of Norman Wells.

Farewell! *Sandy Jane* **Crew**

CHAPTER TEN

BLACK GOLD TOWN

With everything found and a hammer 'to boot', I set about my new job of nail−pulling till a boat appeared. "*Distributor* is expected down river any day now," said Bob Douglas, my native assistant. "Say, how'd you like a bear hunt tonight after work?" "I've learned never to say 'no' to anything in the North," I returned.

It was the most unusual 'bear hunt' I had heard of. We were to visit the town dump, favourite haunt of these quadrupeds, in search of a change of diet. With 'kerchiefs pulled over the head for protection from pests we headed into the sun, batting mosquitoes right and left.

It was along this stretch that we accosted a quaint− looking figure. "You're about to meet the most capable prospector and hunter in the vicinity," whispered my friend as the man came close. Loping along the trail, red−and−white handkerchief pinned to his peaked hunting cap, streaming out behind him to disrupt the mosquitoes, he looked not unlike an Arab returning from the hot sands, 300 Savage rifle in hand. "Not a derned thing in sight...not even a dead bear track!" said Hammer Nelson, his face ruddy and weatherbeaten; a dead mosquito resting where time's wrinkles and a quick hand have caught him. "Nice night fer walkin' if them damned pests would skat!" he said, swinging his arms in defence and reshouldering his rifle. "He's a great guy when you know 'im...always travels alone...came here in

My New Role−Carpenter

1920 and has never found anything of any value in his prospecting, so he says," spoke my friend as we reached the scene of the prospective hunt. An hour passed. Hammer had been right. Nothing appeared; so we sauntered home in the deep purple of evening, the Mackenzie below, wide and swift, heading North without me.

That night I found myself bunked with another veteran of this district. "Amos Schellenberger's my name...bin here since 1918. I have a tradin' post half a mile above the site of Norman...made my pile and now I intend to go Outside to Stratford, Ontario, my old home. Guess I'll only visit...probably wind up prospecting in northern Ontario or perhaps come straight back here and do some...I dunno?" he sighs, lying restless in his bed. "Just can't stop lookin' for gold. I'm like a lotta other guys...when they retire or quit they die. An' I'm only 65...too young to do *that*!" he laughs. "About women...I fully intend to make up for lost time," he adds, the devil sparkling in his eye. 'The mind certainly plays tricks on us all,' I think, and venture with a question. "Are you going to procure a wife and have companionship in your later years, Amos?" And in a squeeky voice: "It would be nice to have a cook...but I'm too old," he adds, having thought it over momentarily, as though admitting time had overtaken some things. The overworked maxim again proved itself. In the last dim halls of consciousness I vaguely hear him muttering, "...knew of the Norman Oil...long time...staked original claim...squeezed out..."

The entire population of the Wells live, work and play as a fraternity. It is an Imperial Oil Town, superintended by Mr. McInnon. Nothing is taken too seriously, so as the next day passed I began to feel one of them. Work became pleasure, surrounded by the gradually ascending deep blues and greens of the Franklin Mountains to the east and the distant Mackenzie Range sloping to the northwest. With each nail extracted from the timbers I felt one step closer to the Klondike. There was no turning back now. I was well on the *Trails of '98*.

So the day of parting for good with the *Sandy Jane* came. Hearing her whistle, it was the signal for me to drop my hammer and make for the shore. I waved and thought I saw a figure answer from the wheelhouse, as the Little Lady pushed upstream at a considerably slower pace than she had come.

Edmonton 1208 Miles

At this point in the river the Mackenzie is about four miles wide. On the far shore one may still see the abandoned Camp Canol, from which millions of gallons of oil were pumped through the mountains to Whitehorse, Yukon. A brief shower. The fog rises to the summit of the Franklins. A mauve sun strikes the tops of the hills while the valley, not set afire, lies cool and dark. It is semi—virgin and pleasantly aloof as it entices the eager heart of the adventurer.

"There she comes!" cries a voice in the main street. It is July 7 and the *Distributor* arrives with its long—contemplated beer barge. It is the second time I have been where the most important occurrence and predominating thought of the citizens is for the universal beverage. "Boy, am I dry!" chimes in another voice. "Let's see, now...how many months is it since...?" and he begins to count on his fingers.

As the midnight sun continued to illuminate the country, a chain—gang passed carton after carton of 'fluid gold' into the local refrigerator. "Only two hundred more cases," said the foreman, Frank Willox, "and per'aps you'll get your reward?" One a.m. and the good—natured foreman kept his word.

When characters like Jim McCauley, Angus Hooker, Charlie O'Neil and Amos Schellenberger get together over a drink, there are bound to be some tall yarns. This morning, early, there were some.

"Why ain't you at your Great Bear Lake trading post, mindin' yer business?" one poked at Jim who retaliated. "Jus' cause the boats in doesn't mean it's all fer you soaks!" Laughter filled the room. Amos, in a bragging mood and with such eager listeners, piped: "I'm gonna spend all my time romancin' when I hit Outside...yessirree...I'll make up for the lonely bachelor years I've given this here North!" "Your wolfin' is all in your head, man," retorted Jim. Undaunted, the former, at the thought, blurts, "You show me a skirt and I'll show you want I can do!" As most male gatherings so often climax with a feminine trend, this one was no exception. But let me narrate, as close as memory allows, the story that preceded the confab regarding romantic abilities.

The Gin content had slowly come near the bottom of the transparent bottle. I strained to grasp what truth lay in the tale which, as it progressed, became coloured almost beyond imagination. I had begun to hear the story earlier, along the river. Each setting, each chase, and each death had been varied. Every settlement was desirous of claiming the bloody ground where the Mad Trapper fell. 'Here, surely, will be an interesting version,' I thought, eyeing the motley group, who at this time felt in exceptionally high spirits, as the story of The Mad Trapper—Johnson, unfolded. "Damned Indians," said one, "didn't and still don't like some of us whites...robbed Johnson's traps...said he'd shoot hell outa them one day...that scared 'em!" "Course he'd been robbin their traps in turn...an' tossin' the traps in the bush," chimed another. "Aw he was bushed!...just plain bushed...you gets that way in time...why lookit you mugs!" he roared, coughing consumptively with an overdose of laughter. "Them Indians gotta seek the arm of the law to lean on," shot another. "Then what happened?" asked the Cheechako, impatiently.

"The Redcoatsh vizzhited hish cabin, they did. Johnson threatened em' and he flourisshed hizh pistol...and before he could finish... "Yeah...and the trapper shot it outa his hand...but he swore he'd be back as he left," said Jim. "Johnson by now had developed a hatred for the Redcoats who interferred," came Charlie. "But they came back… and brought a home—made bomb. They blew the hell outa the guy's cabin…but he outsmarted 'em…climbed under the bed…and when one tried to enter he shot the flashlight outa his hand." said Angus. "Then he built a tepee in the snow from which led a path into a snowbank. Johnson built a cave behind and put a slit in it for his rifle barrel. Obvious thing for the police to do on return was to pepper the tepee. They did, and thinkin' they would surely get 'im, relaxed their vigil a bit…then the Mad Trapper ups and fires…winged the officer in the knee and brought 'im to the ground!"

"This called for a quick departure," added Amos, "and the police were in hot pursuit…mile after mile, all over the bloomin' countryside. Johnson weren't so dumb, though…he circles behind and shoots at 'em. Shot holes in their pots so's they couldn't eat…wings a Mountie, but mind you he never touched the others in the posse, an' beats it again…then in comes Wop May into the picture." "Yeah," pipes up Jim again, "he was pioneering in the air about then, in these parts…damn good pilot, too!…he follows from the air for a while but then he had to go back for more gas an' loses the trail." "How about zhe caribou tracks…he walkss in zhem for milessh an zhey loozz him again," came the uncertain voice amongst us. "And don't forget how he turned his snowshoes backwards too…that fooled 'em plenty for awhile! They got his pots and cooking utensils, though, and finally his food got low…they say he was eating squirrels?" added Angus. 'bout that time it was that Wop spied him from the air, circling a hill…he directed the posse the other way an' when they met 'im they let 'im have it!" Too bad…too bad…he was just another one of us poor no—good Northerners," laughed another. "The law claims to have shot him (course they have to) but I heard it was some good marksman on the possee…never could find out exactly."

"Not that Johnson had no intention of giving up…starve him as they tried…they found dead squirrels in his pockets…he musta been bad off…anyway I for one wished he'd made the Yukon, where he was headin' for…mighta given us more to bull about!" He laughed at his joke, and the laughter spread through the gathering. "Anyway I admired him for his 'trapper justice'; he proved his point, and he got his reward too! I hear they didn't blame him altogether when they investigated…but ain't he lucky…he don't have to beat these cussed mosquitoes anymore…jus' think of it!" This was too much and the hour was too early. A last good belly—laugh all round brought the Johnson Story and the party to a close. Amos was already asleep. The Cheechako showed them to the door and followed in the path of his room—mate.

CHAPTER ELEVEN

A CHANGE OF SKIPPERS

The day before, I had queried the Skipper of the newly arrived Hudson's Bay boat, *Hearne Lake*, as to passage. Being a man of few words he let the matter stand. Today enlightening words came from the usually silent gentleman of the weatherbeaten countenance. "Yes," he said, "you will be going with us to Aklavik as a paid member of the crew!" This was one time when I wished a man to say no more. The financial larder would be well stocked for the journey through the mountains. There was no doubt of this now. Back on the job I scarce remember pulling a nail. I was already miles away...down the Mackenzie River.

Hudson's Bay Company's *Hearne Lake* and Captain Ilyea

"Three days...five, ten, fifteen, nineteen dollars and twenty−seven cents," said the pay clerk. "Thank you," I said, clasping the money and rushing for the billet. It was but a few minutes before the sleeping robe found its rightful place, and with "Luck, Lad" from Amos, I headed for the docks with my gear.

Flopping down in the galley to catch a breath I heard footsteps on the companionway. It was the Skipper come for his p.m. cup o' tea. Spotting the reclined carcass he spoke: "You're a paid member of the crew now...better commence your duties!" The short siesta was too good to last, so hundreds of oil barrels felt the rough caresses of another pair of hands. Joining us for the remainder of the trip was a government agent, Stan Bailey, and his guide, Hugh Cunningham, dealing with the Indians downstream.

Stan Bailey and Hugh Cunningham

Supper was hours in coming around; but with it came the humour of the cook. Aches of the day were soon forgotten. Ed Grey is an owl−eyed, bony little man who once stowed away to this country from his native England. By all verbal characteristics he is a Cockney; but upon accusal he denies the fact with the defensive, "I was born out of the sound of Bow Bells?" "I used to chef aboard the boats from New Haven to Dieppe on the Channel run," he says with pride (as though making up aristocratically for his present position in the crude Canadian Northland).

Quite adept at contenting the crew I heard no complaints. So my first meal passed with the new crew, spiced lightly with the Cockney's wit. Little did we know this was only an introduction to his humour.

Night came; the parade of gasoline barrels ended. It was a tired looking crew that streamed into the galley for tea. The cook went unnoticed; the plates and pots soon emptied; the crew crowded into the small quarters below the decks. We were earning our passage without a doubt.

Seven o'clock comes with the clang of a bell. With the ferocity of one who has had a restless night and desiring to avenge his mosquitoed slumber by spitefully hitting the iron railing with the clamourous bell, the cook triples the obnoxiousness of his unmusical weapon. So we clamber to the deck in order to hit the 'first sitting', greeted somewhat pleasantly by the sun, splashing yellow over the entire countryside. "Hotcakes and eggs...take 'em or leave 'em!" invites the cook. Enough to satisfy any sailor, we leave the table, contented. "Shove off!" yells Captain Ilyea. We 'cut' the shore cable and the *Hearne Lake* falls into the waiting arms of the huge Mackenzie. It is eight o'clock. We are once more on the *Trail of '98*.

It was not long before I met the crew, coming into conversation as we rubbed shoulders or sat around the mess in the galley. Alec Swanson, an Icelander, veteran of more southerly waters and once a 'homesteader' on the Prairies, proved to be a good−natured Mate. Having a Prairie background in common, we were often to leave our Arctic voyage and travel to the 'Dust Bowl' or dwell on the fierce blizzards or perhaps the harvest season coloured with its traditional post−threshing barn dances. These were invariably interrupted by a shift in the riverbed or some duty that must be performed during the course of the day.

Captain Ilyea has spent his lifetime on the waters of the Mackenzie River. He probably knows these waters better than any other man. To watch him, there is little doubt that he is happiest when at the helm, craning over the canvas windbreak around the open wheel to read the ever−changing waters below. As the weather changes so does his headgear, varying from the straw hat worn when the Arctic sun is its hottest, to the felt fedora with rounded crown, or his soiled cap. In truth he is a human barometer. I was to remember one day well, when all three in turn found their way to the plump Skipper's head. I was the midwife at each operation.

Summer he spends with the *Hearne Lake*; the Mackenzie; the hot, Arctic Midnight Sun; blue skies; lazy white clouds; torrential rains and glorious sunsets comparable to those venerated by the Manx from the Isle of Man − claimed to be the world's prettiest. Because of the perpetual daylight the Skipper spends long periods at his favourite position (some as lengthy as eighteen hours) coming below only at such times as sleep and fatigue overtake his better judgement; tea and biscuits oftimes sufficing his desires. It isn't hard to understand his love for the Big River and its every−changing scenery. Winter, I understand, is spent in the city on the Outside where a warm fire and many books are his constant companions.

In truth, he is a modern Alexander Mackenzie, discovering the Arctic each year, on a river that is never twice the same. It is not hard to understand this man's simple desires, as he masters the scene from his favourite position at the wheel.

The Ramparts

The Carcajou Mountains rose to our port side, adding their graciousness to the day's pageant of colour. Afternoon brought the Sans Soult Rapids upon us. A short distance before the swift waters it was necessary to 'tie up' some of the barges. One at a time is the only safe way of cheating the turbulent rapids.

We 'shot' the Sans Soult in the late afternoon, the Skipper's tongue protruding at each hidden reef we passed as he leaned well forward, scanning the beguiling waters, clutching the helm in his certain manner. Depositing our barge we returned and attacked the rapids once more with another part of our cargo. When I next awoke the Sans Soult were well in the rear and nimbus clouds overhead were reeking vengeance and rain upon us. We lay tethered to the bank, the choppy Mackenzie splashing about our craft. Wind and rain abated so we continued down the river. Soon the banks, port and starboard claimed our interest. We had come about fifty miles from the rapids and a pleasant surprise was in store for us. We were to view the Ramparts in all their splendor, as did Mackenzie from his birch bark canoe one hundred and fifty−eight years ago.

The Ramparts are a majestic rock rising sheer above the murky Mackenzie; their stratified shades running a gamut of pastellated colours finally merge into deep purples and black; the latter giving one the thought that perhaps it is oil seeping from the banks as so often it does in this rich countryside. Sulphur fumes rising from springs in the vicinity deprive the scene a certain pleasantness, as we pause in preparation for the coming rapids and the narrow channel through which we must pass.

It was while engaged in this delay that a lone figure in a canoe approached us. He shut off his motor and, using his paddle as a rudder, glided toward the Hearne Lake. Coming alongside, I noticed that he was not a white man. "Well I'll be...good morning Mr. Jackson!" said one of the crew reaching for the rope that was thrown to the rail. This was our impromptu introduction to one of the only black trappers in the country.

Trapper Jackson

"Jus' thought as ahd pay youse a short visit...don't see many folks along now. By the way, ah brung ya some fresh Arctic Trout for ya dinner." At this the cook's eyes bulged. He had been complaining about fresh food. Reaching over the side he unhesitatingly accepted the precious gift and made off to the galley. A finer example of Northern hospitality could not have been demonstrated. As his 'kicker' passed out of hearing again one of the crew leaning next to me on the rail said: "Now there's a fine man; came from the U.S.A. years ago...he and his wife live quite happily together off the land."

Pushing our way through the Gate of the Ramparts, opening like a huge portcullis into the castellated walls, the watery courtyard becomes wider. Huge amphitheatres, void of all players, lay nestled in narrow ravines where spruce and grass dare to come down to the shore. As though Zeus, perturbed on Olympus, had acted by throwing a thunderbolt, a sudden flash of sunlight appeared through the overcast, adding finesse to the pageant; we passed gallantly through to the settlement of Fort Good Hope just beyond.

Gate of the Ramparts

Fort Good Hope

Good Hope doesn't vary from other villages we have passed along the winding course of the Mackenzie River. High on the starboard bank a Mission appears. Lake a welcoming beacon the spire points skyward and a distant traveller knows that people and hospitality are not far away. As we pull into shore on the afternoon of July 10th, a stream of Indians arrive at the water's edge to witness the 'event of the season' when the first cargo of merchandise comes from the South. One by one they seat themselves for the occasion at a point of vantage on the banks above, not unlike Outside children viewing a circus procession.

So the audience was settled and the players began unloading the heavy freight with the aid of two−wheeled handcarts and the frequent assistance of an energetic Indian boy.

Curiosity at First Annual Boat Arrival

It was here that I first noticed the increased size of the average canoe, overturned near the water's edge. They were mostly twenty−two−footers. Then I remembered we were only thirty miles from the Arctic Circle. Already the waters of the Big River had gained considerable momentum. This then was sufficient reason for the increased size. Again I reflected upon the year 1789 and Mackenzie's heroic return from the North. 'How could he possibly have made it when it is all some of the motored craft can do to buck the wind and current for hard−fought miles?...and he in an open canoe!' was the bewildering thought that haunted my brain each time I glanced from the freight to the swift river. I was to grow more in admiration of the explorer as we carried on downstream.

Captain of the *Capstan*

Fort Good Hope boasts an old Roman Catholic Mission, a group of immaculate Hudson's Bay buildings, a few plain wood and log structures and an Indian camp of teepees and cabins behind the main townsite. From the Mission came the Fathers to cast their salutations as we worked. 'Time for a rest,' I told myself, dropping the sack of flour. I engaged in conversation with the holy−man, Father Robin. "Keep movin!" came a voice from aboard..."we've gotta get off and scram," it added. At this I carried on a broken conversation with the priest, dropping each 100 pound bag, snatching a few words, and returning for another. "I am Father Robin," he said, holding out a welcome hand. "I have been here thirty−five years in the Northwest Territories...all over," he motioned with an arm's sweep. "You mus' be sure to see my mission...it is built entirely of wood; the nails are wooden pegs too," he smiled, trotting off to check his awaiting supplies. At that moment another priest made his appearance, and with the same formula for work and hospitality, I exchanged greetings with the man. He was Father Prettier, but a year away from France, his home being in Relsteng.

Then came a lull. With a plan already formulated, I left my handcart and ascended the steep bank. The unique Mission lured me on. Once inside I met the Fathers and heard the history of the church, the altar and the exquisite paintings adorning the walls. It was built in 1870 by Father Segeun, who arrived in the country in 1861 and died in the year of 1901. His early efforts were aided by Father Pettitot, who joined him in 1864. The latter was a scientist, skilled also in many

74

fields including that of art. This is displayed with proud dexterity on all walls of the interior in almost animated plaques of religious events. I was later told by another priest of the map drawn by the Father who travelled the entire area of Arctic Red River to Norman Wells by sled. This same district had since been aerial photographed. When compared, the two maps proved to show little variation.

"Both original Fathers, feeling their work was completed, returned to the Outside, where death eventually overtook them," explained Father Robin. "Father Pettitot went back to France, where he lived a few years before death. Father Segeun, who became blind before he left, died shortly after his farewell to the country that had taken so many of his years," he continued. "You see that altar...that is the work of Father Colles, not with us anymore," he

Annunciation and *Burial of Jesus* by Fr. Colles. Fr. Prettier (R)

said rather regretfully. "But you will meet him in Arctic Red River," he replied pointing to the highly coloured altar, each small detail completed by hand. "There also is his work." He pointed to the *Annunciation* and *Burial of Jesus,* which is not quite completed. Said the priest: "One day, I presume and hope, he will return and finish it?" I too hope he will return before entering the Immortal Halls of the Oblates, and paint the missing crown upon the owner's head, thus completing the magnificent work.

The Ornate Altar by Father Colles. Father Prettier Kneeling

Turning, the Father points to the furniture built by another contributor to this artistic interior. "His name is Brother Ancel," he says, cabinet−maker by trade. His work includes those paintings on and about the altar and this chair, carved completely by hand. "Looking more closely at the article one is convinced it is equivalent to any turned out on a lathe today. Time and comparative solitude can bring out much of the art within people. Here, I thought, was the perfect example of masterpieces shining in their own perfect light. "And to think the Brother had never before taken a paint brush in his hand," he marvels. "He later died at Fort Chipewyan," he ends, reverently.

The door opened and flooded the painting with dancing light. "Oh! It is Brother Minet who has been with us for some nine years or so. Now you have met all of us," he finished. Taking a last glance at the beautiful interior I turned to the door.

**Father Robin and More Exquisite Art
Within the Old Log and Wooden—Pegged Mission**

Already feeling slightly guilty at my departure from the boat I bade the religious men adieu. "Send our regards to Father Colles," one shouted as I made a retreat back to hard work. The door had closed on the finest example of Northern art I was to see. Slipping past the decaying graveyard I gave a fleeting glimpse at the rustic, aged, wooden crosses bearing both Indian and white names, and hurried back to the hundred—pound sacks of flour.

It was at the settlement of Fort Good Hope that I first realized the severity of the Northern Indian mortality due to the scourge of the Redman — Tuberculosis. Figures taken from the Father's records tell their own sad story.

Below I reprint tables over the period of the last ten years.

YEAR	BORN	DIED	NUMBER OF CHILDREN THAT DIED
1938−39	15	18	6
1939−40	12	13	7
1940−41	18	5	3
1941−42	11	18	7
1942−43	19	22	13
1943−44	13	12	10
1944−45	9	29	17
1945−46	12	13	5
1946−47	12	18	5
10 years	121	148	73

Very seldom it was that I cursed the Land of the Midnight Sun. The evening of July 10 was one of those times. Judging by the elements it was still Thursday; but my fatigue told me it couldn't possibly be so. It was six p.m. that I last looked at my watch. Now as I turned my wrist the timepiece said it was five a.m. All this time it was bright as day. "You can go to your bunks anytime," said the purser, as the last piece of freight hit the muddy bank. "Life isn't worth it!" I cursed, flopping on the sleeping robe fully clothed. I was not taking a chance. This was too good to be lasting; and what seemed minutes later a raucous inescapable voice hollered down the companionway, circulating through the lower deck: "Get the hell outa those sacks!...we're shovin' off." Thus we saw the light of the Midnight Sun from the sea−end of a cable. We cast off at this ungodly hour of the day, little caring whether it be morning, noon or night. "Might as well have breakfast while you're about," suggested the cook in his most sarcastic manner. This over with, a more bedraggled crew could not have been seen, making for their bunks, hoping that the next few hours might be called their own.

As good fortune had it, they were; but unable to segregate myself from the hateful bags of flour and sugar I re−walked the gangplank in dreams. It was no wonder that I felt tired and irritable when the light of afternoon found me through the small porthole.

An undisturbed, uneventful journey had brought us to Thirty Mile Point. Sudden storms had forced the Skipper to 'tie up'. Now with optimism he renewed his position at the wheel; closing the five−mile gap between us and that parallel we crossed the Arctic Circle at the mouth of Loon River. We were within the 66th parallel, in that vast territory known as the Arctic.

Sleep and the next day brought us midway on our two−hundred−and−twenty−mile run to the next settlement. The weather suddenly turned cold and dull with foreboding clouds lurking overhead. It was the first time in my life that my breath had turned frosty on July 12. There was no doubt about our global position. The Thunder River (sometimes called Traviar) poured its welcome self into the Mackenzie. A cabin broke the monotony of spruce trees and dirt banks.

"That's Clarke's cabin," commented Willie, the Improved Scotch 'Breed. One assumed that it was the Clarke family that waved us past at a steady 12 miles per hour. "Ship ahead," yelled the Mate, and those interested in seeing a change of scenery came on deck to watch. The Cockney, taking the opportunity of leaving his hot stove, appeared at the rail. "Yes, the *Slave River*," I heard him mutter. Without a doubt the master of the galley of this boat had some thought in mind, for he too appeared at the same moment, a white−clad figure waving from the rail.

They could quite easily have been brothers acknowledging one another's presence across the muddy span of the Big River. With the same curiosity satisfied, both figures disappeared to their respective depths below.

Action at this time was more than welcomed by the crew. It was Alec, the Mate, who sounded the next event. So once again those interested came on deck to catch sight of a black grizzly running from the riverbank to the bush.

CHAPTER TWELVE

LAND OF THE MIDNIGHT SUN

Four—thirty in the morning—it could have quite as easily been noon—we rounded a bend in the river and a Mission came into view. Long before the *Hearne Lake* came to rest, the entire community of men, women and children lined the hilltop, curiously watching our flotilla of laden barges approach the shore. We had reached Arctic Red River, under the warm blaze of the Midnight Sun, situated on a round, green hill overlooking the Red River and its tributaries.

**Arctic Red River
Above the Circle**

Lifeline of Barges

A general murmur of unintelligible chatter and laughter drifted down from the rows of bronzed spectators. They see humour in many things; this time I didn't know just what it might be. Perhaps they are just glad of the 'event of the season'. I was beginning to appreciate these native performances as much as they appeared to enjoy our short visits.

Old R.C.Mission and Artist Father Colles

The New Church

'Another heavy cargo to unload; another dash to shore to meet my man, Father Colles' I mused, as the native deckhand, Frank Stewart, ran to the pivot ashore, making fast the cable. Then over the rise appeared a man in blue denim overalls. A hasty introduction and Father Colles was soon confirming the stories garnered at Fort Good Hope, relative to his abilities with a brush and palette. A short, bespectacled, rather youthful man, he spoke up without hesitation. "Oh, that!" he said upon the mention of art... "I'll admit I learned most of my skill (if you can call it that?) at the Fort, but I do remember vaguely dabbling in Europe. Yes, I remember many things when I look back. I like it here so much that I seldom want to think of the Outside...the wars and so much grief. I too had compulsory army training in my youth...I have been in the North ten years now...six of them right here," he said, patting the ground with a foot. Very satisfied with his life North, he says, in defence: "Where else can you have twenty−four hours daylight a day?" I scratched my head in agreement, retorting: "Yes, but that doesn't mean you have to stay up that long!" to which he replied with a laugh: "No, but we Northerners do our sleeping in winter!"

Following the praise of his surroundings, he continued with snatches from his life. "I am from Paris...it is very beautiful there." And in the moment of reflection, the beret, pallette and brush seemed to become a reality within sight of the Eiffel Tower. "We have so much time to think about things...too bad the world is run by money and such a severe economical system that continues," he thinks out loud, momentarily detached from his present surroundings..."but I have so many things to keep me busy that I do very little art," he digresses. But from what I saw on the Mission wall at Fort Good Hope, my contention is that his heart lies more with the arts than he will admit. With a smile he says: "One must have all day to paint if one is to be a painter." Agreeing on the talent wasted because of the Almighty Dollar, I remark: "I must hustle to my barge−unloading to earn money that I might eventually write this!" Catching the significance, he laughs pleasantly and my meeting with another of the talented Oblate Order of the North came to a close. Thinking, I returned to the river and the barges bathed in the mauve rays of a sun that hovered on the horizon, refusing to set.

11:30 p.m. and our shift ended. Eight vigorous Indians exchanged places with a tired crew that sought rest. Only the odd curse from a restless sleeper broke the quiet below the decks as the chorals of the Indian canines echoed and re−echoed far down the Red River.

A four a.m. 'cast off' is never executed with smiles and light banter: Sunday morning departure was no exception as sleepy−eyed deckhands groped about for the never−ending cables that must be wound by the capstan to the deck. This done, the geometrical representation of the shortest distance between two points (deck and bunk) was illustrated with haste. So all was soon quiet aboard, except for the monotonous drone of propellers churning water.

Sunday morning on a Mackenzie riverboat is quite different from that hallowed day elsewhere. Nine o'clock saw to this as Mr. Swanson−the Mate−yelled another beckoning below in the imperative that originated with the Skipper at the wheel. Self−satisfying curses, careless tugging of 'shoepacks' (type of Northern footwear with leather tops, rubber bottoms) and a dash of cold water over the face filled in quick minutes before the deck was reached. One consolation: the sun was shining brilliantly.

"Separation Point!" yelled the Mate as we hit the deck. We had reached the junction of the Mackenzie and Peel Rivers. "Gotta stow a coupla barges...takin' a quick trip to McPherson." I had hoped to miss none of the settlements enroute to Aklavik: I was especially curious about our next stop. How! Why! When did Fort McPherson adopt this solid Highland monicker? I was shortly to find out.

Brushing these irritating question marks momentarily aside, I concentrated whole−heartedly on the landscape. The topography had changed. Mountains loomed luringly in the distance, snow capped and blue; scraggly spruce trees gave way to robust pine, some of which, unfortunate enough to be too close to the bank, hung halfway between erection and a watery grave. (Their strain will be relieved next year when as much as fifty feet may disappear from the dirt embankment and form a mudbar at some other point in the river.) Indians paddled lazily about in their canoes, chattering unintelligibly in their Loucheux tongue about the Big Boat, perhaps? A thin wisp of smoke rose from an open fire high up the bank, losing itself in the endless ceiling of blue. Squaws, in front of their white tents huddled about the smoke, slapping occasionally at mosquitoes, and the opaque murkiness of the Mackenzie gave way to the transparent blue of the Peel River. "Lookit!...clean drinkin' water for a change!"cried Raymond George, ex−trapper, deckhanding on board. My own thought found words. This I knew would be appreciated by the entire crew, who for days had been forced to stare helplessly at dirt particles in the drinking water.

Coursing our new waterway I stood by the galley entranced with the sudden change in the verdure. It resembled more closely one's Outside impression of the true North. Also enjoying the vista from our moving home was a man with whom I had not become too well acquainted. The barriers soon dropped when he remarked on the surrounding beauty with which he seemed quite familiar; the Scroll of the Years rolled back to his youth, the Moving Finger pointed to his fiftieth year, sailing up and down the Great Lakes.

"Peace River Jim" Cornwall

"Peace River Jim" Cornwall, as he is called, must have sensed a kindred soul, for he began unhesitatingly: "I am 78...going on 79," in his slow−talking manner, his distant look that of a veteran traveller, unchanging as he probed into his past. "Later I went south to the Mississippi and New Orleans, quite a town then," he adds, revealing some adventure that failed to find words. "While there, another ne'er−do−well and I, with our own boat, started gun−running to the Insurgents of Venezuela during the Revolution. While crossing the swamps (part of the plan after hitting shore) and clinching the deal, we were held up by bandits and robbed of our payroll, no small sum," he admits. "...I was shot through the leg...managed to tie a handkerchief about the wound...I got out of the swamps...some of the men died of yellow fever; I was only slightly dazed. When I got outa that I was all rarin' for another adventure...you know what it's like when you're young and carefree!"

One incident gave rise to another and the Colonel went on to relate his early days in the North, where he finally wound up for sometime. "At Waterways me and a partner organized the Northern Transportation Company, running boats down the Mackenzie...later I became owner. At the time we started, the Hudson's Bay Co. were our rivals; hauled only their own freight...thought they had the country sewed up!" he laughed loudly, adding, "ours was the first commercial line." Today it still competes in similar manner under different hands.

"I branched out later and had many trading posts scattered throughout the country...in fact, it was to one of these that Johnson (you've heard of Johnson the Trapper?) came to buy an outfit. It was in the McPherson district. One day, a strange man (I say strange, because most lone trappers are a little 'bushed'−the degree varying with the individual) came to my post. I thought him rather quiet, more so than most men who want to talk about anything after being alone for months−on− end!" Here the Colonel digressed to say it was okay for a man to talk to himself if he wants to, or to seek human companionship by means of conversation whether it is'hot air' or not. "But when a trapper says nothing, I am suspicious of him. It is one of the greatest of human instincts to crave the company of others, and any trapper out for months at a time will invariably desire this....

Knowing bushmen, I thought little of the man's not given to conversation...sold him an outfit...directed him to the Rat River when he asked where some good trapping ground could be had, and bade him adieu." The tale continued as we turned many bends, all decorated with spruce and pine, meeting the shore, the only interruption, an occasional dull 'thud' and 'splash' as another ton of dirt, breaking away from the banks, hit the water below and disappeared. Now and then, against the din of the 'screws', Jim would raise his voice, or perhaps I would miss the thread of the conversation, almost yelling (his hearing isn't what it used to be), for I did not want to miss any detail. So another version of the most−spun tale farther North wove its own original pattern into another debatable design.

"I later heard he built a cabin here on 'open ground' but the Indians, caring little for strangers, especially Johnson himself, didn't like the idea. Johnson's retaliation was a threat": "I'll blow hell outa ya if you don't stop molestin' me!" This brought the R.C.M.P. on a routine visit when the natives complained.

"Now the law was represented by a young man who, upon trying to enter his cabin, was rebuked, the trapper saying: "Despite hell or high water, I'll stay in this cabin!" This gave cause for a report to higher justice, whereupon the officer in charge paid a visit to the site. Johnson, seeing the holster on his hip and apparently not at any time liking the law, (it appears he must have had a legal obsession or was perhaps running away from something) thought they were coming for him and pumped shots into the policeman...then the merry chase began!" he said dramatically.

"They hunted him like a dog," said the Colonel, getting a little excited, "an' finally shot him," with a not altogether sympathetic tone.

He finished his version of the tale, heard up and down the river, by adding: "They called me as a witness to the enquiry at which all I could add was: "I only knew him as a man from over the mountains to whom I sold an outfit...and he went his way."

The hours rolled by in the company of the Colonel as more yarns and incidents came forth. It became an unforgettable day as the stage and Northern players passed in procession. "What about the Rat River Portage?" I inquired, with thoughts on the *Trail of '98*. This brought mention of the Northern Bard—Robert W. Service. "I once met the poet in Edmonton...routed him all the way down the Mackenzie, through the Rat, Little and Big Bell Rivers to the Porcupine and Fort Yukon."

Here was the information I had been trying to find for a month. With the details firmly fixed mentally, I continued to listen. "Be sure to look for names of Service and Emerson Hough carved on a tree...it's on the worn trail." (Look as I did later these landmarks were not to be found. Time had dealt them their end, I presume). "Oh yes, about our meeting...Service had heard I served in the Great War along the Upper Salient at Ypres, and being himself a veteran of that area when he served as an Ambulance Driver for the Red Cross, decided to look him up. Service and a companion made a very successful trip," he climaxed.*

At mention of John Hornby, another northern character, Jim chuckles: "Oh Jack...knew him well...why I remember..." and the Barren Lands eccentric was bared before me. "McPherson comin' up!" cried an interrupting voice. The meaty reminiscence into Peace River Jim's past came to an end as we prepared to dock. The veteran of fifty years (off and on) in the North departed for the galley and a cup of tea. I was about to face the ordeals of a deckhand once more.

As usual our Indian hosts had gathered in rows along the bank. So far this was the greatest single gathering along the rivers. It being Sunday, one would presume this to be

Reception at Fort McPherson

the chief reason for the wholehearted turnout. Scarce had we come into view than the Indian Telegraph had commenced to work, and now, as we touched sides with the shore, the hillside was bristling with natives. Reflecting again on the voyage of Mackenzie, I think how often he met such gatherings, not always quite so peaceful, trying in their superstitious way to turn him back, but in vain.

Work this afternoon was made enjoyable with the welcome assistance of several young 'bucks' who flocked aboard, some asking many questions, others just staring solemnly at the unloading procedure; but for the most part the majority eager to assist the white men. With this unexpected assistance I was able to slip away for awhile on my usual 'mission of curiosity'. Clambering up the

*See R. W. Service's autobiography—**'Plowman of the Moon'** re. this trip and accompanying humour.

sandy bank I reached the summit, paused for breath and came face to face with a gallery of squatted squaws, their papooses riding rumble seat style on their backs. A few old men puffing contentedly on their pipes also watched the youths expend their energies and the whites strain at the bulky cargo as it passed from barge to bank. "Ohhheeee...−Dazzio...lookie Dazzio!" shrieked the giggling squaws as I approached. Children in fright of the Whiteman's whiskers scattered in all directions, some crying; others seeking the comfort of mother's arms. The aged braves solemnly drew another puff on their pipes. I kept going toward the village.

Loucheux Indian Squaw

The 'Improved Scots' of McPherson

Fort McPherson is the most English−speaking settlement we had visited so far. From my new position on the heights I beheld, not a Roman Catholic Mission, but, an Anglican Church. Inquisitive, I asked of the Oblate Fathers and their Mission." No priests here now...all gone...small church over village," said a tawny offspring. This then must be one of the first Indian settlements to be converted to the Anglican faith in the Mackenzie District. As I later travelled westward the Roman Catholic Missions disappeared altogether. Some years ago the race between the two sects to convert the Indians was quite intense. In my travels I soon discovered that the Oblates had been most successful on the eastern side of the Mackenzie Mountains separating the Northwest Territories from the Yukon; and the Church of England to the north and west. So I thanked the native boy and headed for the immaculate house of religion.

A woman busied herself with picking flowers and tending her garden as I neared the manse. The minister's wife, I thought. Dropping her hand−spade the good woman raised her head as I approached. She must have deducted I was 'foreign' as she prompted: "everything grows wonderful here," followed by, "would you like to see the interior of our church?" Interested, I followed her within. It was all very neat. White walls were hung with pictures; pews neatly arranged awaited Sunday evening. I felt it in every way equivalent to those Outside, but on a considerably smaller scale. Swinging through the outer door the minister's wife said: "Be sure to see the graveyard," and disappeared. It was an unusual request; but nevertheless I felt there must be someone of importance interred there. In the vestibule a holder overflowed with pamphlets, and a stack of well used prayer books displayed their petticoats.

Loucheux Indian Brave

Outside once more, my feet turned to the south side of the church. A white picket—fence surrounds the graveyard dotted with many gravestones, crosses and monuments. And then I discovered a mound of importance. In a single plot four graves lay side by side. It is an R.C.M. Police plot and the men are the heroes of the McPherson—Dawson Patrol. Later, a native son told me that at the moment of burial there was considerable controversy between the padre and others. The man of religion had set his mind on an identical burial for all, while his opponents desired that the youngest, Kinney, who (unable to stand the sight of his frozen companion) committed suicide, should be buried outside the plot. The padre, notwithstanding the disagreement, won the verbal dual; four crosses arose from within the burial plot.

The narrative leading up to this scene I was to hear later, in its completeness, from an aged Indian, Charlie Stewart, who guided the search party to the horrible scene of death in the frozen North.

Burial Plot of R.C.M.P. Lost Patrol

At this point I was determined to decipher the reason for all the Scotch names within the area. It was from an aged Indian who spoke fairly good English that I found the first threads of the story. "Many Scotch fellow he come from Outside," he said, with a mixture of his Loucheux tongue. "He trade with me and other Indian at the Hudson's Bay post...then he wanta love and raise big family. So you see now they call um 'Improved Scotch!' He smiled his widest smile and puffed his pipe as though satisfied with the unique explanation. It was cause for much laughter; but I was left wondering just who had made the 'improvement'.

The main feature about Fort McPherson is the people. They are said to be a branch of that widespread Loucheux Tribe of earlier days; but are content to call themselves McPherson Indians. Most of the settlement can speak and understand English quite well. Besides this they have inherited many Scottish characteristics from the much inter—marrying with that hardy race. Fine facial characteristics, neatness and politeness, honest character and a contagious sense of humour are some of the few assets of the new generation of 'Breeds. "They're more reliable than any of 'em," complimented an oldtimer once when the question arose, "just sprinkle a little of the Heelans in 'em and you don't have to worry." His name happened to be McTavish.

There is a rather humorous saying in the Canadian North, up and down the rivers, or wherever the white men live in communion with the natives of the land. "If you stay here over three years, you either go crazy or marry an Indian woman," it goes. So if it held any truth (and I never once doubted it) it is quite understandable why the English and Scotch pioneers, coming out as Hudson's Bay factors or immigrants seeking their fortunes in the New World, have settled to the customs and habits and taken on dusky partners as wives. Indeed, it is no country for sophistication and propriety. One must live as the country demands.

So I discovered why such men as Firth and McLeod have brought such names as McPherson and Peel to the Canadian Northlands. And I was to learn more about this interesting mixture as we travelled down the Mackenzie with two Improved—Scotch deckhands.

Much noise from the beach rose to the heights of the village. My perusal over with, I hastened to the scene of activity at the barge. The din I discovered was the result of a practical joke played on one of the local natives assisting at unloading. In their light—hearted manner the squaws and braves on the bank didn't hesitate to see the humorous side of it all as the fellow picked himself up from the muddy shore. 'Yes, there is no doubt of the Scotch in this lot!' I told myself, tucking a timber under an arm and falling in line again.

All hands aboard, (happy at the thought of moving again except for Willie Firth, who was tempted to jump ship at his home port) the cables are loosened on shore. As the capstan let out its squeaky music of motion I lean on the bar with the two 'Improved Scotch' 'breeds. When the last yard of cable winds aboard I think to myself, 'McTavish wasn't far wrong!'

Into the Peel Channel once more, this time with the current; it was only minutes before the shouting throng were out of sight and hearing. Willie Firth, wishing he had 'jumped', lay thinking on his bunk. I mused at the reminder of my informal swim. The sun had been so hot, the unloading so strenuous, that I had come to the conclusion: Indians or no Indians, I'm going to have a swim! Within view of the entire population the Cheechako dove into the cool waters. This caused quite a ripple along the line of spectators, who apparently have little use for cool water on hot days; I don't doubt the Dazzio (whiskers) will stay fixed in the minds of the people of Fort McPherson. Well out in mid−stream the mosquitoes kept their distance and we soon arrived at our waiting barges.

CHAPTER THIRTEEN

IN THE PADDLEMARKS OF ALEXANDER MACKENZIE

Twenty days on the water; it seems like months as the monotonous churning of thousands of gallons of muddy water continue, driving us on...on...into the Arctic. Already I feel the energizing effect of the perpetual daylight and the resultant loss of sleep. The sun does not set; but at late evening is merely a burning nucleus from which a host of pearl—grey clouds fall out, like plumage from a peacock's tail, split by the dull red rays of a Midnight Sun. The growth along the riverbanks becomes denser and greener against a background of snow—capped mountains. *"A hundred miles beyond lies the Yukon," chides the voice of Adventure. 'Give me time...give me time,' I answer.*

Morning found us at Latitude 67N; longitude 132 W. "We're west of Vancouver today," said the Icelander. "Is that what accounts for the tang in the air?" I retaliated. "Wouldn't doubt it...wouldn't doubt it a bit," he replied, eyeing the trading post that was coming into view. No large settlements inhabit this region of the Arctic. Only a few individual traders are the middlemen between the Outside and Inside, located at strategic points. Pulling into the mosquito—ridden shore, it was Toby Larsen, second engineer off duty, who gave a shriek whistle. A wizened, unshaven man came down to the boat in response to the summons, slapping at mosquitoes and sandflies right and left as a cloud of them followed him from his cabin to the shore. "Don't bring any more of 'em down here!" yelled Raymond the ex—trapper, speaking for an early risen crew, in no mood to combat a foe so early in the morn'. Such was our introduction to Carl Betz.

A consultation between the cargo boss (Harold) and the lone trader followed, amidst the mosquitoes. As I listened and watched the hopeless gestures, I sensed something was up. "Sorry, Carl," came the two words of finality from our man, who with an armsweep signalled the Skipper to go astern. I gathered that freight charges must be paid before traders can obtain their goods. "He has a standing freight—debt. No money, no goods!" said Harold returning to his office.

Maybe the season was tough? Perhaps the trader was too lenient with his credit? Whatever the circumstances, we were soon headed away from the shore, downstream, which also meant a brief respite from the insistent mosquitoes. Lulled by the drone of the twin engines, warmed by the hot Arctic Sun, the Cheechako settled abaft, in one small sense glad of the unfortunate circumstances.

We have been coursing the Peel or Middle Channel, which branches to the left from the Mackenzie River at Separation Point. The entire waterway is gradually breaking up to form a huge inundated area which is known as the Delta. Each river, stream and creek seems over—anxious to reach the Arctic and contribute to that larger body, like vassals helping to make one mighty being; and for their efforts receiving nothing but obscurity. Fitting in its application to the situation came again to mind the words of a poet who probably had never heard of the Mackenzie Delta.

> "Why hurry little river,
> Why hurry to the sea?
> There's nothing there to do,
> But to sink into the blue...
> And all Forgotten be."

As we rushed to the Beaufort Sea many more rivers joined us in their hurry, forsaking their own clean riverbeds for the muddy waters of the Peel Channel.

The sky this morning looks like a great wad of carelessly—pulled, cotton batting with bits of blue appearing through the interstices. Spruce, pine and vegetation come nearer the banks, while mountains still hug their precious, little crowns of snow. The Cheechako could not wait to accept their flaunted challenge and pass through their midst. With these surroundings and thoughts, the challenge still unheeded, we pull into another isolated cabin nestled high upon the south limit of the river.

It is the home of the Harrison family who run a mink ranch. This fact was felt for the next hour. No amount of yelling brought signs of life from the cabin. "Perhaps the hour is too early for them?" suggested the purser, as he set out to climb the steep bank. Some minutes later life appeared at the summit. "You can start on those sacks first," ordered the voice. We started amid a flurry of curses.

It was not so much the freight as the narrow path that inclined its way up the almost vertical, dirt bank of the river. Every other step sent a foot of earth, with a splash, below; and with a hundred pounds blocking the vision (we were forced to carry the bags in our arms) I daren't imagine the result should two feet of dirt suddenly decide to part with the bank. Added to this possibility were the pestilent hordes of winged—life, who at any moment might originate a counter attack, sending a pain—ridden deckhand and his sack of meal to the bottom of the Peel Channel. A swim at this hot stage would, no doubt, be appreciated by all; but to enter the water so ignominiously just wouldn't do. The freight had come too far to be jettisoned in such a manner.

With these odds against us we gritted our teeth and struggled up the decaying slope, pretending to ignore our playful pests. An hour later, with a shirt full of meal husks, a hundred pink swellings about the forehead and face, I sat down on a sack, beat. Mr. and Mrs. Harrison and daughter came out to thank us, the daughter bringing forth three, blond, muskrat skins. These being very rare, she would not part with one, talk as we may.

At this point a swim interested me more than anything else. Arctic waters in July are very different from the southern lakes and rivers. In fact, they never really 'warm up'. Heedless of this, I stripped and plunged, swam a fast circle to keep the blood circulating and clambered aboard the barge feeling ready for another hour of hundred pound sacks, but not along so doubtful a path!

I was rid of the husks and mosquitoes; the barge slid into the Peel once more. I felt a mood of keen appreciation for the beautiful surroundings. Noticeable, as warm as the sun is, was the slight chill in the air caused by our proximity to the Arctic, where, perhaps the ice floes had not yet receded? When the winds blow from this direction it is best to make for the galley or find a southern nook amongst the cargo. I chose the latter course, residing for the next few hours in a close communion with Nature, the trees, clouds and sky continuing their indefinite scenic play; the plot forever the same, but the characters ever—varying. The sun, beating its Arctic tattoo, soon put me to semi—dozing, and in that state I found myself subject to its imaginative effects. *I crossed the Sahara with a camel safari...heat beating down...beating down...no water...days to go...heat...merciless sun...God I'm thirsty!* "All out!...deckhands!"came the Mate's harsh call. 'That's me!' I accused myself. Jumping up, I realized it was noon. Another quaint, log cabin stood to port, back apiece from the shore. The largest team of dogs I have ever seen barked a welcome as they strained on their leashes with excitement. From the shack came: "Hullo there!" followed by its tall, gangly owner, Ed Rystad. He is Norwegian and has "done a little of everything," he says, "includin' some prospectin' on the local rivers. Now I'm settled in the tradin' business...don't mind it a bit working for Mister Lang," he said, as we made ready to unload another cargo.

Conversations must be short when there's work to be done; and once again the endless stream of 100's and 50's began to flow from the barge to shore via a narrow gangplank that creates another competitive obstacle. Dog—food, a popular feed for the canines when the fish is done, comprised a goodly portion of this trip. A half hour later brings an end to the dog—food, flour and sugar sacks and the pleasant meeting with another Northern character. Ed smiles, glad of our visit to his lonely outpost, waving us on our way. Lang's Trading Post disappears: the

**The *S.S. Distributor*
Last of the Mackenzie Sternwheelers**

scenery levels off slightly; mountains loom to the left in the noonday haze. We cannot be far from our own destination—Aklavik.

As afternoon passed the air grew colder. There was no doubt whatever of our Arctic proximity. Four o'clock brought us 'round a bend in the curvacious channel to a straight stretch, a good half mile long. Then we saw the first signs of a settlement. High aerials, houses, boats, a Mission and the standard, white buildings of the Hudson's Bay Company came into view. The *S.S. Distributor*, last of the Bay's sternwheelers, passed us, heading south. The distance shortened. I had heard much about the village of Aklavik and the recent Firth River gold−rush commencing at this point. I was eager to see the town and its people as they were to see the arrival of the *Hearne Lake*.

CHAPTER FOURTEEN

CROSSROADS OF HUMANITY

"It's Aklavik...all out!" came the voice of the Mate. He did not have to yell loud, for we were all on deck anticipating this arrival. The banks were lined with sundry folk, including Eskimo, Indians, Whites and what looked like a bountiful mixture of all three. With almost the exuberance of McPherson these far northern people turned out; and as we ran the cables ashore, making fast the barge, the friends of the crew swarmed aboard for a greeting.

Aklavik N.W.T. from the Mackenzie River

**Oodles of Loucheux
Awaiting the First Annual Boat**

The Indians of Aklavik are a branch of that widespread tribe—the Loucheux—first encountered by the Cheechako in the region of Fort Good Hope, to the south. At one time they occupied the area from the source of the Peel River to its basin and junction with the Mackenzie; the entire area north; the entire Yukon basin from the mouth of the Pelly River down, except for a small strip at the delta where the Yukon pours itself into the Bering Sea.

Loucheux is the French for 'slant eyed' or 'squint eyed'. French—Canadian traders who noticed this facial feature, similar to the Eskimo, dubbed the Indians thus. In past years the Indians and Eskimo spent half their time fighting one another, and the other half trading. Surprisingly enough, the Indians adopted many features of Eskimo life including: the caribou skin shirt (long—tailed in front and back); the thatched, domed sweathouse, banked with snow in winter and having a hole for a smoke outlet in the roof; the straight—sided, flat—bottomed, birch canoes; and the Eskimo sled—sometimes preferable to their own toboggans. However, times and customs change. So nowadays we find the influence of the Outside predominant in clothing and canoes, although the women still cling to their full—length, parka—dresses that make Indian and Eskimo difficult to distinguish. The descent of the Loucheux has been traced through the female side, giving rise to the conclusion that at one time they were possibly

Indians in High Arctic Garb

matriarchal? In the year 1858 the Hudson's Bay Company took a census of this tribe, which totalled about 1,179. Today there are only 700 Loucheux left within the borders of Canada.

**Indian Woman
with Baby in Back Pouch**

Aklavik being the terminus, it was necessary to hire a host of Indians to help with the cargo. "You don't have to work if you don't want to!" said the Purser to the tired crew, "we're hiring some of these muscle−bound natives who have slept all winter!" It sounded like the music of Heaven to my ears. I had noticed a large family sitting and leaning on oil barrels−their point of vantage as the boat arrived. 'Surely they must be Eskimo?' I thought, slinging my camera into a parka pocket. Out of curiosity as much as anything, I approached the long−dressed group. They all smiled coyly, the mother propping the little−one erect for the family portrait. Then I recognized the Indian features which gave way to slight traces of Eskimo. Slightly confused, I chose to call them 'Breeds. All that day I was confronted by the same problem, mainly, I suppose, because they all dressed similarly in their elongated, fur−trimmed parkas so necessary in this Arctic region. However, when the sun shone hot and the parkas still remained, I became filled with more wonderment.

Over−anxious to meet some genuine Eskimo, I approached a boat tethered to the shore. It was named the *Saucy Jane*. "Hello there!" I shouted, boarding the barge by the usual rickety gang−plank, in typical informal manner. A few guttural sounds were spoken in response, by what I took to be the

mother of the family aboard. 'Jackpot,' I said to myself, 'a real Eskimo at last!' Motioning to the children who gazed from within the schooner, she begged them come forth. All was not set yet. The pretty daughter was combing her long, black hair (she must have sensed the significance of the open camera and inquisitive Whiteman). A final command from the mother brought the damsel from her toilet. As bashful a group as I had yet contended with, they stood through the ordeal. I thanked the family as best as one (ignorant of the Eskimo language) can, and debarked from the *Saucy Jane*, convinced that *this* time I had an Eskimo on film.

**Jackpot!
My First Eskimo**

The sight of coal barges along the waterfront gave ample reason for questions. We had not hauled coal north. Where did it come from? The answer came from the local trader, who said: "Used to be a mine worked steady in the hills...shut down...but some of the fellas found it and bring out a little...not the best, but anything goes in these parts, you know!" By now I did; and realized that some future date may see huge plants belching black smoke on to the white snows of the Arctic.

In quest of more personalities, I walked through the village. It was on this jaunt that I met Mrs. Jacobson. All Eskimo are happy people, but this stout mother was the happiest I ever met. For five minutes we exchanged banter; for five minutes she laughed, till I thought her cheek bones would never drop to the serious position. With smiles I was introduced to her two daughters who spoke good English. "We are only visiting," said one, who had been through many grades at the local mission school, "and we are going back to Banks Land very soon." It was a choice meeting;

and here I formed a lasting impression of these simple—living Northerners. They are truly happy Eskimo.

Supper was a gay one on the evening of July 15th. We were augmented by friends from the shore. As the conversation became * warm the northern humour found its rightful place amongst us. All seemed happy about the Skipper's decision to visit the Arctic shores, for it was the first time for many of us. The cook, with his Cockney accent (he still insisted he was born 'outside' of the sound of Bow Bells), was in top shape, bringing laughter to the table with his subtle brand of jokes. "The mosquitoes down river wear snowshoes and parkas (they had been getting larger as we proceeded north), and I can hear them saying, "We're going to enjoy whitemeat for a change from blubber and Eskimo," he went on. Not content to let us enjoy a good mouthful, he followed up with the lighter side of his early life. "Oi 'ad a goat wonce...'an doos ya knoo, 'e yused to loike tins...whoi'e were even foussy about the labels...wouldn't eat anyfing but the best! And 'e 'specially loiked broightly—colored

Mrs. Jacobson, Happy Eskimo

ones." Amid a galley of laughter and spray of tea from the remote side of the table, he continued to mention the time his animal was tethered in the backyard. "There 'e were...couldn't even get into any mischief 'e couldn't...that is until I leaned ova the fence to talk to the neyba...when the dirty...snook oop be—oind me, 'e did, and let's me 'ave it! Oi got ova that, but the next toime oi see 'im 'e 'ad chewed the sleeve off me coat 'angin on the line. Each toime the wind blew 'is direction 'e would grab a mouthful...oi, it were real Scotch tweed too, it were!" was his adjoinder, as though inferring the goat's choice of tins was adopted in this instance too. By now the galley rocked with laughter, the atmosphere was completely merry and imagination took a loose rein over every cup of tea.

The last gentleman to speak was a guest. All I remember them calling him was 'Red'. One gathered, as he spoke, that he had spent some time in Aklavik. Renewing the northern adage that, "if you're here more than three years you go crazy or marry an Indian woman," he said, with a whimsical smile, in response to the question of his time in the country: "Guess it's about time I found me a long—haired, washing machine!" which added the spark to the explosive humour that had congested in the galley of the *Hearne Lake*. 'Chow' over, the northern gathering dispersed and went about their business.

Aklavik is the converging spot for Eskimo, Indians and White men. It lies on the port bank of the Peel Channel about 100 miles from the shores of the Arctic Ocean. Here the Eskimo (more often called 'Huskies') come, in their many and varied boats, to exchange their winter fur—catch for such necessities as they take back with them. Having been in constant contact with the white man for the past half century, they now live with many of our commodities, including: tinned foods, clothing, boats and engines, rifles, stoves and coal. Because of the barren nature of this lower country and the fact that the waters have been 'Whaled out' of certain Arctic fish, some ingenious natives have turned to the Whiteman's mode of heating and cooking. It seemed rather ironical at the time, for an Eskimo to be needing coal to keep his igloo warm, or to cook with; but then I remembered this was 1947.

The village faces south—east towards the Channel, which at this point is very wide and swift. Many streams make Aklavik a veritable island in the heart of the Delta. It is comprised of a Roman Catholic Mission, house and school; a hospital with operating room and four trained nurses; a radio station built up from a wartime 'ham' station; a large Hudson's Bay Company trading post; several independent traders—including Peffer, Strong and Jim Jones; a post office;

Forty years later I was to meet the son (Roy Inglangasuk —meaning 'laughter') of the daughter who was combing her hair —his mother. Roy and I have a standing joke: "I knew your mother before you did!" I have since enjoyed her company when she visits down from Aklavik N.W.T..

dance hall and theatre; Anglican church; a couple of restaurants; army aircraft—used for mail—plane and emergencies; and a Mounted Police Detachment of three constables and a corporal, under Inspector Kirk.

'Your main mission…have you forgotten, mortal? reminded the Goddess of Adventure.' 'Don't rush me!' I told her, not meaning to be rude. I was enjoying the pleasant atmosphere of the settlement. 'The *Trails of '98*…you can't get through the mountains alone, you're only a Cheechako, remember!' 'Yes, I know…don't rub it in…won't always be that way,' I told her. Suddenly I took heed of her promptings. 'A companion to travel with…why not find one now?' Thus prompted, I set out to seek what looked to me like a stalwart fellow with a load of optimism and an adventurous spirit. 'Should be easy in this place,' I comforted myself, and set off.

Seeing a likely—looking fellow with a girl on his arm, I stopped him and asked, suggestively: "Do you know anyone who would like to take a trip through the Rat River Portage?" His eyes brightened, as ideas flashed through his mind. But as quickly as they had come, they departed. His girl friend looked at him; he at her. Then, as though coming to earth again and realizing his responsibility, he said, halfheartedly: "Sorry, but the wife doesn't want me to go…we were married a couple of weeks ago!" Understanding, I thanked him, asking at the same time what gentleman adventurers lurked in the tribe. There must be one, I knew. Thinking a moment, he suddenly said with sureness: "See Malcolm Firth…why he'd jump at the chance…and he's the best hunter in Aklavik!" With these recommendations I made for a tent on the riverbank, in search of my 'Improved Scotch' friend.

Pulling back the tent—flap, I peered inside, asking simultaneously: "Is there a Malcolm Firth dwelling here?" Someone stirred, yawned, and said "yeah…hey Malcolm!…wake up!" The form moved…turned over…hesitated…threw back the cover of a robe…wiped his eyes and yawned…then looked at me. "Are you Malcolm Firth?" I enquired. "Yes, come in and sit down!" was the imperative invitation. I did so. We exchanged words for a few minutes and he beamed at the gentleman's agreement. It went: "I'll supply the grub and gas; you can bring your canoe and 'kicker'. We'll travel a good pace, such as to enjoy the trip, and if you're tired, tell me; if I am, I'll tell you frankly. I like a guy who can go another mile when it's necessary—O.K.?

Before I had finished the proposition it was agreed upon, Mister Firth smiling in his native way but asking one question: "How much do I get?" Promptly, I said: "I'm not a rich, American tourist with money to burn. I'm working my way through the country. We'll share the difficulties 50—50 on everything!" Without further mincing of words and deciding (I guess) that here was a trip paid for all the way, he replied: "I've always wanted to see on the other side of those mountains (the same range that had been challenging me for the past two days in the Yukon). When do we leave?"

There had been a hint of a possible trip to the Arctic port of Tuktoyaktuk; it was confirmed at the supper only minutes before. This I was determined to see. So I informed my friend of a possible two—day trip. "That'll give me time to get rid of some of my stuff. I'll be ready when you get back," he replied, saying: "I'll be back in two days at the latest," I backed out through the flap, beaming with success and the feeling that 'the world had me just where I wanted it!' Never had plans gone so smoothly. Here I was, 20 days north of Yellowknife—a thousand miles away, with plans complete for the next month. The Gods were too kind; but perhaps they thought: 'Lady Luck and he are too good a team to split?'

As it happened, there was no delay when the final day arrived. But let's not rush ourselves. There's the Arctic Ocean to see yet!"…

That night was unlike any other I had ever seen. As the Midnight Sun hovered on the horizon at twelve—thirty, a softball game still progressed on the bank of the Peel Channel; Eskimo, Indians, 'Breeds and Whites of both genders, yelled their encouragements, socked the ball and slid to the bases with all the enthusiasm of an American pro—league team; Indian squaws, chopping wood, sent the ringing sounds of axes through the village; the young daughters hauled water for morning from the local well; a group of carpenters continued to raise their structure, heedless of the hour. I rolled into my sleeping bag, more than satisfied with the events of the day, wondering what the Arctic Ocean would look like on the morrow.

CHAPTER FIFTEEN

LADY LUCK SMILES AGAIN

Morning didn't come, it was there all night, bright as day! But 7 a.m. did (all too soon) with the *'clang'* of the cook's bell. This cunning individual had found a sure means of averting a second call. It was quite simple. On the down swing of the bell he would hit the iron railing which ran about the deck, giving an added resonance to the already unpopular bell; and then on the upswing it would *'clang'* clearly. Unable to stand for long the discordant effect which vibrated in every corner of the little vessel, the crew would dash up, cursing whoever happened to be foremost in their morning vocabulary. Sullenly trooping to the galley, the sleepy group would assume their regular places, eating the first meal of the day in comparative silence, paying little or no heed to the cook's jokes; that is, if he himself was in any mood (which wasn't usual till later in the day) to be witty.

"Wakey, Wakey!"

It was noon before plans and unloading were complete. The Skipper, a very restless man in port, had been pacing the deck frequently this morning. The Mate, with no special orders from his direct boss, checked the barges and cables. The Purser, discharging the final cargo to its resting place, hastily checked his list, ticking first here, then there, sensing also the Skipper's impatience. "That's it!" he yelled, in a voice that split the moment between inaction and action. "Cut the cables...release this barge!" cried the Mate, assuming fully his rightful position. Figures darted from boat to barge to shore...cables were released...audible groans came from the capstan...the Skipper surveyed the waters from his lofty position at the wheel. He wore his straw hat. With more than the usual speed the last cable came aboard. The barge lurched. Mud oozed up from the Channel bottom. We were afloat.

A few miles brought us into the Aklavik Channel, which in turn flowed into the Mackenzie again. At 11:30 a.m. the swift Middle Channel accepted us without hesitation. The scenery changed little, but noticeable was the growing paucity of trees along the hillsides. Day passed into evening; evening into night, as the spruce cast their long shadows across our bows. Clouds hovered close and the circle made by the horizon seemed only a short distance away. In truth, one had the feeling of being at the top of the globe.

It was six a.m. when the cook brought us to the deck with his unmusical tones, exactly one hour ahead of schedule. "Orders," said the Englishman going about his duty. That was that!

It was a pleasant morning notwithstanding the hour. Mountains and tall spruce had given way to flat lands on portside and a ridge of bare patched hills to starboard. Dried logs, washed ashore, lay in the sun, basking not unlike unconventional beachcombers in their nudity. We were about halfway to Richards Island. Out of the spruce appeared a large white house and a hip—roofed barn adjacent, surrounded by a collection of small buildings. "Reindeer Station!" called the Mate, "no stop till the return trip," he added as it slipped past.

It was ten a.m. when the Cheechako first glimpsed the sprawling Arctic Ocean, its tumultuous waves dashing into the Delta. "Tie her up," said the Skipper to the Mate, descending to his cabin. I stripped to the minimum of clothes necessary to preserve certain dignities and settled behind the pages of Conrad's *Argosy*, in a sunny corner beside the galley vent. With the surrounding nautical atmosphere, the *Nigger of the Narcissus* came to life, interrupted only by sporadic laughter, emanating from the galley below, as it rose and passed through the screened opening. The Cockney was at it again.

How long I read and how long I slept was a mystery. But all of a sudden loud words disturbed me..."Say, did you hear about the beavers they exported to Australia?" asked the voice, continuing,

Swabbin' the Deck

"when they went to work on the ironwood trees it broke their hearts!" A loud burst of laughter (mostly on the part of the cook) streamed upwards in its effort to escape through the ventilator. So, rudely awakened, I shifted my position to another part of the boat and continued my siesta under the hot sun. I think a smile crossed my face at the reflection of the sounds that had come from the galley.

Some hours later the waters abated. We continued our run into the Beaufort Sea, on the right of Richards Island. All was going too well when suddenly we stopped. Our course is never twice identically the same. The water was four feet deep; our draw was four feet. We were grounded. I glanced at the placid Skipper to see his reaction. He appeared momentarily bewildered, for he could go neither back nor forward, but just churn volumes of mud with each effort. As though disappointed at breaking his record of not becoming sandbarred this year, he became slightly perturbed.

Land of the Midnight Sun

"Drop Anchor!" commanded the Skipper, at one in the morning. And the day spent itself on Tugiuksuk at the mouth of the East Channel. Chilly winds and the appearance of a white whale (Ogipuk) clarify our northerly position. The Midnight Sun hung, a round red ball, a foot above the horizon.

As forecast by the cook, the mosquitoes were having their change of diet—and didn't we know it! There is a magnetic attraction to beauty in this part of the world. Its sunsets are rich; its winds so invigorating; large volumes of space lie in whatever direction one looks. So many times in the past months I had seen the moving effect of clouds shot with the brightening rays of morn, their tops reflecting daylight; the bottoms grey, opaque.

It was my dislike for the many, winged pests that drove me from the beauties of an Arctic morning to the disorderly depths of a deckhand's cabin below. 'You can't have everything!' I consoled myself, as I prepared for bed, slapping at a hounding mosquito.

A long sleep and a close, sunny morning brought us to the deck, from where we observed the work of our assisting small boat. Clusters of willows, pushed into the Arctic mud, identified our course amongst the shifting sandbars. The mosquitoes, bigger and better, also realize the beautiful day in which to do their dirtywork. So, covered with Skat and Beat It (popular brands of repellent), the morning found us 'sounding' our way along the coast with marked poles; from the front barge, each deckhand takes a half—hour shift, signalling the footage, by means of fingers held at arms length, to Captain Ilyea on the vessel behind.

In this manner of sounding, signalling, sounding, we crept across the northern waters. Then all of a sudden a hundred grey—white fish surfaced, paused a split moment, and plunged into obscurity. "Whales ahead!" someone called from above. "White whales!" Years of imagination now became a reality as I watched the sleek, grey forms rise, turn their white bellies to the sun, and fall off sideways into the depths, only to reappear a thousand yards away. We had run into a school of Ogipuks. Among them was the occasional, huge, black monster; one of their few brothers that have not been 'whaled out' by greedy Whalers at the turn of the century. "Them's 'Huskie' Whalers," said a native pointing to some fairly large boats with tall masts scattered

amongst the ice floes. And a page from a Jack London novel turned into reality. Thus we wound our way along the irregular shoreline, to starboard, keeping it always in view, ever watchful for the sight of the Eskimo settlement.

Sounding For Bottom

The first sign of life that did come into view was the tall mast of a ship, rising from a barren shore as though stranded. Then a small cluster of buildings made their appearance. At five o'clock we lay off shore, waiting for the signal to enter the natural harbour through the narrow but deep channel to the village beyond. It was July 17 that the *Hearne Lake* and its crew left the sprawling Arctic Ocean and slid alongside the log wharf of Tuktoyaktuk. There was no doubt

whatever of our being in the land of the Eskimo, or 'Huskie'. There on the dock to greet us stood four smiling males. At first glance I turned to the Mate and said: 'Do you think we've missed out on a good joke?' "Don't be foolish!" he retorted, smiling, "they just know the right kind of wrinkles to wear." I soon discovered this pleasant characteristic of the folk who inhabit these bleak shores.

Tuk–tuk (as everyone calls Tuktoyaktuk – the place of the caribou) was once named Port Brabant. It is situated above Kitigazuit, on the eastern side of Richards Island, about 200 miles from Aklavik between the 69th and 70th parallels. The surrounding countryside is very flat and barren, but for a short, mossy grass. It is primarily a trading post, exchanging food, dry goods and hardware to the Eskimo for their furs and sea–food brought in from the large district to the north and east. It contains a Hudson's Bay Company post, Roman Catholic and Anglican Missions, a few scattered dwellings and an odd array of boats–including the *Fort Ross*, which plies the coastal waters to the Coppermine district, farther east.

Four Happy 'Huskies'

Among the handful of people in this northern village are the Huskies, 'Breeds of varied ancestry and a few Whites who run the post and Missions. Jumping ashore after unloading our cargo, I set out to meet some of the local people. The first I accosted was a young lad with an ear to ear smile. "Hello there!" I welcomed, figuring that words would be in vain, but I was mistaken. "Hi...what you do here?" he returned. "I'm with the boat," I said, "I'd like to meet a real Eskimo and have a chat," I added. "I'm an Eskimo...my name Tom Oscar," he replied cordially, continuing..."I just come in from whaling...many Ogipuk out near big–ice,"he pointed to the coast. So we had our chat. I discovered the Eskimo people, (for some reason) delight in compiling their name from the Christian names of individual Whitemen they have known, with no limit to the number added. Before I departed, I wondered how many of this interesting people had added my name to their already long 'monikers'?

As the Mission boat, following us from Aklavik pulled to the shore, a heavy−set, bronzed individual debarked from the launch. Gazing skeptically at him and his family I said in all frankness: "What brand of Eskimo are you?" Equally frank, he replied: "You can see I'm not Eskimo," smiling one of those contagious smiles that display a characteristic set of perfect teeth; "I am the son of an American Whaler...my mother was an Eskimo...but this is not all my family," he continued, surveying his trailing flock. So I met another of the strange combinations that have been moulded in this land of surprises. He joked for a moment and the six juniors, bedecked with full smiles, trailed off behind their father to their driftwood house.

**Hudson's Bay
Arctic Freighter—M.V. *Fort Ross***

One Eskimo's Family

Because of the little growth in this district the homes are built of driftwood that washes up on shore, or is gathered from the rivers farther south. Some, however, are half wood and half canvas, while a few are just tents banked with moss. The Hudson's Bay post is the only bungalow in the settlement and with its clean, white appearance supplies strong contrast to the rest of the village.

Ambling amongst the variegated structures I paused momentarily outside a tent. "Who are you?" I asked of the native, squatting beside her fire. She giggled and coyly turned her head. No response came from a second attempt. Trying my hands, I failed again to make identification as the lass giggled louder and sucked her finger. I had never before been in such a predicament with a woman. 'There must be some way?...surely you can figure out something!' I told myself. But I told myself wrong. For five minutes I ran the gamut of names, foods, and other common nouns, swinging my hands and arms, till from a distance I must have looked like a Frenchman in a foreign country for the first time. All I received was a large smile and another round of bashfulness. Had a girl who attended school at one of the missions not turned up, my efforts would have been completely in vain. However, acting as interpreter, she introduced us and explained: the girl was from the Coppermine tribe, to the east, and just visiting.

It was not till later that I fully realized my mistake: I had been circling the fire in an effort to capture the coy damsel on film; but that was impossible, all the while she acted so bashfully. 'Why was she thus? Surely a woman loved to have her picture taken?' I asked myself. "The blue tattoo is a sign of beauty and marriage. She thought you were down on your hands and knees proposing, and she's already married!" I kicked myself and went my way.

Tatooed for Beauty

Noticeable to the southern eye are the parkas that are worn winter and summer. They are made chiefly of lined cloth or duffel, thigh length and invariably trimmed with wolverine fur—the best frost repellent. Some, however, are of caribou skin and have the pants to match. Here it was, the middle of July: a hot sun beat down from directly above. It was the first day of summer and already they were preparing for winter.

Almost anywhere in the village one can hear and see sled dogs, barking and straining on their leashes with anxiety, as though wishing for winter to come and their masters to drop harness about their shoulders. Well—fed and energetic, they characterized the typical Eskimo huskie—considered among the people as part of their most prized possessions. As one old trader once said: "They sometimes worship their dogs more than their womenfolk...cause without 'em they can't get very far!" As I looked at the vast expanse of white, I agreed with him on one point. "They'll pay as much as four or five hundred dollars for a good lead—dog that'll take 'em anywhere," another had commented. Certainly in this country the old maxim about a man's best friend has been proven a hundredfold. Eyeing a barking team, enroute back to the boat, I couldn't discern faithlessness on any one of their faces. A shrill hoot from the boat's whistle and I knew my pleasant visit must come to an end.

Once more aboard the *Hearne Lake* we waved a parting to a smiling group of 'Huskies', slid past the *Fort Ross*—grounded for repairs—and were again riding the waves of the Arctic Ocean, flooded with the evening light of the Midnight Sun. The ice floes had receded a few days prior to our visit; perhaps they would float back and seal up the coast in a short while? Pondering the shortness of summer in the Arctic, I stole a fleeting glance shoreward. An Eskimo knelt in the pink light, gutting an Ogipuk. I turned into the still breeze and pulled the parka over my head, pleased with our visit to the happy Eskimo of Tuktoyaktuk.

The trip from 'Tuk—tuk' was not without event. At 8:30 we had pulled out under sunny, Arctic skies. At 1:00 a.m. we were riding at anchor...fogbound. We had made good time along the coast; but as we approached Whitefish Point the fog began to roll in from the north as the warmth of the sun disappeared. Enroute we were busy constructing buoys out of oil drums, sand bags and lengths of rope. These were to be dumped in the south channel, by Richards Island, above the estuary of the Mackenzie, replacing the willows laid in the down—trip.

Suddenly it became a race as we cast the drums to leeward. Fog slowly encircled us like a silent, writhing monster. All the drums were not laid yet. The Skipper, we could see, was anxious to reach the river channel before operations became obscured. "Drop another!" he commanded from the wheel above, a slight wisp of fog hiding him for a short moment. The Mate, checking each before its descent, said: "O.K....let 'er go!" and I flung the sand bag over the side, in company with the red drum tossed simultaneously by another deckhand. "Three more to go!" shouted the Mate to the Skipper aloft. The fog was upon us...its thickening tentacles in the first stage of envelopment. Scarcely visible were the waters ahead.

Captain Ilyea looked concerned. The Mate had us prepare the next buoy. We wait patiently for the next bunch of willows to slide by. The Skipper circles...approaches the brush...cuts the engines...looks below to Swanson—the Mate...hesitates, then..."Drop another!" *'Plunk'*...and the Arctic waters gain another floating object. "Two more to go...anchor...sleep...crew pretty tired...unloading...sounding...irregular hours...day and night...," I heard the Mate impart to the cook who had come from the galley more out of curiosity than to spread humour.

"One left!" yelled Swanson, a few minutes later. "Drop her!" came the pleasant reply from the Skipper, who had just made a change of headgear. With zest we counted in unison, "One!...two!...three!" *Splash!*...some bubbles and a few widening rings marked the last of the buoys. A future course was laid for the boats. "Now maybe we can get some rest?" sighed Willie, hardly visible in the impenetrable fog bank that had closed in.

A moment later, as though entering the gloomy halls of Erebus, we were in the Mackenzie River, completely obliterated by swarming, twisting banks of mist. "Doesn't look like she'll clear...drop anchor!" said the Skipper, his sou'wester all that was visible through the mist. The words drifted like Siren music to the crew below, who watched what seemed like miles of chain turning out behind the anchor. With a last jerk the clanging iron stopped. We were at rest.

First thought of all was a cup of tea as we made for the galley in one body. No one lingered long in the galley this morning. No one gave ear to the gay Cockney, who, not having laboured with the crew, was at his best. One thought remained in the minds of all as the pot gave its last drops of warming tea. One by one the men streamed to the lower deck and waiting bunks. 'How long could we sleep?' No one knew or cared. Just sleep was all that mattered.

"God...dammit"...a guy can't get any sleep!" were the first words to greet me the next day. 'What time was it? How long have I slept? Couldn't be too long because I felt very groggy. It was only a few minutes ago we dropped anchor,' I thought. "What's up fellas?" I queried, rising to an elbow. "Gotta go again..."came the disgruntled reply, abetted by my own suppressed curses.

It was three−thirty a.m. Swanson was in the wheelhouse. The Skipper had gone to bed after a twelve−hour vigil at the helm. "Pull in the anchor...we gotta get to Aklavik...fog's gone for good!" was all the Mate said.

This done, I slunk below, taking up where I had left off when that unholy volley had met my ears a few moments before. Feeling confident that the next arousing would not come before the cook (armed with his clamorous weapon) would begin his breakfast call, I ungeared my mind and settled into a still warm sleeping bag, hoping I could pick up the thread of the pleasant dream that had been started.

How I slept through the Cockney's bell tolling I will never know; but feeling like a new deckhand, I met the almost−vertical rays of the sun at 10:45. It was one of those indescribably, peaceful mornings, when even the motors were scarcely audible as the screws churned against the current in the southerly direction. Word passed amongst us that we were to stop at Reindeer Station in a few minutes. So I parked on a bench in the sun, more than content with the world, just watching the works of Nature in the Arctic. The river resembled a mirror−reflecting the spruce−bordered banks in perfect symmetry, till our wash erased each scene like a mad artist in disgust with his latest landscape. The spruce (like a well dressed platoon) were ready for inspection, the occasional tree leaning or fallen from the bank, like a faint partisan overcome by the heat.

We were about halfway between Tuk−tuk and Aklavik when the shoreline ranks were broken by a pier, leading from the water to a neat group of buildings in a clearing. We had arrived at Reindeer Depot−headquarters for the entire reindeer herd of Northwestern Canada.

An interesting story of tragedy, adventure and the final success of a handful of men, and 3000 reindeer−travelling a proposed route of 1200 miles, came from many lips, before my departure to Yukon Territory. The facts gathered together sound something like this: By 1925 the natives of the Canadian North had gradually become impoverished by a scarcity of game and an adoption of the white man's mode of living. Something had to be done. Already actual cases of starvation had been reported from the Hudson's Bay area. Contact was made with the Americans in Alaska and an agreement was reached with the Loman Brothers Reindeer Corporation. They would sell the required amount of 'deer to the Canadian Government, which were to be herded across the northern wastes to the desired destination.

In 1926 Alec Porsild and his brother, equipped with two dog teams, sail and odometer (for measuring miles) set out on the proposed route the reindeer were to follow. Along the Bering Strait it became so cold that five of their dogs froze; but they finally reached Aklavik in early April. From here Alec went via Edmonton to Ottawa to report on the success of his findings−two and−one−half years after his original departure from there. He had covered 15,000 miles by every possible mode of transportation. With him, he also brought, possibly, the largest single collection of botanical plants, numbering about 20,000 in all. On the basis of this report an expedition was encouraged and organized.

In 1929, final arrangements were made by the two governments to herd 3000 'deer across the North. Alec Porsild then went to Lapland to select the herders and their families who were to look after the reindeer when they arrived at Kittigazuit, the final destination. He chose three 'Laps' with families and, in 1931, while the herd was already on its way, he proceeded to Aklavik with them.

The great migration started. Andy Buhr, Dan Crowley and 12 specially trained 'Lap' and Eskimo herders moved eastward with their 3000 herd of reindeer, about to tackle the 1200 miles of rugged northland. In 1929 they left Baldwin Peninsula, in Kotzebue Sound, north of the famed gold rush city of Nome. The herd, travelling all at once, moved very slowly because they fed as they moved. The best day's distance ever was 30 miles, while a steady 15 mile average was accomplished all the way.

After some time on the way unforseen incidents began to happen. First, the herd wanted to return to their old grazing grounds. Storms arose, dispersing the herd. Many young were lost or crippled, and much time 'went with the winds' too, as the handful of men endeavoured to circle the herd and keep it together. Then, to add to this, wolves appeared. Sneaking out of the blinding snow, they would lay low the 'drifters' and further demoralize the priceless herd. Incidents were told where the maddened Laps and Eskimo would lie in wait at the rear or side of the herd when they suspected wolves. At sight of the howling, killing beasts they would ski directly at them wielding huge, wooden clubs. In the deep snow they were able to exact a heavy toll amongst their enemy, where the wolves had struck. It was a serious loss, but in retrospect it was spoken of in the spirit of a game.

Large rivers comprised the next difficulties. In order to cross them it was necessary to wait till freeze−up, furthering the delay that much more. Then after they did freeze the difficulty was to drive them across without their slipping on the smooth surface and breaking their legs. Some, in fright, halfway across the surface, would panic and cause a stampede and further loss of time. Whenever caribou migrations were near, large numbers of the herd became mixed up with them and lost. Gradually their numbers were lessening as the years flitted by. In spring and summer the entire herd rested for some weeks to allow the fawns to grow ready for travel. Thus more time elapsed.

Across regions never mapped they finally arrived at the Mackenzie Delta−80 miles from their destination−in 1933. Freeze−up came. There was no grazing on the islands of the Delta, so the herd had to be driven on moonlight nights as well as through the day. It was a tough winter. Two days on the ice and a blizzard came up. The whole herd stampeded back to their old grazing ground. Then, because of great stretches of bare ice on which there was no footing, long detours were forced. One ingenious Lap, feeling pity for the animals, conceived a plan. With anything he could find sharp enough to chop ice on one river, he mustered together the small band. All day and night they picked, scratched and scraped a jagged surface on the sheen ice, while the women kept hot food and broth on the stoves for the men. Fatigued and closer to death than life, the group led the herd on to the ice; one by one they followed their leader to safety. It was a glorious rescue and they found their well−earned sleep.

Over eight miles of Delta they finally made their way, the Laplanders holding their strange power over the animals. It was 1935 when the unique migration reached Kittigazuit on the eastern shores of the Mackenzie River, 150 miles above Aklavik. Andy Buhr, now 70 years old, and Dan Crowley−the Loman financial agent − admitted having covered three times the original distance of 1200 miles. The herd numbered 2,500 of the original 3,000 on arrival.

Meanwhile the reserve had been chosen by Alec Porsild: it was 6,600 square miles on the peninsula above Aklavik; bounded on the west by the Mackenzie River; north by the Arctic; and south by an inland waterway called the Eskimo Lakes−almost a complete chain running from the Arctic to the Mackenzie Delta. This peninsula, 200 miles long and about 40 miles wide, was free from predatory animals−except perhaps the occasional Barren Ground Grizzly or Polar Bear. There were no wolves whatever in the vicinity. It was here that the reindeer had to be herded most effectively, lest they revert to their ancestor's (the caribou) migratory habits and escape from the peninsula.

So in 1935, five−and−a−half years after the start, probably the greatest man−conceived migration came to an end. The Lapp families could go back home and the white men could go their way−all pleased because they had saved the lives of many. As a result of their efforts, in July 1946, the original herd of 2,500 that arrived safely, had multiplied to 15,000 in 11 years. The experiment had proven a great success.

Two gentlemen had come down to the pier's end and stood waiting for their supplies. "Messrs. McGinnes and Morrison...how are you and your reindeer?" asked one of the crew. "You know we couldn't be better," replied the Scotsmen, both beaming with curiosity. "Have you a parcel?" asked one. "It should be marked 'rush' and 'essential', if I remember correctly?" said the second.

A short exchange of banter and we handed them their cargo. "Here they are," said the Mate, "five cases of beer and a bottle"...check. "Keerect...check," replied the Scotsman, receiving the precious cartons. "Many good times!" yelled one of the crew as we pulled away. "There'll be no doubt of that now!" returned a voice from the dock and we left the two waving in our wake. Our new pilot, John Stuart, was reading the waters correctly, aloft; beside him stood the Skipper in his favourite position behind the wheel.

**Alec Stefansson
and Otto Binder—Reindeer Herder**

It was eight–thirty when we turned again into the Aklavik Channel, churned by a westerly wind. Four hours later we docked in Aklavik. This meant the end of the line for me. I suddenly became aware of the fact. "Comin' to the dance?" inquired one of the crew, wasting no time in debarking. "It's at Peffer's Hall." Word had reached the crew on arrival, of the big event. 'Just the change you need,' said my other man. So we spruced up a bit...a comb here...a shine there...a brush off. Heedless of the percentage of whites that would be in attendance we made for shore, ready for what may come. Sleep, this time, could wait.

**Alec Stefansson and Family (left)
With Hunters**

**Messrs. McGinnes and Morrison—
Traders, Reindeer Station**

CHAPTER SIXTEEN

LANDLUBBER

Mr. Peffer is a prominent trader in the vicinity and has built a hall which is the community centre for all. Here the movies (changing very seldom) are shown; dances are held and sodas or ice cream can be obtained at the bar in an anteroom. Squaws bring their papooses, the elderly braves smoke their pipes and lounge in chairs while the young 'bucks' and their gay, long−dressed partners two−step, reel or Red River Jig their way about the hall to whatever music the settlement can produce. Be it only a mouth organ, they will shake a leg to its tune; and how they can dance as the music enlivens!

The violin and guitar that comprised the orchestra this morning could be heard well down the street. So I had no trouble locating Peffer's. My shipmates were already engrossed in a lively two−step; I was determined to join them, beard and all! A bashful row of Indian girls stood alone along one wall. None were very tall, but that factor mattered little at such informal gatherings. I saw one dusky maiden on the sidelines tapping her foot to the music. I made my decision.

We were soon bouncing, hobbling, circling and mostly enjoying ourselves, much to the glee of two old squaws who, not unlike two cackling French hags venting their feeling each time the Guillotine fell, gave forth in their loudest native laughter at each circuit we completed. Dazzio was making them happy; the girl, I hoped (for I could not see) was feeling jolly; and I certainly felt lighthearted, for I had not danced in a month.

More reels...two−steps...jigs, more smiles from the squaws; a light lunch; a chance meeting with the humourous, 'bushed' trapper, Red Anders (who keeps the community laughing at his doubtful stories and gay pranks), the gradually ascending Midnight Sun, all told me it was time to carry a tired body and two sore feet back to the boat.

Next day was an eventful one. The first duty was to square away with Curly, the assistant purser: "...forty−eight, forty−nine, fifty!" He checked the crisp wad of bills and handed them to me. "Ten days and overtime," he explained. Adding this to a bulging wallet, I realized a total of $141.00 for the Yukon adventure which was to come shortly. Next I packed my bags and brought them on deck. With a round of good−byes, I climbed over the rail of the *Hearne Lake* and left the Skipper and crew, wishing them in turn a good trip south. I thought I saw envy in more than one face as I slipped from the gangplank to shore. I was once again a Landlubber. A month and 1500 miles lay in my wake, since the sunny day when the whistle sounded our personal farewell to the town of Yellowknife. The Yukon and the overland *Trail of '98* lay ahead.

Aklavik was humming with Firth River gold−rush talk and excitement this Saturday morning. I was curious to know why. Any sort of news travels fast in the North via the Moccasin Telegraph. Five minutes and I knew the tale. It appeared some natives, desiring to awaken the dormant spirits, embarked on a wassail of 'home brew'. Now anyone who knows the modern natives (Indians and 'Breeds) knows the potency of such clandestine concoctions. Well, in the melee a tent was ignited and burnt to the ground. This of course meant a breaking of the police routine. A roundup followed and a goodly collection of offenders were apprehended. Was my man amongst them? I wondered, fearful of any delay.

Quickly, I dashed to his tent. Entering, I asked abruptly, "Are you still rarin' to go, Malcolm?" "Damn right!...sooner the better...but I still have to get rid of my dogs" I smiled with his optimism; this was the only thing that mattered just then. We were as good as in the Yukon. "Should get away by tomorrow," he continued, to which I reiterated: "I'll be ready," backing out of the tent.

Knowing the need for certain preparations, I headed in the direction of Jim Jones' trading post overlooking the waterfront. It is adjacent the Post Office that occupies a portion of the whitewashed log building. Entering, I found the low interior filled with groceries, clothes, bolts of brightly coloured cloth, a rifle, some skins, beaded moccasins, shells and many trinkets at which a group of squaws looked wantingly.

**Grubstake at
Jim Jones Trading Post**

My motive was to exchange all unnecessary equipment for food, thus lightening the load for the thousand miles of Yukon we were soon to traverse. "Hi, fella"...who are you, behind that hair?" he asked lightly; "name's Jim," he added, proferring a well−used hand. Jim, anxious to be on such a trip, almost to the point of envy, exchanged the wares and came forth with many a suggestion discovered the hard way during his trapping expeditions. These I devoured greedily, as the grubsteak began to look quite substantial. We checked: tins of meat, stew, fish, fruit, butter, two loaves of bread (for the first day), hardtack biscuits, jam, honey, peanut butter, sugar, flour, baking powder (for Cheechako bannocks), tea, coffee, cocoa, klim, tinned milk, porridge, macaroni, rice, a dozen eggs, noodle soup, gum, half a dozen chocolate bars, raisins and matches. Here it is proper to mention the bottles of Skat, Beat It and Skeeter Skatter that found their rightful place in the packsack. For, remember, it was July and the mosquitoes love this month and its usual sunny days. This antidotal adjunct, with the aid of a fast growing beard, I felt, would discourage the largest brand of mosquito the Yukon could muster against humans. I was to learn different later. The grubstake in order, my pack cut to a minimum, there was nothing to do but enjoy the settlement of Aklavik while I awaited events. The *Mackenzie River*, *Hearne Lake* and *Watson Lake* riverboats had all left for the South and another cargo. It would be a short season...one more trip perhaps? I felt alone in my observations. 'Peffer's trading post is busy; 'guess'll drop in...see what's doin,' I said to myself, the boardwalk ringing rhythmically through the village with my footsteps. In the man's absence, Mr. Strong was bartering with some Indians, aided by an interpreter. Sucking on his saxophone pipe he muttered: "...rats 80 cents...how many?" The interpreter began trading in his native tongue. Back and forth he looked, paused and spoke till Strong, his pipe in the side of his mouth fully−gripped, thought a moment, then nodded. The deal was finished. Another Indian moved forward.

'Eighty cents,' I thought to myself. 'What an insult to any fur bearing animal!' and it can produce a dozen of its own kind too!' It was not the trader, but the ever−tilting scales of Outside economy. Russians had flooded the market with cheaper furs, they said...muskrats wouldn't be as popular this year, claimed the stylists...coats were getting shorter...the war, you know. 'Bah!...economy, what is it?' I asked myself. 'What is economy when the life of a beautiful little animal is at stake?, so far away from civilization, too! A loon chided from a nearby stream. I could have wrung its neck! (had it not been such a beautiful though annoying bird.)

The Hudson's Bay Company store was completely lit, revealing from the outside a well−stocked post. It was Saturday night, always a busy time in any village, town or city. Funny about custom isn't it? I walked on past, not wanting to hear of another muskrat skin sold for 80 cents. I began to like these animals more and more at the thought.

Night (according to the hour and not the atmosphere) soon came. I found myself observing the famed Northern sun, at it arced low toward the horizon, from the Anglican Church belfry. From this vantage point I recorded a host of new impressions. Aklavik is nestled between the curves of the horseshoe bend formed by the Peel River winding its way broadly and calmly from the mountains, behind which lies the Yukon and the Klondike. These purple masses are clothed in early morning mist; huge clouds sleep within their upper vales, their extremities showing like the feet of some white giant, too long for his bed; their ominous presence is enough to arouse the challenging spirit within a body−a challenge to penetrate within and seek its strongly−guarded wealth.

The town seems more awake than asleep; its roofs shine after a quick shower; the grass dances with the dew. The nocturnal sounds are many, penetrating the vast surrounding silence. Indian dogs raise their mournful cries to the moon: an infernal engine pounds monotonously; an Indian girl passes below, carrying water for morning from the river; a mixed group of Indians play a vociferous game of softball, casting their long shadows on the riverbank; another dusky maiden swings an axe at an obstinate log, while her younger Loucheux sisters swing out on a roundabout—their mothers possibly walking and talking along the waterfront, dressed in their long, fur—

24 Hours of Daylight Aklavik, N.W.T.

trimmed, parka—like dresses; a youthful Indian lad glides down to the water's edge, jumps into his waiting canoe and pushes off silently, paddling into the distance of morning; the Midnight Sun at its lowest ebb disappears behind a grey cloud; a clamourous motorboat buzzes off into the fading rays of the sun; all other launches, schooners, rowboats and canoes lie with their noses sniffing the shore. My silent vigil ended with the rasping echo of a saw (pushed by two energetic women) which drifted through the village at the unbelievably—light hour of 12:30 a.m.

Next day being Sunday, I found my friend asleep and still not ready for the journey. "Malcolm!...get up!...we've gotta go!" I exclaimed, with mustered anxiety. "Get out!...I'm sleeping!" "Tired...not today...too much to do..." and he curled up like a dog; not another sound came from the ball of clothing. That was final. I knew better, by now, than to go against a native son's word. Sooner or later he would tire of this inaction. Human nature and I plotted with one another. We would try him tomorrow. For today?—more visiting. Where?—the hospital, first.

"Good morning a..er..o?" said Nurse Hawkin, trying desperately to identify the body behind the whiskers. "Oh, just call me Cheechako*...I haven't seen the Fall ice come in yet," I explained. We started our tour of the well—equipped hospital. The patients—Indians, 'Breeds and some Eskimo boys, rushed from the far north for treatment, all appeared happy with their lot. "How's the food?" I asked, and the broadest smiles coming of course from the Eskimo were sufficient response to anyone concerned. Some time later we viewed the modern operating room. It was there I met the second of the nurses. "Miss Clarke," said the first. "How do you like it here?" I forwarded. "haven't time to complain...anyway, we all like it." The third I met in the outer hall. "Miss MacDonald...a curious Outsider, wondering how the sick get well in the Arctic," was the well—placed introduction. "You just can't keep the Scotch out of the North country!" I remarked, momentarily flashing back to the settlement of Fort MacPherson. It was laughter that broke up the party and followed me to the door.   *A person in the North who has not seen the ice come in and go out.

Anglican Church, Aklavik N.W.T.   **Softball Under the Midnight Sun**

July 20th was getting sunnier; the mosquitoes suspiciously deficient. This indeed made foot—travel pleasant, but somehow I refused to relax my vigil. I felt to make sure of my Skat (mosquito lotion) in a pocket. It was there. I smiled to myself. Outside the Mission residence, I met Father L'Helgouach. "What're you doing outside zees time of day...do you want to get eaten up by our friends?" "Funny, Father, but I haven't seen any yet. Do you think they are banding for a mass attack on the new brand of meat that has come to the village?" "Could be my son...could be,"he smiled, adding: "Zey like young people, for zey have more blood...zey have drunk all ours zese last years..ho!..ho!..ho!, he laughed; and it was so contagious that I took up where he left off and didn't stop till by belly ached and tears trickled down to my beard.

Father L'Helgouach

Anxious (like most of the priests) to divulge their life and travels, he continued in accented voice: "I am from Brittany...I 'ave come to ze Norzwest Territories since 1933, to Coppermine and directly west of zere...zat countree is beautiful...I enjoy my life zere wiz the Eskimo and Indians so much...I weel go back some day I hope," he finished, leaving me disturbed, for I had not time to go east in one season.

Inside the Mission I met the plump Father Raymond who had just returned from a holiday in France. "We get them once in many years...it is our only big break, so we make it a good one," he explained. One of the larger missions along the river, it contains two Fathers and four Brothers and a boat crew travelling north from this base. While speaking the Father was interrupted and thus I met Brother Deslisle. A young man, he said he was of Quebec two years ago. The Father showed me the comfortable interior and with a little coaxing deigned to have a photo taken. "Do you want one slapping mosquitoes or unnatural," he suggested. "I'll just take it outside an' git, if they're back again!" I replied, saying goodbye to another veteran priest of the Great North.

Roman Catholic Mission
Aklavik, N.W.T.

Father Joseph Turcotte
and Mission Boat—*Santa Anna*

Waterfronts have always intrigued me. The Peel Channel winding calmly but surely to the Arctic in front of the Mission, was no less. There at anchor lay the *Sant Anna*, recently arrived from Smith with freight for the priests; and the *Immaculata*, with mast and boom sheered of all sail. "Who does the sailing?" I asked of a 'Breed boy on the bank. "Oh, the Fathers do everything!"he exclaimed. One would have thought they were God themselves by the irregular tasks they perform. I began to marvel at these modest men.

Descrying some activity by the pier, I made for it. A roughly clothed man in a small rowboat was trying to push away from the pier. By his beard, I knew him to be a priest. "Having trouble!" I asked. "Yes, this stubborn boat, she want to stay home...I want to go?" came the broken French accent. A quick exchange of conversation followed: "I left France 36 years ago, coming to Fort Rae...Resolution...Bear Lake...now I am here...for fifteen years...for fifteen year now I am fisherman of the Mission...that is where I go now, to tend my nets." "With a push, the boat bearing Benedict Myer was soon in mid-stream, bobbing its way to the fishing grounds.

Monday, I was more restless than a lion in a circus cage. My companion was nowhere to be found. Had he betrayed me? Did no one want to accept dogs for the summer? There was nothing more to do but wait. 'Wait!' I reminded myself, 'why you've lost two days already!' 'What's two days? asked the Patient fellow. 'Fifty miles!' came Impatience 'and a million mosquitoes less!' 'Oh, relax...it won't be long now.' Semi-consoled, I resigned myself to the Fates.

A while later I was glad of this delay, for, had it not been so, I would never have met Carl Gardlund. The name is nothing irregular; he is probably little known outside of the district. But the legend of Albert Johnson— the Mad Trapper—is sung wherever there is a guitar, and told wherever eager ears are ready to hear an Oldtimer spin a few more strands to his yarn. Gardlund happens to have played the important role in the North's greatest man-hunt. He was the only person to stick with it from the start to the grim finish when the Trapper was brought to bay. In his own words he told me snatches from his memory.

Carl Gardlund of 'Trapper Johnson Fame'

"I was an original member of the posse organizcd to assist the Mounties...we musta' covered hundreds of miles...that Johnson was sure smart...turned his snowshoes backwards...shot our pots full o' holes...walked with a caribou herd (that time we really lost the trail; but always we found it again)," interjected the tall, slim Carl, removing his pipe—into the bowl of which he poked a thumb. "Never could see the man...we weren't too anxious to either, in case he saw us first and took a few pot shots...funny though," he reflected..."he never would shoot us...only had a grudge against the Redcoats: he winged plenty of 'em too before we finished." By now I had discovered the reasons for the hunt which he took for granted. Surprisingly enough was the similarity of the many stories, touched here and there by the artistic hand of the northern narrator. Here now I listened to the genuine tale in all its vividness. "*Zing! Bang!*...we had just rounded a bend and were met by a volley of bullets..."hit the snow!" someone yelled...(mind you, we did). When we got up and brushed ourselves off, there was one crippled Mountie and a lot of mad posse, I'll bet you...guess that was the closest. I still think Johnson was havin' his fun scarin' hell outa the rest of us, but always layin' fer the police...musta had some crime record or an o...what's that high-filutin word you use Outside?" "You mean an obsession," I enquired. "Yeah...that's it...sump'n on the mind. Anyway, when along comes this "Wop" May guy, purty good pilot they say, an' he circles round and round above...I bet Johnson got a real surprise, then, Ho! Ho! That did it...he daren't light a fire for fear of bein' seen from the air. Then one day after we lost him again, (Wop had gone back for more gas) the plane circles a hill...and whad'ya know!...there was our man Johnson, roundin' it in an open space...too late!...Wop had caught sight of 'im and came back to signal us. We caught what he meant, so we circles the opposite way. Then the action really started...rifles was splittin' the air somepin' awful...I felt a close one and ducked fer a tree...Mountie beside me went down to his knees, hit in the leg. Then just as quick as a beaver can duck in the water, the shootin' stops. Not a sound anywhere 'cept Wop with his plane above...we were sure Johnson was done fer...we saw him go down; but you could never tell...he was full o' the damndest tricks I ever seen (an' I've seen plenty in my time). So we snuck up on 'im. Sure 'nough, he lay dead. We found some dead squirrels in his pockets...he sure musta been frantic the last few days!"

He paused a moment, as though the story had actually ended, puffed a mouthful of smoke and looked at Red Anders and myself listening intently. "Who actually shot the man?" I asked abruptly. "Well," he continued, blowing the smoke at a swarm of mosquitoes, "the posse had no warrant to kill, so naturally credit for the killing has gone to the Police." "Honestly," I said, "who really plugged him with the final shot?" He glanced from the pipe he was cleaning, a twinkle in his eye, but refused to commit himself as the slayer of Albert Johnson, the hunted man. Because so many had shot at the fellow the credit (or discredit?) could not be claimed by any one man. Gardlund, being a crack shot and the man still standing after the last Redcoat had been brought to his knees, we are left to deduce the final outcome.

The story is told here in the original ballad concocted by the people of the North country.

THE MAD TRAPPER

There's a legend of old 'bout the Scarlet and Gold
That they always get their man;
But did you hear of that Trapper Down North
Who didn't give a damn?
It was on Rat Crick by Aklavik
There was nothing but ice and snow
Where the trapper turned madman and earned the name
Of the man who defied the law.
The Indian stated 'that man he'es got bushed
He'es hang up our traps on em tree
He'es pointum he'es gun say for us go away,
I'm tell you that he'es crazee.
Sure he'es got baby slipper and also gold tooth
And he'es steal lots of fur from our traps,
So we come to the Red—Coats, for to catchum the t'ief
He'es think all us Injuns are saps.'
'So King and McDowell to enforce the law
Made the trip through the cold Arctic night.
It was fifty below as they mushed through the snow
In the Land of the Northern Lights.
To check up his license would be their excuse
And to see if he had such a thing,
But they got a surprise when they called at his door,
"Open, in the name of the King!" Then the leaden mosquitoes
started to hum,
One hit Constable King in the chest,
And McDowell crept up and pulled him away
To a spot where his wound could be dressed,
Then he headed his dogs back to Aklavik,
Eighty miles in a race with Death,
And he covered the trak in twenty—one hours,
As the cold north wind near froze his breath.
'U.Z.K. calling, for the R.C.M.P.,
The voice of the Northern Lights
For the Trappers and Mounties; report here at once,
Be prepared for you may have cause to fight."In response to the
call Constable Millen came in
And with trappers they formed a small posse.
They'd sure get him now, and he'd pay for his crime.
They'd show him the Mountie was boss.
After four days of travelling they came to his shack,
But were met with a volley of shell.

Inspector James called to smash down the door
For the trapper would shoot till be fell.
As the darkness befell them they made further plans,
They would shatter the place with a bomb.
Came the first rays of dawn they carried it out
And the shack was as quiet as a tomb.
There Johnson was lying as though in a daze,
And his eyes were wide open with fright,
But the posse couldn't kill, like he, in cold blood,
And again the posse pulled for the post.
But when they returned the trapper was gone
"They'll never take me," was his boast.
Now the hunt's getting stronger and Riddell joined in,
He knew every trail in the North,
And they followed their foe, through many miles of snow
Till again they'd fight for their worth.
Till Gardlund fired and Johnson fell,
They thought he had paid for his crime,
But Johnson was waiting, his rifle cocked,
And shot Constable Millen this time.
Straight through the heart and murder was done
"An eye for an eye," was the cry
"So go get your man, alive if you can
And to get him be willing to die." Now an airman joined in,
"Wop" was his name,
He would help in the search with his plane
To follow the trail to the Big Divide,
But was fooled by the madman again.
"Yes, the trapper had back tracked at fifty below
Then discarded his snowshoes, but why?
So the caribou tracks would cover his own,
Very soon he'd be ready to die.
For the end was in sight after two weary months,
And the odds were too great for one man.
They'll get him this time, ther'd be no mistakes,
Said, "We'll take him alive if we can." .Down Eagle River they
meet once again
And Sergeant Hersey was shot
With lead through his chest which had punctured one lung
And they questioned...Was he dead or not?
But they got the mad trapper with six deadly shots
And he'd paid for his crimes with his life,
And the North's greatest man−hunt had come to its close
A hunt filled with misery and strife.
The firing had long ceased when Wop May flew over
And reported the trapper dead.
And airman and mounties and trappers too,
Prayed thanks to be rid of the dead;
But the trapper had suffered apart from his wounds,
He was frozen on hands, feet and legs.
He paid here on earth, will be pay once again?
When we meet at the great Judgment Seat.
      ......from: **Songs of the North**, by J.W.

Albert Johnson's final resting place lies directly across the street from Stan Peffer's trading post. At one time the grave lay on the outside of the sheepwire fence; but now it shares equal rights with the many others. Weeds have overgrown most of the plot. Above, inscribed on the two spruce trees that provide a living memorial, is the shortest of epitaphs: "A.J."—burnt into the bark by a thoughtful admirer. Here ends the tale of one of the North's greatest and longest man—hunts.

Carl Gardlund and Red Anders

The tale had come to its end from the lips of Carl Gardlund. Now Red Anders, always ready to lark, threw his arms about the manhunter's neck and laughing in his inimitable way from behind a fiery red beard said: "I'm an old 'un too...but I didn't chase no mad trapper...come into the Yukon in 1910 working on the Cordova Railroad...an' here I am still fit as a fiddle an' rarin' to go! How's this for a posse!" I couldn't resist the combination of trapper and marksman, so the shutter fell on real Northern character.

On a short visit to the radio station I met Red MacLeod. During the war a small unit of army personnel were stationed in Aklavik. Among them was Red—a 'ham' operator. On the long days and nights when the Arctic was frozen over, he set to work with odds and ends which, after much trial and error, took the shape of a transmitter. The idea of such a northerly broadcasting station took effect. Now it has become a recognized transmitter with Red in charge of the army unit stationed there.

"Take a squint at these," he invited. Completely covering the wall were 'ham' cards from all over the world. "By the time I visit Aklavik here again you should have the whole interior papered with 'em," I replied. Much impressed, I left the station, tripping lightly to the music that poured from the loudspeaker to all parts of the village. The squaws had music while they worked this night; I was played to sleep, not by the monotonous music of mosquitoes, but to the sweet strains of an Irish lullaby.

Monday had come and gone; we were still part of Aklavik. The Midnight Sun was getting lower by the night; this was not a good sign. 'Today must be the day!' I had decided, for it was already June 22nd and the *Trails of '98* were long and rough.

Stamping anxiously over to the 'Breeds' dwelling, I poked my head within, determined to bring the situation to a point. "Malcolm...,"I began. Before I could say more, he interrupted with, "I'll be ready by noon!"—the most musical words to greet my ears in three days. By all appearances, Tuesday was to be the eventful day. Aroused from the temporary slumber, my optimism and adventurous spirit virtually leaped as I made haste to check the supplies.

I found everything in order, "...but surely we must have forgotten something?" 'Let's see now...' I re—checked. 'Can't think of anything forgotten. Oh well,' I mused, 'there's enough food so we won't starve...that's the main thing!' Satisfied with the final check I ambled over to the R.C.M.P. barracks for a visit before departure. Along the north end of the main street overlooking the Peel is a collection of whitewashed buildings surrounded by a fence of the same colour. In the middle of the fence is a square corral—like arch on the cross beam, on which are printed in old English the words: ROYAL CANADIAN MOUNTED POLICE. Passing through the arch one is confronted by a square, centred with a flagpole, surrounded by half a dozen log and frame buildings constituting the office and dwellings of the entire force.

"Good morning Constable," I said, elated with the recent decision to continue my journey. "Thought you'd be gone from this mosquito lair by now, Cheechako?" "Today's the day," I retorted "and you can have your brand...they tell me they're larger in the mountains...be able to see them coming and duck...what's more they won't be able to squeeze between the whiskers so easily!" I chuckled. "Well, anyway you're just in time for some real flapjacks...wanta take a chance?" asked

Constable McKinnon. One never says 'no' to flapjacks in the North; one is never expected to refuse an invitation to dine in the North; it is just plain, bad manners in the North! So I accepted.

After breakfast, I met Inspector Kirk, his wife and child, Corporal Baines and wife, the other bachelor—Constable Eddie Phelon. It was a Scarlet and Gold send off; with the taste of flapjacks in my mouth, I made for the waterfront, where, a canoe should (according to plan) be waiting.

I was not disappointed when the river was reached. There, pulled ashore, a 22—foot Peterborough sniffed the muddy bank. Nothing to do but load it and push off. Piecemeal we dragged the packs, sacks and sleeping bags from Jim Jone's trading post to the prow. Then out of the surrounding blue sky my man conceived a notion. "Gotta say s'long to my father across the bay." Next minute he was paddling against the current, leaving myself standing helpless on the shore. 'What next?' I asked the Powers—That—Be. They refused to answer.

It was not noon yet. I could wait; but oh, the torture of delay. The sun shone in my favour, so I parked on the bank for a short siesta… The sound of voices awakened me

Ready for the 'Rat River Portage'

from my dreams. It was two p.m. Shaken into reality, I realized I was not in the Rat Portage; I was still in Aklavik! I had been deceived by the heat. "Get in!" commanded the native, prying the nose from the mud. I knew for certain that the final moment had come. "Where's the gas and oil?…and say, we have no towline!" he exclaimed suddenly. I remember, very distinctly, two people swearing loud and blatantly.

This was too much! With more than a vengeance I dashed up the bank, bought fifty feet of rope, collected the oil and started rolling the gasoline drum toward the boat. "If anything else is forgotten, it's just too damn bad." I said, in a frenzied sweat. "Let's push off before we think of anything else!" yelled the 'Breed. In one—hundred—percent agreement we launched ourselves at the mud which had to yield the bow of our canoe. Squuuishh!…it gave; splashh!…a paddle spanked the water; a few minutes past two we waved to the people gathered on shore. Jim Jones was there. "Jim'd a sure loved to make it three," I turned and spoke to my companion who must have seen the envious look on the trader's face. "Yeah, I noticed," he spoke softly…"but two's company." I felt warm all over. We were two afloat.

CHAPTER SEVENTEEN

A HALF–BREED, A CANOE & LOADS OF OPTIMISM

The Mackenzie River District had been beautiful and its people very hospitable; but I was obsessed by the lure of the western mountains and what I had always imagined, from the artists' and poets' conceptions, to be a much more verdant land. 'You will soon know,' came the voice of Assurance as our 'kicker' brought us ever closer to that grand, purple challenge that reared out of the west.

Upstream we churned, through a well–known shortcut discovered by my companion while 'ratting' (muskrat hunting). From the Peel we turned into the Huskie Channel about 12 miles from Aklavik. On either side stood tall spruce and pine, grassy banks, and countless streams pouring their goods into the larger channels to form a vast inundated area—the source of the Mackenzie Delta.

**Lazarus Edward's
Cabin on Huskie Channel**

Lady Luck (my standing girl friend) was with us in the canoe. She had not deserted me in months. As the monotonous drone of the motor became sweet music, I felt she must be appeased. I scattered some hard–tack biscuit crumbs on to the waters, uttering as I did so my prayer for 'good luck', saying: 'This is all we can afford to part with, oh bountiful Lady, so please bring to us our rightful share of good luck.' The mileage had reached twenty when the motor coughed, spat twice and wheezed itself gently into silence. We glided to a stop. Someone must have spoken out of place. "Did you swear recently?" I asked of my friend. "No. but I'm sure an' hell goin' to right now!" And he did. The discoloured echoes quadrupled in the hills and returned with emphasis. I daren't (and needn't) say a word, but waited for the verdict. It came after much tinkering. "Drive shaft's shot, broken in two!" came the disheartening news. "We'll have to go back...I think I know where there's one to fit it," he added, reaching for a paddle. Lady Luck had divorced me. 'You were too tight with the crumbs, I'll bet, or maybe she doesn't like the Northern bread?' I told myself. "What are you saying?" asked the 'Breed, hearing me speak. "Oh nothing...nothing at all," I covered up, for he wouldn't understand the fickle Goddess, anyway; I reached for the other paddle.

We turned about. Soon two paddles were forcing ripples in the sheen surface, the miles fast decreasing as the current pushed us from the rear. "How about supper?" asked Malcolm, cooled off since his verbal bout with the hills. "Coming right up," I replied. "What would you like?" "Oh, the small meal will do," he joked. So sardines, hard tacks with jam and butter, and cold cocoa, eaten from the top of the gasoline barrel sufficed for supper as we drifted back to Aklavik.

**My 'Improved Scots' Companion
Malcolm Firth**

As we approached the cabin of Lazarus Edwards, a brilliant idea comes to us. "Maybe he has a rod?" my friend questioned aloud. "If so, it'll sure save time and energy," I encouraged. "No one home," yelled the 'Breed, on perusal about the grounds: "no use...have to go all the way back!" In the light of evening and the sound of buzzing mosquitoes that chanced to find us in mid−stream we floated leisurely back, past familiar scenery.

Reaching 8 Mile Stretch the sight of a bark tepee emitting smoke brought life and action to the rear of the canoe. "I could sure go for some smoked fish...paddle hard into shore!" We tied the canoe and climbed the mud bank, the smell of fish growing stronger. "Welcome Malcolm, what you do here?" invited the squeaky voice of the weazened old Indian who invited us to some fish and tea.

Each choosing a well−smoked strip from the rack, we entered the tent. A tea pail stood already warmed on the stove. We squatted on the pine boughs which sent their aromatic smell throughout the interior. The usual informal native introduction followed and my friend Firth said: "Charlie Stewart is the Indian guide who helped discover the Lost Patrol between Dawson and McPherson." The warmth of the tent soon overcame my tired friend. Too interested for sleep, I quizzed Charlie about the tragedy. This he began to spill in broken phrases, his active mind turning back the years to 1910. Thirty seven years had not marred the tale which became vivid as he paused only for reflection, a breath, or just another bite of dried fish...

The Dawson−McPherson Patrol was inaugurated by Corporal Mapley in the year 1904−1905. In 1910 Francis Joseph Fitzgerald was promoted to Inspector and was informed in May that he was to command this patrol; but this year it was to be travelled in reverse. While stationed at Herschel Island−the farthest north police post−he made his plans during the summer. The trip, no doubt, appealed to his spirit of adventure. As a result of long experience he formed the opinion that dog trains played too much for safety; that their speed was sacrificed by the heavy loads of food carried; that men in superb physical condition could travel quite easily on less. Pondering these points, he turned his own team from the post in late November of 1910. He arrived in McPherson a few days later where he commenced to outfit for his patrol. Flour, bacon and corned beef were cut below their usual minimum by a total of 80 pounds or more. Other supplies were also cut. This brought some headshaking; but not on the part of Special Constable Sam Carter whom Fitzgerald had employed as guide, or the other two members of the new patrol−Constable George Francis Kenney and Richard O'Hara Taylor. Nevertheless, on December 21 three dog teams of five dogs each pulled away from McPherson post bound for the old Klondike city of Dawson. It was the Inspector's intention to spend an enjoyable Christmas at the other end upon arrival. All appeared well until the Mounties failed to show up for dinner on Christmas Day. Still no sign of them on New Year's and the entire month of January. It was presumed some difficulty had arisen and the quartet had retraced their steps to McPherson. Still no news on February 5th...10th...and then on the 20th word came through.

Esau−an Indian from Fort McPherson district, arrived in Dawson City. He was immediately questioned about the patrol by the police. "Have you seen anything of our men between here and McPherson?" came the blunt interrogation. "Yes...me with patrol for few days...Fitzgerald hire me to helpum along a way. On first day January he pay me wages...him say I no needed any longer!"

The Patrol was then ten days out of McPherson. It should have arrived in Dawson in late January according to Esau's information. "Do you know why the Patrol is not here?" they continued to pry the man. "I can no say...maybe misfortune, no?" This was the conclusion the worried group had come to. Said Superintendent A.E. Snyder of Dawson: "No faintheartedness would have forced our man Fitzgerald back...of that I am certain!"

News of the apparent tragedy having been forwarded 'Outside' to Commander Perry, he telegraphed an urgent message to Dawson in February: "Send well outfitted party search for Fitzgerald. Go through to McPherson if necessary." Snyder, who had anticipated such notice, was ready and replied: "Patrol leaves for McPherson today."

Under Corporal W.J. Dempster the search party comprised of Constable J.F. Fyfe, Special Constable F. Turner and Charlie Stewart−the Indian guide who sat beside me in the aromatic tepee narrating the gruesome story. They were equipped with three dogteams of five dogs each.

Constable H. Brackett was to leave also, with a team of horses, hauling the heaviest part of the outfit over the first fifty miles. Snyder's instructions to Dempster the previous day were clear and concise: "You will leave tomorrow morning for a patrol over the Fort McPherson trail to locate the whereabouts of Inspector Fitzgerald and party!" So the patrol got under way at last.

"On a March 2nd," began the aged Indian, in accent scarcely discernible, an' Corporal Dempster (him a good man) wif um two more mountie and many dog...leave power plant at Twelve Mile River...we seen come to top of mountain," he gesticulated in a broad sweep of an arm, "...but me no see life...no policemans in sight! One day...two day...free day...many day we travel over deep snow. When the police say it is 12th I find um faint trail in snow...(my eyes good still, but too old to travel much miles)...Mounties don't see it, but I show um and then we rush...rush like sled race...along Little Wind River." "Was it Fitzgerald? and which way was he going?" Dempster asked his companions. They could not tell. "...we lose trail...find um again...lose much...then (he paused for a pull at the dried strip of fish, and filling his mouth he continued to chew and talk)...it dark...nightime...we camp in timber. Suddenly I find strange camp!...not too old...many tins all over...butter and corned beef. I know at once it Mounties by corn beef and then I see um flour bag on which white man letters...Dempster say it say R.N.W.M. Police—Ft. McPherson." He spat out a soft piece of fish, and continued..."All a mens happy...we wanta go quick, but mus sleep good for long travel next day...Dempster say he sure of his suspicions...he, I know!..."

March 13, they pushed on and found another of the lost patrol's camp. From the proximity of the two, Dempster concluded Fitzgerald had failed to find his way over the mountains and retreated one camp each day.

"...next day, we find more camp...lose trail for time, but always with good eyes (he pointed, more with pride than in bragging, for he was a humble Indian) I find um in snow..."

March 14 they picked up the last trail, Dempster not in the least bit worried as to the successful return, he discovered three night—camps within fifteen miles. Grave concern had mounted in Dawson City; now it did likewise with the search party upon this discovery. Dempster thought to himself, 'if only 5 miles a day, then the situation is serious!' "...then many fresh camps...all close..." He blinked, leaning towards me as the action of the story sped closer to its anti—climax. "...we all get excited...dogs too whimper, and wanta go fast..."

March 15 they stumbled on an important clue. In a lone cabin on Mountain Creek, Dempster found a toboggan, 5 sets of dog harness, the paw of a dog, and most sinister of all, the shoulder blade of a dog from which the meat was stripped...possibly eaten? Although startled at the find the Corporal still felt inwardly sure of the patrol's safety.

"...Next day we travel like um wind over snow...reach cabin on Mountain Creek...I know well" (he prided himself on his knowledge of the countryside) "there, verce bad!...veree bad!" he said ominously...we find sled, much harness. And frowning slightly, "dog bones...not meat on em...baaaad!"

By now the fish Charlie held was half eaten; Malcolm snored from his relaxed position on the pine boughs; the warmth from the tiny firebox filled the tent comfortably; I felt as though I had discovered a lost Mayan gold mine. Time began to mean less to me as I became part of the country; certainly I was in no rush to desert Mr. Stewart, who had at last found someone really interested in his aged yarn. I shifted my position slightly. I listened intently.

"Next day, we find no more bones...distance go quickly...me say about 25 mile um day for three days. Then we come to Colins Cabin, 50 miles from McPherson... There was no trail to cabin...but we know Fitz there all right... Inside many dog bones on floor...then I watch Dempster...he look up...reach to high beam...findum bag of mail...we crowd 'round, glad...think all safe...sure."

Corporal Dempster had discovered the Despatch Bag and the Mail Bag which had been cached for safe keeping by Fitzgerald, who was lightening his load for the dash to McPherson. 'What a close call!' thought Dempster; '50 miles to go...and with only one dog team!' They relaxed with that reassuring thought on the night of March 20. ..."morning and we go about ten miles, when I see objects in snow beside trail...Look!...look Corporal...see in snow ahead!" I say...and he think they still just lightening load...now I think different...no so good I smell! We find tent, stove and things..." Forty miles...thirty and then the comforting deductions of Corporal Dempster were shattered.

... "More miles and then we all in fear...there in snow is toboggan, two harness. I know now it too late...see blue hanky flutter from tree on shore of river. Corporal, he see too at same time...his mouth drop, for it well known Mountie signal. We climb bank...I push back willows...baaaad!...I feeel sooo bad for frozen policemen...one um frozen thin...other holden rifle in his hand, pointed at head where bullet hole and much blood show...I'm anxious look for other men...cannot be far. So we split um party and I go with Corporal fast..."

These were the frozen bodies of Corporals Kinney and Taylor. Dempster took in the details: Kenney had starved because of his pinched features and emaciated body; Taylor, the youngest and a new man to the country, unable to stand the sight of his frozen companion staring at him day after day, had blown out his own brains with his rifle, which he still clutched in a shrivelled hand, in death. Dempster concluded they had been given the remaining mouthfuls of food and the bedding, while Fitzgerald and Carter had gone ahead in a mad dash for the post—thirty miles distant. "...We go and leave others to watch dead men...we have trouble to find trail, but I spot eet after while...I know where they try go. Next day we are ten miles farther—only a good yell from Fort; (he smiles at his exaggeration) when see snowshoe stick up in snow...hole broke ice and footprints go to shore. I 'member I say to Dempster..."Lookee snowshoe!...go through ice...mus' be camp to dry feet close," and I run fast ahead to bush...then we see more bad news...I find camp...there two Mountie frozen same as others. One him prop on elbow like this (he illustrated)...he look across the fire at other like alive," he spoke in short, terse phrases and half to himself he trailed off with "baaaad!...baaaad!"

Dempster's conclusions were confirmed this day. The two Mounties had struggled ten miles and collapsed. Carter had died first and Fitzgerald — concious of his duty as an officer—had folded the man's arms and placed a handkerchief over his shrunken face. With a charred stick he had written his will on a scrap of paper. It read: "All money in despatch bag and bank, clothes, etc. I leave to my dearly beloved mother, Mrs. Mary Fitzgerald, Halifax. God Bless all." F.J. Fitzgerald RNWMP.

This completed and only death to claim him, he stretched out—feet already frozen—leaned on his elbow, looking gravely at his frozen companion. Cold death gradually overcame the adventurous Inspector. It was in this relaxed position that Charlie Stewart, the Indian guide, had found him.

"...We covered the bodies with brush...and quick (like moose travel), he interjected, "we go to McPherson that night...tell all the people...they grieve much for they could have sent help so easily had they known the Redcoats did not reach Dawson...it was too bad!...too bad!" he finished, poking the fire and throwing away the empty fish skin.

With two Indians and dog teams Corporal Somers was dispatched from McPherson to the scene of the tragedies. On March 25th he returned with the frozen bodies of the Lost Patrol. March 28 Reverend C.E. Whittaker officiated as the four rude coffins, covered in black, were lowered into a single plot in the local graveyard. Five fellow Mounties fired a farewell salute. Today the grave still stands, its epitaph commemorating the heroic efforts of the ill—fated McPherson—Dawson Patrol of 1910, which has long since become one of the legends of the Canadian Northland.

On the 30th Corporal Dempster left for Dawson, arriving on April 17th after much haste. Here an investigation into the tragedy disclosed the causes of disaster as:

1. The small quantity of provisions taken on the patrol.
2. Want of an efficient guide.
3. Delay in searching for the lost patrol.

Three entries found in Fitzgerald's diary, left where Kenney and Taylor died, told in writing the sad events of the trip.

> Jan. 17:   Carter is completely lost and doesn't know one river from another. We have now only ten pounds of flour and eight bacon and some dried fish. My last hope is gone, and the only thing I can do is return...
>
> Feb. 3:   Men and dogs very thin and weak and cannot travel far. We have travelled about 200 miles on dogmeat, and still have about 100 miles to go, but I think we will make it alright.
>
> Feb. 5:   Just after noon, I broke through the ice and had to make a fire: found one foot slightly frozen. Killed another dog tonight, have only 5 dogs now, and can only go a few miles a day. Everybody breaking out on body and skin peeling off.

From the evidence it appears a struggle endured for about a week following this entry and then in a lonely camp in the frozen wilderness it came to an end, even before Esau had arrived in Dawson with his scant news.

"That's the whole story," said Charlie, one hour later, rising from his cross−legged position. I straightened out my own legs and crossed to my sleeping friend. "Malcolm!" I nudged him, "we've got miles to go if we hope to regain our lost time." "Damn!" he cursed, wiping his eyes, "you're always waking me up...where's some tea?" Another cup of the already−warmed tea and we made our exit from the pine−smelling tent. Seventeen dogs in Charlie's charge stretched and barked in expectation of food. A yell brought silence in which I shook hands with the old Indian, thanking him immensely for his story. My partner, grabbing another piece of fish from the rack, trotted down to the waiting canoe as he munched. In the

**Charlie Stewart−Indian Guide
to the Lost McPherson−Dawson Patrol**

prow, I turned and we acknowledged Charlie's wave from mid−stream, the paddles gently spanking the murky channel. Late evening saw us pulling into the familiar shores again. Still later the rounds of the village were made in quest of an Evinrude driveshaft. "Where'd you find that?" I asked of the native returning with the goods. "That doesn't matter!" he smiled. It so happened that an exact fit could not be found; but that doesn't daunt the people of the North, who, like the Prairie farmer, are quite skilled at improvising. At two o'clock the 'Breed looked up and sighed "That's got it!" the makeshift shaft was in place, stuffed with a dozen tin shims. Inwardly I doubted its reliability; outwardly I daren't show anything but optimism. It would have been futile to dispute the arrangement; my man was sure of his handiwork. 'We shall see,' I comforted myself as we bedded down for a short nap.

Six−thirty came too fast. It was our idea to make an early getaway and avoid any embarrassment caused by the return. Replenishing our fuel supply with five more gallons and not forgetting yesterday's plight in the mosquito bog, I bought some more Beat It, intent on winning the next onslaught. With nothing more but for my friend to pull the cord on the 'kicker', I held my breath. If miracles do happen, one happened then. "*Yi!....Yi!....Yi!*," shouted the smiling native as the engine sputtered and caught. I was all smiles as we slipped against the channel, away from the sleeping settlement.

We soon passed our friend Charlie, tending his nets, this time for keeps...into the Huskie Channel, past Lazars Edwards' cabin by noon. "I won't feel right till we pass our old mark," I yelled above the steady din of the 'kicker'. "If something does happen, we'll keep on anyway," Malcolm shouted forward in agreement. John Robert's cabin farther along...kicker still pounding steadily...mosquitoes still biting and Big Andrew's cabin appeared at the mouth of the Rat River. This was a significant place. Here we would pick up the *Trail of '98*−fifty years too late to compete with the human stream that sought the wealth of the Klondike, via this entry, but only hours behind them in imagination. *'Surely we will overtake some stragglers at Destruction City,'* I thought, revelling in the history of the past. It was nine p.m. *"Exactly three months to the day since we left Fort Edmonton,"* I said to my partner as we slid past the lopstick (tree with only its upper branches, used as a marker) which for fifty years has looked down on thousands like us. "Hold on; ready with your paddle while I run 'er in...don't wanta hit the bank!" he responded. We forsook the swirling waters of the flooded Huskie Channel for the tranquility of the Rat River. It was not peaceful for long as our motor echoed along the narrow winding channel. The river was teaming with wildlife. A muskrat scrambled for shore; a rabbit appearing momentarily on the bank as though to see who the intruders were, turned and cracked its way through the underbrush. A duck, its evening peace disturbed, 'took off' with a splash ahead of us, flapping its way into a westering sun. Bang! and my ears deafened with the report. Splash! the duck was no longer flying. I turned to see a broad native smile. "Fresh meat for supper!" came the words from somewhere amongst the wrinkled countenance. "Now you've disturbed everything for miles," I replied, thinking more of beauty than of my belly at that time. "From here in its survival of the fittest! ...you'll see," he came back. "Well, you look pretty fit to me," I retaliated. Caring little for words, he finished with: "So do you from here!...grab a paddle...we'll save this gas for later." The echoes died; a bend in the Rat River claimed us; all was silent but for the dripping of water from paddle stems.

Destruction City—Rat River Portage
Trail of '98

As the cool of the evening creeps on, the spruce trees cast their long shadows across the winding stream. "Can't be too far now," said the 'Breed, checking our crude map drawn up by an Indian friend who was quite familiar (so he said) with the Rat Portage. Then we rounded a sudden bend and floated out into the open. "Must be Destruction City, but I can't see any landmarks," Malcolm added. "Maybe it's completely destructed!" I suggested, looking at my watch—12 a.m....."You and your dry wit...and at this hour!" he replied without humour. "This is it!" he cried suddenly, pointing to the swirling river washing down from the mountains. "Landmark or no landmark, it is obvious that our trail ascends," I agree.

So in the early hours of a northern mid−summer morn two weary figures made camp; prepared a hasty meal; pitched their 'mosquito bar' and crawled within: *one thought he heard the sound of whipsaws, hammering and much exchanging of words...it was the year 1897 at Destruction City, where hundreds worked day and night preparing caches and winter camp or making ready a lighter craft for a quick dash to the Porcupine, Old Crow or (if lucky) Fort Yukon− across the mountains enroute to the fabulous Klondike.*

Destruction City was appropriately named. It was here that the Argonauts destroyed their larger boats, barges and rafts that had floated them north on the broad rivers, for small craft necessary to forge the narrow but hazardous Rat River climbing gradually to the summit of the distant mountains. "Most of us prospectors followed the same procedure," said Oldtimer Frank Foster at Old Crow, later. "We'd burn our boats to reclaim the double clinched nails. It was the only way you could get them...impossible to pull 'em out," he added, thoughtfully, "With the aid of whipsaws we'd slice the local trees into planks and set about building our new ones. We were all busier 'n a pack of beavers and we certainly mus'ta resembled them, gnawing and hacking at those trees: hardly a one left in the vicinity when I departed." That's why we could see no sign of the once−flourishing settlement. Nothing remained to suggest human habitation on the right limit of the riverbank − caved in with the years and washed away with each spring flood.

"There was quite a settlement here," Frank (puffing contentedly on his pipe) had said. "Some of us pushed on, but many, deciding it was too late in the year (late July) to continue, built cabins and caches. They had been on the move since the first day of Spring at Waterways! 'Why the rush?' thought many, 'if the Klondike is as rich as they say it is!' "It was not uncommon for two men to pool their resources and energies, thus enabling them to relay their individual loads of 1,000 to 2,000 pounds up the Richardson Mountains with more haste."

So the air was rent with the ring of axe and the buzz of saw as Destruction City grew and the population increased with the gradual influx of Cheechakos from the South, in the fall of '97. These were the audible echoes heard plainly above the buzz of mosquitoes and the gentle ripple of a mountain stream bubbling over the rocks on its journey into infinity. This was no dream. We were part of the stream of adventurers on the Trail of '98.

It is accepted by northerners that the mosquitoes, no—seeums and sandflies are the curse of their country. Somewhere, somehow, these pests crept past the well—anchored mosquito—bar covering me from head to foot. Scratch as I could and kill wantonly as I did, the relentless squadrons punctuated sleep with their drone, the advance signal, the dive and their final accurate bombardment followed by the irritating itch and throb. Had the waters been less cold, gladly would I have picked up bed, 'bar' and all and dumped my entirety into the stream to rid me of those pests of pests. Once they discovered the inner sanctum of my sleeping robe I yielded. At some time in the early morning of July 24th, the Cheechako, unresisting, gave up to the messengers that bore him to another land where pests abounded not.

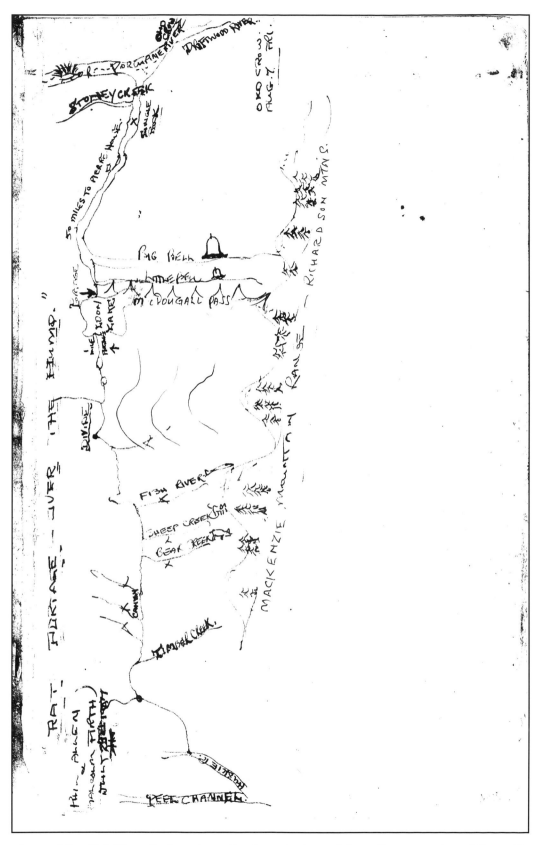

A montage of the Rat River Portage 'over the hump', gleaned from the memories of the natives of Aklavik, and sketched in the authors well—worn diary.

120

CHAPTER EIGHTEEN

THE RAT RIVER PORTAGE

**Cheechako Still
—But Learning**

**Malcolm
Stop for a Smoke**

One sleeps heavy under the warm sun at this time of year, and it was not until late morn' that its fingers prodded us to the awareness of another day. Minutes found the hungry Malcolm kneeling in front of a frying pan over the fire while I chose a pre—breakfast swim. Refreshed, I raced nudely to the protecting smoke of the fire. Our obnoxious friends had not deserted us! I fought the hordes with Beat It, Skat, Skeeter Skater and both hands. The smoke from the fire, though suffocating, proved better than all five. "When'er we gonna get away from these infernal intruders?" I asked my native friend for consolation. Munching on a hardtack, seemingly undisturbed by the mosquito on his nose, he replied: "As soon as you get into this grub and we both hit for the center of the stream." "Center of the stream?" I asked. "You'll find out!" he cut short. I tapped one of those dozen eggs, miraculously unscathed, on the edge of the pan, brooding over his last words. 'Oh, well, you can expect anything from here on,' came the inner voice. And still another challenged, 'it's adventure your looking for, isn't it?' Overanxious to be on the way, camp was broken and left to the insects. We turned from the smooth creek waters at the junction and were claimed by the rapids of the Rat River, rushing from the heights. "I'll go ahead with the rope...you hang on to the nose of the canoe!" said my friend, breaking the silence. A moment later, with water circling my knees, I realized what 'the center of the stream' meant. Once wet I felt my old optimism returning. We were on the move again. A glance from the fore—end of thirty feet of rope brought a smile to my face and a look of agreement from the native. *We joined the cursing, grunting, groaning, splashing procession of humans pitting every muscle against Nature's odds, as they forged their way slowly to the summit. Destruction City and its ghostly population faded in our wake. We were greedy for miles; all were hungry for Gold.*

Up the gradual twisting slope the hills and growth increase. The countryside becomes ever—more enticing. Both parties, over anxious for the next bend and its hidden treasurers, forget time and rest, splashing periodically in the cool water to evade the heat and the mosquitoes that have found us in mid—stream. *'Tracking' (a means of one pulling a long rope attached to the prow of the canoe, held by the other in midstream, steering it through the rapids and rocks) thus, we find ourselves deep in the hills past the southeast end of the mountain range stretching from Aklavik. Hour after hour we continue, each thinking his own thoughts till one too good to hoard, finds words and the silent spell is broken. In such an abundance of beauty as the country disgorges, it is almost impossible to keep within one's impressions, strong and silent as a man might think he is. "What do you think of it now?" enquired my friend, who must have noticed my absorbed silence. "My God but it's great!" were my first words. "And to think there's a whole Yukon and Alaska full of it!"I added, gazing intently into the distance. Slowly, our independence gives way to a combined independence. We were beginning to accept the other with that confidence built up from co−operation.

'Tracking' up the Rat River   **Malcolm**
Sharing the Ordeal

Thursday was hot and mosquitoless. "Strange," said the 'Breed, "something's in the wind!" It was moments like this that sent a twitch inside me: What was he sensing? "There's a forest fire somewhere ahead! " he blurted, catching sight of the previously unnoticed haze to westward. 'Could it be in our path?' I asked myself. "No wonder the damn mosquitoes have beat it," he added, "they're afraid of getting their wings singed or their asses burned!...Well, anyway, it's one time I welcome a forest fire," he finished, satisfied that it was many miles away.

The current becomes swifter as we ascend; rapids increase as they break over the hidden rocks, tossing their white manes to the winds; the riverbed provides treacherous footing as pebbles turn to rocks, sharp and slippery. For every 'riffle' (rapid or rough water) there is a compensating 'bench' (smooth water), where it is sometimes possible to use the 'kicker' aided by paddles. This alone gives us strength for the next exertion. "Got five gallons of 'kicker juice' left for these, " came my friend, as I assisted over the 'bench' with the paddle, "but we'll have to go easy...there's a thousand miles of water where we're headin'. " "Better save it for real hard times," I suggest, and with agreement after slight thought, Malcolm retrieved the remaining paddle from the canoe bottom. "Can't hold her!" I yelled to my man thirty feet ahead, as we tackled the next 'riffle'. Water splashed and frothed about the prow of our craft; feet, unable to secure a firm hold below, slipped hopelessly about; I clung to the bow as the Rat River encircled my waist. I saw his white teeth gritted. He wound the rope over his shoulder and leaning backward took the full shock of 800 pounds. Momentarily it held. "Get a foot−hold...quick!" came his voice downstream. And I did. "Now hang on till I reach you!" he shouted. It was gruelling, those seconds that it took him to work his way back along the rope. "I'm with you...now both together!" he shouted, panting, across the bow. And with the strength of close union we drove the prow into the rapids, edging slightly toward shore. It was the silence at the other end of the rapid that brought words. "Gotta watch on them kind," said Malcolm. "But, I think you've learned okay." It was this more than the conquest of the rapid that warmed me. I was receiving the acid−test of approval. "Let's tackle that long bench," I suggested, feeling the strength of success, "and we'll eat supper, gosh knows we've earned it," I suggested to my companion. "Good idea," he agreed, grasping the other paddle. this did not last for long. I couldn't understand why it was so difficult. It looked flat. So we tracked close to shore. Reaching the destined point, my friend commented: "Look back and you'll get a surprise." "Let's eat...I'm tired of your northern illusions," I reiterated, thinking less of paddling and more of food.

It was 5:30 p.m. when we dropped our grub−box at an old campsite. "It was a white man's camp," muttered my friend on close inspection. "How the hell do you figure that?" I asked, slightly annoyed at my own ignorance. "Because of the pole at a 45° angle from which he hangs his teapail. You don't catch many natives doing that, " he explained. This learned, I still wondered who the white men were, for the singular honour of being the first white man through this year fell on my shoulders. Again my friend came to the rescue with native cunning. "It's last year's fire." *I was satisfied to think of it as belonging to a prospector on the trail to the Klondike. As I rebuilt the fire I was with my own kind again.*

**800 pounds uphill
Along the 'Rat'**

We joked raucously, talked of gold and women mostly; and of McGuire's tough luck spilling his grubstake in the rapids further down. 'Too bad,' came the voice from the flames, 'but he won't be givin' in...not that stubborn Scotsman. He'll catch up, you'll see...' "I doubt it," I answered. "You doubt what?" asked Malcolm, greasing the frying pan. Startled back to 1947 I replied, stammering, "er..o..a..I doubt whether the fire is more than a year old... " "I oughta know, I've lived in the country all my life!" he retorted. "Well, what's for chow?" I asked, slightly embarrassed and quickly changing the subject, for what did he care of the *Trails of '98.*

The scenery is becoming more verdant and enticing with its many shades of green, including, oddly, the emerald of Ireland, where new shoots dare to spring along the riverbanks. Hills recede in varying colours till they appear purple, finally black.

All day we travelled under a hot sun clad only in short pants and leathertop boots. All day we have co−ordinated the mental and physical in the slow process of realizing an age−old dream. One month ago today I left Yellowknife. Now the talk and boast is a reality as the native with his Cheechako friend struggle in the very heart of it all. Never satisfied to pitch camp while the day is bright and young, we continue for two hours more. At nine o'clock we pull into the spruce−studded shore for the night. Sunset is round and red, the smoke from over the mountains dimming it, and, fortunately, obliterating our friendly pests − the mosquitoes. *About 45 miles inland from the site of Destruction City, two of that vast horde of Argonauts make their second camp, well initiated to the ordeals of the trail.*

"How'd you sleep Cheechako?" queried the native next morning. "If it isn't your darned mosquitoes, it's sore muscles. Maybe one of these nights I'll win!" I replied. "You'll be okay in a couple more days...by the way, what does the canoe look like?" The previous day's travel had been rough. With each rapid came the sickening scrape of canoe on rock. Many times there was no alternative but to ease the 800 pound load over the shallower riffles or between boulders that scraped the belly of the Peterborough. This we both knew meant trouble later. I did not know at the time how it would be met, but never once doubted the ingenuity of my 'Breed companion who had already matched his wits with difficulties and won.

"Only four tears," said Malcolm, overturning the 22 footer. "Bring me the Ambroid (an orange paste for patching canvas on canoes) and let's get this thing watertight...it's mid−morning already." So I observed, and saw another difficulty overcome. But the Ambroid would soon be gone at this rate. What then? Little did I realize the surprises that were in store. It was 10:00 a.m. when water spanked gently the bottom of our lady. The benches grow longer and stronger as we rise. An hour, and the river overflows its banks, the entire area inundated by onrushing streams. It has been raining above and now we feel the full force of the waters, rushing, coming from miles to challenge us. The bank disappears. Walking is impossible. "Get out of this one," I challenged my companion, who looks unperturbed. "Just hand me the rope when I round each clump of willows!" he says, swinging through the water to a knoll. *Inch by inch we pull the canoe, hand the rope ahead, move to another clump of growth, slip waist deep into the stream, curse...and all for gold!*

"Now what?" I yelled over the tumultous current, coming to a dead end. "You're tallest...coil the rope around you.. <u>swim</u>!" shouted back the native. With no alternative, but sure of my stroke, I started. There was no bottom. The current, anxious to wash me downstream with the other debris, roared and churned in anger, seemingly jealous of my headway. *Splash!* and a huge portion of the bank dropped into the swirling mess. "Watch out behind you!" yelled the dripping native from the far knoll. I turned in time to dodge a tree, uprooted, racing for nowhere in particular, bearing down on me. 'Two more strokes,' I told myself as the water, filling my leathertops, pulled me down. "Grab that willow!...quick!...the canoe!..., I heard in punctuated phrases. 'Made it!...easy now or you'll uproot it,' I told myself. A broad smile met me as I stood dripping on the far knoll, surrounded by the murky waters, chewing away at the muddy island. Words were unnecessary. I was weathering the test. I had won! It was then that fear disappeared. I was challenging the elements and liking it. "That's gettin' pretty bad," I said to Malcolm as he reached the knoll in the canoe. He said nothing, as though considering it no worse than any other ordeal on trail. The incident over, I concluded that there just wasn't any easy way to live in the North. It's all the same−tough!

There is a standing maxim oft' spoken by the oldtimers, who are happy to think their country is not plagued, like so many others, with exploiters. It goes: *The North does not choose its people; it merely eliminates the weaklings!* More than once I asked myself why I was continuing. Each time the voice of Pessimism was sternly answered with this axiom. It was thus I spoke as I stood dripping on the willow patch. Was I not meeting the qualifications of another kindred soul raised and tuned to the frequency of the northern elements? Was he complaining? No!

"Grab a paddle...I'll try the engine...grab willows if it coughs... " cried Malcolm from the rear of the canoe. A *'sput'* followed by a confined roar came unexpectedly. We moved ahead, water forcing the prow at an angle. A paddle forced it straight again. The shore neared. "Take the rope and jump!" yelled the native. The engine stopped. Another figure leaped ashore, restraining the wild canoe. And then in the silence of a willowed−alcove a voice panted, "Nice going...we made it!" We were still the victors.

Another treacherous spot where a thousand rivulets rushed to join the main stream; another drenching as we clutched sporadic willows −the only means of getting ahead; more fumbling, spitting water and cursing everything; wet, we dragged ourselves up the mud bank for a rest and a well−earned lunch.

With no desire to camp any night till we feel justice has been done to the day, we pack the teapail and cups, making ready for two more hours of water...water...water. The terrain turns into a chain of long rapids, each with its diabolical undercurrent; each with its hidden, piercing rocks. Malcolm, pulling up front, stoops and excitedly yells: "Look at this!...I know who it belonged to...a man who came to Aklavik last year...a Dr. I believe...was taking the Rat Portage," he continues, holding up an orange sole of a discarded running shoe. "He wore a size nine or ten." I check it and it is a nine. "Then we are on the right track," I yelled. "No doubt now. And I've seen some timber cuts along the shore too, " he confided.

Ten o'clock. We shiver ourselves to shore. A six−foot driftwood fire soon turns the atmosphere into a veritable Hades and the two adventurers into devilish−looking creatures casting their grotesque shadows on the waters. The day and the meal have been hard−earned. As we sit around the fire talking and supping tea, we reach some enthusiastic conclusions. We are sure we are on the right trail. Earlier in the day we passed what on the map was marked Timber Creek, branching off to the northwest. We had stuck to the largest body of water. Malcolm had caught sight of landmarks. "Why don't you tell me these things?" I ask, as one left out of a secret. "Just didn't wanta get you all excited," he smiles over his teacup. "By the way, I saw a saw−cut stump a mile back, some broken willows and an old tree scar, if it'll make you feel good. And you see that log you're sitting on? Notice the end?" "Well I'll be"...I stammer, "it's notched like it belonged to a cabin!" "Say, you're learning fast, Cheechako...it probably got washed into the river." "Bet it belonged to a '98 er's cabin," I suggest. "Could be...it's old enough," answers my companion. "Better check the day's damage, now that our bellies are prepared for the shock, " he adds, turning to the beach. "Not bad," I comment, as we turn the Peterborough over to dry. "Only four new holes and two old ones."

It was midnight and no time to worry about anything but sleep. On a plateau between two branches of river we pitched our third camp, 55 miles from Destruction City and 120 from Aklavik. Contemplating a sunny morrow and no mosquitoes, we curled up in our sleeping robes beside the dying embers and soon darkness claimed us.

Signs of the *Trail of '98*

I awoke at 2:30 a.m. to the patter of raindrops on my brow. Our delusions of no rain quickly vanished. Covering my head, I returned to slumber. The Goddess of Rain, apparently offended at my neglect to notice her soft touch, now beat down heavily. Her awakening was more than rude; it was wet, damnably so! as it snuck through the snaps on the side of the robe. Unlike my friend, I was unable to stand the insomnia. I arose and busied myself with breakfast, drying what clothes I could under the hastily slung tarpaulin.

By noon, neither the sun nor my native companion had arisen, but the mist vanished up the mountainside, the rain spitting only occasionally. Time brought rain, which in turn brought my drowsy friend to his feet from the saturated bedroll in which he was curled. Over lunch we talked optimistically. "Two days and we should hit the Canyon," said Malcolm. "I won't be happy till we hit the Little Bell," I reiterated. "You and that river," he exclaimed, "but say, it will be nice to go downstream for awhile, eh?" So we dreamed away the day; patched the canoe — this time with cloth and Ambroid; gathered wood; and mostly sat by the fire in the shelter of our 'tarp'. I refused to offer a libation to the Goddess above because of her rude awakening. Envious, she poured her best torrents down upon the solitary encampment lost in the heart of the mountains.

For two days we 'ate it out' on the small island. The swollen stream rushed past in the wrong direction. The clouds rose and fell, depositing rain at random. I retaliated with indifference, and having nothing else to do, nestled in for a reading bout with Joseph Conrad and Robert Service. Certainly, the surroundings were appropriate. In no time I became lost, forgot all about the Goddess and heeded not her wrath. As I read the works of the Scotch bard, I suddenly felt akin to that homeless tribe of vagabonds who prefer the Battle of the Elements to the Battle of Mankind.

Such were the long, wet hours passed under a backdrop of canvas fronted by a twenty—four hour fire. We both knew this could not last for long. Our grubstake was for two weeks only. Impatience was already growing strong on the first day of inactivity. Perhaps I should give in to the Goddess? 'No!' cried the voice of Conscience: 'Save your food for the journey.' This, I knew, was good advice.

I was awakened to Sunday by a 'hotfoot'. At some time during the night I had stretched to full length and as the embers slowly ate away my sock I was unaware of it, till too late. *"Yeeeeeeooowww...!"* split the early morning silence. "What's that?" cried the 'Breed, erecting himself in his sleeping bag faster than I had ever seen. I snuffed out the toeless sock. He exclaimed: "I thought it was something important...a bear or sumpin?' unsympathetically, turning into his robe and curling into his former position. "Not so loud next time," he muttered. That was the last I heard till morning.

The incident did break the monotony of waiting. Next morning, the rain had ceased. We dried clothes, sleeping bags, packsacks and tarps all day while waiting for the two feet of water to recede.

Then it happened, as though tired of waiting for our prayers: blue skies and a persistant sun poked its red nose through the clouds! We were more than jubilant.

Drying Clothes in the sun

Our hopes reawakened, we have supper and dash to the hilltop to view the morrow's destination. An hour later we overlook the river winding its way toward the Yukon. "There's the creeks marked on the map," cries Malcolm, all smiles. "We'll make the Canyon, which must be just around the far bend, our destination, eh?" he said, looking for assent. It came with enthusiasm. Thus, with the destination firmly fixed in two minds, we turn from the panorama of water, trees and mountains, recrossing the muskeg and 'niggerheads' to the hillcrest overlooking our wake. It is one long series of twisting, turning riffles and benches. "Thank gosh we've put them behind; but they do look kinda nice stretched out, don't you think?" I interrupted my thought, wondering if the surrounding beauty had an equal effect on my generally silent companion. "Sure do...I'll never leave this country...I'd be lost without it all," he replied.

We descended to our valley camp amid this splendour. With joy we observed the receding waters. Warm from the long walk, I felt the sudden urge for a swim. "After all that rain!" was the only retort from my bronzed companion. The evening was dry and we prepared for a quick getaway in the morning, come what may. It was a wonderful thought to sleep on...we would be on the move again.

CHAPTER NINETEEN

A WHITE MAN & A HALFBREED

Next morning the waters had gone down considerably. Said Malcolm: "The Indians wouldn't travel in such weather." "Well, I'm a whiteman!" I replied. "And I'm a half—breed," was his adjoinder. "Then what're we waitin' for?" came the obvious deduction. So the comparatively early hour of 7:30 found us wading in the stream once more. With heads lowered and the silent routine of tracking accepted, we soon put the miles to our rear.

Noon. We rounded the wide bend facing the west and the mountains, viewed the previous evening. The Rat was still high and its rapids became more treacherous. Because of this, it was necessary to stop. It was a plain case of either patch or bail. Already tired of the latter we decided on more permanency. But here a difficulty arose. We had run out of Ambroid!

Undaunted, Malcolm said: "We'll take these tins and gather some sap from the local trees." Having stripped considerable trees in the vicinity, our find was put in a tin and heated. Clambering atop the overturned canoe, with the precious fluid the 'Breed sealed the leaky underside of our Peterborough. Here I was convinced that nothing would stop us from crossing the Yukon if every emergency was met with identical resourcefulness. Lunch over, and our vessel once more seaworthy, we slid it into the stream, loaded, and continued the fast pace. Two days of time and food had been wasted. We began to realize the grub—distance we had yet to go. Who knows what may happen along the way?

Malcolm
Patching Peterborough with Pine Pitch

The '98ers are with us, struggling through the indefinite waters, their shoulders bent, legs weary of the continual beating from rushing water and wind. "Is all this consarn gold worth it?" I heard a voice ask. "Would you rather be a wage—slave like your brother, all your life?" retorted another in answer. Then I heard unprintable language drift on the cool wind as a figure disappeared beneath the rapids ahead, only to reappear a dozen feet away, his canoe aground on a spiked boulder. They streamed out in a long, thin procession behind too, and I thought I saw a woman amongst one group. "That's what I call guts,"said one of our party, knowing it to be beyond the usual fatigues of a good male. "God bless 'em," I added, turning to the waters ahead. How many perished? is a burning question. I'd much rather let imagination take its cold census.

"Cabin ahead," shouted my tawny friend, at the river—bend turning west. "I'm going to do some visiting...haven't seen a white man for a week," I answered. With a daft look he accepted the statement, pulling our craft to the shore. *Almost expecting a dishevelled, 'bushed' Argonaut to appear at the door, I am ready with a greeting. But alas, the door is off. No human greets me with that hospitable welcome of the North, "Come on in!"* Soon, I hope we may exchange such a greeting which is the clove in the pie of any such lonely journey — that true welcome of people, unabashed and sincere. In the North everyone is a friend until some act puts him in the other camp, unlike the wary business life of a city, where no quarter is given from the start. Perhaps this can be a definition of the North? Its simplicity is worthy of a good solid definition; but then again, suppose we let it remain as virgin as its vast territory, devoid of all formulas and man—made definitions? We shall each call it what we will, however we receive and are received by it. And let it not be too harsh (if harsh at all), for this is still the land of the free—man, the pioneer, the follower of the frontiers...

A thousand thoughts approach the mental mirror, stand momentarily in self observation, and pass on; some content with what they have seen; others dubious; and many that are neither here nor there, as the vast space without gives one time for introspection. This, I presume, is what finally makes a man 'bushed': the thinking alone...till soon the Outside world becomes so many fantasies and the realities are the next bend, the next tree or the next cloud—the essences of survival; simple, yet complex enough to absorb the wayfarer's entire self.

I can quite readily understand the eventual aloneness one must feel in so vast and quiet a land. This alone sends men mad— referred to as 'bushed'! Then again, let us consider 'bushed' as a common word for a man who has enjoyed too long the freedom and lack of self—discipline conventionally forced upon we dependent individuals, too wound up with the cares of the universe to enjoy true freedom — the thing most sought after by man and so seldom found. Here I give all credit to the adventurers: Scots, Irish, English; and all those who have invaded the realm of the Indian, sought habitation and have, more than any other people I know, found freedom.

"Come on over here...I've found something!" were the words that brought me from my thoughts. Approaching the voice I beheld another cabin. "Anyone in there?" I enquired. "No one but termites," replied Malcolm. A bunk, intact, fills one corner and a larder at the rear of the cabin stands empty. Leaning a foot on a log it crumbles completely, convincing us of '98 vintage. Agreeing on the possible antiquity of the once cozy dwelling, we leave the cabins to their ruins and whatever ghosts of the past that might haunt them at night, feeling that someone besides us has been here, regardless of time. It is a consoling thought as we make for our wet highway once more.

Aware of the change of scenery and vegetation I leaned 180 pounds on the towline, the mind occupied with the thoughts of an Argonaut headed westward for the fabulous Klondike.

A Much Welcome Cup o' Tea

Four—thirty and we are enveloped by this new scenery. Satisfied with progress, we stop for a quick refresher—a pot of tea. It is not much, but that 'something' we look forward to, to break the long hours and give us a little boost. Content and inwardly warm we agree to try to make this a record day. So we proceed again, alternating rope and bow, water consistently above the knees, numbing, till the limbs have no feeling and walking becomes a clumsy habit.

It is natural for one to hold a fear for unknown rapids. Having shared five days of cold familiarity with them, their white mystery gradually exposed itself. They are like barking dogs guarding the forbidden territory of their masters; in the main, loud, and oftimes concealing a mean streak under the surface. But as Malcolm showed me the key to the secret, I felt not unlike Ali Baba, needing only to say the right words to gain access through the rocky barriers. As the white foam churned about my waist, I openly smiled in abandon; had someone been close, they might have heard challenging words mingled with the vociferous backtalk of the mad waters. The Cheechako was catching on.

With this lack of fear, and an increasing abandon, two figures and a canoe moved through the afternoon sunlight into the quiet of evening. Nine and one half hours of trudging brought them to a halt, and camp, on a high mossy bank. They had set a record as planned. Perhaps at this point, an excerpt from my diary will describe best the situation.

It is 8:15 p.m. and we are in full view of the ever—enticing mountains — looking like so many Madonnas, each surmounted with a halo and girdled about the middle (Saturn—like) with a ring of mist. Behind us lies the river, roaring with rapids as it loses itself in pines. At three m.p.h. we must have covered 25 miles, bringing the total to 145 miles from Aklavik.

We are still looking for two creeks on the left limit, and the Canyon, past which we are praying for easier going. Malcolm has found an 8' x 10' x 3' tent at the deserted Indian camp nearby and as though aware of this fact, the Prophets sent a deluge of rain... With the mountains to the west—so near, yet so far — and the rocky river east, I could quite easily be in Calgary, till looking up I see across the fire the weatherbeaten, bronzed Malcolm supping on his favorite brew of tea. Putting Conrad and the thoughts of the day aside, I settle into my Five−Star−Eiderdown on the softest mattress on which I have ever slept—a bed of moss two feet thick!...

It was the softest bed till the numbness of my bones spoiled the night. 'Travellers cramp' or 'trail fatigue' is a common northern ailment, whether it is from over exertion, the dampness or just what, I cannot say; but as I awoke each hour on the hour, I could not find my limbs! They were asleep, but aching. There is only one remedy for this: get out of bed, circle the tent once or twice and swing the arms as you go. With such interruptions I was forced to postpone my enjoyment of sleeping on moss. But it is fair to say that in the intervals when sleep did occur it must have been enjoyed. Morning found us (one very irritable) cleaning away the breakfast foods, packing the packs,

**We find No Gold
But a Priceless Tent!**

folding our precious tent with dexterity and shoving the canoe into the cold waters, by eleven o'clock. Our determined destination was the illusive Canyon. Looking back I still think it was one of the toughest of our ordeals, slipping into the icy waters on this bleak, grey morning. As though afraid to come out we continued doggedly until 4:30 p.m. when the entrance to the Canyon yawned largely down at us. We stopped for a pot of tea.

Fully rejuvenated and lured on by the Canyon, we dallied not. Steep banks of solid rock towered above us like Cyclops who at any moment might hurl a volley of granite at the intruders. We tackled the turbulent rapids, massed like guards before a drawbridge, guarding the very interior with their lives. With no thought of retreat we plowed into the midst of the frothing foe with more caution than ever. We had not had a single spill in the entire trip. This was no place to ruin a good record.

"Watch it!" cried my short friend from his semi−submerged position at the end of the towline. Glancing up I saw him slip suddenly, the line becoming limp. The canoe swung free, its bow−to which I clung−swung outward carrying the Cheechako with it! I struggled, refusing to let go of the undulating nose. We were losing ground. My feet slid helplessly on the slimy rocks somewhere beneath that churning water. Ten feet...the rope grew taut. I dared look upstream. There was Malcolm, braced as solidly as the Colossus, his white teeth gritted and gleaming. How he assumed that position so fast I will never know; but once before I had watched the native's agility, so I concluded he had taken a plain header forward after the lost rope and

Cheating the Rapids Again

with luck retrieved it, regained a footing, and braced himself for the 800 pound shock. "We've cheated them again!" I yelled exultantly. But with victory still in the balance, he returned: "Don't be too sure...got'er tight yet?" At that very moment the Peterborough, straining against the line in four feet of water, bobbed like a broncho, slapped its nose on a rapid and dunked the Cheechako head and all. We had not won yet I knew, rising to the surface only to see this time a smiling face. Unamused, I received the words: "I've got her okay...now make for the shore while I hold it!" Slowly...inching a little...losing a foothold...regaining ground...'water's sure cold on the chest...gotta get there...legs sure numb...two feet...got it!' I said to myself, covering that unreliable stretch of riverbed.

A pause for breath. Another warm smile from my friend and I needed no further encouragement. Sometimes the less spoken the better. This was one of those times. We both knew how close it had been. We sat down before the next watery battle and agreed to watch closely for another eager rapid anxious to claim an object. "Don't wanta bust our record, do we?" I commented.

Within the Canyon is a geologist's paradise. It's high walls are lined with a variegated display of rock strata ranging from light to dark, as though some giant prism was reflecting its rays on to the sheer face. Orange increasing in intensity to reds, purples and browns predominate nature's colour scheme. Had I been a geologist and not an author, I know for sure that I would have spent hours just looking at the contents of that cold face. As it was I stole many glances, (whenever I dared) as we forged our way through the treacherous waters, gaining an artistic impression of these beautiful cliffs, despite the discomfort of being saturated to the neck in cold, mountain water. If I should ever retrace my steps I shall do so as a geologist, or with a colour camera, and do justice to this wall that is so expressive of Nature as painter and architect.

It was 7 p.m. as we came out on the other side of the yawning chasm—the victors—into the mountain mists and smooth waters. As though testing our stability and perseverance, a last swift rapid had blocked our exodus; but with continued luck and well organized co—ordination we beat the villain, leering at us and spitting foaming waters from its jagged—toothed mouth. Well tutored by this time in the School of Rapids, we took every precaution, headed straight into the largest swell and with an "O.K." from myself (shouted over the din) I felt for hidden rocks, buoyed up simultaneously over the crest of the pounding rapid. A moment later I was approaching a beaming face as its owner pulled up the last feet of line. "We sure beat that one!" panted my man Firth. Chuckling aloud with the feeling of success, we turned to the calm waters that lay ahead.

We were feeling quite satisfied with ourselves by this time. As our reward we snatched a rest, a tin of sardines divided two ways, a pot of tea and a hard tack with jam. We hesitated to look at the canoe's underside. But the lot feel to me, so look I must. To say the canvas was holey would be an understatement. It was ripped, torn, frayed and about all other calamities that could befall a Peterborough, loaded with more than half a thousand pounds, slapping the rapids of the Rat River. In fact, the bottom was shot!

Our vanity melted with the sap that we collected for a quick repair job. It was far from adequate. We would have to keep on the move, bailing as we went. "Anyway," sighed Malcolm, spreading the last precious molten fluid to our lady's bottom, "we made our pre—destined destination!" "That's a pretty big word for a native to be using, isn't it?" I asked, concealing a smile. "Well, I heard you use it this morning, and I'd hate to say who you resemble with all that hair on your face!" We both broke into hearty volumes of laughter that echoed and died in the surrounding mountains. Our feet turned upstream...

Not only did we succeed in our boast, but by late evening many more miles added themselves to the day's tally. It was not until the energies of the day were completely spent that we submitted to a huge driftwood fire, aromatic pine boughs and the delicious taste of food cooked over an open fire. Complete contentment was ours. It had been hard—earned.

As the dry wood cracked—its red—hot sparks igniting the night like tiny meteorites headed for earth—we gloated over the days mileage, which subtracted twenty more from the total. We were (according to a rough calculation of water miles) about 165 miles from Aklavik. It was over the lowering flames of this fire that our accent fell heavy on the Bell River; it couldn't possibly be very far away now? But like all adventurers, who are confirmed optimists and sometimes inclined to be over−imaginative, we beheld the much lauded river just around the next silhouetted, silent line of hills. Little did we realize our mistake; the North was playing her deceiving hand well. However, our minds were subtracting from the distance ahead rather than adding to that in the rear. This in itself was a healthy sign, a healthy thought to sleep on as the hypnotic fingers of slumber massaged gently our tired eyes.

On July 30 one week of this amphibious travel had been completed and 165 miles were a thing of the past. 165 miles of mosquitoes would never have to be trekked again! It was a consoling thought. On the western side of the valley a rock projecting like a lone sentinel drew my attention. With very little imagination it accepted the form of an Indian brave, gauntly looking westward (as I have always envisioned the redskin) discerning the morrow by his God − the sun−as it sets in all its splendor. Having made the Canyon the previous night, we felt quite content; but this day, as each new bend was sighted and approached, a general anxiety arose as we doggedly pursued our water−course in the direction our silent Indian was looking.

It could have been the sudden appearance of the sun, warming and encouraging, that had enlightened us, for when it ran its short course into the clouds at 2:00 p.m. we became aware of its absence and the encroaching dampness. It was not long afterwards that we passed gradually out of the surrounding mountains into hills punctuated with short rapids and long benches. The latter are the 'quiet waters' mentioned in northern jargon−a sort of reward for defeating the rapids. As we progressed with the aid of paddles over these waters an abundance of trout appeared, quite tame, as though unconcerned with truant officers intruding on their peaceful schools.

High in the Mountains

The going is much easier now as we find the banks accessible because of fast receding waters. As 7:30 comes around, ending a twelve−hour day, we pull up for our sixth camp. For the last hour I have wanted to stop, but, with that pride of the adventurer, I desist in mentioning the fact. 'If your five−foot−six−inch friend can hold out, I guess you can,' exclaims Conscience. I take heed of the well−chosen words. The previous day it had been my suggestion to continue when fatigue overtook my man; with gameness he had consented. Remembering this, no more was said to myself or friend till we stopped. Then I spoke. "How do you feel Malcolm?" "Tired...damn tired!...but we made the high hill!" "High hill?" I asked. "Yeah, see it?...I've been trying to reach it all day!...how far do you think we made?"

"About thirty miles," I replied, pausing to note the time and multiply by our average 3 m.p.h. rate, "but in future let me in on your schemes!"

A Stand up Meal on the Trail

CHAPTER TWENTY

THE STAMP OF APPROVAL

"I didn't think you could do it," came out of the blue with all suddenness, a satisfied smile possessing the native's face. Smiling inwardly, I accepted the stamp of approval. It was the greatest thing that could have happened to the Cheechako that day. Compatability is a must if one is to travel with the natives, born to the ordeal of the trail. It is a singular honour for an Outsider, born to the ways of civilization, to receive this stamp. So it was that two became one in spirit, "...and I've outdistanced many a man with longer legs than I," he added. I knew my legs were longer than his.

The great Outdoors being the only life the natives know, it is little wonder they can travel the speed, distance and subsist on the little (tea, drymeat and fish) they do, taking it with or without a grain of salt. We who are nurtured to comfort and ease, lack in the vital requisites: will power and independence that they thrive upon. Nature has decreed that it is how the body is tuned. Should they exchange places their skills would carry them well. But alas, who would want them to leave the surroundings they so colourfully fit into? One who knows them is quite sure none would dare endure the pettiness common to the Outside. Yes, they are content with their lot; content with what little gossip and news seeps through the invisible barrier of their land as though from another world apart.

The order of camp upon arrival at the chosen spot is invariably the same. First comes the fire − abetted with a shot of 'kicker juice' when wood is wet; then the teapot−hung over the licking flames; a tarpaulin is slung; and finally, clothes dry while chow is prepared. After this anything goes.

So it was that the duties had been seen to and the supper found its rightful place. I lay nonchalantly on a soft bed of spruce boughs (we were favoured with no moss this night). I watched the mists playing tag around the mountains. Malcolm, still munching supper, broke the prolonged spell of silence. "I would much prefer some dry meat and a pot of tea to all this...I can go farther on that than this stuff!" "Well you certainly do all right with your share," I challenged; but I understood his secret desires for his native trail diet. "We've both gone plenty far on this stuff...what you mean is, you're getting the urge for barbequed caribou ribs," I teased, reliving moments before on the Great Slave arm. "Now you're talking my language," he smiled, licking his lips, from the remote side of the flame. "You know, we're going to make a Sourdough out of you yet," he remarked with hope. There was nothing I relished more than that thought.

Hours of such dreamy conversations sometimes passed as tales of cities and trails mingled with the evening and the dying embers. "I remember one winter...," he would begin, and end with some close call with Death. "And the skyscrapers of New York..." I would return, knowing full well its clear picture could scarce be fathomed by one a part of the North all his life. "Why, only last winter...seventy below...a few fish...dogs buried in blizzard...twelve days...came out of that one too," he said this night as the stars winked down at us in disbelieving fashion. Thus laying in the plateau aware of the proximity of the lakes the voice changed to talk of the morrow. "It's the Little Bell or bust!" we agreed wholeheartedly. Then the topic switched to the past. Mileage was brought up to 200. This retreat slanted toward the two Americans soon to follow the route. "They'd better have a guide," said my swarthy friend. Again I had cause to smile inwardly at my bronzed companion, his determined features profiled in the fading embers. Did I not have with me the keenest bushman in the district?

The last day of July dawned sunny. I awakened from the best sleep in a week. Through the open tent flap I lay contentedly, watching the sun flood the mountains and rocky streams, sparkling as they rush over the surface pebbles, chattering endlessly their favourite vagabond lullabies. The mountains each display all or one colour to extreme, as an invisible hand disrobes them of their fluffy mists: a woman removing her white petticoat. Emerald is the green splashed by the artist in the vales between two purple giants, reminding the traveller of Eire. Still at other times when it is dull and uncertain, the sun shining on the farthest hills, one is taken momentarily to the Highlands of Scotland, where the winds, rain, clouds and sun rush inconsistently in and out of the lochs. Oh, what a fickle country, this! She woos you, leads you on, fascinates you with her teasing dances, flushes your cheeks with her soft, windy fingers, and then disappears, leaving you with only a memory…but an everlasting memory, to be sure.

For days we have been adding to the patches on the canoe bottom. Such is our post−breakfast duty this morning. But search as we may, we can find little sap. "How'd you like to bail with me this afternoon?" joked my likable companion as we pushed the Peterborough into the turbulent stream. "Well as long as I know we're both doing it," I retorted, stepping to my accustomed place in the bow. "Suppose you check the grub?…I've got a sneakin' hunch…," asked Malcolm. "Funny, I have the same feeling that we're soon going to live on your desired diet." "I knew you'd get to see things my way in time," he muttered, seemingly hoping the check revealed little or nothing. The census of the grub box showed a very limited supply. Then with an exclamation befitting the appearance of the Goddesses of Food and Wine, my mate shouted, "Lookit that!…see it up there!…it's a gull!" "Lo and behold, so it is," I sighed. "But wait!…what good is a gull? I'm not that hungry!" I retorted. "Why you Outsider, you greenhorn, you Cheechako, you…don't you see? We're about to reach the lakes soon. We both know what that means." We did. It was the good omen I had waited for the gods to send. There was no doubt in our minds now, or so we thought! Knowing the habits of ducks and geese at this season we felt no anxiety about the food situation. But our worries turned to another misgiving. Our canoe was now obsessed with a steady leak. The hopelessness of continued patching sensed, we resigned ourselves to bailing. With as much water in the canoe as ever, and four sore arms, we made an early halt at 3 p.m. at the site of Bear Creek. We had to have a spot of tea.

All day it had been an endurance test, but the memory of the gull lingered in two minds. "Gee, it just feels as if this tea is going down into my veins," chimed the 'breed, whose face was hidden behind the bowl from which he drank. "You're lucky," I replied, "just think how much longer it's going to take to reach my feet!" This was a natural sendoff, and a slim moment later the fire sizzled as it received the remaining tea. Two figures, having found their numbed feet once more, walked to the water's edge, looked at one another, and without words slid into the chilly depths… It was an endurance test, no less, as the pregnant waters reached their maximum gestation, giving us such labour pains as to force us shoreward to the warmth of a quickly constructed camp. But it was only a false alarm. We were to bear no fruit till our struggles were exhausted… On again, bucking water, eating up mile after mile more mechanically than natural. We were forcing a march, head lowered, back arched, rope taut as we plod…plod…looking down at the waters passing over the multicoloured pebbles…looking up only when the course of the stream changed perforce, to see a stony point diverting the aqueous underfooting.

As the hours pass by without any changes I amuse myself with the idle thoughts that invade the mind, unaffected by the bodily torments. With one's weight against the line, the feet groping over the multi−sized rocks in their own crude rhythm, unseen, one can travel in the past: places galore…faces that pass in close columns…and the plot of civilization which, viewed from this unique 'Inside' position, appears so foolishly obvious. Is it because one is not caught in it? Is it something intentional, built according to the whims of man's mentality…until now we have the many passions, greeds and violences thrown into an airtight scheme so that to relax and breath freely one must go outside of it and look in on the game? Foolish thoughts, these…but, nevertheless, thoughts.

Such is the freedom here that the sudden release from all ties puts one to observing, thinking, weighing and ever−deducing.

Art plays its glorious part too. The beauty, intrinsic, gives leave to none but constructive thoughts. One becomes possessed with the feeling that he could paint an endless canvas (though no brush were held before) hemmed in by the mountains−solid, pyramidical stone creatures that could quite easily be the mouldings of some prehistoric giant in a moment of doodling, but certainly beautiful in Nature's present design. What vapours rise slowly from out of nowhere, form small, borderless masses...gaining...gaining in magnitude, until a mass of conical stone is surrounded by a lei left dangling carelessly about its neck, while each transient mist merges in a farewell communion before becoming clouds, seeking further ventures in distant places. Rain. Drip!...drip!...drip! Will it never cease? Have we not spent more than a week surrounded by water, wagering every day on sunshine that somehow we feel won't appear? Time to quit for the day. We pull our battered lady to the bank of the scurrying Sheep Creek. "Well, we tried," says Malcolm dejectedly. It is seven p.m. We can no longer stand the cold waters racing at us in their impatient anxiety to become part of the lower Rat, the Huskie, the Peel, and finally their deathbed — the Arctic Ocean—where they become commonplace, lost in the mass...no more the lone wolf, free to prowl with the sureness and success of singleness of youth...just so much more solvent dissolved into the elemental mixture called an ocean, the change accompanied only by the addition of salt, as though the wound were not sore enough without this!

Not yet have we camped in such an ideal locale. We face to the south, the exposure presenting us with a variety of mountains, equal in stature and grace to the Rockies without their crowning white nightcaps. However, snow lying in the vales still defies the bending rays of what was a midnight sun fast disappearing behind the revolving globe. Words cannot justly describe the unexpected view in which we have flopped, wet, tired and hungry. The panorama resembles a well−kept golf course in the centre of which a huge green, purple, pyramidal hazard, smaller than its brothers and sisters towering above the amphitheatre, has been set. Running headlong at this display is our river, bubbling, chattering, not unlike Tennyson's *Brook*:...

An Ambrosial Amphitheatre

"I chatter, chatter as I flow
To join the brimming river;
For men may come and men may go,
But I go on forever..."

...almost as though running completely under its green roof; but verily it turns at the base, a water hazard running east from the golf−course edge.

This is our day's reward, a paradise ventured upon, visited only by transient Indians on their winter trail to the hunting grounds and the few adventurous Whites who dare defy the *Trails of '98.*

The appetite for beauty sated we turned to satisfying the one for food. Supper was for the most part eaten in silence and soon passed, the victim of two over−hungry wayfarers in this Land of the Spruce. The local mosquitoes, apparently unfamiliar with the brand of repellant we were using (Beat It), persisted in their two−point landings wherever skin protruded from clothing, eventually meeting death. Some, however, more cunning than their fellow fliers, hit home. In exasperation I chose other methods to defeat them; surrounded by our wealth of beauty they were ignored as we supped our evening tea, the conversation becoming as mellow as the evening. We lapsed into one of those moments of ultra−satisfaction, complete felicity, or incomparable bliss that so many verbose writers have spoken of. By rights words would destroy the setting as the Cheechako squatted, surrounded by pines, mountains, sky, a sparking campfire and a good companion with whom to exchange pleasantries. Nevertheless I shall attempt to give a word picture of the hour at dusk somewhere in the vast North.

It was a funny thing that the trend of the conversation seldom got around to the opposite sex, as is the wont wherever men gather. Having become saturated with this beauty I ask myself: 'Is it perfect? Is it complete?' I think a moment of what more a man could want for comfort. It is here that a woman crosses my mind and departs as hastily. I have come to my conclusion: 'Not even a woman can add to this unusual display of Nature. I am content.' Then, feeling aware of eyes studying me, I glance across the fire. The owner of them asks pleasantly, "What're ya thinking' about...some female, I'll bet?" "Well, to tell you the truth, I was for about one swift second, but I dismissed her quickly. Came to the conclusion this is perfect just as it is." This, indeed was a very bold statement to make, for me who had been in a man's country for four months. "Have you ever been in such a perfect spot?" I furthered. "Been in plenty of places nice as this...but it is kinda pretty, ain't it?" he uttered, dropping his glance to the fire again. I am convinced it must be so, when two males, usually reluctant to mention such things, can agree as we do. "I'm going to turn in," are my Improved Scotch friend's last words for the day. I am left to relax by the fire in solitude, dwelling on the North and its many virtues. As long as the elements keep the 'undesirables' on the Outside, the prospector, trapper, and trader will go gladly about their daily lives unhampered by all the peculiar pettiness elsewhere. One is overcome by the feeling that one never desires to see this country change. As the '98 *Gold Rush* played host to the strongest and robbed the weakest, so will the elements continue to entertain only those who are hardy and willing to admit that <u>they</u> rule and are the real masters of the North.

Ending my reverie I prepare for another night on ambrosial pine boughs. I soon become aware of the teapot boiling gently over the coals, the mosquitoes' monotonous buzzing and the river chattering nocturnal nothings to the deaf mountains...sleep overcame the Cheechako.

August 1 dawned bright, accompanied by a nor'wester. I had fallen asleep! The light of morning now gave us an opportunity to explore the plateau. Malcolm, with his calm accuracy, followed a slim trail through the soft green moss and for the moment I felt as though we were messengers of goodwill, trodding the royal plush carpets to the dais of a foreign king. Stumbling over a 'niggerhead' the illusion quickly disappeared. I came face to face with the moss and some delicious blueberries. It was minutes before I deserted that spot. Finally, we came to the deserted Indian encampment that my friend had so uncannily sensed by the thin, twisting trail through the moss. Noticing nothing exceptional about the locality, I listened to Mister Firth expound on its advantages. "There are often sheep on the mountain range running north," he pointed, "that's why it's called Sheep Creek. When they hunt them the men circle the base of the mountain...climb slowly, quietly, stalking the animals...they can see the slightest movement from their lofty position...flee with much speed at the slightest movement...sometimes purposely attracted while a party ambushes from a higher level...they are delicious eating," finishes the tawny 'breed, his eyes lighting up at the thought. This meat has long since been considered an Indian delicacy, much prized.

"Over there," he points with sudden familiarity, "is our Fish River that we've been looking for. Certain to be plenty of fish there. I've heard of it much, before. You've seen the berries too?" he remarked. Then it dawned on me what he was getting at. Here was plain Indian savvy. When the caribou and sheep fail to run, fish and berries can always be relied upon. What more could an Indian desire? or for that matter anyone travelling as we were?

The Indian settlement, deserted, inanimately tells of much ado at one time. Moulting caribou skins lie where they have been carelessly discarded; rusted stoves and pipes lie strewn about the moss; a broken Edmonton Pure Lard box still gives a hint as to the reliance upon the Outside for some commodities; a single muskrat trap dangles from a tree, while a Swede saw swings from a branch, awaiting the return of life to the neglected campsite.

Our scavenging is complete to the tune of one rusted Yukon stove; five lengths of pipe and a lid for same; a teapot (black as usual); two handfuls of spruce sap and some precious nails embedded in a discarded wood carton. We return to camp eager to patch the scarred canoe and be on our way.

"That's the last of the sap," I ejaculated, scraping the sticky tin. Eyeing the gaping holes, too large for sap, I scratched my head, asking but one question of the busy Malcolm. I had no time for more as he threw me the boards, saying: "remove the nails and I'll show you!" in his usual confident tone. I did and he did. Standing back from our labours a few minutes later, we beheld the abortive spectacle. There, looking like some antique rescued from a junkyard, lay our Lady, reclining proudly like some prima—donna of the beach, waterproof (so we thought) for the time being. Once more the never—get—stuck principle had been applied and we were on our way.

After two hours of rounding willows, foot by foot because of the swollen waters, at times scaling the dirt banks which threaten to slide us into the river as they collapse, we pause (more out of curiosity than anything) to climb a hill. Malcolm, smiling down at me, gives away the secret. 'A smile like that can mean only one thing,' I tell myself. Reaching the top in close pursuit I am awed with the expanding vista. I had told myself correctly. Far to the west lie the mountains responsible for pouring torrents of water in our path. The Rat River is about to straighten out as it ascends its last miles to the Loon Lakes—the flat plateau between two maelstroms of water. In the distance to the east winds the snakelike river, choking, suffocating what growth its slippery body entwines, mercilessly slithering toward the Peel Channel and the final haven of its kind—the Arctic Ocean. To the north are more massive mountains clothed in endless sizes of spruce and ringed with the abominable fog that deters the strengthening rays of the sun.

Amongst an unimaginable abundance of blueberries, low—bush cranberries and a hundred other varieties, we drank greedily of the westward view. Silent minutes passed, the 'Breed content with his thoughts; the Cheechako absorbed in his own. Then, like all feasts, the end came. Fully inebriated and pleasantly sated, we turned. There was no more time to waste on ogling at Nature's latest strip—tease. We were almost to the lakes...and then 'down—waters'!

An hour later our anxiety dies with the numbing waters. Pulling at a spruce grove, the situation is soon remedied with a pot of tea and a hardtack. It is surprising how little it takes to change the mental outlook. But it

Loon Lakes At Last

does, and gritting our teeth, mustering our willpower, we step boldly into the cold waters with dry clothes. It is not until these torturous spurts that I fully realize why an Indian refuses to travel in such weather. It is not even fit for a Halfbreed, leastaways his White companion. This we could not endure for much longer. So at 8:30 reason drew us: we pulled our Peterborough to shore unable, but undaunted in our efforts to reach Fish River. Camp was constructed. We shelter from the persistant rains, determined to put the waterway miles to the rear on the morrow—our eleventh day. Wet feet pattered on our newly acquired tent; but our latest amenity of home life—the Yukon stove—glowed red as it warmed another hearty meal and the interior. We soon forgot the downpour. Spirits were high. We were definitely cast in the optimistic mould. One would think that after a long, cold, six hours in mountain water the hour of eleven would find two weary bodies abed. This was not so as another day neared its end and two hunched figures huddled near glowing coals, sipping piping—hot tea. It was a peculiarity I discovered, that the physical man was beat but the mental fellow became too active for sleep—his imagination probably kindled by food, fire and rest. So midnight invariably found us batting mosquitoes and 'shooting the bull' over our beverage. It was thus this night as we calmly reflected upon the merits of the day.

"We sure cut the mustard today...and in an ordinary season the Little Bell would have felt the pat of our paddles," says my tawny companion, slurping a hot mouthful of beverage. "Guess I was too optimistic and overquoted the distance," I replied with frank admittal of our shortcoming, "but we'll be there tomorrow for sure,"I make up, as though to restore our vital optimism. Immediately the subject switches to a most pleasant memory when Malcolm says: (as though the dancing witches of the fire have hit his inner senses, commanding words) "Wasn't that a treat...the view from the hilltop?" And the day came forward...the plod...plod...plodding of feet...the climb to the hilltop for no better reasons than curiosity and to warm numbed feet...the endless monotony of plopping one foot in front of the other...the welcome, intermittent fires, the delicious blueberry patches—fresh with dew still sparkling on them. The view of the Rat levelling off into a sane stream at last...the emerald laying placidly at its terminus...the key opening our door to the Little

Bell River...thoughts of duck dinners as our grubstake lessened...the triumvirate waterways identified on our crude map, pouring down from a centralized group of mountains: Bear Creek, Sheep Creek and Fish River...the echo of the native 'let's get down to it!' as the shadows of even' lengthened... the final plunge into the stream, swollen with all the youthful floods and minor creeks, seeking their stowaway passage to the Ocean, possessing the zeal of youth, as without restraint they cut their reckless, swollen path, rushing hard at us...and now the warmth, the friendliness, the success; oh, the contentment of it all!

"GOLD!"
Said One
　　　　　　　　　　　　　　　"FOOLS GOLD!"
Said another...A Creek Full Of It!

"Gold!" said the only other voice within miles, next day. "Who are you kiddin'?" returned the other sardonically. Tracking came to a standstill as two Argonauts, eyes lit up, examined the petrified substance found in the creek bed. "Shall we stake it?" asked the other quizzically. "Hell no!" was the answer, "there's a whole Klondike full of it up ahead...stick it in your pocket and let's get going!"

'The Trail of '98 was a reality now...we had 'struck it'. On...on we fumbled with our burden, well ahead of the main stream of prospectors. Our determination to reach the Bell had put us almost in the lead. There was yet Finnigan, MacDonald and Cuthbert to overtake. They were sure a going concern; the Scotsman—the backbone of the crew with his 280 pounds...always said he could beat any man at tracking. Well, we were doing alright for ourselves...we'd show the impetuous Highlander! It was not till later that we realized it was pyrites we had discovered. It was 'fool's gold' alright, and they didn't hesitate to let it be known just who the fools were...was the laugh of the camp for sometime. Anyway, the laugh was worth its weight in gold them days...'

So continued our endurance test of rain, sleet, wind and icy mountain water. Any good mother would call this foolhardiness; but isn't it this that eventually makes sons into men? There were moments when we felt ahead of our time. It was inevitable; but nightime always brought us to ourselves, and laughter to our lips at sight of our grotesque beings and weird imaginings. There were our days of extremes: all in all, they were pleasant extremes.

The sun seemingly answered our complaints as it held its own against a cloudy attack from the nor—west. Fleeting minutes of brightness encourages us at any time. Time brought us winding and twisting to the confluence of the Fish and Rat rivers. An impossible stretch of water lay in our immediate path. There was only one thing to do. We must portage. Imagine our joy when we discovered a well—worn trail across which some thick willows were stretched. People had been here! And not so long ago. We were on the right trail. There was not the slightest doubt about it! It was the keen observance of my friend who had first spotted a fire and castoff tins thereabouts — the labels still intact. From this evidence he was led to the partially concealed portage. So that's why I received a reprimand when I tossed tins in the fire to burn! It was trail language, left instead of a note. The Cheechako was slowly learning the courtesy of the North.

Five hundred yards is not by far a long portage, but it was the first we had encountered that made it difficult. Thankful to those who had come before us, we slid the Peterborough over the logs and willows; backtracking for the precious poles; pulling, heaving our Lady for another fifteen yards; backtracking again…more grunting…curses loosed at the overhanging willows that slapped the face insultingly…minds set on maximum yardage…encouraging words across the bow…the end of the portage…water again. We lay for long minutes on the grass, perspiration running in all directions, chests heaving rapidly. "That's only a start," smiled the 'Breed from his perch atop the overturned canoe. Here was something I would have to get used to, I thought. "I'll not be discouraged," I smiled back. "I was hoping you'd say just that…now hand me some more sap for this goddamn canoe's bottom." he asked congenially. I knew two still thought as one.

Our Lady was indeed in bad need of repair. In fact, as I stole a glance at her unshapely form I felt certain misgivings. Would we reach the Klondike? Would we capsize in some large river and lose everything? 'Foolish thoughts…with that man beside you?' came the inner promptings of Conscience. I glanced toward the native. In his independent manner he had turned the canoe over, melted our collection of hoarded spruce sap and applied his original skill to another repair job. As I had done many times before, I watched with curiosity as my man went about his work. His energies seemed unbounded, and never once did he show signs of laziness, except on wet mornings when it was not fit for an Indian to arise and greet the day. Then he had a right to be lazy! "Gimme a hand and we'll push 'er into the water," said Malcolm, climbing down, his work looking like an artist's palette after a painting.

With a much more watertight canoe and a fixed destination—the Loon Lakes—we resolved to put miles of stream behind in our attempt to reach and ride the calm waters so long deserved. We had yet to beat the many curves, the sudden swift current of the single channel and the waters that welled and overflowed to the willows on both sides. The situation at this point looked impossible. What strategy would my native friend draw from his inexhaustable reserve? "Looks grim," I said, in an encouraging voice spiced slightly with doubt. Then the answer came. It was staring us straight in the face. "The kicker!" smiled the 'Breed moving quickly. "Why save the gas for the good going? Let's get to it first!" he added. I took little convincing as I said: "I'd plumb forgotten about it…guess we haven't hauled it and that obstinate barrel of gas 200 miles for nothing…give 'er the works, Malcolm!" This he did and brought slight moanings from within the Evinrude. Hopes subsided fast. *Cough!* They rose again. *Sput!* Doubt reigned. *Brrr!*…and a sweat—begrimed face spread with its broadest smile yet. Waters churned into froth at the stern of Our Lady. "Now try and stop us!" yelled the native, above the roar, at the onrushing waters. The next few moments were hectic. "Watch the current…keep a hand on a paddle just in case…willows if…if motor stops…" I heard faintly over the motor's strain. I sat ready for anything, in the prow, paddle in hand like a modern Hiawatha on a stormy night. *Crash!* and water slapped starboard. *Splash!* it rose in a spray wetting everything. Ducking, I lurched, the canoe swung left…willows brushed my face, slapped me into madness, and with that latent energy designed for moments of such emergency, I thrashed back. "Grab them…that's it…pull…pull… for God's sake or we're under!" All this is memory now, but the words remain with me—the encouraging shouts of a partner at the right time. Blindly I wrestled with the lashing foe; one hold brought another, till, with a complete surge of energy gathered for a last onslaught, I layed 180 pounds against the willows and the stream. We moved forward…slid into an alcove…and not till I slumped to my seat was I aware of the silence. The engine had cut. Then I had pulled the entire load out of that mess! A feeling of dizzy satisfaction overcame me. "You're learning, Cheechako…you're learning," said the voice from the rear, calmly.

However, we had still not beaten the foe. Waters still seethed as they raced by, spitting tiny globules at us insultingly. It was this that brought action within the Peterborough. "By God, I'll not be beaten by a two—bit strip of water!" cursed the 'Breed. "And furthermore," I added, "I don't like the way it spits!"

In agreement we stirred from our positions of momentary rest. It was then that an overhanging branch flicked Malcolm's hat into the muddy waters. Jumping for shore I raced along beside it. A quick glance and I saw hat, canoe and native—the latter two heading downstream in reverse. Why this sudden decision on his part I could not fathom. Was he mad? No, he seemed to be holding his own, even though backwards, paddling like one in trouble. Miraculously keeping the canoe from tipping or grounding he shouted commands from his precarious position, inaudible to my ears as I floundered, thrashed willows, vainly running the shore−gauntlet. Too late! The hat disappeared beneath the hungry waters. I slipped; in a mass fell to the muddy bank, feet flying in all directions. 'Malcolm, what's of him?' was my first thought upon realization of my own helpless position. Soon on my feet I glanced riverward. There in midstream, clinging desperately to an overhanging limb, his shirt pulled out of pants and his feet toe−holding the canoe, clung Malcolm. It was so funny it rated a laugh. "Ho! ho!...why all the fuss?" I chortled, "it's only a hat." Seeing little humour he retorted: "It's not the hat...bad news travels fast in this country!...someone might think I have drowned should they find the hat..." he spoke, breathlessly. "Anyway, get me outa this damn position...'taint funny!"

So another very important lesson came to light. As we continued, overcoming the pestilent river at this point, Malcolm still showed signs of deep concern. He was still unsettled about the hat. It was a serious matter, I decided.

Eight−thirty found us just short of our goal. "Oh well, not our fault this time," I reflected. Nine hours labour was but a memory. Camp lay on the approach to the lakes: a castellated, richly−coloured mountain, our silent companion guarding the verdant valley within. The Divide separated us from the Little Bell River. Tomorrow we would be within cursing distance of it. "We're a cinch to win," I said to my silent companion. He just looked blankly, as though the phrase was foreign; the hat was what still bothered him.

Here it was that I decided on a food census. I had suspicions of the situation becoming acute. Arraying the odd assortment of packages beside the fire I checked them aloud to inform my partner of our situation. Doubts met confirmation. The larder included 1/4 pint rolled oats, 1 handful macaroni, 3 tins fruit, 1 tin vegetables (as near as the labeless tins could be judged), 1 lb. tea, too many coffee beans, half a dozen tablespoons cocoa, 1/2 tin Klim, one tin Reindeer brand milk, salt, a little sugar and some curry powder which, thrown in with the macaroni, would do wonders making the least hottest of Mexican dishes in a favourable way. Such was our culinary state of affairs.

"Prepare yourself for the last good feast till Old Crow," I suggested to Malcolm, mixing the cocoa, the smell of macaroni and curry rising from the blackened teapail. "I won't be sorry when it's gone...I could sure go for a caribou about now, real trail−grub that stuff," he piped, a twinkle in his eye. He was unperturbed. I would be the same, I promised myself. 'After all he's been worse off than this and is still ticking,' I convinced myself. We lived almost as one; we would starve as one!

Heat from the scavenged stove permeated the dampness and found its way into the opened sleeping bag. We had finished our last full repast. I had sprinkled crumbs on the flames as a libation to the Goddess of Food; surely she would spill food from her Horn of Plenty in the path of the Argonauts? The click of dome fasteners closed the warm robe around the Cheechako. I felt indifference towards our grub situation which worry would not replenish. So we'll starve, and have fun doing it! I challenged silently...and night enfolded the ninth camp−245 miles from Aklavik.

Sunday came 'round again, this time sunny. We awoke under the lee of our castle mountain, glistening copper in the morning sunlight. "There's the old avalanche they used to talk of," pointed the native. At the base of the mountain the landmark looked not unlike a wide, white canoe pulled carelessly on a rocky shore. It was pleasant 'breaking camp' in the sunlight for a change. With a rhythm we made ready to dunk the canoe and ourselves once more. Then tragedy played its hand. We were vulnerable. Somehow we had aroused the wrath of Zeus. The heavens rumbled. What had we done? Then I remembered not having poured tea on the flames with the other libation. I said nothing to the 'Breed. The wrath of heaven was enough for now! Rain fell from overhead; it blew from the sides; seeped from below. Damnable rain drowned us and our aspirations. With saturated optimism two rugged forms pulled away from camp. The only inducement lay in the west. Broad blue mountains challenged us to scale them. Consciously we were drawn by these loadstones, rain or no rain. We were too proud not to accept their challenge.

Weary of tugging, groaning and pulling our twenty—two footer we resort plutocratically to the 'kicker'. Its noise, not heard for many days, becomes beautiful marine music. Unfailing, it brings us to noon and the two remaining channels. Unanimously we choose the port route. Ours is a free waterway to the lakes. More twig pulling, pushing and paddling gives us our final reward: exultation equal to that which must have been Balboa's, as he gazed over the blue Pacific from "high on a point in Darien". We emerge on to the Loon Lakes.

"The closest I've ever been to God"...
August 1947
Looking over the Loon Lakes to McDougall Pass—Richardson Mountains: 'Height of Land' between the Northwest Territories and Yukon Territory...on the Trail of '98

CHAPTER TWENTY ONE

"HEAVEN CAN WAIT"

We were literally poured into this Utopia. Standing there, spellbound, overlooking the panorama, I felt closer to God than I had ever been. I had found my Utopia. I was at peace with the world. Looking into the west one could see the MacDougall Pass lording it over the galaxy of lakes in the foreground; in every other direction mountains clothed in evergreens and long grass rose from the valley, surrounding this little bit of heaven as though it were a mountain village of Tibet, isolated from the world and not wanting the presence of infidels or outsiders. Berries and flowers in extravagant profusion coloured the hillsides; ducks coming and going in an endless procession of V's left their ever–widening circles spreading over the mirrored lakes. A glorious silence hung over the variegated amphitheatre as did a multitude of fluffy white clouds, descending to merge with the equally–white, snow crowns on the mountains. Two white swans playing wantonly on the waters below brought the scene to perfection.

"The Closest I've Ever Been To God"

There is no greater tribute man can pay than silence: awed, I paid homage to the Powers–That–Be, as a cold ecstatic tingling crept up my spine and burst into a multitude of sensations in my brain. All things truly worth enjoying are comparatively shortlived. My spell was broken by a shout from my companion. "Come out of it. . . we gotta be on our way!" Saturated with satisfaction we descended to those glorious depths below, not unlike kings about to survey closely our newly discovered realm. . .

Vigorously paddling across the first body of water we are surrounded by scenery which possesses the grandeur, variety and colour of the most regal of robed ranges. They are crowned with faint patches of snow, as yet unmelted by the sun. It is our second paradise along the Rat River; the first (if you remember) at Bear Creek some miles back.

**A Castellated Mountain
Guarded Entrance to the Lakes**

Here it is concluded that a man could live in close communion with Nature, forgetting an Outside ever existed, surrounded by caribou, mountain sheep and goats, ducks, geese, beaver, fish, and an overabundance of wild berries and valleys of silence. 'Maybe', I think, 'in the Great Age that scientists plan ahead for us, individuals will have seasonal fruit–farms buried within these solitudes of the North, reached only by helicopter?' But as she is beautiful in her virginity–having had no more than a few thousand eyes glance at her pure form, unraped by the crushing weight of a modern world—so she will remain for many a day.

Clouds came and went, hovering, dallying, changing from rain to billowy cumulus as often as a woman changes her apparel, and with the same tantalizing grace. High above, to the North, a castellated mountain guarded the entrance to the lakes, while to the east a rampart constructed in Nature's perfection and resembling somewhat the man—made wall of China, twisted and turned in a similar manner till it reached its summit. As we twisted and turned likewise along the confusing Rat below, these pallisades changed position, each view as imaginarily impregnable as the last.

**Malcolm
Contemplating our Next Move**

**Goddesses of Beauty and Hunger
Were Both Appeased**

We paddle into the second lake and are soon swallowed up by a third. This is too much luck all at once but we accept it avidly. "Looks like we won't have to take any portages," says my friend, smiling broadly as though having fooled the Devil himself; ". . . it's one time when we can thank the rains. " Then and there I recall all my previous curses at heavenly dew. Though not completely forgetting them, I say a silent something in thanks that Nature can be so remunerative at such a critical time. Indeed, she was soon to repay us further for that unspoken thought in the form of food.

Feeling quite familiar with the lakes from previous talk in Indian circles, my man Firth says: "It is probably the first time in years that the first portages have been omitted. " "It was all on account of my libation," I answered. "Your what?" he quizzed. "Well Lady Luck has saved us much energy this day," I substituted for an explanation. He smiled his 'one—and—only' in perfect understanding. Then we struck a cul—de—sac. "Why don't you keep your mouth shut!" cursed the native, paddling in reverse. I reached for the other paddle. . .

It was our headlong desire to ride Loon Lake that made us momentarily neglectful. After much seeking along shore, 'mongst willows and weeds, an inconspicuous channel, overgrown completely with foliage, quietly informed us we could forget all thought of portages. It was a wonderful discard; but sooner or later we were bound to be caught shorthanded. However, this thought did not much bother us. Hadn't we reached the lakes? Were they not beautifully still but for the ripple of our paddles and the ever— widening circles left in the wake of a fleeting duck? We were in Paradise and we knew it. The appreciation again was silent.

We were still on the third of the lakes. "Don't move an inch!"commanded the native, squatting below the rim of the canoe as he reached for the rifle. I sat like a bronze statue at this latest and oddest behest, hardly daring to breath lest I be blamed for disrupting some well—laid scheme of this impetuous man. "Now duck quick and have a look,"said Malcolm, releasing me from my acquired moulding. "Good gosh!"I exclaimed, "they're beautiful! But what're they doing here?" I added. There, near the far shore floated two large swans, their majestic appearance enhanced by each movement of their graceful, long necks. We were not alone in our kingship over the lakes. Then I remembered my friend, realizing his thought at once. "But they're too beautiful. . . I could never do it," I uttered in answer to his questioning looks. "You remember our last meals, don't you?" asked the Breed, making ready to depart as we worked our way gently toward another part of the shore. How could I forget? Why, even now my stomach was complaining in undertones. We had finished the last of the oatmeal with a few grains of cocoa for breakfast and the macaroni mixed with dirt for dinner.

"Don't make a movement!" said my friend again as he jumped for shore. "I don't know about you, but I'm damn hungry," were his last words as he crouched low and made off along the shore. While I waited for the inevitable report of a rifle a host of ideas ran through my mind. I came to a sober conclusion: there is no law in the Northland when one is hungry. This is one time when Beauty must be sacrificed for hunger. I ceased my battle with Conscience. We would appease two Goddesses and win favour in their eyes with a small libation if luck was with us. Yes that was it; the Goddesses of Beauty and Hunger would both be appeased. Bang! came the echo across the lake a half hour later. In all that time I had seen my companion only once as he darted past an opening. I had every confidence in him. Gazing lakewards I realized I was with the best hunter in these parts, as the natives at Aklavik had said. Another report and a splash of water. We were the kings of the watery realm. For the first time in my life I was to dine like a king. It was not a time for sentiment.

At seven that evening our water journey ended. It was not Mother Nature that had decided this issue. It was a beaver dam. We had not bargained for animal interference; but there it was: as strong a piece of beaver architecture as two men in a canoe could face. We faced it in admiration rather than with curses. They remained dormant. We had held the hand of Luck all day. Mortal effort proving too little, we failed to pull the canoe over the top of the six−foot dam behind which lay a threatening amount of water that, if released, would play havoc with us in a serious manner. So we concluded the final round to the craftiest little woodcutters of the North.

There are repasts that hang vividly in the halls of Memory of us all. Receiving that place of honour in my own mind was the evening meal this night as the pot boiled, the frying pan sizzled and two over−hungry adventurers, excited by the whiffs of cooling meat escaping into the night air, tore huge chunks of tender meat from bone, uninterrupted. We dined on the undisputed 'meat of meats' that perhaps even few kings have had the extreme pleasure of eating. Supper over, we set about pulling the canoe over the 300−yard portage, ready for the waters of the next lake on the morrow. Then we relaxed before the leaping flames of an open campfire, the taste of supper lingering on palates. "That was sure delicious, wasn't it?" I commented casually, at the same time picking a piece of the fowl from between two teeth with a twig. "Yeah," came the satisfied reply; "it's better'n all your tinned food. " "I agree with you this time," I ended. Both slipped into individual worlds of the mind, I reliving the trip as we vacated the treacherous Rat River for the smooth bosom of the placid lakes.

Thump! came a hollow sound from the nearby creek. By now, familiar with the antics of beaver, I knew one was slapping his tail in inimitable fashion. "Bet he's smelled our smoke and decided on a little play," said the tawny Malcolm, glancing up at the sound. This, I learned, is a habit with the sporting beavers. So we chased him down the creek in vain, the willows cracking and snapping, informing him of our whereabouts. As we burst into the open Mister Beaver swam lakewards, leaving only a widening V in his wake, plunked his tail once more and disappeared into the depths. The joke had been on us!

"Ever heard of beaver jealousy?" asks Malcolm examining the neat, solidly constructed beaver−home on the shore. "New to me," I answered, noting the reinforcing mud paddies placed with dexterity over the domed willows felled by a

Beaver Damned!

145

single bite. "I'll bet he and his family have the run of the entire creek," adds the native. "They're like that," he continued, "and watch out for'em in early spring. . . they're very wild after hibernation. " "Well, if they can bite through bone like they do those willows I'll leave my beaver visiting till this time of the year. "

Back at the campfire I again enter the realm of thought, recalling vividly the many events of the day. . . the old portage marks on the banks of the lakes; places where the foliage was broken and a narrow path showed where less fortunate seekers had been forced ashore by low waters. . . the occasional tin can, bark cut or dried pole, marking the trail as we neared our present campsite. . . then the obvious canoe marks where the keels had worn a hollow in the moss, and as we passed over them on this, our first portage, the sundry thoughts that entered the mind. *How many groans were uttered? How many raised eyes to absorb the rare mountain majesty so generously displayed before the observer of Nature—the Architect? The Trail of '98 becomes the Trail of '47.* My companion pokes the embers which spark and flee from the prodding stick into the darkened atmosphere. Once more with the ripple of water as our Northern Lullaby, the dying embers as our warmth, and beauteous thought of travel downstream on the Little Bell sometime on the morrow, we turn in; still the two optimists who are ever anxious to see what lies beyond the rim of the next mountain.

First Portage Between the Loon Lakes   **'Tump Lining' in the Wake of the '98er's**

With August 4th came sunshine to brighten the day and our hopes. Breakfast consisted of fowl cooked the night before. By the look of things we were going to be eating swan for the next few days. I hoped with each meal that it would not become a commonplace. We were soon tackling the last of our packs over the portage in relays, slowly bridging the gap between us and our waiting Peterborough. Then the awaited moment came. Water slapped gently the bottom of our Lady as we paddled across the fifth lake. We landed at a berry patch. Our swift passage was slowed to a stop. It was a full twenty minutes before we tore ourselves away from those blueberries, cranberries and (most cherished of all) salmon berries, both well on the way towards a good 'bellyache. ' "But it would be worth it," was the mutual assertion. After some circumnavigation it was discovered that here lay the Long or Mile Portage marked on our crude map. Now our pleasant course of the lakes was about to be paid for in full.

There is one phase of canoeing that no traveller likes— portaging! Having had our first small taste of it we both knew what was coming. Already I was dividing 300 yards (our first portage) into a mile. I wearied at the very division of it. It was no attitude to take at this stage of the game, so I gritted my teeth and, looking with assent at my companion, lurched forward against the pole tied to the bow of the canoe. It was first suggested by Malcolm that we slide the Peterborough on logs in the conventional manner, stopping when the pattern was run and relaying the staves in front for another quick dash. This, however, became too interruptive just at a time when our will had been set for a longer dash; and, of course, the return for the poles wasted valuable time. "Let's just slide it on the moss," said my friend. It wasn't hard to say 'yes'. So we continued. But again the trek became difficult. Both, being of different sizes, the leverage became impossible for the one so tall. to this was added the ups and downs of the 'nigger—heads' which more than often resulted in stumbling and falling. Tempers began to rise; patience grew thin; the sweat continued to pour down our faces, along the neck and, in a very irritating trickle, found its way to the lower regions of the body. It took a 'nigger—head' to change our minds. Both falling into a hidden hole we became furious, unhooked the pole and without a word (as though none found could be bad enough to express the general feeling) we grasped the foremost spar, raised the bow and continued. The lake still looked a mile away. Refusing to be chided by the sight of water I lowered my head, gritted my teeth once again and told my will that we would get there or break it.

Strange is the co—ordination and natural co—operation that is instinctively built up between people who have thrown their lots together for a similar purpose. Ours was a single purpose. With each spurt of exertion came fatigue. But it came together in a look of approval, as we lowered the canoe to the ground to catch another breath of air. Tension was momentarily relieved in straining muscles. "Once more!" was all I heard. That was enough. Grasping the nose of our heavy object, we lowered our heads for the final dash to the marshy foreshore of the lake. "Only twenty feet more," I whimpered. "Don't drop it now!" reiterated my friend. Ten feet soon became five... four... three... two... and with a last lunge we slapped the Peterborough down on the wet ground. We had reached Loon Lake. Nothing else mattered for the moment.

The Dreaded Long or Mile Portage

It was fully five minutes before a word was spoken. Each, flopped in his most lackadaisical position; lay motionless but for the heaving of a breast and the wheezing of air past dried saliva. "Look at the blueberries!" cried out my friend. The two prostrate forms found life. It was, indeed, a prize patch. And I say <u>was</u> with emphasis, for we left few berries in our quick rape, extracting the blue from the comingled colour scheme of the foreshore. Our lust for berries soon petered out as the thoughts of the remaining packs pervaded two minds. We would have to work fast if the Little Bell were to be reached by nightfall. So we made off, across the longest portage I ever hope to take with a 22— foot Peterborough canoe, to procure the remainder of our gear. Breakfast had been slight. We began to weaken under the tedium of fumbling over 'niggerheads', sliding on wet grass and the heavy, awkward loads. It was two hours and five trips later that we sat sown beside our entire load, the largest portion of the Rat Portage behind us. It was hard work. I swore then and there that if I ever had to portage another mile on a bellyful of blueberries and tea, I would "lay me doon and dee!" My will, miraculously, had withstood the test. But we were not through yet!

Precarious 'Kicker' Gas for the Last Lake Dash   **Looking Back from the Loon Lakes**

For all honest ardour there is an equal compensation —be it only self—satisfaction. Our labours were not in vain. Not only did we have the pleasure of skimming over Loon Lake, but we made an equally satisfying discovery on the far shore. We fell into another berry patch. This time it was the Salmon berries! Whoever has travelled in the North must surely, at some time or another, have had the extreme pleasure of eating these berries. They are, without a doubt, the queen of the berry family —orange or deep pink when ripe, standing above the ground on a three—inch stem. In comparison they most resemble the raspberry; when coated with mountain dew stand on a pedestal of their own when it comes to taste. It was in such a patch we fouled. With lust we picked and ate, always looking ahead for a riper one than the berry we were picking. 'This cannot go on or you'll never cross the Yukon,' piped the voice of Adventure. 'But it's Utopia, so why not enjoy it?' I answered back. This retort did no good. It was a belly—ache that finally pushed me on. I was not alone in this either. It was inevitable and we knew it. But this was one time when it was really worth it. Heeding not the ache below, each mustered his strength for the final Short Portage. Afternoon had advanced. We must hurry. I recall once hearing the definition of a boy as: 'a stomach completely surrounded by curiousity!' By now we were certainly aware of our stomach aches; curiousity did overcome both. We ran across the moss and 'niggerheads' dotted with berries, and came to an abrupt halt at the sound of water. It was a little stream trickling its way westward. We must be close? A few more paces and we smiled with the assurance of victors. We had reached Little Bell River. We were in the Yukon!

There is nothing like one success to encourage another. Returning, we portaged the canoe and packs in another five trips. Our sudden aspirations were soon dampened with the weight of the packs. The will was there but the body was not responding with ease. I knew nothing would discourage my native companion who has openly gloated at the sight of water heading downstream. I could not weaken now. With this in mind I withstood the throbbing blood pounding on temples, the sweat rolling down cheeks like blood gushing from a burst vessel. It seemed to say, as it pounded on the brain with dull monotony — the will bucking it with brick—wall resistance: "Gotta go. . . Gotta get there. . . Gotta make it. . . " A sickness came over me and I wished I were dead. My half—breed friend said nothing; but as I stole an encouraging glance accompanied by a forced smile, I saw he too was feeling the weight of the day. He must have been thinking as I; but natives can uncannily conceal their feelings, and it was this that most made me admire my silent friend. He never complained, but forged on and on as though someone had set him on a course and he was forever destined to roll onward until some greater force blocked the charted journey. He was the personification of inertia. I could never imagine him settling down until his motor, too weak to force the body on, broke down. I shall always think of him this way, as he was that day,

'Pot o' Gold' on the Tripod

leaning his small frame against the other side of the canoe. As I returned my glance to the irregular path of niggerheads I knew he felt the same as I. Neither was going to let the other down! Just when the load seemed impossible the sound of an aircraft greeted our ears. We were not alone. There is gripping aloneness that one feels in the hinterlands; this we had already felt after thirteen days in company with only signs along the trail to remind us of others who remained only in imagination. Now an aircraft. . . and people! But alas, it landed, paused a short while, and with gusto roared along the lake, disturbing its mirrorlike surface, scattering ducks and water as it passed overhead. . .

We waved in recognition to the yellow Norseman from Aklavik. Has it been sent to spot us because of the rains which would cause a delay and naturally shorten our food supply? A tiny head looked down from the cockpit. The bird circled, gunned its motor and soon became a speck dotting the western sky over the Little Bell river, high above the *Trail of '98*. . . and silence crept back into the valley.

Crossing the final portage a tripod came into view. Wherever there is a tripod one can be sure humans have been in the vicinity. I had been informed by my keen−sighted companion many times along the way that either Indians or Whites had made and deserted camps where stood similar markings. It is a habit with the natives to prop into teepee form their discarded tent poles or tarp supports. These abandoned signs I learned to appreciate when nothing but Nature overgrew the entire surroundings, leading me to believe that no one had ever passed this way. Approaching this obvious structure I noticed it differed slightly form others. From its peak hung a tobacco tin suspended by a thick cord. We were due for a pleasant surprise. Opening the tin we discover names, addresses and messages of adventurers−not unlike ourselves−who had beaten the Rat Portage. There are no more than a dozen names in all from every part of the world. Here is a humorous touch. . . there a complaint. . . now a word of encouragement asking the finder to write to the above address. We have discovered the Pot O' Gold, although no rainbow is in sight. Nothing could have been more encouraging at this point in the journey, when the sweat poured over our weary bodies and the down waters were so near, yet so far!

As a small tribute, if nothing more, I would like to take the liberty of listing some of those names more legible than others of these souls who dared challenge th Rat River and its accursed portage. And to those two women who pitted their strength against this ornery part of the Canadian North I say: "God Bless You! You enhance the name of Woman. " To all of you who may be carelessly thumbing your way through these pages you shall see that you are not forgotten.

AUGUST 24/1946

W. D. SWEET
EVERGREEN POINT
BELLVIEW, WASH.
(COMMERCIAL PHOTOGRAPHER)

KEN CONIBEAR
10744−122nd ST.,
EDMONTON, ALBERTA
. . . . a fellow author.

and a third member of this party:

JACK HAVENS 12508−GREENWOOD AVE. ,
SEATTLE 33, WASHINGTON.

Others are: F. HAMILTON and N. REIDFORD
printed on an Imperial Oil tag fastened to a white bag.

DR. SLEEN−1939−
HAARLUIN, HOLLAND.

GERALD ANDERSON
WISCONSIN

ROBERT TYSON
GREENVILLE,
NORTH CAROLINA

At 6:30 the last pack was dropped. We sprawled out on the sloping bank of the Little Bell. Looking back, the overcome lakes lay quietly awaiting the next adventurer to challange them. We had come! seen! and conquered!

Malcolm in his eagerness soon began preparing the canoe with sap whilst I set to 'whipping up' what had to be a scanty supper. A cup of coffee and a tin of fruit was the outcome. Once more stock was taken of the grub situation. It turned out to be the remains of a swan, two tins of fruit, some tea and coffee. We were still three or four days from the settlement of Old Crow! It had been my suggestion to pitch camp for the night, beaten as we were, continue in the morning when the scenery would be appreciated. I knew my friend's answer before it found words. "I've waited so long for this moment that I'm not going to stop now!" he ejaculated with finality. there was no sawing the canoe in half in the manner of two disgruntled '98ers who no longer saw eye−to−eye. We didn't have a saw! The journey had been too pleasant and the day's progress too good to have anything come between us. As much as the Cheechako wished sleep he piled into the prow of the canoe. It nosed out on the placid stream, its movement hardly discernible. . . yet there was movement. . . we were headed downstream. The Little Bell had finally claimed us on our thirteenth day. There was no stopping now. As we had entered this Utopia, so did we make our Exodus−poured from the summit along the smooth down waters of the Little Bell. The Yukon was waiting with outspread arms. . . we were coming!

A Farewell Look At the Rat River Portage

A Little (Bell) Stream
Trickling it's Way Westward

CHAPTER TWENTY TWO

THE YUKON AT LAST!

At seven p.m. the waters scarcely move. At eight we speed along, the river gaining momentum, width and depth. The scenery is colossal and grand, no doubt aided in its beauty by the fact that the waters are running with us. Suddenly the river parts. . . a roar greets our ears. . . we are dumbfounded. Which channel shall we take? Leaving the decision to my pal I watch the swirling waters carry us straight ahead, retarding our speed very slightly with a distended oar. "Paddle back fast!. . . make for that stream!" cries my companion as we edge over towards the roar, the channel blocked by a huge tree. "The beavers have been at work again. . . damn them!" yells the native, throwing his entire frame over the edge of the canoe as he forces the water into submission with his paddle. A moment later we pass through and over the beaver bulwark. They have changed the entire course of the stream, creating three channels. In the ensuing silence I reflect: had it not been for the acumen of my Improved Scotch friend we should be miles down the wrong stream. We have won the first round; there is bound to be more.

> "Row, brothers, row,
> The stream runs fast;
> The rapids are near.
> And the daylight's past. . . "

sang the evening breeze, the faint sound of rushing water informing us that rapids were the next obstacle to be met. As the third hour slipped by, the stream had increased to about six or seven miles per hour. A sharp eye had to be kept for jagged rocks. These, we knew, would introduce the rapids. As the breeze foretold, rapids came closer. Rocks piercing the stream reared their slimy heads in the half light of late evening. "This is it!" yelled my half−breed Hiawatha, using his paddle for a rudder. Dumbly I looked at him, overcome by a premonition. "This'll be it, all right," I muttered, sensing disaster. True enough, it was here that we failed. With complete fatigue setting in I could do no more than keep my eyes open. And then calamity came. . . .

Like a crazed gondolier, Malcolm paddled, first on one side, then to the other. "Paddle hard!. . . other side!. . . watch that rock!" came the volley of orders from the rear, to deaf ears. My mind refused to act; the paddle became a piece of wood as I dipped it. "Watch out!" was the last I heard from the native. The impact was followed by a sickening thud! which told us both a rock had bitten into the side of the canoe. By now I didn't care how we stopped. This proved as good a way as any! At ten−thirty, in the dusk of a chilly August evening, two badly beaten adventurers pulled their equally beaten Peterborough through an opening on the bank, to shore. A tin of plums and a pot of coffee was the ration eaten in silence, It was an unusual meal, unspiced with optimistic conversation and good humour. Two figures squatted beside the fire on the high mossy bank overlooking the Bell River. One didn't even bother to reflect on the progress of the day, as was habitual; the other didn't smile largely from across the flames. It had been the hardest day on the Cheechako in all his life. It had been the duo's most successful day; but that did not matter. They were just too proud to admit they were beaten. Sleep was the only thing that would renew crushed spirits. I didn't wait for the embers to die down. Stretched full length in the sleeping bag, atop some spruce boughs and moss, I groaned with weary satisfaction. Every muscle ached and in anger sent its pain through my body. "Thank god we made it!" I mumbled, and the face in the moon peeped through the drifting clouds and seemed to smile. I distinctly heard it say: 'Sleep, my sons−tomorrow shall be brighter'; and the murmuring voices of the Little Bell sang their nocturnal symphony, lulling us into that deserved Land of Sleep.

Ten miles from the lakes and 275 miles from Aklavik we awoke to the warming sunshine of August 5th. A gentle breeze diluted the heat as it played in the pine and spruce branches on the

The Big Bell River   Faster Still and Wider

August Reflections on the Bell   Last of the Richardson Mountains

Our Faithful Peterborough Prodding Pine Points   Geese to Port Heading South

banks of the Bell. With a scant breakfast tucked away we set about repairing the badly battered canoe. The very sight of our overturned Lady brought to mind the old proverb 'haste brings waste'. Ours certainly caused a grave expenditure of time. We counted the precious nails pulled from the occasional broken box we had garnered along the trails. Spreading them well out for a maximum space and maximum strength, we hammered the boards over the battered underside of the Peterborough, carving them off to a crude smoothness. We settled on to the waters once more. At noon we ran the gamut of rapids. Shortly after, with startling suddenness, they tossed us on to the heaving bosom of the Big Bell River.

It was twelve−thirty when our eyes gladdened at the sight of this huge, smooth mass of water surrounded by glorious, towering mountains. Our new river flowed with a determination, swollen so that it washed high on both banks. As we drifted in relaxation the scenery grew even more spectacular. Saturating myself with the vista I concluded that here is where "God planted the beauty that," as Dan the unappreciative trapper had so bluntly stated, "he missed planting in Yellowknife. " All else was momentarily forgotten. According to dead−reckoning, and the word of the native who drew our crude map, we are fifty miles from LaPierre House and about 100 miles from Old Crow. We are as happy a duo as e'er floated with the current of a swift river in a canoe. Some distance. . . and the highest mountains are coated from the neck up with a scarf of frost. To look at them and feel the cool August breeze cutting through one, the mind automatically turns to woollen sweaters, and the skin to goose pimples. However, this wintry spell was not to last as the fickle afternoon gave way to intermittent periods of extreme warmth. Our canoe still leaks, despite the cloth, ambroid, sap, tin and the final acme of crudity−the slabs of wood that we added this morning. Bailing every now and then with the teapails, we refuse to let such a small thing as this disturb our serenity.

All day we are entertained by the creatures of Nature: ducks with their families, thinking we are pursuing them, panic−the mother or both parents fleeing downstream; the bewildered young, cutting their fastest learned pace, splashing the river into foam as they make their immature getaway. Overtaking them, they resort to a dodge into the shelter of the bank, the mother returning, thinking, I suppose, that she has successfully decoyed us. Playful beaver spank their tails on the water with a profound *'plunk!'* seemingly to attract our attention; but before we can get within range, they dive into the depths, resurfacing yards away, a moment later, to chide us with another *'plunk!'.* Muskrats scurry along the bank of small adjoining creeks. Eagle and crow make their heavenly appearance at times. Fish, unused to a canoe over them, pass by nonchalantly in complete indifference to our presence. A rabbit cracks its way through dry underbrush along the riverbank. The geese continue to skim a dozen feet over the canoe, disappearing beyond the horizon in decreasing V's behind their navigator.

The primeval forest could not have been any more representative than this of wild life; and the vegetation could have been in no greater abundance than in these northern backwoods. An inverse deficiency of humans exist in this hinterland; the only signs suggesting their presence at one time− an odd axe cut or a burned and charred log−remains of a fire that once leaped high and gave off vital heat.

"There's a saw−cut on the bank!" shouted Malcolm, as eager as I to clarify our position. *All thoughts hurriedly turned back fifty years to the days of 1898. . . the stream and banks were lined with makeshift craft−some broken, some being repaired, others abandoned; and still others beached in the glow from the fires of evening that leaped towards the black heavens, heralding the end of another long day; days when the cry was: 'gold! gold!. . . gold! at any cost. Get it or die tryin'. Kill to get it. Cheat for it. Gamble for it. . . but get it! and get it quick! Then if you're a damn fool, spend it as fast on liquor, dames and dance. Easy come, easy go! Yes, that's the old tune; whistle it while you can Jim, cause ya can't take it with you. So remember that! When you're old and grizzled and tired, and ya ain't got no gold or friends, then you'll say: 'What a damn fool I've been! But god damn it, it was worth it!−them's good times. And ain't I got the wrinkles to show for it? Well, I'll go to Hell or Heaven Sourdough, by God! They can do what they like after that. Who knows−maybe they'll give me a gold harp to play. Ho! Ho!−and always gold, gold, gold. . . . '*

. . . And the echoes trailed off into the night, back to their half−century−old catacombs; back into the musty volume of the past where the bones of the dead lie scattered amongst the gold that has long since lost its lustre, guarded from the sparkling fingers of the sun by opaque cobwebs, spun from mound to mound of conical coin, coated with the grey dust of the years, awaiting the life− breath of youth to blow away the burden and show it to the world again.

"We'll blow away the dust; we'll expose the gilded substance. We're the youth that can do it". "We can do what?" queried the 'breed, my thoughts having found sound. "I'd be happy if we could just eat a square meal." "Oh, I was just thinking we could pull ashore anytime now that we've reached the big water. My stomach's beginning to hate me," I invented quickly in an endeavor to cover up my day−dreaming. With an unconvincing look Malcolm grabbed his paddle, dug deep into the murky Bell; the prow pointed its way towards shore.

It was five−thirty when thoughts had turned from the surroundings to those of hunger. All day hunger had been ever− present, but in varying degrees. Now it gripped us with a certainty. Our supplies were about exhausted; each meal a mere excuse−a substitute for the real thing. It did not matter what we ate as long as something kept the acids busy. They must be entertained at all costs. We pulled into shore; built a fire. Soon tea was boiling and a grayling, rolled in clay, steamed gently as the heat penetrated the wet earth. "Let's get into it. . . can't wait all day," complained my companion, great expectation showing on his face and a gleam in his eye. I extracted the burned clay from the hot coals, broke it open, and there exposed in all rudeness lay our supper. It presented a much different spectacle than it had some hours before, darting past the canoe, its lithe form silhouetted against the aquamarine waters of the Bell. "Let's pile into the canoe. . . we can eat as we float," suggested my anxious pal, ever intent on speed. Agreeing, I snuffed out the fire, pushed the large craft back into the Bell and, freeing my feet of mud, climbed within. We were a floating dining room.

"What will you have, Malcolm?" I asked, holding an imaginary menu up for inspection. "Oh, the usual," he exclaimed, feigning disinterest. So I passed him a cup of tea. "Now gimme that fish, quick!" he demanded suddenly. So I broke it in two as near the centre as a small grayling can be divided without animosity. In two large mouthfuls the minute creature disappeared. It was the tastiest fish I had ever eaten. "It wasn't much, but it certainly was an enjoyable change from the fowl we've been eating the past few days," I said, licking my lips of the last tastiest bits. A smile lit up the face in the other end of the canoe. Words were unnecessary. Then suddenly I remembered something. "Say, you remember that last food census I took? I'd swear there was a tin of something left!" "God only knows what you've got in that bag," he added as I groped for the bottom of the haversack. "Got it! By gimminy I've found us a treat," I gasped, holding high the labeless tin. "Well open it quick, it may be fruit!" said my agitated friend, as anxious as I to see the contents. I think I said a very short prayer as I punched it with the hatchet, rounded the lip with the hunting knife. . . from the Horn of Plenty spilled pale halves of pears. "Fruit!. . . it's fruit. . . and pears at that," I shouted joyously. Four bulging eyes followed the contents from that tin. . . and an echo came back from the hill. . . "pears at that!".

The current gradually weakens with the increased body of the stream. The cold of an autumn evening sets in. The time has come for the real treat. Unanimously we agree to try the kicker. I watch helplessly as Malcolm vainly tries turning the impossible engine. (I say impossible because they <u>are</u>. If there has ever been anything more exasperating created by man than an outboard motor, I would not care to know of it!) A numbing chill sets in upon us. *Sput!* coughs the engine. "God damn!" curses the Breed. *Sput! Sput!* coughs the engine again. "Why you dirty. . . " curses the native again, cutting himself short to rewind the starter cord. The canoe swings idly amidstream. Groping for the pliers, my native friend, maddening at the uncooperative engine, sets to work undoing things. While in this mood I never interrupt. It's never wise where 'kickers' are concerned. Chilly minutes pass. Tossing the tools in the canoe bottom, at the same time uttering a muffled curse, Mr. Firth, as though in final exasperation, pulls the starter cord with compiled strength. *Sput! Sput! Sput!* cough. . . *whirrrrrrr* cries the engine, its propeller churning the water with all the eagerness of a two−year−old pounding the turf at the starting post. We are off. Smiling like boys who have succeeded in mischief, we listen to the music of the motor which propels us around into the current again. Resuming my position in the prow, rifle cocked for signs of fowl on the waters ahead, I wait patiently. My reliable companion, huddled by the engine, waits patiently too, with misgivings toward the Evinrude. Despite dual doubts, the engine continues for three hours, bringing us to the shore of our twelfth camp. On a mossy knoll overlooking the lazy Bell river we recline amid congenial conversation, guests at a rare feast of two young geese, bagged from the prow of the canoe. "Let's kill the works?" said my friend, questioningly. "Agreed", came I, reaching into the pack again. From it I withdrew the last tin, its label long since a part of the Rat River Portage. With the impatience of burglers rifling a safe, we pried into the obstinate tin with the hunting knife. Then came our final surprise. No fruit as suspected; but a can of corn to accompany the luxury of geese! Knowing this to be our last feast for some time, perhaps, we took our time spreading the chews evenly between the enjoyable figments of conversation. It was a most memorable evening.

According to guess and the crude map, LaPierre House was just around the corner. Here we would gaze upon an abandoned Hudson's Bay Post, no longer expelling its flour, bacon and beans over a soiled counter to hungry Argonauts. However, it would intensify my longing for some greater sign than a saw−cut or a chance lopstick, to bring to life the *Trail of '98*. Imagination was growing hungry for a stimulant. At that moment it was caught by the *Spell of the Yukon* as the sunset struck the water, still and quiet as the stately spruce that in every direction hemmed us in from the Outside world. We were a part of God's country. The silence was mystifying. How could so much be so quiet? I was overcome by a feeling of utter insignificance. I was a nothing surrounded by everything. . .

A galaxy of stars is our roof this night as we lay thinking in our comfortable sleeping robes on a spring of moss. It is one− thirty; the only audible sounds come from abdominal regions where faint rumblings remind us of our gluttonous repast. Created was an aura of thoughts devoid of words. 'What part does woman play in this scheme, so complete in itself?' asked a voice from within. A chain of thoughts shunted back and forth: 'working with Nature. . . no time for other beauties to pervade. . . yet at times conversation, as most conversations do, turns to the gentler ones. . . ' A crazy loon sounds his insulting call as though saying, 'fool!' 'fool!' I turn a deaf ear to all sounds; forget all thoughts and soon become a part of the silent night.

Dawn. Two weeks after our departure from Aklavik. Again swan predominates the bill of fare; again the curry powder and salt mixture is passed around; once more tea without sugar−but with a last drop of milk forced from the Reindeer tin resourcefully−is downed. Too, the last slab of butter that we had been eating with meat (for lack of something better to put it on) met the same fate as all the other grub. We had kidded our stomachs once more−so we thought!

At nine−thirty we paddled away from shore, only because of a lame 'kicker' pump. Remaining, was about two fillings (one gallon) for a final splurge, at such time as the muscles became weary and the pump an entity. It was more valuable to us than gold. Its potentialities were priceless. "We're probably the first to take the Rat Portage with a 'kicker' on behind," says my usually silent friend, analyzing instinctively my thoughts. I looked at him as one does a mystic−awed. "And it's certainly 'paid off' in many a tough place so far," I added, rather obviously. But man is inclined to be thus in his simple appreciation of things. I was only a mortal; I had a right to be thus.

Noon. The last of the meat disappears. 'From here on we will live on nerve and such food as the country shall give up,' I tell myself, half−heartedly. Myself says nothing. No LaPierre House comes into view (we later learned that it is completely obliterated from the water by years of growth) on the right−hand bank. So, naturally, we doubt the markings on the map: FIFTY MILES TO LAPIERRE HOUSE. However, its absence is compensated by an abundance of living things. Then, ironically, my friend adds: "The Crowfoot Indians seldom inhabit this rich looking vicinity. It's hard to believe when you look around, ain't it?" "Sure is. . . why if this leaky canoe and that two−bit engine gave out this minute I wouldn't mind staying a wee while myself," I add mirthfully, but with a touch of that sincerity that comes from the close communion with Nature. A year later I wished I had done so; but alas, time ever moves us forward with it.

The drizzle that persisted didn't help our spirits any; but the sight of many fish swimming past the canoe enlightened both parties. We at least had an idea of what might be for the next meal. Consolation was also derived from the fact that Malcolm knew people in Old Crow. At this point it didn't seem more than a day's distance. How wrong the human judgement can be at times!

One o'clock and we pass Single Rock, the only granite face to appear. Its sheer face unmistakably tells us our position. One— fifteen we discover Stoney Creek, emptying itself into our already swollen river from the port bank. "It can't be far now to the Porcupine," I said, looking questioningly at my native friend. I somehow suspected he witheld certain information learned at a former date. This was one of his many tricks of the trail. But they were always for the better; always designed to preserve valuable optimism, our most vital weapon against the continued onrush of pine, spruce and water. Suddenly, at that moment there was no withholding anything, for I saw the look of surprise on his face as he said: "There's your Porcupine River, now!"

CHAPTER TWENTY THREE

THE SONG OUR PADDLES SANG

Indeed, it was the most joyous moment of the day. It was one−thirty as we slid from the Big Bell into the murky Porcupine flowing past its delta. "This is it!" said Malcolm, assuredly, pointing to a peculiar tree silhouetting the sky with its naked stem and bushy top. It was a lopstick − the indubitable marker of the *Trail of '98.* "And see on the right bank," I motioned excitedly. He turned to view the end of a fish net dangling from its tethering pole and a tripod of spruce left in obvious fashion by the owner. Another of those intensely gratifying moments, when one feels he is not the only wayfarer, embraced us. We returned the momentary affection with the thought that someone would present himself from the cover of the bushes and say, 'hello there!', or mumble an Indian phrase which at least kindles the imagination and satisfies the soul of those who crave more company than their own. But no one stepped from the bushes. No life could be seen along the huge river. Glad at last to view the waterway that would float us clear to Fort Yukon, we reached for our paddles, assisting the canoe around the wide bend. We gained all of one mile an hour for our effort. At six miles an hour we would soon be exchanging tales with the people of Old Crow, we thought. Little did we know what was in store for two over−optimistic gentlemen adventurers. Forced on by the tantalizing thought of Old Crow and the pangs of hunger that began gnawing at our waists, we eventually pulled ashore at five−thirty p.m.

The Bell Meets the Murky Porcupine River   **Camp on the Porcupine River**

Chewing on the Last of the Bones

Tired and beat, we drank the last of the tea which was at least hot, picking at some discarded bones that I had decided to pack along 'just in case'. The latter yielded some soup, no meat. But the imagination was beginning to come into play about this time. (This proved to be half the battle, but more often an obstacle when one was hungry.) As one−half an hour had spent itself we departed, time becoming more precious with the decrease in food.

Encouraged now by the sun, which appeared in all its setting splendour, we laid our weight on the paddles, putting many miles to the rear. It was eight o'clock when we next spoke to one another. We had promised ourselves not to use the 'kicker' till necessity − that is, extreme fatigue − prevented paddling. It was then that I heard the words I had been so silently waiting for as the monotonous *dip. . . swish. . . dip. . . swish. . .* of the paddle became an aching monotone. "Let's use the kicker, eh?" "Those are the sweetest words I've heard you say all day!" was the exacting reply. Before any more could be said, the roar of the engine drowned what words might have been exchanged. Two broad smiles told a whole story. The miles retreated in our wake. Our extreme joy became more contagious as I pulled the trigger on an unsuspecting goose; a watery struggle ensued. By the time the bird had fought his last we were upon him. Reaching out as we passed the spot of his last twitches I laid a hand on the fowl, throwing it carefully into the bottom of the canoe. "They won't starve us yet!" I purported, with a thought towards the wrathful Goddess of Plenty who was of late being most unkind. We continued downstream. Nine−thirty and the sound of a river brought us to the alert. Is it the Driftwood River so soon? It can't be!. . . and it wasn't. The Porcupine merely widened in acceptance of more water. We reclasped our paddles in acceptance of the fact that the 'kicker' was useless − at least till our master mechanic could bring the water pump into play once more.

The scenery is broad as it levels out in the manner of land stretching away from heights, the hills unable to grow into mountains. Dark blues and greens mingle in a confusing mass as they do in reflections of a prism, and the pines clothe the entire scene as far as the eye can see − as though Nature too can feel its own cool autumn night. The only life we see are the geese trying (successfully) to keep ahead of us. It is worth a curse, for we need another goose if we are to have enough dinner for two. Somewhere along the way is Salmon Cache where we hope to meet a living soul. Oh, how we feel the need of a third party to mellow the conversation. For thirteen days now we have conversed. 'How long will this suffice?' I asked myself. A faint voice answered. 'Till someone else comes along, you fool!' It was time that someone appeared. Of this I was quite sure.

I have forgotten to mention the fact that our crude mechanic, Malcolm, in some manner, forced life from the stubborn 'kicker'. This we had enjoyed for some time when *sput! sput!* . . . *kuh . . . kuh . . . kuh . . . kaput.* Silence is truly golden; but we both saw red! Peeping into the small hole, I awaited the verdict of Malcolm. "Juice's all gone," he said most wryly. My spirits fell like the comb of a beaten rooster. We abandoned all hope for the night at eleven p. m. A cold wind and rising waves encouraged two weary and numb boys towards shore, rowing like never before that day, as thought of fire and tender young geese that lay ready plucked, awaiting only the sacrificial pot. Shore, we were coming!

At a speed of about ten miles per hour and each of the two half gallon fillings lasting for three quarters of an hour we felt sure we were within fifty to seventy−five miles of Old Crow. We had to be! Resigning ourselves to this fact, we pitched camp thirteen on the left limit of the Porcupine. It was not long before the molecules of goose were permeating the air. Then another smell drifted on the breeze to sensitive nostrils. "Malcolm," I said, "there's onions around here someplace, and I aim to smell them out." "Well go ahead if you're that hungry,"he answered curtly. "It's not so much that," I retorted lightly, "but a little variety will help to preserve us both a little longer. Anyway, we need some greens. . . we don't want to "spit out our teeth like stones!" "Who spits out their teeth like stones?" Then I remembered that he was not yet a connoisseur of Robert W. Service, although I had caught him flipping his way through the first page, out of curiosity. "Oh it was a habit of the gold− rushers," I explained. "You see, they didn't have any dentists along the trail, so they'd just let scurvy set in and spit the bad ones out when the gums softened." He looked at me quizzically. I made for the wild onion patch, smiling to myself as my back turned on the native. 'I'll even our score yet' I told myself, reflecting on previous figments of his Scotch−Indian imagination. The Goddess of Hunger was soon appeased. Malcolm crawled into the tent, his snores indicating perfectly that his day was run. I was left alone with the elements.

A habit too well established for me to neglect even in the North — that of brushing the teeth — proved compensating this early morning. I knelt beside the murmuring river. Its only accompaniment was the faint brush of the bristles on enamel. As I spat the white mixture into the accepting river the small blob of tooth paste slowly disintegrated; became part of the whole. Then I was caught, fixed where I knelt, and became a silent part of that other whole surrounding. A light pink, purple, and white−gray sunrise pervaded the eastern sky behind a single row of wind− blown spruce on the opposite bank, silhouetted like silent sentinels of the morning watch. A ghostlike breeze whisked through the trees speaking softly. Hair blew about my face, the ends slapping the cheeks in challenging rebuffs; I remained immutable. I was lost to things mundane. 'Why do men leave this country when they may enjoy such soul− satisfying sights?' asked the inner man. The outer man heeded him not. Herein lay the *Call of the North*, the *Spell of the Yukon* and the *Beckoning of the Lone Land.*

All animal and bird life had long since been throttled by the curtain of night. My necromantic spell came to an end. It must be late? I cupped my hand over the luminous dial of my wrist watch, adjusting my eyes to its temporal glow. I had gazed for a full half hour. I was completely satisfied. 'Sleep will be most enjoyable', I thought, tramping through the weeds to the tent. In those pleasant moments of retrospection before sleep, I reflected on the passing events of the day: the sorrel bull−moose who stood in the foliage of the riverbank, gazing in all curiosity at the object which floated towards him; the brief moment in which we enjoyed the beauty of this stately beast, holding head and horns high in challenge to those invading his verdant domain; his fleeting, rounded rump rippling as he trotted into the brush and disappeared; the plentiful beaver plunking their flat tails playfully on the waters, all the way along the river; the ducks having succeeded under the guiding tutorship of their parents in the rudiments of flight and water travel, heading south for the winter. I mused at the flounderings of one immature duckling, churning the waters of the Porcupine in his dilettante efforts to elude the twenty−two foot 'duck' pursuing him.

A deserved sleep found the calendar turned to August seventh and the hour hand turned to eleven a. m. It was a very pleasant morning but a most unpleasant breakfast consisting of two boiled goose skeletons, some wild onion and a pot o' tea. It didn't last long. The getaway was quick. We slid over the still waters under an azure sky smothered with large, white cumulus clouds. The river was as large as the Mackenzie in spots, its current oftimes as hasty. "Wait'll I see that Indian who drew me the map!" said Malcolm, realizing Old Crow was, as yet, miles off. "Me too," I said in semi−disgust and wholehearted agreement. So we set our hearts upon reaching people and our paddles to serving their fundamental purpose — the kicker having 'conked out' for good. My legs felt like they were still crossing the Rat Portage. The canoe leaked badly. We gave our everything to the paddles as I sang softly, to drive away the devils of despondency: "Row brothers row, the stream runs fast. . . " and "the *drip! drip! drip!* as we *dip! dip! dip!.* . . " to the rhythm of the two paddles cutting the still waters following the *whissshhh*, as they skimmed over the aqueous mirror for another slice.

In a moment of rest I chewed another bitter mouthful of coffee beans. "Have some more coffee" I said to Malcolm, jokingly. "You and your Goddamn sense of humour," he returned indignantly. "Can't you forget about eating?" "Well I can," I answered, politely, "but my stomach's growing to hate me more every day. It's starting to talk back already, in fact!" I added, wondering as to the makeup of a native digestive tract. "I suppose mine ain't!" he retorted. I felt relief at the words. I was not alone in my discomfort. "As for your beans," he shot suddenly, "you know what you can do with them. . . ?" Silence fell over the river again.

The day passed rapidly. Our stomachs would not stop reminding us, in guttural tones, of food. We were getting desperate. The sun bobbed through a hole in the ceiling. Spirits rose. I disrobed, eager to make up for the previous deficit. It was too good to last; cold again. Wind and waves challenged us for one and one half solid hours. Clouds blew in. We donned our woolens and parkas. A short stop at noon. A cup of coffee. A faint rise in spirits. Digestive organs were appeased for the nonce. Claimed by the river. . . "look, a lopstick!" cried Malcolm. "Gee, but that makes me feel good," I commented, my stomach forgotten completely. "And some cut trees," I pointed later, catching onto the Indian methods, little by little. Then the most pleasant revelation for days — a cabin on the estuary of what was supposed to be Driftwood River. "Did you feel that?" I asked the native. "Feel what?" he replied. "That faint breeze a moment ago. " "You must be gettin' bushed," he retorted in disgust, as though I had wasted one of his precious minutes. Yes, I was sure of it! I felt the breeze and heard the faint rustle of my Lady Luck as she resumed her place in the centre of the canoe. We were three. We would make it. My lady had not divorced me!

At five—thirty our stomachs demanded we give them a rest. Their muscles were working without repayment. So they went on strike. Rest is one of Nature's greatest cures. In a short while our ailment took a back seat. We resumed our positions in the canoe. "We'll paddle day and night," Malcolm said emphatically. "Yea," I agreed; "no use camping when the larder's empty." So we resigned ourselves then and there to perpetual motion. We arranged to sleep and keep watch alternately, drifting with the current when fatigue overtook us. There was no more to say or do. We paddled in silence, joking only occasionally about the undertones that emanated from the hungry regions. It was yet to be a more exciting day.

At ten—thirty, as the dimness of evening fell over the Canadian Northland, the excitement started. "Look ahead, Cheechako, a feed of young, fat geese!" "You mean you hope they will be" I dissented. "I'll get every one of them," he returned in his ever confident manner. I somehow knew he would. He reached for the rifle. Directed only by sound we closed in towards the bank. *Bang!*. . . and a goose flopped limply on the waters — wounded. Malcolm had spotted the family with his keen eyes, silhouetted against the water, as we neared. *Bang!*. . . and they scattered, some swimming for shore. Next moment another report split the night air. Another was felled, drifting listlessly downstream. They could not get far, and in all probability would just drift with the current. Our concern turned momentarily to those racing over the shore. "Beach the canoe. . . quick! I'll give them a merry chase, the bastards!" cried the Breed. I had not yet hit the shore when my companion, looking for all like his ancestors, leaped over the prow in hot pursuit. His lithe figure grew dim as his footsteps faded. He was gaining on the awkward looking, gangly—legged creature, ducking and spreading its wings in a manner resembling a glider trying desperately to find flight. A loud report rent the eery Arctic stillness. The goose failed in his getaway. We both knew it was not pleasant; but when one is hungry life takes on an entirely different perspective. As if suddenly becoming aware of having only one bird between the two of us, we raced for the canoe in a frenzy. Water was slapped in unmeasured strokes. "We've gotta overtake the floating birds!. . . by now they may have gained the shelter of a bank," panted Malcolm. Twilight was almost dusk. "There's one!" I shouted, leaning over the prow; the nose of the canoe seemingly turned itself, so sudden was the reflex from the man in the stern.

Fortunately they had not sought the sanctuary of the riverbank. Still in midstream, they floated helplessly with the current. *Bang!* the bullet found its mark. We would have a goose apiece! The next shot put us into the ranks of plutocrats. A third fowl was tossed into the canoe with its brethren. Overjoyed with success, all was laughter and humorous quips as the imaginary feast took place while we made for the shore.

Under a fantail sunset of pastel pink, mauve, violet and blue, we cook and feast sumptuously on Nature's fresh products. Malcolm, in his desire for fresh meat, wasted no time dangling his bird over the flames — the smell of scorched feathers saturating the air. With it, though, is the smell of singed goose as the feathers, burning off, expose the tender limbs. Wanting to enjoy mine to the full, I set about plucking the bird. Soon the smell is too much for both of us. We drool slightly in anticipation. All day we have had nothing but coffee grounds to chew. It is unbearable. It was a matter of minutes before my native friend withdrew his fowl, tore off a limb, and was ravenously tearing shreds of hot meat from the goose. If sounds expressed enjoyment, there was no doubt about my companion's state. Meanwhile, I was busy plucking. The native laughing at the Cheechako's convention, the scene continued. I could stand it no longer. Burning the remainder of the feathers off, I melted the grease in the pan. . . severed the legs off the bird. . . dropped them into the sizzling fat. . . and put the remainder in a pot to boil! I had already learned the virtues of boiling rather than frying food while on trail. But it was the mere memory of a fried leg some days before that tempted me to the latter. I was soon eating the legs as my friend licked the last of his bones. Justice had been done to his complete bird. Contented, he settled to consuming cup after cup of steaming tea. I, not content to let good enough alone, hung patiently over the intoxicating aroma rising from the pans. The wait was plain torture. One hour after the canoe met the shore I was licking the last of the bones. Re−energized, the world certainly looked wonderful.

Two more contented people could not be found along the entire waters of the Porcupine River. Our conversation became scintillating as we huddled about the dying fire. We were impatient to tackle the awaiting river with our new found vigour. "Well, whad'ya say we get on the way?. . . or have you finished with those bones yet?" said Malcolm. Sensing his eagerness, I threw the burning embers into the river, which was instantly lit up by a thousand sparks. Then a white cloud of smoke arose from the charred, wet log starting its course downstream. Another followed. . . and another, keeping the same interval between its predecessor till one by one they disappeared into the shrouding darkness. Kicking sand over the remaining ashes we turned towards the pointed silhouette riding the shore. Our faithful canoe was waiting. . .

Dip. . . dip. . . dip, scarcely audible but for the drip of trailing water − the only sound in the ghostly stillness. Never before have I heard such a quiet − like one in a vacuum. The sunset leaves the trees silhouetted against the clear, northern sky where its rays are commencing daybreak again. While above, to the southeast, a three−quarter moon looks quizzically down upon two adventurous paddlers, reminding them that they are still a part of a vast universe (an infinitesimal bit) but none−the−less a part of the scheme of things.

Gradually the symmetry centers on the shoreline between water and sky. It slowly grows longer on the shore side. Dawn is approaching. The moon fades. . . I doze inside my sleeping robe on the canoe bottom, aroused only now and then by the tap of a paddle on the canoe's edge. My native is at work. He had chosen the first lot. In these moments of interrupted slumber the happenings of the day flash across the tabula rasa: passing Driftwood River. . . a cabin − the first real sign of life. . . crossed poles left by a thoughtful passer−by. . . the chase after the geese. . . those delicious moments when teeth sunk into flesh. . . the gay aftermath. . . and now the gently swaying of a canoe on water. . . the scrape of the paddle against the side. . . the warmth of a sleeping bag. . . oh, the contentment of it all! We had come seventy−five miles down the Porcupine since Tuesday noon. On the morrow we hoped for a sight of Salmon Cache and a Friday dinner. Then Old Crow would not be far, surely?

Invariably imagination and reality present both extremes. I had no idea just how pleasant sleeping in a moving canoe could be. I awoke the next day to be greeted by a hot sum and a favourable wind. I could quite easily have been in Venice, aboard a Chinese Junk or punting on a sunken Indian Lagoon. We must have drifted miles under the guiding hand of my native gondolier. The scenery had changed completely. At some time during the smaller hours of the morning his silent vigil had ended, for there he lay, ashore, sleeping heavily inside his eiderdown, unaware of the penetrating warmth of the day.

Dinner saw the last of the remaining goose demolished with a pot of tea. We were under way again at one p. m. "You didn't see the frost this morning, eh?" was his first query of the day. "No," I answered, dumbfounded. "The canoe and the berries were all frost coated!" he teased. "You were so darned busy counting coffee beans in your sleep you missed it!" he chuckled in his Improved Scotch fashion; "it was sure pretty." For the moment I felt he should be the author, then I remembered his cutting remark and decided not. "Lay off that coffee tune will ya!" I never wanted to drink another cup of the stuff again. With these remarks August−the−first got off to a pretty good start.

Good time was made. The sun remained hot. We again found ourselves at the bottom of the food supply. We drank goose juice, tea and coffee at intervals, to break the mental and physical fatigue that accompanies long hours of paddling. Thus the day wore on. . . but where was Old Crow? "Look!" cried Malcolm, jumping up in the canoe and pointing to the distance. Two thin pillars of smoke rose vertically towards the Yukon sky and disappeared. Never have I been so totally inspired by smoke. The effect was contagious. Both found a hidden reservoir of energy which propelled us around bend after bend. "It can't be forest fires," reasoned the 'Breed; "they're out. . . see the bank," he pointed. A blanket of black spread itself over the entire starboard flats, hanging limply over the water's edge. So here was the source of the smoke, blowing east two weeks ago, that we saw from Destruction City. With each bend our optimism faded. I pretended it was a mirage; my friend had his own idea. We paddled in silence. Calm waters continued; hills to the fore gradually appeared blue with distance; thin wisps of smoke appeared sporadically, only to tease us with their fleeting dance. I refused to take it seriously. Who knows, maybe we were getting 'bushed'. It was five−thirty when our next surprise made its timely appearance. A cabin reared up on the right. Life! Food! Was this a mirage? It couldn't be; the sun was not that hot!

Inside the cabin we found all the answers. There was no sign of life; but it was encouraging to see recent mail addressed to DAVE LORD − OLD CROW, lying on the table. As for food, we found some of that. Sugar, Klim, cocoa drainings, a box of Van Camp's 'delicious 30 minute beans' and two inches of molasses in a deep tin. (Gosh knows how long it had been standing there?) Like two elated French chefs we set about planning our new bill−of−fare. Then we came across another letter addressed to MOSES LORD (the son) − OLD CROW, from the U. S. A. What bountiful rewards the cabin divulged. They were enough for now. We knew we would discover Old Crow very soon. But it could wait till we dined. . .

The repast was held on the beach with as much ceremony as two hungry adventurers (who had eaten nothing all day) could muster. Opening my bag of before−dinner−rituals, I started: "For what we're about to receive. . . " "Well, let's receive it quick!" cut in Malcolm, "lest some eagle swoop down and get it first." Four hands made a grab. Highlight of the victuals turned out to be the Van Camp beans, which, true to the label, took thirty minutes to cook and two minutes to down! Hot and nutritious, they hit the spot. If no one has ever paid tribute to a bean manufacturer I would like here to thank Mr. Van Camp personally, for unknowingly having tinned that delicious family of beans. Oddly enough I had never heard of this brand before, but certainly thanked him openly that day; and since have been attracted by the colourfully wrapped tins. "They're common up here with trappers and prospectors," said the native. This very fact proved itself in the cabins of the Sourdoughs I was soon to meet along the *Trails of '98.*

"The fire came close to ruining the cabin and that meal," I ejaculated, examining the caches at the rear of the cabin, up to which the charred, black carpet stretched. "Was sure close," was all Malcolm said. With the cabin yielding all it could, we turned our backs on the caribou horns above the door and made for the beach. The cabin watched us in silence as first one climbed into the Peterborough. . . then the other pushed as the canoe scraped gently over the pebbles of the shore. . . in he jumped, leaving ripples circling about the spot where his foot was withdrawn. . . two paddles rose and fell as near to unison as possible. . . slowly the speck was absorbed into the afternoon sunlight towards the two blue hills that were to lure it on for hours.

It was fully eight−o' clock before we pulled up again. The smoke columns had disappeared; Old Crow still hadn't appeared. Hunger again began to let itself be known. This was silenced with a cup of Postum gleaned from the odd assortment in the cabin. Reasonably content, we continued to paddle towards the elusive hills where we felt sure Old Crow lay at their feet.

Hours passed. Another cabin appeared, dilapitated, looking like a '98 leftover. Out of the riverbank protruded net sticks. Then. . . at the confluence of the Crow river flowing in from the right and our own waterway, a net! Our first thought was fish. But alas, as we pulled it in, an empty net greeted us. "Let's beach and have a look around," suggested Malcolm. I desired more than anything, something to cheer me up. "A fresh footprint of a man in moccasins. . . and a dog!," I yelled, snooping about the shore. These are too fresh to disregard," I suggested, but my friend was already off in the direction the toes pointed. 'Perhaps we will run into a fish camp' I soothed myself. I could practically smell it already. The footprints petered off into the bush. No man! No dog! No fish! We re−embarked on the smooth but dirty waters, abetted by the Old Crow river tumbling from the north. Not a sound filled the air except the short, intermittent breath of the wind. "Did you hear that?" I asked, a tingle racing up my spine. I froze at the paddle. "You hearin' things again?" insulted the 'Breed. "Now I know you're bushed," he added, just as uncomplimentary. 'Did you really hear something? Do you think he might be right?' I asked my inner man, not wanting to admit that the great aloneness (the long absence from ordered society) might be getting the best of me. I listened again. I waited, tense, for confirmation. Long, silent minutes passed seemingly into the realm of hours. Paddles flicked the waters, now restless in the rising wind. I could hear my heart pound beneath the wool sweater against my skin. Then it came. . . the faint howl of a dog drifted on the winds, hesitated but a second. . . and passed on up the river. I froze in the prow of the canoe like an Indian warrior hearing the far−off war whoop of an age−old enemy. For a moment I said nothing, then turned my head slightly to watch my silent companion. He was standing motionless, his head cocked to the west, his paddle dripping in the canoe. My confirmation had come.

"Something up, Malcolm?" I asked, shattering the surrounding stillness. "I thought I heard a dog bark!," he said, moving not a muscle. "Oh? You must be joining me. Let's get bushed together?" "Paddle, for God's sake. . . we're just about to Old Crow!" he said, preemptorily. I turned, grabbed my paddle and, one stroke behind my swift companion, laid one−hundred and ninety pounds of brawn against the Porcupine. This I did, not out of respect for his command; I was showing silent appreciation that two were one again, in thought and action. 'Yes' I replied to inner promptings, 'a man's best friend is a dog!'. It was the most pleasant sound we had heard in weeks. In our mind's−eye we saw a tent, a hot stove on which a light brown bannock cooked slowly and an Indian family. . . people! Imagination is a wonderful thing; reality was even more so. "Look!. . . a tent!" cried Malcolm. ". . . and a red−roofed building," I added. ". . . and a light!" he shouted, like an overjoyed boy. We both laughed aloud with abandon. Smiles crossed our faces and remained. Oh, what a discovery! Oh, what a delightful moment! Oh, what a precious memory!

Paddling − as though the very Devil himself were pursuing us with lowered trident − we rounded the last bend and pointed the nose of Our Lady at the faint group of buildings gathered in the dusk on the starboard bank. Two minds and two bodies became fused in a single purpose. Two paddles dipped the waters as one. Even the canoe seemed to sense our dire need for complete harmony as she obeyed our every caress. We were an inexorable trio.

As we approached, streams of people came to the top of the high bank, silhouetting themselves against the sky. Some waved in royal welcome to the Cheechako and the native. It was an unforgettable moment as we drew to shore behind a row of bobbing launches, inboards and barges, tethered to stakes on the bank. One third of the village looked down form that steep cliff. They were utterly and completely awed at the motley strangers who crept silently out of the night. In true Indian fashion they waited patiently for us to acknowledge their presence. It was exactly eleven−thirty on Friday, August 8th − seventeen days from Aklavik, a good 300 miles to the northeast. We had waited too long for this moment.

CHAPTER TWENTY FOUR

WE REACH OLD CROW!

'Hullo!. . . 'lo there!. . . Hi!" came the excited voices as we reached the summit of the dirt bank. We faced the awaiting throng. "Malcolm!," cried a bronzed fellow, pushing his way to the fore. "Whatchoo do here?," he enquired. Hearty handshakes began all around with each Northern introduction. "My friend," said Malcolm, introducing me to one, then another of former hunting companions. My man was certainly popular. Then a girlish voice cried: " Oh lookit, dazzio!" Laughter rent the night air. I was the carefree butt of an Indian joke and I gained a new nickname that followed me till our trails parted. "You can look after yourself all right, eh?" were Malcolm's last words as he fell in league with the natives—a customary habit with the halfbreeds. "I'll do okay—looks like I'll have to," I retorted, looking toward the log, Mounted Police quarters. There, I knew, I would find a white man.

We Reach Old Crow

The door of the post opened and a ray of yellow light slanted into the exterior darkness. I introduced myself to the stocky gentleman silhouetted against the warming light within. "Corporal Kirk is my name, come on in!" he invited. Standing within the modern interior of their combined home and police post, I felt 'bushed' and, rather awkwardly, proceeded to the kitchen. There I met his diminutive wife. "I suppose you'd like a good hot wash?" she suggested. "That'll do the trick," I said, from behind somewhat soiled whiskers. So I washed as I described the trip, climaxing it with the mention of the dog whose bark had been our final inspiration for the day. "That was the sweetest music I had heard for a long time!" I insisted.

Mrs. Kirk was by this time cooking and generally preparing the table for a meal. "Will bacon and eggs suit you?" she queried, laying the plates on the cloth. "Can't think of anything nicer," I emphasized, rubbing the mass of wet whiskers briskly with a towel, reflecting on the coffee grounds, stale Postum and goose—gipper diet I had been subjected to for the past few days. It was all a beautiful hallucination. Surely I was dreaming? But no! here I was seated in a kitchen, conversing while a good woman busied herself about the stove flipping the bacon, turning eggs and gently patting potato paddies. Then I realized my friend had been partially right. There was no doubt about it. . . I was 'bushed!'

With restraint I held myself from rushing the frying pan. It was no Siren song, but truly a Siren aroma that tantalized me to no end. I imaginarily chained myself to the chair. Social ethics demanded I do this. I had no crew to secure my bonds; no wax with which to plug up my nostrils. I was alone in my plight. "Pull up a chair, son, it's ready," said the cook. then, I realized I had passed through the rough waters of Temptation. The sailing from herein would be pleasant. Indeed it was. This was, without a shadow on the dim recesses of doubt, the most welcome meal I have ever sat in front of. It was spiced; spiced, with the congeniality of the kind people. They unravelled many yarns about the North and the settlement, before I wiped the plate with an extra piece of bread. "You're very resourceful," noted the Corporal's wife. "I think I'll always be, after that trip through the Rat River Portage," I returned, smiling contentedly. The atmosphere slowly acquired that unrivalled pleasantness one associates with Northern hospitality and Northern people. I was one meal and two friends closer to normalcy. But, here I must confess, I could have eaten that delectable dish thrice over.   Perhaps, in this remote surrounding, here was a small part of D'Arcy Arden's so desired definition of 'civilization'? I began to think there was something to it after all.

There was much ado about the village of Old Crow, in the heart of the Yukon, this night. Corporal Kirk was busy sending and receiving messages to and from his 'ham' set which has gained more that the reputation of a 'ham' station in its valuable link with Outside activity. A plane was expected at any minute, I was informed. A sick woman was to be taken Outside to a hospital. The table was set for a hungry pilot. I only hoped his appreciation would be half of my own. That would be enough. From the doorway I saw a green and red light, remaining parallel, coming up river, flickering like two technicolor stars, slightly misplaced. A wild roar signalled the plane's arrival. The pilot was gunning his motor before landing. Interrupted, our sociable union came to a close.

A long, thin beam of light sliced wantonly the black Yukon night. Corporal Kirk was waving landing instructions to the pilot of a small craft, with a flashlight. Silence filled the valley. A group of Indians gathered along the bank, stood motionless. I could hear myself breathing. Then a loud *slap!* told us all the pilot had made a successful landing. a roar from the single engine brought life and movement to the group. Gunning up to the bank the pilot stepped out, tethered his plane and climbed to the summit. Smiling broadly, he showed his pleasure at such a warm reception on such a chilly night. I knew exactly how he felt. Had we not similarly arrived only so short a time before? Would he appreciate the warm victuals that awaited him in the Corporal's kitchen as heartily as the Cheechako had? Eggs and bacon shuffled past my mind in a tantalizing procession. This would never do! So I prepared for another night in the open, unrolling my sleeping bag on the tall grass in front of the Anglican Mission.

"You're not going to sleep out there, are you?," asked a feminine voice. "I can't imagine a nicer spot," I replied to the unrecognizable figure in the darkness. "You'd better come over to my cabin. . . you can sleep on the floor. . . it'll at least be warm," she insisted. "Sorry," I retorted, emphatically "I might suffer from claustrophobia and I might get worked up in the night and make a heap of noise moving myself outside. Thanks, anyway," I ended, spreading the eiderdown to full length, chuckling to myself at the thought of its soft invitation. Such was my unusual introduction to Mrs. Steele, wife of the Northern Commercial Company trader. It was not long before a flood of yellow light streamed out of the police−post door. Figures followed it. Voices came next, on the breeze. Much activity commenced about the plane. The sick Indian woman was loaded aboard. An overwhelming roar split the heretofore reigning silence. The fading echo of the machine left me standing in the silence that rushed back into the valley. "Mission completed" I said audibly, recalling life on a bomber station in Yorkshire, England, three short years previous.) A soothing satisfaction overcame me. Completely fatigued, my thoughts dwelt on sleep. . . the obvious crown to set off a most wonderful day. Among people and friends once more, I crawled into my sleeping bag on the grass, below the guardian, white belfry of the weatherbeaten, log mission. The breakfast problem had been looked after. Hospitable Mr. Kirk had said, as I left the post: "Get lots of sleep. . . I'll call you at a late hour in the morning for chow. " Cares of the day slowly vanished, and as the stars winked down at me I winked back with the full significance of that age−old custom. . . and the stars went out. . . .

"Bacon and eggs are ready!," said a familiar voice, a hand tapping me on the shoulder. 'What a beautiful dream' I thought to myself in the semi−doze that follows a heavy night. I must not have responded readily, for another shake of the shoulder brought me to my elbow, rubbing my eyes in the brightness of this August morning. "Breakfast's ready. . . bacon and eggs!" said the Corporal, sauntering back to the house. I glanced at the time. It was eight−thirty. The rest of the village had scarce awakened. It was not unlike the other Indian settlements where bedding is late and rising equally so. I had not stirred once all night. Not even the howls of hungry Indian dogs could have disturbed that slumber. Then, wide awake, I remembered, "bacon and eggs!". I jumped up quickly. Nothing would keep me from that bacon and eggs inseperable combination.

There were four of us seated about the table in the kitchen: Corporal Kirk, his wife, Constable Webster and myself. The constable had just arrived at the post, so the topic of the village proved interesting to both of us. Many tragic incidents were related, alleviated by more humourous occurrences than one would expect in an Indian village in the heart of the Yukon. I discovered Mrs. Kirk to be not only a wife; but mother, nurse and midwife to the entire tribe. She said in her modest manner: "It keeps me busy and I have assisted practically every birth and know every child born since the year 1934, when we first came to Old Crow". As for the Corporal—his time is

devoted to the radio station, sending his reports, including those of the weather, fishing, cutting wood, caring for two, large dogteams and taking his usual interest in the affairs of the tribe.

Post—breakfast found the Constable initiating himself to these duties with a double bladed axe and a wedge which apparently was necessary for splitting the ornery, pine logs stacked beside the police post. He was soon joined by the Corporal in their first task of the day. Mrs. Kirk was 'lighting into' a big washing. I left the two mounties swinging four blades in the air for an inquisitive snoop about the Indian encampment.

Old Crow Looking East on Porcupine River

Chief Peter Moses

Northern Commercial Co. and Mrs. Steele

As close as I could discover, the Indians of Old Crow belong to a dismembered branch of the Tena (Takudh) tribes with a mixture of that widespread breed, the Loucheux (sometimes Loochoo), who inhabit the Mackenzie area, and a smattering of the MacPherson tribe who have come west from over the mountains. They are, from all aspects, a good breed of folk. While exchanging words with the Chief—Peter Moses, a surprising fact came to my attention. He does not allow his tribe to drink; and not a drop can be procured in the village. The Mounted Police Corporal backs the Chief one hundred percent in this measure, having direct control of all liquor entering the settlement. I later discovered that those desiring to break the unwritten law could travel to Fort Yukon, 300 miles west on American soil, and have a wassail. But one thing certain: by the time they reached Old Crow, upstream, they would be dead sober and ready to abide by the rules of the tribe!

It was along the main street (or better—path) that I met Chief Peter Moses talking to a friend who leaned on a saw, relaxing momentarily from the work of cutting winter wood. I sensed there had been much activity about the village as the morning progressed. Coming close, the Chief, as though reading my unspoken thoughts, explained why all the hammering and general excitement. "There is to be wedding. . . big wedding. . . Potlatch. . . and dance," he said slowly, "only if my natives have dance hall constructed by Monday," he added in reasonable English. The fate of the wedding date lay in its successful completion. Would I attend? I surely would, I emphasized; adding that I would even bring along my horn and aid the orchestra. "Good!", he replied, smiling broadly, the wrinkles creasing his tawny, weatherbeaten countenance. "You are a good man and friend. . . we shall look forward to seeing you there. "There would be no doubt on my part. Here was a real live Indian festivity. . . and a Potlatch! Only the sick, I knew, would not be in attendance. I didn't intend to be sick this day. It is not every day one from the Outside has the opportunity to witness an Indian wedding. With the thought of the gay celebration forthcoming I left the Chief where I found him and continued my morning ramble. It brought me to the Northern Commercial Company trading−post.

Behind the counter I met Mrs. Steele, wife of the trader who at present was on his return from Fort Yukon with supplies. They are the only other Whites in the village and have two children who play at large with the younger natives. "Hello there!", she welcomed in a cheery voice, "did you sleep well on the grass?", she smiled. "Never better," I replied, beaming at last night's reflection. I watched the Indian interpreter go between a squaw and the good woman. Back and forth filtered the conversation, the squaw adding her personal life (it seemed) to the narrative which must be understood as business in these parts. One must be patient with these natives, I gathered, and certainly Mrs. Steele has learned that virtue. Finally, looking to her husband who all the while had said nothing but now nodded his head in approbation, the squaw smiled and said a word or two to the trader's wife. The sale was completed by the interpreter. Quiet reigned within the cluttered post. "You'll want some homecooking while you're here. You're welcome to eat with us," she broke in, as I surveyed the tinned goods lining the shelf. The squaw received her cheap print dress and parted with her indifferent husband. I accepted the invitation, adding: "After those trail meals it'll be a pleasure to remunerate a good cook. " She flushed slightly at the suggestion, replying, "It keeps us alive anyway!. . . well, time to close for lunch. " "That's good enough for a Cheechako," I replied. She bolted the door and we crossed the riverbank to the immaculate dwelling of the Steele family, flooded in bright, morning sunlight.

Dinner this day was another of those unforgettable repasts that one−now quite accustomed to the crudity of the North−was destined to remember, in contrast, for a long time. While the steak sizzled in the pan we sat and talked over a 'shot' of Calvert's whiskey, paving the way for the delectable dishes that were soon to follow. Now in the proper mood I received the warm welcome: "It's ready when you are. " I was ready.

Real potatoes (a rarity this year) steamed beside the well− done steak; appetizingly coloured vegetables surrounded the whole; home−made baking powder biscuits and canned figs followed. It was a veritable banquet for the Cheechako. If this was hospitality of the North what would it be like in Dawson City? It was weeks before I was to know.

The night wore away in pleasant conversation. I conveyed the latest news from the Outside in exchange for the adventurous tales of the Steele family years spent at St Michael on the Bering Sea. Then the Hit Parade−the first popular music I had heard in months−brought the theme to the Outsider once more and the evening to an end. It was a glorious refresher. Already I felt less 'bushed'. I would be able to meet the Outside soon with defiance.

It was late when I left the neatly furnished bungalow, declining an offer to sleep on the floor. "I still prefer the grass, to which I have become quite accustomed, thanks," I replied to the invitation. I slipped into the night.

It was early in the morning when the rains drove me into an empty tent. They also brought a visitor. A stray Indian dog entered, curled up beside my warmth and we both departed for the realm of Sleep, soothed by the satisfying groans of the canine. I was not alone.

Sunday morning. I awake to find my newly found friend gone. I breakfasted in the cabin of John Kendi, son of the Anglican minister. The night we arrived he had asked me what I desired most in the way of food, realizing the difficulties we had overcome. "A brown bannock oozing with butter,"I had said, unhesitatingly−for many's the time Malcolm and I had talked of its good points while chewing coffee beans on our downward trip. Now like a wish come true, I sat across from John and his wife, behind a beautiful bronzed bannock and a heaped plate of fresh fish. As we exchanged pleasantries I though to myself: 'an Indian never forgets!' As I fulfilled that ardent wish I knew that one white man would 'never forget' either.

Sunday in Old Crow means church, as it does elsewhere. I combed four months growth of hair and whiskers as best one can, all set to call on Mrs. Steele and family. I had previously arranged to escort them thus, in the absence of the head of the house. As we made our way along the bank towards the ancient, log house–of–worship, the bell peeled from the belfry. It told us to hurry. With the fold I reached the door, the object of many wondering Indian glances. I thought I guessed their questioning looks, but dispelled all thoughts with my best Sunday morning propriety.

As a family we entered the mission of Old Crow. Once inside I was aware of the custom of placing the woman on the left, the men on the right. I had noticed this in the Roman Catholic Mission at Fort Rae where I attended my first native service.

**Church of England,
Built in Archdeacon MacDonald's Time**

Baalyum the 'medicine man' is the usher. Seriously taking it upon himself he sees that all find a seat. Finding room on the other side for my host, he turns to me. I feel it a personal favour when he finds room for the Cheechako next to the Chief. Then he returns to his position in the center of the aisle. Comfortably seated, the eyes of the multitude off me, I notice a medal hanging from the chief's breast. This I intended to inquire about later.

The last bell sounded eleven–thirty. The service began. It was the most colourful and unforgettable service I have ever attended. It began in the manner of all Anglican services as Julius Kendi and his assistant, both bespectacled, assumed their places at the fore. All began the singing of a hymn in their native tongue. Baalyum, ever thoughtful, saw my empty hands and passed along his books which, of course, I could not read. But I followed the phonetics which rose and fell in their musical Takudh interpretation. Then as we resumed our seats again the old log church filled with the chant of Indian prayers.

Archdeacon MacDonald, one of the pioneer missionaries of the Yukon Territory, is responsible for the translation of the Anglican Church books. To him go many blessings from the tribe. It was a habit of the missionaries of the Church of England to follow the Hudson's Bay traders to the most distant of outposts. In the summer of the year 1862 Archdeacon MacDonald arrived at the Hudson Bay post of Fort Yukon as chaplain

**Rev. Julius Kendi, Wife Martha
and 'Big Joe' Kay–Assistant**

of the lost and missioner to the Tena Indians. He was a scholar, a Christian gentleman and an industrious worker. He taught the Kotch– a–Kuchin, or lowland people; the Tena of the Munna plain; the Gens de Large of the Chandalar; and even the Gens de Butte or mountain men from the distant Tenana, the first principles of civilization and Christianity. He also translated the scriptures, church service and songs into their own rude tongues. He taught them to read the holy book; to conduct the ceremonies of his church with understanding and decorum. They listened with respect and interest when he talked with them of the land from which <u>he</u> came, only existing in their imaginations, far beyond the mountains that bounded their horizon. They confided to him their secrets of the forest, mountains and streams. As a result of his keen interest his influence has long survived his death. An example of this, given by Judge Wickersham in his writings, verifies this point.

He writes: "An Indian family from Tanana River country came to Eagle City in the fall of 1900 to visit with relatives in the Tena village about a mile upstream from Fort Egbert. During the winter the father died and was to be buried on a Sunday. Came the eventful day; the Judge found the Indians gathered about a rough box—coffin resting on two poles laid across the open grave. The observer, interested in seeing how the poverty stricken fold conducted a burial, and also curious as to their view of the hereafter, watched the proceedings closely.

A young man of 28 or 30 came forward to conduct the funeral services. He held a book from which he read at some length in Indian tongue. At regular intervals the audience responded in unison, apparently understanding his words completely. It was a Christian service conducted with all the demeanor the Archdeacon himself would have used.

At the conclusion of the ceremony the Indian, busy trying to console the mother and her three youngsters, was asked what book he used and what church he represented. He said: "the book of Common Prayer and Administration of Sacraments and other Rites and Ceremonies According to the Church of England. "

The book was translated into the Takudh tongue by Archdeacon MacDonald in 1873 for the use of the Tena (Takudh) people residing in Fort Yukon and the MacKenzie River districts. The Indian had been taught to read it by the missionaries of the church at the Fort and it was generally used in the region on all proper occasions. This Sunday morning I was witnessing an identical usage of the holy books in the hands of the full—blood Indian Julius Kendi and his helper Big Joe Kay, converted to the Christian faith. Both appeared scholarly in their spectacles, reading passages aloud in their musical dialect, receiving similar well—tuned responses from the sincere congregation below. As I listened to the singing of the last hymn, the sound of one especially good voice attracted my attention. It came from the pews on the left where the squaws and their daughters sang heartily, while the other children and papooses shuffled in their restlessness. Although the voice could not be traced, the thought occurred to me at the moment: 'how wonderful it would be, should someone teach them the rudiments of music'. For certainly they could raise their voices well against the chorals of their white sisters of the Outside. A basso profundo to the right challenged the soprano to the left and the hymn ended.

With the reading of a letter of thanks to the people of Old Crow from a former parishoner (now in Dawson City) and the announcement of the final banns of the marriage to take place on Monday—to which Mr. Kendi added: "should the construction of the hall be completed by that time, a Potlatch and dance will be held there,"—the service ended. Only a few departed. I waited, intrigued. Holy Communion commenced. Row after row took their place in tens before the altar. Wine flowed and the tiny squares of bread accompanied it elsewhere. Julius Kendi uttered his blessings in Indian phonetics, waving his fingers over each head in turn. It was my privilege to

take it with Peter Moses. Then came time for our row to go forward. I knelt beside the Chief before the beautiful altar. It was exquisite. Nowhere have I seen such a variegated display of native talent. The beadwork covering was made exclusively by the natives of the village. It added to the colourful array of bandanas and moccasins now lined beside the Chief and the Cheechako, accepting the prayers of the Indian minister. The sacramental bread and wine was passed and the Indian minister paused over all our heads. He said many words in his native tongue. They must have been good prayers, for even my Lady Luck heard them. She stayed by my side for many weeks to come. Another row followed us to the altar as we resumed our seats. Soon the ritual ended. Communion finished with the singing of a hymn. As the last strains echoed through the ancient structure we passed into the sunshine of Sunday afternoon. It was my privilege to engage in conversation with Chief Peter Moses. It was then I brought up the subject of the medal.

The Chief Wearing the O.B.E. Medal

Of this he was far from reluctant to mention. In split phrases he said: "It is the O. B. E. . . the British Empire Medal, which my tribe receive for their so kind donation of one–hundred pounds ($500. 00 approximately). . . . we give to the blitzed–you say? he asked patiently; ". . . children of Britain. . . far across waters. . . many miles!", he said, waving his hand and looking in the dim distance beyond Old Crow as though he might see that land. "I understand, Chief," I replied. "I was there too. . . many miles away. . . and saw that country and its people. " He smiled largely, glad of someone who understood. "You did well," I terminated. I was later told by Corporal Kirk that the money was handed to him tied up in a handkerchief–close to $500. 00 in all. Strolling to his cabin (not unlike E. Pauline Johnson strolling with her tillicum, Chief Capilano, who used to tell her many tales of yester years), I accompanied tillicum, Chief Peter Moses, and he told me much. He spoke of the delegation from Ottawa which came personally to thank his people for their generosity. This he shall long remember. His son shall remember it also. And his son's son shall be told the tale of the white men who flew in the 'great bird' of Goodwill to the village of Old Crow, high in the Yukon, to thank the mighty Chief and his peaceful, kindly peoples for their generosity to their white brethren.

We reached the clean comfortable dwelling of the Chief. I was introduced to his wife; I also met his young, adopted son from Fort Yukon. As we talked my 'tillicums' told me the tragic story of the recent loss of both their sons–one twenty–five, soon to become chief in his father's footsteps; the other a mere boy of eight years: "some day to be a good hunter too!" pined the Chief. Again this cursed malady has struck! But we are both happy now. . . we have a son to inherit the title of Chief. . . that means most to a Chief!" he added, running his fingers through the curly locks of black hair on the head of the young boy. "Yes, some day I may pay another visit, and maybe I shall be welcomed by the Little Chief too?" I said, directing my glance from Peter to his son. He turned to his son and said: "You will remember the dazzio (whiskers), my boy. . . treat him good when he returns. . . " "Maybe then the caribou will be running and you will feast too!" came his afterthought. (This year the animals failed to run by the village).

My visit was by no means a short one. Opening an old trunk — like something out of *Treasure Island*–the Chief brings forth some pictures. Among these are the photos of the delegation who brought the medal to Old Crow. Another depicts the monetary presentation to a bombed–out child of London, broadcast direct from the B. B. C. Official papers and notes of thanks clutter up the trunk. The chief insists I read them. Scanning them I realize the pride with which he wears his medal on every tribal occasion. They are words of sincere gratitude from far and wide. Looking back on history, whoever would think that the North American Indian would come to play

Chief Peter Moses, Wife and Adopted Son

so noble a part in his simple but sincere way? Digging to the bottom of the same trunk Peter's wife emerges, bestowing best wishes upon myself, handing me a piece of lavish beadwork as a memoir of our acquaintance. It was a beautiful neckpiece–part of a dress made in her youth but never finished. This I cherish to this day as a personal gift from my red brethren in whose country I was nurtured; in whose vast expanses I first learned to love the simple way of life of God's children.

I could not leave without a picture of the Chief, sporting his medal proudly on his left breast, in the company of his wife and young son. "Would you eat with us?" asked Peter Moses, after the shutter clicked. It was hard to say no but I declined because of other arrangements. "We shall all dine at the Potlatch, together," I reminded him. He smiled in understanding. "I will see you. . . ," he replied in futurity, waving from the doorstep. His son waved too.

I made off down the crooked path towards the village centre. In the distance I could see an old Indian standing on the edge of the riverbank, his legs spread apart, hands behind his back, gazing intently over the waters flowing swiftly by. I recognized the form as I came closer. It was 'Steamboat', aged Steamboat; too old now for the hunt but spry enough to be the forecaster of the weather, tides and approaching parties from his elevated position above the river. Perhaps, I reflected, this is how so many were aware of our recent approach from the east? That I never did find out. But the keen eyes of Steamboat (named, they tell me, because he was once pilot on one of the larger riverboats) stand him in good stead. He is still of invaluable service to his tribe at Old Crow.

At the halfway point I met another familiar character of the Old Crow tribe. He is Malcolm MacDonald—son of the Archdeacon — who married an Indian woman, as is so soften the custom of whites who have stayed for long in the North. We immediately engaged in conversation, he anxious to know more of the Outside. It was during this informal talk that he brought forth a receipt.

"What is this?" he inquired, "they said I had to pay it!" And I surveyed the piece of paper. It was a Poll Tax receipt for $5. 00. I explained as best I could, but had to sympathize with him at the absurdity of such a measure. Here he was, 300 miles from the nearest large post situated on any accessible river, namely the Mackenzie or the Yukon—the large waterways leading to civilization, where he might cast his vote. . . and more than likely hundreds more miles from the nearest Polling Station. How long do such things go on till something is done about them? Exasperated no end, I dismissed all thoughts of the incident. We switched to more pleasant words about the village and his highly respected father.

CHAPTER TWENTY FIVE

AN OLD SOURDOUGH

It was this same afternoon that I was guided along a well worn path, hemmed in on both sides by brush. My escort was Mrs. Steele; my destination a sourdough cabin. The good woman had informed me there was someone in the village whom I must meet, seeing my interest was in the stalwart gentlemen of 1898. Curiosity aroused, I accepted. "He's full of stories and can tell as good a tale as the best of them," she claimed. I thought to myself at this, 'Oh, oh! you'll have to do plenty of sifting to get near the truth this time, I'll bet!' This, I might take liberty to add, was becoming quite a habit, growing with each Northerner I accosted. Well, come what may! my mind was in gear. I was in the mood to listen to any length of well−spun yarn. The path was swallowed up by an opening. A cabin faced us. We knocked. A voice from within shouted: "Come on in!" We entered. It was a comfortable cabin, once part of the old Hudson's Bay buildings at LaPierre House, floated downstream and now deposited along a narrow trail at the west end of the village of Old Crow. In the rear room, apparently the general gathering spot for company, I was introduced to the gentleman who spoke pleasantly from behind sunglasses. "A cheechako just off the *All Canadian Trail of '98*," said my female escort. "Thought you two would have something in common. " "Glad to meet you, son, sit down awhile!" He paused to resume his former position of comfort in his favourite chair. "What brings you this way, my lad? Don't you know the Gold Rush has been over a long time?" "It's just started," I differed; "and with every Oldtimer I meet I realize just how much gold is still around!" "Oh!, the philosopher breed, I see!"he deduced. "Well that's a mighty good thing to have as a constant companion. . . why, when I was comin' along the trail just out of old Fort Edmonton. . . " The key had been inserted; the lock sprung; now the door creaked open gradually. . . my moment had come. As Frank Foster spoke, his mind turned back the years like so many pages of a long novel. Once more I was on the trail of GOLD. Yes, the Klondike was rearing its glittering head again like a gilt−edged Hydra about to challenge the adventuresome Herculean Cheechako with its hidden potentialities. It had already been overcome from the east by the man from Portage La Prairie, Manitoba. Giving Age the right to hold the floor, Youth listened intently. And the tale of his own quest and struggles came forth. . . "I'll start at the beginning," says Frank, launching wholeheartedly into the past, careful to preserve his literary sense, dramatizing what he thinks deserving of drama, meticulous as to every detail. "I was born in Bradford, England, and after leaving school knocked about knowing and feeling the meaning of work. " With this case−hardening commenced, the cry of GOLD! (not yet an echo) came to another's ears. We next find Frank at Athabasca Landing with a complete outfit, all set for the Yukon. It was the spring of 1898 − April. "May 24th found three others and myself nicely at Fort Smith". At this point he says he remembers certain dates very vividly, recalling also an oldtimer, McKinlay the Trader. "Could this be the father

Sourdough Frank Foster
Fascinating Story Teller

of my skipper on the Sandy Jane to Norman Wells?," I asked, linking the past with the present. "Yes", said Frank, pausing, "quite likely it could be". He continued. "We were the first boat to leave the Landing. But such luck and speed as we were having could not last. It didn't!," he said disgustedly.

Here the tone adjusts itself to disappointment as Frank speaks on. "Great Slave Lake dealt us a cold hand. . . ten miles from Resolution the breaking ice forced us ashore. . . sadly we watched boat after boat pass, headed for the Yukon. This was probably the most discouraging moment I've ever had," he admits, thrashing out the pain mentally as the words continue to flow. "There was every kind of boat, scow and barge on the river. . . one I remember from Chicago, it was sent out in parts and built at the Landing. . . it was a sternwheeler. . . I heard later it never got through." Pausing, as though groping for a distant memory, he adds: "There was another one from Detroit. . . she was O. K. " Frank's first round had been fought. He was still holding his own. I was still his ever−intent second. Here he pauses to stuff his pipe with a rich tobacco from the hexagonal glass jar on the table at his right, then continues. . . "there were many men from the Pullman Shops in Chicago. . . an old Sea Captain (and upon my interpolation). . . yes, I do recall two women. One went by the name of Hoffman, later Currie and now Mrs. Charlie Olson. . . I don't know how many more she's murdered," he adds wittily. "How come you've missed the Big Question?," I interrupted. "Oh, I couldn't see marrying an Indian like so many of the Oldtimers have. . . although I've had the question popped at me a few times," he confesses. Men of Frank Foster's age talk of, but are past the age of bragging about womenfolk.

Out of nowhere I suddenly find myself back on The Trail, portaging three times past that historically impossible turmoil of water over which no one has floated and lived. We are at the Fitzgerald Rapids. "A large white cross, in memory of the two priests who were caught in its narrowing circles, stands just at the head of the rapids," I interrupt again. "Oh", says Frank, picking up a new scrap of information with avidity, "that must have been since I passed. "

"July first Hay River was behind; also Providence, Simpson and we landed at Fort Norman. "I marvelled silently at his memory for dates. "I have times fixed firmly in my mind still," he continued. He must have read my thoughts. It appears July found the party still behind the rest but out of the Mackenzie into the Peel River. . . past the Huskie Channel. . . and finally poured into the narrow but swift Rat River under the lopstick on the left limit. It was only a matter of hours before the party (still four) arrived at Destruction City. Frank continues: "Here camps and caches were forced because of the uphill grind to the Lakes. This took considerable time. . . by now some outfits decided on a winter's stay here. " Another pause for a draught on his pipe. "Undaunted, our party burned the boat for the nails alone. . . Not an original board did we save! The nails were double clinched, so we just burned the old barge and planed boards from a nearby spruce thicket, but," he concludes, "we had thirty−hundredweight to haul in the small boat. . . some made three trips all round to relay their packs," he interjected, possibly thinking in terms of his own luck. As Frank strikes another match the dimming past slinks forward. "I had a complete outfit myself, from the ground up, and just joined the others." He thought pensively a moment. "But that Tom Boon's uncle was so damned impatient, I almost felt like pulling out! " adds Frank, getting himself excited all over again. "He was rush! rush! all the way. You with your diary," glancing my way as I hurriedly scrawled a few of the facts, "remind me of a rather humourous but tragic incident. I recall my own, rather cumbersome record, getting ducked several times. . . and finally lost in the Rat River. It was a sad loss. . . but it was so big I had to toss it in the grub box or elsewhere. . . and when we tipped once it must have gone under. Anyway, about the end of August we reached Loon Lake and it was frozen," he digressed, having surmounted the ordeals of the waters below, "but we pushed our way through and found rollers and some skids on the portage which some forerunners had used, by the look of it." Here it was my turn to sigh at the thought of our own twenty−two foot Peterborough canoe dragging over the miles of niggerheads and moss. Frank continued. "Someone had even taken a spade and pick and dug out the Little Bell so they could round all the bends. This made our descent fast. . . Our boat was worn out, so we burned it and built another at a thick spruce grove along the Bell. . . soon we were descending the Porcupine."

At this point I asked Frank about the aged 'lopstick' confronting the river at right angles. This he recalled plainly. Fifty years had not marred one small marker on the *Trail of '98*. Arousing a new set of memories, my words gave way to Frank's. "LaPierre House was there then, but deserted; its Hudson's Bay Co. buildings with their Red River frame still standing," he reflected. (A puff of smoke and Frank continued as though completely unaware of my presence, just speaking his thoughts aloud.) ". . . There was no Old Crow then, but we passed the spot and reached the deserted Rampart House in September. . . we were frozen in!. . . we had no idea about the weather, as no one had been this way recently. . . we camped in a blinding snowstorm. A few days later the sun shone brightly and everything melted. We repacked our boat and hit for Fort Yukon where we eventually had to stop. . . we holed up in one of the N. A. T. Company buildings. Then a feeling of certain calm after the stormy struggle permeated his words. "Here I made more money than I ever had," he rejoiced again at the thought of his youthful earnings. "They wanted $8.00 a cord for cutting wood and wanted a thousand cords cut. . . I was rich!. . . rolling in dough!" he emphasized, removing his pipe and toying with the sunglasses. ". . . none of the others had ever seen an axe, but I had been using one for years. . . I was at home then and went to work on the trees right away. However, I was soon laid up like the other three because of diet deficiency. . . you remember our sole diet was tea, coffee, bacon and beans!. . . well, there was a doctor there who, realizing the vitamin deficiency, prescribed boiled pine needles. Boy, oh boy!. . . it worked wonders! The word soon spread all over the Yukon. . . and everybody beat their scurvy, but quick! This same mixture of pine juice cured we four and all were soon in action, just like four beavers chewing at them trees."

"Winter over, and with money in pocket, I boarded the *John J. Healy* in the spring of '99. I was a deckhand with all the others who were unable to book passage. . . that was sure a good way of gettin' themselves a crew," he laughed heartily at the thought. I joined him in this, for it tickled my imagination greatly. So Dawson finally loomed in sight. "But", says Frank, "giving this city the once over and still feeling mighty restless, I took the opportunity to sign on as Day Watchman. . . you see, I figured all the good claims were staked and wages on the boat were as good nearly as shovelling that damned pay−dirt for someone else. . . not only that but I was anxious to see what Nome held in store for me. . . but I was a month too soon for the big strike there," he sighed as though his Angel of Good Fortune had frowned down upon him again. "Can you beat that. . . one month from being a king!. . . gold under my feet and I didn't even know it!" he muttered, working himself into his small, mental frenzies at the teasing thoughts of his past. But picking up with a thin thread he smiles, saying: "Promotion came fast. . . soon I was Second Mate on her. The First Mate was fired when she ran aground on the trip, and we all moved up one," he chuckled, as though having fooled the very Devil again. This part of his past amused Frank so much that he entered into convulsions at the thought of the fancy names they were given with each promotion, which amounted to the same in the end − WORK. "Anyway", he adjoined, "they sounded good and made you feel you were someone even though you knew damned well you were still just another gold−seeker." Back to Dawson, Frank set up a winter cabin with Tom Boon and upon looking the 'fair city' over again, decided to work on #5 with old Judge Dugas − a Frenchman who at that time was (as most every one was) in the glittering gamut. "Some dredging was in process," Frank says, " and this was the real work, shovelling a pile of mush many feet high. . . but we got good pay."

Finally we have reached the Argonauts' Paradise. Frank settles in to describe Dawson with its wine, women and song. . . " and there were some fine beauties,"says the oldtimer with a slight, lascivious respect, adding after a pause in which any number of thoughts could have occurred, ". . . mind you, they were not all 'on the row', as we called it. . . the stage girls were darn swell women, good actresses and artists at the Opera House. . . yes, the House (oft' called the Auditorium or Palace Grand Theatre by early prospectors) was a great place! I recall one night my pal and I went. . . I think the show was called *"SWIFT WATER WILLIE'S BRIDAL NIGHT"*? ". . . . . *Yeeeeeeessss,* that's it!," he assured us both. "Boy what a show! I had to return that night to my cabin out of town, but they told me later the show lasted only one night. . . I can understand that, too!," added the old prospector, smiling, with all the Devils in Hades dancing upon his features. It was at this point in the narrative that Frank mustered his most imaginative thoughts, and in true northern fashion might have added considerable colour to what actually happened, if it did? However, I didn't want him to lose my confidence so I let the tale continue uninterrupted, wondering just how much to believe. He continued. . .

"It was a surprise to everyone in the hall, but they enjoyed it. It brought down the house!". Leaning closer over the arm of his favourite chair, as though in the strictest confidence, he said: "For some time the shows had been good and clean. . . but this fellow Mulligan, the bad actor, sure changed things." Then I listened to the spice of the Yukon entertainment world, discovering that as the curtain fell on the 1st scene the police rushed along the aisles to the stage. . . too late! But they closed the show. With finality, Frank says: "And there were women in the audience too!. . . but they loved it all!"As Frank Foster leaned back in his easy chair the curtain fell on what could or could not have happened in the wild days of '98.

"Jack London?". He takes a deep puff and replies: "I saw him but didn't know till later that it was him. I was unimpressed. He was not tough or suave like so many of the people at that time, but stocky and boyish with curly hair. . . but this I will say: when he took the stage he held it! He could talk about anything and hold his own." While on the subject of the current literary gentleman, he said: "I did talk with Joaquin Miller but he was suave − altogether different from Jack."

With a sudden switch in his chain of thought, the grey−haired man asserted: "Gambling was wide open and the cashiers in the saloons would pinch five ounces or so with their thumb if you didn't watch; but I saw that right off when they shook the poke into the blower to weigh it. . . no, they never gypped me," he says with a chuckle, as though that was something in those days. I guess it was!

So '98 and '99 came and went, like Frank who signed on with his pal Tom Boon under another skipper aboard the John C. Barr − the only steel boat on the river. "It wasn't more that tin, but she went as steel, that steamer," laughs Frank whose contagious sense of humour never disappeared during the entire conversation. "We made a quick trip to Circle before freezeup, in the late fall of '99." The turn of the century saw Foster headed north and east, eventually stopping at Rampart House to cut hay for $8. 00 a ton. "We got our money, but I guess that hay is still stacked there!" he jokes. Since then Frank has done a little of everything, finally settling in Old Crow where he has been since about 1936.

As the narrative came up−to−date a knock on the door served as a conclusion to the adventurous wanderings of another Sourdough. A stooped figure, clothed in a zippered windbreaker and a once white fedora with a brim sadly drooping, entered at Frank's beckoning. A pipe protruded from the midst of a walrus moustache which moved slightly as he said: "Hello Frank. . . how's things today?" in his slow, French−Canadian drawl, much less effervescent than that language is usually spoken. Age was beginning to slow his processes too. But one thing: it never retards the youthful imagination of these freedom−loving pioneers of the North − Argonauts of 1898. "Dave", said Frank as the former assumed what must have been his customary place upon such visits, if the showing of comfort suggested anything: "I'd like you to meet a young Cheechako who just blew in over the same trail I did about fifty years ago. . . whadya think of that?"

"Always glad to shake the paw with anyone of guts enough to do what we did in the gold rush!", replied the French−Canadian. "Dave Lord is his name, came over the Chilkoot Pass from the west. Not only that, I'll tell you a funny story about the man," he ribbed, Dave apparently knowing what was to follow.

"Do you know what happened?" Frank asked as though I might know some small part of the tale. "This dang fool Dave, here, hears about a Frenchman, new in the country. So he ups and hitches his dogs and mushes a few hundred miles to where he's living. . . ho!ho!ho!" laughs Frank, unable to suppress his mirth, leaving me on the brink of a possible laugh too. ". . . well anyway, he arrives at the Frenchman's place and whadya know?. . . ha!ha!. . . the dang fool suddenly realizes he's been in the North so long, he's forgotten his native tongue. . . ho!ho!ha!ha!. . . the two couldn't say more than a few words and gesture with their hands. . . so Dave re− harnesses his dogs and hits back for home. . . and the trip was all in vain. . . ho!ho!ho!. . . " laughs Frank at the thought. Tears rolled down his face. Dave rubbed his own eyes clear, coughing consumptively over his foul pipe. My stomach could stand no more of this contagious Foster humour. Echoes of laughter died amongst the cobwebs in the remote corners of the ceiling.

The topic momentarily turned to the *Trails of '98,* Dave vivifying his entry via Skagway, Lake Bennett, Tagish, Windy Arm. It was Service's Trail come to life in a log cabin in the heart of the Yukon. After a short comparison of entries Frank says: "I rather enjoyed my long, scenic trip. " I (now somewhat recuperated from my own ordeals of late) agreeing to its charms, am confident I shall weather the other entry before many more months have passed. The topic turned to the weather and the morrow's wedding. We were back to 1947 in the neat, log−cabin settlement of Old Crow buried in central Yukon Territory.

CHAPTER TWENTY SIX

THE PRETTIEST WEDDING

Monday, the eventful day, dawned bright as the hammers of the natives, busy erecting the dance hall, rang through the Arctic air; shavings fell to the ground as the building slowly rose. Would it be finished in time for the Potlatch and dance? This was the burning question. In fact it soon became the talk of the entire settlement who (whenever the occasion permitted in their daily chores) would pass by and cast a questioning glance towards the busy natives swarming over the log structure. It became so contagious an event that I found myself watching the race with time. I put my odds on the Indians.

So the afternoon arrived and the wedding was upon us. With exactly the same arrangement as of the Sunday church service all streamed into the interior of the rustic chapel and resumed their places. With identical solemnity and Church of England ritual the two main figures listened to the binding words of Julius Kendi. What must have been 'I do' was spoken in Loucheux. The boy slid the ring over his new bride's finger. Only then did I realize Rowina Moses and Moses Lord became one. It was the most colourful wedding I had ever witnessed. As they turned down the aisle from the altar, the full significance and colour of an Indian wedding, performed by a full blooded Indian of the Anglican faith in the High North, became a reality. It was a far cry from a bygone era.

The bride wore a white veil over her head. A similar dress flowed to her feet which were wrapped in her very best moosehide moccasins, elaborate with beadwork and trimmed with ermine. In her arms she carried a colourful bouquet of flowers. The groom, although clad in his native moccasins, wore a well pressed green suit and looked only slightly different from a youth on the Outside about to give himself up to a woman. With all the

**Wedding of
Rowina Moses and Moses Lord
Rev. Julius Kendi, August 11, 1947**

solemnity of a White marriage the guests garbed in their gayest colours looked on. The aged church gave forth its couple. Rice, confetti and beans (thrown and shot by younger hands) rained all round. Knowing they could not 'Get Away' far, the couple accepted the punishment in good spirits. When the photographs were taken and the rice ran low, the two, running for a narrow trail, made off in the distance, still pursued by the urchins of the tribe slinging their chastising pellets. I secretly wished they had run for a hidden canoe and paddled off down the Porcupine. This would have been Romance in all its Indian splendour!

Three shots split the stillness of late afternoon. It was the prearranged signal for the Potlatch. I had been biding my time awaiting future events. Now I would participate in a real Indian Potlatch. Originally the Potlatch was for the male hunters only. It was a wild repast in celebration of a successful hunt. The animals were barbequed wholesale over large, open fires. These feasts lasted for days, sometimes accompanied by weird native dances which, arousing the primitive passions, led to a frenzied state of mind and often collapse. In days of yore it was the custom to have a feast when a boy killed his first caribou. This was a sign of his Manhood. When he bagged his first moose it was a sign of eligibility for marriage. This too had its accompanying feast.

The present—day Potlatch has taken on a slightly different shade. We gathered in the community hall in response to the signalling shots. White guests sat at a small separate table—the most venerated position of the feast. Next, at a log table, sat the males, young and old in accordance with their tribal status. Then came the women, sitting on what few benches remained vacant after the males were seated, the majority squatting on the floor at the extreme end of the hall holding, or carrying on their backs, their papooses. Finally the children, restless as any youngsters at a party, clambered about on the floor with food darting in every direction.

The ceremonial repast was commenced with a speech by the Chief from the centre of the table. In solemn manner he spoke and gesticulated much. They tell me Peter Moses, with long and sincere apologies, explained the absence of the traditional dish−their native caribou. It was his foremost wish that the white guests and the newly−weds sup of this animal. Hunters had looked far and wide for signs of the migration; but alas!. . . none were to be found. It had been a bad year in more ways than this. What was wrong? Was the Sigalie Tyee angry? No matter, we would feast on other victuals concocted by the tribal women. The Chief expressed his extreme pleasure at being able to entertain the white guests with food and hospitality. Finally in many more words, some accompanied by his warm smile, Chief Peter told of his great delight that Moses Lord and Rowina Moses were now man and wife. He bestowed upon them much happiness, many long years together and many babies to carry on their name and customs of the people. Much clapping, we settled before our hearty Potlatch.

Course upon course was set before us. I made the unique discovery that Indian women and girls can cook a variety of appetizing dishes−a far cry from native drymeat and fish. Soup was followed by fresh fish prepared in numerous ways with sauce. Boiled and roasted meat of many kinds came forth, some the product of tins, others from the caches where cured and dried meats lay for further ripening. Vegetables, as though streaming from the Horn of Plenty, passed in close procession along the length of the table. Beautiful young maidens, dressed in their very best, served second helpings over the proper shoulder. For a couple of hours their pace scarce slowed between the empty plates and the Table of Plenty. Warm bannocks oozing with butter shared a place with the freshly baked bread. Then came the dessert. Variegated dishes of jelly, trifles, cakes passed by in lavish parade. The variety brought temptation. Tea and coffee completed the repast. Everyone had eaten heartily. The Halfbreed and the Cheechako long remembered the week before and this eventful day. A final speech of slightly less length than the first brought the Potlatch to an end.

It is customary for the women to bring the eating utensils with them. As I prepared to go I could not help noticing them each filling their bowls and dishes with remnants of the feast, passing into the night towards their individual cabins. 'There will be no waste in Old Crow this year,' I thought. 'Perhaps caribou will run next year?' I sincerely hoped so, for I saw just how much it means to these people. Maybe my next traditional feast would be honoured with caribou?

I slipped into the night, away form my very first Indian Potlatch.

At ten o'clock another volley of shots rent the air. I listened closely. Then it came. Thumping feet told me the dance was under way. The hall had been completed! My odds had been well placed! Not wanting to miss one colourful event of this day, I cleaned up as best I could and made haste to the newly−erected dance hall.

The weird crescendo of thumping feet rose like the haunting beat of a tom−tom through the village night. It was luring the youth and the aged with its passionate throb. Who could resist that Siren echo wafting through the chilly, August air. I too was caught. I fell a victim to its rhythmic spell. I passed beneath the gables of a row of faintly−silhouetted log cabins. Then I caught sight of a ray of orange light leaning carelessly into the black night. It directed my footsteps towards the noisy hall.

Entering, I discover the source of the beat. It is the moccasined fiddler's foot thumping time to the accompaniment of a guitar. This is the entire orchestra. 'They certainly know how to make up in volume for their deficiency in numbers,' I said to myself−now a part of the goings−on. As each fiddler tires a fresh one falls into his place and the *Red River Jig*, quadrille or a variety of square dances, continues. Here and there a fast one− step of two−step is inserted. The motley crowd changes. Intermittent intervals find a 'general resting' following the energetic Indian capers. For all, it seems like an endurance test between musicians and dancers. At this point it was hard to tell who was winning. Certainly it was not I!

Unaccustomed to such warming paces set by the orchestra and held by the dusky little maidens (as Frank Foster is wont to call them), I am soon forced to join the ranks of the squaws sitting about the circumference of the hall, in silent observation of their pretty daughters. Smiles on furrowed faces turned back the years to their own youth and their own gay times. It was at one of these rest periods for the Cheechako that the bride and groom entered the sanctuary of gaiety. The evening wore on. I watched them in their new−found happiness. I felt sure that Dave Lord and Johnny Moses would be quite proud of the union of their son and daughter, for they matched well. They did justice to one another and to the music played in their honour. Again I sat on the sidelines exchanging remarks with an aged squaw. She told me the dance would, in all probability, last till dawn; that in the old days it was not unusual to prolong them for two or three days. Realizing the completely fatigued state they must have been in, and the already tired one I was in, I joined forces with the orchestra in a number.

For all the chuckles and looks of awe, my clarinet might just as well have been a piece of pipe. It was that much out of place in an Indian orchestra. Despite looks or chuckles, I took a deep breath and launched into the prearranged number. The guitar, the fiddle and the feet were with me. If I remember rightly, it wasn't good, but it was loud. That was satisfactory to the audience. How we finished on the same beat is one of those imponderables. My friends improvised even to the number of beats in a bar. Somewhere among that maze of notes I became lost. Undaunted I continued to force sound from my musical weapon. I was no to be outdone by guitar, violin or feet (the latter were my greatest competitors, thumping so that the hall vibrated). Then in an all out chorus−the maidens on the dance floor swirling in widening circles, their many dresses and coloured petticoats rising and falling−it was every man for himself. As we neared the finale I could hear nothing but foot beats. I glanced down. I was an offender too! Then as suddenly as we had started all three instruments and all six feet came to a quick halt. Only the shuffle of moccasined feet filled the hall; there was no one participating who did not have sweat running down his or her face. That would have been impossible. I wiped my brow; disassembled by instrument and thanked the band−boys for my first privilege of playing with an Indian combo. Smiles from them and the dancers showed approval of the Dazzio! (whiskers). I was wet, tired, but happy. I waved goodnight to the squaws and their enjoyable daughters and made for my teepee, exhausted.

The arrival of the Northern Commercial Company boat with its Skipper−Steele, on Tuesday, prolonged the eventful weekend. This meant work for idle hands; gasoline and food for the settlement; and another bout of Northern hospitality for the Cheechako. I strolled casually to the embankment; gazed along the line of sweating natives lugging thirty−gallon wooden cartons of gasoline to the summit. It was then I spotted the skipper giving instructions from the deck of the flatboat from which this endless stream of drones poured. I descended.

I felt I knew the man just by his genuine handshake; the handclasp was inversely proportional to his size. Mr. Steele is a short, plump man by no means soft as of outward appearance. Garbed in his blue denims and greasy ski−cap he cuts an odd figure. As we talked he did not once stop his energetic duties as skipper, but continued to yell instructions in an apparently serious manner, adding to this a few words definitely in need of censorship. Seemingly used to this verbal onslaught the natives varied not their pace. As one said to me later, rather perplexed: "I don't know whether he means it or not?" Such was the desired psychological effect. Glad of an opportunity to welcome a white stranger from the Outside, Steele insisted I come to dinner this evening. As happy as he to meet my own kind, I accepted whole− heartedly.

So it was that the best whiskey came forth from its 'rainy− day' seclusion; the piquant odour of a baking roast left the stove to roam; an aura of hospitable warmth permeated the room; and the conversation flowed freely as it eventually turned from the proceedings of the day to the succession of wars in the past decade in which both had served in the ranks. Such conversations are bound to travel to certain depths in various directions. With these depths well probed my host, with the ring of familiar names, towns, streets, and 'pubs' in his ears, declared we 'warm the cockles' once more, and then settle to the delicious process of eating. "The roast's well done already!" hinted the feminine voice from the kitchen, cunningly not wanting to interrupt reminiscences; our unheard toast to the fair lady and her cooking was about to be answered. Like matter, we changed from fluids to solids.

Justice had been done to everything, including a post—dinner conversation inspirited by the foregoing pleasures. I had brought news and tidings from the Outside world; they had contributed their wealth of information on the North. Then with that reluctance that comes to us all at intervals—to depart from especially satisfying company and surroundings—I chose the line of most resistance and left the family to themselves. I had an obligation to fulfil. I had promised to visit the cabin of Baalyum—the Medicine Man.

The night was still young as I weaved in and out, seeking his abode amongst sombre dwellings strewn about at random along the riverbank. I recognized the tumble—down porch. I knocked. With his ever—ebullient welcome and smiling countenance I was invited by Baalyum into the interior, where sat his wife and Big Joe—the minister's assistant. Conversation commenced with the 'dazzio', the recipient of much kidding; veered to the recent tribal activities; stumbled and fell into the mundane abyss of the weather. However, it recovered its fall and stopped at Baalyum and his medicinal capabilities.

With a sly smile on his face he says: "I can make the caribou run. . . and also make the salmon run!" I showed doubt in order that he explain further. Later when probing his mystics elsewhere I learned that he once sold his information for a price; but I would say now that the average young brave is not as gullible as his tribal ancestors were before the appearance of the Whiteman.

"You had better make sunshine tomorrow or you will hear form me," I said to Baalyum, smiling at the thought of the formula. Beaming confidently he replies: "Baalyum make good medicine today. . . he will make it tomorrow too!" "He'd better!" I threaten, "for the Cheechako had decided to leave the settlement on the morrow!" At this the entire gathering breaks into convulsions realizing the obvious impossibility of making such magic. The laughter dies. "I will show you some of the Whiteman's medicine," I said, reaching for his pouch lying on the table. "This is the Midnight Sun," I point. "Now I shall show you why it does not go to bed in the summer. " Leaning closer he and Big Joe watch

Baaylum—Medicine Man and Wife

my explanation with awe. Handing him back his pouch I conclude the illustration, smiling largely from my seat before the table. It is the only smile in the cabin. Looking up form the crude diagram and his tobacco pouch, Baalyum rewards the 'dazzio' with the simple but sincere words of a bewildered medicine man who admits he has learned a new kind of medicine. "You are the first man to ever tell me that!" he confesses benignly. I was humbly honoured. One can never leave an Indian family without accepting some offering. Already a kettle of water hissed on the stove. Baalyum's wife brewed a pot of tea. We sat for awhile and chatted. It was getting late when the sorcerer's meeting came to a pleasant close. "I shall return tomorrow and take a picture of Baalyum and his wife. . if he should be so kind as to make such sun medicine?" I suggested. "It will be so!. . . it will be so!", he assured me, following the author to the door. I slipped away into the night a little bit wiser as to Indian medicine.

Visiting among the natives extends, as a rule, into the early hours of the morning. Tonight I intended to keep to the rule and make a promised call. John Kendi, son of the minister, had insisted I serenade his wife and he with some favourite tunes before our departure westward. I had not intended to forget the visit because I realized the importance to an Indian of a Whiteman's promise. Small as it was, I felt it might mean much.

I was not wrong in this thought. I was expected. To my enjoyment as I entered the Kendi home—bereft of all its children by the merciless T. B. —I beheld the Chief sitting contentedly in one corner. It was to be a merry occasion. I perceived the ingredients already. With no persuasion I pieced together my instrument, to the amazement of the gathering. Never before had they seen anything musical quite like this. 'It will be interesting to note their response to the first note', I thought. The inevitable resemblance to a migrating 'honker' was noted, but the requests soon followed.

Piece after piece brought a memory, a thought, which in turn found a voice for more. The party went well till a most unusual request brought laughter to the cabin and an end to the entertainment through natural causes. Noting the Chief in a moment of silence I politely asked: "What number would you like to hear Chief?" He thought for a moment. After a long drawn−out silence he lifted his head and said: *"ONE MEAT BALL!"*. The silence of a Yukon evening was broken with wholesome laughter which for minutes must have passed out of the chinks in the cabin and over the Porcupine, fading in the distant hills beyond. . . it still came from within as I, unable to control my mirth, dismantled the instrument and returned it to its case. Rather than have my company think I was laughing at them and not with them, I prepared to go. It was thanks that followed the 'Dazzio' out of the door this time. He thought 'how wonderful their appreciation of small things, and how at home he felt with the most virgin tribe of Indians yet encountered. He departed all smiles.

At a safe distance from the cabin I said to myself: *"ONE MEAT BALL . . . ."* Another burst of laughter echoed through the Yukon night . . . and a faint voice laughed back.

CHAPTER TWENTY SEVEN

GOOD AND BAD MEDICINE

Wednesday dawned dull. Baalyum had not made good medicine! He would hear of this! Malcolm, who I had seen very little of since our arrival, must have been well cared for by his native friends, for, in good spirits, he stopped me in front of the village. "Hello, Dazzio!. . . all ready to go?" he asked, eager, I could see, to continue our delayed journey westward. "And eager!" I ejaculated. "We'll need a couple crates of gas and some grub. . . I'm gonna sell the canoe and get rid of some gear!" "What's up?" I questioned, "lemme in on your schemes sometime, will you?" "Didn't you know, we're going down the river on an inboard scow!. . . Johnny Kendi's gonna adopt a son at Fort Yukon. . . we're leaving soon!" "Well, thank God!. . . no more patching and bailing!" Malcolm smiled in complete understanding; he departed to strike a deal somewhere.

Adventure was calling us both again. We did not resist it. It would not be fitting for the people of Old Crow to send a guest away without some showing. So it was that I had another invitation for a send−off dinner. "We can't let you leave on an empty stomach," said Mr. Steele, calling me to the house. Northern hospitality flowed again. Like the 'fatted calf' ready to be shipped to Fort Yukon, I clasped the hands that had welcomed me so warmly, bidding goodbye to the Steele family−both the inner and outer man well contented.

**Frank Steele Family
and Loucheux Helper**

Paying a final visit to the Kirks, who had so graciously received me first, I bade them the very best. The memory of that life−saving meal still lingered in my mind. It lingers yet to this day. A yell from the scow told me plainly that all was in readiness.

A gang had gathered on the riverbank. There was much ado in the thirty−five foot scow below. "Well, Paul Ben Kassi!" I shouted, recognizing a fiddler from the dance. "You're going to travel in a real boat now. . . and get there!" he added, glancing at our own canoe drawn up on the beach farther down. I smiled. He would be good company. "Johnny and Martha Kendi going, too. . . and another friend." "Don't forget Malcolm," I said; "He's almost a part of me now!" "We got him too. . . here he comes now. . . all set, Malcolm?" A broad smile told me the deal had succeeded. I knew instinctively we were ready. My native companion jumped into the rear. "Sold the canoe as it stood in the water!" he said, all smiles. I tried to imagine the look on the buyer's face at his discovery of the improvised bottom. "Well, that's that!" I sighed . . . and the engine coughed.

I was struck by the talk of the 'friend' who was accompanying us down river. He had sold out his trapping interests in the village, destined to work for the Whiteman in Fairbanks, Alaska. The latter explains in full the conversion of the modern Indian from his natural way of life to that of the Whiteman. He talked of 'big money' which failed to impress me; I personally felt a certain sympathy for the fellow. How quickly he had sold his heritage, his bond with Nature−the preserver of the Indian. How slowly I was learning his way of life, his secrets of survival when ordinary human odds are discounted. Little did he know how rich I was getting; how poor he was getting. The outboard lapsed into a steady roar. . . white smoke rose above the churning waters behind the barge. . . we headed into midstream.

Catching sight of Baalyum amongst the multitude of people I yelled: "Your medicine is lousy, Baalyum!", and a drop of rain fell on my face. He waved his hand frantically in recognition of the 'Dazzio'. "Something go wrong. . . me try hard!" came to me on the wind. I smiled to myself, waving a last friendly gesture to all. 'He has an answer for everything', I said as I settled amongst the caribou skins on the floor of the barge. Fort Yukon, we were coming. . . The engine throbs its way through the rain; we continue to wind our way along the swift waters, eating our meals aboard, the natives taking turns at the rudder−bar. Verdant scenery gradually wears off giving way to crags rearing themselves from both banks. We have reached the Ramparts−rivals to those on the Mackenzie. Coloured rocks in grotesque shapes, looking not unlike works of some crude sculptor, rear their irregular shapes and with a little imagination take on the appearance of familiar historical busts.

The 'Ramparts'
Porcupine River From 35 Foot Scow

Paul Ben Kassi and
Peter Tazia on the Bow

Skipper−Paul Ben Kassi
Through the Ramparts

The Ramparts
Looking Back Towards Old Crow

We passed through the Canyon, emerging on the other side into welcome sunlight. This was an unexpected blessing, for Malcolm and I still felt we had our share of water in the Rat Portage. Spirits rose. We continued, seemingly gaining on the western sun, our attitude disturbed only by the occasional flock of ducks or geese venturing close enough to be good targets. At eight o'clock we arrived at Rampart House, the Canadian−American boundary line. Beaching the scow, we had that pleasant feeling of the discoverer trodding on foreign soil. At last! we stood on American soil.

I was especially curious to view the remnants of what D'Arcy Arden had told me was a one−time flourishing trading post. The story goes that one Dan Cadzo, a man who liked a big show and the centre of activity, decided to build himself a large mansion at Rampart, where he could enjoy all the amenities of home life and be his own little king at the same time. This dream became a reality as the fur trade boomed in the ditrict. He even constructed a cable car which could haul goods from the shores of the Porcupine and thus eliminate certain physical labours. I am told that he was very fond of beverages other than water and wouldn't hesitate to 'bend an elbow' with the next man. It also came to eager ears that this was the enjoyable manner in which he "shuffled off this mortal coil" during one of his wassails, leaving the trading post in the hands of his squaw wife. Money meant nothing to Dan on his sprees, I gathered, and he spent generously in his ostentatious display. All this had been related to me as I stood looking over the little, deserted settlement. I pieced the Indian's phrases together and saw quite clearly the man's life. Today his dream—home still stands, lonely, empty, boarded—up, a home fit only for mice and ghosts.

**Rampart House
Home of Dan Cadzo**

Climbing to the top of the embankment I came face to face with a metal cone which, upon closer scrutiny, divulged the words UNITED STATES-CANADA BOUNDARY. In the greying twilight my mind flashed back over half a century to the rugged figures that erected this very marker, and perhaps on some equally dim evening trudged further north along the 141st parallel of longitude. Continuing up the gradual incline towards the dull cluster of buildings, my footsteps

Old Rampart—Alaska

brought me to a weatherbeaten church, indistinguishable but for the Gothic windows crudely boarded over. Forcing a way past the obstinate door, I beheld stained glass windows still intact, reflecting their prism of light onto the floor laden with the dust and filth of years. Some unpolished pews lined the side. "What's this?" I said, stopping to pick up a picture frame. It was a photo of Bishop Stringer—well—liked early missionary in the Yukon. I dusted it off and stood it upright on the table. I distinctly heard him say: "Carry on, my son, your mission is a worthy one." I passed from the uninspiring interior that once echoed with the combined Sunday chorals of Indian and Whiteman; but the echo of the Bishop passed outside with me. There was no turning back; I had to carry on!

Going towards the deserted mansion one comes upon a once active Mounted Police Barracks, the dried white caribou horns surmounting the doorway telling its age. A small detachment once lived here, but with the decline of the gold rush and the eventual desertion of the trading post, it was abandoned. Behind this rotting frame lie a group of low—built cabins with deteriorating caches falling off their perches. The buildings are a molasses colour from age and upon close examination reveal a not—too— distant occupation, for they are littered with caribou hides and horns. Within each is a rusted stove (probably the original) brought upriver in the very early days, some the worse for wear.

Crossing the creek, which has ceased to be active like the rest of the settlement, and climbing the opposing bank, I come face to face with Rampart House itself. She resembles a Queen reduced to poverty; a two—storey, gabled mansion clothed in a faded coat of green and white, looking haggardly to the west. No sound of boisterous, good times have echoed into the night for many a year. Only Dan Cadzo's Indian squaw kept her family and what life she could, thriving, after his death. Then she too deserted the site. This accounts for the remaining inanimate occupants: bedposts, chairs and boxes. Beside the house are more weatherbeaten buildings that comprise the trading post. Forcing the door I enter the two—storey house of business. Thick oak counters line two walls, their showcases empty but for a few large coloured beads, cheap trinkets, once traded for furs to the Indians. The fixtures suggest anything but poverty within the post. Still inquisitive, I climb to the upper storey. There, strewn across the entire floor lie moose, deer and caribou antlers in great profusion. Yes, it had certainly been a rich district at one time.

There is something fascinating about decayed and ancient dwellings; but there is also something repulsive to bring one back to the present. With this feeling I left the cobwebs in charge of the past and groped my way outside to the fading dusk of the present. In the open again I heard a peculiar sound. In the eery twilight I turned quickly. What is that? Then I knew. The wind, blowing through the exposed ribs of a skiff, deprived of its skin—covering by Time and now denuded atop its stage, proved a veritable *Harp of the Winds*. It was the accompanying funeral dirge in the Dead March of Rampart House.

This was not the only exposed craft that had not seen water for many a year. As I slid down the embankment towards the welcome fire and smell of cooking meat, I stumbled across another set of equally bare ribs of larger calibre. Beside them lay their rusted motive power—a widely dispersed array of rusted engine parts. The cable and cable car shared the same inactive fate. The dream of them had become a reality, but now a decayed mass, waiting to return to the source of origin of all things.

The evening meal was cooked and mostly eaten by the time I reached the campfire. Wading into a chunk of caribou, speared with a hunting knife from the boiling pot, I soon caught up to the rest. A few minutes later John's wife was cleaning dishes. I smiled at Malcolm. He smiled at the Cheechako. Both reflected: we realized then the beauty of having a woman along; had it not been so, they would have been given a quick flush in the river and a similar toss into the grub box. Our realizations were warranted. Had we not done this very thing in our tired haste through the Rat Portage? Sometimes (admittedly) the freedoms of the North are carried to extremes. But the Cheechako and the Improved Scotchman owed no one an apology. I glanced across the fire and the native still smiled. The last dish found its clean self in the grub box. Supper was over.

The Porcupine claimed us at eight—thirty; darkness claimed both at ten. Not a soul had we seen en route. Understandable was our extreme pleasure at sight of an Indian coming down to the water's edge at midnight in answer to our *"Haloooooooo. . . ".* We had reached Old Rampart—the original site of the boundary line till confusion forced it further east. "Pull ashore," said Paul; "we stop for the night!"

A quick exchange of greetings and we all made for the warmth of the cabin. Here I discovered who the dark shape was that had come to welcome us. His name was Dave John. In turn he introduced us to his wife and family. This over we set about to eat, drink and make merry with a violin and clarinet—which my unkind friends told Dave I was concealing. This served to arouse his curiosity the more. He demanded that he hear "this funny thing. " With no alternative I fetched the instrument: I began to play songs at random. It was in such a moment as a song loosened his mind that the tragedy of the family came forth. Dave said: "I have lived here fourty—one years. Last year," he continued in his best English, "my family was eight. . . this year is four!" He took another drink as though trying to forget. I

Dave John
Old Rampart

waited patiently for the answer that I knew would come. "T. B." he uttered in capital letters. "Two die. . . two are in hospital. . . we are just four now." He half lowered his head; too strong to cry; too drunk to laugh.

This would never do! So I played a lively tune and the subject changed itself as his wife danced forth from the other room. Indian welcomes are never half−hearted. This one held to the rule as ample food, cooked by Dave's pleasant daughter, was placed under our noses. Climaxed by a basin of berries it was complete. Sleep was the obvious item on the program. It had been a long day. Even a sleeping−bag on the floor felt soft. Heavy breathing and the odd snore filled the cabin. . . . *Bang! Crash! Thud!* and the cabin vibrated with the pounding of fists on the door. "Lemme in! I'll shoot the works of you!. . . lemme in!" and a volley of unprintable curses followed the command. "What's up?" I asked, jumping from my sleeping bag in one, ordinarily impossible move. "Someone forget the party's over," came a hollow voice from the darkness. It spoke of fright. "I'll go out and tell him to go on back to bed. . . I wouldn't mind some sleep myself!" I said impatiently. "No! No!. . . he mad. . . he might shoot!", stuttered another voice from within. The banging continued. Round and round the house beat the intruder with fists and feet. Wilder and wilder beat my heart in an earnest desire to shut him up. "He had too much good time. . . he mad!. . . you stay way!. . . you no understand!" I understood−too damned well! It wasn't the first time I'd seen an Indian lose self−control 'cause he was crazy enough to get himself all 'hootched up'. It's been going on for years. Ever since the white man introduced malt, beans, raisins and contributed his personal recipes to the easily− swayed redskin. It was just another debauch. It would have to end. I was sleepy.

Dave John and Family
Good−byes

I strode to the door without the support of my colleagues. Someone had to convince him we were friends. I slid into the night. The door−latch clicked behind me. I must face my inebriated adversary. Feeling not unlike a Mounted Policeman must in a critical moment I spoke: "Hey! come here. I want to talk. . . I'm a friend." He approached awkwardly and I commenced talking. I did not stop for a half−hour. Topics ranged from the caribou run. . . to the Porcupine river. . . to the fishing. . . and finally in a psychological moment I remembered something. 'I'll try it, and quick!' I told myself, still unable to convince the fellow.

"We have pancakes and syrup this high for breakfast," I motioned with both hands, remembering his words of some hours before. His eyes brightened. I was on the right track. I daren't slacken now. "This high," I added, spreading my hands farther apart. He smiled broadly. It was his favourite dish. "Now!," he said bluntly. "In the morning," I suggested. "This is fit for owls only at night. . . Whiteman and Indian eat many, many flapjacks in the morning." And I continued to pour syrup over them.

A momentary pause and words confirmed his decision. "Okay dazzio" (he recognized the whiskers in his stupor). . . "but two of you come sleep in my cabin." I gulped. What next? hadn't he threatened to shoot us? Oh well, I consoled myself, I can't think of a pleasanter exodus. It'll be quick. I convinced another of us that it would be safe with numbers. "Okay. . . we go with you," I said briskly, smothering all qualms. So, mustering all the courage of a Mountie backed by the law, I picked up my robe. The three of us, receiving 'good luck' from the remainder, peeking from the cabin door, crossed the browned−grass. We entered the other abode. Flopping bed and all on the floor we listened to some music scraping its way through to this distant outpost. It served with words as detraction. The log hut was verbally full of pancakes, imaginary syrup ran off the plates, over the table and coursed its way along the floor. Insomnia had overcome two of us. The third mumbled. . . snored. "We can go to sleep now," I whispered to my friend. "Thank God!"he whispered back tiredly. Minds relaxed and out of gear we must have followed suit. The sensitive fingers of Sleep stroked our eyeballs gently.   Morning came early. A ray of light slanted through the window. It was seven o'clock. I woke my friend. The third snored heavily. "We'd best get out quick. . . the memory's sometimes not a good thing." He was dressed and out the door before me. The third did not stir. Over pancakes − only twelve high!−I listened to jokings of the night before and sporadic scraps of the one−time historic post. "It was one time a Hudson's Bay trading centre. . . graves still up on hill. . . you want to see maybe?" he said. The pancakes decreased. Breakfast, without our boisterous friend, was over. Dave and I started the climb.

We wasted no time in reaching the top, Dave still the good Indian walker he has always been. I hoped for something ancient. Eyes brightened when Dave stooped to the grass, retrieving a grey wooden slab, soiled with age but still maintaining its original shape, carved by some crude northern hand into a facsimile of the real thing. The deceased was not forgotten. Peering close I read:

SACRED TO THE MEMORY OF
JAMES SIBBESTON,
NATIVE OF ORKNEY,
POSTMASTER H. BAY. CO.
DIED 14/MAY/1879.
AGE 61 YEARS.

'Twenty years before the Gold Rush!' I thought. All I could utter was "My!" "old, no?," was Dave's question to my reaction. I agreed. We glanced hastily at the remains of the picket fence and other rotten slabs which were unreadable. We descended.

 The clock was creeping closer towards noon. We must be off. Shaking hands with all, we clambered into our usual places in the scow. A *'put! put!'* from within, in response to the feverish turning of the heavy inboard's wheel, brought looks of satisfaction to all faces. Fort Yukon would be next! As we pulled away from shore the figures of the John family stood waving on the beach for some time, like marooned folk watching the last sign of life disappear before the silence set in on their solitude.

Scene Along the Porcupine River
To Fort Yukon

A Trappers 'Cache'
Safe From Prowlers

We were soon passing out of the Ramparts into an illuminating sunshine which chased away the gloom−clouds. Under such conditions this mode of travel was very pleasant, much more so than paddling a canoe on an empty stomach in the rain! "Look, a bear!," cried an Indian. As the discovery stimulated us another voiced hailed another bruin. Malcolm reached for his 30/30. "Three of them!" I shouted, a little too loud for hunting's sake. Paul threw the rudder bar. We circled for advantage. Malcolm raised the rifle. *Click!* and he cursed. Our circle neared completion. "Where's the bullets?"asked the frustrated marksman, feeling in his pockets. The

188

situation was tense. Two black bears and a cub—and no shells. A second circle, this time smaller. Tension mounted. Nothing was said. The bears turned. . . loped into the brush from whence they had come. "Dammit!" cut the silence. It was enough. We completed the circle as though nothing had happened. Well, nothing had, except that I had visions of lying in front of a fireplace on the soft fur while the animal still wore it. I checked my imagination, slumped back against the scow slightly disappointed, but ever watchful towards the banks. My optimism was not to be dimmed.

Along the Porcupine we splash—twisting, turning, dodging the sandbars where they appear. "Raise the rudder—bar!" cries the pilot, "sand bar ahead!". But it comes a shade too late. The bar thrashes, water bubbles, the screw scrapes bottom.

The engine cuts. "No damage!" says the native voice from the rear. We continue with added precaution. Many aged dwellings appear and now and then a 'stage' elevated high off the ground breaks the line of spruce alongshore. 'Ahhhh. . . we are on our *Trail of '98* again', I soothe myself. 'Klondike, I'm coming!' A cabin lazily puffs smoke skyward. . . signs of life. . . "That Charlie Martin's", says John, eager to inform me of everything. A body waves from the shack. We pass on. . . .

A small collection of huts and tents appear. "Burned Paw," says my fellow tillicum John Kendi. "There is a legend. . . " "Tell me!" I ask. A brief pause. . . his thoughts find words. "Many years ago there was a trapper. He cannot get home to his woman. . . too far. So he make camp. Building big his fire he lay down to sleep. . . the fire dies to ashes. . . a bear prowls too close while he is sleep. . . he burn his paw. So you see they call it Burned Paw," he ended casually, looking to me for assent. "I see. . . . " I add this to the growing list of legends stored in the archives of my mind.

"The Village, that is what they call it," said John later as another settlement appeared and as quickly disappeared in our wake. It was five—thirty. Time for a rest and food. Beaver, given to us at Old Rampart, was to be the main course. My palate was about to experience a new thrill.

Supper. . . a lowering sun. . . once more the river claimed us. Another in the increasing gamut of cabins dotted a clearing. "Joe Ward," said my alert informant. It is a pleasure to find one who is eager to divulge knowledge at anytime. My man knew I wanted to share. Another cabin. . . silhouetted against the western sky, high above the vertical dirt bank. The river was coming to life. I was especially eager for a verbal exchange along the way. I was looking for more Frank Fosters, more David Lords, more remnants of that heroic band of Argonauts. Ten—thirty. . . time for a rest. We were welcomed at a cabin by the occupants who showed signs of desiring company. Invariably the case in such isolated spots, we reciprocated with our own enthusiasm, glad of a break from our chilly, open scow.

We entered Schuman House. "Mr. and Mrs. Joe Herbert," said my friends in introduction. "This is our Dazzio who travels much across the North. He goes to Yukon with us now." They chuckled at five months growth of whiskers; I smiled from behind them, for I was enjoying the perpetual joke as much as they. Relaxing in the warmth given off by a red—hot barrel heater, I scrutinized the room in my usual silent observation for peculiarities. Ancient calendars, stained and rolling at the corners, told of parted years; a painting of Christ betrayed the influence of the missions and the Anglican Missionaries; a bead—work holdall adorned another wall, its exterior studded with pins, needles and other feminine effects; a Coleman gas lamp hung from a rafter doing an excellent job of illumination.

Confluence of the Porcupine and Yukon Rivers Fort Yukon, Alaska

Soon the kettle boils. The table is set ready for another repast. We dig into the hardtack and butter; dry fish and dried, tinned salmon (appetizingly pink), followed by tinned pears. Conversation jumps from one to another of us till finally the tale of the trip over the mountains comes to the fore. With interpretation the speech becomes a confused Indian—English chatter, the intermittent laughter our common denominator. With only one complaint arising from old Joe, who bemoans his broken leg which will not heat, the enjoyable hospitality comes to an end. Next door to Sleep I am aroused from the well—worn curves of my seat to face the night, and its merciless August chill, with my companions.

The family, including the son, daughter and their howling dogs, wave from the bank till their forms become a part of the night. Our coughing engine is all that disturbs the vast silence of the Alaskan countryside. The swish of a flock of ducks and the solitary flight of a single goose, close to the canoe, are the only attractions as the night wears on. At eleven—thirty we are ninety miles from Fort Yukon. The last I remember before sleep overcame me was my companion boiling some beaver over a gas stove in the front of the scow. The ordinarily exciting smell of this and boiling coffee failed to arouse my sensual desires; but the rhythmic throb of the inboard soon satiated my appetite for slumber. . .

My first impression on the morning of August 15th was that of a 'V' of ducks heading south. With it the artists' conception on calendars became a reality as they winged away, fading into infinity against a fiery sunrise. It was eight a. m. We were but a few miles from our destination. Breakfast was eaten on the move. I settled to viewing the scenery which levelled out even more with the increased speed and size of the river. We were being rushed to somewhere. An hour later it came! Emerging from the mouth of the Porcupine, we were poured bodily into its confluence with the Yukon River. *The Yukon River!. . . the waterway to Dawson City! 300 miles to the Klondike! My Columbian voyage took on a new meaning. Gold!. . . the gold of Bonanza, Hunker, Eldorado, Last Chance, Gold Run. . . awaited the Cheechako. Three hundred measly miles between me and the wealth of the Klondike. 'Well, nothing will stop me now even if I have to paddle all the way!' I thought, trying not to show my excitement to my companions. Freezeup's a long way off, too. 'You're well ahead of the majority coming through the Portage,' encouraged the voice of Adventure. I was determined to share some of that wealth.*

Extremely swift, with a regular Delta spreading fingerlike in all directions, the dirty waters splash against the clean—cut banks of the Yukon river. A breeze sweeps across the delta from the north, making our navigation slightly difficult. As it crosses diagonally the wind throws waves against the starboard side. "Hold the bar!. . . ease into shore," shouted one amongst us. Another obeyed.

CHAPTER TWENTY EIGHT

THE LAST FRONTIER

Ten a. m. and we pull under the lee of the high embankment beside numerous other scows—some submerged, others submerging and still others slapped by the rising waves. A first impression would lead one to believe it was carelessness on the part of the owners; but a closer examination shows the scarcity of beach, which for the main has been washed away by the spontaneous onslaughts of the mighty Yukon. Stars and Stripes fly over the Fort. There is no doubt. . . we are in Alaska. Not unlike its founder, Alexander Murray, we debark from our scow, seeking a suitable site upon which to erect our camp, one hundred years later.

**Fort Yukon, Alaska
From the Porcupine River**

It had been our pre—arranged plan to cling together till Fort Yukon was reached, whereupon future plans would be decided upon. Would Malcolm venture Outside with me? I wondered. Arrived, we dispersed, each going his own way. "See you around," said my native friend, making off towards the Indian village on the north end of the Fort. The improved Scotchman and the Cheechako had come a thousand miles together. What adventurous future lay in store for them? My prime obligation upon arrival was to deliver the mail put in my charge at Old Crow. I discovered the lowly, log building at the end of the main street. Upon its facade was inscribed:

POST OFFICE FORT YUKON

North of the Arctic Circle.

I was standing there with a handful of letters when I realized my extreme northerly position in the world of mails since the day the Penny Postage was inaugurated. I posted my obligation. I was a free man again. The huge sign CARTER'S attracted me. Entering the store, it is obvious that

"The Mail Got Through"

I am in a branch of the 48 states when a young man greets me with a burst of slang. "Hi stranger — what's cookin?," he enquires, more in friendliness than curiosity. "Just livin'" I retaliate, furthering his curiosity. "There are enough Stars and Stripes in here to establish a 49th state! — why even your Indian beadwork's gone crazy with flags!" I blurt frankly, giving the place a once—over. "Funny, but that's what some of 'em want. Most of us like our little bit of God's country. We don't want no fighting unions and power politics to ruin our peace. . . 's'bad enough Outside. . . you know they've forgotten how to live. . . course maybe I've been here too long?. . . but you get a different outlook," he adds, after a thought. "Most of all we like our own laws. . . they fit the country. No! I wouldn't live Outside now, but I do like the occasional visit. . . reminds me how much I wanta get back!" Then his mind came back to my presence, having rambled through the thick maze of happenings and events that confirmed his love for Alaska. I understood how he felt, exactly. We chatted a moment (the Cheechako accounting for the whiskers and generally bushed appearance) and his friendly welcome made me feel already at home. America has long been known as the land that accepts free men with open arms. I felt that welcome here.

My second but minor obligation was a visit to the Northern Commercial Company post. Swinging through the door, I introduced myself and said quite frankly: "Now which one of you is Bart?" "That's me!" said the glassy—eyed man, sucking on a half—smoked cigar. "What can I do fer ya?" "I bring good tidings from Steele at Old Crow," I said. "Oh, he made the trip without mishap? Fine." We settled down to a round of banter. Invariably you'll find the two in their unmistakable, turned—up—brim, U. S. Army fatigue hats, very busy or 'shooting the breeze' with their casual visitors. With the sudden need to fill a rush order our confab ceased. "Anything we can do for you, let us know," said the trader over his shoulder as I strolled from the post. Such were my friendly introductions to Fort Yukon, Alaska.

Liza Henry
Closing North Commercial Trading Co. for Season

Sternwheeler _"Barry K"_
At the River Confluence

I learned the riverboats were not running this year and the price via hired craft was outrageous. I still had some 300 miles to go. This left but one alternative. I would visit a bush pilot! At the tiny airstrip I met a gentleman rubbing down his private plane with affection. "Are you Ed,?" I asked. He turned from his glistening, blue craft to see who I was. "Yes, Ed Badten's the name—how are you?" he exclaimed in friendly northern manner, extending his hand to meet mine. An enjoyable conversation followed, wherein I learned he was not the Ed I was seeking. I was talking to Reverend Ed Badten, the flying Pentacostal missionary. "Oh! Ed Toussaint's your man!" he laughed, aware of my unconventional plot. "He should be back tonight!" Thanking him, I returned to the main street for a look around. I could wait till tonight.

Fort Yukon is the oldest, English—speaking town in Alaska and was founded by Alexander Hunter Murray on June 26, 1847. He was an immigrant from Scotland to the United States, where he became principal man with the American Fur Company. For years he wandered the Southern States and one spring he struck north from the Missouri to Old Fort Gary, where he changed his allegiance to the all—powerful Hudson's Bay Company.

Now senior clerk appointed to the Mackenzie area, he commenced his journey via the Churchill, Athabaska, Slave and the Mackenzie rivers, arriving at Fort Simpson. He took from the trader his daughter as his wife. They continued from here to the Peel river, landing at Fort MacPherson.   There he wintered and the bold trader formulated plans for a most important mission: building a Fort on the Yukon river. On June 18, 1847 in a boat fashioned at LaPierre House along the shores of the Big Bell River, which flows into the Porcupine, Murray, some voyageurs, British servants and a few Indians started downstream. Of every turn and twist in the river Murray took bearings for precise records of the new country, to send to his chief. June 20 he concluded he had crossed the boundary to Russian Alaska. Little did he know he was 50 miles from it. Following an exciting journey through the Ramparts, they came to the confluence of the Porcupine with the Yukon on June 25. But alas! The successes of the day were hopelessly shared with mosquitoes.

Murray wrote: "I have been in the swamps of Lac Pouchartrain and the Belize; along the Red River (Texas) and most parts of the Gulliniper country; but never experienced anything like this. We could neither speak nor breathe without our mouths being filled with mosquitoes; close your eyes and you had fast, half a dozen." Murray chose a suitable fort site. It stands today but there are no remains with the exception of the graves of a few Hudson's Bay employees. Having chosen this site he wrote "I began plans for Fort Youcan as I sat smoking my pipe, face smeared with tobacco juice to keep at bay the damned mosquitoes."

Shortly after his arrival he learned news of his dreaded rivals—the Russians. From a party of Indians who had traded with them, Murray learned they were armed with pistols and supplied abundantly with beads, guns, powder, pipes, kettles and knives; that they traded first for the furs from the tribes with beads, then knives, and if necessity demanded, dogs.

Then came to Alexander Murray startling news: the Russians promised to come up the river with two boats, not only to trade but to explore the river to its source, believing that he was on their territory. 'This was not very agreeable news,' said Murray. So he decided to keep a constant lookout in case of surprise.

From the annals of the Hudson's Bay Co. come an interesting account of The Man, Alexander Murray, and his work at Fort Yukon. 'The idea of retreating never crossed his mind. He had already discovered that the district was well stocked with fur—bearing animals and was the hunting ground of many Indians whose allegiance he thought he could win.' Murray's journal says he told them his party was very different from the whites farther down the river, who, 'only came once a year to take away their furs and cheat them with useless goods'. He added that his company intended to build a permanent fort among them and would supply them with guns at 20 beavers instead of 25 or 30 they had been giving to the Russians; and the same quantity of beads for 6 beaver, as the others had asked for 12 or 15. His 'speechifying' ended, Murray began building a Fort in earnest. 'I have determined on building a fort worthy of the country,' said the doughty pioneer; 'stores and dwellings made of solid timbers, the picket walling in front, not 'pointed poles or swabs', but good— sized trees shorn of their bark, squared on two sides to fit closely—14 1/2 feet above ground, 3 feet under. The bastions will be made as strong as possible, roomy and convenient. When all this is finished, he cited boldly: "the Russians may advance when they damn well please!" It was on July 1, with the plans well under way, Murray reported planting the first potatoes at the new Fort.

The Hudson's Bay Company historian, writing of Alexander Murray's first year, quotes: "Life at the Fort ran smoothly enough and Murray might never have found a complaint if it had not been for the one Big Bad Wolf—the Russians. As it was, the Russians created a dark cloud on the horizon that he could never long forget. Every little while his peace was rudely disturbed by hearing that his rivals had outtalked him with this band or that and stolen his trade; or moved farther up the river; or may pay him a call any day. He wrote to his chief that he was used to the strongest kind of opposition while in the south and "likes nothing better than a row; but I am exasperated at not having enough of or the right goods with which to compete." Also lacking instructions, he was in a quandry as to know how he should act in the event of the Russian arrival. "They may order me to leave the country; perhaps try to force us from it should we persist in remaining; and I should be very sorry to involve the Company in any difficulty with our Russian neighbours." In 1848 Murray, after and absence, returned to Fort Yukon with his wife. He continued service in various posts of the Company in Canada after his exodus from Fort Yukon in 1850. In the year 1874 this stalwart adventurer died at Old Fort Gary.

The trading post at Fort Yukon flourished until 1869 and was never molested by the Russians, although Lubeen—a trader at Nulato—made one trip on fur investigations up the Yukon River in 1863.

It was in 1867, on May 27th, that the U. S. purchased Alaska from the Russians. Captain C. W. Raymond of the army came to determine the Fort's exact position. The astronomic observation was determined as west of the 141st meridian. After all these years the Stars and Stripes were raised above the Fort where it had often been thought the Russian flag might flutter. The Hudson's Bay Company traders were given their orders to vacate the American soil.

It was in the year 1862 that the Reverend Robert MacDonald, the Anglican missionary to Fort Yukon, found amongst the Indians he visited, gold. From his reports professional gold seekers began their trek into the Northlands, arriving about 1872. The first to arrive at Fort Yukon was a party of eight, three of them the famed trio: Harper, McQuesten and Mayo. They landed July 15, 1873. Quickly establishing themselves as agents of the American Fur Company, they built many settlements along the Yukon river. Too, they found the majority of gold centres in the interior with the exception of Dawson and Fairbanks, Alaska. From the great mind of this bishop emanated the first translation of the Prayer Book, hymn books and Bible in the Indian tongue. Today, a century after Murray's discovery, the population is about 500. The Fort is still the centre of the huge area of northeast Alaska, reached by plane and boat. Unique about this town it its 'hangover' from the early days—the use of the .25¢ piece as the smallest coin. Fur trading is still the chief business. Fort Yukon boasts proudly the Hudson Stuck Memorial Hospital—one of the most efficient within the Arctic Circle; a radio station, airfield, Roadhouse, three stores, theatre and the district Federal Offices under jurisdiction of a Marshall. Above these buildings one still sees the Stars and Stripes fluttering from the flagpole—82 years later.

**Main Street
Fort Yukon, Alaska**

My ramble was brought to a halt by the sound of an Aeronca overhead. Instinctively I hastened to the Toussaint cabin. Here I met Ed's wife. She, also having heard his plane circling, was preparing his supper. It was the good omen, the winged eagle, telling her he had beaten the weatherman and would be ready for some warm 'chow' by the time he reached the house. Two waited eagerly for his appearance this afternoon.

He entered the cabin, greeted his wife in the conventional manner and apparently weary, slumped into his favourite chair, glad to be home again. It was then that my presence called for an introduction. I shook hands with likable Ed Toussaint.

The bush pilot is a hefty, middle—aged gent wearing leather windbreaker and 'cowpuncher' boots. His bushy head of hair, slightly receding, crowns the other extremity. As he strokes the ears of his excited pooch I explain my mission and my dwindling state of affairs. In no time he says: "Sure I can give you some work and then I'll fly you to wherever you want to go!" If it hadn't happened once before on the Outside I would have sworn this could only happen in the North! What few worries I thought I had, dissolved. Ed follows with: "You'll have supper with us?" "I sure will!" I assented, overjoyed at the opportunity to exchange conversation and humour with other kindred souls.

Ed Toussaint not only runs a private airline but maintains a cold—storage plant constructed by himself. It is powered by a D4 Caterpillar engine which also produces the electricity for the entire village, wired by this versatile Alaskan bush pilot. The cooler is one of those phenomena that just doesn't seem to fit into the scheme of things. For is this not the Arctic, where freezing is a byword and the tundra is solid at a depth of three feet below the surface, all year round? Have the Indians not kept their foods fresh all this time by natural methods? These were the two obvious questions that I or anyone might be likely to ask upon inspection of Ed's cold storage facilities.

As the evening wore on the conversation was interrupted many times by a knock on the cabin door. Each time it was answered an Indian or his squaw made an appearance in the doorway, asking for the key to get his or her frozen fish or chicken. "You mean they go for chicken?" I queried. "You bet!" said Ed emphatically, "they're getting educated—that's the third one who has called for it tonight." Another odd fact about the gradually changing North was filed in the pigeon—holes of my mind. The hour was late when the warmth of the cabin was vacated. I slid into a starlit, August evening, hardly aware of being within the Arctic Circle. Walking through the village (as I was wont in the evening before bed) I sauntered past the Roadhouse. The usual poker game was in session in the front room, the hunched figures gathered about the circular table plainly visible from the dusty street. Tinny music blared from a brightly coloured juke— box, reaching a crescendo with each exit from the front entrance.

I passed Mrs. Roberts' bakeshop where she was kneeding the dough for the morning's batch, and carried on in the semi— darkness towards Carney's Hall—the favourite hangout for the younger set of Indians and 'Breeds who, after the evening show, linger about to dance to the tunes played by a local self—taught fiddler, should he be around. If he is not in attendance they exchange adolescent banter, kidding and laughing as normal young folk find time to do. Turning about, I retraced my footsteps past the Roadhouse where the posture of the players and the stance of the onlooker would lead one to believe that the game had not progressed one hand. The juke—box is silent for want of a stray quarter—the settlement's smallest coin—one of the few remaining vestiges of the early days of the country. At the thought I now remember vividly the words of one irate Oldtimer in Dawson as he fumbled for small change: "Pennies, nickles and dimes are a big pain in the neck!. . . oughta be done away with!. . . never heard tell of them in the old days!" he climaxed, finding the desired change.

Enticed by the lights rather than the craving for something to eat, I ambled into the Coffee Shop; sat down at the counter. Two other figures were seated, talking in loud tones and laughing spontaneously. "How's the situation here?" I enquired, easing the scrutiny that was directed at any new face within the camp, especially one clothed in a full beard which might suggest any number of things. "Not bad!" said the plump, dark, young man to which his companion—a gnarled, emaciated fellow with a grey, walrus moustache and a similar coloured hat (both stained from constant usage) added, after apparent deliberation: "Yes. . . yes' t'ings is not bad," the last two words convincing in their musical, Portugese

**The Authors Cabin
While In Fort Yukon, Alaska**

lilt. What little ice there is to break when people meet in the North was broken. Attention was divided three ways, I contributing episodes of my trip at this point to ears eager to hear of a new experience or a new yarn that might give the older—spun fabrics a temporary rest. So it was that an enjoyable hour flashed by with Vladjimer Peterson — proprieter, and Tony Rose—the Oldtimer whose irregular figure can be seen here on any late evening settled in a chair, 'shooting the bull' over a cup of coffee. More than satisfied with the events of the day I said goodnight. Tony retaliated good—naturedly: "Ve vill be here tomorrow." I slipped into the darkness once more, making for my cabin overlooking the Yukon river just to the rear of the shop. Trust Ed to see that his visitor would be comfortable during his stay! A double bed and spring mattress awaited a tired traveller. The Cheechako was about to indulge in luxury.

From what I saw and heard on that first day, I knew that Fort Yukon held much in store for me. The '98ers were increasing in number as the distance to Dawson decreased. So I continued my perusal of the village in quest of its character and difference. This morning found me at the northern end of the village, gazing at a circular sign above a long, many—windowed log structure. It was the Indian School; the sign on the belfry read:

U. S. NATIVE SERVICE SCHOOL
FORT YUKON ALASKA.
LAND OF THE MIDNIGHT SUN
LARGEST VILLAGE ON THE YUKON.
NATIVE POPULATION (1946) 413
WELCOME!

Fascinated by everything that Fort Yukon was, my eyes caught the hospitable invitation: WELCOME! I was prompted to visit the Indian Agent at the adjacent home. It was here I met Mr. William C. Beach who is in charge of the teacherage. A short talk and I was shown his prize possessions—two rare Indian axeheads. I had come at an inopportune moment. He was packing to leave for the Outside. He had waited a long time for this. About now I was beginning to understand the feeling. "Hope your trip to the Outside will be as eventful as mine,"he said, at the door. "There's no doubt about that!" I added with a smile, my hand jingling the last coin in my pocket. I politely departed.

**Jackie Schuman
With Bundle of King Salmon**

Daniel Horace and Fish Wheel

Too numerous to detail are the interesting characters I met this day. But feeling I must mention them because of their geniality, I shall do so. Dwarfed Jackie Schuman, a familiar figure, apt to be anywhere in the village at any time, stopped me in the roadway from the Mission School. Saying little more than his favourite, overworked phrase "good deal"—picked up, no doubt, from the G. I. 's stationed in the vicinity during the war—the diminutive figure insisted I visit his cabin before departing. I consenting, he said once more: "good deal!" and made off with a bundle of King salmon under his arm. Daniel Horace explained the intricacies of a Fish Wheel lying inactive on the bank of the Yukon and the author realized how enjoyable fishing could be with such automatic contraptions. This meeting led me to his cabin where I was introduced to his pretty wife and their young papoose, kicking energetically as it swung to and fro in an improvised hammock. "I give you bead work for shirt?", he asked. "You mean the one I've got on?" I exclaimed. "Ya. . . ya—even with holes in elbows!"And I thought of the thousands of mosquitoes that had dive—bombed their way through those very openings in the past week. Here was an excellent opportunity to foil the dirty, little pests. "I'll do it!" I said unhesitatingly, remembering I had another in my pack. So there and then the Cheechako disrobed, bartered and pulled on the parka that hung over his arm. A cup of tea and three friends richer, I left with the standing Northern invitation to return.

It was late in the morning by the time I reached St. Michael's Mission. I bore good tidings from Old Crow. The Fates were kind and I dined royally with Mr. and Mrs. Files in the heavily—beamed interior of their spacious, log home. From inside one is inclined to be transported to England where oak beams, antique furniture and fireplace are the fashion of the country estates; one glance out of the window convinces one that this is not the cultured beauty of that "precious stone set in the silver sea," but the ever—rugged, wild beauty of Alaska. Dinner was spiced with the local tales of adventure, climaxed with the historic climb of the travelling minister—Hudson Stuck—to the summit of Mount McKinlay. Since, I have heard many times of the dare—devil climb by three inebriated Sourdoughs. It appears they were participating in a few rounds at the local bar when the challenge was thrown amongst them. Like true Scandinavians, always ready to accept a good contest (and, of course, by this time, amenable servants of Bacchus) they started their strange mission there and then, girded to the loins and fortified only with several more bottles of the best Alaskan whiskey and an oversized Stars and Stripes which they were to plant on the uppermost peak.

What would have been a Swiss Dilemma, miraculously turned out to be a Sourdough Success. Yes, they made it! All three ascended, raised the flag and descended under the benign influence of their co—partner—Alcohol. She enticed them to the summit; she deposited them safely at the bottom; she left them in the charge of her rival—Sobriety. It was while under her care that the three began spinning the fabric of their yarn which today is legend in Alaska. It can be heard in any log cabin when the north wind heaps snow against the windows and a log fire crackles inside. It can still be heard, too, from the lips of the one of that reckless trio who still lives to spin the original version over a 'quick one' to Cheechakos who are wont to doubt the veracity of such occurrences; and who most always leave a wide margin for Sourdough improvisation—a common trait of all tale— tellers of the North. I left no margin as every day I began to hear of these *"strange things done in the Midnight Sun"*. I was becoming a Sourdough myself.

The 'Old Church'
Built in 1850 (Circa)

Anxious to survey the entire village I promised a return visit and headed for the Old Church—one of the original buildings built after the mid—1800's. Nearby stands the New Church, its logs painted a deep brown, its roof surmounted by a belfry, bell and cross. Here is truly the Contrast of Time. William Salmon, consistently harbouring a pipe between severe lips was the next of the Indian population I was to accost. Always dressed the same—in his mate's cap, heavy windbreaker and colourful moccasins—he cuts a picturesque figure, opposite in proportion to his fellow tribesman, Jackie Schuman. He insisted I visit his cabin to view a moosehead, his greatest pride. always inquisitive I accepted the offer.

It must have been a monster; but alas, his taxidermy has decayed to the extent of a head—minus horns. It must have been a proud day for him when he dragged his moose into the village. Although Time has almost destroyed his prize possession, it has not lessened one iota the pride of Mr. Salmon who, on the slightest provocation, loves to exhibit his relic to all who should come within radius.

Back at the Coffee Shop I met Tony Rose. This time the story of his life flowed rather incoherently as he stroked his grizzled, handlebar moustache. Tony is a Portuguese from San Francisco. In May 1897 at the age of 26 he departed for Juneau, finally landing at Skagway, Alaska on May 17th. Boating his way to Dyea, seven miles away, through the spring ice, he recalls some 85 other craft—each averaging about six men. "Dey vere like seals floundering amongst da ice floes," he described, "all bustin' demselves to git ahead and up da Pass." the famed, treacherous Chilkoot Pass was rearing its rocky head in imagination again. I listened intently. Destined to fall in league with the thousands of other gold— rushers, Tony entered the Chilkoot. "Da overhead Tramway helped a bit for dose fortunate enough to have da filthy lucre," he said enviously, "but once over da summit on da oder side a roughlock (a brake over the sled runners) and G pole vere necessary to descend da slopes or ve all slip an' pitch headlong to uncertain depths," he added dramatically. (A brief pause to mention those who pursued the Dalton Trail across country by horse, thence into the Lewis River for a 300 mile boat trip to Dawson City.) Back again to pick up the dropped thread he continues. ". . . Ve remove da roughlocks at da bottom and use dogs, or just plain haul our loads by hand. . . it vere spring now. . . Spring of '98 dat I never forget! Da lakes vere slushy in daytime, frozen at night. Sometimes ve vould have freezing veather for a few days and den ve'd go like hell using G poles and creepers!"

So they progressed over Lake Bennett, Tagish, Windy Arm to Caribou Crossing (now Carcross). "An abandoned village of half a dozen houses," he adds in reminiscence (a brief pause) ". . . dem lakes vas just full of fish. . . you could put your net anyvere under—and da fish vere good too!"Then he toyed with his whiskers for a long time. "Each and every vun of us had lots of it. . . ve figures about a year's supply (I was desperately trying to follow his thought). . . PORK AND BEANS AND BACON!" he shouted, as though suddenly prodded by the Goddess of Vengeance. "Ve had lots of it. . . " he trailed off. "Den I come down here (Fort Yukon) and see pack of geese dat make you deef," he continued. . . " you'd have to get out of bed and fire a shot so you could get some sleep!"was his adjoining hyperbole. (Here he stroked his handlebars vigorously, reminiscing all the while.) When Tony next found speech we were shifted to the Mississippi district of the U. S. A. He said: "I recall da time da migrating birds stopped at da Alkali Lakes. . . Dere vere so many feathered animals dat you could step on dem, after dey'd become unable to fly 'cause of bloating from da alkali." he added, somewhat amused. "Farmers transferred birds to artificial lakes and vere successful in recuperating most of dem". He smiled largely, the handlebars rising and falling, getting a personal kick out of the predicament of the fowl—and perhaps his gross exaggeration? And we swerved to the left on another beautiful digression.

"Poor girls took to dancing. . . " I mentally darted back to Dawson City, to what a month later I discovered to be the Auditorium Saloon and Dance Hall. "Each had a pouch for tickets on her side. . . you could have a drink and da bartender vould give dem a ticket for each male patron successfully guided to da bar." Their take for the night was in direct proportion, apparently, to the number of such tickets within the pouch at evening's end. "Some of dem girls in Fairbanks dey vere perfect girls!. . . vork hard as da men going over da summit!. . . cook for you. . . vash your

Author and Scythe
'Earning Passage'

clothes. . . help all dey could on da vay down from da top (a pause and a twist of the handlebars). Dey would hook on vith da men at da boats. . . Didn't see no oldish vomen doing dat—dey vere all 15, 20, 22, 25," he added, a twinkle in his eye at the thought of these young, budding women who had slipped into the past with his youth. "Dey vould eventually marry some miner. . . follow him up to da creek." His mind wandered back to the original thought and with finality he emphasized "dancing vas da only recreation!"

Several minutes elapsed as we drained the chilling coffee, Vladjmer holding the floor momentarily. The subject became more timely, dealing with his logging concern on the remote bank or the Yukon River. It was a pleasant diversion, but I knew Tony, given a moment to gather his imagination and wit, would again try to lead us back fifty years. My reward for patience came when a lull punctuated the conversation. It came with the mention of his partner who took the long trek with him, and had only recently gone on that longest of all journeys—The Great Trek, leaving only Tony to deal with earthly things till the two might rejoin one another on the Great Ethereal Creek, to continue their beloved prospecting. "Joe Roberts (and I cocked an ear to the left) was twenty four, just finished 'is country school. . . lived in Antiok, California. . . he was seventy—four ven he died last May, 1946. . . buried in Fairbanks," he said regretfully, lowered his voice and head in subconscious respect for the deceased.

"Ever strike it rich?" I probed, as I was wont to do with each Sourdough, to see how the Fates had treated them. "Many's a time I vas on the verge of making millions; but not having experience in the mining game, I missed," he exclaimed. "But maybe eef dey have some rich creeks in Hell I meet Joe and ve strike it rich, maybeeee?" he laughed boisterously; we all joined in heartily. The Coffee Shop shook with vibration.

Bewhiskered, grey and slightly white on the extremities, Tony cuts a profile saturated with character. "You miss old Robert,"I said more in assertion than interrogation. "Ohhhhh yaaas. . . " was his Fabian reply, "I never knew heem to tell a lie. . . he believed only in the truth. Often times ve spring a gag just to have a leedle laff. . . but I only done it once on old Joe for kind of amusement. . . dat vas da last time. . . he deed not like eet! He died at seventy−four," concluded Tony in memory of his long−time friend Joe Roberts.

I heard many tales of Whalers deserting their ships on the Arctic shores and heading south for the goldfields. It was just before Tony hobbled off to bed that he mentioned very briefly one such individual. "His name is Abe Shaeffer, a Canadian. He desert. . . yaaas. . . but I don't know eef he get rich or no?. . . he entered the Yukon via Rat Portage. . . settled at Old Crow for awhile, den Fort Yukon. . . he's now in hee's eighties. . . fine old man. . . he come before I to thees hole. . . but ve love it. . . ve wouldn't go elsewhere!"

The evening had begun by the time Tony decided he had an errand to run. Tired from listening to the detailed expoundings of the characters of Fort Yukon, I retired to my log sanctum, pleased with the exploits of the day. I was growing to like the Fort, its variety of characters and especially the variegated sunsets that spilled themselves through the small window, cut from the logs, to illuminate the cabin in that interval between day and night when it is neither dark enough for a lamp nor light enough to hold intercourse with a small−type newspaper. It was just as well, for I might have missed that solitary, silent session with the sunset as it spilled the remainder of its pot of daily paint in a variegated mess of pastelated colours on to my face. August had half−run her long course and the colour schemes of Nature's Western Painter were more than a pleasant surprise. It was one of the last of her torch dances before she closed her western door on another successful fall season. I soaked it up physically; I drank deeply of its appetizing draught; I captured and stored it as it assuaged the sensuous portions of my mind−stored it in the treasure chests for less beautiful evenings than this.

My work had already begun. I was 'grubbing' brush on the site of Ed Toussaint's future home. Whenever the sun poked its bright face through the racing clouds I would drop my scythe or hatchet, substitute instead my camera and find legs. In this manner I had managed to pass a day, lacerating the young willows and vigorous spruce, dodging off intermittently (as though lured to crime by Old Sol) to fulfill my reasons for being here. Was I to be slave to a scythe? Would a double−bladed axe command my energies? No! I was here to meet the people, unrehearsed.

CHAPTER TWENTY NINE

ECHOES OF THE PAST

I awoke to a sunny Sunday morn and a Sourdough breakfast of hardtack biscuits abetted with the remains of the tinned goods bought at Old Crow. "The seventh day thou shalt rest!" With this in mind I relinquished all thought of brush−cutting. I would be a slave to no one or no thing. Free man for a day! I smiled to myself. Free, then, to continue my ramble about the village, I turned my feet in the direction of the old Hudson's Bay graveyard. It lies just off the left hand side of the south−east trail leading from the settlement. Fumbling through the brush I came upon the immaculate, wooden markers of a hundred graves. Surely these were not what I was seeking? My doubts were confirmed when, at the remote end of the plot, I spied a heavy chain forming a cordon about a grey, stone monument in company with a half−dozen ramshackle picket graves. Ahh! I sighed, feeling like a pirate discovering hidden treasure. I read the epitaph on the bronze plaque−a part of the cold, silent monument.

**Hudson's Bay Co.
Historical Graveyard**

IN MEMORY OF THE PEOPLE OF THE
HUDSON'S BAY COMPANY
WHO HAD DIED AT OR NEAR FORT
YUKON BETWEEN THE YEARS
1840 AND 1870,
MANY OF THEM BEING PIONEERS AND
DISCOVERERS AND EXPLORERS OF
VARIOUS PORTIONS OF THE
YUKON AND ALASKA.
ERECTED BY THE
HUDSON'S BAY COMPANY 1923.

**SACRED TO THE MEMORY OF
ERIC WARDS H. B. CO. SERVANT
WHO WAS DROWNED ON THE
18th OF MAY 1867
AGED 21 YEARS.**

I said to myself: '1840! wow, that's 110 years ago!' Such archaic things have always been a stimulus to my enquiring mind. I was right at home with Antiquity for the next few minutes. Climbing inside the guardian chain I give close scrutiny to the faded names, dates and epitaphs on the plain boards that serve to mark the hallowed spots of a few of the North's early pioneers. Here I see a dim 1865, flashing the mind to the pre−gold rush era; there a faint word M−A−R−Y; but no stranger shall ever know her surname. Although crude, some art has been applied in shaping the wooden headpieces, some of which are rounded, gabled or bevelled. Certainly the northern architect was extremely thoughtful. He has served Art well. He shall sit righteously in the Ethereal Halls and receive generously the favours of the God Apollo. Then I find one still readable on which is the story:

Could it have been the merciless Yukon River, which does not give up its victims? 'Could be' answered the voice of possibility; and I remembered the splashing waters that have washed away the banks, the original graveyard and forced the townsite back many yards each year. To my mind also came the rather humourous description of the spring scene in one Sourdough's own colourful words. "Ye should a' seen the sight. . . it were like a reg'lar procession o' the dead as the casks sticking out o' the bank were finally loosed and floated north we' the river!" As he chuckled over the memory of the sight, another smile had crossed another countenance. Two other slabs, discoloured and sadly warped, spoke in their fading letters:

SACRED TO THE MEMORY OF
SARAH JANE SIBBESTON
WHO DIED ON THE 30th DEC. 1865
AGED 3 MONTHS

and

SACRED TO THE MEMORY OF
ANTOINE MOOLE H. B. CO. SERVANT WHO
DIED ON THE 22nd OCT. 1868,
AGED 41 YEARS

Before leaving this northern Elysium I paid silent tribute to the many other headstones. It was among this motley collection that I perceived painted in fresh black letters: O' BRIEN 1861–1938 and the oldest of all: J. C. WERLINE 1856–1940. Turning, I thought aloud: "Life has surely been good to you fellows! Wonder if I'll still be kickin' at 80?". . . and the spruce trees slowly closed the pathway to the graveyard.

"Hello there!" said a voice. I looked to see a squat man in a battered fedora – one hand under his exposed suspenders, the other holding a long cigar – sitting on the rail in front of an old log building. Verily, he looked the Pater of Plutocracy. "Whatch' doin?" he enquired in straight forward curiosity. "Jus' lookin' around," I replied casually. I shook hands with Bill Carney, proprietor of Carney's Hall –the entertainment centre of Fort Yukon. It serves as theatre when the films periodically arrive, and community hall for dancing, or other recreation. Billy, in his slangy American drawl, says he has been here many years and does well. "Say, I suppose you run the film backwards the second week for these Indians?" I suggested, giving full rein to Imagination. He smiled at the thought answering: "Oh, it's not quite that bad!"

**Bill Carney's
Hall of Entertainment**

Bill Carney is typical of the type of American businessman who struck it fairly well in the last decade when movies began to talk and slot machines were the fad. Yes, Billy belongs to the America of the last decade when Hollywood was billing new stars every week, silent pictures found their voice and that country embarked on its vast voyage of exploitation. Truly, he is a vestige of a gay but bygone era.

"Have a look inside?" he asks. I assent. We enter. With the air of a successful man, Billy points to the walls. Here in rising tiers are the silent movie billings and brightly–coloured, illustrated show cards dating back to the time when I was but a thought.

AL WILSON featured in *THREE MILES UP*; HOOT GIBSON starring in *BURNING THE WIND, CLEARING THE TRAIL AND BORN TO THE SADDLE*: TED WELLS featured in *BEAUTY AND BULLETS, BOOTS AND SADDLE*, and the stirring *THUNDER RIDERS*. On another wall is a group of FRED HUMES favourites: *RANGE COURAGE* and *HANDS OFF*. A current author was REX BEACH, who compiled the *MICHIGAN KID* and *THE FOREIGN LEGION*, which I vaguely remember at a much later date. Not to be outdone is the JACK HOXIE placard – *THE FIGHTING PEACEMAKER;* ROY STEWART, playing in *ONE SHOT ROSS* and the favourite BILL CODY in *SLIM FINGERS*. Among the musicals reminiscent of the last decade are THE COHENS and *KELLY IN PARIS*. Finally, a beautiful card in colour, surmounted with bold letters spells: *BACK TO GOD'S COUNTRY*, by a much-favoured author in our home, JAMES OLIVER CURWOOD; I am brought up to date, being in what I have since termed 'God's Country'.

All the while Carney had been watching from the other side of the Kelly table as I darted from placard to placard, commenting on each as I gave it close scrutiny–a sort of running commentary. He knew them all as far back as the posters went and at times I felt he wanted to recall the days which have slipped so quickly into the past. I suppose it does give a man satisfaction to look back sometimes; I'm sure I gave Bill Carney the opportunity to slip easily into reminiscences.

"I left Illinois for New York and finally landed here on July 9th, fifty years ago!" said the theatre man. He mentions briefly his trip to Alaska via Skagway, White Pass and Whitehorse. "Which proved quite eventful. . . and I have resided here ever since. . . was in partnership with Charlie Urban, and this is our original theatre," he added, chewing a small portion of his cigar from the end and spitting it across the room. "I married a native and my two girls are going to school Outside." "Maybe we'll have time for a game of Kelly before I leave," I suggested as I passed the sign: SHOW .75¢. Billy replies; "Glad you dropped in. . . come around again. " "I will," I said. Feet sidled up the dusty street towards the Roadhouse.

Passing the Northern Commercial Company's store I met Liza Henry stocked high with goods. His laden scow awaited him along the banks of the Yukon. His wife sat waiting too. "Where to?" I asked in all friendliness. "We go for a season,"he replied. I was left wondering how long 'the season' might be as I eyed his packs. Deep inside, the adventurous fellow wanted to ask if there was room for another. But the voice of Reason spoke up: 'We have still our mission to complete. . . Time and we will move too!' The street still beckoned.

Lunch. I paid another visit to the Indian section of the village. As the most intriguing parts of cities are their foreign sections; so the most interesting part of these settlements is their Indian village, the original settlement that now assumes the subordinate role. It was here that I accosted Albert Peter rounding a bend with a light canoe slung over his shoulder. He looked overmuch like he was just returning from some adventure; but in truth he was just departing. "I'm heading for Salmon Creek," he said in response to my query; "they're waiting for me now!" So I followed him to the bank where a heavily laden scow, equipped with a high horsepower kicker and occupied by what appeared to be an entire family and a team of dogs, awaited his person. Jumping aboard, the party was complete. The sound of a motor lashing water echoed their departure for the season. As they faded with distance

**Albert Peter
Headed for the Hunt**

another party appeared in their wake. I recognized Liza. He had finished his business transaction and was headed for 'the hunt' too. I waved and he recognized the figure of the Cheechako. Little did they know that part of me went out with each boat; that my spirit was sitting beside them. "But what the hell good is a spirit without a body," I said aloud. An Indian woman looked to see to whom I was talking. I blushed beneath four inches of whiskers. I kicked myself gently and departed.

It is romantic to see Indians on their way to the woods. It is as though they are going home again—home to the Great Wide Wilderness. They are happy; they chatter much; they laugh gayly. One would think it had never happened before. They are so much happier than when hugging the shelter of the settlement—the idleness of which soon drives those with thick blood to the wilds. I wondered, watching them depart, the exhaust vapour billowing through the churned wake, 'when would they return and with what?' Talk of moose had been rampant in the village of late. Oh, would I were there to see them return, successful hunters, with perhaps the largest moose of the season? Maybe one whose head would exceed that of William Salmon's prize. It would be the talk of the village for months. I secretly hoped Albert would hold the singular honour. For there is still a sense of manly pride within each tribe towards the most successful hunter. Indian traditions do not die young.

Indian Cabins Along the Yukon

Mary Crow, Mrs. Roberts and 'Old Fannie'

Previously I had an invitation from diminutive Jackie Schuman to visit his cabin. This I decided to do while in the Indian settlement. A long row of identical log cabins faced me. This meant one thing: I would knock on each door till my man appeared. It proved lengthy but my patience received its reward. I not only met the little man, but what turned out to be probably the most interesting women of the tribe. I had caught them in an Indian Talking Bee. At this moment I came to the conclusion that our female sex is universally the same. The conversation came to a close and with more than average female bashfulness they cowered at my presence. Bearded I was not exactly the ordinary Messenger of Goodwill. A disarming remark from my short friend put them all at ease.

'Old Fannie', as she was introduced to me, is the oldest Indian woman in Fort Yukon. She is 84 and still active. In the ensuing exchange of banter she told me in her few English words that she well remembered the coming of the '98ers in their headlong search for gold. She would be a budding, young woman herself about that time. I was introduced by her to her two friends, one of which I discovered to be her daughter, Mrs. Roberts. She is the Chief's wife and quite proud of the fact. The other woman was Mary Crow. In the sparse English that we all knew, we exchanged more words. Finally I took to laughing; Fannie laughed; her friends laughed; and I laughed some more. . . and so on. We did (however little serious ground we covered) have a laughing, good time. I parted in this happy mood as they waved excitedly from the door to the Dazzio. The bewhiskered messenger had also found goodwill!

Indians are very rhythmical people, who, if interested in something, are quick to catch on. My first awareness of this came at the church service in Fort Rae, where a vocal justice was done the hymns. Later the fact was again noticed in the Anglican church at Old Crow. Now whether music or rhythm has anything to do with carpentry is debatable; but the ability to 'catch on' lies within the body of one native of Fort Yukon. He is Paul Soloman, carpenter.

Knocking at his door, I waited, glancing as I did so at the new porch. 'Could this be an Indian home' I thought. 'You must be at the wrong house!' was the reply. He was wrong! A bespectacled gentleman in a striped, blue suit and white shirt invited me inside to meet his family. I was shown the self−made domicile trimmed with modern curves and finishes. Meanwhile I listened intently to the tale of his life in general.

"While on the trapline when I was younger I spent nights in different cabins. At each cabin I keep so many books. By the time I had made the rounds something was learned from each. You see now?" he enquired, eager that I know of his early efforts. "Most of them were textbooks on carpentry, which, for some reason, fascinated me. When the war came North it brought work. I leave my trapline and choose the life in Fairbanks, Alaska. Here I eventually become foreman on the construction gang." Hardly able to believe the words, I inserted: "You mean you had many men working under you?" "Yes! yes. . . I tell them what to do!"and he smiled a broad, honest Indian smile. "Well, that beats everything!" I said in my surprise. He smiled again and I knew he took this as a compliment.

I was now convinced of the adaptability and transformation of what was essentially a hunting race. Time changes all things; it definitely has, the North American Indian. 'If Hiawatha could only see his red brothers now!' I said to my inner man, 'he'd leave the Happy Hunting Ground and come down to advise them personally.' But then maybe he too would not understand their present role in the scheme−of−things? I left the home befuddled.

I met Charlie Lola, bedecked in an old Mounted Police hat and the loudest backwoods shirt I saw in Alaska. For photography's sake I stopped him. Hardly amused at what he obviously thought was an odd request, he complied in his sombre manner. When the deed was executed we both went our ways with but a word of parting. I was after colour. I knew I had it this time.

My day was far from full yet. I realized this when I met Len Short. (He is one man who can talk for hours, and tell you things you didn't know before.) Aware of all his faculties he can quote the exact dates of the most important episodes of his life and those of memorable historical incidents, names and places. I had been told I would enjoy his company. It began and ended thus.

Len Short
Story−Teller Par Excellence

Len is a small, dumpy man who can invariably be found sitting in the sun on his favourite chair outside the littered, log cabin he calls home. Atop his head you will see one of the two or three hats worn according to his feelings toward that article of apparel that day, or perhaps the prevailing weather? In his hand is his faithful cane, that he says: "has so far not let me down!" This substitutes for his "bum feet", as he calls them now.

It was a welcoming voice that said loudly 'Come in!'. I entered the low, log shack. "Make yerself at home, son!" I accepted the proffered chair, stretched my legs to full length and did so. I let Len do the talking. As he spoke I sensed his greatest satisfaction was to hold the floor. With that inherent quality for entertaining, I gladly gave him full rein. I was about to go on a mental travelogue with an adventuresome narrator. Oh, how nice to hear of other's travels!

"I was born in Little Egypt, Southern Illinois," he started, "where corn grows high. . . born on Lincoln's first election day in the year 1860. . . I never did stay at home. . . I ran away as soon as I was able to make a living. . . never could get along with my stepmother!"I said nothing as we both looked out the south window: Len a few thousand miles farther south than the Cheechako. ". . . I went to Texas, then Oklahoma. . . hunted buffalo in Montana. . . came north next . . . never done any Indian fightin', although they scared me a couple of times. The only thing that would tame an Indian was to kill the buffalo. . . they had to stay home then!," he said, with a note of triumph likely to be first−hand experience. ". . . Sitting Bull tried to raise hell at Wounded Knee. . . I was in the North then," he added, as though fortunate. "Monkeyed around one place and another trapping, hunting, till the Riel Rebellion, in which I scouted for Colonel Otter. . . here I met Bob Wilde, cousin or some relation of Oscar Wilde, the English Poet. . . I remember him well. . . he had the reddest complexion of any man I've ever seen. . . Burke and Wilde later had a ranch in Battleford. . . he was one of the original 72 policeman there. (here he paused to spit a wad of tobacco at the tin near his left foot). Hitting it, he continued. . . .

"I left Battleford for Jackfish Lake−you remember it?," he queried, hearing I was from North Battleford. "Yes, yes. . . very well, used to swim there in my younger days," I recalled. Satisfied our common factor was intact, he carried on. "In the winter of '84−'85, when the Rebellion broke out, I was laying in the guard room, (I had been in Saskatoon when the Queen's Own Rifles arrived) and I sure got a kick out of one homesick boy writing to Montreal. Why, right then he thought the Prairies were No Man's Land!" he interjected. Getting back to the Rebellion, he said boldly: "All the killing that was done was one old man of 75; and he committed suicide! They claimed they killed half the Indians of the West!"Having heard other interpretations of the fight in my younger days in the actual vicinity of the uprisings, I began to doubt his authenticity; but letting him tell the tale in his own manner was my object; also I have not tried to alter any quotations lest I should detract from the beauty of these Oldtimer's phrases and thus spoil their imaginative creations. so let the truth be known and the tale remain as spoken!

". . . I remember Bluebottle, the cartoonist, on one of his current sketches. . . the caption under the drawings of some officers crouched under an ammunition cart was: :THE PROPER PLACE FOR OFFICERS IS WHERE THE AMMUNITION IS THICKEST! At which he chuckles with unbounded glee. Another incident in his digressive talk was the mention of Dicken's son, who came west from Fort Pitt as an Inspector in the Mounted Police.

Leaving the Rebellion as was, Len took me along his life path to Edmonton, Alberta. "The first name for Fort Edmonton was Beaver Lodge," he recalls. "I stayed around here a year or two and then came down to the Athabasca country, an 'indentured servant' of the Hudson's Bay Company. I was 23 when I first saw the Hudson's Bay Co. trademark in Medicine Hat stamped on a package of goods and had to ask what it meant. I'll never forget the look I got for my ignorance," he chuckled again (Another pause for a second shot of tobacco juice at the stained pail beside his rocking chair.) His marksmanship never varied. "Yes, I remember that year well. . . it was the year the winning wheat at the Philadelphia show was grown at the mission in Fort Chipewayan. Anyway, I worked the H. Bay Co. boat 'Graham' from McMurray to Fitzgerald about five summers," he said with renewed enthusiasm, as though he had relieved himself of an obstacle with the emitting of another stream of juice. Digressing, to add that he was in Edmonton on Queen Victoria's Jubilee, I silently marvel at his keen memory. He continued to astound me in his physically aged, but mentally acute, manner.

"Bill Clarke, Harry Anthony, Ernest George and I winter−trapped in '97−'98. Anthony had started with dogs to head north in 1889. Clarke made quite a piece of money running boats through the Grand Rapids, while George was homesteading between Edmonton and Sturgeon Lake where he sold out for $1000. We broke up after that year. Anthony beat it somewhere. . . George returned to his native England. . . Clarke and I stayed on, built a home−camp near Hay River and continued to look for furs, just when things had been looking good for all of us. Oh well, it always seems to go that way,"he sighed, spat, and continued after a slight pause.

"In the summer of '98−'99 we went to the Continental Divide, up Root River to Great Rose and thence along the south fork of the Gravel River, then we headed for Alaska. We figured that according to the Indians we were three days from the McMillan river near Dawson." Re−enacting the meeting with the Indians, Len quotes: "What's on the other side?" To which the reply was: "Ain't no other side. . . two sleeps and you come to flat plateau covered with lakes, much grass, willow." "Them damned Indians mixed us up so much we daren't take a chance, so we returned. But one thing I can tell you, son, is I believe it's in that area that the Glacier started its motion spreading the gold as far south as Red Deer, Alberta−speaking of gold, I wasn't particularly interested in the Klondike Rush and never have forsaken huntin' for gold minin'. Anyway an old trick I learned was to singe a blanket and then filter my gold through that; just another of the many wrinkles,' he added, momentarily proud of his discovery.

Came the summer of '99, Len and Co. built a boat near Hay River, from where they proceeded to Fort Norman. "Here we added a two−year supply of newspapers; headed for MacPherson, but dumped off here, with our already heavy load. . . newspapers from damn near all over the world; damn near a ton of 'em!" he mused. "With this we raised a canvas 'water sail' on a pole with rocks at each corner and below the boat. The wind was fair part way, but dropped. Later a 'Huskie' (Eskimo) boat came along and towed us to the Peel River post of Fort MacPherson. Here, with delight, he mentions the incident of the ton of papers:

"Firth, the Hudson's Bay factor, dumped all the papers on the floor of the post. You should have seen everyone. They went paper−happy. . . grabbing a *Daily Express* here, a *Manchester Guardian* there, a *New York Times* or a *Toronto Daily*. They all went mad for news more than a year old! Even the Indians went berserk grabbing their share, their many children racing all over the pile in gay delight. What a happy moment that was for everybody. I hadn't felt the least bit sorry we had brought them. The show was sure worth it. "

"Leaving our old boat we bought a Peterborough canoe and continued down the Huskie Channel into the Rat River to Destruction City. There was no one here at the time. So we continued up the waters. You bet it was tough!" he admits (reliving certain agonies.) I too felt those selfsame agonies in my own bones still! ". . . and to make it tougher I had with me an old man of 75 I had picked up at Fort MacPherson. He broke his wrist to complicate things still more. But about 60 miles up the Rat near Trout Creek we overtook the party that had ditched the old man. I sure told 'em a few things! We passed on. . . sure showed 'em!" "MacDougall Pass gained, we continued to LaPierre House; fourteen days later we arrived on the Porcupine River at Fort Yukon, bucking headwinds all the way" (another shot at the stained tin with the same degree of success) ". . . I worked on the *Little Victoria* and and then went to Eagle City. There, under the government contract, I cut timber. This lasted but a very short time, when the stampede to Gold Run−a tributary of the 40 Mile−caught me. I was never out for the 'gold trick'" he said, with reassurance. "At Deadwood I saw them picking it out of the bedrock crevices with teaspoons and it never excited me a damn bit!," he adjoined, emphasizing his favourite adjective. "I only know of one man who got out of Deadwood. . . and that was with a shotgun. One barrel was loaded with currency; he banged the hammer off as a ruse. Even he was held up three times before he got out. But he fooled 'em with that shotgun!" A large laugh, shaking his corpulent belly, preceeded another brown bull's−eye. He settled back in his rocking chair to continue his narrative.

"My first time in Dawson was 1903. . . no '04? Well, 3 or 4," he decides, for the first time failing to be his previous, precise person. Len Short is wonderful proof that the mind need not grow feeble with age; and as dates continued to roll off his brown− coated tongue, I marvelled at the plump, little man in his eighties. "I remember buying 40 pounds of maple sugar for .10¢ a pound, and two cases of bacon from a gent in the street for $2.00 a case. Each contained 24 pounds; but the only fault with it was it was too damned thin! You could almost read through it; it was the finest I've ever tasted!" Len thinks he's been to Dawson twice and knows he spent most of his time in Beaver River−about 100 miles below Fort Yukon. "I ran a wood company for the N. C. Company for three years; then a Roadhouse at Beaver Village in 1913. In 1926 I sold out for a fox ranch. Went broke!" he exclaims, "then I retired and I'm still broke!" His smile broadened to its utmost with the latter. He sighed an occasional sigh and groped for more words, plunking his hunting hat at a cocked angle upon his grey locks. "If it wasn't for my legs I'd still go trapping − not alone, though, like I used to. In fact, I'm goin' in a canoe this fall after a bull moose, legs or no legs!". I admired the boast which may or may not have been fulfilled. One never knows what might happen in the North.

Len's (like so many other prospectors) total asset is his $40.00 monthly pension. However, on this he enjoys life in his one−room log cabin, surrounded by many native and white friends, welcoming the intent ears that will listen to his adventurous tales of an excessively−active life. If you are lucky, he may happen to open the trap door to his food cellar and retrieve a bottle of his precious homemade headcheese.

With the entrance of Jim Jackson—Len's close friend and special news bearer—I gave up the only other chair. Hours had been fleeting; but they were enjoyable, enhancing hours split only by Len's pause to sigh or spit a bronzed stream tinwards, never missing; enjoyable pauses too. The screen door banged shut on Fort Yukon's most scintillating character, Len Short—an oldtimer who in all his travels has never seen salt water; unlike Balboa he probably never will.

Night had begun its descent when I stepped outside. I headed for the Toussaint cabin surrounded by the echoing howls of a score of Malemute dogs. It is the music of the North; nothing can change its mournful wail; it is an accepted part of any Indian settlement. Reaching the welcome light in the cabin window, I entered. "Ed won't be returning till Tuesday," said Virginia, his wife, as I shut the door on the night. This meant more willows to be slaughtered; but they would have to wait till the morrow! The night was still mine. I relaxed for two hours in the warm atmosphere of a Northern cabin, made homelike by the deft touches of a woman who has forsaken civilization for the glorious spaces of the North.

It was the Coffee Shop that next claimed me on my nocturnal ramble. This was an inevitability, for unlike Odysseus, unequipped with a mast to tie myself to, I became easy prey to the Siren building; Tony Rose was the enchanter. A night wasn't complete without an adventurous bedtime story spun in his inimicable Portuguese fashion. I was caught; the spell lasted till the sunset (yellow, mauve and pink) cast its weird prismatics through the north—western window. It had been a grand day, saturated with living tales of men who have dared to live dangerously. My cozy cabin on the banks of the Yukon River awaited my presence. The door closed on another chapter and a Northern sunset.

Monday came, and found me again in company with two sizes of axes and a scythe of huge proportions. The sun shone warmly upon a back stripped of clothing to the waist. Ed Toussaint had gone to Fairbanks. I would cut brush till his return. The sun beat down; the scythe swished in rhythmic semi—circles; hours of pleasant toil passed; noon found me ready for a break. This time I chose a visit to the end of the settlement. I was seeking another Oldtimer—Len Curtiss. He was one of the 'musts' I had been told to interview. It was a brief moment after I knocked on the log—cabin door, that his wife, a local teacher, said: "I'm so sorry, he left four hours ago! He's gone down river for the season." So the tales and experiences of another Sourdough are left unwritten. However, she did say he entered the country in the early days of '97. Invited in, I sat listening to her life which has also been quite eventful.

"I arrived at Prince of Wales Island in 1909; then went to Summer Straits, Cossiosca and Chican, where I was the only white woman; thence to Fort Yukon in 1910. My baby was one year old the day I left. It took us eleven days to go over Eagle Pass. Frank Foster and Mrs. Burke were on this trip undertaken by dogteam. Guess I'm one of the few white women who has dog—teamed, flown, motored, boated and all but walked and swam into Fairbanks!"

**Mrs. Roberts
The Grand Lady of Fort Yukon**

Speaking further of the ascent of Mount McKinlay, she mentions the burning of the original mission which destroyed Hudson Stuck's films of his climb and also the original history of the Hudson's Bay Company at Fort Yukon. A sad loss these, indeed. Sorry to have missed her husband and son by so short a time, I thanked her for what information I received, but I was unable to obtain a picture of her husband from her. With this I shut the door on the galaxy of pin—up girls surrounding the walls. I was again tramping the main street of Fort Yukon. It was beginning to know the heavy tread of my feet.

Mrs. Roberts, short, bespectacled and with her silvering hair curled tightly, had just shut the oven door on another batch of bread when I pulled the screen−door open. I entered upon her invitation to "Come in!" Single handed she bakes all day; with the satisfaction of knowing one's cooking is acceptable (as every woman so wishes) She said: "During the war they were lined up at eight a. m. and I didn't shut the door till eleven at night!" "I understand you've been in the North for many years," I suggested, hoping her tale would flow as the sap in the fall, thus saving the need for obvious questions. I must have won her favour more readily than did the late Ernie Pyle when he once paid a visit to the grand old lady. She said of him: "Although he aggravated me from the start, we became solid friends. He was the lousiest reporter because of his irregular approaches. I guess he was quite reticent and just a little afraid he might offend. He was a little on the chummy side−that was in 1936 on his visit here. Since then we were very good friends and corresponded wherever he went; he always answered my letters. Last, he told me he was going to Italy, then Okinawa (she paused as though in respect) where he met his death." Mrs. Roberts pulled up a chair in front of me, crossed her arms and took me back in her life to the San Francisco 'Quake and Fire. From here we travelled forward in a logical sequence. "I didn't know where to turn or run, as the streets opened up and the buildings were swallowed. It was horrible!. . . hundreds of people dying, buried alive or running in the first direction their feet would take them! I remember seeing one whole building that was many stories high slip into a fissure, its top just sticking above ground. It was horrible!. . . and then the fire!"

Continuing, she said: "I came from Portland Oregon, direct to Alaska by steamer, then on the train through the White Pass to Whitehorse and from there to Dawson in an open boat." Speaking of the ordeal she continued: "There were about 110 boats we called the Mosquito Fleet in the race to get to Dawson first for the 'discovery' on the Anoka River on May 12th, 1912. We were pretty well last−my husband, brother−in−law, baby girl of four and myself." She described their following the ice, in ecstatics. "My daughter thoroughly enjoyed the ride too; ours was a good−sized rowing boat; some boats ahead reported us lost but we were on the Main Channel while others took the Slough Route. We made it in good shape; no trouble whatever. I just sat and watched the beautiful, white clouds drift by in the blue sky; oh, it was pretty! Mind you I took a turn at the oars and rudder with the rest. In all it was like one big picnic all the way down!"

In 1920 we came to Fort Yukon, doing mining and prospecting just before freezeup, and trapping in the winter. We had a long trapline and 'swamped' our own trails and 'cuts'. When Bergland (my husband) took sick in 1925, I trapped alone for ten years and cared for my five little ones." This would be hard to believe by someone who had not met the ambitious little woman; even today the way she unceasingly turns out fresh bread for a livelihood is ample verification of her feminine stamina.

Speaking of rigors of mining, she continued: "I 'shovelled in' and 'panned' till I was nearly exhausted. But here in Alaska you had to work shoulder to shoulder with the men in order to get your season's work done. It takes women with strong character; Alaska is not a country that is kind to women. If you don't take what is handed to you and go ahead, you go down. I've seen the soft, simpering kind; as anywhere else, if there is indulgence in self−sympathy, you are lost!"

Arriving at the present, she said: "I believe the day of hardship in Alaska is over; I guess I wouldn't know a hardship if I met one; I've never known what it is to have things easy. If something had to be done and overcome, it was all in a day's work. It has been a thrilling adventure all the way. I have baked for five years now," she continued. "I like it and do make a living. My daughter has her own trapline now,"she added, pointing to a picture of the lassie clad in furs behind a healthy looking dogteam. Her daughter truly inherited her fortitude. "My two young boys were drowned in the Yukon," she tells me; "rather an unfortunate accident!" Her face draws tense at this and I suspected more than the dear old lady wished to tell me. Changing the subject quickly, she said brightly: "I have written a book of my life trapping in the woods. It's too bad Ernie died, for he was going to help me publish it." It couldn't help but be an interesting account, as our short conversation proved immensely so. With a pie tucked under my arm I shook hands with this gracious lady. The screen door shut behind me on Fort Yukon's most interesting woman.

Bad news travels fast. Talk in the streets had it that a skeleton had been found, washed up on the bank of the Yukon. Could it be the missing Mrs. Beach? This was the burning question. All

209

wondered. An autopsy was called. After several hours the skeleton was discovered to be male. In all probability it was the adventurous Cheechako from Seattle who, alone, left for a northern tributary some time previous and had not been seen since. So the mysteries go on in Alaska.

'Don't you think you've done enough for one day?,' asked the voice of Devilment in its most chiding tone, after another hour of work passed. 'Well I hadn't looked at it that way!' I responded. 'Come to think of it, I have done enough! What right had this axe and scythe to demand my company for so long? I'll seek company that gives me more than blisters in return! Yes, I'll have no more to do with you today! Take that!' I threw the tools earthward. I was a free man again. I would visit Jim Jackson and so complete my calls on the Oldtimers. . .

Jim Jackson
The Eloquent Swede

Invited into his cabin, I sat on the well−worn slope of the chesterfield. Jim was at first reluctant to talk because of a certain natural distrust for Outsiders who invariably return hospitality with twisted tales. I assured him I wanted only the true background of the men of '98. Convinced, his words were soon flowing prodigiously. Putting his thumbs behind his suspenders like a sage, he began: "I sailed in on an eight−ton schooner with George Whitman to Ketchican in 1899. Reaching Skagway, I worked on the White Pass for a couple of years then headed for Dawson in 1902. Prospecting in the Mayo district for 18 months, I re−visited Dawson in 1904. Fall of that year I went to Circle City and across country to Fairbanks October 1st. Then came the Anoka Stampede; but I never made a strike". Restless as a new father, he walked the room, paused and continued: ". . . went Outside to Oregon and did some drilling; then to Nome steam−shovelling for two seasons with the Pioneer Company. Finally I made another trip Outside in '16, and d'you know. . . I made up my mind then! I'd rather starve to death in Alaska than work on the Outside!" I understood well, for I too had become slightly nauseated with human nature. "But I intended to return with renewed interest and start swinging all over again. It was my challenge. I must accept it." Back again we find him on the Copper River working for the Jumbo Company of Googanhimes. . . "1917 I was with Ididerod and in 1921 returned to Fort Yukon by dogteam−800 miles in all! Then I traded on the Porcupine with my brother at LaPierre House for twelve years. In 1924, when my brother died, I moved to Old Crow. For twenty−six years I have traded on the Porcupine River. I sold out, moved to Fort Yukon where I've resided since. . . and do you know thy've all been my own trading companies!". Here I sensed Sourdough independence full blast.

"I wouldn't be any other place,"says the Swede. "I got a pretty nice home in Europe; but I haven't been to it in 60 years. I left in 1888−or damn close to it anyway. I was born near Wisby. . . I'm the last of the family now. . . have high blood pressure. . . must hang close to the hospital. Nevertheless I live quite comfortably." With a sudden abruptness, opposite to his first flow of words, he ceased talking. He had seemed very glad to have confided in someone. Now that they knew, he was satisfied. He deigned to have his picture taken.

We parted. Even now I think of Jim as I first saw him −sitting on the counter of the Northern Commercial Co. store, kidding the gullible Indians until they called him names. It was his work, his hobby and his pleasure. He enjoys it immensely because he understands the Redman.

Funds had reached an all−time low. How long could I hold out? Well, frankly I didn't much care. Hadn't my guardian Goddesses and my Lady Luck stood me in good stead? Well they could do it again! I wasn't going to worry my head over a thing. Anyway, I had some leftover grub from the river trip. That would suffice. It would have to!

From this precious larder I dole out a half−tin of beans, a small piece of dried beaver, some raisins and a cup of tea. I am getting used to these Sourdough suppers. My intercourse with food over till the next day, I walk through the village. The street is still dusty, the Roadhouse poker table completely surrounded and a fiddler 'swings' it to native rhythm at Bill Carney's. Not particularly interested in anything, I seduce the Coffee Shop. My Portuguese friend expounds at the counter. His topic is Christopher Columbus. I adopt an adjacent stool.

"No, that's not how come the man found America!,"he ejaculates, twisting his moustache excitedly, offering his Northern explanation. I say Northern, because having lived in these regions too long, one is liable to over—develop the imagination. Tony has been here too long! However, he forwards his version in all seriousness. "Christopher heard about America from da Norvegians who pirated along da coast of Europe. He found dis out ven drinkin' vid da boys in some of dere dens of in— ini. . . how you say dat?" he asks, turning an eye to the Cheechako. "Oh! you mean iniquity?" "Ya! Ya!," he beams, then lowering his eyes in recognition of my presence, he assumes his most serious story—telling look. "Yas, he peek up his information at dese iniquity houses." Smiling with apparent grammatical success, he continues. . .

"He feign a trip to India to get badly needed lumber for Portugal; but when he reach da Cape he, instead of turning south and east, he turn west for America. But ahaaa! Isobella later catch hccm quick and land hccm in jail for being so original!" Insisting he is right, but receiving volumes of protest from all listeners, Tony bangs a gnarled fist on the counter and pushes his faded fedora tighter on his head. I had heard enough of exploration and discovery in the half—hour display to dream myself around the Horn. So, amidst this humourous display—following the lengthy discourse about the year 1492—I slid to my cabin to catch up on some neglected notes— calligraphic and sonorous. Had any one looked in later and heard the laughter they might have wondered. The Cheechako was just reflecting on Tony's original Columbus adventure.

Tuesday passed without event—except for the stripping of the virgin field, till it looked cold in its semi—nudity. A walk through the village and the usual pleasant exchange of banter in the Coffee Shop concluded a fourteen—hour session with Nature and her obstinate underclothing. Still Ed had not returned to tear me from my rapacious task. How I longed for the sound of an aeroplane motor as I swung that scythe!

Next morning a knock on the door brought me to a sitting position. A word brought a young Indian boy within the cabin, saying: "Here's the fish my dad said he would catch you. . . where shall I put them?" For the first time in my life I was awakened to be the recipient of two fresh fish. I smiled as he set the pail on the floor and departed in the bashful manner of these people. I had given the boy my fishing kit the night before. His dad, tickled with the gesture, promised to catch some fish with it for me. The word of Fred Paul, like the word of all other Indians I met enroute, was kept. Such is the Indian reaction to common decency and friendliness.

I had high hopes of leaving this day. Already I felt the free and easy life of Fort Yukon was gaining a beachhead on the heart soil. This would never do. As I worked in the field swinging the scythe in a certain rhythm, changed only with the presence of a hidden root which would send a body—shaking jar up the entire handle, I was visited by many native friends. "Why do you do this, Dazzio?," one would ask. Fine opportunities to steal a rest on myself, I would sit on a log with my friends. There I would explain the intricacies of the Whiteman's dollar—bill. An Indian loves nothing better than a good joke. As I delved into dreary economics they would catch the idea and share my present predicament with humour.

So the day was punctuated with friendly visitors, some condescending to cement relations with libations. Under a hot sun behind a dull scythe it would take a good man to say 'no'. I was not the best of men this day! One by one they came and went, extremely pleased that someone should travel the hard way and be interested in them. For all work there is a compensatory pleasure. To the Cheechako the natives were that pleasure.

The sound of a plane brought my strenuous efforts to a halt. Leaning on the scythe, I looked heavenwards. I caught a glimpse of yellow. Ed Toussaint was getting home from Tanana notwithstanding the wet and wind. We would leave tomorrow! Eager to finish my job, I ploughed into the last cluster of willows at the corner of the field. Ed soon arrived on the scene. Pleased with the progress, he said: "Call it a day and let's get some grub; I'm hungry!". With extreme pleasure I dropped the scythe. With the same pleasure I gave a last glance at the double—bladed axe. I was through with these implements of destruction. No more would I be their slave. I was my own master again. Not only that, I was a guest of their owner. We departed for supper.

With the goodwill that pervades the atmosphere when friends enjoy food and drink, supper gives way to the latest gossip from the west, humour and the proposed trip on the morrow. "Where do you want to go? Anywhere you say!," asks the generous bush−pilot after the repast. "I'd like to pick up the *Trail of '98* at Circle City," I reply. "That's only ninety miles!," exclaims Ed "but just as you say. Then we'll look for you at eight−thirty tomorrow, breakfast will be waiting!"

Having some odds and ends to clean up, I scamper about the village in pursuit of them. One is a quick visit to the Hudson Stuck Memorial Hospital. Here I have the good fortune of meeting Dr. Dososway−the French doctor, and her assistant−Miss Davis. Both show apparent signs of fatigue. Guided through the well− equipped interior I fully realize the amount of work necessary to cope with the local tuberculosis situation. Indeed, there is a big job ahead for both of them. At the other end of the settlement I finally discover pretty Nellie Cadzo, daughter of the ostentatious Dan Cadzo of Rampart House. To my surprise I find she is just married. So that's why all the commotion in the village last night! Native wedding−bells have rung again in the village. My visit in Fort Yukon is complete. Tomorrow I will be a part of the 'beyond' again, headed for civilization. Oh how full and complete life is! Wedding bells! Laughter! Travel!

Morning. Under the bright sunlight I slid down the steep embankment and had my last wash in the murky Yukon. Saying farewell to <u>my</u> *Little Cabin* I forced my gait to the Toussaint's log home. Breakfast was ready at eight−thirty; the pancakes had disappeared by nine; at 9:01 Ed kissed his wife Virginia and we headed for the waiting Aeronca; 9:15 Fort Yukon was but a memory−a very pleasant memory.

Hudson Stuck Memorial Hospital

Nellie Cadzo
Daughter of Illustrious Dan

Ed Toussaint
The Generous Bush Pilot

Back on the *Trail of '98*

CHAPTER THIRTY

AIRBORNE

Airborne, we circled the farthest west trading post of the far−reaching Hudson's Bay Company. Glancing below I beheld a wonderful panorama of spruce−studded land cut carelessly by the meandering Yukon River which split into a vast delta as it headed westward towards the Bering Sea. It was an unbounded forest of water and spruce. Then suddenly it gave way to a foreign body−a small white blotch on the otherwise natural landscape. Ed, leaning back as best he could without shifting his weight, yelled above the engine's steady drone: "That's the Arctic Circle marker!", at the same time pointing a gloved finger at the almost invisible object below. "I'll circle so you can read it!" Without further words we dived in an arc at the immaculate target.

**The Delta
Alaska**

As we flashed by I caught the words A−R−C−T−I−C C−I−R−C−L−E on a white circle a hundred yards in front of a low log cabin. So we left the northern regions and followed the river's irregular course towards the 66th parallel. It was at this point I first felt I was deserting my newly accepted hinterlands for the womb of civilization. Instinctively I could feel it coming closer.

Pointing out of the right−hand window of N. C. 83528, Ed directed my attention to a crooked trail sunk in the forest floor winding in a crude parallel with the river below. "That's the old mail route. . . sled dogs. . . cabins. . . few miles. . . " were the jingle of words that forced their way to the rear seat. Piecing them together I nodded in acknowledgement; and we resumed our former postures so as to distribute the weight equally. The only other sound besides the straining engine was the frequent *whirrrr* as the wind cut a strut. The propeller flashed in the tilting rays of the sun. I was very happy!

Mountains loomed enticingly in the distance. Somewhere within their midst lay Fairbanks. 'But I must not get ahead of myself,' I thought, looking below eagerly for our immediate destination. Still nothing but water and trees; trees and water, going in the opposite direction, giving way to smooth−looking sandbars left high by the abating waters. My thoughts found words, but in another mouth. "They look like good landing fields, don't they?" After yelling my agreement the pilot adds: "But they're deceiving . . . tried one awhile back. . . emergency. . . not so hot!" They must look tempting, I imagined, when the fuel needle points to E.

**Circle City
Once the "Paris of Alaska"**

About this time I began eyeing the tobacco tin on the floor, open and waiting. The air pockets increased; my stomach was trying hard to tell me something. I pretended not to hear it. I tried not to believe the suggestions transmitted to my mind and re−directed to my mouth. Had I not been in the Air Force four years without such mishap? I tried consoling myself by concentrating on the phrase 'its 90% mental' so oft repeated by one who seemed to neglect the physical being. I looked to the mountains for diversion. I could not fool myself any longer; I must weaken! I did, and I felt much better−although bemoaning the loss. It wasn't every day that commenced with pancakes!

It was Circle City that made me forget my troubles. There below lay a collection of buildings. I had reached the famous Gold City−once called The Paris of Alaska. We circled once, casting a vulture−like shadow over the houses. We bumped along the runway that was no more than a mown field. Taxiing back to the low building the engine spluttered, coughed, and silence filled the air; but a drone filled my ears. Feet stepped on terra firma once more. I had bridged the gap in the *Trail of '98* caused by a deficit of riverboats. The land trail was about to commence.

It was with a mixed feeling of reluctance and eagerness that I shook hands with Ed Toussaint. It was the end of a good friendship; the beginning of a new adventure. "You might need them," was all he said, with a smile. My hand felt heavy. Glancing down I espied four, shiny, silver dollars. I had completely forgotten my state of affairs; I shall never forget that gesture. It was the true spirit of the North. I waved a last farewell as the propeller groped for air. With a snort the little, yellow fly carried Fort Yukon's best bush−pilot home. He had left me. He was returning to his wife.

Ed Powers
Proud Pump Possessor

Echoes of the spring in Yellowknife sounded: "Look for the Old Opera House if you get to Circle City," came the voice of D'Arcy Arden. I was here, now, in the City. I would look first for the weathered house of entertainment. Oh, it felt good to be with the '98ers again!

Passing along what could only be the main street, I thought sure I saw my first real sign of civilization. I came face to face with a gasoline pump. Gasoline pump? Wasn't this near the Arctic Circle? Was I really 'bushed'? No! there it stood as red as life−blood itself, in front of the N. C. Company post. It did look utterly out of place. I entered the store. "Well, where have you been, Daniel?" came the voice of the factor from behind the counter. "Name's Ed Powers," he added, extending a hand. "Just call me Cheechako, show me the rest of this elongated *Trail of '98,* then call me Sourdough," I replied blandly. "Confidentially," I asked in a whispered tone, "is that a gas pump or am I really bushed?" "Well I'll be! Yes, that's as far north as they plant 'em. She's our pride and joy!," he exclaimed in mixed surprise and elation. "About the Operee House: you'll find what's left buried in the south bushes yonder, he pointed. I would not let D'Arcy down after all! With that I ventured forth.

Near the shore of the Yukon is the original log Roadhouse; the faded antlers of a once large moose still hanging above the door in silent welcome. I have always interpreted them in this manner, for to me they suggest warmth and hospitality. Who would not treat their guests with friendship who would lure them within by such a door−piece? So I entered the cold, lifeless structure.

Years of dirt, dust and decay littered the place. A small bar that once echoed to the clink of tumblers stood at the rear, its top covered with a coat of dust, its brass rail torn from the roots. *For the moment I was leaning carelessly against its shining facade, one foot cocked on the highly polished rail. Beside me lounged my northern brothers−some shoddy, others clad in buckskin coats−all bewhiskered. Some carried on in a vociferous orgy at the end of the counter. I listened intently to one of the thousand yarns that have crossed its scarred face, from the lips of one just in from the goldfields. We clinked our glasses to 'good health', I slid from the bar attracted by the* flight of stairs leading to the upper storey. In reality I ascended the broken staircase. A similar spectre of decay greeted me. Two windows looked out towards the Yukon River—one to the north, the other to the east. But it was the wall that attracted my attention. There I glimpsed the corner of a newspaper. Since my childhood I have delved into old papers with avidity, seeking the excitement of the past. With the same appetite for news of the old city I tore off a strip of the printed wallpaper. Lo and behold! I found treasure! The tainted newsprint read: BOSTON SUNDAY GLOBE JULY 9, 1905. What I learned from the stained record was that in those days one could procure a gallon of Old 56 'Rye or Bourbon for $3. 00 (express prepaid); Lager was $1. 25 a dozen (no charge for bottles) and a corner grocery store was selling for as little as $150. 00. Times have certainly changed!

Satisfied with my wallpaper exploits I turned to go when another much fresher—looking newspaper on the floor caught my eye. Stooping, I withdrew it from its half smothered resting place. I read:

FAIRBANKS WEEKLY TIMES SATURDAY 29, 1908. (In exciting headlines I found what I was looking for.) ANGRY LAWYER KILLS PIONEER!. . . COMMUTATION OR REVOLUTION: Unless General Stoessel's sentence is commuted, revolt will occur; cossacks are being held in readiness to prevent outbreak. . . REVOLT STILL IS WIDESPREAD. . . Portugal is still in the throes of revolution from one end to the other; expect trouble in Lisbon.

And in the largest letters of all on the second page of the four—page weekly I read:

SWELLEST DANCE EVER HELD IN FAIRBANKS! Obviously notwithstanding the worldly upheavals the North was having its gay times.

The chill within reminded me of the warm August sun without. Shuffling my way through the rot I descended the creaky stairs with caution. 'I must see the town and be on my way to Fairbanks,' I reminded myself. 'Why the rush? Time, time, its all yours to make!' came the promptings of Patience. 'Yes, you're right! why should I rush?' Whistling, I made my exit under the moose antlers, turned into the warming sun and adopting my easiest gait swung down the overgrown, south path winding its way along the riverbank.

The path wound through the willows, by a detaining raspberry patch, and past a log cabin. There in a partial clearing stood the remains of what was once a fine building. The Old Opera House was giving its last performance—a scene from Desolation. Not one sign suggested that this might have been a place of merriment. Its roof no longer kept out the rain; its facade no longer advertised the billing in gaudy colours; but in the main aisle a clump of grass and weeds were the silent audience. I turned my back on the last act of DESOLATION: its stars—TIME and FROST; its bit—players and extras: WOODPECKERS, SPARROWS, TERMITES, ROT and DECAY. How many more years will it rest in quiet decomposition? How many weeds sould rear their obnoxious young in this historic environment? Will it reach it centennial? I think so, silently.

An Indian woman stooped over a washbucket arrests my attention as I saunter along the path back to the city. Her name is Lucy Roberts. We talk for a few minutes, I gathering that life in the settlement is not too bad. Smiling, she turns to her washing; I turn to the road. Among the other natives, one is liable to meet Lucy Crow busy drying fish on the racks beside the house, or perhaps enter the cabin of Rosalie Joseph, wife of Stanley—the Chief. Once inside you will find it sparsely furnished. On the wall hangs a picture, faded with time, but beautiful in its antiquity. She is the Budweiser Girl of 1904, advertising Lager. She, without a doubt, must have been extremely popular in these parts in her day. After forty—three years she and her product look as inviting as ever. Laughter, the inevitable Indian sign of goodwill, follows me from the door. I leave the Budweiser Girl to grow old gracefully.

Walking by a team of Malemute dogs (the common breed used in this section of the country) tethered in the sun by a slowly rotating fishwheel, I came to the shore of the Yukon. A noise above turned my gaze skyward. The air was black with herons, circling, shrieking, a few moving off when sufficient revolutions were completed. It was a fascinating sight; and since, when mentioning Circle City, I was asked by one old Sourdough: "Do the herons still circle over the river there?" Assenting, I deduced that the huge birds were an accepted part of the landscape, familiar to all Oldtimers who shared the early days of Circle with them. Nor could I leave the city without accepting the people's hospitality. Back on the main street a voice from the N. C. store hailed me: "Have you had dinner? If not, come on over!" I had not and I did. Arms were soon reaching in all directions as we devoured a bachelor's meal. My hosts loved their almost isolated settlement, working without 'eagle−eyed bosses hoverin over them, 'taking five' whenever they felt like it. ' Since returning to the Outside I have many times envied their independence. It takes guts to live with Nature as they do and develop that kind of philosophy.

The sound of a truck brought the last forkful of my dinner to its goal and myself racing to the door. Maybe I would see the much−talked−of Fairbanks this day? A government dump−truck was stopping for gas. "Ed and Gordie'll take you to Central. They make the run back every day," said Mr. Powers. Thanking my hosts for their cordiality, I convinced myself that Ed and Gordie were my men. It didn't take much convincing, for with broad smiles they beamed at a bewhiskered Cheechako looking like a hermit come out of a self−imposed exile. Ed said: "Sure, jump in!" I didn't hesitate. A cloud of dust put my waving friends and Circle City to the rear. The day had reached four o'clock. 'Fairbanks or bust' was my newly adopted slogan.

Riding in the rear of a dump−truck is usually grim. This time it was a joy. I counted the endless Mileposts, F 160. . . F159 C1. . . F 158. . . −C2. . . winding up steep grades, past narrow precipices, always surrounded by thick spruce and pine from which came the cool, aromatic breeze of late afternoon. Then we came to a halt in a little village. The milepost read F 129 C 33. We had reached Central.

Riley Erickson
The Affable Roadhouse Proprietor

A long, two−storey Roadhouse caught my eye. Here was the logical place to find information. Stepping past the mileage signs on either side, I entered. The interior was dim but as my eyes bacame used to the surroundings I noticed a pot−bellied stove, several well−used chairs in a semi−circle about the room and a table cluttered with innumerable current publications. A counter lined the far side. Behind this I perceived a little man sorting tinned goods on the shelves. This must be Riley?

The Roadhouse at one time catered to one and all, giving beds and meals. Times have changed this considerably where good roads make stopovers few and far between. Riley Ericson is not as spry as he used to be, either. So it is his home−the meetingd place for the town's 'bull sessions' around the warm stove; and a comfortable place for a weary proletariat to lay their heads when stranded, should Riley accept their faces.

"You Riley the Irishman they tell me about?" I enquired of the man. Wheeling from his display of tins faster than a man of his age should, he sputtered: "Why, you young pup, I'll have you know I'm a damn good Norwegian! and furthermore. . . . " By now I roared, in company with the men behind me. The little grey−haired man, taking no offence, saw the humour and joined in the laughter wholeheartedly. "Well what can I do fer ya, stranger? Look like ya might need a meal and a bed; one thing sure, you need a shave!" at which smiles passed all 'round. "You guessed it, Riley, except, the whiskers are staying there!" I chuckled.

"You can sleep upstairs tonight if you like. . . and if you want supper you can have some with me. . . it's comin' now," he said, heading for the kitchen. These words were more than music; they were a Symphony in Hospitality. It was 'Bust'. Fairbanks could damn well wait! There was no hurry; furthermore I sensed some characters within the building who might tell interesting tales when darkness fell and the stove glowed. So, I made myself at home with the Sourdoughs.

Three places were set; three bowls of steaming pea soup awaited. Nick Knudsen was the third party. As we ate, he, noting my curiousity, rolled back the years, telling his life story between bites and gulps. About six foot six with a youthful (almost boyish) look, one would never suspect he is 72. Born in Aalesund, Norway, his first stop was America. The year 1900 found him in Skagway, Alaska. By then the White Pass Railway was established. So Nick boarded the train for Lake

Bennett. At this point he raised his head from his plate, swallowed and half smiled. This was a sure sign that something amusing from the past was forthcoming. It did. . . " . . . ve drank coffee und ate doughnuts und cake for 95 hours ven da train continued to get drifted in. It vas March," he said impatiently, "ve took our hand sleds, Yukon sleds und pulled dem to Lake Bennett. Ve continued to Dawson und sometimes ven da trail vas good ve made as high as forty miles a day." In his slow deliberate words, clinging to original strands of Norwegian, he added, "Ve reached Dawson City on April 10. Dere must have been 25,000 people in Dawson und de mines vere vorking full blast, den. I vorked in mines und on claims on a percentage und came da spring of 1905 I left, floating to Circle City in an open boat. Den ve took pack trail to Central; und since I've been on creeks mining, und to Firbanks in 1907. Dere I stay a few years und den come back here. Und here I am!" he said with finality and a big Scandinavian smile.

Supper finished. It was not until the dishes were being attacked that I learned the story of the little grey−haired man with sloped eyebrows and a pipe forever dangling from the right side of his mouth. As he crossed the large kitchen in his slightly−stooped, slow manner, putting away a pot, retrieving a dirty knife or looking for a clean dishtowel, he narrated an account of his past.

Alf 'Riley' Ericson began life in Olso Norway in the year 1860. His father, at that time, was the only organ maker in the city. He naturally wanted his son to carry on the trade. But not unlike the Prodigal Son he declined the apprenticeship. Weren't half of Norway seamen? Which half would Riley fall in with? It became a touchy point at home. Then one day at an early age, like a good Norwegian, he went to sea. His 14th and 15th year found him a veteran of whaling expeditions to Greenland and Iceland, member of the 100−man crew aboard a whaler. "Ve sailed most of da time, but sometimes dey vere part steamer," he said, the pipe riding up and down on its crease in his lower lip. "Ve vent to da Arctic on dis trip for da old vales−called da Bottlenose. Dere ver Swedes, German, Scotch and many valers of all countries. Dey vould each kill dere own, put dem in a pile and mark wid a flag for identification. Da rowboats vould leave da main ship wid four men, stearer and harpooner." Placing a dish on the shelf, he returns to the sink, saying, "Big ice moves between Iceland und Greenland. . . ve pass through, rounding North Iceland, vere da sealing (all brown) took place, on our vay back. Ve vould be gone about five months."

Knowing his new craving to go to sea, his father wanted him to join the navy. But his year at sea put an end to the thought of such organized sailing and between the ages of 15 and 16 the noble plans of the pater were shattered completely. A rough sailor, Riley rounded the Horn, landing at the port of 'Frisco in '79. 1882 and '83 found him Codfishing in the Aleutians, mainly near Schumican. In 1886 he left the rough and tough Port of 'Frisco for Astoria−the first town on the Columbia River where he says: "Ve fished for King Salmon−da best salmon in da world! Later I became a member of a life−saving station on the Columbia Bar. Den da gold lure got me and in 1897 I entered da Chilkoot Pass, headed for Dawson. I vasn't going to stay in Yukon und Alaska long; I vas yust going to make $10,000. 00 and go home to Astoria. But I stayed here a year and den vent to Fairbanks in 1903 coming down in steamer name *Oil City* in twenty−one days. Ve ran into every sandbar in da country!" Stacking dishes on the board he continues. "I took to mining around Fairbanks and den took a 'Lay' on No. 4, den one year on No. 1, both very good producers. Done all right; made about $20. 00 a day for myself, but ve didn't have any left ven ve got t'rough. I used to be fond of dancing; it vas a $1. 00 for every dance, and you can bet dey made da dance pretty short. I never vent to town very often and vas far from being a Two−Step Louis" (The man who danced 175 times to *Turkey In The Straw* in one evening). Then Riley digressed to the year '97 again. "Ve vinter at da head of Lake Bennett and in da spring of '98 sailed to Dawson."

"Yas, (at the mention of Jack London), I saw him in 'Frisco and later in Dawson." And as though his mind were a grasshopper he jumped back to the city of Fairbanks. "I stayed here from '04 till 1911, and at one time owned #No. 6 Discovery. Fortune? I never had da fortune! Had money to buy a boat and head for Deadwood; I paid $5,000. 00 for it. So No. 6 didn't treat me too bad. I stayed here from 1911 to '26, where I 'placered' on Deadwood Creek. I remember how ve veeled da dirt out in veelbarrows und den vorked it," he reflects at the old procedure.

The dishes dried and put away, Riley finishes his life story in a few short sentences, glad to reflect on the past but just as eager to let it rest where it is. "I came to Central and bought dis Roadhouse." Then as if something were suddenly remembered, he added: ". . . my real name isn't

'Riley'. It vas before I came to 'Frisco' aboard an Irish vessel near Gibraltar dat some guy mistook me; and I've been called it since!" Here he is, still catering to a Cheechako and Sourdough clientele, content to cook for Big Nick and himself and share the company of their favourite Scotty − Sandy. Another pet, the local horse, knows too, where kindness is proffered and at such visits receives a handful of oatmeal, a lump of sugar and a scratch behind the ears. Such was the setting of Riley's Roadhouse on the evening of August 22.

Nick Knudson
Norseman and Pet Horse

As the evening proceeded and the conversations around the stove changed, a short, thin−faced man with pointed features slammed the door of the Roadhouse behind him. The topic changed to himself. Brushing the soiled fedora to the back of his head, he slanged away in a drawl characteristic of the southern States. Tom Kennedy had dropped in to cast his usual remarks. But tonight as he turned to go he spied me. "Hello, Crusoe," was the disarming remark that brought a smile to my face and a handshake from Tom. "Doin' anything? Haw'd ya like to tramp dawn the road to ma cabin? We'll have a short one when we reach it!" Open for excitement, I assented.

Had you been standing in the Alaskan twilight this evening you would have seen two bedraggled−looking figures, falling accidentally into step, make their way south along the semi−lit road. You would have seen them stop beneath a sign some hundred yards distant. It read: Circle Hot Springs 8. Had you been with them you would have turned as the arrow suggested. You would have smelled the sweet aroma of pine, whisked to the nostrils by a chilly evening breeze. And as you trudged south with them you would have heard two kindred souls delving into Likes and Dislikes, Life and Death and the Joys of Being. You would have heard too, the odd gripe enter the confab and be dismissed quickly; the night was all too conducive to Good Thoughts. Oh! but it was great to be alive; you would have been alive too! Darkness had fallen by the time we reached the tiny graveyard on the right of the road. Tom pointed to each grave in turn as we passed along the mounds. "Buried 'em all meself! Here's the latest−I had a hard time fitting him." I suspected his talk to be tinted with some 'B. S. ' when he said he was from Texas. I have never seen it fail; but I love it and try hard to believe the stretches of imagination − so simple in their origin but so fantastic in their final complexity. He continued to relate the characters of each, building up the tougher ones, not omitting a shooting here and there. When we finally reached the end he pointed to a hole not quite six by three. "Got another one this week," he said, with the air of a man in an official capacity; "he was a swell guy!" as though he had known him from birth. The graves, some dating back many years, had been moved from an old location. Tom somehow seemed to forget this fact in his new acquaintanceship with Death. I listened enraptured.

"Well, whadya think of 'em?" he interrogated. "I just hope when it's my turn I'll get extra consideration for my length. And another thing: I hope you won't be the one to bury me!" Bursting into laughter he slapped his denim pants with a whack, saying, "Let's get to the cabin; got a surprise, remember?" . Frankly, I hadn't forgotten; and by the time we reached the low, log shack I can honestly say I needed a bracer. August nights are chilly anywhere; but here in Alaska they have a special sharpness and foretell winter in a very certain manner. It was this sharpness that called for an antidote. A cutoff took us over a rough path, only recently cut through tall trees that let in a narrow stream of light from the sky. "Even have to build my own road too!," says Tom, stumbling over a clod. Crossing a rickety culvert we reached his little, log cabin in the pines. It consisted of the usual shack and cache (which stood 14 feet above the ground, because Tom, having once had his store destroyed of furs, harboured a pet grudge for the Wolverine). In another cache I saw a masterpiece of craftsmanship, weighing but a few pounds, lashed entirely with sinew. The sled was so constructed that it would bend when going over 'niggerheads' (common in the district) without breaking. Tom also has a pet aversion for bears. He takes great pride in showing me his log beartrap and the shavings within, carved by his latest victim who was a tremendous lover of freedom. "None of 'em git outta here once they're in!," he smiled confidently. I had not the least doubt as I surveyed the neat structure. "They really catch themselves when they reach for the meat and the log door drops behind them!" chuckles the trapper, seemingly eliminating himself from the dirty work entirely.

Trappers lead a somewhat lonely life, lost in their own small struggle with Nature and the Wilds. Till recently Tom had a mate who lived with him. "But," says Tom, "he ran out on me an' got hitched," like it was a crime. I felt his loss personally, for here he is alone with his vast amount of books which could never take the place of one live friend. He shows me the picture of his ex−pal, putting it back on the shelf as much to say, "well, he was a nice guy!"

"Here, have one," he said, the warmth from the fire just finding the interior of the cabin. So I warmed my cookies with a good brand of Scotch. Tom followed. How many times this was repeated I cannot remember. But in half−an−hour we had trapped the country of every kind of fur; improved the system of government; put women in their place (which I daresay we failed to find) and were deep in the psychological aspects of life. The oil lamp lent a pleasant glow to the low structure. It is a common habit of men who frequent public houses, after a certain saturation, to lean closer over the table and clandestinely try to convince the others that one's ideas are most sound. We must have looked not unlike two of Soapy Smith's henchmen plotting some new scheme over a 'snifter' as we huddled closer with each 'nip' till our noses about touched and our convictions found easy acceptance.

The warmth from the stove, the glow from the oil lamp and one other glow made the whole world the nicest place to live in. It was with a start that I raised my head from the huddle. "How'd you like to stay the winter and trap with me? I'll show you the ropes. We'll have a great time! How about it,?" he encouraged. For a moment I nearly said 'yes'. Then my Guardian Angel touched me on the shoulder and said: 'You have a goal to reach by October, remember?'. 'Yes, it is August already isn't it' I replied in thought. She agreed that Time was fleeting. She vanished from whence she came; and there was Tom in her place waiting for the word. I'm afraid it didn't come but I said I would like to. I told Tom what my Angel had said. "Well, lesh av ano'er," he retorted distantly. He raised it to "Good Friendship" , passing me the remnants. I said in a less unctuous voice: "My spirit is with you but the body has to keep moving." With this we ended our innocuous imbibing.

The blackness of Hades when the fires are out (if ever) swallowed us. Arm−in−arm, we stumbled along what was none too good a trail, Tom dangling his 30−30 from under the other arm. The hour was either late at night or early in the morning. I don't remember. But I do recall a loud explosion which sent a red flame heavenward and started a ringing in my ears. "A SALUTE TO THE DEAD!" , yelled Tom, raising the rifle to a proper saluting angle, and with the same loud report let go another blast. It echoed through the still night indefinitely, till space claimed the last faint sound and a gholstly stillness hung over the graveyard scene. Right then I hoped the dead forgave us for our untimely din; but it was all in order. Had we not honoured them? Had we not done the proper thing? Then came the parting of a short but genuine frienship. With a few intelligible words I shook goodbye. A ship that passed in the night, I slid into the seemingly impenetrable darkness. *Bang!* and another throaty yell was carried to me on the breeze. That was the last I heard of Tom Kennedy. I turned and headed for the Roadhouse. I often wonder as to the destiny of that solitary, salty Samaritan. For Tom without a partner is somewhat like a gem without the sun.

The night air was bracing. By the time I reached the long, log shadow looming up along the roadside I was ready for sleep. Riley, Patriarch of the Roadhouse, sleeps lightly with one ear out for his clientele. As I fumbled for the doorlatch I heard his tiny voice from within: "Who is it?" . Consoling him with my identification, I tip−toed to the second floor, chose one from the long line of cots and hastily crawled between clean, cold sheets. In the moments that passed before that Beautiful Unconcious Sleep, *I visioned the room filled with rough, bearded men. They were cursing the very day they came North, calling down the Creator in uncensored language for giving life to mosquitoes and in the crude tongue of men starved of affection conveyed their individual impressions of the weaker sex. How many Sourdoughs had flopped on this very bed, exhausted from long fruitless days on the gold creeks, or, perhaps, just stupid drunk! But whether the ghosts of the Sourdoughs frowned on the nocturnal intrusion of a Cheechako or not, he little cared. He had earned his bed, his place among them. Then out of the eery dark their faces appeared and disappeared in aged procession; they never all passed; were never all counted. . .*

It was eight o'clock when Morning called me. I descended from the archaic attic to a mess of bacon and eggs, the aroma of which had already penetrated the upper story. Riley and Nick assumed their usual places at the table. Coffee was poured. A light−hearted conversation started the day off on the right foot. Strayed pieces of their lives that had been misplaced in the continuous shuffling of Time were fitted into their two respective pictures. They no longer remained incomplete puzzles. It was a pleasant breakfast which ended like all pleasant breakfasts should. It was with a feeling of desertion that I shook the huge hand of Nick and the conversely small palm of Riley. Both are truly Sourdoughs of the Old School and are as much fixtures of Central as is their stolid, log Roadhouse, the center of most male moots. As we squared away the old sailor said: "Never mind about paying me for the bed. " Yes, this was the North speaking again. I had heard its generous, genuine voice before. We parted. I repassed the sign saying: 'Fairbanks 129 miles', caught a glimpse of Riley's Model T Ford−dating back to the early '20's, parked under a rickety shed and I was once more on the Open Road basking in the sun that rose unimpeded towards its zenith. I thought: 'The World is mine again! How sweet is Life! How good are people! How wonderful the Open Road, flooded with warm Sunshine! Oh! the explicit Joys of Living!' An arrow pointing south halted me. 'I have seen you before!' Now let me see (deep thought) it wasn't so long ago, but when? Aha! It is all clear to me now! 'Last night; yes, last night; now I recall. Should the ghosts of the dead haunt these parts I shall hold you responsible.' "It was you who so directed us yester' even!," I said scoldingly, but inwardly reharvesting those joyous hours spent in company with the trapper. Then like an enquiring Greek standing before the Delphic Oracle I asked one short favour: "Where to now?" It pointed to Circle Hot Springs without even the low mumblings of an oracle. Time was mine. I would obey its silent behest.

Too far to walk, I seated myself down on the roadside facing the sun, extracted my well−worn volume, *The Complete Poems of Robert W. Service,* and waited with the patience of the philosopher for the traffic that was bound to appear. While in this state of perfect composure I became aware of an univited guest. His name I do not know; his manner, anything but friendly. I turned a page on *The Man from Eldorado.* The movement of my arm sent my guest racing to safety behind a car wheel. Over and over his determination to get a sniff of me ended in the same performance, and a similar failure. His extreme annoyance was then accompanied by barks of anger. It was this that came between 'Service' and me and in similar annoyance I barked back at the irate canine.

One usually associates such events with an unhappy ending. It was not so. The lady of the house came forth boldly, lured her dog from beneath the truck and snapped the leash to his collar, at the same time looking at what must have resembled an outfielder from the House of David, with a more than suspicious eye. Now I have never liked suspicions. So, sensing her doubts, I forwarded an introduction by appealing for a glass of water (the sun was already at work). The best part of an hour passed. I slipped the refreshing 'ale' as I read. I was alone. My canine friend was suspiciously silent. Again I was interrupted; but this time pleasantly so. "Would you like a ham sandwich?," was the direct query. Now who can say 'No' to a pretty, generous housewife whose husband probably loathes ham, dislikes the way she cuts bread and seldom compliments her on her culinary caprices. So the next few minutes were spent between 'Service', the 'ale' and the sandwich; the dog, feeling somewhat cheated, looked more woebegone than a St. Bernard, from the extremity of his leather leash.

Before the sandwich was finished my man had arrived. Throwing 'Service' into the kitbag and the breadcrusts to the dog, I climbed into the auto. We passed the graveyard, scene of the solemn salute the night before. An inconceivably large smile spread over my entire countenance. Although the driver said nothing, he must surely have wondered at my sanity. What was there to smile at? That, he will never know! Five miles closer to the mountains that reared themselves in a glorious green backdrop we were hailed by a group of Siwashes encamped along the roadside. Then a hotel came into view. Here was the famous Hot Springs of the Cold North. Their mystery I was bent on discovering.

'Hot Springs in Alaska?' I ask myself—the Unbeliever. But there they are, streaming from the embankment behind the hotel; steaming as their sulphurous contents trickled into the pumphouse to be treated and pumped to the swimming pool below. Circle Hot Springs is one of those wonders of nature that keep the world curious. They certainly attract inquisitive tourists to Alaska. I spy a shack labelled SHOWERS. I look within. Therein lies a small pool, designed especially for those who like to soak. I think of a busy day. I see a mental picture: a Congeries of Corpulence wallowing in the warm waters. I leave the pocket— sized edition of a Roman bath. I am in the sunshine of Alaska once more. "Fairbanks, you will soon claim me!" , I say as I turn my back on the neat row of cabins, the gabled hotel and the Hot Springs. I shall detour no more. Thus decided, a moment later I was riding the rear of a truck, face defying the breeze, miles diminishing with rapidity. My mute companions—cabbages and potatoes—express their disregard for trucks also, flopping hither and thither with my own lurching body. "What care I with whom I ride?" I shout joyously to the breeze as we tumble merrily in happy unison. "Fairbanks and Bust!" I ad gayly. Then I remember something for the first time. I feel my pocket. Yes, it is true. But haven't I looked at Truth unabashed before? "O ho!," I say to the cabbages. "A ha!" , I shout to the spuds. "Who cares!" I yell to the winds as they lash my face with a four—month growth of hair. Notwithstanding the conditions we are a happy lot in this truck on this day.

The dim distance diminishes. . . a graveyard (another smile). . . corner sign. . . left turn. . . fresh highway bordered with spruce, poplar, willows. . . a river. . . wooden bridge surmounted with thin, white caribou antlers. . . sign below: FAIRBANKS! Oh! I can hardly wait! *Already I form pictures: clusters of log shacks, dejected trading posts, Sourdoughs lounging in the streets.* How wrong I was! How my mind had cheated me. Who had misinformed it? On, on, over the bridge. . . a broken—down squatters cabin. . . weeds sprouting from the roof. How close is 1898, yet how far! as the shack contrasts itself with the new highway. It is an unmitigated mural of Time itself. On. . . on. . . is there no end to the Open Road? Crooked Creek. . . Boulder Cr. . . Porcupine Cr. . . Mammoth Cr. . . up hill down dale. . . Berry Dredge (the only remaining wooden dredge on the creek). . . finally a stop, Miller Roadhouse. Herb Kerns, a lad from Wyoming, is certainly putting the miles behind us to the satisfaction of everyone. Even my friends the cabbages seem to realize this as they grow less impatient; the potatoes too, settled themselves in a corner in motionless resignation.

The Steiss Highway between Central and Fairbanks is a series of hills and dales; sunshine and shadows; culverts and creeks. Each trickle of water has been named by some gentleman of imagination, or, for personal reasons, perhaps, bears his own moniker with fading pride. Bare hills rise gracefully into mountains; a creek, its belly torn by a destructive dredge limps its way, bleeding to the valley below. Up!. . . up!. . . to Eagle Summit. . . Eagle Spruce; down. . . down. . . to Chatineeka—a Roadhouse; up again. . . to Glacier Pup; down again. . . to No Name Creek (the easiest name to remember). . . Medicine Cr. . . Sourdough Cr. . . Faith Cr. . . Cripple Cr. . . U. S. Cr. . . Perhaps Cr (looking like neither a river or a stream). . . Ptarmigan Cr, first of the bird and animal names, as though the dubber changed suddenly from his subtle humour to his love of wild life. . . Grouse Cr. . . Moose Cr. . . McKay Cr. . . Boston Cr. . . Bell Cr. . . Kopana Cr and the Fairbanks Exploration Dredge—its prehistoric, monstrous form wallowing awkwardly in the creek below. Beside us rises and falls the snake—like multi— million dollar pipeline syphoning water to the dredges when the creeks are low, its head always invisible; its corrugated belly wiggling amongst the willows; its tail never ending.

Picturesque is this Open Road, stretching into infinity towards the famous gold town of Fairbanks. As the distance is cut in half by the Chatanika, we climb. . . rise corkscrew—like to Cleary Summit. From here, on a clear day, the fortunate traveller may be treated with a rare, but distant view of Alaska's highest mountain—McKinley. I did not know my Lady Luck was tumbling with me amongst those vegetables! It is an exceptionally clear day. It is the will of the Gods that I behold McKinlay's crown, faintly etched against the western sky. Oh, how thankful I feel for all past libations! How good to receive one's reward for consideration! How sweet to give and to take! And weren't we to drink to Bacchus when we reached Fairbanks; to toast and appease him from the first saloon? Oh, Glorious Gods and Goddesses! You have rewarded humble me so fully! No more will I scatter hard— tack on the waters of the Yukon for thee! No more shall I pour stale coffee over the Northern moss for thee! But I shall appease you all with a Vegetarian Offering! To Lady Luck, Optimism, Adventure, Hospitality, Goodwill, Friendship, Reason. . . and to all you greater and lesser Gods and Goddesses I offer my humble tokens: 6 cabbages and a sack of potatoes; and upon the first saloon floor I shall spill precious drops of the best Alaskan Whiskey! No more shall you frown upon the Cheechako! No more shall you vent your wrath upon the Dazzio! We shall all be appeased. . . . Oh! happy day!

Once over the summit a zig−zag trail carries us to Birch Tree. The road levels off considerably. A host of monstrous, gold dredges clutter the creeks like so many wild animals sniffing amongst the earth of the riverbed, pawing here and there for signs of golden vegetation. Behold! a log−framed sign. Our caravan comes to another halt ovelooking the Tanana River Valley. Bold, gilt letters proclaim themselves!

"DISCOVERY CLAIM"

The first Gold Discovery in the Tanana Valley was made here by Felix Pedro July/22/1902. Pedro Creek. I am hot on the gold trail again. The pages of history turn back; the wheels of our truck turn ahead. Evening falls. The sunny illumination of the day fades. At last! flickering lights in the distance. A city awaits with outspread arms and twinking eyes. A multitude of disconnected thoughts come and go like the breeze that brushes my face. Is it true? Am I imagining all these lights? Surely neon hasn't invaded this Last Frontier with its commerical gaudiness? No it's a mirage! I don't believe it! I'm 'bushed'!

CHAPTER THIRTY ONE

CIVILIZATION AGAIN!

Fairbank's Main Street

**Alaska Railroad
Engine #1–Fairbanks Station**

A lurch. . . screech of brakes. . . cabbages, spuds and I tumble forward in an anonymous agglomeration—a huddled, humiliated heap in one corner. Apologizing for my weight, I arise from the pile of bruised vegetables. It is eight o'clock, August 22nd, exactly four months from Edmonton, Alberta. Sighing, more with fatigue than exhilaration, I shape the words, "Fairbanks, I've reached you—broke!" . I swear the last word just came of its own free will; I was faced with stern reality once more. But who am I to worry? "Well, this is it! You're in civilization again, Cheechako," said the southerner. "Civilization," I gaped; "Define your civilization!" , came the far—off challenge of D'Arcy Arden. "I don't want to," I told the voice of Prompting. "I just want to watch it, test it, share some of it, laugh with it! Can't you understand?"

I think to myself: 'so this is that other world we think of so often when the pines creep closer; the waters chatter away to themselves; when stalking Silence fills the vacant valleys and a sombre Solitude overcomes the Wayfarer of the Wilds. ' Having been in the Hinterlands a few months one begins to wonder, as I, about civilization, at the first sight of bright lights. As the neon colours of Fairbanks glittered their gaudy welcome I began to wonder if I were not 'bushed'. There was the feeling of being foreign, and at the same time a feeling of warmth, emanating from those lights. Remembering that things remain the same, it is we who change, I shook off all doubt. With full beard and complete confidence I would face the city. I climbed from the truck to the cement sidewalk below.

We strolled down the main street which bristled with gambling joints, taverns, juke—boxes—belching their tinny music from opened doorways; G. I. s and girls arm—in—arm; innumerable theatres—their multicoloured billboards shouting: SENSATIONAL! ACTION— PACKED! MURDER!; dashing, checkered taxi—cabs; huge buses pulling into the sleepy, half—lighted depot.

**Rogge Brothers
Sourdough Express Since 1898**

223

We stopped in front of the Mecca, its soft lights beckoning like tempting, illuminated Sirens to would—be passers by. "About that saloon and our promised libation?" I said to my friend, harbouring a duel thought. "This is it!," he smiled pushing through the varnished, chromium—plated entrance. We found two vacant stools. I sat momentarily, watching with lust the hundreds of brands change colour with the changing lights. "What a wonderful lot of libations!" I said to myself. Herb waved the bartender.

"Why, hello there Moses! Where've you been?" came the first onslaught from behind the bar, from a face corrugated with the right kind of wrinkles. "Far enough away to want a quick one!," I replied, eyes giving the only clue as to how the face was reacting to his choice of humour. "What'll ya have?" , he followed quickly. "Two whiskey, straight!" , I commanded, adding "I promised it to the Gods" . "You did what?" "Say, Herb is this guy bushed?. " "That's for him to answer, I guess," was his unconsoling reply.

Eyeing the shot of amber fluid glistening mercurial in the transparent glass, I became violently Grecian. My friends turned to Gods; the neon to a blazing fire; the tavern to the Halls of Bacchus. "Drink!" I shouted to my friend and the bartender (who had surreptitiously become equipped himself) ". . . to all the Gods and Goddesses past, present and to come. . . and to our friend Bacchus I spill precious drops on the floor (despite the janitors)." With no more words I tilted the glass. Drops fell floorwards. Then three glasses clinked musically, their tones but a slight interval apart. Three heads went back. Three glasses simultaneously emptied. Three distinct 'ah's could be heard. The best Alaskan whiskey followed the course of the cabbages and spuds. My libation was complete. Surely the Gods were appeased, for the forthcoming days held much in my favour.

Now, how Omar ever entered the ensuing moments is still a mystery to me. In fact much of that post—libation period remains vague in memory. "Drink! for Tomorrow we may be ourselves with Yesterday's seven—thousand—years," was the last distinct toast I can remember. Never was Time, Place and Company so conducive to Goodwill. But it was not Goodwill that ushered us out the door; the janitor was receiving his end of the libation. Apparently the hour was late.

"Off Limits"
Fairbank's Red Light District

"You wanta shee the town? All right!," I recalled. A million, harlot stars winked down at the Cheechako. Two Big Dippers poured an endless stream of sparkling water from their bowls. Orion drew his mighty sword and swung it challengingly. I distinctly saw the heavenly vendor placing his bottles along the Milky Way. I winked back at the glittering galaxy in affable approbation. Always eager for Adventure I asked no unnecessary questions. "Thash right!," I said. We turned along Cushman Street. A post blinked a dim 4th Avenue down at me. We turned into a short, narrow street lit only by sporadic, open bulbs. The cold night air brought back all that had gradually departed.

The avenue was studded with tiny houses. Each possessed a large bay window through which could be seen a multi—coloured juke box bubbling and changing its subdued tones for another kaleidoscopic, colour combination. Each contained a chesterfield and chairs and the welcoming atmosphere of the best of homes. In some, men chatted and raised a drink with their hostesses. Here was where the 'good—time girls' were carrying on the work of the harridans of 1898. Here was the Isle of Iniquity—object of so many controversial radio broadcasts. Yes, Fairbanks is in every respect a frontier town. There is not the slightest doubt about this.

Executing our Exodus from the other end of this unique Street of Sin, cement sidewalks claim us again. Footsteps direct us to the truck. I am tired, vaguely familiar with the city, and broke! 'Oh well, the night is still mine,' I say, patting my faithful sleeping bag. I spread it out amongst the cabbages and potatoes. In this vegetarian company I am soon miles away from all cities, in a land where the feet never tire and cement sidewalks are never heard of. . . .

A thousand route miles and two months from Aklavik I awoke to a new kind of life. The routine of the day had commenced: cars rumbled past; the sound of screeching brakes split the morning air; people hustled to work. Indeed, I felt foreign. 'I must rehabilitate myself again,' I thought. There must be a job awaiting me somewhere; and there has to be a breakfast before that job is tackled!' I bade farewell to my nocturnal companions ready for the market when it opened this morning. I found myself a part of the main street once more. I paced the sidewalk in front of the cafe several times before I brought myself to the decision. 'It doesn't matter what you do, but it has to be something—and quick!' Without further debate my mind was made up. I entered the Model Cafe. Five minutes later I had a job and was sitting behind a plate of bacon and eggs. It is surprising what food can do to a man. I was again on top of the world where I felt I belonged. What self—respecting man isn't, with a mess of food before him?

We must have been the oddest duo of dishwashers the cafe had ever seen—an Eskimo girl and a bewhiskered adventurer. Ne'er were two people greater misfits. Nevertheless the combination worked harmoniously and we both sensed that neither belonged there. How she had ever exchanged her previous healthy outdoor life for such drab labour I cannot understand. But it is one of those drastic changes of a modern world. I revelled in the experience, for the North had taught me something precious. I had learned to love and respect common labour. I had learned of the virtues of good, honest work. In this rugged part of the globe it is a must! So enthused had I become with life that I shone with pride the interiors and exteriors of the garbage receptacles. Each glistened from its proper corner at the rear of the eating house. Then one day a glance bothered me, and its Yankee owner said: "Hey! take it easy, Canada: we've gotta work here after you go!" Was I to thwart my artistic pride? Was I to shun what the North had taught me? With a laugh I understood the remark. As I became at home in the city my vocation changed. I said goodbye to dishes and the garbage pails on which I had been made specialist. I found myself in that healthy outdoor element again. I was working under a hot Arctic sun which caressed a shirtless back with its energizing fingers. I was now a Hod—carrier.

Life in Fairbanks is a busy but pleasant one. No one works too hard; money is plentiful; and one can enjoy a beer, sitting on a foundation in the main street when the construction boss sees the job is going well, and the sun is reaching its noon. So the days passed and I got to know the city, to meet some of its interesting characters. I began to hear tales of old Sourdoughs, without whom Alaska would be a colourless picture. They are the nucleus from which the present has grown, and invariably the conversation turns to these pioneer gentlemen who involuntarily take a back seat and wonder at the modern Cheechako who have invaded their rugged realms. I began to hear yarns about 'TWO STEP LOUIS' SCHMIDT, who bought

Ladd Field
Army Airforce Base

champagne at $15. 00 a bottle for his and his girls' baths. But he is most remembered for his love of the dance. It is told in bold words how he danced to *Turkey In The Straw* 175 times in one evening; how he danced three fortunes away before he died, only recently, a pauper. Louis will always be remembered in Dawson, Fairbanks and most any part of the Golden North. Men like him invariably are. Then came unbelievable tales of 'THE CRAZY SWEDE', 'SWIFT WATER BILL' GATES, JOHANSEN of ELDORADO, LINDEBURG THE NORWEGIAN, ROBERT SHELDON, EIELSON and the imaginative JACK LONDON. Yes, I was really hot on the *Trail of the '98ers.*

Fairbanks is a modern American city just below the Arctic Circle. It harbours two airports: the municipal—Weeks Field, and the Army Airforce base—Ladd Field. All day a thin procession of tiny coloured craft rise. . . circle. . . fall. . . rise. . . circle. . . and sometimes disappear into the distance, maybe on an emergency run, perhaps taking a prospector to the bush, or an eager sportsman headed for his first bull moose. From the other side of the city Flying Fortresses zoom low over the housetops, loaded with a full crew training for an uncertain future, and fade as they become part of the colourful countryside. A shining monster swings low, drops its wheels and skids to a rubbery halt. Another cargo of civilians make their exodus from its innards, anxious to see the most−talked−of city in the North. There is no doubt of the future of Fairbanks. It is a Crossroads of the World!

Along Second Avenue one sees the newspaper office of the *News Miner,* which spreads the white and black sheets far and wide, giving special mention to those hardy pioneers−the Sourdoughs of Alaska. Nearby is K. F. A. R. , which sends its vibrations along the air waves. A special program, *Tundra Topics,* keeps the isolated trappers, prospectors and Indian villages in touch with friends whom they have not seen and may not visit in years. Here you are likely to be welcomed by genial Allan Walker and charming Margaret Benedictus who will throw a volley of questions your way; and if perchance you are listening to the radio the next night you will quite likely hear mention of your adventures over *Tundra Topics* − the modern modification of the Moccasin Telegraph−which informs the hospitable folk across the North that you are safe and sound. This surprise and pleasure was mine as I sat in a local taxi−stand and heard justice done to my own unforgettable trip. Before leaving I was shown a map on the wall of all points, so far, receiving K. F. A. R. transmissions. They form a complete web over the entire North, reaching as far as the remote points of Aklavik N. W. T. and Point Barrow. K. F. A. R. is truly another of those indefatigable servants of the North.

Along the main street one also catches sight of several taverns, including such descriptive names as the Mecca, Wonder Bar, Silver Dollar, Vet's Club, Johnny's and Hill's Cocktail Bar. It was one night that I felt especially alone. In quest of noise, laughter and music, I pushed my way into Hill's. Shuffling past the bar, a poker game, and a large crap table over which two digits tumbled, a spontaneous roar filled the air in company with cigar smoke and the clink of silver dollars, I reached the back of the hall from whence emanated the music. I sat down in perfect relaxation. Tune after tune came from the trio at whom the listeners threw silver dollars, yelling for more requests. The entire atmosphere was one of gaiety. I soon forgot the cares of the day, sipping on a Tom Collins, exchanging remarks with a G. I. whose appetite for company was similarily satisfied.

As the week went by I came to know Gadget, the friendly pianist; Chuck, who, hunched over his drums, utters the odd unintelligible guttural and an occasional scat song with gusto; and modest Johnny Rice who plays a very neat trumpet. I came to know also that it is music, above all, that makes the world go round. By the look of some of the couples it was undoubtedly spinning!

Again the pleasure was mine another night when Solitude drove me to Hill's with my own horn tucked underneath an arm. "Do you mind if I blow a number with the band?" I asked the busy bartender. "Hell no! glad to have you! Have a good time!," was his unhesitating response. It was not long before the band increased by one. The Gloom Bug was chased out of Hills. In precious moments of retrospect I can still see Gadget, with a half empty glass on the piano top, singing sentimental songs to lonesome soldiers who shower her with silver dollars just to hear their favourite request: I still see her merry men of music gathered about her. Yes, Rudy Hill's was indeed a homey place.

I have forgotten to mention a first inpression of civilization as I entered it once more. It seemed cold compared with the simple friendliness of the Oldtimers and Indians. I had no place to stay, no money, no job. . . no nothing, in fact; but lots of nerve, optimism, guts and good vocal organs. 'However,' I consoled myself, 'with luck this will be remedied and you will be in Dawson in a week!' It is not so much the unfriendliness of cities, but the cruelty of them. They demand money and labour, whereas one is the guest of the settlements in the hinterlands, and at worst drymeat, fish and tea are proffered by the Indians in their friendly manner. It was most interesting to note the two, so close, yet still so remote from one another. Too, my predicament had not been singular. For on the Sunday I had met three young Americans on Second Avenue, trying desperately to sell their canoe and 'kicker', which had been lugged thousands of miles from the U. S. A. Their ambition was to hunt goats before they returned. Finance was also curbing their

Destiny. But with a few hearty laughs at the Powers—That—Be, we all forgot things monetary and enjoyed the sights of Fairbanks. Thank God there is no price on Nature's head of beauty! Indeed, what a sad world it will be the day She is forced to harlotry; forced to sell her virginial beauty to the rapacious hand of man. Oh, joyous Nature! How gracefully and fully you expose your shapely limbs; how precious little do we sometimes see you. But ah! this day, how greedily our eyes sought your divine form; how we drank you in like scintillating wine! How we thanked you for your natural generosity! We were penniless, but Life was sweet.

Work and sleep became the order of the day. I raced Time once more in order to raise the necessary amount for the 'flip' to Dawson City. The only future flight was scheduled for the following Tuesday week. It would be September 2nd. The season was fast advancing. As compensation, I enjoyed the intermittent hospitality and visits to surrounding points of interest. Fairbanks from the first was a friendly city; but lo! I heard another voice. Temptation was again rearing her feminine head; but no! I would not dally. She would not be catered to! Dawson was calling still louder. . . .

Creamer's Dairy Farm

Crossing the Chena River, along the banks of which huddle many variegated craft, one passes Creamer's Dairy. It looks more like a model in its perfect setting—the Holsteins grazing in the Alaskan pastures — second only to Ireland for greenness, stretching towards the pine—clustered slopes of the distant mountains. About five miles along the winding river, studded with waterfront homes, the University of Alaska is reached. It overlooks the valley proudly from its heights, as though knowing that the future will see its graduates turning their knowledge to productive interests of the fertile valley below.

**Eilson Building
Museum of Natural History**

A new Administration Building has arisen on the University site. It is the Eielson building, named after the 'pioneer flier' who crashed with his mechanic while attempting to rescue men and furs from an icebound Russian ship. He was formerly a school— teacher in Alaska but gave this up for the air, and the job of flying the mails. Eielson made the original flight from Fairbanks to McGrath. (It was in this same tragedy that Bill Lavery took part, and for his efforts received the Order of Lenin for which he still receives a small pension. I understand for some reason it has been delayed. With concern Bill has written the authorities across the Bering Sea regarding this. . . but we are getting away from the subject!). Eielson is royally remembered by all the early inhabitants; the people have given him a worthy monument.

Within the modern structure an entire floor is given to the Museum of Natural History—the most complete story of Alaska to be found. It includes everything from ancient Mastodons, Musk—Oxen, Kodiak Bear to the exquisite bone and ivory carvings — made and designed by the Eskimo. The story of the Great Gold Rush and its accompanyng days is painted, carved in wood and preserved in the old inventions of the time. One of these is the first automobile, built by Robert Sheldon, an early pioneer, who, it is said, had never seen an automobile—but he built one! He later ran a tourist line from Anchorage to Fairbanks with a wierd fleet of aboriginal autos.

Seldom is gold taken from the surrounding creeks with the pan in this day. Dredging is the commercial process that has replaced the colourful Sourdough who once bent over the edge of a stream, swished the sand and water till only faint colours remained in the corner of the sloped pan, at which a bewhiskered smile of success would cross his face and the efforts renew themselves with silent encouragement.

As I continued a couple of miles past the University I came upon a huge monster gorging itself in the bed of Ester Creek, excreting its 'tailing piles' in the rear as it moved forward for a fresh bite, inch by inch, on its own pond. I was looking at No. 10—the largest dredge in the valley, busy at its ravenous work of extracting gold. It is an unbelievably enormous, metal monster manned by a crew of half a dozen. As though a brother in enlargement, across the way swings on of the world's largest draglines—Bucyrus Monighan. Feeling quite unimportant under the shadow of these busy mammoths (not unlike prehistoric animals feeding quietly in the creekbed) I, primitive man, gazed at their superiority, and marvelled. Completing the placer picture were several geysers of water. At the base of each stood a man turning the stream on to the bank, stripping it away and thawing as the process of Hydraulicking made ready for the two grazing monsters. These long, opalescent plumes created a thousand rainbows as the sunlight hit their fine spray and the colours danced on the earthly Milky Way. Verily it was Yellowstone National Park momentarily transpiring in Alaska.

#10 Dredge
Largest in Esther Creek

Hydraulicking
Stripping and Thawing the Creek

One of the Worlds Largest Draglines
Esther Creek

Earning My Passage as a Hod Carrier   **Time Out for a 'Stubby' on the Main Street**

My sightseeing tour was complete. I settled at making my plane fare to Dawson. I commenced work as a Hod Carrier with such men as buck, Tom, Bill, Max and Dempsey−Jacks−of−all−trades who erect buildings with every success. They hailed from all parts of the States; one, in his unmistakable Texan drawl, entertained us with such rough stories as only an ex−cowpoke from that hot state can tell. They might have been 'Bulldust,' but, mingled with northern humour, it proved a spice in the everday meal of labour. If I never work under a more congenial boss than Matt I will be satisfied. Without fail, at some timely moment of the day he would appear with a brown−paper bundle under his arm, and, calling a break, would sit and drink Stubby's with us on our rising structure in the main street. Work can be such pleasure. Here I credit all men like Matt who make it that way. So the days passed. . . .

Before the week was up I became one of the citizens of the city. I began to meet its interesting galaxy of people. There was Francis King−correspondent of the *News Miner;* an intellectual imbiber called Grigsby−an oldtimer in the hospital who dreams he will be back on his homestead, but never will!; a hospitable Norwegian family named Carlson and famous '98er Martin Pinska of the Sargent and Pinska Trading Outfit−well known in the early days of Dawson where today his antiquated warehouse still stands, carrying his name forward with Time. Martin was celebrating his eightieth birthday. With his bright coloured suit and bald head flashing in the sun, he walked down the street, a man twenty years his junior. I thought as my stay grew ever−short and three new jobs presented themselves: 'Fairbanks is sure good to a Cheechako, I'll hate to leave it!' With this thought in mind I made arrangements to leave the next day.

Labour Day Parade   **Labour Day Fireworks**
A.F. of Musicians−Local #481   **September 1, 1947**

Labour Day in Fairbanks is something worth seeing. The splendiferous parade of floats include all of the unions. These are: Musicians, Hod−carriers, Bricklayers, Painters, Carpenters, and the Plumbers−carrying a Chick Sale outhouse on which is printed SQUATTER'S RIGHTS; and a bountiful bevy of Queens−all of which pass through the hot September streets. The night is filled with fireworks which totally outdo the Northern Lights in their wierd illumination, rising and falling above Griffin Field. No cost is spared to put on this show. In consummation the local band, playing only the National Anthem, decide it is not enough. So, packing their horns and the bass fiddle along the main streets, enter Hill's bar. There a jam session takes place and the night is split with jazz. It is a good finale. The hour is late; I am satisfied; I saunter home tired; I settle into my sleeping bag with beautiful thoughts of the Klondike passing through a tired mind; I say: "Fairbanks, you have given me work, you have entertained me royally, but I must go! The Trail calls. . . . "

Paying my food bill for the week, I am slightly short. 'Something's got to be done!' I think. "I'll rouse it up before noon," I say. His reply was: "I promised to help you the day you arrived broke, so we'll cancel the works and call it square, O. K. ?" There was nothing more to say. So I thanked John Klopfer who had initiated me to Fairbanks (and garbage pots!) and made for the airport. I was about to desert Fairbanks, Alaska, for the Yukon.

**The Author
Flying with Bill Lavery Airlines**

There is nothing like a heaping plate of flapjacks to start the day off right. With these firmly under my belt I made for the airport. Detentions are a common rival to compete with these days. It was the noonday sun that frowned upon us as the warming motors roared their insults to the cloudy heavens. It was then that I met Neil Watten−Bill Lavery's congenial pilot. The slight gentleman with receding hair and a pleasant, bronzed countenance said: "You must be Mr. Allen?' smiling contagiously. "Looks like it's Dawson for sure tody!," came the indirect answer. I am feeling over−eager at hearing motion and not being a part of it. "Climb in and we're off!" he yelled above the din of the rotating propeller. I slammed the door on the last piece of luggage and the only other passenger−Miss Kate Bowyer, an Englishwoman from Suffolk who travels, works and travels more, in her curiousity to see the world. I was not alone with unconventionality. "Belts O. K. ?" asked the pilot. Receiving full assent Neil pushed the throttle ahead with gloved hand. At 1:40 p. m. we became airborne.

From high above the clean−looking city of Fairbanks one catches a wonderful panorama of pine−studded land cut by winding rivers and guarded by snow−capped mountains looming majestically in the distance; the Tannana River, curving lazily into the heart of the city, exuding from the other side as it winds towards the northwest in company with the Delta, Salona, Wood, Nenana, Toklat and Katishna rivers. . . somewhere beyond the limits of the eye, pouring its amassed volume into the Yukon River in its hurry to join the Bering Sea. Following the course of the Tanana through the uncertain weather we pause over Big Delta through which runs the famous Alaska Highway. The scenery is exceptionally pretty, the river spreading its tentacled fingers at Delta.

Along the Tannana River over Big Delta

Our course changes to an easterly direction. Nealy Lake trading post and an Indian village come into view on the right. Two tents far below are the only landmarks intruding upon the profuse pines. The sun suddenly throws off its blanket of grey clouds. The vivid,yellow, autumn colours below spring to life. 'Yes, fall is creeping slowly over all the land,' I think. but the time element is forgotten as a fluffy cloud passes close alongside; at the same time an air pocket throws us down, then up, with pleasant sensations. In the dual role of pilot and guide Neil points to the small settlement of Chicken; then Walker's Creek—the original home of which was Boundary; finally we approach 60 Mile to starboard, scene of another early gold strike.

Aha! we have beaten the rainstorm! The clouds no longer suck up thin vertical columns of earthly moisture to their ethereal realms. We cross the mountains, radiant and encouraging beneath the low−lying cumulus clouds that follow the rain. Passing through a huge rainbow as though entering a prismatic heavenly gate to a city of minarets, spires and domes rising in pearly luster, we round a bend at the forks.

A city flashes into view. It is Dawson! At last! We have reached the Klondike in the Rush of '47, in the wake of the long, thin, straggling line of gold− hungry prospectors. No Argonaut ever looked more avidly at Dawson City than the Cheechako at this moment! Hastily the fantasial minarets, spires and domes of Imagination turn into the realistic chimney pots and log cabins of Dawson City. 'Dawson City! At last I have reached you!'

Dawson City
Klondike at Last!
on the *Trail of '98*

CHAPTER THIRTY TWO

50 YEARS LATER!

All at once there were not enough windows in the aircraft. But the multitude of longed−for first impressions remain to this day whenever the infallible mirror of the mind flashes back to that bright, memorable August afternoon: the white 'scar of the slide' high above the city, below Midnight Dome; the idle wharf; the grey, corrugated, tin Fire Station along the waterfront; the immaculate Bank of Commerce−workshop of Robert Service, the Yukon Bard; the clean−cut, wide, streets characteristic of early frontier towns, dotted with ramshackle buildings of eaglespread architecture; its silent ghostliness−the aftermath of a gold boom town; its neat layout and surprising look of cleanliness; the lazy confluence of the Klondike and Yukon rivers; the sharp left turn that put us below the summit of the bordering hills in the Klondike Valley; the narrow stream of water (once the rushing Klondike River) that trickles through the 'tailing piles' stacked in wasted, wandering waves which pass out of sight beyond the next bend; the pools of stagnant water cut off from the main stream, reflecting our winged image as we pass overhead. . . .

Oh, how full of vivid imaginings those fleeting moments were! The city sprang to life; the narrow, wooden sidewalks rang with thousands of restless feet; people floundered in the streets through the mud, walking heedlessly over the carcasses of dead dogs and horses that littered the path; vociferous drunks yelled and fired off sixguns into the air in careless abandon; here and there a woman, amongst the bewhiskered mass of males, daintily lifted her farthingale above the mud; tinny music escaped from the swinging, saloon doors which seldom had a respite; heavily−laden rafts bumped the shore wherever they could squeeze in amongst the variegated craft, while other late arrivals strung to infinity up the Yukon River. The unmistakable sound of building came from behind First Avenue; minute figures carrying heavy packs toiled up the Klondike Valley; a rickety flume along the hillside spat its watery contents through a sluice below; a thousand, tiny figures mulled in the creekbed, shovelling, panning, cursing. It was one ambitious ant−hill of activity and the human ants were wrestling for their prizes. Oh! but it was alive! it breathed! it excited! It was Dawson City in the year 1898!

An air pocket jarred me fifty years ahead. . . I was with Reality again.

A short distance up the Valley a branch in the river turns south. Neil points to a schism in the hills. "There's where Bonanza lies," he says, words creating another picture on a senstive tabula rasa. *I see gold−hungry prospectors scrambling into that narrow tributary in one headlong rush; I see the glitter that lights their eyes as they pull from the creekbed their grotesque−shaped nuggets, God's pure gold left in the wake of the Great Eruption, washed down to the valleys below. I see the Con− men, shysters, parasites pilfering prospectors of their hard− gotten gains. Oh, what a golden orgy!* "Below," interrupts Neil, "on one of them hills. . . two foreigners staked. . . jest. . . people wanted a good laugh. . . greenhorns. . . by God struck it rich!. . . worth millions. . . had the last laugh. . . ho! ho!," came the sporadic words of the pilot over the engine's roar, followed by his healthy laugh at the thought. I too smiled, little knowing how many more such precious moments I was to have in that valley below.

A bridge crossing the Klondike river. . . Bear Creek−a small settlement of Yukon Consolidated employees. . . more tailing piles and surrounding hills. . . then seven miles from the mouth of the Klondike the motor is cut. . . 4. 05 (two and a half hours since 'take off') we glide to a stop on the C. P. A. landing strip. We are greeted by a seldom−used hangar, the wind whispering in the tall grass, and a few cows grazing unconcernedly. Immediately we become objects of keen interest to the sand flies and gnats who seem to ignore the fact that summer is over. The plane is tethered to its groundweights. No sign of life. . . the aromatic Yukon air. . . a short wait.

The local taxi driver, George Chapman, having heard the plane fly over the city, arrives. Howard, the customs agent, serves his brief inspection. We are bundled into the taxi. Motion again. . . an old log Roadhouse. . . the winding trail over the tailing piles. Behold! we are spilled into the most famous Canadian city. She alone of them all was the sole witness of history's greatest Gold Stampede! We are in Dawson City, Yukon−pulsating heart of the fabulous Klondike!

George Chapman−Taxi Driver

Storing my baggage I settle to the circular, leather seat in the rotunda of the Royal Alexandra Hotel. In its uproarious days of infamy this house of hospitality was better known as the Exchange. It is warm; it is homey; it bespeaks an intriguing past. As I sit feeling the aura of contentment I behold three life−size nude paintings hanging on one wall. They are masterpieces of expression−face and body. Not content to appreciate art from a distance, curiosity compels me discover the painter. A close scrutiny of all and I find a faded signature in a bottom corner of one of the paintings. It reads faintly: H. Delamotte 1892. Already my search for Dawson's character has begun. Curiosity has me excited. The story behind the nudes was not long in exposing itself.

"See them pretty gals?," pointed the oldtimer to the sufficiently−adorned wall; ". . . come from the Barbary Coast of 'Frisco. . . pilfered in the rough days after the Great Fire. . . packed to Dawson over the pass. . . sold to the proprietor,"ejaculated the Sourdough in excited memory of wilder days. "Kinda pretty, eh?," he finished with a wink and then (as though his younger self) added: "Could sure do with some of that round these parts now!". We both laughed heartily; in the ensuing silence formed our own opinions of God's most beautiful creations.

Truly, the Three Temptresses have found a perfect resting place; they brighten the dull interior of the ancient hotel; they do not go unheeded! For, even the slightest connoisseur of art is tempted to look twice.

So the moments passed as I slowly became oriented with my new surroundings. *The ancient bar in the back room gave itself up to the occasional visitor. The dozen−odd Flora Dora Girls came suddenly to life, leaped out of their picture frame, and commenced to go through their gay paces, can−canning to the noisy din of cheap music, drunks and the accompanying raucous laughter; a bottle hit the floor with a splintering crash; gold dust poured down the back of a dance hall floosie, fell and scattered itself amongst the sawdust on the floor; a woman−starved miner made a thrust at a pretty leg as the end chorine swung it temptingly over the edge of the stage; a fresh burst of laughter filled the hall at his foiled attempt and at her next swing which sent him careening backwards over a beer table.* The laughter is real! Am I dreaming? Then I awoke quickly from the past. . . .

Laughter floated through the rotunda from the cribbage table where Ed Trana pegged a dozen; Sam Broughton sat talking over old times, close by, with another veteran of early days; an aged Sourdough puffed contentedly on his pipe which gave a momentary spark to the dim corner in which he sat. This and the silent pictures that surveyed us, impervious to time, was all that greeted the Cheechako who arrived fifty years late for the Rush. The hotel was here; but the song, the dance and the unbridled laughter had long since departed from the Flora Dora. However, Ed and Sam are pleasant fixtures as are the paintings; at any time of day or night one of them can be found cleaning the floor, emptying the spitoons, serving behind the bar, playing cribbage, or stealing a catnap on one of the soft, leather chairs. I felt the feeling of warmth and security in the rotunda of the Royal Alexandra. Fifty years had not deprived the old building of its hospitable nature. That will never change.

Adjacent is the Flora Dora Dance Hall, where the famous troupe can−canned gaily to the sheer delight of the women−hungry males, loaded to the hips with gold dust and to the eyeballs with liquor. Repairing to that hall of gay repute I sit in company with the pilot and the proprieter Harry Gleaves. The history of the building in its heyday comes forth as Harry points to the carved name set in a floral harp above what is now the kitchen door. It spells in capital letters:

FLORA DORA

Royal Alexandra Hotel
and Flora Dora Dance Hall

The memorable dance hall has changed in fifty years to a dining room; but fortunately for late comers two things remain, obvious signs of antiquity—the fourteen foot tin—covered ceiling and the original bar, now the lunch counter at which we eat. This is solid oak and if the Alexandra is erect in fifty years the bar will undoubtedly still be in use. Trying to imagine the number of whiskeys that passed over its shining surface I am brought back to the conversation which sounds of the Isle of Man. Harry Gleaves is a young—looking man, the fact concealing his actual age. He is a Manxman, born on the Isle of Most Beautiful Sunsets; he came to Dawson City in 1912. So that's what accounts for the three—legged emblem of Man sewn on the Union Jack that flutters in front of the stately, white building! He smiles in smug satisfaction at mention of it and we discuss his homeland to his great joy. There is nothing an Irishman, Scotsman or Englishman likes to talk of more than his homeland. So it is natural that the Isle of Man should be the current topic with Harry. Back to Dawson again, Harry says: "You wouldn't believe it but once eight hotels filled the block!". Time has rotted all but the stoutest—the Alexandra — and she is preserved for use out of only five of the originals in the entire city. With the meal and the conversation coming to an end the jovial Manxman says: "Here's something to remember my place by," handing me a printed slip. It is a complimentary menu. It being the most unique bill—of—fare that I have ever laid eyes upon, I feel it deserves a printing here.

ROYAL ALEXANDRA
HOTEL FLORA DORA DANCE HALL
. . . .
ARCADE CAFE
Harry Gleaves. prop.
Dawson, Yukon Territory, Canada.

. . . .
MENU
Special Lunch and Dinner, $1. 25
SOUP
Gold Hill Vegetable Soup
FISH
Arctic Trout, Fish Wheel Style
BOILED
Ham and Cabbage, Nigger Jim Style
ENTREES
Young Moose Steak, Whiskey Hill Grill,
Eldorado Caribou Cutlets, Last Chance Jelly,
Combination Cold Lunch, Iceworm Salad,
Lamb Chops, a la Bob Service,
Young Moose Liver and Bacon, Bonanaza Style
ROASTS
Leg of Grizzly Cub Bear, Diamond Tooth Gertie's Delight
Legs of Young Moose, Nugget Dressing
Prime Ribs of Beef, Sourdough Style
Leg of Pork, Trail of '98
COLD
Milk—Fed Chicken, Beef Tongue,
Sugar—Cured Ham,
Pure Gold Salad, Pay Streak Dressing
DESSERT
Glacier Pumpkin Pie, Midnight Sun Apple Pie, Klondike Ice Cream
EXTRAS
Sliced Tomatoes .50¢, Cucumbers .50¢, Lettuce .25¢, Ice Cream Sundae,
Pick and Shovel Flavour .25¢, New York Milkshake .25¢, Malted Milk Shake .25¢,
Fresh Cow's Milk .25¢, Orange Juice .25¢, Tomatoe Juice .25¢, Pineapple Juice .25¢,
Grapefruit Juice .25¢, Apple Juice .25¢,
Asparagus Tips, Skookum Jim Mayonnaise, $1.00,
Hot Moose Sandwich and Yukon Vegetables .60¢,
Hot Moose Hamburger Sandwich .60¢, Tomato Sandwich .35¢,
Cheese Sandwich .35¢,Moose Sandwich .35¢,
Northern Light Tea—Midnight Dome Coffee
THE LAND OF PURE GOLD AND SUNSHINE
—Mush on—
. . . .
With the Compliments of
"The House of Gleaves"
In the Heart of the Golden North"

With this I departed for a stroll along the boardwalk, footsteps echoing back and forth between the old structures of First Avenue. The September was bracing and as the sun disappeared completely behind the high hills that secluded Dawson, I found myself tired but satisfied with the day. I checked in at the Occidental Hotel. It too smelled of the past—its bar, its ancient pictures, its worn, heaving floor. Entering Room 11 on the second floor of the rickety structure I welcomed the sight of a clean bed. There was no happier man ever climbed into that four—poster than the tired Cheechako whose heart was set on becoming a Sourdough. He was in Dawson City, the Heart of the Klondike, at last! Night fell. . .

**No Happier Cheechako
In Room #11**

Like on so many other mornings of this unpredictable summer I opened one eye to see rain flattening itself against the window pane. Not the most pleasant reception; I dragged myself forth, determined to greet the city with a bright outlook.

I felt it a gross insult to start the day with anything but Sourdough Hotcakes. I was in Dawson. I would do as the Sourdoughs do! Justice done to the traditional breakfast, I felt ready to meet the world. The door of the Flora Dora slammed shut. The boardwalk rang again with firm, determined footsteps. Thus I commenced to see Dawson—its warped and twisted buildings faded with the years; its dance halls and saloons crudely barred; but the echoes of the past began to escape from each structure. They dared to whisper their fascinating yarns.

It all started on August 17, 1896 when squawman George Washington Carmack was returning to his home in the Indian Village on the confluence of the Klondike and Yukon rivers. With him were his native friends 'Skookum' Jim and 'Tagish' Charlie. Prior to this they had been accosted by Robert Henderson, prospector, while salmon fishing at the confluence. He was returning from a visit to Ogilvie with supplies. On invitation all headed for Goldbottom to stake, where Henderson had recently made several fair prospects. This done, Henderson prompted the trio to depart over the Divide via Bonanza, where the prospector suggested they prospect the gravels there and inform him of any finds. Lo, they struck exceptionally rich deposits; they staked Discovery claim and those adjacent to it. Failing to notify Henderson, the excited trio headed for Forty Mile to file their claims.

Sometimes good news travels fast; this was one of those occasions. In no time at all the Fortymile miners and thousands of 'Outsiders' from every walk of life stampeded over mountains, through passes and along rivers towards Dawson City. History's greatest Gold Rush had commenced!

One Judge was heard to say in the early days: "There's never a law of God or man runs North of 53!" *I began to feel this as the imaginary, rough figures tumbled from the saloons into the street, so crowded that one was forced to walk part way in the ditch. From here I saw the character who, having made the wager that he could walk the entire length of the main street on dead dogs and horses, proved his point and collected the gold dust! Yes, it appeared before my very eyes, I swear it!*

Last Trip of the Overland Stage

Then swiftly the street takes on a barrenness. The sun throws long, shadowy lances across the broad thoroughfare. Footsteps on the boardwalk halt. On the left in a vacant lot stands one of the original Overland Stages—buckboard style −, its last rough journey to Whitehorse completed. How many times it was pulled at a gallop down the dusty street! *How the coarse, bewhiskered driver yelled his crescendo at the sweating beasts of burden! How many precious letters fell to the platform in a heap as the stage pulled to a stop in a cloud of dust! And how the jostled female passengers ranted as they ascended from the stage to the terra firma of Dawson Dity!* Now its wheels turn no more; it has come to rest in the tall grasses, securely braked by overgrowing weeds, sadly neglected.

Across First Avenue one catches sight of the Firehall, grey and sombre, its original, ancient steam engine adorning the front with its many pipes, valves and tank, all highly polished, reflecting the morning sun. Immediately adjacent in an immaculate coat of white paint stands the Candadian Bank of Commerce. Here then is where the Northern Bard—Robert W. Service—spent some years as a 'wage−slave teller' and, I daresay, many hours thinking of words to rhyme with other words, that eventually came forth as *Ballads of a Cheechako*.

Dawson's Original Fire Engine

Workplace of the Wage−Slave Teller Robert W. Service

Bank of Commerce−1st Ave.

Original Home of the Northwest Mounted Police

Continuing along First Avenue with the swift Yukon close on the right, we come to Turner Street. On this corner stands a large, two−storey, grey building fronted by two old cannon. It is the R. N. W. M. Police (now called the R. C. M. Police) barracks constructed in 1901, still in excellent condition but with only a few of its many rooms resounding to the footsteps of the Keepers of the Law. At one time there were stationed here and along the Klondike creeks some 100 police who maintained a high standard of law and order in the rip−roaring days when Dawson was adolescing. Many of these men left the ranks of the Argonauts to joing the ranks of the Mounties, carrying on the work of the original Yukon Field Force which numbered but a few in the territory.

Behind the barracks are the stables, jails and storage buildings, much as they were in the past, forming a square; some, boarded up, have served their purpose. Today the small detachment of police live in the adjacent, log quarters. Beside these looms a stone monument erected to the memory of the Mounted Policeman—Fitzgerald, Carter, Kinney and Taylor who perished on the Fort MacPherson—Dawson Patrol in the year 1911. It is a constant reminder of what can happen to those who travel in the North, ill— equipped and falsely guided, when the mercury drops to an uncomfortable low.

**Cairn Memorial to the
Lost MacPherson—Dawson Patrol**

**Plaque to the
Memory of the Patrol**

**Andrew Jorgenson
Tales from a Root Cellar**

Walking over the top of what looked like a field of weeds we were halted by a smothered voice which uttered words indistinguishable. A body emerged as though from a cave below. "Hullo thar. . . whatcha doin?," it enquired. "You might a put a sign up so's we know where we're trespassing!," I laughed, jumping from the roof of the root cellar. I shook vigorously the hand of Andrew Jorgenson, another old Sourdough. "Come on in Cheechako and have a talk. . . got time,?" he invited. "I make the stuff,"I returned. We entered, underground. Seating himself on an inverted pail and inviting me to do likewise, I shifted a bulging spud, sat on the sack of potatoes and listened to the oldtimer joke about the past. As the chilliness grew so did the warmth of the conversation. "I was born in Jutland, Denmark, and came to Canada in 1886. In '98 I came through the Chilkoot Pass—at the time of the snowslide. It was horrible. . . about six women died there too. Some men lived after we dug dem out and it was odd dat when a man fell backwards he lived: but dose who fell forward died. When we rescued some, the live men were as white as corpses. Dere was me fellow dere. . . we worked till it dark an' next morning we returned and dere was a man still alive!" Pausing momentarily to hand us a carrot, he continued. "Dey all had a hold of a rope and we followed it. . . da last man stumbled but dere wasn't snow enough to bury him. Dey were all taken down to Sheep Camp. (he doubles back to the 'slide, saying excitedly) "It started with a storm. . . snowed

239

all night. . . slide started about 11:00 a. m. . . . we could hear it roaring," he blurted with the anxiety of one at the actual scene. "It was April and dey had been warned by da Indians. . . . Too bad!. . . Too bad!," he tapered off.

The subject turned to his version (every '98er has his own slant on all historical episodes of that time; some tremendously enlarged with the fading years) of Carmack, the squawman, and his lucky find—Bonanza. Quickly he digressed to the amazing yarn of Charlie Anderson who had a claim on 60 Mile. At the time of the rather humourous incident he was at 40 Mile. With $800. 00 in his pocket he became extremely intoxicated; upon becoming himself once more he found a bill of sale in his pocket but no money! Approaching the police on the matter the disgruntled prospector was told it was legal for him to prospect his claim No. 29. With no alternative he commenced work. To the surprise of all in the vicinity, and mostly himself, he became a wealthy man overnight. He'd struck pay—dirt. "But alas", says Andy, "he was a fool and married a whore. She got the works. He died penniless. She had her pimp right there on the claim—the foreman! The Andersons went outside and bought a beautiful home in California. . . I understand they paid $300,000. 00 for it." Smiling, he says: "Then she hired a big negro. When Anderson came home the man said politely: 'Missy Anderson will not allow Mistah Andeson in de house!'" So, we are left to guess that the lonely prospector with lowered head made his way North, back again to his unharming Klondike, life's lesson learned.

Flitting with grasshopper mind to Skagway, the Scandinavian relates vividly the episodes of the town's number—one thug, Soapy Smith. But this will come later. Then with another jump he began: "I was down at the Forks when it was telephoned there. (we felt a tease here, but he continued) It was about a man who killed his wife because for $50. 00 she gave herself to another man about the saloon. A spotter told him and he, infuriated, walked into the room and shot her. The other man ran down the stairs to the saloon, his pants dangling around his knees! Yes, there were some great old times in them days! I remember the man who went to Circle City to sell his claims. His wife got in league with the dance hall crowd in the Flora Dora. He got wind of the goin's on and dey tried to deter him from finding her room. . . He had men on his side too. . . finding da room he shot his wife and den himself!"

With this tragedy, told in equally effective but hardly Shakesperian fashion, came the end of the Sourdough's yarn in the cool root—cellar. The sun's rays were slanting through the door when we emerged beneath the inverted horse—shoe. We bade adieu to the grey—haired Dane of 82 years who so eagerly regaled us as he revelled in the past. He returned to his potatoes. We made for the Klondike river. . . .

Oldest Sourdough in Dawson City

Arrived at Craig Street we passed the general store of F. G. Caley, who proudly boasts the "Biggest little store in the Yukon," and came to the entrance of the Klondike Valley. At any time of day if the weather is fine you will inevitably see an old Sourdough sitting on a crude bench in front of his log shack that he has inhabited for years; legs stretched out in comfortable fashion as he views his favorite stream—the Klondike, which talks to him in his solitude as it scurries by his door. He is likely to be chewing a wad of 'snoose', expectorating at intervals, sending a brown stream into the dust of the road; perhaps soiling with the trailing drops, his already shiny pants. Likely he will ask about the latest news in town, although he uncannily knows everything that is going on. Perhaps his unique position at the gateway to the once fabulous creeks is the key to his knowledge? Certainly all important traffic passes this way.

His name is Louis Salvey, a native of Alsace Lorraine. Louis proudly claims to be the oldest man in Dawson, with four score years and fourteen behind him. "Old Houser died recently and the honour fell on my shoulders," he says modestly. "Never smoked five—cents—worth of tobacco in my life. . . guess tht's why I'm so healthy," he prides himself. "I first saw light on a December 14th morn. My father was a drunkard who sold the farm and I had to go to work at an early age. . . it was hard mind you. . . then I decided to come to America. Here I spent three years. Then I went to Wrangell, up the Stikine River to Teslin Lake working on the government trail: that was in 1895. Later I packed grub for the Hudson's Bay Company to a Mr. Harland of Telegraph Creek, with six horses. Then in the summer of '97 I drifted with a pair on a raft to Dawson; we were three days trying to get ashore and finally we jumped off and ran over the ice at Lousetown! I've been here for fifty years," he concludes, spitting a spray of chewing tobacco into the dust and stretching his legs.

Louis philosophically says: "I'm not going to live too long now," and glancing over the river as though at the years before its current swept him here, he continues, "A fortune teller in St. Paul told me I would live to be 102. . . it was at a Barnum and Bailey Circus I saw there." With a lucid but wandering thought, we find ourselves back in Dawson as the old man continues. "Pretty good hotels and gambling houses established when I came to the city: you could put a whole poke down and lose it all in a minute. It's one thing, I never gambled and danced. Mined on Hunker and Sulpher Creeks. Here I am, perfectly happy, single and free, and I can look for hours on a nice day at my favourite sight—the Klondike". After a momentary pause, his eyes towards the hilly horizon, he exclaimed: "Say! would you like a row over to Lousetown?"

Leaning on his crooked cane for security's sake, Louis hobbled from his bench. We followed him down to the river. Climbing into his rowboat tethered to a stout willow we pushed off, Louis at the oars, looking not unlike the weatherbeaten seamen in the old masterpiece — *A Helping Hand*. We were at the mercy of the Klondike current which at this point rushes turbulently to join the bulk of the Yukon. But the Sourdough knows his river! "Can I give you a hand, Louis?" I asked obligingly. Insulted slightly, he said directly: "I've been rowing it this many years and I still can now!." He dug deeper with the oar, forcing the prow against the current in a retaliatory stroke. I had said the wrong thing at the right time! I knew it. It was there and then that the Cheechako learned to respect Sourdough independence.

Grunting occasionally and turning to 'break in' with one oar upstream, the 94—year—old Sourdough brought the 'flat bottom' safely to the opposite shore. We were in Lousetown—home of the 'good time girls' who played an essential part in the wild drama of the Klondike in the boom days. To those who preferred propriety it was called Klondike City. But even today, seldom did I hear other than the colourful title befitting such a licentious town.

As legend has it the original Red Light District (something long since associated with frontier towns) was along Third Avenue. But as the city became larger and more respectable it was forced back an avenue, to Fourth. Time soon changed this;

Entrance to Lousetown

with the vote against the District, it moved across the Klondikeriver. Amusing are the incidents related about over—inebriated prospectors, feeling the necessity of other company, throwing their weight and a small boat against the Klondike. One receives them with the respect due to Romance anywhere; and they are spoken, in words closely akin to Chivalry, how the darkness swallowed the prospective customers.

Funny, yet tragic, was many a return trip. It appears that invariably a few more drinks were tippled on the remote shore according to custom. Tired, and past the normal state defined by the word 'drunk', the return voyage was attempted. But alas! The Klondike, ever vigilant for prey, swallowed many a debauched individual, saturated with the requisites of the Hedonist. Their worries (if they ever had any) were over, for the river flowed into the Yukon which does not give up its victims! This in turn led to the final deposting of the strumpets, sometimes titled the 'Goddesses of Virtue', to the site of Klondike City−alias Lousetown. Here they lived in their tiny shacks, reached from Dawson by an over−head trolley from which swung a box. Here, there was little danger of the most−times inebriated individuals falling to the waters of the Klondike below. Assisting them too, was a nocturnal gentleman who loaded and unloaded his strange cargoes, receiving his fee, and a tip possibly on their return trip, should the night have proven propitious to the adventure−seekers.

Homes of the 'Good Time Girls'   **Propriety call it
'Klondike City'**

Walking under the gable of what was originally the station for the Klondike Municipal Railway and pulling the bell cord which sends a dull ring from the rusted bell, we proceed to the interior of the point, overgrown with weeds and brush but revealing its secrets where the inquisitive dare to look closely. Across a thickly overgrown glade we walk under the overhanging willows, punctured by spears of sunlight which set afire the coloured leaves strewn carelessly by the wind along the path. Latching the swinging gate behind us we we enter the limits of Lousetown. It looks at first like a lost, Indian temple, its distorted cabins gasping for air and light through the years of growth.

'Scotch and Soda' Thanks!

A 'jerry', twisted bedposts that once were white enamel, a soda squirt and a collection of odd−shaped and different coloured whiskey bottles told their own tales. The gay thoughts at recalling the lively era overcome the sadness of decay and ruin. Along what must have been the main (and only) street half a dozen bizarre buildings−Ghosts of Time−face the Yukon River catching the last rays of the setting sun which brings them momentarily to life. Here, where once gaiety and laughter could be heard at any hour of day or night, potatoes, carrots and turnips grow in rows up to the boarded buildings. A solitary Oldtimer lives in his shack and cultivates his garden. He is the uncrowned King of Lousetown−Severian Beaulieu−who entered the country via the Chilkoot Pass in 1895, proceeding to 40 Mile where he struck it rich and sold his claims, continuing to Circle City and finally Dawson in the *Great Rush of '98.*

Behind the buildings, parked where they last stopped, are fancy buggies—some, once aristocratic black, others more gayly coloured. Beyond is the remains of the brewery; its broken boiler abandoned after the last stoking. Three engines of the Klondike Municipal Railway, antique in design, stand overgrown with brush, rusting with age. Who would think they once steamed up the Klondike Valley on their narrow—guage, connecting the distant creeks with the gay cities of Dawson and Klondike.

Chewing on fat carrots, we followed the route where the iron rails once lay; crossed a sturdy bridge over a gully; came unexpectedly upon two coaches. Well preserved, they give a better conception of the comforts travellers had when the 'boom' was at its height. *Climbing in we hear the conductor cry: "BOARD!. . . BOARD!. . . FOR DAWSON CITY!" Our iron horse panting and puffing, we arrive at the station house once more. But the railway bridge over the river is washed away. . . .* Faithful Louis, in no rush to do anything, waits patiently at the water's edge.

**Severian Beaulieu
'King of Lousetown'**

Going Overboard on a Buck Board   **The Broken Brewery Boilers Last Batch**

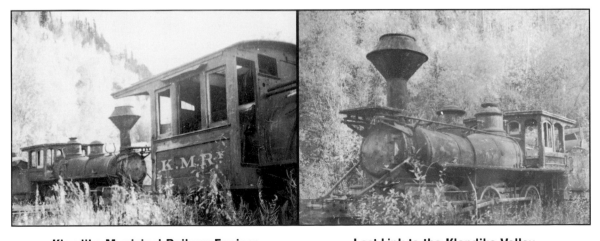

Klondike Municipal Railway Engines   **Last Link to the Klondike Valley**

Iron Horses Out to Pasture

**"Board!...Board!...
Last Trip to Klondike City**

With Louis' complete mastery over the tricky Klondike we reach the other bank slightly below the point vacated on the remote side. We have deserted the decayed site of the once gay Klondike City—better known as Lousetown. No darkness shrouds us, no carefree laughter, no overhead trolley carries us across, no tips do we offer the watchman for our nightly adventures; we merely tether the boat and resume the path leading to the log cabin beside the road, once more.

"How'd you like it?" queries the old Sourdough, resuming his position on the wooden bench, gazing into the west. "It sure must have seen some great times," answered the Cheechako reflecting on what he had seen. "It did. . . yes, it sure did. . . ," and Louis was back at the turn of the century. So we left the oldest man in Dawson with his 94 years, his outstretched legs and his soiled pants, staring contentedly over his Klondike River into the westen reaches of the past. Dawson has been his home for fifty years. Somehow one cannot help but vision this veteran sitting on this same bench for any number of years to come, waving his hand at passers—by bound for the gold creeks of the Klondike.

CHAPTER THIRTY THREE

THE YUKON BARD
ROBERT W. SERVICE

Robert W. Service and the Klondike are as inseperable as ham and eggs. Walking north along 8th Avenue one comes to a tiny, log cabin with an overhanging roof sheltering the veranda. Above is a bleached set of welcoming moose antlers. Here is the home of the Yukon Bard, standing as it did the day the poet bade *FAREWELL LITTLE CABIN!* – the poem that hangs on the front porch, placed there by the citizens of Dawson following the departure of the poet for the wars.

Entered, one discovers the front room simply furnished with writing desk, chairs, pictures and a well–worn pair of

**Robert W. Service's
'Little Cabin' of Inspiration**

snowshoes. Best of all are the slogans scrawled on the walls, carelessly. They read: DON'T WORRY WORK! DIFFICULTIES ARE STRENGTH TESTS – DOWN THEM! And another of the poet's coined maxims: REBUFFS ARE ONLY RUNGS IN THE LADDER OF SUCCESS. The other room is a bedroom. Covers and a patchwork quilt clothe the wrought–iron bed; a stove on which sits an antique teapot and a cupboard near the south windows complete the scant furnishings. A door opens into the garden at the rear. Tempted to feel more closely the atmosphere, and slightly footsore, I lay down on the bed. I am overcome by echoes from the *Spell of the Yukon* and *Ballads of a Cheechako*. Indeed, the poet must have spent a comfortable two years, after leaving his wage–slave job at the bank, just living, while he recreated the spirit of '98.

Some men know where to find contentment. As I close the door on the *Little Cabin* I think: 'Here is one man who has found it!'

With this I sauntered down the hill to 5th Avenue, wherein lay the Administration Building. Bronze plaques have always enticed me to read their dull lettering. So lured, I glimpsed closely at the one beside the front entrance. It read:

YUKON GOLD DISCOVERY

To the memory of the indomitable prospectors and miners who, braving extreme dangers and untold hardships, crossed the Chilkat and Chilkoot Passes into the unexplored valley of the Yukon, and thus paved the way for the discovery in 1896 of the rich gold fields with which the names of Robert Henderson and George W. Carmack are inseperably associated.

Erected 1931

It is a fitting tribute placed in a fitting spot –the entrance to the Mining Recorder's Office.

**Gold Discoverers
Robert Henderson and George W. Carmack**

The day had nearly run its course. As evening set upon me I cast long shadows down the main street. I was looking for a place to stay. "You might try Smitty the artist, he's a right guy. . . lives in a cabin up on the top o' the hill," said the grizzled oldtimer, noting the sleeping bag dangling from one hand. So I swung into the Souvenir Shop, the windows displaying a variety of mastadon ivory and northern oil paintings. "Sure, you're welcome," followed the firm handshakes and I knew Dawson City hadn't changed in fifty years. Thus I met the Smith Brothers—Mel and Vic.

Administration Bldg.—Dawson, Yukon Territory

An hour later, panting, I reached the end of King Street; climbed the incline road leading to Midight Dome; and stood over-looking the world's greatest gold—boom city. In that precious moment of solitude I felt the Great Aloneness and Ghostly Silence that enthralls the North; saw the swish of Northern Lights across the sky; watched the twinkling of a thousand stars and the flickering of the lights of Dawson City (not to be outshone), the only other movement. A cool wind from nowhere brushed a hot face. Refreshed, I turned up a narrow trail to the yellow square of light that was to spell *home* for the rest of my stay. Smithville claimed me. . . .

A warm cabin, a cup of coffee, the wit of my new acquaintance Vic and I felt a citizen of the Gold City. 'Turning in' on the floor I read the travels of *Ogilvie's Early Days in the Yukon* till the flame flickered, winked and went out. The stars looked down through the window on a happy Cheechako that night as he thought, 'Dawson could not have been more hospitable in '98. ' An Indian dog howled in the distance. . . the stars went out. . .

White Pass and Yukon Route Dock

S.S. Casca
Last of the Sterwheel Steamboats

One in an embarrassed position must find work. The dew was glistening on the multi-coloured leaves, the sun trying hard to force its face over the hilltops, when the Cheechako waltzed down to the sleepy town below. One change had been made in the scene since the night before. A stern—wheeler puffed lazily at the Yukon and White Pass Dock. 'Surely I could get a job unloading?,' was the optimistic thought. Fifteen minutes later the thought was turned into action. The Warfinger looking me up and down assented with: "You look like you can handle it!. " So another handcart wheeled in and out of the *Casca* — one of the fleet of woodburners plying the Yukon River waters to Whitehorse. All day we trudged behind the awkward loads; were it not a city that once blossomed with gold the monotony would have been greater. However, with each load I dared think of the Crazy Swede, the Norwegian and the notorious Swiftwater Willie and other such lucrative individuals. Then the lines of Service would appear!

"Winning meant more than mining then,
And life was a dizzy whirl,
Gambling and dropping chunks of gold
Down the neck of a dance—hall girl."

Oh, but these thoughts were compensating! As the last load of iron bars was laid to rest I was ready to be laid there too!

It was not until that night, after trudging to the heights, pausing to catch a breath and scan the scenery, that I realized the romance of the *Casca*. In the middle of the Yukon she hooted, sending a reverberating echo up and down the length of the valley; slapped the opposing current determinedly with her wooden wheel; and lighted like a Mississippi riverboat, she twinkled her way to the south, out of sight. . . .

Patting my wallet I hoped the next boat would not be too soon for I had many '98ers to meet and a thousand yarns to give ear to. Just then the rising moon flooded the rooftops of Dawson with molten silver as the river rippled past, its current faintly audible where it joined the Klondike. Oh, but it spoke soothing words to me! It made me forget iron, money and hill climbing, such worldly things! How easily that voice lulled me back fifty years—*the same moon glittering on the same rooftops; the same hill overlooking the same valley! Oh, then how its heart within beat wildly: it laughed! it sang! it was beautifully noisy! As the last boisterous sounds of night trailed into the grey dawn of morning, how still that heart became! How heavy hung the Silence! But still the rivers murmured: they spoke to the Cheechako of the glorious past of Dawson; they told him the hour was early. He heeded them. He turned his back on the Valley of silence. The orange square of light beckoned from the rise above.* Never was that view the same and each day I looked forward to the viscissitudes of the Gold Boom Town before retiring to the sanctuary of Smithville.

September 4 dawns wet. Mist encircles the squared, city blocks and unpainted buildings in the valley below. The old landslide's gaping hole below Midnight Dome is plainly visible. Caught by the spell I momentarily expect to see the milling crowds, hear the occasional shot and witness much activity; but much like Rip Van Winkle I see the city as it now is fifty years later — aged, mellow and silently proud of its unpainted state. Paint never made a city; Gold made this one!

Through what Outsiders call the 'grape vine' and Northerners the 'moccasin telegraph' I was kept informed on such characters as I had intended to rout out in time. "Ya oughta see Jack Carpenter . . . he'll tell ya some good ones," came spontaneously from a general conversation. It was in respect that I remembered the suggestion. The day was mine. I would visit Jack. Turning from the vista of low—lying clouds and morning silence that hangs over Dawson till the rising of the sun and the populace, I scuffed down the descent leading to the sleepy collection of buildings below.

I cannot decide whether Dawson is at its best in the morning or evening. One is the silence before the toil; the other the tranquility when day is done. The morn'—wet with sparkling dew, filled with transient clouds that dare to come down from the mountainous heights to the earthly realm with their accomplice, a faint breeze. Evening—the darkness blacker than e'er a coal mine; the twinkling of a million stars that, in their activity, should seemingly produce some sound; the Northern Lights darting here, now there, in careless, unbounded flashes like rays from an acetylene torch—neither green, blue nor white but a weird misture of all three; and their faint swish as one listens closely. No! one should not compare these temporal occasions. Each is part of the day; each belongs to Dawson; the city silently recognizes both. Yes, they must be respected and admired as a part of the beautiful whole.

Arrived at 7th Avenue and King Street I rapped on the old, log cottage—since camouflaged with modern design. I was answered by the same hollow echo that greeted Walter De La Mare's *Traveller,* except no mice scurried in fright. The hour being quite indecent for those who boss themselves, I reconsidered my plan. I turned and headed for the city centre. Dawson, as small as it is, contains a wealth of interest to those interested. With this thought in mind I knew that something would turn up or I would call elsewhere.

So far progressed, the day had been bountiful; but its real bounty was yet to come. Sauntering forth along First Avenue bordering the Yukon, I stood below Midnight Dome encircled by a gamboling, matin cloud. Footsteps had reached St. Mary's Hospital—the home of the aged prospectors who, having found their 'lode' or not, require the services of the Grey Nuns and nurses. These ladies also deter them when the urge to seek gold becomes too strong, for now their bodies are unable to cope with the cruel ordeals. From one within I learned more of the Roman Catholic hospital.

**St. Mary's Hospital
and Old Men's Home**

**From the Sanctuary
The Mighty Yukon Flowing to the Arctic**

"Oftimes when the roster is called one will be absent," he said; "and if the power−that−be could give him the strength to prospect, it's prospect he would!" But alas, the urge is suppressed, the miner convinced his mining days are done. I began to realize the effect of gold on some men's lives, even when the odds are more than twice what they should be. To them it is Life; when the search is not there, there is no life. . . there is Existence. So to those within it is existence, till the day when their souls shall pass into the Eternal Valley of Gold and they become Eternal Prospectors, panning for what made life on earth Heaven; will make life in Heaven (if they ever reach that most revered spot) no more than what one expects in that celestial realm. So may they each receive a pick, a spade, a pan and the liberty to 'stake' freely on God's Eternal Creek.

Seated on the porch railing of the Old Men's Home was Barney McErlane. Born in Derry, Ireland, he left the land of the shamrock for Newcastle−on−Tyne. It was not till years later that he returned home; but soon, with itchy feet, he sought the New World, landing in Boston which, he says: "was very friendly and I enjoyed it there." The year '97 turned up on the calender and the Irishman turned up at Atlin where he stayed for a year, "and could have done well," he said, "had I stayed, but lure took me to Dawson in '98."

Pulling his once−white fedora down, to shield the sun from his face, he commences the conversation in earnest with mention of Soapy Smith and his sledt−of−hand trick, with the $10. 00 bills and bars of soap, from which he received his nickname. Digressing rapidly we are soon back in the Klondike. "I mined Millar Creek for a good while. . . most I ever made was $4,000. 00 out there but I soon put it back in the ground again. That reminds me. . . Harry Boudleer and I always kept a gallon of rum with us. . . it was $8. 00 a gallon then. . . used to have the mailman bring us one every week. Yes, it sure was funny," he chuckles in reflection. "Harry says to me one day: "How about a short one Barney?" Well, without hesitation we left the steam rods and thawing for the shack. You can imagine what went on in there?" he adds, amused. "Do you know what?. . . when we returned the roof over the diggin's was caved in. . . blown right off!. . . this was one time I was under the right star or roof!. . . thanks to our bottle of rum!. . . so you see me lad, being after drinkin' now and then isn't a bad thing!," at which the air was split with laughter. It died; the tale resumed its crooked course.

"I remember my first day in Dawson, you couldn't walk on the street for so many people. I'll never forget the dance−hall girls walking in the street at 4 a. m. It was a fright!. . . Money!. . . Money!. . . Money. . . We had no currency then and there was plenty of wealth. . . Money was no object! Why, I remember some men pounding their rubber, gold containers on the sidewalks to see who could get the most people to go and drink with them. . . no currency then," he reiterated.

"You'd hand the bank tellers your poke and God knows what they'd take out of it!" With the abandon of one from whom they'd taken all his money but was still the happiest man in the world, Barney settled into an easy chair in the sun. "Come on back Sunday, son," he said, "and meet a bunch of the boys." So this son of Eire settled to his siesta in the hot, noon sunshine as I turned towards the broad Yukon, knowing full well that I would return Sunday. Too, I hoped they felt sprightly enough to 'whoop it up' a little in their inimitable fashion.

Reaching the White Pass and Yukon office once more I turned into King Street. On the left one sees the Northern Commercial Store, Dawson's oldest merchants (so they boast); to the right at the end of the block stands the Rochester Hotel—three storeys, faded and with its windows soaped to hide the rude interior. Through a semi—clear pane I dared look past the facade. I beheld a spectacle of disorder, as though a brawl had taken place before the bar and the years had not seen the mess cleaned up. The only things in order were a few pictures hanging squarely on the walls which were coated with the dust of ages.

The Aged 'Rochester' Hotel

**Pearl Harbour Hotel
once the 'Principal'**

Kitty—corner from the Rochester is the Pearl Harbour—one of the five original hotels of Dawson in use today. It was once named the Principal Hotel. Although its name is new the interior is saturated with pictures, horns and relics of old. . . . It is veritably a taxidermist's collection amongst which sit comfortable chairs, chesterfields and a tall, disfiguring mirror which stands full length, giving one a start when passing the bar adjacent. Behind the high, oak counter of the bar you are likely to see pleasant Pearl or her husband Nick—in white shirtsleeves and black armlets—surrounded by a vast array of souvenirs from all parts of the world. It is an English pub set in the heart of Dawson City. With its quiet pleasantness one can hardly imagine the licentious revelry that most surely coloured this bar in the early days. A cool bottled beer drunk from a metal mug, the Cheechako vacated the interior for the sunny street and further perusal.

East on King Street along the same block stands a chocolate— brown building stretching to the lane. Its faded facade (once a bright cream) is quite ornamental in its early, eaglespread architecture. It is the Auditorium, Palace Grand Theatre or oftimes called the Old Opera House. Today it bears the name Nugget Dance Hall. We must see its interior.

**Pearl and Nick
Proprietors of the English Pub**

**Auditorium, Palace Grand Theatre, Old Opera House
Nugget Dance Hall Now**

**Alec Adams
Proprietor of the Old Auditorium**

There is one key to the building. This remains in the possession of old Alec Adams. One is most likely to find the Sourdough at McCormick's Barn having a 'bull session' with some of the old boys. It was there we found him. As he escorted us back to the hall he began his tales of better days. Turning the key we slide into the dull interior. The present is forgotten. Here is where Gaiety and Revelry were unbounded—their faithful servants: Wine, Women and Song. pulling a high—backed chair beside the old Sourdough, we listen *as his mind and voice flash into the dim past, the dullness and chill forgotten as the curtain rises. . . the music blurts forth. . . a row of bared legs turns itself into the can—can as the gay lassies kick above their heads and a roar of approval resounds from the inebriated audience quaffing $1. 00 drinks.* As our own drinks mount up we slide whole—heartedly into the gay atmosphere, for this is Dawson—throbbing heart of the fabulous Klondike, in the unforgettable year of 1898. Slowly the scroll of Time rolls down.

"You could come in for nothing but is was liable to cost you plenty before you got out! You could sit down and have a drink and a girl would tap you on the shoulder, ask if you wanted a dance or if you cared to buy her a drink. You could decline and they'd not bother you. All this while the can—can dancers would be doing their stuff to the gay music of the orchestra in their rear, on the 25 foot stage. Folks soon got tired of all the leg show," Alec continued, "and I'll bet if a woman walked down the street in a long dress there'd be a regular rush for her!" "Of course," I interrupted, "you're speaking for the Oldtimers," in natural defence of modern times, to which he mumbled, "Well, . . . maybe so" in his trembling voice. Dodging quickly into the past again as if it was (and it undoubtedly was) more important to the '98er, he says: "A dance was $1. 50; with a drink $2. 50. On the first balcony drinks ran $20. 00 with the company of a female partner," he added quizzically. "Up top," glancing to the highest balcony in fond remembrance, "$35. 00!" The drink on the floor would be a wine usually; the other Mum's Extra Dry. The bar was on the left side of the entrance, while the gambling took place on the right. The boxes (2) on each side of the stage is where they would drag the so—called Royalty of Dawson when they got too drunk to stay on the floor—and that was plenty often," smiling broadly with the addition ". . . they'd just flop and hang over the box while the music and dancing went on. . . it was some sight, but nobody gave a damn!"

"This is the very hall where Douglas Fairbanks, Pantages and his girl—Klondike Kate, Marjorie Rambeau and Big Fat Billy Bitner got their start. . . I remember them all very well. " Asked about Jack London, he rejoined: "Yes, I remember Jack. Kind of a lean fella. . . he could hold a conversation with any of 'em. . . used to come here sometimes and you could see he was takin' it all in. He was a good boy was Jack! I danced here in '99 when it was first built," he adds, in a last plunge into the fading past. I would put my money on Alec Adams dancing a pretty mean jig today, should the band strike up and a girl tap him gently on the shoulder.

A penetrating dampness, and the desire to leave the remainder of the romantic past where it was, brought us to our feet, Alex changing the topic to the Trail of '98. "Y'ev heard of the fateful landslide of April 3rd in the Chilkoot Pass! Well, I recall the tragedy. . . I lost a pack in the avalanche. So I guess I aughta remember!," he says with emphasis. Alec turned the key (this time in exit) on the dust and chill—silent revellers of a gay past that springs to life each time Alec Adams pulls up a chair beside an interested visitor and unfolds the crisp parchment of Time. Alec is a faithful prospector working his claim on the creeks, "just enough to pay for my keep," he says, "so the government won't take the rest in taxes!," he gloats, maddened at the thought of such indirectness called Justice. And you're likely to hear him curse the day that Clifford Sifton sold Joe Boyle the ground ten miles back from the mouth of the Klondike reaching from summit to summit. "Doesn't pay a man to take too much out!," he interpolates. "I get by, do a little carpentry and odd jobs. I'm quite content," he adds, turning towards McCormick's barn to resume his 'bull session' with the boys. Our feet continue along the boarwalk of King Street. . . it is 1947 again.

Crossing kitty—corner at the end of the block one comes face to face with another relic of early days. A two—storey, grey building, now occupied by others, carries in bold letters the name: Mme. Tremblay's Store. It is a familiar landmark; any Sourdough will tell you about the grand old lady—the first to start an all ladies ready—to—wear in Dawson City, with imports from Paris.

Mme. Tremblay's
First Ladies Ready—to—Wear Shoppe

The *Dawson City "News"* Weekly

Along Third Avenue is the *Dawson City* office which prints weekly the farthest north newspaper in the British Empire. Here one may read the early publication of the *Klondike Nugget* dated July 4th, 1900. However, in the archives of the Administration Building the original publication of the paper on July 31st, 1899 is preserved. In this same year the *Dawson Daily News* went to press with their original edition on September 1. Today a weekly paper keeps Yukoners in touch with local and worldly events. Farther along this avenue the Cheechako came upon two more of the five remaining hotels—the Westminster and Occidental, between which is wedged the popular cafe, the F. and F. At any time of day or night a collection of men lounging in the chairs of the lobbies—some snoring, others puffing energetically on stale old pipes—look into space with that contented look of resignation and old age; still others, legs crossed, bodies bent forward towards the center of the moot, listen intently to who might be expounding from within the circle, on gold, the government or just idle local gossip. It is a last gathering of kindred souls who, in their antiquity, reflect mostly on the past, chiding the youth who might be in their midst with such phrases as: "No, you can give me the good old days!"; or equally as often: "I don't know what you modern youth are coming to!". Such is, and, I suppose, always will be when people have nothing to look ahead to but ample time to look back. It is progress. . . and Life!

The remaining hotel—the Regina—lies on the corner of York and Second Avenue, slightly off the main thoroughfare. I shall always remember an incident connected with this lodging—house. It happened on the day of the arrival and departure of the *Casca* on her last tourist trip 'out' for the season. Standing in the lobby with an old friend named Ed Freeze who by chance I met in this remote corner of Canada and who was waiting to pay his bill for the week's stay, we were accosted by a woman (apparently in charge). She said casually: "What time is the *Casca* leaving?" When my friend retorted in the same casual tone: "In half an hour," she became completely flustered and said to Ed: "Give me a couple of dollars and we'll call it square!", adding as she hurried for her coat, "I've got to leave on that boat!" in a voice suggesting life or death. A few minutes later we saw a coat, a hat and a small grip darting along the street. The hotel was closed for the season!

**Regina Hotel
York and 2nd Avenue**

**Occidental Hotel, F. and F. Cafe
and Westminster Hotel**

R.W. Service Chronology

1874	*—Born in Scotland on January 16*
1885—1888	*—Attended Hillhead High School in Glasgow, Scotland*
1896	*—Moved to Canada*
	Worked on a farm on Vancouver Island
1898—1899	*—Travelled*
1899—1903	*—Worked as a cowboy in Duncan, B.C.*
1903	*—Became a bank clerk in Victoria, B.C.*
1904	*—Transferred to Kamloops, B.C.*
	Transferred to Whitehorse, Yukon
1906	*—Wrote "The Shooting of Dan McGrew"*
1907	*—Published a collection of poems "Songs of a Sourdough"*
1908	*—Transferred to Bank of Commerce in Dawson*
1908—1909	*—Continued to work in bank*
1909	*—Quit bank to write full—time*
1912	*—Went to Balkans as war correspondent*
1913	*—Went to Paris*
	Married Germaine Bourgoin
1921	*—Went to Hollywood for movie of "The Shooting of Dan McGrew"*
1939—1945	*—Lived in the United States during the war*
1945	*—Returned to France*
1958	*—Died at the age of 84*

CHAPTER THIRTY FOUR

THE INFAMOUS BARD

Afternoon had worn itself out. I turned with tired feet towards the heights above the town where 'home' awaited. Suddenly I recalled my morning mission. I would drop in on Jack Carpenter en route.

As the echo of knuckles on wood became a diminuendo a voice from within commanded: "Come in!. . . Come in!" in that imperative, hospitable tone common to folk of the High North. Tracing the source of the voice I found short, plump Jack Carpenter reclining on his bed. "I was just cooking supper and dozed off a bit," he muttered, rubbing his eyes in post−sleep fashion, I, smelling burning grease and simultaneously catching sight of faint blue smoke drifting bedroomwards. "Make yourself at home, son," was the next hearty welcome following our introduction, then the warm invitation "will you stay and have supper with me?. . . all I have is chops and not many potatoes." "About ready for chow myself," I assented. "Have a drink?," he proffered. We did.

I did not know Jack; he knew not I. But the hospitality − it was unbounded! Where was I? Who was Jack? Was I in some Utopian camp? Was he some unknown demi−god? Never before was I so overcome. I braced myself for anything in this strange land. Yes, this was just one of the many "strange things done in the

**Jack Carpenter
Self−Styled Poet Laureate**

Midnight Sun." I felt sure of that! Oh well, I was enjoying myself immensely and if faces tell the truth I was not alone in this. The bottle dry, Jack says, "This'll never do. . . better get a refill!." So I pursue another V. O. from Phil Hickey the local government vendor. Soon gathered around a table of steaming food, we raise another to 'Good Friendship'!. A few bites and another to 'Dawson City!' A moment later to 'Sourdoughs and Cheechakos!'. And that confidence men have in one another, when loosened by the carefee, sweet maiden of intoxication, is felt.

Warmed and internally contented, Jack talks freely. Admitting the bard instinct and a respect for the muse, he divulges some of his lines originated and quoted at various instances in his wanderings as a prospector. The imaginative gent primes himself ready for a tour of his works. "Here's one," he comments and the words flow freer than the beverage had before.

> "A lift on the trail
> With a pleasant smile
> Will lighten the pack
> And shorten the mile. . . .

Do you like that? It has so many meanings. Here's another," he utters, well lubricated and ready for motion.

> ". . . Here's to our mighty Yukon
> Where the creeks run full of gold,
> We are the pioneers who sought it
> But now we're getting old
> We'll buck up and be merry
> Wherever we may be,
> We'll never mind the wets and dries
> So have a shot with me!"

Submitting to suggestion at this point the V. O. cap is removed, glasses klink and two kindred souls oil the gullet again. White haired Jack continues with overpowering hospitality. "Have shum more food, and make yourshelf at home, shun! Howsshh the schop?," he manages, still quite perceptibly. Taking another bite of the the bronzed, pork chop, I assure him I feel at home; that I have plenty of food; that the chop isn't burned. In that clean, cosy kitchen one couldn't help but be otherwise in the presence of Sourdough Carpenter. The last toast loosed the last inhibition (if there ever was any) and the poetry flows freely. Beginning to doubt my own ability and fearing the 'imbibition' of my host, I am put at ease with a spontaneous remark. "It'd shake more'n zishh to get me tight. . . leshh 'ave anozher toasht. . . .

> "Here'sh to the state of your blood
> The all important factor of good health;
> If you health ish good, your blood ish good
> So here'sh to your bloody good health!"

Naturally this called for verification while on the subject of fluids, after which he continued, bubbling over with the inspiration of an Omar. "Heresh one I thought up. . . I shink you'll like it. . .

> "I had a dream the other night
> When everyshing was shtill;
> I dreamed I was a Pearly Cashwell
> A comin' down the hill.
>
> I asked her "watsh the matter?"
> And she began to cry.
> "Don't you know?
> The Yukon vendor has gone dry!"
>
> So Jeckles went to Whitehorse
> To see what he could do;
> And he got another consignment—
> So here's to me and you!. . .

. . . Do you like it?," comes the usual query. Catching the signifigance of the quatrains, I cannot help but submit to the contagious humour of the rhyme. Then we departed momentarily from the muse. "I have shpent only two of my forty yearsh in the North working for shomeone elshh on a payroll. During my proshpecting I discovered gold, lead and named Silver Hill and Black Hill, wishh I shold. Mayo washh my dishdtrict for shometime," he says, apparently reminded of a time when the land was smothered in snow; and he thought of his sister; he returned to his crude form of verse again. Fortunately, by now the toasts were exhausted. So into the rhyme he dived without formalities. . .

> "On this Xmas day
> I am far away
> In the Land of the Midnight Sun,
> Where Northern Lights Are sparkling bright
> And the stars are twinkling above.
>
> It is sixty below
> In this land of the snow,
> Where the mighty Yukon flows;
> Oh yes, it is true I'll be thinking of you
> On Xmas day. . . "

I smiled at the abrupt ending; and Jack in turn smiled distantly at my reaction. The sundry toasts were taking their effect on the oldtimer. He became rather maudlin. This brought forth verse that showed, at some time or other, oldtime bachelor prospectors do think of the opposite sex.

"Your smiles are like the sunshine
And your tears are like the dew,
And your thoughts are a great big garden
Filled with mem'ries, it's love, it's the truth.

With the sunshine on the flowers
Your thoughts are just a care.
We'll make this Yukon beautiful,
And keep our friendship there!"

The evening was advancing; the bottle stood on the table, empty! Jack, yawning, slid into another poem which became less audible as the last verse drew near. "I think you'll go for this one," he said, perking up slightly at the thought of the words. "I call it: On The Alaska Highway:

Come over the Alaska Highway
To this wonderful gold camp.
Where big opportunity awaits you
On every hill and creek
Where you pitch your camp.

You are always sure of a welcome
And a glad hand
Way up in the Yukon
Where a man is a man.

Now buck up and get ready
Mighty damn quick!
Don't fail to bring your blankets,
Your pack and your pick!

Don't remain in Edmonton!
No! No, indeed!
But come to the Yukon
And get in the golden lead.

The trail is damn rough
And muddy you'll bet;
But you're no piker
And you don't mind getting wet!

If you hit a good claim
(As many people do)
Dig in my friend!
That's about all there is to do. . .

. . . . Goodnight, Cheechako," he said cheerily, admitting his drowsiness as his words trailed off unintelligibly.

With this, the small, grey−haired bard (who is neither Kipling nor a Robert Service) crawled between the sheets with effort and closed his eyes on the September evening. Not as able to 'raise them' as he used to, the tipples had their effect. I only hoped, as I washed and cleared the dishes, that the aftermath on the morrow might not be too severe on the Sourdough. Tip− toeing from the house, I closed the door on another of Dawson's unforgettable characters.

The night air was filled with the ring of boots on a boardwalk. I drew up at the log building bearing the letters Y. O. O. P. It is the Yukon Order Of Pioneers—a select few who came into the country as originals over the old trails. (Since, however, with the gradual decrease in numbers, others of later vintage have been welcome.) Their motto "Do unto others as you would be done by»

The Y. O. O. P. was inaugurated December 1, 1894 at FORTY MILE, Yukon Territories. In April of the next year many joined in the stampede to Circle City. To start a new lodge it was necessary to have an order signed by ten Sourdoughs. 1895 their charter was granted and enrollment at Circle reached 200. The winter of 1896 saw still another stampede to Dawson, where Lodge No. 1 was finally transferred. This naturally broke the Circle lodge; but others sprang into being at Rampart City, Alaska, and still later at Nome in 1900. Both, however, became defunct later.

**Yukon Order Of Pioneers
A Sourdough Organization**

Till January 1913 Dawson Lodge was looked upon as the Grand Lodge; but on the first Thursday of that month a Grand Lodge was organized granting the privilege to other lodges to send delegates. It has remained thus since. Annual celebrations of the Order are held on Discovery Day—August 17—the memorable day on which George Carmack struck his Bonanza, which has since become a legal holiday in the Yukon by proclamation.

Upon introduction I entered the log building. The meeting was in session. I was ushered to the lower hall. Feeling at home I surveyed my surroundings. There on a wall hung the first oil painting and frame ever made in Yukon. It was presented to the Y. O. O. P. at 40 Mile in 1894 at their first ball. Below the snow scene reads: STORMY, BUT WE ARE GOING TO THE PIONEERS' BALL JUST THE SAME! 'What spirit! What determination! How typical!' I think to myself.

No Cheechako can hope to gain access to the inner sanctum. But it was my privilege to dine and converse with the Oldtimers after their ritualistic gathering in the upper chambers. Oldtimes were re–lived; trails re–trodden; gold mines re– discovered; and innumerable old yarns, frayed, but with the main thread still holding, were re–spun. A general feeling of goodwill, sincerity, and Northern humour (which must be heard to define) prevailed. A fine gathering of the aged, who are as mentally young as the day they first saw 'colours' in a creek of the Klondike, left me with the

Charlie Evangelista and His Pet Dog

sweet tast of assocation with real men. I was honoured with their presence; they were equally honoured with a Cheechako who dared challenge their hazardous routes into the Yukon. When they are all gone, which shan't be too many years hence, I feel I can carry on their spirit. For there and then they made me a Sourdough!

At the summit once more I stood in the blackened silence looking out over the twinkling lights of the city in neat rows, still illuminating faintly the city of Dawson— asleep. Each night, the silent rows of cabins, saloons and lights told me tales of the old city. Each night I revelled in the thought of such free and easy living when Dawson was adolescing, as I turned to climb the path to the yellow square of light that beckoned me to my own *Little Cabin* and the beautiful other world of sleep. . .

It was while walking towards town next day that I casually met Charlie Evangelista at 512 King Street. Perched on the porch railing in front of his log cabin, stroking a huge white dog, he exemplified a contented Oldtimer. The usual cheery greeting extended, he lapses into talk of the early days with that ease that comes from the memory of only recent events. "I came over the White Pass in '98 and I never went out yet," he said. Stroking the dog continuously, he adds, "Tree times I strike it rich; two times on Bonanza, one time on 60 Mile. . . more that $160,000 taken out of the claims!. . . '98 was all right. . . den we closed claims till 1900." In the same breath Charlie carries on in the year 1898. ". . . Crise, the Yukon was black with Rushers going to Nome via Circle City. Then in the fall of '99 we had the telegraph wire to Dawson. I remember some of the prices in those days," he says, with the usual Sourdough digression that I was becoming used to. "Flour was $2.50 per 100 lbs, milk .15¢ a tin, tomatoes .15¢ a tin, bacon .08¢ − .10¢ a pound, electricity − for the water pump used in mining on the creeks − $24.00 per day, wages for the men were $7.50 a day. Saturday night I'd have a 'poke' and it would be this full," he voiced with gesticulations, "but because of this high price of electricity I couldn't make money. . . and then I had to pay the wages. It sure went in a hurry!," he sighed. "I get by now," he concluded and I left the gnarled, little man in the waistcoat and bashed, felt hat, stroking his silent canine companion affectionately.

George Fulton, in charge of local mails, was my next visit in making the rounds of the Oldtimers. Engrossed in work when I entered, he pushed back his chair and, in a voice that deprived him of many years, commenced talking (upon suggestion) of his entry into Dawson City. Meanwhile his wife brewed a pot of tea. He recalled quite vividly the trip over the White Pass and eventually over the Whitehorse and other rapids before the Gold City was reached. "A young girl of 20 to 21 wanted to come along with us on our raft. We agreed but told her of possible dangers. However, she was unafraid, sitting there as we coursed the rapids, wrapped in a black coat. . . she was the nicest piece of stuff wrapped up in that skin!", he reminisced, his wife smiling amusedly at both of us. She was undaunted! With us there were three men; but when we got to the Canyon and the Rapids, one of them chose to walk around." This incident brought to mind the tale of 'Swiftwater Willie' Gates who was nicknamed because of a similar detour when things looked too rough. "But, in spite of him and all, we made it!. . . yes, right the way to Dawson!" he climaxed.

Tea was served and arrangements made that I might accompany the Sunday mail run on the Loop Trip to the Klondike Valley in order to meet the Argonauts who still live along, and pan the sites of, the famed gold creeks; some indomitably persisting in extracting from the earth 'colours' enough for subsistence. It was an exceedingly pleasant meeting; a generous gesture for the morrow. I descended to the town in the seemingly endless search for the nucleus of Dawson's wonderful character.

Along Third Avenu on the corner of Queen Street stands a faded, brown drug store. Entering, we meet chubby, good−natured Dr. John F. MacLennan one time dentist and now sole druggist, and his congenial wife. Among other things, they too like to chat about the good old days. Mrs. MacLennan has a rare album of equally rare pictures that depict the rugged, wild, early days of the city, completely. Browsing through the pictorial contents she introduces us to such notable characters as Apple Jimmy who paced the main street with the apple−

Dr. J. F. MacLennan−Druggist and Wife

cart which earned him his living. Klondike Kate, well known to early pioneers for her general mien and popularity with all, plus her stage ability at the Auditorium in its glorious days, poses on a bench in the street in carefree manner with Jimmy who doesn't appear to mind it in the least. Next in the gallery of pioneers comes a shot of Bert Daryl who lived in a cabin with MacLennan for years. He was a lone hunter who, when winter came, took up his gun and a small bag of salt for his annual trek to the Arctic coast. "On one of these trips he had a strange meeting," says Mrs. MacLennan. "From somewhere in the distance, Amundsen, who was exploring the northern reaches at the time, said he heard a far off whistle." "It turned out to be our solitary hiker on one of his visits north. Again the same whistle was heard the following year. Once more Bert came into view and presented himself. He became known for his unusual solitary exploits; and on one of these shot a Musk— Ox which he took to England with him when he forsook the Canadian North!"

Corporal Dempster of the Royal Canadian Mounted Police shares a space in the crowded album. Famous for his adventures with the Force, a picture depicts the return of one such patrol from the tragic discovery of four comrades who perished on the MacPherson— Dawson Patrol in 1911.

Smothered from head to foot in furs and frost, the man is scarcely distinguishable. Still another corner is occupied by Solomon Albert who died at the ripe age of 82. He once froze his feet in an overflow. Remembering the cave of a bear in the vicinity of the accident, he smoked the animal out, killed it as it made its exodus, cutt off its feet and put them over his own. "Both were amputated," recalls Mrs. Maclennan, "and I remember how he would ride his bike all around town with his stumps, followed by his faithfu dog."

Next is a snapshot entitled 'Oshiwara' or 'White Chapel at Midnight 1900'. It plainly shows the 'good time girls' leaning from their small shacks in Lousetown, looking for 'last prospects' at the hour of 12 under the bright light of the Midnight Sun.

Over the page we see Turner Townsend and his team of five shorthair dogs. He was the proud owner of the fastest dogteam in the Klondike—an enviable honour in those days; Boundary Line on the Chilkoot Pass in '98 shows the thousands of packs hauted laboriously to the summit on the Long Gold Trek; The Goddesses of Liberty Enlightening Dawson—a unique photo of the strumpets sawing their own wood in the street; the Cheechako Railway to the Dome, making its first trip on September 31th 1901; 'Swiftwater Willie' on Quartz Creek with his harem of three wives, lolls plutocratically in front of his cabin. He preferred to walk around the Whitehorse Rapids, saying bluntly to his companions faced with the frothing waters: "I'm gonna walk!"; the old Exchange— now the Royal Alexandra; fourteen teams of horses and their drivers hauling along the Klondike Valley; Last Shipment of Gold from Dawson City September 14 1898, containing 1 1/2 Million dollars in gold bricks, shipped by the combined Banks of Commerce and North America; another bullion photo showed the last shipment of over 1/2 million dollars from Whitehorse April 6, 1905, shipped 350 miles; then one sees the *'Sinking of the Dawson'* — one of the original riverboats plying the Yukon waters. Finally the character, Walter King, "who was never sober from year to year; never got into trouble and always had a beer bottle in his pocket as he pushed his hand cart along the street," says the druggist's wife. "He would do anything for a bottle of beer!"

With this the priceless album fell shut. She talked freely of her own early days and those of her husband. Repairing to the upper regions of the building we had lunch, which completed the cordial round of hospitality. Whoever visits Dawson in quest of its history must visit the MacLennan Drug Store before they can truly say their search is complete.

While visiting Dawson City one is bound to hear some of the thousands of delectable stories that are still told about the uncut days of '98. As I roamed about the city I chanced upon some of these, a few of which remain vividly in my memory. They still talk about THE CRAZY SWEDE who had the best claim of all. He was called this because of the nonchalent manner in shich he would throw his wealth around the dance halls and saloons. But he was no different from many others whose sudden wealth went to the top of their anatomies.

'SWIFTWATER WILLIE' GATES, who received his nickname when he refused to run the Whitehorse Rapids in a canoe but walked around them, was noted for his polygamous tendencies. He was the proud possessor of three wives at one time. Generous as well, he used to throw banquets and put $100. 00 bills under the plate of each guest. This could only happen in Dawson City in the year 1898!. . .

You'll hear too of JOHANSEN OF ELDORADO who paid a girl her weight in gold to keep house for him. She left after one night, taking the gold with her! They tell too of LINDEBURG— THE NORWEGIAN LAPP who used to buy $500. 00 gold pieces and throw them like chicken feed to the hungry men and women stranded on the beach at Nome. . . then there was the enterprising saloon keeper who, realizing the scarcity of newspapers, had his papers (as often as they arrived) read by a gent from atop the bar. Each was read, from front page to want ads, to the assembled miners. There was not the slightest doubt of booming business in this saloon on paper days.

One night as the Cheechako sat in the rotunda of the Royal Alexandra on First Avenue, an Oldtimer buttonholed him into listening to some yarns. This he did with avidity, leaning closer, so as not to miss one word of the previous tales to be passed on for future generations to read. The first was of ONE− EYED RILEY who won $17,000. 00 at a poker game in Dawson. Heading for the Outside with his gains he arrived at Whitehorse, whereupon he immediately engaged in a crap game. In three passes he lost $3,000. 00. Thinking Lady Luck had given him the brush−off he moved on to Skagway. Here, suffering from an identical 'winning hunch', he became involved in games of chance. Cleaved of his last dollar he turned back to Dawson City to rehabilitate his lost fortune. This was the case of many who fell easy prey to such vultures as Soapy Smith and their illicit card games or walnut− shell tricks. But all the while there was more gold in Dawson, what came easy went with the same reckless abandon.

Humour of a slightly different colour arrived with the narrative about the Englishman. Having come to Dawson via the Edmonton Trail, he landed in the city at a bad time. There was an acute shortage of fresh fruits and vegetables. Broke, but with a goodly supply of marmalade−which he loved as only an Englishman can−he was in popular demand. Nightfall found his complete supply gone; his pockets bursting with money!

In the winter when the cold isolated settlements and cabins, the popular sport of the miners (in order to retain their sanity) was the reading of what newspapers, labels and words of any kind or language they could lay their hands on. These would be committed to memory, including such items as the want ads. Then a verbal competition would result. "We got pretty good at it!," said one Oldtimer, tickled with the present− day abundance of good reading. Then too, was the clamorous auctioneering of a pretty miss by a bartender. As she walked the bar in scant clothing, to the delight of the women−starved males, he shouted figures: pounded his hand on the bar; pointed to the last bidder; and called another preposterous monetary figure. Winter was coming on and the prospectors, ever in need of a good cook, would bid outrageous figures for the charming lassies who, on the other hand, were delighted to exchange their services for the warmth of a miner's cabin. So the bidding would end with a boisterous shouting; a clinking of coin; and the lucky prospector would leave with his hard−won damsel. These are a few of the strange things that actually happened in the fabulous days of the Gold Rush of '98. Perhaps there will never again be a day of such strange times; such strange breeds of men; such strange actions? That alone is the shielded secret of time.

Strolling past the Royal Alexandra of an evening, I had noticed a heavy−set gentleman in a cap and thick windbreaker. He wore a walrus moustache which smothered the pipe that periodically dangled from within its midst. This day as I sauntered along King Street the same figure waved a Yukon welcome. I approached the cabin. His garb had changed to a touque and a scarf, loosely hung around his neck. Suspenders covered a grey, wool shirt. The pipe remained the same.

"Hullo, dere!," he hailed; "Come und see vat i'f gut. . . you can hulp me, no?" I doubted whether my services would be accepted; but I agreed to have a look. What I saw amused me; it must have been a source of amusement for the inventive− minded man. There in the centre of the room, occupying the majority of space, stood a large wheel, innumerable cogs and many levers− mostly all of wood. "Eet ees my latest invention. . . eet ees a poomp for da mine. . . you th'ink eet vork, no?. . . maybe I make lotsa monee und gedt a patent, no? Ve see!. . . ve vill see!. . . sometime I vill be great, no?. . . eet ees a great eenvention, yes!." Although I looked at the work of days skeptically, I could not help but admire the man's efforts, his ambition to invent and

Jan Wetzl
World Traveller and Inventor

his undaunted faith in his originality. For one who had no tuition, his imagination was not the least lacking. The blueprint and its working model were ample proof of this.

Jan Wetzl was born in Hohenstaat, Moravia, on August 15th 1867. In 1892 at the age of 25 he was just out of the military. That year saw him commence his round—the—world journey with $. 04 in his pocket. "On foot I pass trough Vienna, Budapest, Bucharest, Odessa, Tefleck, Caucasus to Akatarenbourg in S. Russia, Samara, Turkestan, Saratoga on da Siberian border to Irkusk, Omsk, Harbin, Vladivostok," he started. "I used da sign telling of my vorld tour da hard vay only to Budapest. . all over Austria I had de best reception. . . und in Vienna a grand duchess gave me tirty dollars und bought me new shoes und clothes." at which he chuckles. . . . "Eet was hard een Siberia all right. . . I vas all da time lost! Dere vas no roads! In a horsecart," he continues, puffing a foul cigar. "Ya!. . . Ya!. . . I go up to Kresno, Jinks. . . from dere to Yakutsk. . . und from dere on I vent to Sredny Kulimsk carrying a shot gun und a rifle." Asked about Siberian wolves attacking, he chortled, "Ya!Ya!" in his usual introduction to speech, "Crise, after ten o'clocksa dey started *ooh. . . ooooohhhh!*. . . und Siberian bears dey go at you too if dey are hongry. I hud four reindeer pulling my sleigh vid a horse on da lead. Da horse I sold at Mihny Kulimsk, den vent on to Tshimiske. . . Ya!. . . I sold my horse dere. . . vas trade eet for a sled. . . da people vas all right. . . but too many races, Ya!" he said solemnly.

"All over Siberia, too many languages!. . . eet vas hard to get around. Very few spoke Rroosian bud I got on vith vat I peek up on steamboats. Eet vas not much deeferent dan Bohemian. From here I vent to da Bering Sea, Bering Island and North Siberian Island. I vas on da road to go as far as I could over da Arctic to Greenland und Scandanavia, den home!. . . but I only vent half way. . . no grub. . . so I could not make eet over da ice. . . so I make my home dere by da Eskeemo in a cave. . . no houses dere! Eet's son— of—a— bitch country! No go as I vas. . . most trappers near dere. . . but two or tree left. Dere dey die off for dere vas not enough game. Ve buy grub vich vas very high, from da Valers. Tirty year I stay dere on many islands. If da Eskeemos move to islands, I move too!. . . . Ya!Ya! I catcha da fur and da grub. I sold to Roosian und American Valers, den I buy a gas boat from a valer for fur. I hud goot Eskeemo captain und pilots. . . dey know every place goot. . . und I go to Nome for grub and sell fur".

The cigar had come to its Waterloo; was snubbed and tossed away. In the gloom Jan continued to roll out the tabloid on which his wanderings were permanently imprinted. . . .

". . . From Siberia I vas crippled in da legs. So I go to Karlsbad Hot Springs in Austria by Nome, Vancouver, Halifax to Europe. . . I vas freezing on da feet und rheumatism. From dere I come to da States and Canada. I vent to Edmonton vid all kinds of money. . . but I mees da boat at Athabaska Landing, da last boat vanting to go to Aklavik, Herschel Island and eventually back to Siberia vid a Valer. I take da shortest vey.

So den I vent from Prince Rupert to Dawson over da Vite Pass. . . . Ya! Ya! Ya!," he blurts in anxious memory. ". . . I hav no visa at Eagle City so I could not get trough. . . so I come back to Dawson. . . Und so I am here!" Here Jan is 80; happy in his inventive mind; existing on a government stipend of $24. 00 a month. "I make invention to trap vid a gramophone," he starts again, chuckling at this latest thought. "I steek a peen een da yong bear and foxes ass, und ven dey howl da gramophone catch eet. . . . Ho! Ho! Ho!" he blurts out unbounded, convincing me how he used it successfully.

Jan, like many other men with 'inklings' towards invention, is combating perpetual motion theories in the form of a pump used in the summer to wash the gold with water caught from the mountain streams. "Now I am vorking on an irrigation poomp, see? (He stretched a weird looking blueprint, hand drawn, in front of me. The maze confused my unmechanical mind). . . . Eet ees for da dry contrees like Australia. . . maybe I do beesiness vid dem, ya?" he finished with a 'ya' that made its way through the hoards of 'no's' that had been his habitual ending. As I left, I knew he felt he had a friend he could confide in, for he promised to show me some cherished belongings he had hidden in a trunk.

Promising I would return to help him dismantle the gruesome— looking wheel that weighed a good two hundred pounds, I left the gloomy, single—roomed interior. I was to see more of the lonely Oldtimer. Once again night was upon the Cheechako.

Bear Creek Settlement   **Tailing Piles Left By Dredge**

#3 Gold Dredge   **Steam Pipes Thawing Perma—Frost**

Hunker Creek

Loop Trip #1

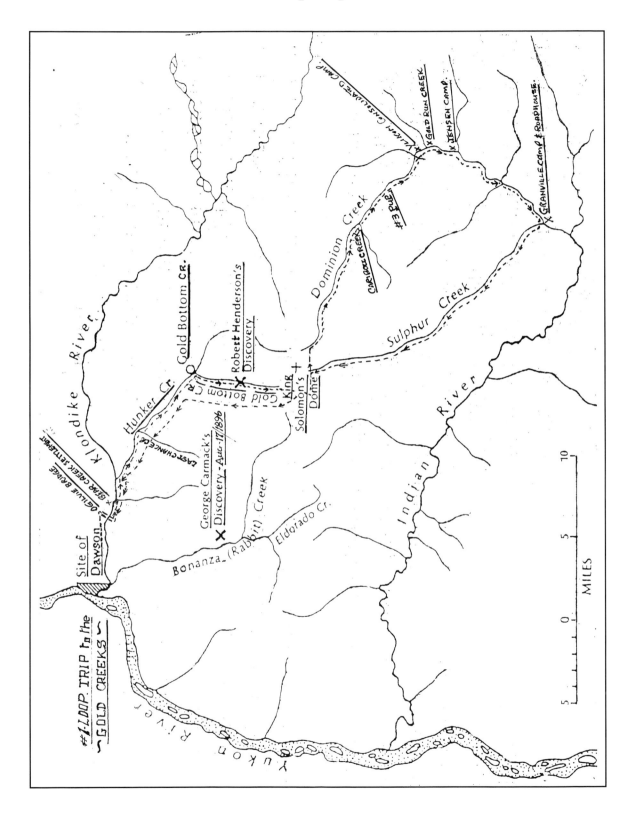

CHAPTER THIRTY FIVE

LOOP TRIP
TO THE FABULOUS CREEKS

Sunday dawned doubtful. Low flying clouds met me at the top of the hill overlooking the valley "peopled with silence", asleep at this hour. As I walked below they scurried on their way, teasing me into building up false hopes of a sunny day. It was 7 a. m. but I knew when the sun bobbed its head over the surrounding hills these transient balls of grey batting, twisting their silent way down the slopes, would disappear. So I entered the Royal Alexandra, ordered breakfast of flapjacks and coffee and awaited Les—the mailman who was to be there on the hour. A young man dressed in tall, brown boots into which his pants disappeared, a couple of thick wool sweaters and a peaked ski cap, entered briskly from the chill outside. He slumped on to a stool and ordered a cup of coffee from the waitress who appeared to be feeling the effects of an early rising. 'This must be my man,' I thought; with that sureness prompted only by intuition, I introduced myself. I had met my man Les—the pleasant, young ex— serviceman on the mail run.

Entering Klondike Valley   **Ogilvie Bridge**

Five minutes later I climbed aboard the truck in the company of the driver, Fred Bernier — quite an oldtimer who was working a claim near Granville—and an elderly prospector bound for his home on one of the many gold creeks. Nestled amongst the mail bags in the rear, I rejoiced as we entered the famous Klondike Valley, the wind blowing fiercely over the hood, slapping hair blown backwards into my face. Thus, our motorized unit slid over the miles of tailing piles as we made our mechanized rush towards Bear Creek, Hunker, Last Chance, Gold Bottom—names that sing loud of gold. They almost spoke, as I glanced at the map; told their lusty and lurid tales of men and their hunt for gold. Yes, I was about to meet some of these men who Time has not eliminated from the Argonaut's Race.

Passing Louie Salvey's cabin (the bench vacant for once) we entered the Valley, the faint trickle of a once—fast river heard in the silence of morn at such times as the driver's foot eased up on the gas. Bonanza Creek, most famous of all, pours itself into the Klondike from a south—easterly direction, winding away into nothingness behind a rising shoulder. Next is the Ogilvie Bridge crossing the Klondike River to Bear Creek settlement, wherein not a sould stirs. But as we exit on the other side a grinding noise of metal on rock greets our ears. It is a prehistoric—looking, mechanical monster chewing its way along the creekbed; wading in its own pond of water which moves ahead as its rock dung piles up behind in undulating rows. It is a Gold Dredge—a boxlike structure with a chain of buckets circling in an endless routine; rising, dumping its yardage; falling, digging with a horrible ripping, tearing noise smothered by the gurgle of water, as it splashes up from bedrock with its mouthful of wet rocks, following the same bucket each time into the belly of the dredge. Day and night No. 3 works; its sixty—five buckets singing their grating song, stopping their creeking chorals only for a breakdown, or for a new lip with which to chew at terra firma. Winchman—Jeff Wynem, Bowbecker, Stern Decker and Oiler, abetted by a Bull Gang of three in the daytime, force their slave monster to do their bidding; forcing it to tear asunder the creek bed in the relentless search for the metal of metals—Gold!

A Sourdough Homestead   **Last Chance Creek**

As morning advanced slowly, the sun's rays still gracing the eastern sky, determined to overcome the line of hills that kept it from flooding the Klondike Valley with molten gold, we reached a dishevelled, decaying building on the right, overlooking the thin trickle of water that was Hunker Creek. A sign tacked on the wall bore an arrow. "What's this?" I said, making my way to the ruins. LAST CHANCE CREEK, it said, an arrow pointing to what was once a runner—up to Bonanza, Eldorado and such rich discoveries. In our short pause the ruins told their fifty—year—old tale of gold pans, spades and hungry prospectors; its glamour scarce jaded with the years. A call; the gunning of an engine; a slammed door and a could of dust, gently wafted to leeward, put us along the winding road—lost now and then in a clump of willows overhanging the road. As restless as Argonauts we pressed on in search of greater riches in greater creeks, dumping our cargo of mail as we went. We came upon a mailbox bent with time and bruised with rough usage. Eagerly I awaited the appearance of the first Sourdough, whom I feel quite sure will not miss this

LEFT:
George Elliot
Hunker Creek

RIGHT:
Charlie Peterson and
Andy McConaghy
Gold Bottom Creek

opportunity to exchange conversation with the mailman who makes but one trip a week. My hunch proves correct as the door of the cabin across the road swings open and a stooped figure in a fedora beams like one in anticipation of good news. The mail has been dumped and we pause before moving on, Les knowing the ways of these Sourdoughs. "Ye didn't fergit me, I see. . . thanks son!" said the man as he felt within his box, smiling largely as the hand returned, full. "Probably a letter from me mother, wonderin' when this hyer danged Gold Rush is going to be over!", cackled the ancient prospector. Laughter filled the mailbox and the valley beyond.

Later I was given to believe that the exchange of banter that invariably follows the depositing of the mail is mutually looked forward to. Certainly it is an occasion for the discharging of stored—up humour. Thus I met George Elliot, who had only time to mention slightly his entry into the Yukon via the Chilkoot Pass and his superb intention to live another fifty years in the Klondike Valley. Our stops all day were to resemble this informal pattern, I gathering what little information I could from the Oldtimers at each stop. However, as the visit was for the purpose of getting acquainted with the prospectors, I shall mention slightly each irregular pause; each character as he is and has been for a goodly number of years; and the pointed remarks that make such visits so worthwhile. Next of the creeks is Gold Bottom. Here a one—time, deep—sea captain makes his appearance on crutches. He is Charlie Peterson. In cut—down denims suspended by wide police braces worn over his heavy woolen underwear, he scarce looks the swashbuckling captain he once was. As we enter conversation I disregard the head of fine hair and find myself sailing out of Nova Scotia aboard a vessel under his command. Having deserted the sea for the safe waters of harbour, I found myself once again at 'home' in the Yukon. "The only difference is that I came fifty years too late!" I sighed, reflecting on his adventurous past. Quick to pick up the thread, he said, smiling: "Well, I dunno. . . I came fifty years ago and what have I got?" throwing up his arms in such a way as to challenge security and laugh at the material. An oversized laugh exuded before we shook hands. With crutches thumping on board, Charlie saw us to the door, cursing his supports with: "Damn these shaky timbers! If I only had stronger limbs beneath me!". As he and bewhiskered Andy McConaghy stood together on the doorstep Charlie's canes waved an emphatic farewell. The road put two more of the Klondike's confirmed optimists in the vault of Memory.

**Mailman Les and
Old Sourdough at the 'Dome'**

**The 'Dome' and
Ogilvie Mountains**

From Gold Bottom the creek forks, leading to the Dome—the central zenith 4250 feet high from whence the creeks emanate. From here one can see the winding creeks on either side, losing themselves in the new growth of timber that has sprung up since the early days when, every tree to the summit of most hills was cut for the construction of flumes, troughs and dams—vital in the relentless sifting and washing of gold. In the distance to the northeast a thin line of mountains, capped with snow, rear their peaks, a silent barrier to the lands beyond. They are the Ogilvie Range of the Mackenzie mountains.

Roadhouse on Dominion Creek

**Al Olsen Along Dominion Creek
on Caribou Creek**

Les Steinhilber Loading 'Riffle Box'

A large Roadhouse and some scattered buildings greet us. Their occupants, Joe Fornier and his woman cook who live alone in the once−busy house, appear with rifle, spaniel and a coyote shot earlier this morning. A short exchange of mail and the latest news finds us over the Dome, coursing Dominion Creek. The sun is now master of the valley on both sides of the Dome. As we descend clouds caught momentarily between the sun dart across the fertile valley, their shadows playing tag down the hillside, across the narrow creek and on up the opposite verdant slope, gamboling not unlike Scottish lambs in the Highlands come spring.

It was along Dominion on Caribou Creek that a mail box brought us to a halt. A yell drew us from the cab. It was Al Olson, a grizzled oldtimer, and his young apprentice from New Mexico − Les Steinhilber. "Have a look at this!" they motioned. We gazed at a useless−looking mound of gravel, a bucket full of the same mixture, an open shaft and a crude 'riffle box' crossed with logs of wood. "It's worth from .90¢ to a buck and a half!," said the younger, pointing at the overflowing bucket. "We've been working like hell the last while. . . doing O. K. . . say, what's the rumour about the price of gold rising?". I wondered, as I looked at the crude contraptions, that men can be so happy moiling in the earth, watching the colours form on the riffles as the stream of water forces the soil onward. It is a lure, an enchanting devil that mocks you and says: "Try to find me! And if you do, then try and sift me out!". I was to feel like a traitor before leaving the Klondike; that men of three score should still be charmed by the Gold Sirens, and I, with a young and flexible body, should be an observer. Yes, I felt like a traitor on my day of departure; but after all I was thinking about it; talking of it; and maybe, I thought, 'I shall write about it?' No, you are not a traitor, I convinced myself. . . leave it for those who came first.

I am getting ahead of myself. . . "I've been here for two years," said the bearded New Mexican; "learning all the angles from Al. "And mind you, he knows them all!". With this we talked our way around to the front of the cabin. It was near noon. We weren't halfway through the valley yet! "We gotta be off! The mail must go through!," came the voice from the truck. So we left the old and the new teaching one another the tricks of the trade. No. 3 Pup above Discovery brought two

John B. Norman, #3 Pup Creek

Confluence of Dominion and Gold Run Creeks

Pete Bateau on #3 Pup Claim

more of these optimists into communion with us: Short, tubby John B. Norman, a veteran of the Chilkoot Pass era; his partner Pete Beteau, gangly, clad in rubber boots and with a pipe, constructed somewhat similar to his own physique, forever riding his lower lip. His entry was via the White Pass two years later than his pals. "That the best ya can do fer us?" said the little man in somewhat cockey tones, to which Les, in his best retaliatory words retorted: "Why, you're lucky to get anything!. . . who wants to write to a broken−down Sourdough like you?" Still hurling insults at the departing vehicle, the two men (not unlike Mutt and Jeff transplanted in the Klondike) turned up the path leading through the weeds to their cabin.

They were happy that someone had remembered them. Two such men as these often spend most of their lives together, having that comixture of characteristics that make for companionship. Many prefer to live the life of a recluse; but as we coursed the creeks those sharing their lives with another Sourdough (kindred−souls), predominated. When the Yukon winter settles in and shuts out transportation it is a far from pleasant life for some, alone, with nothing to do but read and talk to oneself for diversion.

Farther along the creek we pass a stately Roadhouse, still neat and erect with all its fifty years. "Belong'd to a guy named Bob Ross and a fella named Fraser. . . quite popular spot a few years ago. . . deserted now though, since they died. . . Gertie, I believe, has taken over," said my driver between bumps. "Gertie?" I said to myself. Well perhaps I would meet her? We stopped. A gaze through the window clarified its lack of usage. It was littered with everything imagineable, as though life had ceased within but yesterday. Ten−thirty. We halt at the Yukon Consolidated Camp for tea and pie which almost seems more important than dumping the mail. About fifty men inhabit the camp, devoted entirely to churning up the creek and extracting the free gold. A second cup of tea and the latest jokes cap the ten−minute stopover. We continue along Dominion to its confluence with Gold Run Creek, pulling up again at Jensen Camp−another Yukon Consolidated outfit. "Got our precious mail,?" yells an impatient young man, slamming the bunkhouse door as our dust settles. "Sure have!", says Les; "and what's more, it's all intact!" With unusual decorum the ration of bottles is doled out to those with the necessary finance. There is no lack of this on

The Gang at 'Gerties' Lunch

Eugene Price, Gold Run Creek

**'Gertie' Melhouse
Proprietor Granville Roadhouse**

such rare occasions; and as the door continues to open and slam, the contents of the box decreases. An empty carton finds its way into the rear of the truck. A short distance down the road we stopped at the mailbox of Eugene Price on Gold Run. With a yell and a run he reached the road, apparently expecting aomething of the gravest importance. We dumped his flour on the roadside with a box of groceries; at the same time handing him his mail. "Gosh, derned lucky this time!. . . you fellas is more'n angels to me!," he murmured with pleasure equivalent to John Norman's feigned displeasure. Sauntering back down the trail, his pants joined to suspenders by means of a nail or two, he cut a pleasant figure of unconventionality.

Granville Roadhouse brought an end to morning. It was noon and time for lunch. "This is going to be one dinner you won't forget!,"said Les, as we arranged for two more and seated ourselves to wait patiently in the rotunda for the call which we hoped would not be long in coming from the 'salle a manger'. Miss Gertrude Melhouse is the proprietress of Granville House. Noted far down the valley for her cooking, she is most desirous of retaining her reputation. With all the post−war vicissitudes her bill−of−fare does not change; accordingly her remuneration for such repast is the same as it has always been−$1.00 per place−a characteristic gesture of those people of the Inside who have retained their sense of values, heedless of the fast−changing, outside. "Come and get it!," came the familiar invitation to feast. We took our places around the spherical table laden with more than enough varied dishes. The centre was crowned with a vase of Yukon flowers sided by elevated trays of freshly−baked buns. Trays of steaming, roasted, wild duck−a chestnut brown, came from the kitchen in the hands of Gertie who insisted on doing things well. "There's one for each, if you can eat it. . . now dig in!" she commanded. We needed no second invitation. Hands darted in every direction; soon the agreeable sound of masticated food, mingled with light−hearted conversation, verified the pleasure of all seated about the table; not unlike Arthur's Knights, some daring to lift their bird to the mouth much as men of the Round Table might have done on a similar occasion. Saxon goblets of wine, however, were replaced by a strong brew of coffee and tea. An hour brought the feast to a close and approbation from the entire gathering. Justice had been done. Whenever I think of Granville I sense a pleasant association with the day we pulled away from the Roadhouse, leaving Gertie, Fred Bernier and the

Fred Bernier, Granville on Dominion Creek   **Hunker Creek 'Tailing Piles'**

motley crowd in our wake; the well−picked bones of her delicious ducks scattered over the table− silent tribute to a memorable repast.

The turn of the confluence of Dominion and Sulphur Creeks brought us to Granville Camp. Some letters and a volley of 'hellos' exchanged, we continued on the weekly run, headed now along Sulphur Creek, back towards the Dome. The Cheechako's silent observation of Beauty takes a rumble seat as we come up a rise to a tenthouse. It is the home of Alphonse Duquette, his Indian wife and family. "Hello, Frenchman!" greeted Les. "How do yu do, Cheechakos?"returned the Oldster. As we greeted one another he sensed my curiosity and spoke: "I leave Monreau twenty− five yar ago," came the accented words, " and last year I spend de wintar in a tent. . . it war near eighty below. . . but we war warm!" he emphasized with that note of pride that comes with accomplishment. We left them in their tenthouse, I hoping above hope that the winter would save its severity till Alphonse managed a log house. The afternoon sun plays on the sheen waters of the dredge pond of Upper Sulphur No. 9. The crude brute lurches back and forth, its neck like that of an awkward dinosaur coursing an arc, pausing momentarily as though suspecting intrusion while it feeds; then back again to its limit on the other side; then a slight forward motion as the 'spud' is lifted and resunk, the mechanical process continuing; all the while the excretory mass of rock− dung piles up in tiers behind the monster. Autumnal colours sprayed carelessly down the bank, meet the creek; a cloud chases another from bush to bush, eventually losing itself in the variegated maze; far down the valley a twisted skein of bright yellow stands out in proud profusion. The Klondike in autumn is beautiful!

On the Dome once more we stood, like the hub of the Edinburgh Floral Flock, looking down the spokes on the colour scheme, broken only by the nude intrusion of a creek forming the hands, the darting shadows of clouds providing signs of movement. Shadows along the handlike creeks lengthened. The hour was getting late. We moved on. Winding back along Hunker the miles of undulating tailing piles became a memory of an eventful day with the old Sourdoughs. Past Bear Creek gold room; over Ogilvie Bridge; under the lee of the cliffs on the right, we reached the entrance to the Klondike. There in his usual position sat Louis Salvey absorbing the last rays of the setting sun. He looked up and waved as we shot by. Thus was our Exodus from the Klondike Valley. I bulged with the golden reward of a day's panning. I had struck 'colours' and the richest lode in the Klondike. I had met the Argonauts of the *Gold Rush of 1898!*

The Loop Trip came to an end at the home of George Fulton, in charge of mails. "Have a good run?"he enquired. "I've never seen so many characters in all my travels!"I replied, adding, "and I wouldn't have missed the trip for anything!. . . sure pretty scenery in that valley." "Dawson's a wonderful place all round, you'll see!" Believing him, the Cheechako turned towards town once more. But he was not to realize the full truth of these words until it was time to leave Dawson City for good.

It was late in the evening that I realized my pockets were empty. Work was calling from its unpleasant realm once more. "To hell with it!" I said boldly, crawling into my sleeping bag on the cabin floor. Slowly I turned the innumerable Klondike characters over in my mind. . . but I never got past Gold Bottom. . .

The Author
Panning for Gold on the Yukon River

CHAPTER THIRTY SIX

I DIG A DITCH

At some time of the day you're bound to see a slim, greying gentleman peddling his white bicycle through the streets of Dawson. It is said that his slow motion has not varied in the last few years. It happened this Monday morn that I saw a white bicycle approaching, at what would be termed a snail's pace. Stopping the City Engineer, I asked for a job. "Sure thing, lad! When do you want to start?" "Seein' as I'm flat broke it'll have to be right away!" was the reply. "Come with me, then; we'll find you a pick and shovel," he climaxed. And a half hour later found an extra hand in the crew laying sewers on King Street.

The day being so sunny I was prompted to ask a favour. I was not too surprised when the easy−going Sam Bluen granted the wish, saying: "Sure, you can take all the pictures you want...we want you to enjoy your stay here...keep track of your hours too!" With that from the boss no man ever swung pick and shovel with greater zeal than I. I thought, as the pick struck something solid a good foot below the surface: 'The spirit of working together has not been lost with the '98ers. How pleasant it would be if bosses on the Outside thought and felt the same.' How intensely I was enjoying my work.

Chatting with the old characters and interesting townfolk who attract the worker from his labours by hurling repartee in his direction, the day was spent in a pleasant association with Dawson's soil and its people. "Hey, Cheechako! Expect to find gold?" "We worked that property in '98, son!" followed by a hearty laugh were but a few of the gay bits that made an excuse for the momentary cessation of labour. My own timekeeper, I decided on an early quitting in order to visit St. Mary's Hospital. This is the home of Oldtimers too feeble to live in their cabins on the creeks; but quite active and aware of a good portion of their faculties. Here would be a gold−mine for long yarns and re−spun tales. I was certain of that.

A ten−minute walk from the White Pass and Yukon ticket office along the Yukon River brings one to the foot of the Slide on Midnight Dome and, consequently, the hospital. On the steps I met Napoleon Marcoux from Vittonaville, Quebec. Absorbed quickly into conversation, he recounted his entry into the Yukon over the Chilkoot Pass in '98, saying: "I recall the landslide; and its a damn lucky thing I didn't get caught in it too! It was odd how lucky we were. I was with four French−Canadians who were green on the trail. Another

I Dig a Ditch

**Napoleon Marcoux
Walking from St. Mary's (rear)**

271

prospector kicked them and their sheep off his site. Next morning it was completely buried. We harnessed the sheep to pull our stuff over the pass, with the thought of killing them later for fresh meat." His mind drifted back to the present, with the successful reaching of Dawson City; his body slowly descended the steps; his feet firmly on the gravel path below; he walked away unhesitatingly. Invariably you will pass him thus, headed for town, clad in his rich brown suit and his fedora, from below which protrudes a pipe belching smoke at intervals.

A Queer Quartet

It was with some difficulty that I pursuaded four of the inhabitants of the 'home' to come forth and arraign themselves for a group photo. No sooner had they lined up in position than one, with an idea of his own, turned and started off. 'Time for a little assistance,' I thought. So soliciting the services of Barney McErline the quartet were finally captured, lined up and shot. Indeed, they included a colourful cross−section of Sourdoughs: Archie MacComb, 78 year old; A.A. Cripp of Bonanza Creek−a veteran of the Chilkoot, having come from New Zealand and Africa prior to this, his birth−place being Tasmania; J. Bill Callette, a Frenchman who ventured into the Yukon in 1897 over the Chilkoot; and Swan Johnson who entered via the Chilkoot Pass also. "I remember vividly an incident on Sheep Trail," the latter forwarded. "A thief was caught, breaking open caches. We gave him a 'miner trial'. And d'ya know when we reached a verdict of 'Guilty', he tried to make a quick getaway!" To this Swan adds in a bloody manner, "We brought 'im down in his tracks! Yes, that was the real justice we had in them days! No two ways about it then!"

**Two Stubborn Oldtimers
George Sutherland and
Maurice Grenier**

At that moment a figure clad in blue denim overalls appeared at the front door. "Come on out for a picture!" I begged George Sutherland. Maurice Grenier, who himself came into the country in 1902, said: "What fer?" "We might drop dead any minute!" At which point he was assisted to the region below the steps. Old George, as he is sometimes called by his many friends, said as we coaxed him to be still: "I must be 94 now...can't you find some younger man to take a picture?" Calmed at last by an onslaught of questions, he revealed his birthplace as the State of Maine; his trip aboard the *Rosy Lea* and his entry through the White Pass on the 6th of June 1898. George is heralded as one of Dawson's oldest inhabitants running the eldest, Louis Salvey, a close second.

The ordeal overwith, George came close. With short vision he glanced upward. A large look of surprise crept over his countenance. He retorted emphatically: "If I had your youth and body, I'd still be out prospecting for gold!...oh ho! Look at the whiskers too!" he cried, bringing into focus the Cheechako's overgrown Imperial.

It was then that I looked towards the crowning hills of Dawson and thought: 'Maybe you should be!' I felt momentarily guilty. It was true, that the longer I stayed in Dawson, the more I heard told of Gold, the keener I got about the few passing fancies that had stirred a corner of my curiosity. But they were growing to be more than passing fancies. I was slowly getting caught in the golden web of imagination. Everything was beginning to take on the aspect of gold. Was I about to be caught for good by its enthralling tentacles; its beguiling lure; its Siren song? So the second oldest Sourdough in Dawson City left me standing, staring, thinking. The voice of age had spoken to the mind of youth. But reason interrupted.

From the balcony of the hospital one commands an excellent view of the Yukon River, the afternoon sun's rays glancing off in blinding flashes with each undulation. At times when the river is quiet its surface is a mirror reflecting the towering hills in symmetry. It was such this afternoon as the heat beat against the veranda. But the symmetry was suddenly broken. A sternwheeler, belching volumes of smoke, slid noiselessly along the left of the axis — that thin line where the water and the land become one and the same—and docked. The *Casca* had been expected. Now here she was. I began to see myself leaving Dawson City. The thought was not a pleasant one. I

**Yukon River
From St. Mary's**

had come to feel a certain at—homeness here that I had not felt elsewhere; a strange liking for the depth of character of its inhabitants, their open friendliness, sincerity and profound hospitality. Disturbed thus, I left my new acquaintances at St. Mary's and headed along First Avenue sloping towards the heart of Dawson.

"Sorry, full crew!" said the Mate of the *Casca*. With a feeling of inward joy I received the verdict. I could not work passage aboard her to Whitehorse. I would have to wait for the *Whitehorse* or *Klondike* riverboats. This would allow me a couple more days association with this pleasant city. Inwardly the Cheechako smiled. Along King Street he turned once more to his cabin on the heights commanding the finest view of the famed city of '98, tired; but overwhelmingly pleased with his associations of the day.

Morning found the sun spanking the remote hills. 'Just the day for a climb,' I told myself. Whoever has scanned the slopes from Dawson must have thought to himself: 'I wonder what the view is like from the Dome?' So the thought was born. I accepted the challenge. I would tackle Midnight Dome. Now Smithville is part way up the summit, so feeling quite smug I shouldered a kit bag and turned up the slope! The day belonged to me!

Sacred to the memory of the people of Dawson are the Northwest Mounted Police who died in the early days of the country. At the top of the first hill one comes face to face with rows of immaculate headpieces in the plot reserved solely for these men. The exception is a single grave representing the original Yukon Field Force. Noticeable, too, is the early age at which the majority of these law—keepers died; and understandable is the era in which they perished—1896 to early 1900—the rough years of the Great Gold Rush. Youngest of the sixteen was Constable Edward Flett, who died February 15th, 1899 at the youthful age of 20. Could he have been shot? Was he drowned in the merciless Yukon? Did he freeze in the cold of winter? Was it scurvy? These are but a few of the probable questions that arise in the mind of the onlooker reflecting on his age. As we tip our hat, turn and tread silently away, we say to ourselves: "They May Rest in Peace!" For the Gold Rush has come and gone...and Peace reigns over the Klondike Valley.

Northwest Mounted Police Graveyard

Charlie Schwege—Buried Overlooking His Creeks   **Yukon Order Of Pioneers Last 'Stake'**

"It Got Their Man"

David Snygo

Pushing through the surrounding bushes, I came out on the top of the hills forming one side of the Klondike Valley. There below lay rows of inactive waves, tapering off at the confluence of the Klondike and Yukon Rivers, isolating lakes of water—each mirroring the transient clouds in turn. These are the endless rows of 'tailings' that Time and the Mammoth Dredges have churned and redeposited. As I stood thinking about modern processes of "moiling for gold" my eyes fell on the weatherbeaten remains of a grave. 'At least one Oldtimer got his wish,' I mused; 'buried on the slope overlooking the Klondike, where he once knelt with a rusty pan, sifting colours from the water and alluvial sand.'

I felt glad that he could not see what Time has done to his Klondike Valley, where the romance of panning has been replaced by drudge of the dredge. The Cheechako turned his back on the plot of Sourdough Charlie Schwege who died on June 29, 1899, aged 58 years. I turned my feet in the direction of the Dome.

Varied were the men of the Trail of '98 and their gravestones speak the last of many. Stumbling through the brush I came upon another—that of David Snygo of Boleman, Sweden. Crossing the dirt road more gravestones confronted me. Would I never reach the summit? Truly, I felt I must review the dead as I had done the living in the city below, for did they not all contribute their part or their lives to the making of history? So I walked between the hundreds of crosses in the Y.O.O.P. graveyard, centered by a giant cross bearing the letters R.I.P.; the past flashing across the tabula rassa, quickly replaced by the thought of the present and future. It will not be many years before the last of the originals join their fellow men; and the tales will become legends; and the legends history; and the history of this Gold Rush soon overcome by the cobwebs of time in the attic of antiquity. 'How fortunate I am,' I think, 'to meet the living remainder; to hear the true story from aging lips!' I said a few words and departed.

274

Yukon River—Heading 1600 mi. to Bering Sea

Dawson from Midnight Dome

Victor Peterson
Y.O.O.P.

Indian Village of Moosehide

Climbing to the Dome is not difficult but it is quite steep, necessitating frequent pauses. With each pause the panorama widens, the trees thinning, and the wind dares to challenge as it whistles around the Dome. It is noon when the shack crowning the heights is reached. I sit down for the final pause to view the pageant of the Valley, 1500 feet below Midnight Dome. To the south stretches the mighty Yukon, dividing, reforming into one swift mass, disappearing into the distant hills to the northwest. It wends its way, past the Indian Village of Moosehide, 1600 miles to the Bering Sea, forming an archipelago on one island on which lies the neat farm of the Roman Catholic Sisters who supply the hospitals with fresh milk from their herd. To the north, lying just under a thin layer of cumulus clouds, can be seen the snow—capped Ogilvie Range of the Mackenzie Mountains. To the east one catches an overall glimpse of the Klondike Valley; a dredge moving slowly in the creek below; miles of 'tailing' piles, the rock dung of the huge, prehistoric dredges wallowing in their wet creeks; Bonanza—once the richest gold creek of them all— branching off to the southeast; and directly below, the rectangular blocks of Dawson City cluttered with their odd assortment of crude dwellings, looking, I imagine, no different than they did in the early 1900's. The only movement: the ferry crossing the Yukon periodically, creating as it docks a modicum of activity on the wharf.

The dredge, like a tiny ant, moves slightly at its gorging work; the ferry recrosses the river; the wind blows hollow, melancholy sounds through the broken—down, tin shack beside me; the warmth of the sun continues to pour down upon us.

I could have sat reflecting on Dawson's past for hours had not the wind been so persistent. Heeding it, I descended the other side of the Dome, intent on visiting the village of Mooshide the Indian encampment a mile downstream from Dawson. The steep trail took me past Suicide Point. One wonders how many dejected gold−seekers came to such an unfitting end here? Personally, I could not see any of this hardy breed of people giving up so easily. 'Give in' are words they have never known...and I thought: 'It must be just a name!'

Saturated with the fragrance of autumn in the woods and the firm sound of crunching leaves underfoot, I enter the narrow path arched with yellow ochre. As the leaves give way a cabin on the left takes their place. Thirsty by this time, I approach the old abode whereupon a figure bent over in the garden patch attracts me. "Hello, there!" I shout in usual welcome. "Welcome son! ...welcome!" comes the hospitable reply from beneath the grey, walrus moustache.

The Optimist

As I sat and talked with John Lawerence, who continued to pull and clean his turnips, he told me bits of his life. Arrived at Skagway December 22, 1898, he proceeded to Atlin, where he says in disgust: "I found nothing and went out again! It was tough, for we had to pull 450 pounds apiece on hand−sleds. Back in Vancouver I got the urge again and this time went through the White Pass on the railroad, in 1900. I'm 81 years old...still I'm able to cut my own wood...I've always done it...and always will!" he adds doggedly. I had not the least doubt he would.

John Lawerence
The Optimist

Chewing on a juicy turnip, I listened while he switched to mining talk. "Used to allow us ten days to stake our claims...anything over ten miles away we were given one day for every five miles...." Then came a distinct change in mood. "I recall now some nincompoop sold Joe Boyle and Frank Slaver the land from summit to summit and ten miles back in the Klondike Valley. With added fury as though the past was this very day, he says: "I built, and thought it a good place to prospect...and it was!...till I found there was a concession on it! Say, would you like something to eat afore you go?" he enquired, quickly and effectively forgetting the disconcerting deal. "Sure 'nough, and I wouldn't mind a turnip with it," I accepted. So we discoursed while I downed turnips, beets, baking powder biscuits, a raisin−and−fig mixture of his own and spruce tea with sugar. (The latter, a Northern beverage designed in the early days by a doctor to prevent scurvy and sickness from lack of greens, is commonly used by some of the Sourdoughs for tea.) Old calendars and pin−up girls provided the ancient setting for the equally aged tales that spiced the meal. With this I departed, proudly possessing a present from the man: one of his original, rusted gold pans which he insisted I take.

Equipped thus, I followed the path which lead to the Mission door. Receiving the greetings of the quaint English schoolmaster−Mr. Bridge − wearing a black beret and a monocle, I was informed that, school over at three o'clock, I could secure a lift upstream with some Indian boys. My transportation settled, I perused the native settlement and soon discovered its populace: a few women and a herd of unruly children, the smallest of whom breaks into tears at sight of the Dazzio or bewhiskered white man. The men, I learned, were out fishing and hunting. Among the pleasant associations I remembered two squaws who, coming originally from other parts of the country, asked me about their friends. Having met some of them, and relatives along the Mackenzie River, we had a common factor. So I related the latest in true 'moccasin telegraph' fashion to eager ears.

Some Unruly Children Having Fun

The 'Dazzio' Pleases and Frightens

An Indian Meat and Fur 'Cache'

The Popular Native Fish Wheel

**Jim Hughes
From Argonaut to Fisherman**

It was the school bell that brought our conversation and my disport with the papooses to a close, and the rush of tawny youngsters from the depths of the Mission School. We shoved off in a rowboat manned by two Indian boys who seemed very confident at bucking the Yukon waters. Taking turns we pulled our weight against the river, passing the White Pass and Yukon ship graveyard to starboard. Here the *Julia B.*–a once proud sternwheeler plying the river–and a companion vessel rot with age, their keels mere skeletons picked bare by the greatest of all vultures –Time.

Tracking for a few hundred yards, we pulled up to shore under the lee of a rack loaded down with a large supply of drying fish. Following my young native friends (two I remember as Peggy and Henry) we entered the log home of Jim Hughes, which, once inside, smelled not unlike the other surroundings. Coffee and bread smeared with sugar were served by the Oldtimer to the intense delight of my friends. As they munched, he spoke. Jim is another of the old gang who tackled the Chilkoot Pass in '98. Since, he has turned from mining gold all over the country to catching King salmon, whitefish, greyling and pike for a living. With tell–tale traces of sugar around each mouth, my native friends gathered themselves together and our short stay with the fisherman found us once more crossing the swift current. Finally, not unlike the ferry seen from Midnight Dome, we pulled into the wharf, 'home' in Dawson City again.

Supper in the Arcade (Alexandra) and an exchange of yarns in the hotel adjacent, brought nightfall down upon me. With thoughts of the trip to Bonanza Creek on the morrow flooding my mind, I trudged upward to Smithville; that ever–pleasant view of Dawson at night, illumined by the flickering lamplights; the flash of the Aurora Borealis across a jet–black sky; its swish and the faint sound of the Yukon River the musical lullaby. A small square of orange light suddenly lit the darkness...flickered momentarily...was snuffed out as the door closed on another complete day in the heart of the Yukon Territory.

Author Trying Out His Gift Pan for 'Colours'

Home Again to 'Smithville' Dawson City

Loop Trip #2

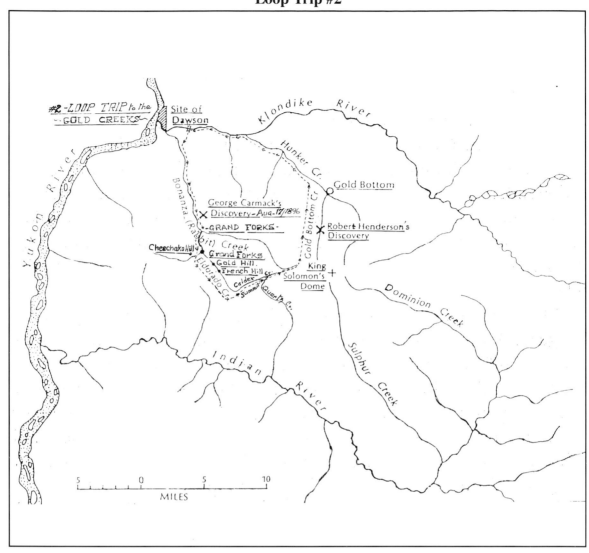

Finally...
Phillip Finds *His* Bonanza!

CHAPTER THIRTY SEVEN

BONANZA RICHEST OF ALL...

As usual, the transient clouds of morning were making their way 'round the midriff of Dawson's pallisading hills, gamboling till such time as the sun would force them to become an invisible part of the atmosphere. Whistling with the light lilt of the free, I trudged down the road to King Street. It was seven o'clock, the regular time for the mail run, as I accosted George Chapman, dumping the last sack of mail into the truck for the other mail—run to the creeks. A quick "good morning" and we climbed aboard.

Entering the yawning mouth of the Klondike, I sensed something missing. There was no sign of Louis Salvey sitting in front of his log cabin! Already the idiosyncrasies of Dawson were becoming familiar to me. But on realizing his age (and furthermore, the sun, in which he loved to bask, was not shining this early) the hour was conceded to Louis and sleep. Crossing the Klondike River we slid past a famous 'cut' on the left limit where the Argonauts had tried to penetrate the ridge between the creeks, but were baulked. Bonanza was ours! More intense than on the previous Loop Trip did my interest become as we broached the unknown. No prospector could have gazed on the world's most famous gold creek with more lust than I. But the lust differed in that it was to meet the remnants of that heroic band—the survivors of the fifty—year Battle of Bonanza.

The Cheechako's lust commenced satiation at the mail box of Harry Leamon. A native of Camden Town, London, he came to the Klondike in 1899 over the Chilkoot Pass. Looking far below his three—score—ten and more, he greeted us with that excess of cordiality common to Yukoners. Even his dog seemed to sense friends and in a sincere wag he too greeted us with that love for man that only a dog can proffer.

Running the gauntlet of legendary hills and tributaries we arrived at the site of Discovery Claim, staked by George Washington Carmack on August 17, 1896 and the adjacent claims staked by his Indian friends 'Skookum' Jim and 'Tagish' Charlie. It was here that Robert Henderson suggested they look on their way over the Low Divide from Gold Bottom, where he was panning. This they did, and to the amazement of all, found large nuggets along the stream from which they hurried to record their claims at Forty Mile. Unfortunately they neglected to inform Henderson, who, when he did find out about the discovery, learned the entire area was staked. However, he is credited with the find and should be regarded as the real discoverer of the Klondike.

Harry Leaman
From London, Eng. to the Klondike

"3 Bootleggers of Bonanza"
John Struger, Mike Papovitch, Phil Burich

Close to the forks of Upper Bonanza and Eldorado we stop at a group of ancient buildings. Immediately three oldsters emerge for their usual bout of levity with the mailman. A quainter trio of characters I have yet to see. "We're the Three Bootleggers of Bonanza," pipes Mike Papovich, smallest of the group, clad in oversized breeches which sagged on overworked suspenders…"that's what they call us around here." His companions of long standing are John Struger, who became affixed to this part of the world in 1908, and Phil Burich of 1910 vintage. Mike, it appears, preceded

Peter Brown
Postmaster of Grand Forks

John Drabeson and Ted Watch
"…We got to strike sump'n soon!…"

his friends in 1905. "We still scrape enough out of these damn creeks to earn a living," says one of them as he bundles the mail under his arm and we prepare to go. As I cast a fleeting glimpse at John with plaster over his nose, it is not hard to imagine the early years when tempers flashed and fists flew. The Bootleggers of Bonanza waved us out of sight.

The scenery along most of the creeks is the same. A new growth of trees and shrubs is successfully replacing the once lush growth that rose to the summits but which was completely destroyed for the construction of flumes, bridges and buildings when the Great Rush was on. From Bonanza we course Eldorado Creek to Grand Forks. Hobbling from his picturesque shack, looking like a by−product of the Buccaneer days, the postmaster comes down to meet us. He is Peter Brown, a native of the Shetland Islands, who came into the Yukon in 1900. A short discourse found another Sourdough pigeon−holed in memory.

Next in the galaxy of faces came two more Oldtimers, John Drabeson and Ted Watch. Toying with his tobbaco pouch, the former said: "I came in over the White Pass from California in 1900…and I been here since." Ted originally came from Hungary, travelled the U.S.A. and he too, in 1907, was deposited in this historical valley below the Calder summit. "Heard of French Hill, Cheechako?" asked John, abruptly, "and Anderson, the man who worked for it?" "Not yet, but I'm listening," I returned, anxious to add to the growing store of Klondike history. "Well, it seems he got himself pretty well plastered…so much so that when he awoke he discovered, in place of the $200.00 in his pocket, a claim deed. It was for Nos. 26 and 27 below Eldorado. Broke and with nothing better to do than work his new 'find' he started in. And do you know what happened? Before that man was through moiling he took $3,000,000.00 from that hill!…yes sir!…so I say the moral behind it is: maybe it pays a guy to get hiself 'corned up' occasionally so's someone can do him a like favour!…some of 'em's had all the luck…but me and Ted here's not givin' in yet…we got to strike sump'n soon!…It's written in the stars!" "There's Gold Hill over there," said Ted, suddenly voicing his story of the surroundings. "She was a beautiful find for some of 'em…rich as they come!…see them old buildings yonder?…them's the site of the old schoolhouse…and say, you've heard of Cheechako Hill?…well, it's below there a bit," pointing generally in the direction from whence we had come. "It's quite a hill too. At one time Cheechakos came up the valley lookin' for diggin's and just for a lark a bunch of Oldtimers, doing too well for added competition, said: "You aughta stake the top of that hill…should be rich!"

With hearty laughs all round they went back to work, amused at the gullibility of greenhorns. There's a standing proverb about the 'last laugh' which turned out too true here. The Cheechakos made thousands and the last of the tale is still heard when winter closes in on the Klondike and the barrel stove becomes the hub of the social wheel. "Yes, they shore cleaned up, some of 'em... and believe you me, one of these times those Yukon stars is gonna look down on Johnny and me and wink kinda big like, 'cause we intend to 'get it' before we kick the bucket...and it's there just a

waitin' fer us, too!"All smiles and chuckles, the two bundled their mail in their arms; Ted pushed back his black stetson firmly on his head; Johnny waved and shouted something inaudible as we pulled away from their rustic cabin. We jolted over the crude trail to the Forks.

Arrived at the confluence of Calder and Quartz Creeks, we stopped for another short 'bull session' with the local inhabitants. A small hint of the early days brought the past of 'Duly' Cameron to the fore. The year '98 saw him entering via the White Pass where he was stationed with the police for some time. As the Rush continued he moved on to Bennett, Tagish and finally to Whitehorse with the H Patrol, which travelled regularly to Kluana—a distance of 167 miles. Although the years have bent him he is still active, describing his early days with the vividness and clarity of his brother Sourdoughs all along the creeks. With him lives his partner, Steve Groshell, who recalls vaguely that about 1900 he entered the Yukon; years before that he migrated from his home in Jugoslavia.

'Duly' Cameron and Steve Groshell

Quartz Creek
Towards the 'Dome'

Ogilvie Range of (the) Mackenzie Mountains
from the 'Dome'

Having reached the end of the run we turned up Quartz Creek towards the Dome, from which the never–tiring view of the surrounding creeks is seen in all its autumn splendour. Little did I know the pleasant surprise that awaited me on this return. As I entered the Rex Cafe for supper the last two years slipped past as a voice cried in wide exclamation: "Well hello there!...if it isn't Phil Allen under all those whiskers!" I was in league with an old travelling chum, Ed Freeze, who served with me in the R.C.A.F.

The next few days renewed my association with a pick, the many Oldtimers and my old buddy who, with the cessation of work on the gold creeks for the season, deigned to continue the westward trek with me over the *Trail of '98.* But how was I to leave Dawson City? The boat crews were complete. "There must be a way; there is a will!" I told myself. "There's got to be!" As we

'Tailings', New Growth and Prospectors Cabins   **St. Andrews Church—1901**

Barney McErlane
From Derry to Dawson—1898   **The Unknown Sourdough**
and His Best Friend

Midnight Dome and the Mark of the Slide   **Vintage Dawson Loghouse and Model–T Fords**

trudged along the waterfront, hands in pockets that jingled a little from the results of honest labour, a voice interrupted the conversation. "How'd you like to pan a little free gold?" "Gold? Where?" we interjected with aroused interest. "Right in front of you...under the floor of this old saloon," said Alec Adams. "I mind the days when the stuff didn't mean a damn to anyone, mostly the drunks in from the creeks...yes, they'd be tighter'n an old fashioned corselette, tipping the dust from their pokes down the back of some dance hall floozie...and laugh!...they'd laugh like hell as the damned stuff fell in the sawdust of the saloon or through the cracks in the dance floor. A man can make plenty panning the dirt beneath the floor...go ahead and work it if you like," said the gnarled Oldtimer as he pulled down another portion of a once vociferous saloon.

Gold! We accepted the challenge. But just then a figure came rushing down the street. "If you still wanna go to Whitehorse we got room for you...one of the crew's gone to hospital...step it up, though!" panted the ship's messenger. As if one Goddess of Kindness was being replaced by a still more generous woman, I was forced to make my decision. And just when I had my first gold strike! Time and the Season accounted for another form of gold. Such was my vicissitude.

Public School—1901

That night was to be my last with the Sourdoughs. 'I may never see these faces again!' I thought. "We shall celebrate!" I said. And celebrate we did! Invariably, those who fall in company with Tom Tracy—

the light−hearted Irishman with the contagious humour−are bound to celebrate. His life, so it appears, has been one long succession of celebrations, studded here and there with enough honest labour to salve his conscience. With each pay check his dream of his own farm is shattered; with each debauch his dream is resurrected. Tom is the Corsair of Confliction. So the farm passed back into the dream world and emerged a greater dream...but celebrate that night we all did!

Then in the darkness of night the Cheechako waved farewell to Jan Wetzl, the Bohemian, and his pal, Ed, who was to follow on the next boat. It was in the moment before we shoved off that I met the last of my Sourdough acquaintants, 'Mac' MacCush. Night watchman for the White Pass, he was there on the dock, his hat brim unknowingly turned up, to see us safely away. In his Scots brogue which does not let down his native land, he said: "I was wi' the Royal Northwest Moonted Police, and huving two or so years to complete me time, ah wanted budly to go north during the Goold Rush. When my time was up I received an honourable discharge and began looking for gold. Ah made noo real strikes and

**Sargent & Pinska
Early Trading Post**

eventually gave it oop. And herre ah am!" In retrospect, he says: "The people we hud to keep lawful were a goot lot and niver go' into too much trouble...of course there were the sharpies and gamblers−bu' then, noo one cou' ge' oot o' Dawson. We patrolled wi' posts every few miles to Whitehorse via Stewart, and we'd meet in relays und return ta our base on such patrols." He concludes convincingly as the hoot escapes from the boat's whistle. "Ah woodn't leave this country−it's grrrreat!"

Dawson to Whitehorse

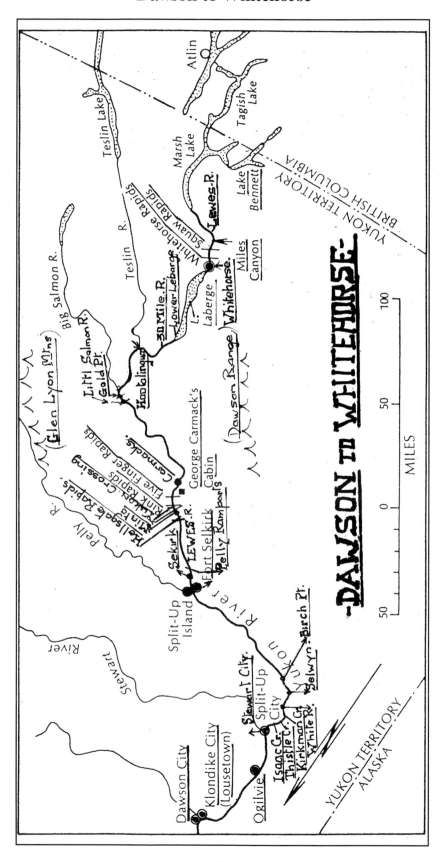

CHAPTER THIRTY EIGHT

ON THE TRAIL

The impatient Skipper finally getting the O.K. from the Mate, the creeking capstan hissing as it tightens the barge cables, and the nondescript crew hustling in every direction, we gradually lengthen the black distance between the *Klondike* and the wharf. The splash of the sternwheel slapping the Yukon, churns it into a froth, tinted yellow by the light from the stern lamp; the hiss of alternate white and black smoke puffs from the stack, throwing small black particles of soot on the deck below; the thud of heavy logs—fuel for the boiler—being dropped in the lower deck, is pleasant river music to all ears. One last, long whistle echoes back and forth between the banks of the Yukon River; the Skipper is in the wheelhouse; the pressure is up to 180 pounds. We slide past the Bank of Commerce, its unmistakeable square structure silhouetted against the faint illumination from the street lamps. Thoughts of Service and his years spent within the bank as a 'wage—slave' teller creep from the night; and with them the Spell of the Yukon.

"There are hardships that nobody reckons;
There are valleys unpeopled and still;
There's a land—oh, it beckons and beckons,
And I want to go back—and I will!"

As Service said: "Goodbye, Little Cabin," so did I think of his words in saying my own farewell to Dawson City.

"The shadows enfold you, it's drawing tonight;
The evening star needles the sky:
And huh! but it's stinging and stabbing my sight
God bless you, old cabin, goodbye!"

**S.S. Klondike
Steaming on the Water *Trail of '98***

Dawson City was but another very pleasant memory somewhere behind us in the Yukon night. As I sank into the welcome bunk after the final 'woodwatch' a hundred cheery faces of Dawsonites paraded before my eyes; one in the manner of the '98ers spoke for the many, saying: "You'll be back!....You'll be back!" I vaguely remember answering the Sourdough sage with: "I want to come back—and I will!"

The sun shone brightly; the enormous pistons played a pleasant duet; the yellowing autumn leaves told me the Season and I were well on the way. *On the Trail of '98* (in reverse) *we are once more with the prospectors, bucking the swift waters of the Yukon River.*

Stewart City to Port

Soon, on the port bank, there appears a fair—sized settlement. As the shore cables are drawn taut we discover it is Stewart City. Here is a two—storey Roadhouse, a collection of Hudson's Bay buildings dressed in their usual white with red collars and several other abodes scattered along the bank. It boasts a post office also, being an important junction at the mouth of the Stewart River for traffic to one of Canada's leading silver, lead and gold mining areas—Mayo, 175 miles up river.

Several creeks and rivers flow into the Yukon in the next few miles. One of these is Isaac Creek, fifteen miles from Selwyn. Here are the remains of a settlement sprung into being when gold was discovered in the Shushana country in 1913. Thistle and Kirkman Creeks have their short histories too. The former is the prospector's question mark, for here immensely rich pockets have been discovered which in time peter out. For optimistic prospectors the real 'pay streak' has yet to be found. However, prehistoric buffalo have been found in the creek. An amusing incident occurred in the fall of 1903 on Kirkman Bar. Seven boats became stranded at one time, the *Canadian* spending the winter where she lay. This brings to mind the rather humourous incident at another bar during the '98 Rush when rafts, barges and makeshift craft came down in an endless stream, many becoming hard aground on sandbars. One scowman, when asked what good fortune kept him from becoming similarly stranded, replied: "I couldn't get on them because they were all occupied!"

White River, next, has the singular distinction of being the only glacial stream to enter the Yukon in this area. Its name comes from the white sediment that it carries with it. Also huge, copper nuggets weighing two or three hundred pounds have been discovered here.

Night time. The black curtain is drawn once more on the varying performance of the Yukon. Through the eeriness a pin—point of light shines towards the *Klondike*. Someone waves a flashlight. Our master—beam probes the dark waters ahead. A buoy bobs up six feet from shore, a white flag surmounting it. All this means but one thing. A plank is tossed ashore; the Mate prods his way through the dark with a narrow beam; an elderly man appears out of the night after what resembles a conversation of fire—flies as flashlights conglomerate from all directions; both figures climb aboard; the plank is pulled to the deck; a hoot escapes from the whistle; the sternwheel churns. Once more the swift Yukon resists us. The *Klondike* has welcomed another passenger.

Selwyn, a busy place in the early days, is often remembered in connection with Bob Henderson—one of the discoverers of the Klondike. A tale is told of woodcutters having a special rate on the riverboats. Bob, in response to the purser's demand for credentials as proof of his vocation, is reputed to have shown his hob—nail boots. The ruse worked successfully, the boots were loaned to his friends. Result: All got the special cut—rate. Rather less humorous, it was here that another of the river tragedies occurred in the fall of '99 when the *Will H. Irving* and the Steamer *Stratton* both caught in an ice jam and sank.

"Woodpile!....Woodpile!...." The echo passes through the lower deck, the Mate expressing himself in no uncertain terms. The crew roll one by one from their bunks in indignant resignation, pull on their pants, cursing simultaneously all things including the Mate. We make for the upper deck. Minutes later the Purser, garbed in his red shortcoat and black, peaked hat, armed with a metered stick, appears on the foredeck. We pull slowly towards the starboard bank. There is no doubt whatever about this stop. An endless pile of four—foot, pine logs await our visit, to be taken on as inanimate passengers, only to be thrown relentlessly into the firebox from whence they pass up the stack into the air, and finally back into the soil where they had their origin, their purpose served. How futile it all seems! And at this black hour of the morning! But feed our female gourmand we must. So Birch Point—less twenty cords of wood—passes joyously into our wake. The Mate ceases his callous orders. The crew resume their horizontals. Inertia overcomes the lower deck. Silence, but for the persistent pounding pistons, is master of the *Klondike*.

Yukon is an Indian name meaning 'big'. Where the Lewes (the upper Yukon) joins the Pelly from an easterly direction the waters are just this, combining to form a waterway (the Yukon River) that continues some 1750 miles to the Bering Sea. Across from this junction lies the old Hudson's Bay Trading Post—Fort Selkirk, built in 1848. Its history has been a far from peaceful one. Tragedy met the post and trader when in 1852 the Pelly Indians sacked and burned the post, which was never rebuilt. In the eventful year of 1898, 112 militia were sent here over the Teslin Trail to guard gold shipments from Dawson; but later were relieved when the Royal North West Mounted Police were established. The log barracks once housing these men stand in their antiquity, silent tribute to a noble force. The present settlement includes a detachment of R.C.M.P., a Church of England, a Roman Catholic Mission and the Hudson's Bay Company Post, re—established in 1938.

Silently we approached the historic site; as silently we slipped past it into the grey dawn of another day. Next in the gamut of villages comes Selkirk, 178 miles from Dawson. It is important as a trading centre of a very rich, fur country extending to the Pelly, MacMillan and even distant Peel district.

Intense cold and dense forests, which ward off the bleaching rays of the sun, are presumed responsible for the excellent quality of fur found in these areas. Another characteristic of the vicinity is the growing of hay and grain, which has been successful for many years. Horses and cattle have also been raised, then shipped to Dawson and other parts of the country. Noticeable from here looking up the Pelly is the extinct volcano—possible home of the volcanic ash strewn along the banks in so many places. Across the river stand defiantly, the Pelly Ramparts—huge pillars of volcanic rock, the formation of which geologists report is quite recent, resembling other diamond—bearing strata. Relieved of a ton of freight the 'wheeler grunts, puffs clouds of smoke and slaps the Yukon with its wooden hand. The sun tries hard to brighten the day but succeeds only in illuminating the vivid colours along the high—treed bank. Thus we ply our way up, up, up the tireless Yukon in a never—ending land of water, trees and hills...

The word 'hell' has long since been uttered in damnation of things. It is quite reasonable to believe that one skipper, in his continual bout with the next stretch of river we enter, decided to lay forever his curse upon the waters. So we have the name Hellsgate attached to that part of the river where the waters rush, in their eagerness to pass through a narrow gap, and spread out beyond—at one time leaving no navigable channel. This would not do. So dredging has taken (as someone once remarked) "the Hell out of the Gate", consequently resulting in a navigable waterway. As we drew the *Klondike* through this Northern Charybdis the Sirens sang; the waters churned and seethed; the wire cable snapped and the crew cursed. "Grab it quick!" commanded the

Hell's Gate Rapids

Mate, as the slippery cable (frayed where it broke) slid towards the prow. A clatter of feet and shouting voices mingled with the excited imperations of the Mate and the Skipper, who poked his head out of the wheelhouse to guide the disorganized humanity below, filled the still Yukon air. Victorious in the obstacle race, someone wrestled with the snakelike rope tethering it to a nearby stancheon. "Got it!" he yelled. The Mate relaxed under the scrutiny of his boss—the Skipper above. Many "hells"were uttered in the succeeding half hour as the Mate, fumbling with the stubborn cable, fashioned the facsimile of a splice. The crew, all this while staring helplessly at the Mate (still under the watchful eye of the Skipper) suddenly came alive. The splice was finished. The Mate had cursed his last curse at Hellsgate. The winch steamed and groaned. The captain turned. The cable held. The Mate gave orders. The Skipper smiled. The *Klondike* moved forward...we had beaten the Hellsgate Rapids!

High above the river can be seen glimpses of the Overland Trail as it dips and curves in accordance with the irregular topography. This, we are told, is the Skyline Pieces, because of its elevation. So for the first time on our water route we caught sight of the land trail to Whitehorse, one hundred miles shorter in length. But I, not unlike the Argonauts of '98, felt the warm satisfaction of discovery by water as each new bend was rounded. It was the original and only route to Dawson City. It was the Trail of '98!

Morning. It is dull. The scenery is much the same all along the river which narrows then widens into more channels. The clear, open sky—hued with blue and faint brown—tries hard to lift its oppressive burden of overcast clouds, then retires giving up a hopeless struggle. We arrive at Minto, twenty miles from the last post, to find that one of the most sensational murders in Yukon history was committed in the vicinity. The setting was the Yukon; the murderer O'Brien; his victims: Clayson—a Skagway merchant; Olson—a government telegraph lineman; and a third named Rolf. 'Mushing out' over the riverbed *Trail of '98* with their gold, the three were assaulted.

They disappeared. Anxious relatives, not hearing from their kin, informed the police. So Detective Walsh was dispatched to the scene. Following their trail from Minto he discovered where the murders had taken place; also the hole in the ice through which the bodies had disappeared, about a mile and a half upstream. At the spot where O'Brien had made camp the detective found auger shavings which turned out to be conclusive evidence in the final conviction. It appears the Irishman had bored holes in his sleigh runners, inserted the stolen gold–dust amounting to about $6,000.00 and replugged the ends. With the aid of his dog, who proved to be O'Brien's best friend and worst enemy, the murderer was found guilty. O'Brien was executed–but at a cost of $150,000.00 to the government. Here at Minto we unload cargo, take on thirty cords of wood and depart from the scene of one of the North's more barbarous crimes.

Twenty miles. The *Klondike* reaches Yukon Crossing. It was another of the many police posts in the earlier days. Here the winter Overland Trail crosses the Yukon River en route to Dawson City. It is at this point that the ice jams in spring and fall, adding adventure to mail carrying. The mails, which we know 'must get through' are taken across by canoe with one of its occupants thwarting the ice floes with a pole. Entering an archipelago white stripes are visible in the clay of the islands. We are informed it is volcanic ash which, during a phase of the earth, covered this section entirely. It was just past these islands that events began to happen. We ascended Rink Rapids. Famous places are invariably named after famous men. The rapids bear the name of Dr. Henry Rink–an explorer and authority on the North of many years back. These waters prove to be of less hazard than their appearance might suggest. Safely we reach their head. "For men may come and men may go, but I go on forever," seems appropriate as our never–ending course carries

Through the 'Gate' **Calm After Storm**

Pushing Cargo Upstream to Minto **Yukon Crossing–'Skyline Pieces'**
The Overland Trail Meets the Yukon River

us around infinite bends, only to be met by more hills, more spruce and another stretch of river. To the left lie the Glen Lyon mountains; to the right the Dawson Range. But wait!...the river has gained momentum!...it broadens!...rapids are ahead! We have reached the notorious Five Finger Rapids which also took their death toll in earlier days. So these are the wet executioners of so many brave people of 1898.

**Past Rink Rapids
Glen Lyon Mountains to Port**

**'Dawson Range' to Starboard
Harsh Winter Warning**

**Up...Up...Up... the
Mighty Yukon We Ply**

Five Finger Rapids Ahead!

Four foreboding shoulders of rock rear themselves directly in front of the Klondike's path. How can a craft this size possibly squeeze through the five passages of water, which perspective narrows to mere thin channels? The walls are sheer, composite rock like the shoulders. They spell destruction for the unskilled pilot. Most such men, having spent a lifetime on these waters, accept the rapids with no more than their usual caution. I glanced towards the wheelhouse. Such was the mien of our Skipper as he headed the steamship into the turbulent waters.

Into the Middle of the Fingers

Out of the 'Hand' of the Rapids

**Looking Back With Success
at the 'Five Fingers'**

Westward into the Mountains

Already we have scraped bottom for the cable, necessary to pull us through. We approached the port cliff with extra caution. The manoeuver a success, we hang momentarily...the wire cable turns satisfactorily about the corselleted capstan...the Skipper pulls to starboard suddenly...rapids are met with an equal furore. It seems hours, but in reality it is minutes that we buck the waters...fail!...rush our foes again. All hands stand by tensely waiting to assist the capstan with their brute force—a motley group, each with a section of the never—ending cable in his hands; pulling at his own tempo; trying desperately to keep time with the man in front who uncoils yards of wriggling, wet rope with excited abandon. It is a tense moment. Will the cable break? What will the Skipper do if it does? What will I do if I am pitched overboard? I challenge myself, stealing a quick glimpse of the treacherous Yukon swirling between the towering shoulders. Naturally enough, I think of self—preservation. What thoughts traverse the other minds? Are we not all alike? Does not the unwritten law of self come first, though we sweat and struggle as one with this monster from the riverbottom? Are we not so many atavists in disguise, shedding our cloaks of civilized man in a crisis? I half wait for calamity; wait to judge my fellow man; wait to see how true to Nature he lives—how primal he may get; how the forces within will act. Too, I wait to see my own reaction. Will I, as one judging, be judged? Will I too become primeval? But the crisis never came! Human nature remained unjudged. My thoughts remained unfounded. An extra large puff of smoke...an ensuing grunt, exerted from the effort of discharge...swishing of water against the bows...and our Lady slides past the towering shoulders into the less turbulent waters above. Calm follows storm. Silence replaces din.

Glancing back the watery hand is quite plain, its five tentacular fingers reaching out as though vengefully desiring to draw the *Klondike* back through its hazards into its unpredictable womb; hoping this time to crush the wooden vessel in the cold palm of her hand. But we are out of reach. Charybdis has been cheated again!

The Five Fingers was discovered by Fritz Kloke in 1900. But the most memorable name associated with the days of '98 is, undoubtedly, that of George Carmack—the man who staked Discovery No.1 on Bonanza Creek in the Klondike Valley. Bucking the current another mile the *Klondike* arrives and docks at the town which proudly bears his name. A police detachment, post office, Taylor and Drury trading post, a church, an old log Roadhouse and a score of homes greet the sternwheeler and her crew. Here the Overland Trail comes ambling down from the heights to meet the river in the first junction of the land and water routes.

Hardly had the plank been thrown ashore to admit the Purser to the settlement than we were ordered to 'pull it to' again. A short conversation and a handful of mail was the total exchange. All the while the sternwheeler, panting gently like a hot Saint Bernard thankful for a moment's rest, lay motionless against the bank. A parting blast from the whistle, a solitary figure waving in the distance and the historic settlement passed out of view around a bend. Little is heard of coal mining back−of−the−beyond. Abondoned, a Short distance below Carmacks, lies the Yukon's original coal mine. As the sternwheeler puts another mile behind we sight an old bunker and dock on the starboard shore. Dejected and decrepit in their idleness, they tell of the once active

Carmacks−Yukon Territory

Tantallus Mine, abandoned because of water seepage, since the coal vein ran below the water level. Another mile...a high cliff to the left...a scaffolding and chutes leading to a black hole in the face of a hill. It is the Tantallus Bute Mine. At one time ferns were prolific in this area, their fossils still quite apparent. As a result of the burial of this extensive growth during the world's climacteric, a large amount of good quality coal is mined. Dawson, the chief market, utilizes a large quantity of it for power and heating when the extreme winter shuts it off from the Outside world.

Lone Woodcutters Cabin
Stacked Winter Wood Piles

Above Carmacks
"Wood Up!...Wood Up!"

Stops along the river grow infrequent−only to 'wood−up' with four−foot lengths of pine (chopped by lone woodcutters at isolated spots) or to unload a few articles of freight; or perhaps take on a passenger or cargo bound for Whitehorse. The scenery changes continuously as we ply the river in a sou'−easterly direction; now and then the verdure giving way to close−cropped, grassy hills and groves of spruce trees that come down from the hilltops to the water's edge comingling with the birth of poplar in their fall fashion show of colour.
On past Little Salmon−one of the more prominent Indian settlements in the Yukon. Situated here was a white trading post and a church bringing religion to the natives. Tragedy overtook the village in 1917 when the flu' epidemic all but wiped it out. The resultant graveyard seen from the boat is ample evidence of its merciless destruction.

'Wood up!....Wood up!' came the obnoxious herald of Work. Scenery was forgotten. Ponderous logs were mauled, torn from their neat resting place along the bank and thrown onto the two—wheeled carts that carried them to the nadir realm of the boat. "Look out!...coming down!" shouted each deckhand, rushing down the incline of the lower deck only to stop abruptly (as the Cheechako ducked sideways out of the path of the flying timbers) and discharged his load at the front of the irregular pile, stacking them in haphazard fashion. The Cheechako, adjusting them and stacking the drifters, made haste in the short interval between handcarts. Sweat poured freely; logs bounced wildly; Breeds cursed openly; but the endless monotony continued.

**Little Salmon River to Gold Point
"Wood Pile!...Wood Pile!"**

An observer would doubtless wonder where all the wood was going. But we knew. It was not completely handled yet—not by far! Reloaded and wheeled to the stoker, who in turn would throw them into the maw of the red—hot boiler, they would still claim many hours of our time. The one pleasant thought, however, with a considerably large crew, the shifts were staggered. But the early morning calls were never pleasant. 'What a gourmand,' I thought often as I witnessed the result of our laborious efforts, wheeled endlessly into the bowels of the steamer which every few minutes managed to excrete another empty handcart to be loaded. About the time I was becoming disgusted with the obvious theory of supply and demand which was a sore reality, the Mate yelled from the deck: "That's enough!...let's get moving!"

In all, thirty cords of wood were separated from their family ties. I began to loathe wood. What pleasure it would be to see it standing vertical along the banks once the boat found motion! Trees!..."*I think that I shall never see...*" It was no use thinking; my vocation was as cut and dried as the very logs. How I hoped it was to be the last 'wood up' of the voyage. So settling in a deck chair I flipped the pages of Service's Works.

Twisting and turning the river brings us to Gold Point—a bar in the river presumably containing much wealth. There it lies, awaiting the pluck of some sporting miner, game enough to probe its secret treasures. On...on past Big Salmon to Hootalinqua, at the confluence of the Thirty Mile and Teslin Rivers , once a very important settlement. It was the meeting place of the gold rushers who entered the Yukon by the All Canadian route via the Stikine, Lake Teslin, Teslin River and those who safely scaled the passes at Skagway to continue by way of lakes Bennett and Le Barge. The cabin of Dan Snure, still standing, is remembered by many a Sourdough as the Mecca from which he departed to tackle the one remaining obstacle to the Klondike—the River Yukon.

Passing between the overhanging hills that appear mountainous, a wreck comes into view. It is the old *Klondike*, sunk in 1936; since drifted eight miles downstream. The numerous bends, rocks and bars in the Thirty Mile River once accounted for many a craft and scow manned by Cheechakos, and even experienced water—men. One of the more famous of these is the U.S. Bend, once run by a captain in an emergency without even slowing down—a feat never before accomplished on this section of the river. Narrow and tortuous, the Thirty Mile River soon swallows our steamer. Skipper and Pilot come into their own in a keen struggle to thwart the rapid current. Swiftwater steamboating is gradually becoming a lost art. But as fine an exhibition can be seen on this stretch of water as anywhere else that Sternwheelers are still in existence. Because of the numerous bends and consistant speed of the water, a process of 'jacknifing' the barge ahead of the steamer is undertaken — the First Mate, Pilot and crew working in complete harmony at the approach of each treacherous bend. Manoeuvering such, we enter the Horns—one called the Cape because of the relative difficulties it offers to riverboats. Its precipitous, grey cliffs are foreboding under the gleam of the pilot light which, with insistent probing, reveals the treacherous bends, each in time and in turn. A lone cabin and woodpile fall into focus; are lost in the blackness of the Yukon night. "Thank God!" I sigh, as the latter disappears.

Morning found us sliding from the clear, deep−green Thirty Mile into the still deeper, aquamarine Lower LeBarge. Here was the terminus of the trip for those hauling freight in the early days. In springtime the lake bustled with freighting activity and it was stipulated that those handling the lake work receive their round trip pay amounting to a good two hundred dollars or more at this point. Being a frontier it was not infrequent that the Spirit of Chance invaded the scene; thus many a man cast his lot with the Lady and lost his entire stake, at the turn of a card, to a rival freighter. Once highly populated, a couple of shacks are all that remain of the settlement. With no apparent division the next few miles found us coursing the smooth waters of Upper LeBarge, about 30 miles long and 5 miles wide. The lake is claimed by an Indian named Jim Boss. Legend holds that, during the Rush, some stampeders accidentally went through the ice! As a result this cunning Indian charged them fifty cents a head for bathing in his waters. Such was the 'exchange' exemplifying that strange Indian cunning.

As the Klondike shatters the mirror into a million pieces of spray, behold the wonderful vista from the deck. On every side are mountains, their crowns covered with a layer of frost that has descended in the night; those to port especially display their sheer faces rouged with the stain of various water−levels left since the Glacial Age when LeBarge was one of the main drains for the Great Ice Cap situated in the vicinity of Atlin farther to the south. The lake abounds in ducks and geese which come and go in an endless procession of V's. Far off to the left can be seen Mount Laurier, soaring 5,263 feet into the Yukon skies. Undelayed, we pass into the marshlands studded with poles that one time served as a breakwater. We are on the "Marge of Lake LeBarge!" But a quick survey reveals no 'derelict' which Service speaks of in his *Cremation of Sam McGee.*

> "Till I came to the marge of Lake LeBarge, and a derelict there lay;
> It was jammed in the ice, but I saw at a trice it was called the "Alice May"
> And I looked at it; and I thought a bit, and I looked at my frozen chum;
> Then "Here," said I with a sudden cry, " is my cre−ma−tor−eum."

Behind practically every tale told in the North is a truth (though mostly very remote). The truth, as close as one can gather, behind this muse goes something like this: In the fall of '98 the *Olive May*−a steamboat bound from Dawson to Whitehorse became frozen in, after getting stuck at the head of the lake. Word came to the police at Tagish, then the main post, of a man at the lakehead sick with scurvy. A Dr. Snugden was dispatched to his aid. Upon arrival the medico found misfortune had cheated him of a patient. With the ground frozen and no tools with which to dig his grave, the ingenious doctor cremated the body in the firebox of the *Olive May*, returning to headquarters with the ashes as evidence. Robert Service and Snugden lived together in Whitehorse during the poet's stay there with the Bank of Commerce.

Service, with his license and imagination, chose the boiler of this boat as the ideal spot to fulfill the deathbed wish of the character Sam McGee, who had said: "...so I want you to swear that, foul or fair, you'll cremate my last remains." So, because McGee, a Sourdough of Whitehorse, rhymed nicely with Tennessee, he was chosen to be cremated in words. The 'derelict' has since disappeared. We pass on to the Lewes River.

With the '98ers once again in imagination, we push against the current towards Whitehorse. Rounding a series of long bends the *Klondike* with full steam up, churns its way between the gravel banks. A signal sounded from the wheelhouse usually demands a response−be it an order, a polite signal to the passengers to note a historic spot, or the appearance of a wild animal that dares lope down to the shore to view with curiosity the strange floating monster on the river. So it is that we are called to the upper deck. There to port we see some remains. "What remains?" asks someone and the inevitable answer comes from one of the crew, who, having served much time on the river might easily swap his job for that of a guide.

"It's the deserted Royal Canadian Mounted Police post. At the time of the Gold Rush it was necessary for each craft to obtain a 'clearance' from the police," he explained in detail. "This paper was shown at each such post along the way. In this manner a record of all persons entering the countryside was recorded. Should mishap befall a single individual, search parties would be organized and sent in quest of the missing party." As though a walking guide−book, he finished his expostulation precisely with: "To this system is credited a high quality of law and order which prevailed in this country and not in other pioneer countries."

**Past "the Marge of Lake LeBarge"
We Arrive At Whitehorse**

**Whitehorse
Capital Yukon Territories**

More bends…suddenly buildings. Whitehorse at last! We have reached the end of the line, four days and 460 miles away from Dawson City. As the wide channel leading to the town receives us the landmarks of Whitehorse begin to rear their heads. With a confident *Whooooooooo* − the vanguard of sound from the ship's stack, skipper Bromley guides the *Klondike* past the derelict sternwheelers, *Yukoner & Bonanza King*, grounded for life on the skids of the White Pass and Yukon graveyard; with a gentle *thud!* brings the steamer to a stop against the bank. Sid and Ed, our reliable First and Second Mates, give their final orders to the crew. With a sudden scurry we lay down the gangplank; make fast the shore cables. Then comes that period of inaction that follows action. The last order is carried out. It is journey's end.

CHAPTER THIRTY NINE

THE HOME OF SAM McGEE

Debarking, I felt as if I was leaving an old friend. 'But,' I reflected, 'no more woodwatch!'... No more would I hear those awful words in the middle of the night—Woodpile!....Woodpile! I would be a landlubber again, as soon as that feeling of motion departed. Yes, it would be good to be on solid terra firma once more. With these thoughts I slipped down the gangplank to shore. The Cheechako disappeared along the main street.

'Overland Mail' to Dawson in Winter

**Original Sourdough Home
Front Street**

Whitehorse is the commercial metropolis of the Yukon. It is reached by land over the famous Alaska Highway; by air, rail, and the waterway used exclusively by the '98ers who paused here after their strenuous bout with the waters above. During the war it was the terminus of the Canol Project carrying oil from Norman Wells in the Northwest Territories. Here also is the headquarters of the R.C.M.P. for Southern Yukon, of which Inspector Howard Cronkite is the commanding officer. In the past years the Overland Mail, amounting to about 40,000 pounds of first class mail, left here for Dawson in the winter by horse—drawn sled. The contract was fulfilled by the White Pass and Yukon Route; one of the well—used sleds stands today in First Avenue, reminding us as we pass, of winter freighting—not the most pleasant of jobs when the mercury runs low in the Yukon.

**Where 'Buzzsaw' Jimmy Richards
and
Bill Chantler Reminisce**

Accosting a gentleman, a conversation follows; viewpoints merge; and I am informed that here also is an outfitting centre for big—game hunting. Proceeding along First Avenue, often referred to as Front Street, we see some of the old landmarks. The first is a quaint, two—storey, log cabin with a rugged porch—an original Sourdough home; another—the Regina Hotel running close on the heels of the former for vintage—the rendezvous where oldtimers like 'Buzzsaw' Jimmy Richards and Billy Chantler gather on evenings to reminisce and spin some new yarns.

One is not overly impressed by the exterior of the town; but towns like people are sometimes deceiving; a further perusal is necessary to determine their real character. Traditions, legends and aged structures are what really give character to any city, town or village (besides, of course, its people). Whitehorse, like any town made famous by the *Gold Rush of '98,* has its share of these requisites. Heading west from the White Pass and Yukon Railway Station along Main Street we see the White Pass Hotel, Taylor and Drury's Department Store and The Inn—an old landmark as well as the popular hotel. As I tramped listlessly along, the words of Service's incomparable *Cremation of Sam McGee* ran back and forth in my mind....

"There are strange things done in the midnight sun
By the men who moil for gold;
The Arctic trails have their secret tales
That would make your blood run cold;
The Northern Lights have seen queer sights,
But the queerest they ever did see
Was the night on the marge of Lake LeBarge
I cremated Sam McGee"
Suddenly the thought came to me: 'I will rout out the home of the man Sam.'

**Mainstreet, Whitehorse
Yukon Territory**

Sam McGee's cabin lies on Third Avenue and Elliot Street. It is a small log structure with a gabled roof; a central door and one window comprise the front. Above the door is a horseshoe, which, if associated with good luck, we can say was lacking in the bard's famous character. It later came to pass that "Sam McGee arrived in Dawson some years after the so—called "Cremation" and, stepping to the dock very much alive, shocked some of the townsfolk who were religious readers of Service. They thought sure that he was a ghost." The Oldtimer telling me the incident continued to say that McGee was asked if he was going to let the bard get away with this, to which the "Cremated" retorted: "If Service wants to make a little money on my name, that's his business!" It isn't hard to believe that the poet Service, in search of a word to rhyme with 'Tennessee', chose the solid, Scots monicker of McGee.

Crossing the road to the opposite corner, another log structure excites the inquisitive observer. It is the old Log Church of which Rev. Canon L.G. Chappell is the rector. This church, erected in 1900, cherishes among its clergy the names Bishops Bompas and Stringer,

**Sam McGee's Cabin
Third Avenue and Elliot Street**

**Christ Church
Robert W. Service was Clergy and Secretary**

Rev. H.A. Cody, Dr. C.E. Whitaker and Robert W. Service. In the study of this church the poet penned his *Songs of a Sourdough*. Here also the minutes of the meetings can be observed in the poet's own handwriting when he was Clerk of the Vestry during his banking days in Whitehorse. Proudly it is that the town boasts the environment where he composed his first poems, including *The Shooting of Dan McGrew* and *The Cremation of Sam McGee*, which the poet later said was: "the keystone of my success" —bringing fame to the 'wage—slave' teller of the Bank of Commerce.

Whitehorse, like many other northern towns, has adopted an Indian name. It is derived from the rapids above the town, which, bubbling and churning, resemble the trailing manes of many white horses as they stampede over the rocks beneath. One ancient legend holds that an Indian woman drowned in the Squaw Rapids and her husband, Whitehorse, overburdened with despair and grief, drowned himself in the larger rapids below which now bear his name.

Quaint are the Indian graves on a slope above the town. Here one sees the plots covered with canvasses, tarpaulins, pup tents and frame houses. Within these windowed huts can be seen eating utensils: a battered, blackened teapot, a mug, hatchet, hunting knife or just the usual wilted bouquet of flowers laid in memory. In one, the clothes of the deceased were folded in a neat pile over the grave. I later discovered the Indian superstition behind it all.

Indian Graves
Assure Life in the 'Happy Hunting Grounds'

Apparently the house keeps out evil spirits; while the utensils are placed within for the continued use of the dead in order that they may continue to hunt in the Happy Hunting Ground. Such is the romantic native interpretation of the Hereafter. Unique among the graves is the marble monument of a dog above the grave of John Sidney, who, as near as can be guessed, belonged to the Dog Tribe. True to Indian nomenclature is the adjacent grave, immaculately latticed, on the head of which is printed Big Salmon Pat.

My fifty—five cents would not last very long in a town where meals were $1.00 minimum. So it was that I secured a labour job and a billet, continuing my prowl about the town intermittently during the short week's stay.

In routing out the '98ers one is quite likely to meet Messrs. Taylor and Drury, partners of Whitehorse's largest general merchandise store on Front Street. On an evening with nothing special to do I clicked my way along the boardwalk to the home of Mr. Taylor. Welcomed, I took a seat. As I leaned over the table surrounded by his wife and daughter, a most unusual tale began to unfold itself from the memory of 83—year—old Isaac Taylor. "I left England for Australia in 1891 because of ill health," he commenced his narrative. "I'm a Yorkshireman...they said I would never get past the Red

To the Memory of Indian John Sidney

Sea...but I fooled them. I've been through it several times since then!" While he was mining in Australia in '97, the cry of Gold in the Klondike was heard. '98 saw him well into the interior of Canada, following the old Caribou Trail via Ashcroft. Here he became equipped; carrying on to Cache Creek where he became as quickly unequipped when his horses stampeded. Chuckling in retrospect, he says: "It took me a week to round up my gear!"

It was along this trail that he met his present partner in business, Mr. Drury, also an Englishman who had homesteaded in Ontario. They huddled about the campfire while the pack horses grazed. Taylor eventually reached Skagway where he joined the construction gang of the White Pass Railway which was pushing its way through the mountains. "The foreman said to me (he went on): "Come to the camp and we'll give you a velvet handled shovel after you get some wrinkles out of your belly," to which Taylor, still chuckling, added: "A good way to winter; good quarters and good grub."

Next spring while travelling to a new gold strike from Discovery, near Atlin, he again met his future partner who had wintered at Telegraph Creek. Here they decided to link as Taylor and Drury—General Merchants, opening the original store at Discovery, B.C. which has since branched eightfold.

As the clock strikes one, Mr. Taylor says: "We've been forty—eight years together...a record in partnership, I imagine?" Asked if they have ever quarreled, he retorts: "Drury, the other fellow, is too big for me to fight," at which all burst into volumes of laughter realizing Taylor's size. I discovered that his wife entered the country via the "railroad to the door", as she calls the White Pass R.R., in 1903. She has travelled much with her three sons and daughter in the company's interests on their boats *Kluane*, *Thistle* and *Yukon Roads*. We exchange farewells. "But before you go you must have my recipe for Sourdough Hotcakes; I've used it for years." Accepting the good woman's assurances for successful results and her special recipe as a criteria, I feel I must give the reader an opportunity to experiment with a standard Northern delicacy. The recipe follows thus:

Sourdough Pancakes

Mix thin batter of flour and water.

Add a little rice and macaroni water and a pinch of sugar.

Put in a pail and hang over stove for four hours.

This is the start of the 'leavening'.

"You won't have to worry about it multiplying; then the rest is up to you!" she joked as I made to go. The door closed on a wonderful Oldtimer and his family.

Whitehorse is a nautical town. It is the home of several sternwheelers that ply regularly the waters to Dawson City, 460 miles downstream. With a little imagination one visualizes a port on the Mississippi; the Yukon the Canadian equivalent of that famous southern river. Along the waterfront towards the north end of town is a graveyard. It is a rather unusual burial ground, in that it is reserved for sternwheelers unable to meet the demands of the unpredictable Yukon River. Weather—beaten and deteriorating on the skids in the White Pass Shipyards, where they have become silent sentinels of time, rest the *Yukoner* and *Bonanza King*—two of the original steamboats on the Yukon—silently envying their sisters and brothers beside the docks accepting cargo for a voyage down the Yukon. But alas, they have had their day—each with an interesting, though rather short history.

S.S. Yukoner
Built in 1898, Victoria, B.C.

S.S. Bonanza King
From U.S.A.

The *Yukoner* was built in Victoria in 1898 by the Canadian Pacific Navigation Company and sold to one Pat Calvin at St. Michael for $45,000.00. Departing for Dawson she became fouled by ice, was forced to winter at Russian Mission on the Lower Yukon, finally reaching Dawson June 24, 1899. The trip was not without event, for during the voyage the crew mutinied and deposed the Captain. A court case was held in Dawson and bankruptcy for the Company followed. The *Yukoner* became the property of the British Yukon Navigation Co.; spending her years in public service on the river till her final voyage, in 1903, to the skids in Whitehorse where she now occupies the berth of a lady. Alas, her draft proved too deep for the waters of the Upper Yukon.

Bonanza King, its sternwheel nothing more than an inactive hub with spokes, shares the fate of the *Yukoner*; a cold grave on the waterfront. However, its history is a little less ignominious. Built at Dutch Harbour, Aleutians, in '98 she was a sister ship of the *Eldorado*; both ran the waters of the Upper Yukon as the Flyer Line. Serving for several years the *Bonanza King* was retired for a more modern vessel. Among the more active vessels docking at Whitehorse are the *Klondike*—the river's largest freighter—built to carry concentrates from the Mayo silver—lead mines; the *Whitehorse* and the *Casca*—flagship of the British Yukon Navigation Co. Also wheeling her way through the swift river is the *Nasu Flin*. At present the *Aksala* is undergoing repairs in the shipyard.

**S.S. Nasu Flin
and S.S. Aksala**

Having viewed the dead and the living sternwheelers, we ask: "Which of these romantic craft was first to see the shores of Whitehorse and rub her side gently against its banks?" The answer is supplied by an Oldtimer, W.D. MacBride, an authority on Whitehorse and the surrounding country.

He says in his ever—modest manner, "The *Canadian* was the first steamer to make the trip up river from St. Michael to Whitehorse, a distance of 2,061 miles."

Already it was Thursday. The *Whitehorse* has arrived with the sad tale of the loss of its pilot while stopped at Stewart. It was thought he might have tripped on a stancheon and plunged into the river, which the saying goes: "Does not give up its victims!" But the best news of all was that my friend—Ed Freeze had managed to work passage up—river and was eager for the continuation of our trip through the mountains. So the night was filled with the chatter of grubstakes and the Chilkoot Pass. It was a most memorable night.

About five miles upstream from Whitehorse along the old water route of '98 we come to a huge canyon of precipitous heights. A swirling current rushes between its rock walls. This is Miles Canyon, named after General Miles—an early explorer of this country. We are back in the days of '98 once more...*rushing through with the current on our makeshift raft. Will we make it? Wonder how many drowned before us? As we shoot safely out of the turbulent abyss, we sigh and think of the hundreds less fortunate than us.* Through this very gap came the bulk of the tide of humanity bound for Dawson City. There was no other way. It is with this thought that we silently admire the courage and fortitude of those

**S.S. Whitehorse
Docked at Dawson**

Miles Canyon
Jack London—
Showed his Seamanship Here.

men, women and children who won over these seething waters, waiting for human victims who floundered in her current or navigated themselves into her jagged walls.

Crossing the suspension bridge we come to a narrow path winding up and down the face of the hillside. This is the remnant of the MacAuley Tram. Consisting of wooden rails and carts, it served to transport those who feared the treacherous canyon and rapids farther on. With the rising death toll something had to be done. So this ingenious fellow built his wooden tramway, exacting a livelihood by transporting people and their outfits to the old site of Whitehorse on the east side of the river. It was here that the notorious Bill Gates received his nickname. Arriving at the dangerous point above the rapids on a scow, he developed an extreme case of 'buck fever'! With a sudden exclamation he is reported to have said emphatically: "I'm going to walk!" And walk he did. But from that day on he was known as 'Swiftwater Willie'.

S.S. Casca
Last of the Ladies

Whitehorse Rapids
Next Argonaut Challenge

Back over the bridge we travel along another thinly−defined trail, downstream. Scattered remains are visible amongst the trees: here a rooted rail; there a battered, wooden cart. This tramway running to the foot of the rapids was known as the Hepburn Tram. In imagination..*we wheel on the narrow gauge, loaded down with our outfits; the sound of the pounding rapids just over the cliff remind us of our safety. Halfway between the Canyon and the town we gaze at the famous Whitehorse Rapids*, which were responsible for so many gravestones in the cemetary at the old site. It isn't any wonder! There, in a hundred−foot−wide channel, splash the multitude of white horses, kicking, frothing, sending huge whitecaps of spray into the air. As we stand looking on, *barges and scows tip, frenzied cries rise above the din of the pounding surf. But alas! we can do little. They belong to the Yukon now! The next raft flounders, hangs momentarily on a whitecap, slides into even waters. Its excited crew raise a cry of joy in unison. Success is theirs. They have made it!* Dawson and Gold await. We must awa'. Turning to go, an excited whoop greets our ears. We spy a thin canoe loaded with three−two paddling, the middle one waving his stetson−shooting from the bowels of the white froth. Our luck is their luck. We pass on to Whitehorse through the park dedicated to Robert W. Service.

Whoever passes through Whitehorse must certainly visit the office of Dan MacBride. For therein lies the key to the town. With a short, unlit cigar tucked between his lips and a stained fedora cocked on his head, the Special Representative of the White Pass and Yukon Railway tells us a brief history of Whitehorse; explains the adventures that lay behind the taxidermy in his office; and thumbs his way through a hundred antiquated pictures of the *Trail of '98*. Among the latter are such photos as Dawson's favourites: Cad Wilson and Al Rose; the largest raft ever to be brought through Miles Canyon; three canoemen shooting the Whitehorse Rapids. But our mission was twofold. We desired a map of the Chilkoot Pass; plus sufficient advice as to its dangers, from the Sourdough who has covered every old trail in this part of the Yukon. We had come to the right man!

Back at our billet we surveyed the map; read the adjoining advice; and set about packing the most articles into the least space. Grub, fish, rifle and sleeping bag... all was in readiness for the morrow. Two happier men could not have been found in the Yukon as they talked themselves into the Chilkoot Pass and sleep....

Farewell 'Workgang'
Allen and Freeze 5 and 6 from Left

Gateway to the Yukon

Morning found the sun and the two Cheechakos up at an early hour. The train for Bennett was due at nine. Two hours and we would be on the *Trail of '98* again. Breakfast at a local cafe brought the zero hour nearer. Checking our excess baggage through to Skagway we waited with the curbed anxiety of greyhounds at the starting post. The season was waning. The last tourists scurried here and there, checking timetables, baggage, etc. in order to connect with the boat in Skagway. Whenever a train comes or goes Dan MacBride is on hand to direct tourists and spread his goodwill. With cigar in mouth, as impatient as we, he greeted us and soon all became lost in Northern conversation. It was with a start that we responded to the call: "'Board! 'Board for Bennett!" The time had come. Climbing into the coach with packsacks and sleeping bags we must have done something to Dan, for he said: "I'd give anything to go with you!" in a voice that envied our youth and our freedom. "We'd be tickled to have you with us," was the reply that never reached his ears; for at that moment the bell rang and the engine, grunting vociferously, pawed the tracks towards Bennett. As we slid into the distance I shall never forget the lone figure of Dan MacBride standing on the Whitehorse platform waving one arm. 'You will be with us in spirit if not in body,' I said to myself...and the tracks pointed back to infinity.

Stops are few and short—some merely names that flash by, lurking only in memory: Wigan...Cowley...Robinson...DeWette and then Lewis when a huge cavity yawns below the tracks. Bill Bettinger, conductor on the small train, pipes up: "That's where they tried to shorten the distance between Lewis Station and DeWette by lowering the lake about ten feet. No visible outlet or inlet could be found so they dug a ditch about five feet wide. It didn't last though... the waters widened it to 700 feet and the lake fell about eighty feet and dried up. Sure fooled them!" Minto... Lorne... Lansdowne—more painted sign posts that come and go till finally we pull up to stop at Carcross.

The original name for this settlement was Caribou Crossing—called so because of the great herds of caribou that used to cross this natural ford between Lake Bennett and Nares. It lies 67 miles from Skagway on the north extremity of Lake Bennett. Glancing from the train one sees the *Tutshi*, the immaculate riverboat that plies Lake Nares and Tagish; eventually reaching the southern tip of West Taku Arm at Ben—My—Chree—Manx for *Girl of My Heart* — the Northern Utopia settled and cultivated by Otto Partridge for his beloved wife. During our ten minute stop we see the *Gleaner*—another veteran steamer, and one of the original railway engines reminiscent of early days.

Small Gauge Railroad to Lake Bennett　　　**Beautiful But Turbulent Lake Bennett, B.C.**

S.S. *Tuschi* on Lake LeBarge　　　**Obsolete *S.S. Gleaner*
and Original Railway Engine**

**Where Caribou
Once Crossed**

"'Board!" Our perusal is interrupted. We pass over the Crossing. Along one of the most beautiful strips of lakes and mountains in the North we course to Watson...Pennington, striking the edge of the lake all the way...and at twelve p.m. with a screech of brakes the train stops at Bennett—the end of the line 40.6 miles from Skagway. Here 10,000 people once lived when the town was the scene of boat building in the spring of '98, as the Argonauts made ready for the water route to the Klondike. "You can get yourself a good dinner in the station," says our congenial conductor, "and I think you'll need it too, where you're going!"

Where Faith on the Trail was Instilled

**Goodbye Bennett
Hello Chilkoot!**

So the next hour found us literally gorging our last fresh meal for what we decided would be a week. Paying the long—since established $1.00 for our *table—d'—hote* we thanked the Scots cook; bade goodbye to the conductor; then shouldered our packs. But wait! What is that building on the hill overlooking the lake?

Curiosity is a wonderful thing; in this instance it brought closer the year 1898. Built out of crude logs, its steeple surmounted with a ringed cross pointing into the clear blue British Columbia skies, stands the Presbyterian Church, a silent reminder that where men go they carry Faith with them. A wooden plaque above the door tells the whole history. It reads:

THIS CHURCH WAS BUILT IN 1899 UNDER THE AUSPICES OF THE PRESBYTERIAN CHURCH OF CANADA. DR. JAS. ROBERTSON WAS THEN SUPERINTENDENT OF MISSIONS AND REV. J.A. SINCLAIR WAS THE MINISTER IN CHARGE. AT THAT TIME THOUSANDS OF MEN ENCAMPED HERE, BUILDING BOATS FOR THE JOURNEY TO THE KLONDIKE.

**Looking from L. Bennett to L. Linderman
to the Chilkoot**

Cleaver's 'Casey' Crew—End Of The Line

It was a worthwhile pause, for waiting to go to work was Jean Cleaver with his railway repair crew. "We'll take you up the track to Milepost 35. It'll save you a few miles anyway!" he shouted. So we mounted the 'Casey'; and as its *chug...chug..* grew louder the buildings of Bennett, nestled along the east shore of the lake, grew faint...and disappeared amongst the mountains.

With directions firmly imprinted on the mind we shook hands with the last humans we were to see for a while. How long? Neither knew. I recall vividly the faint *chug...chug* as the smoky 'jigger' continued up the White Pass and turning to my pal said: "Well, let's go!" Anxiously he retorted: "I'm ready." We soon became a part of the scenery flooded with bright sunshine, covered with a dense growth and surrounded by an amphitheatre of snow−capped mountains. We were headed for the Chilkoot Pass on the *Trail of '98* with the same abandon as the fleecy clouds that drifted above on this 26th day of September.

The Chilkoot Pass -

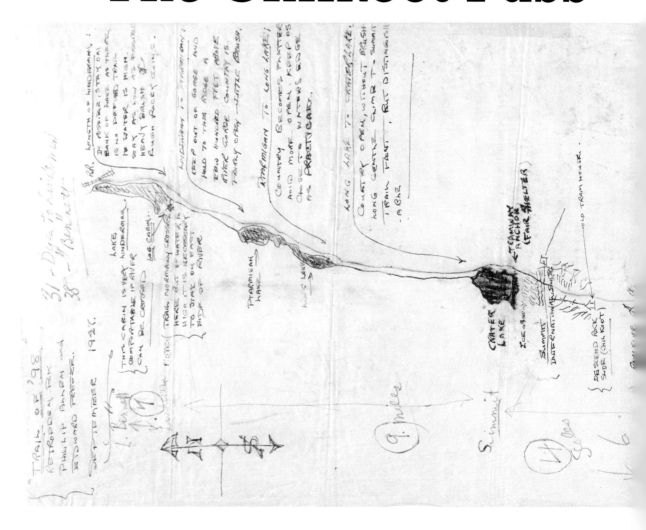

Trail of '98

CHAPTER FORTY

WE CHALLENGE THE CHILKOOT PASS

We stumbled on for what seemed an eon... cursing, damning, condemning the rocks that led to cul−de−sacs when their summit was gained, the gnarled undergrowth that spent its time like a serpent in a crooked growth waiting to trap and choke its every prey. Our only compensation was the beauty of Lake Linderman, mirroring the local mountains in all their rising splendor, which at best was seen only when we raised our heads or paused for inspection. Oh yes! I might add the sobering fact that in 1898 others had suffered the same discouraging trails and kept on. This added determination to our plight. With each step I began to think more of that race of people I had left behind

Terrain Between Lakes Bennett and Linderman

across the entire North. Yes, they earned every ounce of gold they ever panned in the creeks! I found myself biting a lip as I fell with fifty−five pounds strapped to a back that ached with every unsure step. My pal, Ed, floundering behind, seemed at the end of his tether. 'This cannot go on indefinitely!' I thought; and in the year of our ease−1947. It was 7:30 p.m. when the two beaten Cheechakos dropped their packs and themselves to the mossy bank just above the shores of Linderman, reflecting the last vestiges of light across its sheen face. The day was done for them.

Nine o'clock changed the outlook; brought forth humorous retrospection of the day; reflected the dancing flames of a pine fire on to the ebonite Linderman. The smell of woodsmoke mixed with pine and the sight of a rising moon is enough for any man of the woods to lapse into ecstatics over Nature. So it was that the world had us just where we wanted it! Aches of the day gave way to the pleasantries of the night. A snap of dome fasteners in the wooded silence found us deep in our sleeping bags. The faint breeze that arose through the pines, comingled with intermittent snaps from the dying embers, augmented with the faint splash of water on the rocks, sang a lullaby of the woods that would send even the most insensitive man into that ethereal realm of sleep. We were sensitive men.

The smell of bacon permeated the still morning air, accompanied by the occasional ring of frying pan on stone. "What time is it? What's for breakfast?" inquired the second party, rolling over and squinting into the brightness of morning. "Time you met the day and ate some of this chow," was the satisfactory answer, for it brought Ed out where he too could appreciate the beauty of morning on Lake Linderman. Slowly removing her nightgown of fog over snow− white shoulders, Dawn left the lake denuded at our feet. She was a pretty sight, and had we a canoe, her motionless body would have been seduced by our very prow. Oh, how we longed for a canoe!

Looking South Over Lake Linderman

Breakfast is over. Camp broken. Agonizing packs slide into yesterday's sores, giving rise to forgotten aches. We hop along the rocky shore leaving the hillsides to the trees. Sunshine slants over the crest of the eastern mountains sparkling in the bubbles of water left isolated on the rocks, giving life to a thousand prisms. Had the '98ers noticed these silent beauties of Linderman? Or did their every glance perceive Gold? I ponder, retracing their footsteps toward the Chilkoot Pass. "They say that Linderman really gets rough when it takes the notion. Accounted for many a barge capsizing in the early days." "Can't imagine that," says my friend trudging behind, taking in the vista of clear water stretching to the base of the pine−studded mountains. It <u>was</u> hard to imagine Linderman anything but gentle.

James Fortin
Never Made It!

Elias Mountains to the West

Rocks...Snow...and Fog

Saturated with this array of beauty we continued to hop, skip and jump along the rock shore. Then a creek, coming from far up the valley, broke the winding shore line. Cross it we must! So cross it we did! Wading through the knee−deep, icy waters we became temporarily confused. Which was the ascent to the Pass? Were we lost? Which ravine to follow? We would look for debris along the Trail...that would solve the enigma! We were not long in finding ancient signs of life. Among the visible signs of great activity at one time were three cabins. Nearby was a graveyard; the last resting place of a few prospectors who, unable to compete in the struggle for existence, were interred amidst the august setting of Lake Linderman. A metal disc on the cross of one of the crudely constructed rock and log graves bore proudly the name of J. Fortin, dating back fifty years. Yes, the living still remember; the dead are still remembered!

Four−hundred yards beyond the stream we arrive at a deserted cabin. Cabins are so rare a thing in the wild bush that one has to have an iron will to resist their temptation. We are in no particular hurry. (So we give resistance a wide berth.) The inside betrays what the outside camouflages. Many have been this way−some only recently−each leaving a personal message behind. One of the most picturesque slogans decorating the wall is the following, which I feel deserves a hallowed place amongst backroom scrolls.

1930 BANQUET
Linderman Lodge

MENU
Gopher Gizzard Stew
Boiled Gum Boots
Wool Sock Stew
Beans
Gopher Liver on Toast
More Beans
More Beans
Sardine Sundae
G.E. Gallant — Toastmaster
Committee:
Fred Blanchard   Ken Blanchard
Warren Fenn   Jack Conway

No Doubts of the *Trail of '98*

Another cabin farther along the shores of Lake Linderman gives rise to more doubts about the correct trail to follow. On a consummation of suppositions we choose the creek just crossed as possibly leading to the heights. The decision confirmed all round, we turn our backs on the six miles of lake and begin the nine—mile climb to the Chilkoot Pass, the bodies fifty years behind the spirits.

Tackling mountain—sides once again, we keep to the right, ascending higher...higher above the valley. Five—hundred feet above the cavernous, rocky waterway we pause. A well—worn trail is quite plain on the opposite cliff. Is this the *Trail of '98?* Will

Rising to Lake Ptarmigan

our own lead to a dead end? "Let's forget the trail and have some grub," says my companion, (his mind dwelt more on food the next week than on the famous path of the Argonauts). "Very well," say I, pulling a can of beans from the pack—sack. "You'll have them cold like a Sourdough and like 'em!" We don't really mind as long as it is food. So, followed by a round of cookies (and water to wash them down), we continue our inspection of the locale. It is the unexpected appearance of a rusted sled—runner that renews our interest and dispells any doubts whatever of the Trail. Our luck is followed by a succession of discoveries: a horsehoe, Yukon sled, cooking utensils, whiskey bottles, coffee urn, a skull, an iron runner, rotting harness and a galaxy of frying pans. The latter leads one to believe that at this point the prospectors had given up their traditional bacon and bean diet. The former only too well told of the tribulations in the Chilkoot Pass.

Now ahead fifty years, we leave the sundry articles surrounded by blades of grass and moss that dare to snuff them out, coming upon more landmarks of Time; a rock monument erected beside a dilapidated Yukon sled. Is it some humane man's last respect to his noble dogs? That we shall never know. Another rock pillar four—feet high marks the entrance to Ptarmigan Lake. However refreshing in its imprisoned stillness, the lake presents an obstacle in our ascent of the Pass. With no raft, there are two alternatives: to walk around, or ford the channel where the lake narrows before hurtling itself to a watery grave in the steep chasm below. Like true '98ers we choose the latter. Up to our waists in water, packs above the head, we take our chances—the rapids dashing about our legs, threatening, with each step, to catch us off balance and dislodge the Cheechakos from the slippery rocks. Lady Luck has, so far, been good to the latecomers. Would she dare walk these waters with us? Like half—drowned rats we find secure footing on the opposite bank. Three have crossed after all. The waters swirl on without us... Ptarmigan Lake is fed by another, higher up—Long Lake. Rightly named, it is hemmed in on the opposite side by a vertical stone wall. It checks with the map. Luckily we have chosen the right route.

As we trudged up and down the irregular left limit, the only other sounds of life that greeted us were the squirrels, chittering in the pine branches and a snipe wading in the shallow water along the shoreline. Stopping periodically to munch on a cluster of slightly—frosted blueberries, we finally forced camp. It was seven p.m. Night had descended so fast that we had no time to choose a suitable campsite. A propitious clump of moss served the short purpose. So the second evening found us weary, hungry, but ever—optimistic. No one ever enjoyed evening in the wide open spaces more than did the two 'who came late'. As the last faint light of day gave way (after a prolonged struggle) to the inevitable jet of night, a small flicker of flame danced its macabre dance with wood. I imagined a lone, weary prospector saying, as he topped a mountain rise that overlooked the silent valley from some miles distant, and caught sight of the faint patch of light like a lost yellow square on an entirely black, patchwork quilt, "I am not alone this night." A breeze became faintly audible as it blew through the Pass. As it murmured in the brush, *I heard the sound of talk; the careless laughter of men who live hard; and the throb of a thousand footsteps, lightened only by the mental processes working in the brains of the same bodies, turning over the miles in swift succession, picturing Dawson City and Gold....Gold....Gold.* That was it! That was what drove those feet an extra mile when they felt like lead. It was the Gold! Pulling off a shoe that felt heavy, I slid into my robe; but my thoughts were far from igneous fatuous. They dwelt on sleep. Too, it must have come quickly, for I don't remember lowering the arm on which two luminous hands pointed to 9:30...the voices in the valley became silent.

Terrible, Tough Terrain   **Long Lake Arrived**

Rocks, Ridges and Rivulets   **Long Lake to Summit Lake**

Determined to reach the summit this day, we arose to find mists closing in and a slight spraying of rain. Breakfast, consisting of Cream of Wheat, poached eggs (which somehow had miraculously survived the rough climb), bread, marmalade and cocoa, was completed by 10:15 a.m. We broke camp and continued up the gradual ascent which led us through the shallow waters of the creekbed; along the boulder strewn shore; of oftimes to the grassy slopes on one side or the other, to which we clung like mountain goats lest a slip find us amongst the jagged rocks below.

By noon our trials were forgotten as the path, which had become a narrow gully on the side of which rested patches of the first snow, yawned, exposing unexpectedly a small lake. "We'll soon be at the top!...this is Summit Lake for sure!" echoed my friend's optimism.

Time for a rest. So we sat on the moss and relaxed. Like a discarded emerald the tiny body of water lay embedded in snow; illummed at intervals by glorious shafts of sunlight, probing their way through the blanket of fog which is blown through the Pass to the south by a chilly September wind. Behind us lay Long Lake, barely visible through the V−shaped rocks that pass into infinity on either side of which, more rock−at one time molten masses before the Great Eruption−gives way to a few stunted pine and pea−green moss. A few minutes later we dissolve into the narrow passage leading up between the rocks, snow, mist, clouds and summit−our silent, challenging opposition. Rocks...snow...snow...snow...rocks...and a large, aquamarine lake shows through a rift in the clouds. We were mistaken! This is the Summit Lake−Crater Lake at last!

Our trail appeared and disappeared with the casualness of the fog. "We'll never make it under these conditions!" I blurted, losing the path again. "Well, Wise−One, what do you suggest?" came the pointed reply. "Let's look for some more leftoffs−that's the surest path there'll be, O Thoughtless One!" returned the Cheechako, sardonically. So the search for remnants of our forebears began in earnest. As the cloak of mist swung gently to the side, the body of the main *Trail of '98* lay exposed to four eyes. "Look! A sheep collar, horse collar, harness, spades of all shapes, pans, pots, another coffee urn and cutlery to boot!" cried one, with the fervour of a Sourdough finding a lode. The other, finding his 'colours' too, held

**"Like a Discarded Emerald
the Tiny Body of Water Lay..."**

Summit or Crater Lake

A 'Lode' of Abandoned Gold

up the booty.   "More sleds abandoned on the rocks...probably pulled there and left stranded?...pony shoes—all sizes...pipe the whiskey bottles, broken and whole!...well I'll be!—a Hiram Walker label...." "Good choice... good choice... nothing but the best for the Argonauts... definitely good taste!" aired the other." As four feet hit the *Trail of '98,* assured of their tread, two smiles confirmed the excellent taste of the gold seekers regarding one indispensable item carried on the trail.

Finally we are forced to close from the lakeshore. The only possible way to round the waters with a pack is to scale the rock precipices above. Clouds still obliterate our view as they play tag in and out of the nearing Pass. 150 feet above the jagged shores a rift in the clouds brings us suddenly face—to—face with a Tramway House shrouded in mist, somewhat resembling a Sherlock Holmes movie, set on the bleak, Yorkshire moors. So this is where the dangling cable led; but alas, the rusted cable remains idle; a heavy Yukon—sled (its last burden hauled to the heights) abandoned; its timbers, still solid through fifty years of weathering, provide a good shelter. But we have no time to dally. We must push on to the summit!

Tramway House

Rusted Remains of Tramway Pulley

Surprises come one upon the other. Our next is a glacier, green like lime in a transparent bottle, high above on the left slope! Back down to the water's edge we are with the '98ers as the faint path amongst fragments of discarded wood and steel leads to a broken raft on the remote shore of Crater Lake. There is no doubt that this is the easiest method for transit of the lake. But how scarce are rafts in this timberless region? From here on, the climb becomes steeper as faint snatches of the upper reaches appear with the advent of wind, shifting clouds. Lo! A glacier is our next obstacle to overcome. Its surface is smooth. One slip will send us to the icy waters of the lake below. There is nothing to hang on to but our packs. We must cross the glacier. But how?

Gladly Grabbed on a Glacier   **Nearing the Summit**

Remembering the advice of an Oldtimer I pull the hunting knife from its sheath. As I do so, feet part from the ice beneath them. I am headed for the lake below! Jabbing right and left with the knife I cannot secure a firm hold in the ice, which chips away with each thrust. The heavy packsack throws me eccentrically at the slippery mass of ice and snow. Already I think: 'How shall I rid myself of the burden on my back when the waters claim me? Fifty−five pounds will surely take me straight to the bottom!' I had entirely forgotten my companion as I jabbed in vain at

the stubborn ice. Now he came into view. Some distance below me, apparently hearing the commotion, he embedded his hatchet firmly in the glacier and awaited patiently for my awkward descent, with an amused look on his face. Seeing nothing funny about my predicament, I came tumbling past...he grabbed for me! I had already resigned myself to a swim and a possible drowning when all of a sudden I stopped! I hung there, a helpless mass of humanity. Inch by inch we spent the next few minutes crawling to the rocks along the side. On a solid footing once more, the tension of the moment was released. "Boy! That was close," I sighed. "And exceedingly funny," added Ed, the same devilish smile forcing its

Tramway House on the Heights

broadening wrinkles on his countenance. Then, seeing the humour of it all from an observer's standpoint, we burst into loud volumes of laughter which rolled after the mists, down the valley and disappeared. Turning, I threw an insult at the waters that had been cheated, wondering just how many victims the lake had claimed. We continued our eventful ascent.

Scattered at random as we rise are more spades, pans, cans, sled−runners and whiskey bottles; another Tramway House looms silent in a cloud of mist. Turning, we see nothing but fog−immersed rock, jutting here, disappearing there, like so many ghosts of the past daring to appear and as hastily to disappear. A length of thin−guage wire dangles from within the fog. Is the top near? How much more of this accursed climbing? Then (like an answer to a prolonged prayer) a gap of light appears between the two solid rock walls. "It's the top!" I shout to my lagging companion, half lost in the swirling fog. Hands scratched and torn; bodies bruised and sore from the numerous spills; we arrive in the avenue of The Pass looming in the misty reaches above. We work gradually upward...stepping from rock to rock...missing, slipping, sliding, but uncannily holding our own against the rock foe. Packs grow heavier; the summit closer; and optimism strengthened with each rock put in our wake. We must push on to the top!...more clambering...more debris decaying with time...one hundred feet will gain the summit, beat the Chilkoot Pass. Gaining the rusted,

Chilkoot Pass Conquered
4p.m., Sept. 28, 1947

inactive winch−still clutching its length of cable between tarnished teeth−we enter the narrow passage formed by converging, rock walls. One hundred feet soon become ten...nine...eight...two...one.... At four p.m. on September 28, 1947, exactly fifty years late, the two Cheechakos stand 3500 feet high in the mist. The Chilkoot Pass has been conquered.

There are unforgettable incidents in the lives of all of us. I shall never forget that moment as the mists enveloped we two. I thought of the thousands of feet that had passed this spot, glancing at the discarded, rusted equipment strewn amongst the rocks, simultaneously thinking out loud: "They must have been a hardy breed of people!" The year 1898 came suddenly to life. The mists darted in and out of the Pass; clouds descended to meet them and scurry off together; a faint wind whispered through the gap...and it spoke. But it was not the voice of Zephyrus, nor Notus or even cruel Boreas. It was the combined voice of the Argonauts of '98. It cursed the rain, the slipshod trail and the very day they left civilization, with every step of leather on cold, wet rock.

"How many miles more to this accursed place?" a gnarled, old fellow asked. A robust banker, divorced from his roll−top desk, unused to such physical efforts, ejaculated in bitter tones. "That's too damn far for me!" spitting as though to wreak vengeance on the cold, silent, challenging rocks that rang with the clink of metal cleats as a hundred struggling bodies surged upwards like reptiles slithering in the primeval mists. Another, fresh from the protective environs of city life, asked apprehensively: "Wonder if there'll be any claims left to stake on Bonanza by the time we get there?" And a sardonic companion (one of those men who have lived and loved to extremes) said resignedly: "You'll be lucky if you ever get there!" A silence followed, broken only by the crude comment which found its way through the mounting mists, the voice belonging to no one, but striking a common thought: "D'ya t'ink dere'll be any dames in dis here Dawson place when we gits dere?" −freeing itself from one body and easing the burdens of the multitude with its feminine relief.

A lull. The voices ceased. A Cheechako spoke: "You've earned your gold...every ounce of it! And to the women who followed you−God bless them!" he said, hoping as he did so, that as he checked through the Pass in that Last Gold Rush, Sourdough Peter would deem him worthy of entry to all of the heavenly gold creeks where he might stake with the forgotten legion of Sourdoughs. Then suddenly, like a jester at a seance, my heretofore silent companion broke the spell of my tribute to the '98ers. "Come out of it!" "Let's get going!" And fifty years rolled forward....

Lost in the Mists of Time

A Deadmans Gulch Strewn from Summit to Summit...

Surveying the beautiful, hazardous valley one sees the snow−capped mountains rising majestically in the rear, green foothills coming closer and finally a dead man's gulch strewn from summit to summit, with landslide rock of all shapes and sizes. Wanton mists come and go, chasing one another till they become lost in the brooding clouds above, which appear to be debating whether or not they should send a torrent of rain upon the two Cheechakos who dared defy their etheral reaches−the Chilkoot Pass.

CHAPTER FORTY ONE

A WET DESCENT

With that calm that comes after a storm and a coming feeling of elation, we turn our backs to the Pass. Scattered at random as we descend are more spades, eating utensils, harness, sheep collars, whiskey bottles, another broken Tramway House and the International Boundary. With no Canadian officials (as were once stationed at this zenith, in tents) to impede our progress for lack of $500.00 or a year's supply of grub, we set out on the 22 miles to Dyea Harbour. Alaska had claimed the duo. A promontory is reached. Pausing, we see the mist rising to the snow−capped mountains in the distance, falling back into the valley of granite below. Eerie but majestic is the panorama of cloud, snow and rock. We must push on to the bottom. More clambering...the bleached bones of a horse. How he ever reached this height is a mystery; but the bones and broken collar from which the stuffing protrudes, form an apt gravestone and wordless epitaph to a noble beast. We are not alone. Oat husks, a rusted wire dangling from the heights and a rotten telegraph−post littering the path are our silent companions. Tired and sore, we arrive at the Scales−the American avenue to the Pass looming in the misty reaches above. It derived its name from the fact that in the 'Rush' days the packers had to stop at this point and weigh the freight they carried. The charge ranged anywhere from five to sixteen cents a pound for their efforts. This terrain forms a veritable, rock amphitheatre rising from the stream below in a fifty−degree slope. It is fortunate we do not have to compete with the usual twenty feet of snow that lines the slope in winter. Gradually we work our way down, over the slippery rocks waiting to dislodge the step of an unwary trespasser who dares defy their Tibetan sanctuary.

Near the Scales are the remains of a building. Rummaging about the waterlogged timbers, a set of porcelain dishes and cups are found. Such a treat does not come every day on the trail. So it is decided on a repast à la Chilkoot. A toast of cold mountain water is drunk from the immaculate cups to 'our continued success as mountain climbers.' Later it was learned that the Messrs. Fuller and Joppe had a fine restaurant on the site and did a thriving business. Quite likely we ate and drank from the very utensils discarded within the rotting, wooden restaurant when the cry of GOLD! grew faint and the White Pass Railroad pushed through the adjacent mountains. With the falling of rain and night; the shrouding of mists; we made camp under the lee of the Third Tramway House in the rotting remains of the old Fuller and Joppe Restaurant. Time had changed this scene from one of warmth and hospitality to one of entire dampness and discomfort. So with the rains harassing the fire, which was struggling desperately to retain a foothold on the damp timbers, we managed supper, smoked−out like Indian fish. By this time the valley was filled with fog which isolated us on our elevated rock. With boards for a mattress and huddled beneath the collapsed ruins of the eating−house, two Cheechakos (wet to the skin) gloated over the successes of the day; mumbled their complaints as the rain dripped through the cracks in the roof. As more drops gradually snuffed out the last embers of the drowned fire, so did fatigue snuff out the last energies of the two. They fell asleep in a cloud....

For all we know it is the same cloud cloaking us as we greet another wet day. The winds during the night have shown no respect for our shelter, and with their usual velocity, gained by the vacuum effect of the Pass above, have blown the rear out, in passing. In an obviously wet condition we stir, to meet the gloom of this Monday morning. As usual, Cream of Wheat, eggs (the last of which, miraculously, only one is broken), cocoa and marmalade suffice for breakfast. Without further ado we lift our packs to sore shoulders, leaving the ghostly site of Messrs Fuller and Joppe.

Descending the Rock Slide, as the mists ascend, we reach the bed of the Taitya River which is just in its infancy, having only received the rains from the immediate height of the Pass. But it was to become so large as to force us up the mountainside before the next day was over. Plodding along, sometimes in the river, sometimes ashore, we feel the gradual increase in weight of our gear as it absorbs the huge raindrops. "Thank God the trail leads downhill!" we sigh. This is consolation enough.

Perched on a rocky precipice is the skeleton of a Tramway House, its two supports silhouetted against the rampant mists. How they remained erect, carrying their daily load of twenty tons above the stream of humans footing it below, is one of those engineering feats and wonders of the Chilkoot Pass. Farther along on the left limit are the remains of another such Tramway…a mile down the valley we run into brush; gnarled, twisted and stunted—a perfect obstacle matted amongst the rocks. From the heights a hundred cascades tumble out of nowhere, rushing to join the already enlarged Taitya River below.

**Overhead Tramway
High Up The Chilkoot**

Water…Water…Everywhere!

Next comes Long Hill—remembered as the most strenuous part of the entire climb. Prospectors dragged their loads piecemeal to this point in relays, continued from here with the use of 'fall and tackle', thence packed their loads to the very summit. High above a glacier breaks the granite surroundings with its pastel green, now visible…now obliterated by mist. A thousand streams from the mountain sides have gathered in one huge, frothing serpent which rushes at us from above, bearing its fearful, foamy fangs.

It was in one of the many ravines in this locale that the Tragedy of the Chilkoot Pass occurred—the snowslide of April 3, 1898. Life was smothered from 65 victims of the unmerciful, moist, spring snow when, without any warning, the whole valley shook with a thunderous roar. The Indians had not worked for two days knowing that spring in the Chilkoot could not be trusted. However, not heeding their native packers, the Argonauts sought only the upper reaches in their haste for speed; their desire to keep up with others; their lust for gold! When the roar and the wet snows ceased to fill the valley, the death count was taken, as one by one the victims were dug out with spades wielded by hundreds of willing hands. In the melee of the slide many had managed to grasp hold of a rope used for hauling freight to the summit. This was followed by the diggers who, to their great surprise, discovered a few, nearest the bottom, still alive. Encouraged, a new zeal entered the labours as the rope grew shorter; but alas, the fortunate were very few; the remainder buried under as much as fifty feet of slush, suffocated as they clung in vain to the thin rope.

It all started in the early hours of Sunday morning. At 4 o'clock a neighbour came rushing to the cabin of Mr. Mueler of Vancouver, B.C. (a partner of Mr. Joppe), yelling: "For God's sake come and help me!… the Maxsons have been buried in their tent!" Hurrying to the scene with shovels, they extricated the family. Fearing another such occurence, the entire camp was awakened. Later that morning they started, with the aid of a rope, to descend to the lower levels. It happened so suddenly that only some few remember the actual incident of the main slide. Mr. Mueler himself was buried in six feet of snow for three hours. Quoting his story from the *Dyea Trail*, Dyea, April 9, 1898 he says:

"I concluded that we might need shovels to clear drifts and made everyone who could procure one, do so. After this we took hold of the rope and started down with Mr. Joppe in the lead. We proceeded down the trail about a thousand feet below the Scales where we came to the Draw—a low ravine just above the O & I Power House. As we entered it we heard a low rumbling sound.

Someone shouted: "Snow Slide!" I thought it the howling of the wind and answered back to her to that effect. I had hardly gotten the words out of my mouth when I found myself buried to the hips in a solid mass of snow and ice. I did not have time to think before I was pushed over on my side by another mass and covered to a depth of six feet. I realized the awful fate in a moment. I knew it was not myself alone that was buried, but thought that perhaps those on the last end of the rope were not covered and the construction gang, who were ahead of us, would be ahead of the slide and possibly save us... I thought of home and friends (every act and hope of my life crowded into my mind in a moment) but I did not give up hope of being saved. I could not move hand or foot. I was held as fast as if I were in a plaster−of−paris cast. I did not shout or cry out. I realized I needed all my breath and strength. I could hear people near me groaning and praying. In only a few minutes all was still. I became unconscious. I fully realized my position−it was not at all tortuous; but simply that of going to sleep....

When I awoke I found myself on the floor of the Power House; it was some time before I could realize it all happened. I was terribly bruised and black and blue all over; but I feel that no permanent injury will result. They tell me I was buried for three hours. They took out seven, alive, who were on the rope with us; but four of them afterwards died..."

"A singular romantic episode occurred after I was taken to the Power House, which is worthy of publication for the deserving little heroine" (the man narrated, forgetting his own recent ordeal). "Miss Vernie Woodward, who has been on the trail over a year packing freight on her back and managing five pack horses, which she had bought with her earnings, was one of the first to reach the scene from Sheep Camp. She came to the Power House to aid and comfort the wounded and discovered, in the row of dead, the body of Mr. Joppe who she had known for a long time and to whom she was very much attached. When she recognized him her grief was unbounded. She cried and begged for him to come back to life to look at her. She unfastened his shirt, and in frenzied grief began to rub him. She worked upon him, (as only a true woman will) moving his arms this way and that; pressing his chest and breathing into his lungs until three o'clock in the morning. She was then rewarded by his opening of his eyes and speaking her name: "Vernie!" Everybody shed tears of rejoicing. The little heroine and hero were at once taken to Sheep Camp. "Mr. Joppe is out of danger and Miss Woodward is the heroine of the hour."   Another of the personal experiences, gleaned by a Dyea reporter from Mr. J.A. Rines of Maine, is told in his own words: "All of a sudden I heard a loud report and instantly began to feel myself moving swiftly down the hill, and, looking around, saw many others suddenly fall down; some with their feet in the air; their heads buried out of sight in the snow. Then I realized that we were being carried away on a immense avalanche. I never once lost my presence of mind, but braced myself as well as I could and kept on my feet, letting myself go with the slide. When I struck the bottom I tried to run but the snow caught me and I was instantly buried in thirty feet of snow. I was almost suffocated before they dug me out−being buried at least thirty minutes. As soon as I was able I turned to, and helped dig out, many others. I think the slide occurred about 11 a.m. I never want to experience such an awful half−hour again so long as I live; and am thankful to be well and alive."

The slide, reputedly reaching a depth of fifty feet, rolled down some 3000 feet from the eastern side of the Pass. By the time it stopped it covered about fifty acres and was 150 yards in length. All who perished did so by suffocation. One eye witness said the party of about two hundred, descending, reached the fatal spot at a critical moment. Had they been a few minutes earlier, or later, they would not have been caught in the slide; but in all, the true spirit of conmradeship was displayed when fifteen minutes later 1500 men arrived at the scene.

Gazing at an inclined ravine−its trees noticeably bent and broken−we conclude that perhaps here was the scene of this horrible disaster. Close by is a crude, wooden cross set in a pile of rocks. Here is where one faltered, fell, was buried in his tracks. The rest pushed on. So we pushed on with them (the tragedy also our topic of conversation) past Stone House−an immense rock sitting high by itself; deriving its name from the fact that it had an overhanging shelf which afforded some shelter from heavy storms.

A well−earned rest; a tin of beans; more rocks, water, gnarled underbrush that tears at the legs like so many devils reaching from below to shackle and drag us to Purgatory. Devil's Club standing erect in our path, waiting for us to trip, stumble, fall and reach for its thorny support...incessant rains beating down, pounding the Cheechako with their staccato rhythm...anon, signs of life!—ancient ruins half hidden by fifty years of overgrown brush and trees. "Hell can be no worse than those last three miles!" I shout to my friend, adding in utter disgust: "Let's call it a day and wait for the sunshine tomorrow!" More than eager, he caught up, dumped a saturated packsack from weary shoulders and smiled a large smile at the very thought of rest. We had reached the site of Sheep Camp.

Sheep Camp derived its name in the early days from the flock of animals that once camped on the spot for several weeks, their owner enroute to Dawson with meat on the hoof. The town—its single sixteen—foot—wide street at one time boasting two drug stores, a hospital, fifteen hotels and restaurants, two laundries, bath house, numerous coffee houses and lodgings—is completely overgrown with tall trees and twisted underbrush. Finding one hotel (still stubborn in its elemental struggle) half erect, the problem of temporary shelter is solved.

Sometimes the Fates are kind: this is one occasion. Inside we discover two oak bedsteads, as sturdy (except for the rusted springs) as the day they reached this height in the Pass and were assembled within the once—flourishing hotel. With sleeping essentials in order and inwardly contented by a meal of canned food, we stare at the spitting fire as it hisses like an annoyed snake with each raindrop that seeps through the roof; or is whisked under the board shelter by an excited wind; and lashes at the wet clothes hanging above the tongues of flame. We are taken back fifty years as the wind and rain, mercilessly lashing the shack, sound not unlike the echo of a thousand Sourdough voices arising from the makeshift town, all eager, as we, for the morrow or the challenge of the Chilkoot Pass. Darkness falls at six p.m. Three hours later the last story is told. With all the mien of a guest at the hotel, I slip into my robe on the bedstead, wondering as the sparks fly into the night and disappear, the wind caressing the log building, 'just how many other weary bodies have prostrated themselves on this aristocratic piece of furniture?' Verily, I am the Plutocrat of Poverty.

Morning. No breeze; but rain! rain! rain! A bowl of mush. A pack on the back. Our tedious descent was resumed. Winding along the faint trail, more ruins came into view. On the opposite bank of the river we discerned many more decrepit dwellings, all browned with age. Such was our departure from Sheep Camp. Still battling the rocks, brush and water, we passed a pony skeleton— bleached remnants of a beast that fell in its tracks up the impossible grade. Close by is the grave of a man, sunken between two large boulders, the wooden casket open. How paradoxical—the fate of man identical to that of beast in this rough era! On close observation of the round—topped board, serving as a headstone, faint letters were discernible. They read: MAY HE REST IN PEACE. We were sure he would in this almost forsaken valley of the Chilkoot. We soon came upon the well—blazed trail to Canyon City.

The rains deter us from the path. Numerous streams, swollen to triple speed, head us off into the mountainside. Soon back on the trail we hit and miss; plying the inundated valley in our rush to beat nightfall and reach Dyea. We push through Pleasant Valley (which is not so in the downpour characteristic of this season) with its cottonwoods and spruce. Then six miles from Sheep Camp we reach a gap in the bluff along the muddy river. Lettering on a wide blaze says: CANYON CITY. An arrow points across the river. There lies Canyon City across that impossible stretch of water that confronts us. Ramshackle and decrepit, it still struggles against the strangling brush; but only echoes fill the jaded, log homesteads that once compromised the first stop for the thousands of weary gold—seekers.

Fighting the new growth that has sprung up, and grasping our share of hellish Devil's Club, we come upon faint vestiges of a wagon trail in an open clearing. Nothing could have been more inspiring at this time. Goaded on, we find it disappears into bush as abruptly as it appears. Knee— deep in water that fills the natural bed of the trail, we stumble, fall, curse everything cursable (and a hundred things that aren't); meet timbers or a ruined barge (drifted hither and thither from one of the camps) trying in vain to follow the blazing on tree trunks, some hardly noticeable; others freshly cut by some thoughtful person. Hawk and crow suddenly become prevalent, circling and hovering above, seemingly scoffing our sluggishness. "Give those black bastards the works!" shouts my irritated friend. *Bang!* And before the report finishes its reverberations up and down the valley the sky is cleared. All unwanted spectators have departed in haste. A tail feather glides slowly to earth. The valley widens. "Look!...daylight!...blue skies!" Oh! What a glorious feeling it is to be rewarded for one's efforts! Oh! What compensation Nature gives for her tortures! Oh!

The beauty of calm after storm! As we stand there, saturated completely, our eyes drink up the picture of dryness beyond. Two smile largely; two packs suddenly become light; two pairs of feet attack the trail.

The next few miles sees a dense growth of pines, spruce, moss and Devil's Club, forming a formidable barrier but for the blazed trail. Occasionally we come into the open where dual wheelmarks, left by the freighters packing goods to the summit, are faintly visible in the overgrown moss underfoot as they wend their way through the scattered brush, long since grown over the trail.

The Swollen Taitya River

The accursed river, swollen to enormous heights, forces the Cheechakos off the marked trail into the pines; and finally above the water level on the moss bank of the steep mountainside. "This is impossible!...what the hell'll we do?" I yelled, picking myself from a waterhole into which the slippery bank had deposited me. "Let's call it a day...human beings weren't meant to do this!" came the mournful reply. So we fooled the river and put Dyea out of our minds for the day. Slinging a wet tarpaulin, we climbed into the damp bedding. Coughing at the back door of pneumonia, Ed (also emitting a nocturnal staccato with his teeth) informed me, indirectly, that: "Home was never like this!" Naked, I slid into the damp innards of a sleeping robe. "What fools we mortals be!" I sighed; "what discomforts man subjects himself to...and for what?" I found myself asking. But little did either know till the morrow. As the body heat began its dutiful work, a faint smile of satisfaction crossed my face; my friend coughed us both to sleep.

Like two semi−drowned land creatures lost in a primeval swamp, we stirred; shook ourselves; and arose to meet the grey of another day. Steam rose from the waters; the trees dripped their last lingering drops; a hush hung over the entire primordial forest. All about us was eeriness−a contrast to the boisterous days fifty years ago when axes rang through the valley, pack horses snorted as they wended their way upwards and the loud cursings of men split what silence there might have been. Climbing into our cold clothes and eating an equally chilled breakfast we started south again, slipping, splashing our way through the mangled morass. Once on the path edging the river the miles disappeared quickly in our wake. Suddenly we saw the remnants of some pile− driven logs. "This must be the remains of the Kinney Toll Bridge," I suggested, "in which case we are about three miles from Dyea." Optimism leaped. It was not till later that our suspicions were confirmed. It was the site of the 1,000−foot−long toll bridge that crossed the west or main branch of the Dyea River to an island of about 60 acres which is heavily wooded. The prospectors had to cross this on the summer trail up the valley; not unlike toll bridges on the Outside, many a curse must have resounded as a hand reached into a pocket for fare. Such was one of the many bridges constructed at strategic locations on even this−the *Trail of '98*.

A mile from our miserable camp of the night before we came upon the double blazings marking the river−crossing to Dyea. Gazing at the torrents of dirty water that crept high up the bank, we realized the impossibility of such a venture. However, elated by the appearance of the sun, we continued along the east shore. Things were going too well to last. The trail turned upwards and disappeared into the thick mass of vegetation somewhere amongst the lording pines. The mountains claimed us once more.

Arrived at what looked like the top of the trail, we sat down for a rest. Busy picking Devil's Club thistles from badly scratched hands I failed to notice the movement of something that was not human coming up the path. My friend, less engrossed in the prickly business, tried to warn me of impending danger; but having lost his voice with the cold and wet, all was in vain. A prod in the back finally brought me around to the reality of the situation. Just at that moment the animal must have changed his mind. Veering off, fifteen feet away, it chose a lower path. Frozen to our packs on which we sat, we thought of nothing. There should have been a million thoughts. But there we were, speechless, thoughtless—masters of inaction...and at a moment like this, which many times I had relived and acted out in stories of others caught and cornered. But action there was none. The huge, Cinnamon bear lumbered past...disappeared. Visions of the terrible mangling of an Indian boy by a bear in the Pass only the year before brought us to our feet; our minds trying desperately to decide which of the many things to do in such an emergency. Sizing up the surrounding trees in one, swift glance I noted they were all dry. I cursed loudly, then remembered Bruin who might take personal offence. This picture was all too clear: dead branches breaking one by one as the Cheechako climbed just out of reach; the monster pawing at his legs from the foot of the tree trunk. "Oh no!" I exclaimed, living the horrible thought. "Oh no, what?" asked my equally agitated friend. "No, we can't climb...hit the trail, quick!" Neither needed a second invitation or spur. Before we or the bear could change minds, the path swallowed (faster than ever it had done before) two Cheechakos.

Up...down...over a stream...under a fallen log...up again—never once looking back. Eventually, breathless, we descended rapidly to the bottom where the golden sunlight flickered on the turned, autumn leaves. The valley had opened wide; filled itself with a mass of inviting blue and white clouds. How wonderful the world looked at that moment as the rain, hills, thorns and the bear were momentarily forgotten.

Fired with new zeal, we follow the faint, dual wheelmarks submerged in the overgrown moss; losing it here, picking it up again there where the path leads into the open. Then, like a fairy castle appearing in the clouds along the Great White Way, a cabin appears amongst the green foliage. Abiding by one of those unwritten northern laws we enter and make ourselves at home.

"I haven't had a smoke in four days and now I run bang into a pack a Lucky Strikes!" cried my companion, tearing a corner off the container, moaning about the ruination of his own by the rains. "I can chew again!" I shouted with equal excitement, mauling the package of Doublemint. "Gold! We've found gold, Ed! The Gods have answered your prayers of the other night," I said, beaming as I licked the powder from the gum wrapper. "Prayers, hell!" came from behind a screen of smoke. "That was my teeth chattering and I was cursing behind them." The next few minutes were spent in silent reverence—one smoking, one chewing; then in unison we thanked Malcolm Moe (apparent owner) for his wares; determined to look him up and reciprocate generously over a bar should he be in Skagway. (The latter <u>was</u> fulfilled with amusing toasts accompanying the tipling.) So, chewing on a 33 cent package of date cookies, we shut the door and made for the river close by. From here we caught sight of the remains of Dyea City, clearly visible in the morning sunlight on the far shore.

**Malcolm Moe's Cabin
A Lucky Strike for Both**

Here is the famous entry to the Chilkoot Pass, seven miles from the town of Skagway, Alaska. At one time Dyea was a booming port of some 10,000 prospectors, miners, bankers, businessmen, lawyers, faro men, gamblers, shysters, dance hall chorines, prostitutes—people from every possible walk of life; mulling in the streets, drinking in the saloons or cussing the very day they left civilization for the hazardous trip that lay ahead through the toughest pass of them all. Here also was a reserve of 300 Chilkoot Indians eager to pack the white man's load for a fee which at times became outrageous. Those able to pay did so; those without the necessary coin had but one alternative—to pack their own, in relays if they must.

Dyea today is a ghost town—deserted except for a trapper, Al and his wife; Wesley Patterson and his family who have rebuilt an original log homestead; and an ex—New York musician, Ed Hossford, who has taken to the outdoor life as a trapper. The huge wharf—where boats unloaded the cargoes of beans, bacon, flour and such trail essentials—is nothing more than a broken platoon of piles washed by the changes of tide. Still standing erect amongst the weary structures of the city is the notorious Hotel St. Michael, hidden by fifty years of growth. "Should it speak," I am told, "it could sure tell some mean ones!"

As we stood looking back at the Pass, which loses itself in mountains far to the rear, we talked of the innumerable trails used by the Argonauts in their headlong desire to reach the fabulous Klondike. There were the all–Canadian routes–including the Rat River Portage via the Mackenzie River and the Caribou Trail through the heart of British Columbia. On the American side there were many more, commencing in the Alaskan Panhandle through such passes as Takou, Chilkat, Chilkoot and White Pass. It was decided there and then, at the end of our descent, that of all routes the Chilkoot Pass was undoubtedly the most treacherous and surely had the most colourful history. And to think we had successfully climbed it! It was then, upon this realization, that the two Cheechakos were overcome by the glorious feeling of Conquest!

Tired, and not desiring any more mountain climbing, we turned our thoughts away from, and our backs to, the Pass. Amid the reeds and browned grass of the inundated shore a raft made its timely appearance. Climbing aboard–our grunts and groans of launching the half hour before, rewarded–we floated with the afternoon tide, abetting with boards for paddles, no less motley a crew than that of Tom Sawyer. Two headed for the port of Skagway seven miles distant.

As my luck had been unfailing through the past 5000 miles, so it continued as we drifted with the increasing speed of the waters of Lynn Canal. The dim figures of men and the faint sound of machines drew our attention to the port shore. The noise stopped of a sudden. The figures, noting something plying towards them, gazed without recognition. "Ahoy there!" went the shout from our raft as we pulled to shore. "Well I'll be damned!" came a bewildered remark from the rock bank. "Got room for a couple of mad Canucks?" I shouted from the unstable raft that tipped according to our excited movements. "Come on over here and we'll pull you up! You must be all in?" said another. The same awed gentleman who cast the original remark over the waters added: "Where the hell did you guys come from?"

Wesley Patterson's Cabin
Dyea River Valley

Taitya River Meets Dyea Flats

Dyea Harbour and Mud Flats

323

With smiles and handshakes all round we landed in the company of the crew of 'Luddy' Ludwig—construction foreman of the new road to Dyea. Their equipment having broken down, they had decieded to quit for the day, when one spotted the odd—looking shape floating towards them. We were in the hands of Lady Luck and hospitable Americans. The Cheechakos were landlubbers again. As we left the scene of our conversion and traversed the picturesque new highway around the salmon bays, buried in the lee of the surrounding mountains, our adventures of late fell upon interested ears. The town of Skagway, Alaska came into view.

"...An Archaic Raft Made Its Timely Appearance."   **An Alaskan *Tom Sawyer***

Mate—Ed Freeze Rafting on Lynn Canal   **Dyea Harbour and City Ruins of 1898**

Looking Back from Skagway
Lynn Canal, Dyea to the Chilkoot   **Skagway Alaska**
Port of Entry to Chilkoot Pass

CHAPTER FORTY TWO

KINGDOM OF SOAPY SMITH

It was 'Cal' Kalenkosky who spoke up with: "Come on over to my place and meet my wife...we'll treat you proper." Before a half hour was up we knew what "proper" was. Seated beside the hot stove, devoid of our wet, tattered clothing, we downed the special mix of hot brandy concocted in Cal's own style. Pea soup bubbled anxiously on the stove. Soon the shivering ceased. A warm glow permeated the flesh. Laughter filled the kitchen. The events of the journey took on a less grim perspective. Never had such a hospitable welcome come at a more needed time. We were safe in the clutches of a mortal Bacchus.

It was hours before we left the warm sanctuary of the Kalenkosky home, fortified with dry clothes among other things. "Come on down town and we'll meet some of the boys...I think Moe'll be glad to see you both," said our host welcomingly. We followed. Passing along the wet pavement that reflected the neon lighting, we arrived at the Frontier Bar. Entering, we soon became an integral part of the gathering of colourful characters that congregate nightly. We met bespectacled Moe behind the bar. "Wanchya to meet a couple guys who made use of your cabin yesterday, Moe, ...tink dey got sump'n ta say," introduced Cal. "Just wanted to show our appreciation for the fags, gum and cookies you left in the shack, Moe," I spoke up..."they were sure a livesaver!...by the way, you'll find a small remuneration on the table by the cheese the mice have beat you to...and we tidied up and shut the door when we left." "Well I'll be!!!...Those damn critters have done it again...anyway, I like the style of you fellas...not Americans are you?" "No, sir," I ejaculated, "damn good Canadians!" "God, I like the sound of that! Glad too, you respected my cabin...and I'm happy that it was of service to you." With this Moe brought forth some glasses. "The drinks are on the house," he shouted, "and we're drinkin' to these crazy Canadians." Laughter filled the tavern. Moe beamed with the glee of a Patriarch. Glasses clinked. Even Oldtimer Johnny Greshell broke his regular nocturnal habit of one beer to join us.

Hours later the clamour subsided. Tired from the day's ordeal and over−whelmed by the unusual abundance of Northern hospitality, we departed. 'Sharky' Stiles became our new host. Accompanying him to his home, he said: "It's yours as long as you wanta stay." I cannot remember any more, except that the lights reflected on the wet streets seemed to speak; I heard them say: "Welcome to Skagway....Welcome!

**Main Street
Totem Poles**

**Skagway Alaska
Main Street Looking East**

Skagway lies at the joint of the Pan and the Handle, which form the well known Alaskan Panhandle, about 1000 miles northwest of Vancouver, B.C. It derives its colourful name from the Indian word 'Skagua" meaning, North Wind. When on July 26, 1897 it was declared a port of entry, the town boasted one small cabin owned by a retired seaman—Captain Billy Moore. Far from the congested city of some 15,000 people waiting to go over the Passes in 1898, it is now a pleasant little town, sunk in the bowl of surrounding snow—crested peaks, lording over it 4000 to 6000 feet. Outstanding amongst these heights is the A.B. Mountain, bearing the name of the original established order of Alaskan Brotherhood.

A.B. Mountain
West on Main Street

As I mingled with the people of this lazy town I began to feel one of them, performing their daily duties as an accepted lot, free from the hustle and bustle that stirred dust in its same streets in 1898. I accepted the traditions that make Skagway and keep it ranking high in men's minds as a once—booming city that has seen a more prosperous day. I learned of its most famous character who is still revered today—revered for his notoriety as a sleight—of—hand saloon keeper and gunman—'Soapy' Smith.

Among the variegated characters from all walks of life who sought the new—found riches of the Northland was one especially colourful gentleman. Born in Georgia in 1860 of a prominent southern family and christened Jefferson Randolph Smith, he was soon to acquire the much shorter monicker 'Soapy', which followed him through the rest of his life. The upheaval of the Civil War found the lad leaving home and eventually becoming a cowpuncher in the middle—west. While taking a day off from the herd to visit a local town he became intrigued with the sleight—of—hand activity of 'Clubfoot' Hall—one of the greatest three—shell experts of all time. Fascinated with the easy money made in so short a time by such cunning manipulation, Soapy rode back to the ranch, announced his resignation from cowpunching and, with a few borrowed dollars, hit the trail again.

We find him in such boom—towns as Denver, Creede, Leadville, gradually improving his art and meeting the notorious con—men who gradually became his gang. Clubfoot's decision to quit the three—shell game for bigger stuff left Soapy the master of the trade. It was while engaged in his travels that he met Joe Simons from Texas who had the honour of becoming Soapy's most intimate friend. Never at any time after their association did either see the other destitute. Upon the death of his friend in a shooting affray, Soapy bemoaned greatly the loss of Joe. Even a travelling poet put the affair into memorable words. Later, in moments of thoughtfulness, Soapy would often read the poem for inspiration. Thus we see the fabled 'honour among thieves'.

Besides his three—shell art, Jefferson had put into practice his favourite trick. He would wrap packages of soap which he offered for sale at 50 cents or oftimes $1.00 to the crowd of greenhorns or 'suckers' who invariably gathered around his stand for the demonstration. Ostentatiously wrapping some bills of a higher denomination in with the soap, he would ask for a bid and receive one from a 'capper' placed in the audience. On opening the package discovering the bill the 'capper' would wave the contents, crying aloud of his luck. At this point a massed buying took place. Seemingly wrapping more bills, he would substitute previously wrapped packages, or hand the ones containing the bills to other cappers. As the crowd bought and moved on, Smith would set up elsewhere, till, finally, out of soap, he and his 'cappers' would meet elsewhere and split the profits of the day. Thus Jefferson Randolph became widely known as 'Soapy' Smith, carrying on the work of the inventor, Taylor, who first contrived the idea to fleece a gullible public.

As the boom—towns of the Old West became law—abiding places we find the ruthless Soapy looking for greener fields to exploit. Broke and deciding to leave his favourite haunt—17th Street, Denver—where he had become quite a prominent figure, he hadn't quite concluded 'where next?'

when, like at so many other decisive times in his life, incidents just happened and Fate played her hand.

With the arrival of the S.S. *Portland* in Seattle on July 16, 1897, carrying lucky Argonauts, and the resultant disturbing headline in the *Post Intelligencer*—A TON OF GOLD, the Great Stampede to the northland began. News travelled fast to Denver, Colorado. But how could Soapy and his gang go west, broke? The Good Angel beamed down once again on the ignoble crew of confidence men. George Wilder, one of the gang, had been hoarding his winnings for some time. He now generously proffered them so that all might carry on their ignominious pursuits. Not enough for all to go, Soapy chose a mixed sextet from his criminal throng: 'Reverend' Bowers, 'Slim Jim' Foster, 'Red' Gibbs, Syd Dixon and Wilder. They set out hurriedly from their old haunt, Denver, never to return.

Arriving in San Fransisco, they continued their illicit practices. From here they hit Seattle. But on October 1, 1897, were ordered by the local swindlers to move along. Boasting to an old friend met in the streets, Soapy said: "I'm going to boss that town!" Somewhat imbersed, the gang headed for Skagway, Alaska—the last frontier.

Events moved rapidly as Soapy sized up the town. Enlisting more scoundrels into their mob, the gang set up their 'three—shell' games at Skagway and Dyea—entrances and exits for all men and gold to and from the fabulous Klondike. The object of this chance game was to guess under which walnut shell the pea lay. Naturally it was under the wrong one (or none at all) and the Cheechako was done out of his grubstake finance; or the returning Sourdough his hard—earned gold recently brought out from the creeks of the Yukon.

An adjunct to this scheming was inaugurated by Soapy in the shape of an Information Bureau. The inquisitive traveller, railroaded to one of the tar—paper shacks by an informer waiting at the docks for new arrivals, would find himself engaged in conversation with the so—called 'Bureau men'. Suddenly the lights would go out; the gang to their work of rough—housing. Awakening from the ordeal sometime later, the unfortunate gentleman would be sure to find himself on the street, his pockets void of all valuables.

Gradually power began to fall into the hands of Smith. His gang increased day by day. Among the gang numbering some 192 in all, governed by the Uncrowned King—the title bestowed upon him with his rising success—were many doubtful individuals and characters from the underworlds across the States and Canada. There were such men as The Lamb, Blackjack Doctor, Moonface Kid, B.S. Jack, Slim Jim, The Queen and many other unprintable sobriquets. Others included George Williams, Clark (alias McCormick), Charles Compton, J.C. Thomas, E.C. (Poker) Davis, King Warren, J. Collins, Harry Starr and W. Butts (alias Smith).

Soapy's first headquarters was situated next to Clancy's on Holly Street (later called Sixth Street), between Broadway and State. His wide—spread, illicit web was designed to entagle, somehow, everyone carrying wealth. On the trails he would send men to build fires at likely locations where the foot—sloggers, returning from Dawson, would welcome warmth from the cold winds and hazards of the White Pass. Here, the interested would become inveigled into participating in the three—shell game—oftimes called the T.B. Game. Too, it is suspected that many a discouraged 'sharper' used other means of extracting wealth from his victims, for at one time eight bodies were found on the White Pass Trail. Those not apprehended were zealously encouraged to seek advice from the Holley Street Bureau.

The ingenious saloon—keeper also sent his men aboard the steamers to feel out the people and direct them, upon their landing in Skagway, to his little, black, covered shack of ill—repute—the Information Bureau. So the game of robbery continued; whiskey poured into the settlement unrestricted; the drinking palaces increased gradually to the eventual 70; and fresh tales of new discoveries filtered over the frozen passes from the lips of successful prospectors headed for the Outside with their new—found wealth.

Then came the action which gradually began to shape the future course of Skagway. In February 1898 Andy McGrath accused Fay — the bartender of a saloon in Jake Rice's Opera House Block —of a sure—thing game. Indignant, he stormed out, only to return in a few minutes with Rowan—the U.S. Marshall—to back up his accusation. At 10 a.m. as the two pushed their way through the door two shots rang out. The irate bartender proved one jump ahead of them. Two bodies slumped to the floor. The shooting became a mystery; but an investigation followed. It was Tom Ward of Portland who shed some light on the shooting, naming the killer under the promise of protection from J.M. Tanner. All set for a lynching, the townsfolk gathered. The rope was already about Fay's neck. Just then Soapy, hearing the news, rushed to the scene. With his usual diplomacy, he turned the tide of events with: "Who knows whether or not the man is guilty without fair trial?" Convincing them, he turned Fay over to the authorities who sent him aboard the *Walcott* to Sitka for fair trial. Luckily, he was acquitted later.

Meanwhile the storm gathered anew. Rowan's widow gave birth to a baby at 1 p.m., the same day of its father's death. While the folk at Skagway (feeling the tragedy more deeply) demanded justice, Soapy set about to gather a collection for the deprived widow. Again, at the critical moment, Soapy deterred the wrath of a maddend crowd against his interferences, by announcing that he had turned $700.00 over to the widow. Thus he was unanimously accepted by the citizens and lawless faculty without argument. $15.00 more he turned over to the McGrath and Rowan widows. So with renewed prestige Soapy and his men continued, more openly than ever, with their fleecing habits. With a pal, John Clancy, Jefferson Arnold opened his own saloon. This he named Jeff's Place, erected on the site now occupied by the Bank of Alaska.

Office of
'Uncrowned King of Skagway'
Jefferson Arnold Smith

Mysteriously acquiring a roll−top desk, the uncrowned King of Skagway established his headquarters. Despite varying opinions among the people of Skagway, Soapy continued to talk Law and Order. Then with the advent of the Spanish American War, Jefferson Randolph Smith organized the First Regiment of Alaska Militia, writing a formal letter to President McKinley offering his services. Among the many volunteers were dejected gold−seekers and victims of his misrule, seeking a free trip to the Outside. But Soapy's honest effort (for once) rebuked, the group disbanded. Disappointed, Soapy hung the President's return−letter in a frame on the saloon wall, in his ostentatious manner of showing popularity and self−importance.

Time passed. More killings occured on the trails to the Klondike. Again events moved rapidly. Shot from behind, a prospector named Bean died on the White Pass Trail. Then came the killing of a negro woman of the underworld, at which point Mattie Silks−a white woman from the same walk of life−fled back to the States in fright. Out of danger, she accused Soapy Smith's gang of the crime. This led to an inquiry, followed by a Citizen's Meeting from which evolved a poster bearing the results. It was issued by the members of the One Hundred and One, directed by Major Strong, Captain J.M. Tanner, Sam Lovell, H.E. Brady, C.B. Beeson, Henry Shea and W.L. Berbee. It read:

WARNING
A word to the wise should be sufficient. All confidence men, sharks, bunco and sure−thing men, and all other objectionable characters are notified to leave Skagway and the White Pass Road immediately and to remain away. Failure to comply with this warning will be followed by prompt action!
(Signed) Committee of One Hundred and One

Soapy, quick to retaliate in the defence of his so−called Law and Order program, made the following poster, which adorned the local streets.

ANNOUNCEMENT

The business interests of Skagway propose to put a stop to the lawless acts of many newcomers. We hereby summon all good citizens to a meeting at which these matters will be discussed. Come one, come all! Immediate action will be taken for relief. Let this be a warning for those Cheechakos who are disgracing our city! The meeting will be held at Sylvester Hall at 8 sharp.

(Signed) Jefferson R. Smith, Chairman

The result of the meeting led to the founding of the Law and Order Committee—Three Hundred and Three, with Jeff Smith as permanent chairman. In this capacity he printed another poster.

PUBLIC WARNING!

The body of men styling themselves the Committee of One Hundred and One are hereby notified that any overt action committed by them will promptly be met by the law—abiding Citizens of Skagway and each member and his property will be held responsible for any unlawful act on their part and the Law and Order Society, consisting of 317 citizens, will see that justice is dealt out to its fullest extent as no black mailers or vigilantes will be tolerated

(Signed) The Committee

Came to Skagway a preacher of the gospel. His intention was to help clean up the evil doings — tales of which began to spread far and wide. Soapy, respecting men of religion, met the man upon arrival. In the ensuing conversation he discovered the parson's desire to build a church. A small matter with Mr. Smith; he undertook a personal canvass of the town. Soon the preacher received the healthy sum of $600.00 with smiles. By this gesture local antagonism lessened towards Soapy, who now found himself King of the Last Frontier and financial pillar of the First Church of Skagway, Alaska.

Crime had reached its height in the cold spring months of '98. A favourite saying amongst observers became: "When hell freezes over, it will be just like Skagway!" A newspaper about this time dispatched an item throughout the U.S. and Canada, which read:

Seattle, Feb 25. 1898   Officers of the *Noyo* from Skagway today reported conditions of Lawlessness at Skagway as beyond description. Soapy Smith and his gang are in full control. Law—abiding citizens do not dare say a word against the holdups and murders. Meetings are a part of the daily routine. Eight bodies were picked up in the White Pass on Feb. 15.

Soapy had proven his boast to Willis Loomis, former Police Chief of Leadville, that: "I'm going to boss that town!" In a letter to a friend Outside, he wrote: "We have got them licked, and we mean to rule absolutely!" This they continued to do. As the months passed, more atrocities, grafts and swindlings occurred — some within the gang. Shyster lawyers, too, inserted their fingers into the nefarious pie of Skagway.

The entire site of Skagway, for one half a mile of beach and one mile inland, belonged rightly to Captain William Moore—a retired, ancient mariner who had built a cabin in the early '80's and settled ashore. While he raged helplessly, the townsite was split into 3600 lots which were sold. He was left the one lot where his cabin stood. Stubbornly the skipper refused to acknowledge the sale of his land. For this, his enemies wrecked his cabin; looted his treasures gleaned from the world's far ends. Meanwhile the lots were sold and resold again, with the departure of the original buyers for the Klondike, and each successive claimant's departure. Such was the game the land sharks played in the wide—open town of Skagway. (It was not till years of deliberation passed that the old captain received remuneration for the havoc. When it finally came, he received 25% of the value of the original lots).

So the great game continued; more men joined Soapy Smith's gang. Among these latest were Old Man Tripp (alias Tiplett) and "Yeah Mon" Hopkins, who became bouncer at Jeff's Place. This odd sobriquet he received from his long association with Chinamen on the Pacific Coast. 'Yeah

Mon' is a Chinese feast for which the man had a peculiar liking. He had also been a bodyguard for Chinese merchants in the Tong wars.

During the period before the climax, Soapy gained a reputation for benevolence. "Soapy never turned down a hungry man and even staked the dance—hall girls when they were broke," said one who remembered him well. Another incident in the Gold Rush was the shipping of stolen dogs from California to ice—locked Alaska when reports came Outside that dogs were in great demand. However, the majority of them were no good in such a cold climate. Soapy also came to the aid of the hungry, howling canines when food was scarce enough for the residents of Skagway. He commenced an 'Adopt a Dog' campaign. He himself showed a good example by adopting six of the strays. Murmurs of Vigilante threats were heard only occasionally and died as fast as they arose. Skagway was its unusual self for the nonce.

It was July 4 in Skagway. The entire town was decorated with flags and bunting. Fireworks greeted the dawn. Soapy had spent weeks organizing plans, ordering fireworks to come on the boats from the south; building platforms, preparing the order of the parade and deciding on the speaker—Governor Brady of Alaska Territory. He was finally induced by Soapy, who iterated: "He is my friend; he will come to deliver the Independence Day address." Soapy was naturally chosen for position of Grand Marshall.

Besides bragging, that for patriotic reasons (the Spanish American War was on) it would be the greatest show yet, he emphasized the pleasure children would receive from the events of the day. This toned—down the Vigilante murmurs that again ceased to die as they were spoken. Momentarily misrule was forgotten; the entire populace conglomerated in the street for what proved to be the greatest 4th of July Alaska had every seen.

One by one Jeff Smith's plans saw completion. The day came to a climax with the parade before the reviewing platform of the Governor. It was led by none other than Soapy Smith. Crowned with a new, white sombrero, mounted atop a grey, dappled steed, the Uncrowned King was followed by his own Regiment of Militia and numerous floats built by the merchants. Dynamite blasts echoed up and down the valley. As the din subsided, Soapy dismounted, climbing to the platform beside Governor Brady. Following his speech came, probably, the proudest moment in the life of the man from Georgia. Someone in the vast audience proposed 'three cheers for the Grand Marshall'. Three were given heartily…

Night fell. Fireworks ceased to illuminate the dusk. A pleasant hush fell over Skagway. She rested momentarily in peace. Soapy Smith had reached the zenith of his glory.

On July 7 this sleep was suddenly broken. Soapy had started towards his nadir. It was all because of a tired prospector who arrived in Skagway with a poke of gold. He was J.D. Steward, a Scot from Nanaimo, B.C., homeward—bound to build a new home and settle down at last. Unknowingly he fell into the hands of Bowers—Smith's soft spoken henchman who induced him to 'drop in at Jeff's Place and see the eagle.' Stewart, aware of his riches, suggested he drop them for safe keeping at a local mercantile house. Bowers, protesting, said: "They charge a commission and want a rake—off. I know a man who'll change it for nothing." Too good an opportunity to discard, Steward assented. With his $17,000 bucksin poke he plodded towards the den of iniquity. He was about to 'see the eagle'.

Awaiting the man who would change his dust into currency, Stewart 'viewed the eagle'. Turning to go from the back yard, his arms were pinned, his poke taken. The boldest and most reckless crime yet was committed in broad daylight. The Scot, getting no satisfaction from the marshall, Taylor (who it was later learned received a $400.00 bribe from Soapy), referred his story to the U.S. Commissioner at Dyea—Judge Sehlbrede. The so—called 'fireworks' began.

A summons was issued to the merchants. (they had hitherto remained neutral, for 'business' sake.) Gangs began gathering. Denouncement of criminals gained momentum…it spread like a plague; its effect became as deadly. A committee visited Jeff's Place, asking that he do the proper thing—turn over the stolen poke. Insisting it was won 'legally' over the tables, he evaded the reply, saying: "Call again at 4 o'clock and I promise to see what I can do in the meantime…"

Soapy, invited to a meeting presided over by the good Judge Sehlbrede, was given the opportunity to return the gold. Still evasive, he demanded his terms: "If they arrest the accused then I'll see that Stewart gets his gold—provided I can name the guards in case of mob violence."

The resolute Judge, now convinced of Soapy's knowledge of the crime, said emphatically that no compromise would be considered, adding with finality, "now get busy!" Time was surely growing short for Soapy Smith in Skagway...

At zero–hour Soapy swung into the street. He carried no poke, but his Winchester high–power rifle. Throwing challenges at the gathered crowd, he traversed the main street and entered the nearest saloon for a drink. At the bar he noted a shifty henchman. To him he directed his last boast: "this may be the finish, but I'm going to face it whatever happens." Downing his drink, he shouldered the rifle. Again he swung gaily down the main street, fired with his own importance and the glass of whiskey, paying no heed to the warnings of his cohorts.

Meantime the Vigilantes sent their messengers through the town to summon all who could be trusted to a meeting at Sylvester Hall. The purpose (read the call) is to complete the efforts started by 101 some time ago. Gathered, J.T. Hayne, a printer, announced the purpose of the meeting. Thomas Whitten of the Golden North Hotel was elected chairman. As the meeting was about to commence a member cried: "I move we adjourn to Juneau Wharf, because, on looking around at the faces, I see some that, according to procedure, shouldn't be here!" It was agreed. The hall soon became deserted.

To weed out 'undesirables' a group of four men stationed themselves at the foot of the pier. They included City Engineer Reid, Captain Tanner, Jesse Murphy and John Landers. Meanwhile, Soapy dropped in at several spots to bolster the fainthearted. Runners kept him advised on the Vigilantes. Witnesses say he said: "Boys, I'm going to Juneau Wharf to talk to the meeting on your behalf. This isn't my first gamble with life." Bill Tener, bartender, said: "But, Soapy, it'll be suicide!" But the soapman slid out to meet the foe...alone.

"Halt! Throw up your hands!" came the imperative voice from the dusk. Instead, Soapy instinctively raised his rifle, simultaneously recognizing Reid. "My God, don't shoot!" blurted the Uncrowned King, knowing well the man he was facing. Reid, knowing also the meaning of the Winchester in such hands, didn't wait for more words. But, as he pulled the trigger, a mere *click!* come from the weapon. By the time another cartridge had been turned into place the Colt cocked, Smith had time to raise his rifle and fire. Reid, no slouch with a six–shooter, managed to discharge a shell about the same time. Two reports resounded. Two flashes lit the dusk. Two bodies slumped earthward. Reid, however, managed to get another shot away. this was unnecessary, for Soapy was shot through the heart, dead.

Several people claimed witness to the incident. Among those was Mrs. Harriet Pullen—Mother of the North. Out looking for her young son, she saw the affray and screamed. When the shots and her scream faded, two bodies lay at the foot of Juneau Wharf. It was my good fortune to meet still another who claimed to have witnessed the affair. He is elderly Frank Fowler who lives quietly in a comfortable house with his wife; content to dabble in horticulture, and glad always to reflect back to the rough days when his own flower garden was but a mudhole and the house a crude frame building or saloon.

"As Soapy plodded down the street, rifle in hand," Frank Fowler leaned over the table, his wife on the other side..."Reid was sitting on the railing at this end of the dock," he remembered, "as Soapy approached, Andy Street (my partner) and I crossed the road to go to our cabin on the beach. "Don't follow me!" said the suspicious Smith, nearing the wharf. As he came close Reid spoke up saying: "Where are you going?" to which the bewhiskered Soapy replied: "To break up your damned meeting!" "You're not going down!" retorted Reid. "I am," ejaculated the inebriated Smith. Reid, sensing the seriousness of the threat, went for his gun. At the same time Soapy stepped back, dropped his rifle and fired point blank. Reid slid off the rail exclaiming: "I'm shot!" firing, as he did, a shot into Soapy's chest. Both crumpled to the planking, Soapy dropping like a horse hit on the head with a hammer...yes, he sure went down quick—like," said the old Sourdough. With a finality unlike all fairy–tale endings he said: "The gang dispersed—some were caught, others scattered. With the Vigilantes in hot pursuit, they fled to the hills towards the peaks and disappeared...

A voice was heard through the streets yelling: "Soapy's killed!" Then all hell broke loose in Skagway. Outlaws fled along the riverbanks, up mountain trails; saloons were raided. Thugs were slugged. Wholesale vengeance was reeked upon all 'doubtfuls' in the town of Skagway.

"If any crook resists, shoot him down" was the order issued to the mob. When the count was taken, 40 criminals and suspects were off to the City Jail, while the mob yelled for a lynching bee. But thwarting the designs of the enraged, honest folk, the U.S. Infantry under Captain Yeatman reached the jail in time to prevent a raid.

Soapy lay where he had fallen for some hours. Shortly before dawn a widow whom Soapy had befriended in a time of need—after a restless night—enquired as to the source of the din. Upon discovery of the truth she set out in search of the body of Jeff Smith. Finding him prostrate on the wharf, the kindly woman removed the limp carcass to the morgue...

Reid, on the other hand, still breathed. Shot through the groin, he was taken to the Bishop Rowe hospital. In his ever—cool way he said to the doctor, about to operate: "Do the best you can for me, doctor." But alas, the city—engineer passed away on July 20, 12 days after the shooting affray with Soapy Smith on Juneau Wharf...." The words of Frank Fowler died off; his wife nodding in a sort of final agreement with her husband.

Meanwhile, saloons closed; gambling stopped; and Stewart's poke of gold dust was recovered—short $500.00. Those lawless characters accused of felony were sent to Sitka. All others were deported on the British ship *Tartar*. But before they said farewell to the shores of Alaska, a short ceremony was performed by each. The Vigilantes—to keep their own records clean—made each deportee, as he stepped aboard, say that he was leaving of his 'own free will'. Should they every set foot on Alaskan soil again they would be hung to the nearest tree.

So, the *Tartar* sailed, carrying the last of the Soapy Smith gang from Alaskan shores. Soapy's funeral was held in the church that he helped to found; the minister—the very man Soapy had so generously helped on his arrival. The good man chose as the topic of his sermon: 'The Way of a Transgressor is Hard'. He lauded Jeff's virtues and good works—how many times he had come to the aid of the church when finances failed. He reminded those present of the time Soapy rounded up $600.00 in collections; of the $200.00 donation given for the erection of the first church and schoolhouse. Warm with righteousness, the preacher continued to speak highly of the three—shell expert, adding that some of us fall short of what is expected of us by the Maker; and perhaps Jefferson Randolph was one such individual. but in the consummation of the Good and Evil of Mr. Smith he had to admit that the good works had not sufficed to offset his wrong doings. Bestowing upon him his blessings, the minister concluded: 'May he rest in peace.' Four days had seen the fall of Soapy Smith—the Uncrowned Monarch of Skaway—from the greatest heights to the lowest depths.

Today, a mile up the railway tracks leading to the White Pass, can be seen two graves of particular importance. One—barely noticeable amid the trees and dried leaves—is covered with a wire protection through which the marble headstone appears. Its inscription reads:

"My God Don't Shoot!"

JEFFERSON R. SMITH
DIED JULY 8 1898.
AGED 38 YEARS

The original grave farther up the valley was a plain, wooden cross placed by two women on his behalf. But time and people have removed the entire marker. About 1933 a former friend of Soapy's—thomas Kearney of St. Louis—sent a cheque to the late Mrs. Pullen for the erection of the present marble slab. Much more impressive, a short distance away, stands the tall monument in memory of the slayer of Soapy Smith. Its inscription reads:

FRANK H. REID
DIED
JULY 20 1898
AGED
54 YEARS
He gave his life for the
Honor of Skagway

"Do the best you can for me, doctor."

Here is the final resting place of the one man Soapy feared, but, in a careless moment, failed to convince in his last bluff. May they both rest in peace within the sound of Reid Falls, which, tumbling down from the heights above, will go on forever like the memories of both men.

Jack Griesback, present owner of Jeff Smith's Parlour and property, gives more credit than many to the virtues of Jefferson Randolph Smith. One of the Oldtimers, Jack can be buttonholed most mornings between the Skagway Grill, under proprietorship of the chef —Skagway Jim— and Jeff's Museum, to which he hobbles on his crutches, opening the place for such visitors who might be interested in Skagway's notorious past. Having finished his morning coffee and emerged from the Grill, he was accosted by a Cheechako. "And whut kin I do fer you?" he questioned. "They tell me you know something about this character Smith?" I suggested. "Oh, Soapy! Well I reckon"... as we headed along Broadway the colourful narrative began. Unlocking the padlock that guards his most prized treasures, Jack switched on the light. In the rear room stood stuffed dummies of the Smith gang. They include such notables as Smokey Dick, Dolly Baby Ida, Packhorse Bill and Diamond Lil. Jack said: "Soapy wasn't half so bad as they make him out...why, once he even donated $200.00 to the building of the first schoolhouse!...and he would help anyone, but of course (with a slight apology) like all saloon owners he had his following." Jack drew my attention to a clipping that said Soapy was so popular that he was offered the job of Town Marshall. Still in support of the man from whose lurid history he makes his living, Jack said: "The bullet taken from Soapy's body didn't fit Reid's gun!" So, satisfied with the interior of the famous haunt of Skagway's gunmen, blanco and faro men, the Cheechako passed the much used bar over which Soapy received his slug of whiskey before going to meet the Vigilantes. Imaginarily accepting a 'shot' over the bar, I downed it and once more gained the street on my more peaceful mission. Jack Griesback had made his daily visit to Jeff Smith's Parlour.

CHAPTER FORTY THREE

END OF THE TRAIL

A week passed in this hospitable atmosphere of Skagway. The *Princess Louise* and *Alaska* steamships came and went. A thousand bits of information parted from the lips that have been telling yarns and the notorious history of Skagway for half a century. They spoke of the Chilkoot Indians who refused to work for any price on Sunday...of the 38 cents a pound fee for packing over the Chilkoot Pass in 1897, and the later drop in '98 of 5 cents to 16 cents per pound...of Isaac—Chief of the Chilkoot—who organized his tribe into a profit—making business, advertising with such signs as: PACKING A SPECIALTY...and of Don—A—Wok—nearly 80 years old. They told too of an ox killed at Lake Lindeman, the heart of which sold for $7.00, the head $12.50, the remainder for 50 cents a pound.

Came the tales of Skagway, then: I heard of the steamer *Queen* under Captain James Caroll that brought the first Klondike miners from southern ports...of the unfortunate burning of another steamer in the harbour, loaded with horses and hay. About to unload she caught fire, was ordered away from the dock, and finally the Captain at the mercy of a mutineering crew was forced to run her ashore, where, in a few hours, she was but a mere, twisted hulk; her invaluable cargo a complete loss. By July 26, 1897 the town had suddenly sprung to a population of 4000 people in 3 months...how in the latter part of August, during the horshoe—nail famine, as high as $1.00 per nail was paid...of prices at the local blacksmith shop: $6.00 for shoeing a horse, $10.00 for oxen. Unseen today, I was informed of a small settlement called Ragtown which sprang up between Skagway and Dyea...and told of the seventy saloons and gaming houses throughout the boom town with such names as Jeff Smith's Parlour, Montana Saloon, Lee Gathaway's, The Nome, and the original bar in Skagway—The Pack Train Inn that kept the Argonauts well entertained.

**Pack Train Inn
Font of the Famous**

It is inevitable that the tales of the treacherous Chilkoot Pass should emanate here at this Port of Entry. One—by—one they came, adding impossibility to daredeviltry; challenge to defeat; humour to tragedy. One is bound to hear of the two optimists who tried lugging a two—oven Majestic stove over the Pass, choosing later at a high point to abandon the awkward, cooking device. Still today, as unadulterated as the day it happened, comes the laughable tale of the much revered 'Klondike Mike' Mahoney who packed a piano over the Chilkoot. (He must have been an ardent lover of music, or the piano was a midget model?) We hear, too, of the twelve horses that packed toilet tissue over the White Pass Trail to be sold for 50 cents a roll; by the time it reached Dawson City, $1.00. "But little ever got that far!" said the oldtimer narrating the incident. They tell also of the ingenious gentleman who did an original type of prospecting. He packed a grindstone on his back—charging $1.00 per hour for usage and $1.00 to turn the handle if the customer so desired. He oftimes, reputedly, made as much as $8.00 an hour. Heard still is talk of the Chorus Girls that braved the Chilkoot in search of an audience in Dawson City, 600 wet miles away...and tales of the fearless 'Montana Kid'—a noted frontier character who possessed the prize dogteam that raced between Skagway and Dawson. Came tales of the Chilkoot march: how more than 1000 people camped at Sheep Camp in August and September of '98. Hotel rates at the camp were 75 cents for a berth on the floor; 50 cents with one's own bedding. Beyond this point on the trail a meal couldn't be had at any price. Still another described the twenty−five pound sheet−iron stove so commonly used, costing $5.00 in Seattle and sobriqued the 'Klondike Stove'...how a week or more was employed whipsawing timber and building a boat at Lindeman for the final 600 miles of waterway to Dawson City...and the worst tragedy of the Gold Rush of 1898−the landslide of April 3 which killed some sixty−five Argonauts, burying them alive with molten snow and ice.

As the fire died one evening in the antiquated, log cabin; the embers casting our eerie shadows upon the opposite wall, a Sourdough spoke in his aged voice; his stories sought vacant pigeon−holes in the Cheechako's mind. He told of the Royal Canadian Mounted Police, who, strict in their discipline, would let no one over the Chilkoot Pass without a year's supply of grub or 1100 pounds of foodstuffs in all...of the eight steamers that brought 2000 people to Port Dyea in three days. One event especially stood out in his memory and brought to the fore the stories of the day's foremost novelist−Jack London. It was the arrival of the *Alice Blanchard* from San Francisco, including in her cargo of livestock, fifty−two dogs of every breed, (rounded up usually by thieves in southern climes) shipped north and sold for $300.00 apiece. "Dere vas beeg und small, tall und short, tough ones, by God! Und some veek as hell−no goot for da trail at all! Byt I nevere see soo manee dogs at vunce...und fight!..." he remembered vividly. While on the topic of ships he mentioned too, the first steamer−*Excelsior* which was sent to 'Frisco with $175,000.00 in gold ore from the Klondike; and the prime ship to Seattle−*S.S. Portland* which arrived with a ton of gold from the fabulous North, resulting in the *Post Intelligencer* headline: ONE TON OF GOLD! and the consequent *Gold Rush of 1898.*

In all, some 75,000 fortune−hunters passed through the ports of Skagway and Dyea−men and women from every possible walk of life; tired of routine; lusting for adventure; seeking fortunes overnight. Some of the most colourful characters in the entertainment field sought audiences, laughter, handclaps in a land starved of genuine entertainment. When the first piano was borne to Jimmy Ryan's Nugget Saloon it was English Harry Marston−an old vaudeville circuit man who had travelled the U.S.A.−who was pressed into service. As the music filled the saloon and the hearts of the happy mob, the drinks came round and round till, overcome, the maestro sank to the floor under the bench, stupefied. It took more than hard liquor to halt music in Skagway at this time. So another musician was found. As the keys tinkled, the crowd shouted boisterously their requests; still more drinks found their way to the piano top; and another player found the unnavigated path to the floor. This endless round of activity continued for twenty−four hours when at such time, it is said, the piano had paid for itself.

One is likely to hear of 'Diamond Lil' Davenport−one time Queen of the Chicago Underworld. Bedecked in her familiar strings of jewellery, she would sing sentimental ballads and entertain royally in her favorite saloon. Finally, as the years passed, she left Skagway with a fortune. Later, when her beauty began to fade, she became a charwoman in a Seattle Bank. It was here that her life came to an inglorious end in the year of 1928.

Some will undoubtedly remember the bearded Russian who strolled into the camp from somewhere off the Siberian Islands. With him he had one companion−a huge trained bear tht danced and begged for him. When last seen the inseparable pair were headed over the Chilkoot Pass; the bear a beast of burden. Others came from the south. Among them was a negro with a mouth from ear to ear. In this huge cavern he would place three billiard balls (or the equivalent in plaster eggs) engaging a public dying for amusement; collecting his grubstake as he travelled. Came, too, was the small Neopolitan with the strangest cargo to ever land on the shores of this port. He brought with him a host of balloons which, surprisingly enough, he sold to the encamped gold−rushers. Today it is still a guess as to what use they could have been put.

Peter the Apostle made his timely appearance in the frozen North. During his servitude to God and the Argonauts he is credited with saving many lives and minds of those unfortunates unequipped for the ordeals of the trail. A fine, physical being he was truly of assistance to many a fouled gold−seeker. Still another came in the body of the Temperance Lecturer from Portland. In the vilest and most profane language imaginable he cursed every drunkard who fell out of or into the local saloons. In his efforts to purify the inebriated he became quite a problem to the famous Soapy Smith who could, ordinarily, handle quite readily any irregular disturbances. Whatever became of the prohibitionist is still a mystery in Skagway.

Finally, with reverence, they speak of Molley Walsh—the Wonder Girl of the White Pass Trail. Without help in the winter of '97 —'98 she ran a tent roadhouse, feeding and lodging the most persistent and wildest men; remaining as clean morally as the immaculate Alaskan snows. Her memorable work ceased when she was murdered by her husband October 28, 1902.

**Thomas Whitten—1898—Original Proprietor
Mrs. Harriet S. Pullen—1947**

**Alaskan Brotherhood
Camp Skagway #1**

Travelling along the streets of this famous town one sees the antiquity of this eventful era; the stories suddenly fill the empty buildings with life. Among the oldest is the Alaska Brotherhood — Camp No. 1, built in the year '99—its facade constructed completely of small logs and willows; the Golden North Hotel once owned by Thomas Whitten; and now by Mary Pullen—daughter of the famous lady—Harriet S. Pullen, a great story teller and Skagway legend; hostess at the Pack Train Inn—claimed to be the first and original bar of the Gold Rush days, boasting a famous clientele, including such characters as Tex Rickard, Robert Service, Frank Slavin, Peter Jackson, Alex Pantages, Frank Gotch, 'Philadelphia Jack' O'Brien and many others, in its heyday.

**Pullen House
Home of the 'Mothers' Daughter—Mary Pullen**

Spawn of the North

East on Broadway we come to the home of the late Harriet S. Pullen — Pullen House—another of the famous hostels of early Skagway. Called 'Mother of the North' by those who remember her well in earlier days, she was wont to ride to the trains and about the town perched high on her personal stage—coach. Today this very coach rots with antiquity behind the famed hotel; its wheels come to journey's end. The hotel—still elaborately furnished, including a grand piano—contains a priceless museum of thousands of curios and relics gathered over the years by this active woman.

All are bequeathed to her daughter—the likeable Mary! Mrs. Pullen passed away on August 9, 1947 and the author was deprived (by seven weeks) of meeting this northern woman and listening to her reams of imaginative tales for which she was so well known. Nearby stands one of the original dwellings, claimed to be the oldest log—cabin in Skagway. It too is silent but bespeaks a greater day; a livelier past; an unforgettable era.

In Skagway's adjacent creeks one sees the famed *Spawn of the North*, bringing to life the delightful novels of Jack London the adventurer. Salmon, salmon trout, trout instinctively seeking the upper reaches of the rivers after their life term at sea; dying off gradually as their pink bodies turn white, till they flounder no more; lying motionless pieces of rotting flesh, while others pass on…up…up with that instinctive creative desire to spawn. They will always supply food for whosoever travels up the waters that rush down from the passes above—be it 1898 or 1948.…

Before I left Skagway I heard of another memorable character. His name was Martin Itzen— unmistakably distinguished by his busman's hat, gold—nugget watch—chain and walrus moustache. He was the proud owner and builder of the town's street car—the only such vehicle of its kind in Alaska. Martin was known to tell more yarns about the Chilkoot, White Pass, Soapy Smith and his Gang, than anyone else thereabouts. He had one lifelong ambition: to 'go up and see Mae West sometime'—which he fulfilled in 1935, driving his own bus about the streets of Hollywood, each window adorned with a figure of one of the notorious Smith—gang. Later, back at his unique job in Skagway, he died peacefully. His grave today lies not far from those of Skagway's other famous personalities.

It was October that the snow fell about the waist of the surrounding mountains and I prepared to leave. I had come; found no tangible gold; but shared the Northern hospitality. Now it was time to go. So that night I dropped into the Igloo Saloon for the last round of farewells. The Blimp—as the bartender is called—was still bantering about the Yankee Baseball Series; Lundy—a local fisherman and his wife dropped in too; and Albert Jutson with his wife, Mary (two of the remaining Indians of the valley) mingled with the crowd, sipping drink for drink. An unforgettable hour passed in such company.…

White Pass
and Yukon Railway from Whitehorse   **'Largest Nugget in the World'**

The gang at the Frontier Bar were lounging as usual when we entered. Drinks went the rounds; toasts were raised to the departing 'Canucks'; and the street was found once more. Again the lights twinkled on the wet pavement of Broadway. But this time they said: "Farewell".

A hoot from the dock warned us of the 'last call'. We had worked two days, much to the chagrin of the local Immigration Officer, who, with the force of the law behind him, threatened us with deportation. Smiling broadly, we reached the boat five minutes before sailing and, jumping from the taxi, overheard him say: "There they are!" The scene—as the Vigilantes ushered the remnants of the Soapy Smith gang aboard the *Tartar* for deportation—flashed vividly before my mind. However, we were not embarrassed at having to openly admit that we were leaving Skagway of our 'own free will', this October 14, 1947.

338

Waving the usual farewells to the hospitable people gathered at the dock, the ship slid past the leering, thirty—foot skull of Soapy Smith—carved in the rock wall above the wharf by the townsfolk shortly after the death of the uncrowned King of Skagway in 1898. Looking back and seeing the profile of the Law, I could not help feeling like one of Soapy's cohorts threatened with a lynching if he returned. But then I remembered the two—week abundance of hospitality which outweighed by far this trivial incident; and I felt happy. I was heading for the Outside—loaded with a 'find' of Drifter's Gold in the 'moosehide poke' of my mind. I had 'struck' it rich!

Skagway Harbour...
To Lynn Canal...
To the 'Outside'

"End Of The Trail"
Aboard S.S. Princess Louise

As the October darkness swallowed the Princess Louise and the stars twinkled on Lynn Canal, it was fifty years ago that a Cheechako, having left the fabulous Klondike with his hard—earned riches, crossed the rugged Passes to the coast and headed down the Panhandle for home—an acknowledged Sourdough on his last lap of the Trails of '98!

Phil Allen.
July 8th 1949.

...The Howling Winds Swept the Distant Echoes of 22,000 Pairs of Feet Through the Misty Vortex of the Narrow, Rock Gap—The *Chilkoot Pass* on the *Trail of '98*, Re—conquered 50 Years Later, September 28, 1947 at 4:00 p.m., 3,500 Feet High on the Yukon—Alaska Border.

CHAPTER FORTY FOUR

OTHER TRAILS...

 D.S. al ⊕ *Coda*   ⊕ *Coda*

Inside Passage
Juneau Alaska

Down the Panhandle
Wrangell to Ketchikan

Docks
Prince Rupert, B.C.

Railroad Along the Skeena to Terrace, B.C.

341

**Alexandra Suspension Bridge
Over Fraser River Hazelton, B.C.**

**Caribou Trail
Inland Fraser River**

**Cairn and Waterwheel
Hazelton, B.C.**

The New Caribou Trail

**Fort Alexandria
(Williams Lake) B.C.**

**The Fort
Farthest Northwest Trading Company, West**

Indian Ingenuity

Hudson's Bay Company
Williams Lake, B.C.

150 Mile House along the Fraser River

100 Mile House on the Caribou Trail

The Old and the New

Nearing The End
Vancouver B.C.

Old Hotel Vancouver
Georgia and Granville Streets

Harbour Docks and Fishing Fleet
Stanley Park

Inner Harbour, Victoria B.C.
October 23, 1947

End of the *Trail of '98*
6,000 Miles, 6 Months on a Dime

End of the Trail
Victoria, B.C.
October 23, 1947

Alec Stefansson—March 2, 1910 circa—1969

The little—known son of the well—known Canadian Arctic Explorer, Vilhjalmur Stefansson, (deceased 1962) who first reached the Arctic in 1906.   Alec participated in the last of his father's expeditions (1915—1918) remembering well the spirit of his dad whom he had not seen since he returned to the U.S.A.: hoping one day, if money came, his dream might come true. None came.

Alec and his mother 'Fanny' were abandoned completely; Alec supporting her by his inherent qualities as a hunter and leader, till her death about 1946.

Alec—tall, heavy set, brown—eyed, with a determined jaw offset by a welcome smile, as a full handshake assures a friend once made—has enjoyed reading his fathers books. Crippled somewhat, by a right leg hamstring, he still was an expert hunter, raising with wife Mabel a family of six—three of each gender. They continue to bear his famous name over many areas of the Northland.

When Vilhjalmur Stefansson was approached by the author on his return from Arctic travel, bearing pictures and good tidings of desire for son to meet father, the explorer denied any knowledge of an Eskimo family and son. The author was understandably saddened and deeply hurt, (knowing Eskimo love of life) by the illustrious explorers indifference.

Today Mr. Allen still keeps in touch with the Stefansson Arctic family!

"The Two Sourdoughs"
Author and Poet—Attending the 'Sourdough Ball'—at the International Reunion, Vancouver, B.C., 1948

The Author with His Photos, Bert Parker—President (3ʳᵈ from left) and
'Sourdough' Friends at the 50ᵗʰ Anniversary of the 'Trail of '98'

Phil With Canine Friends

L'Envoi

I've squandered the gold that is minted in coin
With carefree and spendthrift hands;
Buying folly, and sorrow, and joy
On the byways of many lands.

But the gold that I've minted from memories,
That I've gleaned from the worlds far ends,
I've hoarded, and saved against the day
When I coould share it with friends.

Don Blanding